Clinical Interaction and the Analysis of Meaning

A New Psychoanalytic Theory

Theo. L. Dorpat
Michael L. Miller

THE ANALYTIC PRESS

1992   Hillsdale, NJ   London

To our wives, Doris and Jan,
and to our friends at the
Seattle Institute for Psychoanalysis.

Published by The Analytic Press, Inc.
365 Broadway, Hillsdale, NJ 07642

Library of Congress Cataloging-in-Publication Data

Dorpat, Theodore L.
   Meaning analysis : an interactional approach to psychoanalytical theory and practice / Theo. L. Dorpat, Michael L. Miller.
      p.   cm.
   Includes bibliographical references and index.
   ISBN 0-88163-146-9
   1. Psychoanalytical interpretation.   2. Psychotherapist and patient.   3. Transference (Psychology)   4. Object relations (Psychoanalysis)   5. Personality and situation.   I. Miller, Michael L., 1947–   . II. Title.
   [DNLM: 1. Cognition.   2. Professional–Patient Relations.
   3. Psychoanalytic Theory.   4. Unconscious (Psychology)   WM 460 D716m]
   RC506.D67   1992
   150.19'5—dc20
   DNLM/DLC
   for Library of Congress   92-22054
                                                                                       CIP

Contents

III
Applications and Exemplifications
Theo. L. Dorpat

Acknowledgments

We would like to express our appreciation and gratitude to the following colleagues who provided us with invaluable criticism and suggestions for the preparation of this manuscript: Dr. George Allison, Dr. Robert Bergman, Dr. Hugh Dickinson, Dr. Kenneth King, Dr. Robert Langs, Dr. Charles Mangham, Dr. Don Nathanson, Dr. Leslie Rabkin, Dr. James Raney, Dr. Herbert Ripley, Dr. Don Ross, Dr. David Rowlett, Dr. Werner Schimmelbusch, and Dr. Lawrence Schwartz.

We also want to convey our gratitude to our patients for the clinical experience that enabled us to formulate our theory. We particularly want to thank those patients who permitted us to use their material to illustrate our ideas.

We acknowledge with great appreciation the assistance of Dr. Paul Stepansky and John Kerr, of The Analytic Press, whose constructive criticism and advice helped us to clarify and integrate our writings. Their excellent editing and organizational ideas transformed our manuscript into a book. Thanks also to Eleanor Starke Kobrin for superb copy editing.

Except for parts of two chapters, this volume is entirely new. Chapter 12 is a modified version of a paper previously published in 1989 in a book titled *Denial: A Clarification of Concepts and Research* edited by E. L. Edelstein, D. L. Nathanson, and A. M. Stone. The previously published parts of Chapter 12 are being reprinted here with the kind permission of the Plenum Press. Chapter 13 is a much revised and expanded version of a paper previously published in 1987 in Volume 2 of *The Yearbook of Psychoanalytic Psychotherapy*. We are grateful to Dr. Robert Langs and to the Gardener Press for permission to reprint parts of the original published paper in Chapter 13.

The clinical material presented in Chapter 9 originally appeared in 1987 in volume 7, number 2 of *Psychoanalytic Inquiry*. It is from the section authored by Dr. Martin Silverman entitled "Clinical Material." We thank the editor of the volume, Dr. Stanley Pulver, and The Analytic Press for permission to reprint this material.

In addition to these acknowledgments, which we share equally, each of us individually would like to mention those individuals who were of personal support to us.

I am most especially indebted to Ms. Jean Keating for the preparation of this manuscript and for her administrative skill in making the writing of this book possible within the context of my professional life.

T.L.D.

I owe a tremendous debt of gratitude to my wife, Jan Sauer, for her understanding patience in tolerating the seemingly endless weekends and weeknights that I spent writing this book and for the many hours she contributed in critically listening to my ideas as they developed. I am deeply grateful to my coauthor and mentor, Ted Dorpat, for his guidance, his consistently helpful criticism of my ideas and writing, and for his encouragement and support of my psychoanalytic training. Whereas I would thank my secretary for assistance in preparing my manuscript if I had one, my Toshiba computer and Wordstar word processing program deserve thanks.

M.L.M.

Introduction and Overview

THEO. L. DORPAT

This book is concerned with delineating what we believe are errors in classical psychoanalytic theory and our corrections and revisions to that theory. To illustrate the clinical significance of our proposed theoretical revisions, I shall present a short clinical vignette to orient and guide the reader through the initial theoretical parts of the book.

The following vignette is only a small portion of a psychoanalytic hour discussed in depth in Chapter 9, where the process notes of the entire analytic hour plus a discussion are presented. The treating analyst, Silverman (1987), provided process notes of four successive analytic sessions. The patient was described as a masochistic single young woman. At first the analysis went well, only later to enter a prolonged stalemate. The process notes reveal a repeated and consistent pattern of interactions between the patient and analyst best described by Gill (1987) as a sadomasochistic interaction. Through a formidable array of highly provocative techniques (including inappropriate compliance, withholding, stalling, and other modes of interpersonal manipulation) the patient evoked in the analyst and others responses of anger, impatience, and condescension, as well as patronizing and demeaning attitudes.

In what the analyst calls "a chilled monotone, drained of all emotion," the patient describes her "masturbation fantasy" about her supposedly imaginary interactions with a "mad scientist." She says, "There's—a doctor—a mad scientist—and his nurse and—he ties me down to—do things to me." Later she tells of submitting like a slave to the mad scientist, and one of the things he does to her is to give her bigger breasts. The discussion that follows describes the marked difference between the classical interpretation of the patient's communication and our interactional interpretation.

Classical psychoanalysis would view her fantasy as a derivative of an unconscious fantasy of endogenous origin and isolated from contact with reality. Many analysts would consider the patient's story of the mad scientist as a transference manifestation. They too would consider this transference as a derivative of an unconscious fantasy and as a distortion of reality.

In our view, the patient's story of being bound and manipulated by the mad scientist is a concrete metaphor describing in visual imagery disturbing aspects of her interactions with the analyst. The patient's narrative is *responsive to* and *representative of* the controlling and demeaning elements in the analyst's previous interventions and the patient's emotional reactions to those interventions. The patient's telling of the mad scientist fantasy contains an incisive and basically veridical appraisal of the sadomasochistic interactions between herself and the analyst. Her account about what the mad scientist does to her is the product of a process of unconscious meaning analysis in which the patient has unconsciously appraised what is occurring in her relations with the analyst and then represented those meanings in her story.

In summary, many classical psychoanalysts would view what she said as a derivative of an unconscious fantasy and having little or nothing to do with her actual interactions with the analyst. In contrast, we believe that her story of the mad scientist unconsciously represents her actual interactions with the analyst and that her narrative is a product of a process of unconscious meaning analysis rather than a process of unconscious fantasy.

ERRORS IN THE CLINICAL THEORY

The practice of psychoanalytic treatment (psychoanalysis and psychoanalytic psychotherapy) is seriously impaired by long-standing errors and omissions in psychoanalytic clinical theory. These deficiencies are an important cause of fundamental and widespread mistakes in the way psychoanalysts understand and interpret unconscious processes and unconscious contents. These mistakes and defects in clinical theory and practice derive in part from an important element in Freud's metapsychology, namely, his theory of cognition.

In what follows, I summarize two of the major errors in the psychoanalytic clinical theories that this book focuses on explaining and correcting. A basic flaw in psychoanalytic theory and technique stems from the mistaken belief that the patient's transferences, defenses, symptoms, dreams, and other distorted cognitions stem from a process in which drive activated unconscious memories and unconscious fantasies are subjected to the distorting powers of the primary process before the derivatives of this process reach the level of consciousness. The central role of unconscious fantasies in traditional psychoanalytic thinking is shown by a recent statement by Kramer (1988), who said, "Psychoanalysis has become the science of unconscious phantasy" (p. 36). The first section of this book provides arguments showing that there are no such psychic contents or processes as unconscious fantasy and unconscious memory and that the primary process is transformative rather than distorting.

The second fundamental error in psychoanalytic theory is that the primary process is cut off from contact with the outside world. For many analysts and psychotherapists, this error is closely linked with a blindspot for interactional dynamics. We maintain that the primary process system is in direct and immediate contact with the external world. Though Freud and many analysts after him considered unconscious fantasy as a major process of the primary process, we hold that one of the major processes is that of unconscious meaning analysis. Unconscious meaning analysis is a constant process in which the individual evaluates his or her interactions with other individuals and represents those interactions in such primary process products as affects, imagery, metaphors, nonverbal communication, and intuition.

In short, psychoanalysts who follow the classical psychoanalytic theory tend to have a serious misunderstanding of what is occurring unconsciously within their patients. One aspect of this misunderstanding is their mistaken notion about a specific process and content (unconscious fantasy) that does not exist. What's more, they are unaware of an important unconscious process in their patients (unconscious meaning analysis) that does exist. In the analytic situation, this function (unconscious meaning analysis) evaluates and represents the patient's interactions with the analyst.

Our criticisms strike at some of the foundations of the clinical theory fully as much as at the metapsychological theory. The same errors Freud made in the part of metapsychology we call his theory of cognition were also made in various clinical theories about defense, transference, dream formation, symptom formation, and other types of psychopathology.

The theoretical revisions we present here have important implications for the clinical practice of psychoanalysis and psychoanalytic psychotherapy. Some previous critiques of metapsychology have had little relevance or impact on clinical theories or on how psychoanalyses are conducted. For example, whether one does or does not subscribe to the theory of psychic energy does not matter much in how one understands one's patients or interprets their thoughts and feelings.

Some critiques of metapsychology have attempted to separate and isolate metapsychology from clinical theory. These efforts appear to have been prompted by the motive of constructing a new and purified clinical theory by extracting the base metal of an obsolete metapsychology from the pure gold of clinical theory. Such misguided efforts to purge clinical theory of metapsychological influences and assumptions have not worked, probably because it is not possible to eliminate the influences of metapsychological concepts and assumptions from clinical theories.

All psychoanalytic clinical theories will inescapably contain implicit, if not explicit, assumptions about human thought, action, and development. These assumptions are mainly derived from scientific fields other than psychoanalysis and are inextricably interwoven into the fabric of clinical theories. Freud's theory of cognition and other elements of his metapsychology were derived from his philosophy of science and from the biological sciences and the neurosciences of the late 19th century. The concepts and models my coauthor, Michael Miller, uses to construct a new model of the mind in Section II come from scientific knowledge and theories about the mind prevailing in this, the latter part of the 20th century.

TWO TYPES OF CLINICAL THEORY

There are extant today two related but different types of clinical theories— the first is the written theory and the second is the unwritten and informal types of theories transmitted to psychoanalytic candidates in training and especially through their experiences with their supervisors and training analysts. How psychoanalysts conduct analyses is shaped far more by their interactions with their training analysts, supervisors, and colleagues than by what they have learned through reading the psychoanalytic literature. In my view, the informal and unwritten clinical theory even more than the written theory has the same fundamental faults addressed in this book.

In writing of classical analysts as a group who share a collective blindspot for interactional dynamics, I am cognizant of creating a straw man, or what Max Weber called an "Ideal type." After all, psychoanalysts, classical as well as others, vary widely in how attuned they are to interactional dynamics. The straw man tactic, in my view, is unobjectionable as long as one recognizes its value for expository purposes and so long as it is acknowledged that the straw man is not designed to describe actual persons fully or accurately. The straw man in this book is constituted not only from my experiences in teaching, analyzing, and supervising, but also from my self-analysis. The blindspot for interactional dynamics is one I once shared early in my career, and I still struggle with residues of this faulty way of thinking.

Early in my psychoanalytic career I mistakenly believed that as long as I safeguarded the analytic frame by adhering to the ground rules of analysis and by maintaining psychoanalytic neutrality, I could devote my complete attention to observing and interpreting what was occurring within the mind of the patient. Then I gradually and painfully began to realize that my steady preoccupation with what was going on within the patient often obscured what was occurring in my interactions with the patient. Now my aim is to shift flexibly between the intrapsychic and interactional perspectives in order to understand and interpret not only what is going on within the patient, but also what is transpiring in the interactions between the patient and the analyst.

With few exceptions, the criticisms presented in this book apply more or less equally to four different spheres: the portion of Freud's metapsychology we call his theory of cognition, the written psychoanalytic clinical theory, the informal and unwritten clinical theory, and finally the practice of psychoanalysis and psychoanalytic psychotherapy. Psychoanalysts give too little attention to understanding, explaining, and interpreting interactions between the analyst and the analysand. Our interactional emphasis arises in part as a reaction to the prevailing and traditional tendency of psychoanalysts to conceptualize both psychopathology and the analytic process almost exclusively as an intrapsychic process occurring wholly within the analysand and isolated from the person's interpersonal relations.

Traditional psychoanalysis looks to the depths of the psyche to unconscious wishes, to the so-called derivatives of the instinctual drives, and to other dispositions for its explanations and interpretations of human cognition, feeling, and action. This nearly exclusive focus on the intrapsychic domain obscures the profound and complex ways in which the analyst is implicated in the clinical phenomena he seeks to study and to interpret.

One of the major goals of this book is to assist psychoanalysis in becoming a breadth as well as a depth psychology by demonstrating the importance of object relations and the interactional perspective for understanding and interpreting patients' communications and actions. Both in theory and practice classical psychoanalysis is a depth psychology but is seriously deficient as a breadth psychology. Continuing with the use of spatial metaphors, one could say that psychoanalysis looks *vertically* to the depths of patient's psyche for the causes of behavior at the same time that it generally fails to look *horizontally* at the individual's interactions with the environment for its explanations and interpretations.

Most psychoanalytically oriented therapists minimize the significance of the intersubjective context for codetermining their patients' transferences, resistances, communications, and even psychopathology. Little attention is given to the *actual* interactions (as contrasted with the alleged unconscious *fantasy* interactions) between the patient and therapist and how the patient *unconsciously evaluates* and *represents* these interactions.

As Balint (1965), Modell (1984), and others have written, the one-person psychology of traditional psychoanalysis stems from a biological model of an organism cut off from its environment. When early in this century Freud abandoned the seduction theory of neurosis, he also gave up attempts to construct a two-body psychological theory. Instead he focused on developing an intrapsychic theory of instinctual drives, internal conflict, and unconscious fantasy. Dissatisfaction with the limitations and problems of the traditional one-body theory has gradually led to the emergence of two-body theories that are known as psychoanalytic theories of object relations. Self psychology, in the opinion of Bacal and Newman (1990) as well as ours, should be considered as a type of object relations theory.

The interactional approach we are recommending and the object relations theories with which it is allied do not replace classical psychoanalysis but are, instead, a necessary adjunct to it. The classical intrapsychic psychology, a one-body theory, and the two-person context of object relations theories are complementary.

THE "FUNDAMENTAL ATTRIBUTION ERROR"

The collective blindspot of psychoanalysts and other mental health professionals about interactional dynamics is not always or only caused by adherence to Freud's theory of cognition or to its applications to clinical theories. There is one cause well known by social psychologists but not by others that accounts for the pervasive and long-standing failure of the mental health professions, as well as the sciences concerned with cognition, to understand situational elements in their explanations and interpretations of human behavior. Social psychologists call it the "fundamental attribution error," which was defined by Nisbett and Ross (1980) as "the tendency to attribute behavior exclusively to the actor's dispositions and to ignore powerful situational determinants of the behavior" (p. 31). I believe that the fundamental attribution error, together with the effects of Freud's outmoded theory of cognition on psychoanalytic clinical theory, is an important reason for the prevailing overemphasis on intrapsychic determinants of affect, thought, and action.

Nisbett and Ross presented convincing evidence for the proposition that a general "dispositional theory" bias is shared by almost everyone in Western cultures. Children growing up in Western countries come to hold an increasingly dispositional view of the causes of behavior because this bias is so thoroughly woven into the fabric of the culture. Psychoanalytic theories, as well as most other psychological theories until a short time ago, embodied this bias toward the dispositional causes of human thought and action and at the same time overlooked or minimized situational determinants.

We hope our contribution will help mental health professionals to overcome their fundamental attribution error through a better understanding of how all human thought and feelings are influenced and partly shaped by the individual's interactions with others. Cognition and affect, as well as overt actions, are determined by one's interactions with others as well as by one's predispositions.

The cognitive sciences have gradually come to understand the contextual and interactional determinants of behavior in humans and other animals. For example, social psychology and developmental psychology recognize that two interrelated variables—the individual's dispositions stemming from past experience, learning, and genetic influences; and the individual's current interactions with others—acting together, jointly determine an individual's experience and behavior. According to our interactional theory, there is no action or communication made by one party in the analytic situation that does not influence and contribute to the experience and psychic functioning of the other party.

AN OVERVIEW OF THE BOOK

This book is made up of three sections. Section I provides a critique of classical psychoanalytic theory and some brief initial proposals for theoretical revisions. It includes studies on Freud's theory of cognition, unconscious fantasy, unconscious pathogenic ideas, and the primary process system. Our examination of the psychoanalytic clinical theories of defense, dreaming, symptom formation, transferences, and psychopathology generally reveals that many of the errors and omissions in those theories can be traced back to their origins in that part of Freud's metapsychology we call his theory of cognition. For this reason, the critique of Freud's theory of cognition in Chapter 1 and of his theory of the primary process in Chapter 2 provide the foundations for our examination of other clinical theories in succeeding chapters.

Section I's criticisms of classical concepts about unconscious memory and unconscious fantasy show Freud's theory of cognition to be obsolete and incompatible with contemporary knowledge about cognition. Psychoanalytic investigations, as well as the findings from such cognate disciplines as developmental psychology, cognitive psychology, and the neurosciences, require some important revisions in the psychoanalytic theory of the primary process. One of the major goals of Chapter 2 is to demonstrate that the primary process system is not isolated, as Freud thought it was, from environmental interactions and influences.

Chapters 3 and 4 conclude that there is little evidence for, and much evidence against, Freudian and Kleinian theories about unconscious fantasy. Arguments against the traditional view of the unconscious as a container for unconscious memories and unconscious fantasies are presented. This "cellar" theory of the unconscious as a container was based on the discredited *copy* theory of perception and memory and other out-of-date theories of cognition that prevailed in the 19th century.

In psychoanalytic writings, the term unconscious fantasy has been used to refer both to an unconscious process and to an unconscious content. Chapter 3 argues for replacing the notion of unconscious fantasy as a process with the concept of unconscious meaning analysis, and Chapter 4 recommends substituting the concept of unconscious pathogenic ideas for at least some of what was formerly called unconscious fantasy considered as an unconscious content.

A major discovery developing out of our collaboration is the idea of unconscious meaning analysis. This new approach to understanding unconscious processes provides an important basis for our interactional prospective and is one of the foundations for theoretical revisions. Our theoretical formulations about this process and the implications of those formulations for psychoanalytic technique are spelled out in various chapters, beginning with Chapter 2.

The five chapters in Section II present a systematic formulation of interactional theory. These chapters advance a new model of the mind as well as an interactional perspective on such topics as defense, psychopathology, symptom formation, and psychoanalytic technique. Our chapters on the interactional perspective in Sections II and III advance a fundamentally new way of listening and interpreting patients' communications. Instead of listening for the so-called derivatives of unconscious fantasies and interpreting them as distortions of reality, we recommend attending to the products of patients' unconscious meaning analysis and interpreting them as the meanings patients unconsciously attribute to their interactions with the analyst and others. What psychoanalysts have erroneously called primary process derivatives are actually, in our opinion, the products of a process of meaning analysis in which an individual unconsciously evaluates and represents the meaning of his or her interactions with others in such manifestations as affects, nonverbal communications, images, intuition, and metaphors.

Chapters 5 and 6 offer a new model of the mind, one that is more consistent with contemporary knowledge in the sciences concerning cognition and human development. Chapter 7 systematically spells out the basic principles of an interactional theory's perspective on defense, symptom formation, and psychopathology. Chapter 8 presents an interactional model of the psychoanalytic process and technique. In Chapter 9 the published process notes of a psychoanalysis are to illustrate our interactional approach and to show how an analyst can decode primary-process products and thus reveal the unconscious meanings patients ascribe to their relations with the analyst.

Section III presents more applications and exemplifications of our theoretical revisions to such topics as transference, defense, self-fulfilling prophecies, and dreaming. For decades, psychoanalysts have recognized that a patient's behaviors and communications may influence the shape of an analyst's countertransference. Only in the past decade or so has some attention been paid to how an analyst's interventions influence a patient's transference. This new social perspective on transference is elaborated in Chapter 10.

Chapter 11 discusses the contributions of philosophers, social psychologists, and psychoanalysts on the significance of self-fulfilling prophecies in object relations, including the therapist-patient dyad. Self-fulfilling prophecies are enacted in projective identification insofar as the subject manipulates the object in such a way as to evoke responses that confirm the subject's prophecies and expectations.

The traditional concept of defenses is essentially an intrapsychic conception with its major focus on the individual's use of protective mechanisms activated by signals of danger and used for defending against the awareness of instinctual drive derivatives. Chapter 12 contributes toward a revised theory of defenses that recognizes the central role played by object relations in the development, internalization, and maintenance of an individual's defensive activity.

Chapter 13 proposes some modifications in the theory of dreaming to account for the significance of unconscious meaning analysis and unconscious perceptions in dream formation. Case vignettes of dreams and their analysis illustrate the inclusion of the products of unconscious meaning analysis of recent interpersonal interactions into the texture of the dreams.

Though many of the ideas presented in the following chapters first saw the light of day in our discussions together over a period of over six years, the responsibility for writing the various chapters was divided. I wrote Sections I and III, and my coauthor, Michael Miller, wrote the chapters in Section II. Each chapter in Sections I and II is complete in itself and can be read and understood without the need to read the chapters preceding it.

Critique of Classical Psychoanalytic Theory

Theo. L. Dorpat

Chapter 1 provides a critical review of Freud's theory of cognition. His theory of cognition was an essential part of Freud's metapsychology and provided the foundation for his psychoanalytic clinical theories on such topics as defense and transference, as well as dream and symptom formation.

A revised theory of cognition is required to correct and modify psychoanalytic clinical theories. Freud's concept of unconscious mental representations (such as unconscious memory and unconscious fantasy) as analogous with the contents of conscious experience (e.g., memories and fantasies) has become not only obsolete but basically unnecessary. As I show in Chapter 1, Freud's concepts about unconscious mental fantasies and unconscious memories were based on his outmoded copy theory of perception as well as other out-dated notions about cognitive processes.

Freud's theories about dream and symptom formation and about transference were derived mainly from his hypothesis about the supposedly distorting powers of the primary process. He incorrectly assumed that unconscious mental representations and other latent contents both in the process of dream formation and in the early stages of waking cognition are distorted by such primary process mechanisms as displacement and condensation prior to their emergence as the manifest content. Chapters 1 and 2 argue for the proposition that the primary process plays a transformative rather than (as Freud believed) a distorting role in dream and symptom formation as well as in cognition generally.

Both empirical and logical evidence oppose Freud's formulation that the latent content of dreams, symptoms, and the like is composed of rational and undistorted cognitions occurring prior to the formation of the dreams and symptoms and in the forms that analysts reconstruct through the analysis and interpretation of dreams and symptoms. Though Freud was far ahead of his time in noting that the products of higher level psychic functions, such as judgment and problem solving, could be represented in dreams, he was mistaken in placing the functioning of these higher level functions in a process and time preceding the dream-work, the process of dream formation. Dreams, symptoms, jokes, among other kinds of cognitions, have only one content and what is "latent" in any psychic content is some meaning that the subject does not initially understand.

Chapter 2 attempts to integrate recent studies of the primary process and presents a revised theory of the primary process system. According to Freud, the primary processes occur within the id, and the major content of these processes is wish-fulfilling unconscious fantasy. In contrast to the ego, the id was conceptualized by Freud (1940a) as cut off from relations with the external world. In both the classical and the Kleinian theories, unconscious fantasies have their endogenous roots deep within the id, where they are considered to be isolated from interpersonal influences. The concept of the id, primary process, and unconscious fantasy are correlative. That is to say, these concepts define each other.

Freud was mistaken in thinking that primary process manifestations stem from unconscious fantasies and that primary process functioning is isolated from interactions with the environment. Recent studies reveal that the primary process system is directly engaged in *actual,* not fantasy, interactions with others and that it unconsciously analyzes the meanings of those interactions and represents them in various primary process products.

The so-called primary process derivatives that are commonly misinterpreted as stemming from unconscious fantasies are actually constructed from the individual's unconscious attempts to evaluate and represent the meanings of his *actual not fantasied interactions* with others. Chapter 4 recommends, as a substitute for the outmoded notion of unconscious fantasy as a type of unconscious content, the adoption of Weiss's concept of unconscious pathogenic belief (Weiss and Sampson, 1986). Weiss and his associates present convincing evidence supporting their hypothesis that unconscious pathogenic beliefs play a central role in psychopathology.

The heart of psychoanalysis—and what distinguishes it from other psychological theories—is what has been variously called "the dynamic unconscious," the "unconscious" or primary process. The overriding goal of this section is to provide major modifications and revisions to traditional psychoanalytic theories about the nature of unconscious processes and unconscious contents. Chapters 3 and 4 present an in-depth study and critique of classical, Kleinian, and self psychology concepts about unconscious fantasy. These investigations conclude that there is no solid basis or evidence for the existence of unconscious fantasy considered either as unconscious content or as unconscious process.

Freud's abandonment of the seduction theory early in this century represented a fateful shift in his thinking, a shift that had profound implications for the subsequent development of psychoanalytic theory and process. Thereafter, Freud and later other analysts focused more on theories about internal entities such as unconscious fantasy to the exclusion of their patients' actual relations in the real world. Psychic conflict replaced psychic trauma as the major theoretical and clinical paradigm of psychoanalysis. In dropping the seduction theory, Freud also gave up attempts to develop a two-body psychological theory. Instead he focused on constructing a one-body theory of instinct, internal conflict, and unconscious fantasy.

When Freud was unable to confirm his theory that hysterical symptoms arose out of unconscious memories of seduction in childhood, he began using the idea of unconscious fantasy as a causal explanatory hypothesis. In his view, unconscious fantasies were the latent content and proximal causes of dreams, symptoms, transferences, and other psychic manifestations.

A major strategy in Kleinian and classical psychoanalytic technique is the uncovering and interpretation of unconscious fantasies and what are mistakenly called derivatives of unconscious fantasies. Unconscious fantasies are commonly viewed as the precursors and the immediate cause of symptoms, dreams, and transferences, as well as other communications. Often, unconscious fantasies are viewed as the exclusive or prime source of distorted and irrational thoughts.

Many of the typical interpretations employed today in psychoanalytic treatment are highly questionable inferences about the supposed existence and causal effects of wish-fulfilling unconscious fantasies. Such interpretations, as well as the psychoanalytic theory from which they in part derive, ignore patient–therapist interactions that, acting together with the patient's dispositions, determine the nature of the patient's defensive, transferential, and affective responses.

As an alternative to the traditional concept of the process of unconscious fantasy, my coauthor, Michael Miller, and I propose the concept of unconscious meaning analysis. The products of this ongoing process of unconscious meaning analysis are what analysts in the past have commonly called primary process derivatives, and they include such manifestations as affects, images, metaphors, intuition, nonverbal communication, and narratives. Holding that the unconscious deals with meaning making rather than with drives and unconscious fantasies, our revisions in theory offer an important paradigm shift from much classical psychoanalytic thought.

Concepts about unconscious meaning analysis advanced in this book are consistent with Weiss's formulations about unconscious higher level psychic functions (Weiss and Sampson, 1986). Studies carried out by Weiss and his associate indicate that such higher level functions as thinking, anticipating, testing, deciding, planning, and setting goals can occur unconsciously as well as consciously.

In his early writings, Freud did not recognize the importance of unconscious higher level psychic regulatory and adaptive functions, and he tended to view unconscious mental activity mainly in the biological terms of instincts, forces, and drive-cathected, wish-fulfilling fantasies. Late in his career, he discovered that higher level and complex mental functions could occur outside of conscious awareness (Freud, 1940a).

Weiss's and Freud's prescient notions about unconscious higher level psychic functions foreshadowed the recent emergence of similar ideas in cognitive psychology. Only in the past decade have cognitive psychologists devised experiments showing that such higher level mental functions as judgments, decision making, and the analysis of meaning occur outside of conscious awareness.

Weiss's theory of higher level psychic functions differs from the one presented here inasmuch as he implicitly restricts his usage of the term "higher level psychic function" to such unconscious secondary process functions as deciding, choosing, anticipating, planning, and the like. The theory advanced here asserts that primary process functioning can also occur at a high level and that one of the functions of this system is the unconscious meaning analysis of events, especially interpersonal interactions.

Chapter 4 compares traditional with contemporary approaches to psychic trauma and concludes that enactive memories of traumatic experiences are not caused by unconscious fantasies but by the biological need to repeat novel, unexpected, and traumatic events. Though the classical theory of defense cannot explain how such defects as developmental arrrests, stalemated mourning, and alexithymia are caused by psychic trauma, my cognitive arrest theory of defense is used in Chapter 4 to explicate their pathogenesis.

CHAPTER 1

Freud's Theory
of Cognition

In Chapter VII of *The Interpretation of Dreams* and in later papers, Freud (1900, 1901) advanced a causal explanatory theory of cognition that used the latent dream as the example of thought formation. There Freud proposed a metapsychology, that is, a causal explanatory theory of dreams and, more specifically, for latent dream thoughts and their vicissitudes. Psychoanalytic metapsychology was based on the exposition Freud gave in Chapter VII, and psychoanalysis today still looks upon it as fundamental.

My examination of classical psychoanalytic theories on such topics as primary process, dream and symptom formation, transference, and object relations revealed that the mistaken ideas in those theories could be traced back to their origins in Freud's theory of cognition. This chapter's review and discussion provides the foundation for the examination of other psychoanalytic theories and most especially for clinical theories in succeeding chapters.

Freud's theory of cognition implies a three-stage process: first, the cathexis and activation of unconscious mental representations by instinctual drives. In Freud's theory, mental representations are conceptualized as internal copies of external objects. The theory assumes the formation of undistorted objective perceptions and their storage as veridical memory images. The second stage includes the transformation and distortion of mental representations through a complex set of primary process mechanisms such as displacement and condensation. The progressive establishment of reality testing and of secondary-process cognition provides, in the third stage of cognition, the ability to inhibit the distorting effects of the primary process and unchecked drive discharge. The third, and final, stage of cognition in Freud's theory essentially involves a partial undoing and restraining of the distorting powers of the primary process carried out in the service of reality testing and adaptation to reality.

This chapter is divided into two parts. Part I examines and critiques the first stage of Freud's Theory of Cognition. Part II deals with hallucinatory wish fulfillment and primary process distortion in dreams, symptoms, and cognition generally.

5

I. FREUD'S CONCEPTS OF UNCONSCIOUS
MENTAL REPRESENTATION

Schimek (1975a) and others have persuasively argued against a basic Freudian theory that unconscious mental representations (unconscious memories and unconscious fantasies) are stored in the unconscious from where they manifest themselves in consciousness in various disguised and transformed ways. The concept of the unconscious as a storage container of specific memories, images and fantasies—the so-called cellar theory of the unconscious—is no longer tenable.

Investigators from diverse fields provide cogent reasons for decisively rejecting Freud's theory that the primary and original form of the unconscious is an ideational one, namely, contents of memories or fantasies, which by acquiring instinctual drive cathexis become causal agents of behavior (Piaget, 1952, 1962; Schimek, 1975a; Basch, 1976a).

Freud's concept of unconscious mental representations was derived mainly from the general neurological and psychological concepts and theories of his time. *Vorstellung,* the term Freud used for mental representation, refers to a concrete object or thing whose image may even be vague and blurred. Such images are conceptualized as the building blocks of mental and psychical processes, beyond the immediacy of perception from which they originate. In contrast, the more complex and abstract relations formed by associative networks between these basic elements were considered in Freud's writings and those of others as thought (*Gedanken*).

This chapter focuses on one kind of unconscious mental representation, unconscious memory, and leaves for Chapters 3 and 4 investigations about unconscious fantasy.

The Copy Theory of Perception:
The Principle of Immaculate Perception

To understand Freud's concept of mental representation we need to first examine his ideas on perception. In Freud's (1900) view, perception is a sensory given and immediately known to the subject—that is, Pcpt = Cs (roughly translated, this means perception equals consciousness). He believed that sensory stimuli, in contrast to internal stimuli (such as instinctual drives), have direct access to consciousness. In accord with the association theory of the 19th century, Freud held that perception is essentially the passive, temporary registration of a specific external object.

In Freud's view, the perceptual apparatus functions like the lens of a camera or the receptive surface of a slate. To keep its receptive ability available for new registrations, the perceptual apparatus retains no permanent traces of registrations; it is "without the capacity to retain modifications and is thus without memory . . ." (Freud, 1900, p. 539).

Such a conception of perception has been called the "copy" theory of perception or the principle of "immaculate perception." Freud's theory of cognition, partly derived from his copy theory, assumed an innate capability for objective perceptions and their automatic storage as undistorted mental representations (e.g., unconscious memories) in the unconscious (Schimek, 1975a; Holt, 1976).

The outdated copy theory implies a capacity for veridical, objective perceptions of external objects and a direct and intrinsic correspondence between the actual external object and the individual's perception of it. According to the copy theory of perception and memory, every perception produces a lasting memory trace, so that the subject's experience of the perceived object continues to endure as a specific memory image or mental representation. For Freud (1925a), memory images in their original undistorted form duplicate the content of the objective perception of an external object. Actually, as cognitive psychologists have demonstrated, memory storage retains information about mental acts rather than copies of perceptions (Neisser, 1967; Norman, 1969).

Though the copy theory of perception was widely held in Freud's time, in recent decades it has been replaced as a result of advances in research on cognition, memory, and perception. Today, the individual is no longer seen as a passive recorder of events, but instead as an active constructor of them. Likewise for memory, a remembered event is a reconstruction.

Freud's copy theory of perception is similar to what Heider (1958) calls "naive psychology," which consists predominantly of common sense assumptions about psychology. In everyday life, most people assume that events that occur before their eyes are more or less photographically perceived. There is, however, overwhelming evidence against the common-sense view that perception is the direct passive registration of the external world (Mandler, 1984; Neisser, 1967). Though scientific studies show that perception is a complicated construction of the external world out of unarticulated sensory information, in naive psychology this complexity is unrecognized.

Along with his contemporaries in psychology and psychiatry, Freud mistakenly assumed that perception is a simple matter of coming into direct contact with reality. Cognitive psychologists now take it for granted that perceiving is an active process in which a person's motivational and structural properties play an intrinsic part. One erroneous implication of Freud's copy theory of perception is that perception is not influenced by past experience and is immune from developmental, learning, and affective influences.

Freud's metapsychology and his theory of cognition were both based in

part on the copy theory, which Holt (1976) calls "the assumption of naive realism" (p. 81)—the mistaken idea that all percipient organisms naturally form phenomenal copies of external reality merely by being exposed to it.
    Basch (1981) writes:

> It is the hypothesis that perception is a sensory given and immediately known to the subject, i.e. Pcpt = Cs. (Freud, 1900) that is both the fundamental and false assumption . . . on which Freud constructed his metapsychology, which, therefore, failed to provide a useful and theoretically sound framework for his findings [p. 160].

To replace the copy theory of perception, I recommend acceptance of the constructivist theory of perception and of other kinds of cognition. The object of perception does not come to us as a sensory given; rather, it must be actively constructed by nonconscious cognitive processes.

Hartmann's (1964) formulations about "primary autonomy" probably stem from the copy theory. He viewed perception as an ego function with "primary autonomy" as nondefensive and noninstinctual, as given by heredity and as guaranteeing a certain degree of "preadaptiveness." Hartmann's concept of perception as possessing primary autonomy from instinct, conflict, and defense is contrary to contemporary investigations of perception, such as those of Westerlundh and Smith (1983), who see perception as an "actualization of ontogenetically acquired meanings" (p. 618). Many clinical as well as experimental studies show that perception as a process is loaded with conflict and defense.

When Freud wrote about thinking and thought processes, he did not include perception; today psychologists most often use the general term cognition to include perception as well as other mental processes such as memory and thinking.

The Copy Theory of Memory

In Freud's theory of cognition, memories are copies of perceptions just as perceptions are copies of external reality. Freud (1925a) wrote, "All (re)presentations originate from perceptions and are repetitions of them. Thus originally, the mere existence of a (re)presentation was a guarantee of the reality of what was represented" (p. 237).

In Freud's view, the whole of the past is preserved in the unconscious. Consciousness, having no memory, can only illuminate the memory images that lie beneath the surface of consciousness.

Today, the cognitive sciences know that the contents of perception and memory are the end-products of active constructive processes. A memory image is not a mere copy or replica of the past object, but, as Schimek (1975a) writes, "the selective reconstruction of certain aspects of past experience in terms of the needs and cognitive capacities of the present" (p. 181).

Freud conceptualized drive-cathected unconscious memories and unconscious fantasies as causal agents, active forces that set the psychic apparatus in motion. Drive-cathected mental representations were seen by Freud as the original and primary way in which drives express themselves. Often in his writings, unconscious mental representations were equated with the drive itself (see Editor's notes, Freud, 1923c, pp. 111ff).

Piaget on Reconstruction Memory

Why is it that humans have no conscious memories of their first years, which are so rich in emotional experiences? The classical Freudian reply is that repression blocks the recovery of early childhood memories, thus bringing about an "infantile amnesia." According to Freud's hypothesis about the formation of unconscious mental representations, the beginnings of memory coincide with those of mental life. He attributed clear, differentiated, and veridical perception to the infant (Freud, 1895).

Piaget (1962) proposed a different theory of memory, *reconstruction memory*. According to Piaget, there are no memories of the infantile period because infants lack the cognitive equipment, such as symbols, necessary for reconstruction memory. Reconstruction memory has its developmental beginnings only after the ability to create symbols has developed and after the development of object permanence (i.e., the ability to evoke the image of absent objects). Piaget distinguished between *recognition memory* (as exemplified by the ability of the infant to recognize his mother) and *reconstruction* (or evocative) *memory* (as exemplified by the child's ability to reconstruct or evoke the image of the absent mother). Reconstruction memory (also called representational memory) is the ability to recall the past in the form of memory images. It is the product of a complex developmental process and is preceded by the development of recognition memory, the ability merely to recognize objects of past experience.

Piaget argued that

> There are no memories of early childhood for the excellent reason that at that stage there was no evocative mechanism capable of organizing them. Recognition memory in no way implies a capacity for evocation, which presupposes mental images, language, and the beginnings of conceptual intelligence [p. 187].

Schemata and Memory

Piaget (1962) discussed the development of recognition memory and the assimilations on which the reconstructions of reconstruction memory are based. He argued persuasively against the theory that unconscious memory is images deposited in the unconscious. In recognition memory, a baby recognizes an object or a person insofar as he is able to react to them as he has done in the past. With the development of abilities for symbolization, reconstruction memory develops out of recognition memory.

It is true that the growing child frequently generalizes his first modes of giving and receiving, of clinging and rebelling, and that there is a striking continuity between these first interactions in the family and subsequent interpersonal and social interactions (Piaget, 1962; Stern, 1985). The facts lose nothing of their clarity by being expressed in terms of schemata and their mutual assimilation, rather than of unconscious memories. Piaget effectively disputed the psychoanalytic view that images formed by infants of their primary objects persist throughout life and that other people are later unconsciously "identified" with their primary objects.

Schemata: An Alternative to the Theory of Unconscious Mental Representations

The concept of schemata is an alternative to the discredited and obsolete cellar theory of "the unconscious" as a repository for unconscious memories and fantasies. (See Chapter 5 for a more complete discussion about schemas.) The data of modern developmental psychology support the conclusion that organized, goal-directed action patterns, which can be carried over to new situations and be modified by them, occur before the young child has attained cognitive abilities for evoking the past in the form of mental imagery (Piaget, 1962; Mandler, 1984; Fast, 1985).

Such action patterns (or sensorimotor schemata) are based on innate reflex structures that become progressively differentiated and modified as part of the individual's interaction with the environment. An event or external object is given personal meaning by being assimilated to such a schema, and the schema itself accommodates to the new experience with an object and becomes modified thereby.

In the theories of developmental and cognitive psychologists there are no assumptions about unconscious cognitive contents (such as memory images or fantasies) preceding those action patterns and regulating them (Piaget, 1962; Mandler, 1984; Fast, 1985). The earliest form of cognitive activity is sensorimotor acts—the sensory event and the motor response constitute one integral unit. It is legitimate to infer nonconscious sensorimotor organizers of action at a preverbal level, without postulating that *behind* the various observable manifestations of an inferred unconscious motive lies an unconscious image or fantasy.

Schemata have their beginnings in innate reflex activities, including the mode of functioning of various organs (e.g., oral, anal, phallic) but they rapidly develop beyond this. Therefore the schema concept should be considered as a psychobiological rather than merely, or only, a biological concept.

The influence of the past is carried on through schemata, not through unconscious memory or unconscious fantasies of absent objects. The fact that a person repeats and generalizes salient aspects of his interactions with his parents to other people, including his analyst, does not require postulating the persistence of unconscious memory or fantasy images of the individual's primary objects. The organized set of sensorimotor, intellectual, and other schemas constitute the "character" of each individual, that is, his permanent modes of behavior.

The general concept of prerepresentational nonconscious organizers of action (as exemplified by Piaget's concepts of schemas and by Erikson's, 1950, concepts of organ modes) has the same methodological status as Freud's concept of unconscious mental representation. Such organized action patterns are modes of doing things and include the disposition to seek or to avoid specific situations, and, as Schimek (1975a) argues, they do not require any unconscious mental representation of past experience as their anticipated goal.

Habit Memory and Representational Memory: Neurophysiological Studies

Neurophysiologists distinguish "habit," "skill," or "performance memory" and representational memory, and they have discovered that these two basically different kinds of memory have different brain pathways (Mishkin, 1982). According to Mishkin, habit memory is served by a corticostriatal system and involves noncognitive links to subcortical structures. Experimental evidence supports the conclusions that the brain system serving habit memory is both phylogenetically older and ontogenetically earlier than the brain system subserving representational memory. As Mishkin indicates, these two parallel and relatively independent memory systems contribute in somewhat different ways to the learning process.

There is reason to believe, then, that the corticostriatal brain system serving habit memory begins to function very early in life and that later (probably late in the preoperational stage of cognitive development) a second system associated with representational memory begins to function independently and in parallel with the corticostriatal system.

Reiser (1984) speculated about a correspondence between the mental and the neurophysiological realms of memory. He asks if there might be

> a fundamental analogy between the postulated principle of dual-parallel and independent-physiologic systems that process two types of learning and Freud's idea of two parallel and independent modes (primary and secondary) of processing information in the mental realm—in both instances one mode older than the other and closer to primitive than to complex cognitive functions? [pp. 117–118].

Further research is needed to test Reiser's promising hypothesis that the primary process is linked with habit memory and the secondary process with representational memory.

Representational memory plays only an occasional and fleeting role in memorial activity. The other, more action-oriented forms of memorial activity (such as enactive memory, epiosodic memory, and habit memory) are carried out automatically and continuously. The influence of the past silently affects all of our behavior, and only occasionally and briefly are humans capable of remembering the past in *addition* to repeating the past. Even more rare is that priceless product of a successful psychoanalysis—the ability to remember *rather* than to repeat the past.

The Neural Representational System

This critique of classical psychoanalytic concepts of mental representations as unconscious memories and unconscious fantasies stored in "the unconscious" does not dispute either the existence or the importance of what Hadley (1983) calls the *neural representational system*. She proposes the neural representational system as a bridging concept between neurophysiology and psychoanalytic theory. From the disparate theoretical viewpoints expressed in the psychoanalytic literature, Hadley has extracted a common denominator for the meaning of representation as used in psychoanalysis, that is, "the notion that transactions with the external world are registered and stored within the individual, presumably in his brain" (p. 16).

Her excellent overview of neurophysiological studies summarizes evidence that such representation does indeed occur within the human brain and that the activity of these representational systems forms the neurophysiological basis for human perception, memory, affect, action, and thought.

Concluding Remarks

Freud's concept of the unconscious as ideational (memory and fantasy) by analogy with the contents of conscious experience has become not only obsolete but basically unnecessary. His theory of unconscious mental representations as causal agents rests on theories of perception and memory that are contradictory to contemporary observations and concepts in developmental and cognitive psychology. The Freudian concept of unconscious mental representations is linked with untenable ideas of psychic energy and instinctual drives. It places a reductionistic emphasis in psychoanalytic theory and assumes that by interpretation analysts and patients can recover past experience in its original form. Evidence from the psychoanalytic situation cannot support objectively true reconstructions of the actual past (Spence, 1982).

II. THE SECOND STAGE OF COGNITION IN FREUD'S THEORY

As I stated earlier, the second stage in Freud's theory of cognition is one in which drive-activated mental representations are distorted through primary process mechanisms of displacement and condensation. The final derivatives of this distorting process attain consciousness as the manifest content of dreams, symptoms, and other kinds of cognition.

There are two main elements in Freud's concept of the second-stage of cognition: the first is his theory of hallucinatory wish fulfillment, and the second is his concept about how drive-activated unconscious wishes become distorted through primary process mechanisms of displacement and condensation.

Freud's wish-fulfillment hypothesis provides one of the foundations of his theory of cognition as well as for his hypotheses about symptom and dream formation. For Freud, dreams, like neurotic symptoms, were a substitute for the presence of wishes or fantasies in consciousness which remain repressed. He frequently wrote about the "complete identity between the characteristic features of the dream work and those of the psychical activity which issues in psychoneurotic symptoms" (Freud, 1900, p. 597).

The same basic formulation that Freud derived partly from his clinical work with neurotic patients and partly from his theory of cognition, he applied to his hypotheses about the formative stages of dream production and parapraxes. He asserted that only sexual impulses from infancy, which have undergone repression, are capable of being revived and thereby furnish the motive force for the formation of psychoneurotic symptoms of every kind and for dreams (p. 605).

Freud's theory of wish fulfillment was not limited to dreams and symptoms; he held that all behavior stemmed in part from instinctual impulses seeking discharge. His causal explanatory theory about wish fulfillment is an integral part of his theory of cognition and the psychic apparatus.

As Freud noted, "the idea that *some* dreams are to be regarded as wish-fulfillment" (p. 134) had been commonplace in *pre*psychoanalytic psychology. His theory differed from previous theories about dreaming inasmuch as he universalized this idea: "The meaning of *every* dream is the fulfillment of a wish" (p. 134). Freud (1933) was aware that the most disputed point in his theory of dreaming was his assertion that all dreams were the fulfillments of wishes. For Freud (1925b), a repressed wish "is the actual constructor [cause] of the dream: it provides the energy for its production and makes use of the day's residues as material" (p. 44).

In his classic *The Interpretation of Dreams* (Freud, 1900) and elsewhere, Freud's intent was to explain dreams as caused by unconscious wishes. As Moore (1983) has indicated, such a causal explanation depends on two testable hypotheses: first, do dreams always express unconscious wishes that the dreamer's free associations to the dreams will reveal? And, second, do such wishes cause the dream to have the manifest content it has? Most striking about many dreams is that they do not, in any direct or straightforward way, express wishes. Counterexamples include all sorts of unpleasant and disturbing dreams, punishment dreams, examination dreams, nightmares, posttraumatic dreams, and the like.

Freud's (1933) explanation of one class of counterexamples (punishment dreams) has not met with general acceptance. He wrote: "Punishment-dreams, too, are fulfillments of wishes, though not of wishes of the instinctual impulses but of those of the critical, censoring and punishing agency in the mind" (p. 27).

Dream Distortion and the Primary Process

To explain the other types of counterexamples, Freud needed some account of how the unconscious wishes that cause the dream to have the content of wish fulfillment come to be so unrecognizably disguised and distorted. He attempted to explain how dreams are formed and how unconscious wishes and unconscious mental representations come to be distorted by a set of primary process mechanisms (displacement and condensation) he called the *dream-work*.

Freud conceived of the primary process as that process which distorts an originally undistorted mental representation or other kind of undistorted cognition. In his view, the primary process accounts for the unrealistic and distorted contents of dreams and symptoms, and he conceived of defenses as opposing the inherent tendency of drives to seek discharge by the shortest possible path. When this direct path is blocked by defense, a mobile drive cathexis will be *displaced* onto contiguous associated mental contents, and the contents of several representations will become *condensed* in order to find access to consciousness in disguised and distorted ways. This formulation is the core of Freud's hypotheses about defenses and the transformation of latent into manifest content in dreams, symptoms, and other contents.

After conducting a systematic review of Freud's writings on the second stage of cognition, on the dream work, and on symptom formation, I conclude that there is no empirical evidence for Freud's theory of the second stage. Also, I was unable to find any place in Freud's writings where he presented evidence for his hypothesis regarding the second stage in his theory of cognition. My conclusions are in agreement with those of Moore (1983), who presents a convincing argument against Freud's theory of the dream-work, which is essentially the same as the second stage of cognition in Freud's theory. Chaitin (1978) also presents cogent reasons for refuting the Freudian theory of condensation and displacement as causal processes.

Freud's theory of the dream-work and of symptom formation as a process of primary process distortion was his unsuccessful attempt to explain how unconscious wishes and other unconscious elements come to be so unrecognizably distorted in the manifest content of dreams and symptoms. Freud's theory of primary process distortion, then, provided one of the foundations of his theory that dreams and symptoms were caused by unconscious wishes. With the decisive refutation of Freud's theory of primary process distortion by Moore (1983), Chaitin (1978), and me, his theory that dreams and symptoms are caused by unconscious wishes also collapses.

Exceptions to the Wish-Fulfillment Hypothesis

Not until 1920 did Freud admit that there were exceptions to the proposition that all dreams are fulfillments of wishes. He wrote:

> But it is impossible to classify as wish-fulfillments the dreams we have been discussing which occur in traumatic neurosis, or the dreams during psychoanalysis which bring to memory the psychical traumas of childhood [p. 32].

Such dreams arise in obedience to the repetition compulsion, which, in Freud's view, is "something that seems more primitive, more elementary, more instinctual than the pleasure principle which it overrides" (p. 23).

The dreams of patients afflicted by traumatic neuroses (for example, soldiers who endured a severe psychic trauma in combat) regularly end in the generation of anxiety along with the reliving of their traumatic experience. Freud (1920, 1933) admitted that he could not identify any wishful impulse that would be satisfied by the repetitive way traumatized persons need to repeat their distressing experiences.

Later, in the *New Introductory Lectures on Psycho-Analysis,* Freud (1933) again acknowledged some exceptions to the universal claim that all dreams are fulfillments of infantile wishes. While retaining wish fulfillment as the impetus of dreaming, he acknowledged that it frequently miscarries. In such cases, according to Freud, there is a failure in the function of a dream. "Failure" for Freud here means, first, that the patient wakes up and second, "there is a failure in the functioning of his dream work, which would like to transform the memory traces of the traumatic event into the fulfillment of a wish" (p. 29). Despite this failure in the function of the dream, Freud (1933) concluded that "nevertheless . . . a dream is an *attempt* at the fulfillment of a wish" (p. 29). In brief, the motive for dreaming is still held to be a wish, but the ensuing dream is no longer claimed to universally be the wish's fulfillment.

The Primary Process and
Hallucinatory Wish Fulfillment

In this section I present some preliminary remarks about the relationship between hallucinatory wish fulfillment and the primary process in Freud's theory of cognition. (A more comprehensive study of the primary process may be found in Chapter 2.)

In Freud's (1895) view, the primary process is egocentrically organized around the fulfillment of the subject's wishes. His first definition of the primary process was "wishful cathexis to the point of hallucination" (pp. 325–326). The primary process, in Freud's view, proceeds without relation to the external world and it functions on the basis of the primary model of hallucinatory wish fulfillment.

Primary process cognition in Freud's theory is hallucinatory wish fulfillment in that some wish is expressed as actualized, not as requiring actualization. Consciousness, or reflective awareness, is not present in primary process cognition; and therefore an idea expressed in primary process terms, whether wishful, fearful, or whatever, is experienced as real, as actually occurring in the here-and-now. Belief is (uncritically) attached to the products of primary process cognition. The well-accepted fact that *some* dreams do express certain wishes as actualized does not constitute evidence for Freud's theory that *all* dreams represent the fulfillment of wishes. Affectively charged ideas other than wishes can be and often are represented in dreams as actualized. For example, fearful even life-threatening traumatic experiences can be represented in dreams as "actualized" or "fulfilled."

In my view, negatively toned ideas (for example, ideas linked with emotions of fear, shame, or guilt) as well as wishful ones can be represented, dramatized, and illustrated in dreams. Just as wishes are represented in dreams as real, as fulfilled or actualized, so also can ideas linked with unpleasurable affects.

Freud formulated his ideas about the primary process in economic terms of psychic energy and instinctual drives. The idea that the motives for, or the meaning of, thought and behavior depend on an energic force of libidinal or aggressive nature has been repeatedly and tellingly rejected by biologists, neurophysiologists, and physicists (see Rosenblatt and Thickstun, 1970; Peterfreund, 1971; Basch, 1976a, Swanson, 1977).

Freud's theories concerning instinctual drives and hallucinations were attempts to establish a biologically based theory of human motivation. Though research in the cognitive sciences has brought such theories into disrepute, other psychoanalysts have continued to look to biology for the foundations of a psychoanalytic theory of motivation.

In recent years some consensus has grown among psychoanalysts and others in the developmental sciences for the view that inborn affect systems constitute the primary motivation systems (Kernberg, 1976; Izard, 1977). Though the fundamental emotions are subserved by innate neural programs, they can be modified by learning and experience. Lichtenberg (1989) reviews the clinical and experimental evidence suggesting the postulation of several distinct motivational systems and they are: 1) physiological needs; 2) attachment/application; 3) exploration/assertion; 4) sensuality/sexuality; 5) aversion (fight or flight).

Bowlby (1969), Lichtenberg (1989), and developmental psychologists argue for viewing these motivation systems as neurophysiological givens as compelling as sexuality. The primary motives are various needs and dispositions linked with innate neural systems, and they are manifested long before the infant has acquired abilities for symbolization such as that required to represent needs as wishes.

Empirical Evidence for the Wish-Fulfillment Theory

To prove that some entity (A) causes another entity (B), one needs to demonstrate a repeated temporal relationship in which A regularly precedes B. No one, including Freud, has done this for the wish-fulfillment theory of dreams and symptoms or other psychic manifestations. There is no solid empirical evidence for the theory that either conscious or unconscious wishes cause dreams, symptoms, or other psychic phenomena.

In analyzing dreams, analysts or other scientific observers have not found that unconscious wishes are located in a separate time and place from the manifest dream. In fact, what analysts and other investigators of dreams do find is that dreams sometimes, though not always, reflect or express wishes, some of which the dreamer is unaware. Though dream interpretation often helps people understand the wish-fulfillment nature of some contents in their dreams, it does not reveal causes of their dreams.

It is not wishes that are unconscious; it is persons who may be unconscious of some wish expressed in their dream or other communication. Strictly speaking, there is no such thing as an unconscious wish. The latent content of a dream, symptom, or any other communication is some wish or other meaning reflected and represented in the manifest content that the subject does not initially understand.

Dahl (1965) describes some childhood experiences of the deaf and blind Helen Keller as a natural experiment and as evidence in support of Freud's model of the psychic apparatus and of the wish-fulfillment hypothesis of primary process thinking. Keller (1908) wrote:

> When I wanted anything I liked—ice cream, for instance, of which I was very fond—I had a delicious taste on my tongue (which, by the way, I never have now), and in my hand I felt the turning of the freezer. I made the sign, and my mother knew I wanted ice cream. I "thought" and desired in my fingers. If I had made a man, I should certainly have put the brain and soul in his fingertips [p. 115].

Keller's experiences of tasting what she wanted preceded her delayed development of language and other abilities for symbolization. I hypothesize that at the time she could "taste" what she wanted to eat (for example, ice cream), she had not developed the capacity for symbolization and thus had not acquired the ability for representational memory or for wishing. Therefore, Dahl's conclusion that Keller's accounts of her childhood experiences constituted evidence for the wish-fulfillment theory is not valid.

Her own descriptions of this early period contribute to the evidence against the view that she had developed the capacity for representing her needs and desires as wishes. During this early, presymbolic period, she had only what she called a "tactile memory" (p. 115). She described the absence and lack of any mental life or symbols in these words: "My inner life, then, was a blank without past, present, or future, without hope or anticipation, without wonder or joy or faith" (p. 115).

In the sensorimotor phase of development, various needs and desires shape the child's experience long before the child can represent those needs and desires as wishes. Helen Keller's inability to represent her needs as wishes and her highly developed, even extraordinary, sensorimotor capacities are exemplified by her statements "I felt the turning of the freezer," "I 'thought' and desired in my fingers . . ." and so on.

In the foregoing discussion, I distinguished between Keller's desire for ice cream and the wish for ice cream, and I argued that she had not developed the capacity for representing her needs and desires as wishes. Some might argue that a desire is a kind of wish or that it implies a wish. Even if, for the sake of pursuing this line of argument, we asume that a desire implies a wish, Keller's account does not constitute empirical evidence for the wish-fulfillment hypothesis. There is no evidence in her book about her early experiences that her desire for ice cream regularly preceded the delicious taste in her tongue or the feeling in her hand as if the ice cream freezer were turning in her hand. In fact, her descriptions indicate that her experiences of tasting the ice cream, of the sensations in her hand and fingers (which felt to her as if she were turning the freezer), and her desire were *all aspects of the same experience* rather than discrete and separable events. Keller (1908) said as much when she wrote, "I 'thought' and desired in my fingers" (p. 115).

Why Freud Did Not Present Empirical Evidence for His Wish-Fulfillment Theory

Apparently Freud did not see any need to present evidence for his theory of wish fulfillment, for at no time did he do so. Perhaps that is why none of the dreams reported in *The Interpretation of Dreams* is explained by reference to the infantile repressed wishes that Freud consistently throughout his career claimed were necessary causal elements in dream production. Jones (1965) made a thorough search of *The Interpretation of Dreams* and found not one illustration of a dream that met the criterion of a reference to a repressed infantile wish.

A number of investigators argue that Freud's theory of hallucinatory wish fulfillment in dreaming is not an inductive conclusion based on the empirical analysis of many dreams, but rather an inevitable deduction following from his theories of cognition and the psychic apparatus (Pribram and Gill, 1976; Fisher and Greenberg, 1977; Edelson, 1984). According to Fisher and Greenberg (1977), Freud came to the conclusion that dreams are wish fulfilling because he believed that all things that emanate from the unconscious are wishes.

When Freud (1900, p. 507) claimed that nothing but a wish can set our psychic apparatus at work, he was not making, according to Edelson(1984) any empirical claim. Rather, Freud was making a theoretical definition, not a hypothesis which can be shown to be true or false. The link in Freudian theory between unconscious wishes, unconscious memories, and unconscious fantasies and the notions of psychic energy, instincts, or drives does not derive from clinical observations or inferences drawn from clinical observations; rather, it rests on theoretical presuppositions regarding the nature of the organism.

A telling quotation from *The Interpretation of Dreams* pointing in the direction of this conclusion is this:

> Thought is after all nothing but a substitute for a hallucinatory wish; and it is self-evident that dreams must be wish-fulfillments, since *nothing but a wish can set our mental apparatus at work*. Dreams, which fulfill their wishes along the short path of regression, have merely preserved for us in that respect a sample of the psychical apparatus's primary method of working . . . [Freud, 1900, p. 567, italics added].

Eagle (1983) asserts that Freud's concept of psychic determinism

> constitutes a claim that all behavior—including behavior such as dreams, parapraxes, and certain symptoms, which were thought to be meaningless— reflects the operation of instinctual wishes constantly pressing for discharge [p. 340].

In Freud's theory of cognition, drives express themselves as wishes, as the seeking of a lost object that previously provided satisfaction. The pathway for drive discharge always starts with the cathecting of a mental representation, an unconscious memory, or unconscious fantasy—originally in infancy as hallucinatory wish fulfillment and later as a "purposive idea," an image of the wished-for object that guides the search for the object in the external world. For Freud, hallucinatory wish fulfillment was the first stage and primary model for drive discharge from which both thought and action were derived.

Freud's Primary Model of Cognition

The primary model of cognition, formulated by Freud in 1900 (pp. 509–510, 533), was summarized by Rapaport (1960) in this way: "drive reaching threshold intensity → absence of drive object → hallucinatory idea of previous gratification" (p. 25). According to this model, when the drive object is absent, drive action is not possible, and a short cut to hallucinatory gratification takes place. Drive cathexis is displaced to the memory of past gratification and the resultant activation of the memory image results in hallucinatory gratification. Freud's primary model of cognition erroneously assumed the storage of undistorted memory images (i.e., mental representations) as copies of perceptions.

In Freud's (1900) secondary model of cognition, the psychic structures of defenses and controls provide for the delay of discharge—the crucial distinction in Freud's theory between the primary and secondary models of cognition. This delay of discharge prevents the short-cut path to hallucinatory wish fulfillment and thus facilitates detour behavior, with its ordered reality-oriented cognition. The *pleasure* principle (with its tendency to immediate discharge) prevails in the primary model, whereas the *reality principle* (with the tendency to delay discharge) prevails in the secondary model.

In the following passage, Freud (1900) speculated about the developmental origins of cognition as wish-fulfilling hallucinations in the hungry and frustrated infant.

> An essential component of this experience of satisfaction is a particular perception (that of nourishment in our example) the mnemic image of which remains associated thenceforward with the memory trace of the excitation produced by the need. . . . An impulse of this kind is what we call a wish; the reappearance of the perception is the fulfillment of the wish; and the shortest path to the fulfillment of the wish is a path leading directly from the excitation produced by the need to a complete cathexis of the perception. *Nothing prevents us from assuming* that there was a primitive state of the psychical apparatus in which this path was actually traversed, that is, in which wishing ended in hallucinating [pp. 565–566, italics added].

As Basch (1976a) reminds us, today there is something that *"prevents us from assuming* that there was a primitive state of the psychical apparatus in which . . . wishing ended in hallucinating"* (Freud, 1900, p. 566, italics added), namely, the infant observations by Piaget and other developmental psychologists that indicate that infantile memory traces are of action patterns. The perception of differentiated objects and the sensory qualities associated with them, as well as the ability to evoke the images of an absent object, becomes a possibility only much later.

Having demonstrated in *The Interpretation of Dreams* that some dreams could be understood as a wish-fulfilling hallucination, Freud postulated a process of dream-work to explain how "normal thought" became regressively transformed before becoming expressed as the distorted manifest content. Believing that infants' cognition also began with wish-fulfilling hallucination, he hypothesized that the same process produced both dreams and infantile thought, and he called this distorting process the primary process. Freud then went on to assume that his understanding of dream formation and neurotic symptom formation provided him with insight into infantile cognition and its development. Basch (1976a) concludes, "This assumption collapses in the face of the evidence that infants' brains do not work evocatively" (p. 85).

Which Comes First—Action or Cognition?

Freud was mistaken in claiming that cognition (for example, wishes) always precedes overt action. For him, action was the enactment of a wishful fantasy—first in infancy, later in dreaming through wish-fulfilling halluci-nation, and then through goal-directed behavior toward the external world. The last Freud called a necessary detour or "roundabout path" toward the fulfillment of a wish. Within the framework of his theroy of cognition and the psychic apparatus, Freud had to postulate unconscious mental images to account for the goal-directed and organized aspects of actions (Schimek, 1975a).

Freud's notion that cognition always precedes action has been proven false by the studies of Piaget and others, showing that the developmental sequence is the reverse of what Freud postulated. Their studies of cognitive development in infants show that cognition begins with and develops out of action and not imagery as Freud would have it. Piaget and Inhelder (1969) demonstrated that action and its organization are the core of cognition. Their investigations revealed that goal-directed action precedes imaging and that imaging itself is an activity (not a "sensation" or an afferent registration). One of Piaget's most important findings is that the capacity for reconstructive memory (recall based on imaging) does not develop until approximately the 18th month of life.

Basch (1981) writes:

> The assumption in psychoanalysis and psychology generally has been that imaging is an afferent, sensory prelude to thought and motor activity; . . . and that the "image" serves as a nucleus of reality around which thought and motor action can be organized. Piaget's experiments, among others, have demonstrated that imaging is not the necessary foundation for thought, but that, instead, action encoded in sensorimotor schema is that foundation [p. 159].

> The manner in which thought is processed by the brain is something we do not fully understand, but we do know that it is not in the form of sensory images. Imaging is an activity, not a sensory given, and its appearance marks the end of infancy, not its beginning [p. 165].

Developmental Studies

Contemporary investigations of cognitive development in infants indicate major flaws in Freud's primary model of cognition. As I indicated in Part I of this chapter, his model erroneously took for granted that the infant has the capacity for the veridical perception and memory of an object differentiated from the global experience of satisfaction (Holt, 1967, 1976; Wolff, 1967; Schimek, 1975a; Basch, 1976a).

Because the infant's early experience of satisfaction is global and undifferentiated, it cannot involve (as Freud wrongly assumed) the perception of a specific object differentiated from other objects and from the self. Therefore, an infant's impulse cannot be the search for a discrete object, but merely the desire to reexperience a diffuse, pleasurable, sensorimotor-affective experience (Schimek, 1975a). According to Piaget (1962) and other developmental psychologists, the hallucinatory revival of an absent object cannot occur in infancy because the necessary memory mechanisms do not develop until the second year of life.

From direct observations and experiments with infants, Piaget (1962) inferred a nonrepresentational stage of cognition that presupposed no a priori psychic image of the object when the object is absent, and he conceived of an epigenetic sequence from sensorimotor action patterns to imagery, symbolic thought, and socialized language. This developmental sequence stands in sharp contrast to the psychoanalytic conception of an innate capacity to form hallucinatory images and of an innate ability for undistorted perception and memory.

In the Freudian primary model of cognition, hallucinatory wish fulfill-ment is the reactivation of sensory images that occurs when action on objects is not possible. In contrast, no such distinction exists between action and ideation in Piaget's theory. In his theory, the earliest forms of cognition *are* sensorimotor actions; thus cognition and action are identical during the early phases of development.

Differences in the two theories are related to the fact that Freudian theory conceptualizes the fixation of experience in isolated traces, whereas sensorimotor theory conceives of this process in terms of schemata, wherein the sensory event and the motor reaction constitute a single integral unit.

The weight of Piaget's (1962) and others' observations, along with that of experimental evidence, points to the conclusion that there is no representation of absent objects before about 18 months. The Piagetian sensorimotor conception states that global action patterns gradually give rise to representational thought and that thought is an internalized derivative of action rather than a substitute for it.

Freud's Theory of Unconscious Wishes and Dreaming

Other tests and evaluations of Freud's theory of hallucinatory wish fulfillment come from investigations of dreaming. Freud (1900, 1901) claimed that the motive force and cause for dreams were unconscious wishes, and he implied that without the wish there is no dream.

Recent research on dreams reveals that humans dream about every 90 minutes, that all mammals except monotremes dream, and that dreaming is part of a complex neurophysiological system (the D-State) not yet fully understood (Winson, 1985). The regularity of dreaming cycles suggests a biological rather than a psychological cause of dreaming. In order to hold to Freud's wish-fulfillment theory of dreams, one would have to propose that the dreamer's infantile wishes somehow become activated every 90 minutes and, as Eagle (1983) put it, "that animals have unacceptable wishes that await the weakening of the censor to appear in dreams" (p. 336).

What about the *content* of dreams? No one disputes the fact that the content of dreams reflects wishes, desires, and fears. However, as Eagle (1983) cogently argues, that dream contents are personally meaningful and made up of our most pressing preoccupations, desires, and wishes

> does not mean that we *wanted* to dream these contents or that these contents were dreamt in order to fulfill certain desires and wishes. It could mean simply that pressing preoccupations and desires continue to influence thought . . . in the dream state. . . . Dreams are not the carrying out of intentions and aims; rather, they are happenings that *reflect* intentions and aims . . . [pp. 336–337].

There is a consensus among dream researchers and others for rejecting Freud's hypothesis of unconscious wishes as motives that cause dreams (Jones, 1965, 1970; Basch, 1976a; Eagle, 1983; Moore, 1984). What is critical in a customary motivational explanation is whether the behavior was intended to achieve a goal or aim set up by the agent (Eagle, 1983). This is not true for dreaming, because the dreamer does not intend to dream such and such and then proceed to dream it. There is neither the reality of personal freedom of choice or the sense of freedom during dreaming. Personal agency does not exist while one is sleeping or dreaming, and the dreamer is not able to control, choose, or intend what he is going to dream about.

Dreams are not *caused* by a person's wishes or other motives. Dreams are not intended actions; rather they are happenings that reflect intentions, wishes, and fears (Eagle, 1983; Moore, 1983).

The philosopher Moore (1983) wrote:

> Freud did not actively bring about the dream of Irma's injection. . . . His dream happened to him in the same way that the death of his father happened to him—in neither case did he bring about the occurrence (which is not to deny, in either case, that he might have had some wishes related to each event). Dreaming is like nondirectional thinking—sudden inspirations,

revelations, or images and the like—in that it just happens without the will or agency of the subject [pp. 49–50].

A similar idea was expressed by Nietzsche (1886) in this way: "a thought comes when 'it' wishes, and not when 'I' wish. . . . *It* thinks; but that this 'it' is precisely the famous old ego is, to put it mildly, only a supposition" (p. 17).

Eagle (1983) holds that psychoanalysts beginning with Freud have overextended motivational explanation far beyond its legitimate boundaries. Eagle (1983) and Rubenstein (1980) argue cogently for the view that certain behaviors, such as dreams, are best explained in terms of underlying conditions (for example, neurophysiological, hormonal, situational, and social factors) rather than in terms of motives and wishes.

What follows is another argument based on logical evidence against the wish-fulfillment hypothesis. If we consider a wish to be a thought (and what else could it be?), then Freud's wish-fulfillment theory of cognition is illogical because the theory entails an infinite regress. The hypothesis that thoughts are caused by unconscious wishes is equivalent to saying that thoughts cause thoughts. An infinite regress is involved because each thought is caused by a preceding thought, which, in turn, is caused by another thought, and so on ad infinitum.

Clinical and Experimental Studies of Hallucinations

Earlier we noted that the experimental research on dreaming has shown that the *occurrence* of dreaming is determined by biological not motivational causes. Clinical and experimental studies on other kinds of hallucinations point to the same conclusion. The classical psychoanalytic hypothesis that unconscious wishes are a necessary causal factor in hallucinatory phenomena is not borne out by experimental and clinical studies of various kinds of hallucinations.

The hypothesis that dreams and other types of hallucinations are wish fulfillments is based in part on inferences from the symbolic content of dreams and hallucinations. Though some hallucinations, such as the visual and auditory hallucinations of schizophrenics, do have symbolic content, other types do not (Asaad, 1990). The absence of symbolic content in such instances makes it impossible to infer the presence of either conscious or unconscious wishes to account for the hallucinatory content.

Malitz, Wilkens, and Esecover (1962) found that most hallucinations produced by drugs (such as LSD-25) did not have any primary symbolic content or intrinsic psychologic meaning. Therefore, the hallucinations they studied did not express or reflect wishes of any sort. The hallucinations experienced by their subjects were those of abstract forms, geometric forms, bizarre forms, colors, and the like. There are other types of hallucinations, such as some of those occurring in toxic and organic states, that do not contain symbolic content and therefore cannot be said to fulfill, express, or reflect either conscious or unconscious wishes.

Penfield and Rasmussen (1950) found that stimulation of the occipital lobe evoked hallucinations of color and abstract forms. Their patients reported flickering lights, stars, wheels, discs, whirling balls, and dancing lights, all in color. There was no evidence that either conscious or unconscious wishes were expressed or reflected in the content of the hallucinations.

Clinical investigations of patients who develop phantom symptoms following the surgical removal of a body part conclude that neither conscious nor unconscious wishes play any causal significance in bringing about the phantom phenomena (Kolb, 1951, 1954; Dorpat, 1971). Researchers generally agree that phantom phenomena are hallucinations, albeit different from the hallucinations of psychotic patients—patients experiencing phantom phenomena have not lost the reality-testing function regarding their phantom experiences.

In one investigation of patients with phantom symptoms, I made the common error of assuming (as Freud did) that all hallucinations represented wishes (Dorpat, 1971). However, repeated interviews with posthysterectomy patients who had hallucinatory uterine contraction sensations revealed that the hallucinatory sensations did not have any symbolic content or express any intrinsic psychological meaning. Therefore, they could not express or represent either conscious or unconscious wishes of any sort.

Clinical reports by Kolb (1951, 1954), Dorpat (1971), and others indicate that phantom phenomena are not ordinarily a psychopathological response. Nearly all patients (98% in one series) develop painless phantoms following amputation of an extremity, and Kolb correctly concluded that the phantom limb is the expected and normal response to the loss of a limb.

Clinical as well as experimental evidence supports the hypothesis that the interruption of sensory input to the central nervous system is a necessary condition for the formation of phantom phenomena (Adrian, 1934; Melzack and Loeser, 1978). A previous paper sketched the broad outlines of a biological theory of hallucinatory phenomena in which it was postulated that the organism has innate needs for sensory stimulation (Dorpat, 1971). When this need is not fulfilled, as, for example, when some afferent nerve supply to the central nervous system is blocked, the central nervous system activates sensory centers and the experiential products of this stimulation are hallucinations. This biological theory of hallucinations is concordant with clinical and experimental studies of hallucinations, phantom phenomena, and effects of sensory deprivation (West, 1962; Asaad, 1990).

Can the Psychoanalytic Method Be Used to Test Freud's Theory of Cognition?

Freud believed that the conclusions he had reached in Chapter VII of *The Interpretation of Dreams* and in his other writings on cognition and the psychic apparatus came directly from his clinical observations. Actually, he imposed on his clinical observations hypotheses he had obtained from the then current, but in many ways erroneous, theories of perception and cognition (Schimek, 1975a; Basch, 1976a; Moore, 1983).

Freud was mistaken in believing he could develop a valid explanatory theory about cognitive processes such as the dream-work on the basis of clinical observations and inferences, because it is incorrect in principle to derive a theory of cognition (perception, learning, conception, and the like) from a clinical method limited to investigating the significance of meaning in thought and deed (Basch, 1976a).

Freud erred in thinking he could use the results of his efforts to interpret dreams and symptoms as evidence for his theories of dream and symptom formation. He argued that the process of dream and symptom interpretation that occurs in psychoanalysis is the reverse of what occurs in dream and symptom formation. In dream analysis, for example, an analyst uses the patient's free associations and other data to reconstruct the latent content of the dream, and Freud mistakenly conceptualized the latent content as preceding and causing the manifest content. The latent content of a dream or symptom is not a discrete and separable entity that occurs before the latent content and causes it. The latent content is some meaning of a dream or symptom the person does not initially understand.

Consider for a moment Freud's arguments in Chapter VII of *The Interpretation of Dreams* for the processes he called the dream-work. There he inferred from certain characteristics of the manifest dream the existence of processes taking place during the dream with these characteristics as their corresponding effects. Freud incorrectly assumed that the phenomena (in this instance certain characteristics of dreams) justified the causal explanatory theory brought forward to explain it. This is a circular argument and not a proof. Rubenstein (1976b, 1980) employed similar arguments to support his claim that the occurrence of such processes as unconscious wishes cannot be confirmed clinically.

Philosophers of science from Democritus onward have insisted that there is no direct logical connection between observations and their postulated causes. It is, of course, scientifically permissible for Freud to have formed hypotheses about the causal processes responsible for dreams and other types of cognition, but these processes must be tested independently of the phenomena.

CONCLUDING REMARKS

In summary, the experimental, clinical, and developmental studies I have reviewed strongly support the conclusion that there is little evidence favoring and much evidence opposing Freud's theories about the first and second stages of cognition.

Studies of hallucinations in waking life arrive at conclusions similar to those reached by dream researchers. The occurrence of hallucinations is determined by biological elements in the central nervous system and not by wishes. The notion of unconscious wishes retains some usefulness as a maxim for understanding and interpreting the content and meaning of some types of hallucinations. A limitation of the wish-fulfillment interpretive maxim is that the dreams of infants and animals, as well as some other types of hallucinations discussed in this chapter, do not contain symbolic content or intrinsic psychological meaning and therefore do not represent or reflect wishes of any kind.

Just as wishes can be represented as fulfilled, in dreams and other kinds of cognitions, so also can fears and other unpleasant affects be represented as actualized in primary process cognitions.

Freud's causal explanatory theories about displacement, condensation, the dream-work, and primary process as a distorting process as well as other elements in his theory of cognition, do not represent inferences *from* psychoanalytic data, but rather, speculations *about* psychoanalytic data. The various constituents of Freud's theory of cognition are, for the most part, a set of untested hypotheses incompatible with today's theories and knowledge about the workings of the mind.

The conclusions reached here about Freud's theory of cognition have profound and far-reaching implications for psychoanalytic concepts about what happens in psychoanalytic treatment. In Sections II and III, my coauthor and I show how psychoanalytic technique has been adversely affected by obsolete ideas in Freud's theory of the workings of the mind and how a revised theory of the mind can lead to more therapeutically effective technique.

CHAPTER 2

The Primary Process
Revisited

Though the demise of Freud's theory of cognition demands major changes in psychoanalytic theory and practice, I believe there is abundant clinical and research evidence for Freud's idea that a special system of thought operates in dreams, symptoms, and disordered thought generally, as well as in the higher reaches of play and creativity. Investigations by Holt (1967, 1976), Fast (1985), and others support the proposition that Freud's descriptions of the empirical varieties of primary process products do describe something unitary. His clinical observations and intuition enabled Freud to discern in his variegated observations a single conceptual entity, which I have called the *primary process system*.

The discovery of two fundamentally different kinds of cognition, the primary process and the secondary process, constitutes one of the most monumental of Freud's contributions. My aim is to provide, through a critical review and discussion of the literature of psychoanalysis and the cognate disciplines, a modified theory of the primary process; and I discuss it from several perspectives, including object relations, development, communication, perception, and neuropsychology. Freud's theory of the primary process was derived from his clinical observations of dreams and psychiatric symptoms and from his concepts about such topics as psychic development, cognition, and perception. Psychoanalytic studies, as well as the findings and theories of developmental psychology, cognitive psychology, and neurophysiology that have been carried out since Freud's time, necessitate some important revisions in the psychoanalytic theory of primary process.

BASIC CONCEPTS AND DEFINITIONS

The term primary process has two somewhat different meanings. As an explanatory concept, it plays a central role in Freud's metapsychology and his theory of how dreams, symptoms, and other kinds of cognitions become distorted. With the collapse of that conceptual edifice as discussed in Chapter 1, the corresponding meaning of primary process as a distorting process has lost its utility. As a descriptive concept, the idea of a primary process system retains promise and usefulness.

A large proportion of our mental functioning is dominated by the primary process system. Not only are dreams largely under the sway of this mode of thought, but also the processing and expression of nonverbal and affective communication, most types of creativity, and nearly all emotional and psychologically founded symptoms, and so on. Many empirical studies support the assumption that the primary process is centrally involved in creative activities (see Suler, 1980).

In Freud's writings the concepts of the id, the primary process, unconscious fantasy, instinctual drives, and the pleasure principle are correlative—that is, as the concepts define each other. He viewed the primary process as taking place in the id, which, in contrast to the ego system, is cut off from perception of and relations with the external world. For Freud, the primary process was regulated by the pleasure principle and it was concerned with instinctual (sexual and aggressive) drives.

Freud (1940a) wrote:

> We have found that processes in the unconscious or in the id obey different laws from those in the preconscious ego. We name these laws in their totality the *primary process,* in contrast to the *secondary process,* which governs the course of events in the preconscious, in the ego [p. 164].

Investigations both within and outside psychoanalysis demonstrate that some of Freud's concepts about the nature and functioning of the primary process are mistaken. The primary process is not restricted to the id, conceived of as a system or locale isolated from interactions with the environment. A major thesis of this chapter is that the primary process system is immediately and directly involved with perception and with an *individual's interactions with the human and nonhuman object world.* The primary process unconsciously analyzes the meaning of these interactions and represents those meanings in such products of primary process activity as affects, narratives, metaphors, images, and nonverbal communications. Until recently, many analysts followed Freud in viewing the primary process as the archaic residue of the infantile narcissistic period, unmodified by learning, as an activity in which cognition is without relation to reality. This obsolete view has been challenged and discredited by the studies of Holt (1967, 1976), Noy (1969, 1979), Fosshage (1983), Fast (1985), Langs (1986a), and others. The primary process is not exclusively regulated by the pleasure principle; and, in addition to sexual and aggressive impulses, primary process functioning is linked with many other functions, motives, and needs.

The primary and secondary processes may be conceptualized as two parallel and relatively independent systems for the reception, analysis, processing, and storing of information (Rogers, 1980). In normal awake adults, these two modes are integrated, and all psychic functions (such as cognition, perception, memory, communication, and so forth) have both primary and secondary process elements, although one or the other may predominate. Recent investigations, which will be discussed later, reveal that the primary process system (in right-handed persons) is linked with the right cerebral hemisphere and that the secondary process is mediated by the left cerebral hemisphere.

The idea of relatively autonomous and parallel pathways for the processing of information is a new one in neuropsychology and neurophysiology, and one that has gained considerable experimental support in recent years. Gazzaniga (1985) convincingly argues that the human brain has a modular-type organization; by modularity he means that the brain is organized into relatively independent functioning units that work in *parallel*. The human brain is not organized as a unitary, monolithic system, with each part linked to every other in some kind of hierarchical manner. Instead of information's being exclusively processed serially, it now is clear from split-brain (commissurotomy) and experimental studies that there is much parallel processing of information.

Our knowledge about the primary process derives primarily from clinical and experimental investigations of three situations in which the primary and secondary process systems are not integrated. They include 1) dreaming; 2) "split-brain" patients who have had a cerebral commissurotomy; and 3) psychopathology, that is, disordered cognition and symptoms.

In discovering the primary process, Freud revealed not only a new language, but also its grammar and method of translation. According to Basch (1981), Freud did not recognize his find for what it was—a "language" or a "code"—but he erroneously assumed it was an infantile manner of thinking wherein primitive images were combined with wish-fulfilling intent without regard for external reality. Freud judged his discovery of primary process by the yardstick of syllogistic reasoning and found it distorted and illogical. Primary process cognition is neither illogical nor disorganized, although it has a different kind of organization and mode of functioning from that of secondary process thinking.

The primary process functions outside of consciousness, though some products of the primary process (such as imagery and affects) may be consciously experienced. Primary process manifestations are most readily observed in dreams, symptoms, and the disordered cognitions of patients with thought disorders. Secondary process is more familiar to us through our everyday introspection, and it predominates in the conscious, rational thinking of mature adults.

The primary process mode of cognition is reflected in people's emotional and intuitive responses and the secondary process system in logical reasoning and linguistic abilities. Primary process thinking is characterized by the absence of a sense of time (timelessness), absence of negatives, representation of parts for the whole, tolerance for the existence of mutually contradictory ideas, references by allusion, and predominance of the visual over verbal mode for representing ideas. In contrast, secondary process thought follows the laws of syntax and logic. It is deliberate, controlled, and predominantly verbal in representing ideas. Adult behavior in which the primary and secondary processes are integrated is characterized by modulated affects, high frustration tolerance, the ability to delay gratification, and overt actions that are intentional and planned to conform with reality demands.

UNCONSCIOUS MEANING ANALYSES AND PRIMARY PROCESS

As a replacement for out-of-date notions of unconscious memory and unconscious fantasy, I propose that an important function of the primary process system is that of unconscious meaning analysis. A major function of the primary-process system is to unconsciously and automatically make rapid evaluations of current events involving self and other.

Primary process products, such as the metaphors, images, and nonverbal communication that appear in dreams, symptoms, and speech are not, as Freud and some other analysts believed, derived from unconscious memories and fantasies. Rather, they are the end products of a process of unconscious meaning analysis of events in which the individual is unconsciously evaluating, appraising, and representing his current interactions with others. The function of both unconscious and conscious meaning analyses stems from the individual's need to ascribe meaning to his relations with the external world and to adapt to it. My coauthor's contributions in Section II present a systematic theory about meaning analysis and the applications of this new theory to psychoanalytic technique as well as to the understanding of psychopathology.

The conclusions reached through meaning analyses play a central role in the following psychic functions: the activation and deactivation of certain schemas, the arousal of specific affects, the initiation of defensive and adaptation activities designed to cope with the event being analyzed, and other psychic activities and overt motoric actions. The subject may or, more often, may not be aware of the content and conclusions of this unconscious process of meaning analysis.

In the past, the products of unconscious meaning analysis were called primary process derivatives because it was erroneously believed that they were derived, through a process of primary process distortion, from unconscious memories and unconscious fantasies. I recommend dropping the term primary process derivatives because, as I indicate in Chapters 1, 3, and 4, there are compelling arguments for rejecting notions about unconscious fantasy and unconscious memory. Another reason for dropping the term primary process derivatives is that (as I explained in Chapter 1) it implies a mental process of primary process distortion that does not exist. As noted in Chapter 1, unconscious fantasies and unconscious memories, according to Freud's discredited theory of cognition, are subject to the primary process distorting mechanisms of displacement and condensation before they attain consciousness as the manifest content.

The mental operations in unconscious meaning analysis involve learned skills, which through practice become automatic and unconscious. In earlier models of information processing, the analysis of meaning was excluded from the domain of unconscious cognitive activity. However, recent research shows that complex processes of meaning analysis, once they have become automatized, can take place outside of introspective awareness. According to Kihlstrom (1987) and other cognitive psychologists, we now know that it is possible to perform meaning analysis on information that is not accessible to conscious awareness by means of automatized, unconscious procedural knowledge.

Experiments on unconscious cognitive activity and automaticity reveal that a great deal of complex cognitive activity can go on outside of conscious awareness. Some cognitive skills such as learning to play a musical instrument or swing a golf club are acquired through experience. When one is learning a skill, the process is initially accessible to consciousness—as indicated, for example, by the novice golf player's overt or covert rehearsal of the body movements involved in swinging his golf club. Later, through practice and learning, the whole process becomes automatic and unconscious.

The unconscious nature of learned skills is shown in the inability of typists, athletes, and musicians to describe their skills to others and by the fact that conscious attention to them interferes with their smooth performance. Learned skills become automatic through practice and their operations are thereby rendered unconscious (Kihlstrom, 1987).

Unconscious procedural knowledge has been described as automatic as opposed to controlled or effortful. Automatic psychic processes are so named because they are triggered by the presentation of stimuli, regardless of any intention on the part of the subject. Cognitive processes that are carried out automatically are performed outside the subject's focal attention. Automatic psychic processes are unconscious, in that the individual has no introspective access to their principles of operation—or even realizes that these processes are in operation at all (Kihlstrom, 1987).

Kihlstrom has summarized the conclusions of recent studies on unconscious meaning analysis performed by cognitive psychologists in this way:

> Experiments on automaticity are important because they indicate that a great deal of complex cognitive activity can go on outside of conscious awareness, provided that the skills, rules, and strategies required by the task have become automatized. . . . Now it is clear that there are circumstances under which the meanings and implications of events can be unconsciously analyzed . . . people may reach conclusions about events—for example, their emotional balance . . . and act on these judgments without being able to articulate the reasoning by which they were reached. This does not mean that cognitive activity is not involved in such judgments and inferences; it only means that the cognitive activity, being automatized, is unconscious in the strict sense of that term and thus unavailable to introspective awareness [p. 1447].

The fundamental change proposed here in the psychoanalytic theory of the primary process has profound implications for theories of the psychoanalytic process and technique, as taken up again in later chapters. The revised theory of the primary process, and especially of the concept of unconscious meaning analysis, fosters a new and richer way of listening, understanding, and interpreting patients' communications. Instead of mistakenly inferring the activity of unconscious memory and unconscious fantasy, mental health professionals should attend to and interpret their patients' unconscious meaning analyses of their interpersonal relations and most notably their here-and-now interactions with their therapists.

Traditional psychoanalytic concepts about unconscious memory and unconscious fantasy imply unconscious psychic contents and processes that are separate from the subject's interactions with others. As a consequence of this view, many therapists fail to understand or interpret the importance of their own contributions both to their patients' experience and to their patients' unconscious psychic functioning. Few mental health professionals understand that their patients are *unconsciously* and continuously evaluating and representing in primary process cognition their interactions with their therapists. (For a similar perspective on the significance of the therapist's interventions upon the patient's experience, see Gill, 1983, 1984, and Hoffman, 1983.)

The following vignette illustrates the clinical significance of the patient's unconscious meaning analysis of analyst–analysand interactions.

A CLINICAL VIGNETTE

In clinical practice the use of unconscious memory and unconscious fantasy concepts often excludes interactional contributions to the patient's communications. For example, in his record of a patient's analysis and his discussions and commentaries on the analytic process, Dewald (1972) wrote about primary process cognitions as deriving from unconscious fantasies of wholly endogenous origin.

The patient was a young married woman seen in psychoanalysis for her neurosis. In the first four exchanges of an hour early in her analysis, the patient described the differences between her experiences with her former therapist, Mr. Harris, and with Dr. Dewald.

> *Patient:* "I wanted him [Mr. Harris] to like me, so I could act cute and feminine and coy and nice. I suppressed all of my hostility towards him. But I know that you'll see through me and so it is senseless. You will know what I'm doing so I can't hide."
>
> *Analyst:* "What comes to your mind about wanting to hide here?"
>
> *Patient:* "I could make Mr. Harris like me but I can't do that with you. So I'm not even going to try. I know that I can't. I feel very hostile toward you, and I don't understand what I'm supposed to do."
>
> *Analyst:* "I think that really you do understand what you're supposed to do here in analysis but you can't believe it. *Patient:* (one-minute pause) "I don't really understand this. Somehow we don't seem to be discussing things and it seems as if I'm doing all of the talking." (two-minute pause) "I think of Mr. Harris and the way he used to support me. But somehow we never really talked about me." (one-minute pause) "I've felt anxious all day. [Elaborates symptoms] I don't know why."
>
> *Analyst:* "Let's see what your associations are without jumping to any conclusions about it."
>
> *Patient:* "I feel as if someone is trying to overpower me. As if they are trying to . . ."
>
> *Analyst:* "What is it that you're afraid to say?"
>
> *Patient:* "As if you are trying to sit on me and squash me."
>
> *Analyst:* "I think this is one of your fears about starting analysis. It's as if you fantasize that you're going to end up in my power and that you're going to be helpless."

Immediately after the patient said that she did not understand what she was supposed to do, the analyst countered with a confrontation that contradicted her opinion. He said, "I think that you really do understand what you're supposed to do here in analysis, but you can't believe it." She replied, "I don't really understand this" and then went on to describe having symptoms before the analytic hour.

One of the most striking and repetitive aspects of Dewald's interventions in this and other analytic hours was their directive and controlling quality. In this session, for example, he asked 14 questions that had a directive quality. At no time in this session did he acknowledge to the patient that her complaints about him might have had some measure of validity. By his repetitive questions, he directed her to continue talking, while at the same time, he either implicitly or explicitly negated the interpersonal significance of what she was saying about his repeated directiveness.

In another effort to assert his control over the patient and the analytic situation, the analyst chided the patient with, "Let's see what your associations are without jumping to any conclusions about it." The patient responded by saying, "I feel as if someone is trying to overpower me. As if they are trying to . . ." She paused, and, later in response to Dewald's question ("What is it you're afraid to say?"), she replied, "As if you are trying to sit on me and squash me." Then the analyst made a transference interpretation of the patient's fear of being squashed, "I think this is one of your fears about starting analysis. It's as if you fantasize that you're going to end up in my power and that you're gong to be helpless."

The patient's image of the analyst sitting on her and squashing her was a concrete metaphor that vividly encapsulated actual aspects of her interactions with the analyst. This image was derived from her unconscious meaning analyses of how the analyst was relating to her and her affective responses to his directive actions. By his interpretation of her imagery as a transference fantasy, Dewald denied that her image of being "squashed" by him had anything to do with their ongoing transactions. The analyst's interpretations in this and many other hours repudiated or ignored the patient's conscious and unconscious communications about how she was being controlled by the analyst's directive interactions with her.

Both Dewald's interpretations in this session and his written discussion about this session ascribe her mounting anxieties about being controlled by the analyst entirely to the emergence of transference fantasies and feelings. It is clear from the transcript of this session and from his discussions of individual analytic hours that he uses such terms as "transference" and "unconscious fantasy" to denote unrealistic behaviors wholly formed from intrapsychic sources and inappropriate to the present situation.

My point about Dewald's use of the transference concept and his transference interpretation is not that he was entirely incorrect in describing the patient's fear of being squashed as a transference fear. There is abundant evidence in Dewald's book that her fears of being overpowered and squashed did stem in part from her childhood relationships with her father and others. My objection to Dewald's transference interpretation is that he ignored the actualities of his interactions with the patient. Her disturbing feelings and ideas linked with the "being squashed" metaphor derived partly from her unconscious meaning analyses of the analyst's controlling and directive interventions and partly from her past experience.

Human experience is shaped by both the past and the present. A person's unconscious meaning analyses of present events are formed out of current interactions as well as from schemata embodying past experience. (The interactional or social perspective on transference presented here is taken up again in Chapter 10.)

By describing and interpreting the patient's communications to the analyst almost exclusively in intrapsychic terms of unconscious fantasy and transference, Dewald failed to account for the here-and-now effects of his interventions upon the patient's unconscious mental functioning as well as on her conscious experience. His exclusive preoccupation with the patient's intrapsychic functioning and her alleged unconscious fantasies prevented him from understanding the products of her primary process functioning and from interpreting what effect his interventions had on her.

EVENT THEORY AND PRIMARY PROCESS

In her successful effort to integrate Piagetian and Freudian concepts, Fast (1985) uses event theory as a framework for formulating theories about the primary process and object relations. Event theory proposes a basic unit of experience and mental structure that represents the *self in interaction with the nonself*. Events are the fundamental units of primary process cognition and are represented in the reflexes present at birth. Each event is an affectively motivated unit of experience. The primary process unconsciously analyzes the meaning of events, especially interactions between self and other human objects, and then it represents the meanings of those events in the products of primary process activity.

In Piaget's (1962) model, the basic units of experience in infancy are actions (e.g., nursing, grasping, gazing) which are registered cognitively as events. Each event can be seen, objectively, to be composed of an infant-in-interaction-with-the-environment unit. The infant's subjective experience is not differentiated into subject, action, and object. Cognition and motor enactment, subject and object are all initially undifferentiated aspects of the same global action event. In infancy, events are enactments in the present of (as yet implicit) purposes, motives, or aims. They are unconscious in the sense of not being subject to reflection. Examples of such events include: infant-grasps-finger of parent, infant-nurses-at breast, infant-focuses-visually-on mother's face. In the earliest psychic organization, similar events are organized together in sensorimotor schemas, which

Piaget demonstrated to be the innate and biological basis of all further psychic development.

Event theory is centered in the idea that development occurs by the differentiation of self and nonself, and it provides an object-relational model for the development of psychic structure. The basic content of primary process cognition is not a self-representation or an identification, but a representation of a specific relationship or interaction between self and the human and nonhuman environment.

The basic unit of secondary process thought is not the event but such characteristics as weight or length, which are abstracted from events. Logical or categorical cognition (the secondary process mode of cognition) far more often deals in symbols, such as words and numbers, rather than action images. The focus of secondary process cognition is not the particular; instead, the particular is represented in the light of the general. The secondary process mode is adapted for communication through reasoned discourse rather than by representation of the evocative event (Fast, 1985).

ARCHAIC AND SOPHISTICATED
PRIMARY PROCESS COGNITION

Investigations of primary process since the time of Freud have increasingly accepted the idea that the primary processes may occur on what Fast (1985) calls a "sophisticated" (mature) level and an "archaic" (primitive) level (Schur, 1966; Holt, 1967, 1976; Noy, 1969, 1979). As Fosshage (1983) argues, not all primary process functioning is primitive or regressed. He defines primary process as a mode of mental functioning that uses visual and other sensory images with intense affective colorations for serving an overall integrative function. The imagistic primary process thought that Kris (1952) describes as accompanying even the highest levels of scientific and artistic creativity can be viewed as a mature, rather than primitive, form of primary process cognition. Archaic and sophisticated primary process cognitions represent the same cognitive mode in which the basic unit is a self-in-interaction-with-the environment event. Both involve experience in the particular and predominantly in imagery. Archaic and sophisticated primary process cognition may be seen in dichotomous terms; any primary process cognition, however, may be examined for the degree of its maturity along the entire developmental continuum.

Fast's (1985) classification of different developmental categories of primary-process cognitions is supported by Holt's (1976) studies. Holt distinguishes between Level 1 primary process cognition, which includes primitive and pathological cognitions and a more socialized and normal Level 2 primary process activity.

Myths, poetry, and stories contain recognizable forms of both archaic and sophisticated primary process cognition. Fairy stories and other simple fictions constitute for children an education into extended forms of primary-process activity and thus provide for the cultural transmission of ways to use higher forms of primary process cognition. Myths have been described as collective dreams.

The distinction between archaic and sophisticated primary process cognition is important both clinically and theoretically, for it is at the heart of the major distincion between adaptive and maladaptive forms of thinking: primary process thinking used "in the service of the ego"— creatively, humorously, playfully—against primary process products as indicants of psychopathology. Because psychoanalytic notions of the primary process as archaic have historically had their base in observations of primary process manifestations occurring in psychopathology, it is high time to emphasize and to delineate the normal functions of this vital system of cognition and affect.

Fast (1985) writes that sophisticated primary process cognition "is a cognitive mode occurring as experience in the present, appropriately placed, however, in such reality frames as memory, anticipation, hypotheses, or fantasy" (p. 47). Sophisticated primary process cognition is centrally a cognition of images, primarily visual but also kinesthetic and auditory. These images occur without confusion between thought and its referents. In contrast to archaic primary process cognition, sophisticated primary process cognition recognizes what is objectively independent of the self. In cultural experience, sophisticated primary process cognition can be employed in those pursuits whose aim is the expression of an idea evocatively rather than analytically, in images of particular events, as in poetry, drama, or fiction. Sophisticated primary process cognition and the secondary process mode of cognition are the two normal cognitive modes of adulthood. Both modes occur on a developmentally mature level and no a priori judgment is possible as to the superiority of one over the other (Fast, 1985).

Contrary to conventional psychoanalytic thinking, archaic primary process cognition is not divorced from reality. Rather, it fails to represent particular aspects of reality as external to the self and undifferentiated from the self. Archaic primary process activity, as observed in psychiatric symptoms and disordered cognition, represents event-centered cognitions, which, because of defense, psychic trauma, or both, have not participated in the developmental processes that result in sophisticated primary process cognition. Archaic primary process cognitions are those the individual has found intolerable to modify in accord with immutable reality (Fast, 1985).

When the developing child is unable to modify reality to accord with his idea (e.g., wishes) and also finds it intolerable to modify the idea to accord with reality, the idea is excluded from the cognitive organization of the self-schema. Such cognitions (or complexes of cognitions) are excluded by defense and constitute archaic primary process cognition. These primitive cognitive activities have the characteristics Freud described for primary process activity in psychopathology. They unconsciously provide substitute gratifications; they are not subject to learning, and they are repeated with little or no change in their basic structure (repetition compulsion).

PRIMARY PROCESS DEVELOPMENT

In Freud's view, the primary process is the original state of mind in infancy and the secondary process, which later develops from it, has an inhibitory and regulating control over the more primitive primary process. In recent years this concept of a hierarchical relationship between the two systems has been supplanted by a concept of the two systems as functioning both in childhood and adult in a parallel fashion. Most authorities now acknowledge that primary and secondary processes exist from the beginning of life and continue to develop throughout the life span (Rapaport, 1967, Noy, 1969; Klein, 1976; Palombo, 1978).

Investigators such as Basch (1981) and Holt (1967), who believe that primary process first develops in the preoperational phase, view primary process as a code or a system of symbols. Their conception of this system thus excludes the contributions made by the sensorimotor stage to the development of the primary process system, especially to those important abilities for regulating affect and for the interpersonal perception of affect in infancy. The onset of the preoperational phase at about 18 months and the emergence of capacities for understanding symbols mark a decisive advance in the development of both the primary and the secondary process systems. From that time forward, the child gradually acquires competencies in the use of sophisticated primary process cognition.

Most investigators, until recently, followed Freud in believing that the secondary process developed after the primary process and after the end of infancy. This traditional view has been challenged by Stern (1985) and Vygotsky (1934), who claim that the essential elements of secondary process cognition, such as abilities for abstraction and categorization, have their beginnings in the first year of life.

Contemporary investigators effectively challenge the Freudian misconception that, at a particular point, the developmental course shifts from the primary to the secondary process and that only the secondary process continues to mature, leaving the primary process in its infantile and primitive form forever (Holt, 1967, 1976; Noy, 1969, 1979; Fast, 1985; Stern, 1985). The primary process never ceases its development, but normally continues to evolve and mature alongside the secondary process. An important exception to the normal development of the primary process occurs in psychopathology where certain complexes remain archaic and sequestered from the rest of the psyche.

The development of the primary processes is reflected in the child's growing ability to assimilate complex emotional experience and master phase-appropriate traumas, to accommodate the self to an ever more demanding environment, and maintain the integrity and cohesion of a self that is gradually beginning to differentiate.

Noy's writings (1969, 1973, 1979) provide neither empirical or logical evidence to support his hypothesis that the organizational modes of the primary and secondary process are, respectively, self-centeredness and reality orientation. Actually, the primary process system at all stages of development is inextricably tied to one's interactions with reality as well as to one's perception of and adaptation to reality. Although the primary and secondary process systems differ in how they receive, represent, store, and transmit information about the self and external reality, they should not be differentiated on the basis of self-versus-reality orientation (see also Rogers, 1980, Fast, 1985).

THE RELATIONSHIP OF CONSCIOUS VERSUS UNCONSCIOUS TO THE PRIMARY AND SECONDARY PROCESS SYSTEMS

Although an idea expressed in primary process terms is experienced as real, it is, in another sense, unconscious. Consciousness, in the sense of self-reflective awareness, is not present in primary process thought (Fast, 1985). The relationship of consciousness versus unconsciousness to primary versus secondary process is not a one-to-one coordination. Not all secondary process thinking is conscious, and not all the products of the primary process are unconscious. Cognition of the conceptual type (i.e., secondary process thinking) may be barred from consciousness as much as can primary process thinking. Bear in mind that I am not discussing here the brain processes by which thoughts are formed but rather the end products of those neural activities. The actual brain processes subserving both the primary and secondary process systems are *nonconscious*. Individuals may or may not become conscious of the meaning of the end products of these two systems, and psychic defenses are one of the major elements that prevent people from understanding the meanings of their primary and secondary process products.

There is much, much more going on in the primary process system than Freud and other psychoanalysts who followed him knew. Cognitive and developmental psychologists alike agree that Freud, by his nearly exclusive championing of sex and aggression as matters of the primary process and "the unconscious," underestimated the extent to which thought, feeling, and behavior are subject to both unconscious and nonconscious influences (Bowers, 1984; Mandler, 1984).

One reason it has taken psychoanalysts and psychologists so long to recognize the important functions of the primary process system in cognition, in perception, and in the individual's responses to external as well as internal stimuli is that the primary process system operates in a nonconscious, automatic, involuntary manner. In both clinical and experimental situations, it is only by inference, not by direct observation, that an investigator may gain some understanding of the complex functions served by the primary process system.

In everyday life, the activities of the primary-process system are only occasionally and indirectly revealed through such predominantly primary process products as emotions, images, and intuitions. People are much more capable of awareness of secondary process functioning and its conceptual verbal products. By introspection and self-reflection, one can retrace the logical steps taken in secondary process thinking to reach some rational conclusion (Noy, 1979). Unlike primary process cognition, secondary process cognition is sometimes (though not always) voluntary and consciously directed. (See Chapter 6 for a further discussion of consciousness.)

THE PRIMARY PROCESS SYSTEM AND THE EXTERNAL WORLD

As I discussed in Chapter 1, one of the major mistakes linked with Freud's copy theory of perception was his concept of the id and the primary process as having nothing to do with perceptions of or interactions with the external world. Today, there is abundant support for the hypothesis that the primary process and the secondary process systems, acting together, contribute to perception as well as to other kinds of cognition (Fisher, 1956; Neisser, 1967; Brown, 1972; Mandler, 1984). Major functions of the primary process system include receiving information about interactions between self and others, analyzing the meaning of the information, and representing and communicating the meanings derived from the prior meaning analysis.

What follows is a summary of Freud's (1940a) final conceptualization of the relations between the mind and the external world as presented in Chapter 8 of the *Outline*. He described the id as the "core of our being" and as having no direct relations with the external world. Within the id the sexual and aggressive instincts operate, and the processes occurring within the id Freud called the "primary process." For Freud, the other agency of the mind, the ego, is adapted for the reception and exclusion of stimuli and is in direct contact with the external world. Just as the id obeys the inexorable pleasure principle, so is the ego governed exclusively by the reality principle and considerations of self-preservation.

Freud mistakenly equated the id and primary process with what was biological and internal in the organism and the ego with what was acquired through experience. This false equation of the innate with the organism's interior and the environment with what is adventitious and learned contributed to Freud's (1923) model of the ego and id. He stated, "It is easy to see that the ego is that part of the id which has been modified by the direct influence of the external world through the medium of the Pcpt.-Cs." (p. 25). In Freud's view, the ego is formed as a result of the interaction of the id and the environment and contains the individual's acquired experience; whereas the id is conceived of as an internal repository of the instincts acquired through the process of evolution and the collective past experience of the species.

The biology of the 19th century, when Freud's ideas about instincts were first formulated, did not appreciate the dynamism and formative interactions that exist between the organism and its environment. Biological studies were dominated by the laboratory experimental method, in which environmental conditions were assumed to be constant. From those studies arose the erroneous idea of an instinct that was cut off from environmental influences. These notions are rejected by contemporary biology, which no longer subscribes to any correlation between what is innate and the organism's interior or what is learned and the environment. According to Lorenz (1965), what is innate is what is not learned; to make learning possible, it must exist before any learning occurs.

The ego, no less than the id, has part of its origins in innate biological structures and mechanisms. Freud's concept of the ego as a structure wholly molded by experience has been effectively challenged by Hartmann's (1939) demonstration that the ego is in part autonomous, as it contains biologically given modes of adaptation to the environment.

The point of this theoretical discussion in regard to the primary process system is to modify our concepts about its locus of functioning and its psychic contents. In contrast to what classical psychoanalytic theory holds, the primary process system is not exclusively concerned with sexual and aggressive drives; and its operations are not confined to the interior of the mind or brain, where it is cut off from environmental interactions. In Section II my coauthor continues this discussion on interactional aspects of psychic development, structure, and function.

FREUD'S CONCEPT OF PRIMARY NARCISSISM

Freud (1900) formulated his clinical observations on the primary process in economic and developmental terms. In his view, the primary processes are developmentally the first form of cognition, and they are formed in a stage of *primary narcissism* in which the infant is absolutely egocentric. The focus of infant experience is exclusively on the rise and fall of its own tension states; it is without any interest in the world outside itself. For Freud, the primary processes are the cognitive mode of this period of primary narcissism, and they proceed without relation to the external world. The primary process, according to the classical Freudian perspective, functions on the model of hallucinatory wish fulfillment.

Freud's inferences about primary process activity in dreams and symptoms led him to hypothesize the origins of the primary process in a period of life when the infant is altogether unaware of its environment. The concept that the infant is uninvolved with its environment even in the first days of life has been vigorously challenged by child psychoanalysts and developmental psychologists. Investigations from the rapidly developing field of infant research overwhelmingly support the idea that infants interact adaptively with both the human and nonhuman environment from the time of birth (Lichtenberg, 1983; Stern, 1985).

In Freud's view, the primary process is, from the beginning of life, divorced from reality. According to classical psychoanalytic theory, infantile thought (i.e., hallucinatory wish fulfillment) occurs only when the gratification of some action, such as actual nursing, is not immediately possible. Piaget's (1952, 1962) development theory, as well as Fast's (1985) event theory, propose that thought and action are undifferentiated aspects of the same event; in other words, in infancy, thought can occur only in the presence of motor action. As Fast rightly concludes, "The primary processes are not divorced from reality but are absolutely tied to it" (p. 43).

From birth onward, infants are acutely sensitive to and interact with their human and nonhuman environment. Rather than becoming aware of an external world, *the child, by differentiating self from nonself, gradually becomes aware that the world is external.* Transitions out of primary narcissism depend on the infant's recognition of a world external and separate from itself. Event theory suggests that this recognition is the product of self–nonself differentiation and that the changes Freud attributed to the infant's becoming newly cognizant of its environment can be understood as differentiation outcomes (Fast, 1985). In short, infants are very much aware of the world around them, but considerable cognitive development must occur before they are able to represent aspects of their environment as external to themselves.

In the following sections, I discuss different ways in which the primary process system is directly involved in perception and other types of cognition. *The primary process system is immediately and directly engaged in the individual's interactions with both the human and the nonhuman environment and in evaluating, representing, and communicating the meaning of those interactions.*

A CONSTRUCTIVIST THEORY OF PERCEPTION AND COGNITION

To replace the copy theory of perception as advanced by Freud and others of his time, Michael Miller and I recommend acceptance of the *constructivist* theory proposed by cognitive and developmental psychologists (Schimek, 1975a; Mandler, 1984). Contemporary studies demonstrate that perception is an *active* investigatory activity and not merely the passive reception of information from the environment or the perceiver's body. The object of perception does not come to us as a sensory given, as Freud (1900) put forth in his copy theory of perception. Rather, the object must be actively sought and constructed through cognitive processes (Brown, 1972). Perception is the construction of meanings, which are constructed from sensory input to the brain, from memory traces, and from the perceiver's motivations and expectations.

The process of perception depends on the combined and integrated functioning of both the primary and the secondary process systems. A phenomological description of perception distinguishes two factors, which in their manifestations are fused but neither of which can be reduced to the other. In meaning, they remain distinct, even though it is not possible actually to separate them as discrete entities.

The philosopher Cassirer's (1960) description of two aspects of perception, thing-perception and expression-perception, are similar to the concepts proposed by Noy (1969, 1979) and me about the secondary process and primary process modes of perception. According to Cassirer, the world that the self encounters is in one case a thing-world and in the other a person-world. In the case of thing-perception (akin to the secondary process mode of perception), we observe the objects in the world as completely spatial, physical objects; and in the case of expression-perception (akin to primary process mode of perception), we observe an object as if it were something "like ourselves." In both cases, the otherness of the object persists. But the otherness of thing-perception differs from expression-perception in the following way: with thing-perception, the other, or "it," is an absolute other; with expression-perception, the other, or "you," is someone like ourselves, an alterego (Cassirer, 1960).

The contribution made by sophisticated primary process cognition to a one's understanding of one's object relations should not be dismissed as primitive or unrealistic. Intuitions, images, and emotions derived chiefly from the primary process system provide an immediate and prereflective awareness of our vital relations with both ourselves and others. Normally, the primary process mode of perception does not deceive. It is at bottom the only means by which we can free ourselves from the vicious circle of abstract thought and make contact with the reality of the self and its relations to both internal and external objects. As I discuss in a later section, mature primary process cognition plays a central role in both our understanding of ouselves (intrapersonal intelligence) and our under-standing of others (interpersonal intelligence).

The role of the two basic modes of perception in relation to external objects also applies to one's perception of one's own body. Noy (1979) describes two aspects of body perception, the *experiential* and the *conceptual* and relates these, respectively, to the primary and secondary modes of perception.

For example, a person perceives his leg in two ways: *experientially,* as something that belongs to him and that he can feel through sensory channels (e.g., touch, temperature, proprioception, and so forth) and *conceptually,* as an objective part of his body that he can comprehend. On the primary process level of representation and perception, one's leg is an experience, and on the secondary level it is a concept. Its total image stems from an integration of perceptual experience and the concept. This double perception and representation pertains to any part of the body, and to other representations and dimensions of the self.

PRIMARY AND SECONDARY PROCESS
MODES OF COMMUNICATION

Investigators of human communication view language as a system consisting of two levels, which can be described as the primary process mode of communication and the secondary process mode of communication. Langer (1942) and Rycroft (1962), describing language as a system of symbols, and distinguish between "discursive" and "nondiscursive" symbols. Bertrand Russell (1940) distinguished between the ability of language to communicate facts and its capacity to express the state of the speaker. Wittgenstein (1921) described two kinds of communication—that which transmits theoretical and factual information and that which transmits values and states of experience. Researchers studying human and animal communication distinguish between analogic and digital communication, analogic communication corresponding to the primary process mode of communication and digital communication corresponding to the secondary process mode (Watzlawick, Beavin, and Jackson, 1967). Although each of these writers uses a different nomenclature, all of them refer to the same two modes—called here the primary and secondary process modes of communication—and all of them regard these two modes as essential aspects of any system of human communication.

Both primary and secondary process modes are present in ordinary conversation where objective, factual (secondary process) information is transmitted by the meaning of the uttered words and where affective and object-relational information is processed by the primary process system and transmitted primarily by nonverbal communication. Nonverbal communication includes body movements (kinesics), posture, gesture, facial expression, voice inflection, and the sequence, rhythm, and pitch of the spoken words. The primary and secondary process modes of communication not only exist side by side, but they complement and are contingent on each other, often in highly complex ways.

The secondary process mode of communication (digital language) has a highly complex and powerful logical syntax but lacks adequate semantics in the field of relationship; the primary process mode of communication (i.e., analogic language) possesses the semantics but has no adequate syntax for the unambiguous definition of the nature of relationships (Watzlawick et al., 1967). Objects can be referred to by a self-explanatory likeness, an analog, such as a drawing; or they can be referred to by a name. The two types of communication are equivalent to the concepts of analogic language (or primary process mode) and digital language (or secondary process mode).

Although human beings are the only animal known to use both the analogic and the digital modes of communication, there is a vast area where humans rely predominantly on primary process communication, often with very little change from the analogic inheritance handed down to us from our mammalian ancestors (Watzlawick et al., 1967).

Although all nonverbal and affective communication is a product of the primary process system, not all verbal communication is exclusively secondary process. Primary process elements contribute to metaphors and other figures of speech. According to Lacan (1968), unconscious wishes and thoughts are revealed by the ways in which a speaker uses language, and the influence of the primary process is most especially found in the use of tropes (figures of speech). For Lacan, the unconscious is structured like a language; and he assimilates the two basic mechanisms of Freud's concept of the primary process—condensation and displacement—into the linguistic axes of metaphor and metonymy.

PRIMARY PROCESS AND UNCONSCIOUS COMMUNICATION

Langs (1982a) has developed a procedure for deciphering what he calls unconsciously encoded messages by using the "trigger" (stimulus) for each communication as the key decoding device. The trigger decoding method is relatively simple, highly specific, immediately dynamic, and alive with cogent meaning. Langs's writings on unconscious communication in both everyday life and in the therapeutic situation emphasize methods for the decoding and interpretation of unconsciously encoded messages.

According to Langs, unconscious encoding is a means by which one forms a compromised, disguised response to an immediately disturbing stimulus. Unconscious encoding serves the dual purpose of coping with disturbing internal and external stimuli through a combination of positive expression, on the hand, and defensive protection and restraint, on the other. Communications that contain unconsciously encoded messages have both a manifest and a latent content.

The classifications "conscious communication" and "unconscious communication" are misleading. It is not that communication is conscious or unconscious, but, rather, that persons may or may not be conscious of the meanings of the messages they transmit or receive. We should not think of unconscious communication as some general entity, system, or universal interpersonal communicative channel. The degree of conscious awareness among different persons about the meaning of a specific communication of their own or others is highly variable. One person may understand the meaning of a particular message, and another person may not. It does make sense, therefore, to classify communication into the primary and secondary process modes of communication, but it does not make sense to classify communication as conscious or unconscious. In describing human communication, the term "latent content" should be used only to refer to those meanings in a person's communication that he or she does not understand.

One should not confuse or conflate what has been loosely called "unconscious communication" with the primary process mode of communication. Often the meanings of primary process products in a person's speech are not unconscious, in the dynamic sense of the word, for either the speaker or the listener. For example, there is nothing unconscious about the meaning of a drowning person's cries for help. The meaning of a speaker's affects, gestures, images, and other predominantly primary process communications may be either consciously or preconsciously accessible to either the speaker or the listener. Only when a person's defenses or other factors, such as brain damage or developmental deficits, prevent the understanding of the meaning of primary process manifestations in his or her communications is it correct to say that the subject is unconscious of the meaning of such expressions.

It is both theoretically and clinically important to distinguish between communications that are preconsciously available for conscious focal attention and understanding and those communications which, because of defenses, are dynamically unconscious for either the speaker or the listener. In everyday conversation, the speaker is consciously aware of only a few of the many meanings conveyed in his or her verbal and nonverbal messages. Many human communications transmitted outside of conscious awareness are readily (i.e., preconsciously) accessible to self-observation and conscious understanding. A moment's self-reflection, for example, may reveal that one's tone of voice is communicating one's fatigue.

THE PRIMARY PROCESS MODE OF COMMUNICATION, AFFECTS, AND OBJECT RELATIONS

The primary process mode of communication is event centered and object relational; it transmits affective information about the state of a person's internal and external objects. The term "object relational" is used here in the broad sense that includes both interpersonal and intrapersonal relations. In "intrapersonal relations," the self-as-agent (the "I") has some conscious or unconscious affective interaction with the self-as-object (the "me"). (Some examples are self-love and self-hatred.)

Using the studies of Tinbergen (1953) and Lorenz (1965), as well as his own, Bateson (1955, 1972) showed that vocalizations, intention movements, and mood signs of animals are analogic (primary process) communications by which they define to each other the nature of their relationships, rather than making denotative statements about objects. One of Bateson's examples illustrates his point. When a person opens a refrigerator and a cat comes and rubs against the person's leg, this does not mean "I want milk," as a human would express it verbally. Rather, the cat's rubbing invokes a special relationship, "be mother to me," because such behavior is observed only in kittens in relation to adult cats and never between two adult cats.

The subject matter of primary process discourse is different from that of language and consciousness. Secondary process communication speaks of things or persons and attaches predicates to the specific things or persons that have been mentioned. In primary process communication, the things or persons are usually not identified, and the focus of the discourse is on the *relationships* that are asserted to obtain between the subject and other persons or things (Bateson, 1972).

Every human communication has a content and a relationship aspect, and the two modes of communication not only exist side-by-side but complement each other in every message (Watzlawick et al., 1967). The content communication is mainly conveyed by language (the digital, or secondary process, mode), whereas the relationship is transmitted predominantly nonverbally and by affects in the primary process mode. Wherever relationship is the central issue in communication, secondary process communication alone is insufficient and usually inadequate. This is so not only between animals and between man and animals, but in many other situations in human life—combat, courtship, and love, as well as in nearly all interactions with very young children.

Emotions and moods are *modes of relating* in which we are attuned and responsive in one way or another to the world. Affective states such as anxiety, joy, and boredom bring disclosure and reveal how we are related to others. Often emotions are dismissed as internal states having nothing to do with one's relations to the world. On the contrary, emotions and moods both express and illuminate the nature of an individual's interactions with the human and nonhuman world. The primary process system usually operates quietly and wordlessly, providing one with a background of emotions, intuitions, and images that are often mistakenly isolated from one's perceptions and responses to somatic and environmental stimuli. Affective responses are often minimized or discounted as "internal" or "subjective" and therefore unrelated to the person's ongoing interactions with others. Actually, the mode of apprehension in affective states is neither subjective nor objective, but, rather, comes before distinctions of subject and object.

The implications of these principles of communication are enormously important for psychoanalytic listening and interpreting because the particular object relations and introjects revived or enacted in the therapeutic situation are conveyed predominantly by the patient's nonverbal and affective communications with the therapist. Affects communicate the nature, meaning, and intensity of a person's object relations.

The interrelationships discussed here among affects, object relations, and the primary process mode of communication provide part of the basis for a much-needed psychoanalytic theory of affects. Psychoanalytic writers tend to agree that psychoanalysis lacks a systematic theory of affects.

This deficiency exists mainly because, although the ego has been viewed as the locus of affects, the sources of affects have been conceptualized as drive representations, instinctual derivatives serving as safety valves for drive cathexis (Rapaport, 1954). The classical instinctual drive-discharge theory of affects views affects as arising from within the interior of the mind, as though this interior (or id) were cut off from relations with its environment. This obsolete conception is belied by important scientific advances in our knowledge about the development of affects and about their object-relational and communicative functions (Modell, 1984). For example, there are many studies from psychoanalysis and elsewhere about the transmission, the "contagiousness," and the "dumping" of affects in both large and small groups, including the analytic situation (Basch, 1976b).

THE PERSONAL INTELLIGENCES

Words by themselves do not constitute the basic data of psychoanalysis. What endows words with personal meaning and what constitutes the primary data of psychoanalysis are affects (Modell, 1984). The ability of one person to "know" the mind of another rests on one of the earliest kinds of perception: the capacity of the infant to recognize and respond to the affective state of its mother and, conversely, the capacity of the mother to understand the affective state of the infant. This ability to perceive and respond to the affective state of another antedates the development of symbolic functions and persists after the acquisition of language (Basch, 1976b).

Competency in understanding the affective state of another is, in my opinion, the foundation of what Gardner (1983) calls interpersonal intelligence. Gardner discusses and delineates two kinds of personal intelligence: intrapersonal intelligence (knowledge of the self) and interpersonal intelligence (knowledge of others). Primary process meaning analysis is, I believe, the central psychic function employed in both personal intelligences.

Intrapersonal intelligence involves chiefly one's examination and knowledge of one's own feelings; interpersonal intelligence looks externally toward the behavior, feelings, and motivations of others. Gardner describes interpersonal intelligences as *"the ability to notice and make distinctions among other individuals* and, in particular, among their moods, temperaments, motivations, and intentions" (p. 239). Although an intuitive knowledge of ourselves and our public knowledge of others are of tremendous value in everyday life, the significance of those competencies—

indeed, their very existence—has been ignored or minimized by nearly all psychologists and other students of cognition.

Using information from a number of different disciplines, Gardner presents a convincing case for the theory of multiple intelligences and the existence of seven relatively autonomous intelligences. (The seven are linguistic, musical, logical-mathematical, spatial, bodily-kinesthetic, interpersonal, and intrapersonal intelligence.) Previous approaches to intelligence, the I.Q., the Piagetian, and the information-processing approaches all focus on certain kinds of logical or linguistic problem solving. All fail to address such mental competencies as the personal intelligences and creativity, which cannot be explained by or reduced to linguistic or logical abilities. For example, I.Q. tests do not measure the personal intelligences, although they do provide some measure of logical-mathematical abilities.

Each of the personal intelligences has its own characteristic neurological representation and line of development. The neurological literature, especially clinical reports of patients who have suffered brain damage, indicate that both interpersonal intelligence and intrapersonal intelligence can be destroyed or spared in relative isolation from the other varieties of cognition (Gardner, 1983). The frontal lobes and the right hemisphere (in persons who are right-handed) are associated with the personal intelligences. Defects in these areas of the brain interfere with the development of the personal intelligences and can cause pathological forms of intrapersonal and interpersonal knowledge.

My clinical experience suggests that sophisticated primary process cognition is a prime ingredient in the personal intelligences and that impairments in these psychic competencies are linked with archaic primary process cognition. Research on the relationship between primary process cognition and the personal intelligences would be eminently worthwhile. Some testable hypotheses come to mind. For instance, I strongly suspect that competency in doing psychoanalysis or psychoanalytic psychotherapy depends on one's degree of competency in the personal intelligences as well as mastery of sophisticated primary process cognition. In working as a therapist as well as a supervisor of psychotherapy and psychoanalysis, I have repeatedly gained the impression that clinical acumen and competency is founded on sophisticated primary process abilities.

THE ANALYST'S USE OF MATURE PRIMARY PROCESS COGNITION

The analyst's use of his own sophisticated primary process cognition is a vital investigative tool especially valuable for the understanding and interpretation of the patient's archaic primary process cognition.

Imagery, intuitions, emotional reactions, and the like are the products of the analyst's unconscious meaning analysis, and the analyst's self-reflective evaluations of these manifestations may provide a valuable means for understanding the patient's archaic primary process cognition. The analyst's visual imagery often is an illuminating and highly effective tool for encapsulating vital information about affectively charged interactions occurring within the patient and between the analyst and the patient.

Because the primary process system represents interactions rather than abstract ideas, imagery may be a particularly useful mode for the therapist to attune to the event-centered nature of the patient's primary process. The Chinese proverb—"A picture is worth a thousand words"—describes the values of imagination and imagery for representing salient intrapersonal or interpersonal relations.

The empathic analyst's creative use of imagery may capture what is still inarticulate, inchoate, and undifferentiated in the patient. In such situations, the analyst's conscious imagery and intuitions may be congruent with the meaning unconsciously expressed in the patient's primary process cognition. The value of the analyst's conscious imagery rests on the similarity (and not the identity) between the analyst's imagery and the functional mode of primary process in the patient. Much more than secondary process cognition, the analyst's conscious imagery is similar to the archaic primary process cognition of the patient in two important ways. First, both kinds of cognitions concern concrete events and actions rather than abstract ideas. Second, both sophisticated and archaic primary process cognition can process and represent information more rapidly than secondary process can.

What in the past has been called regression in the service of the ego may be identical with, or at least include, a person's ability to suspend attention to secondary process cognition while playfully attending to the products of the primary process system. The rapidity of the primary process system and its diminished requirements for conventional or logical association may lead to creative and novel combinations of apparently divergent ideas. Self-reflective thought and secondary process mediation and revision may, of course, be necessary to complete and refine the products of sophisticated primary process cognition.

A VIGNETTE ON PRIMARY PROCESS AND SECONDARY PROCESS MODES OF COMMUNICATION

The ability to understand affective (primary process) communication is retained by brain-damaged patients who suffer from aphasia and who have lost some of their capacities for understanding words. Oliver Sacks (1985), a professor of neurology, provides a fascinating account of a natural experiment about the responses of hospitalized brain-damaged patients to hearing a televised speech by former President Reagan. Patients with aphasia resulting from left-brain damage met Reagan's speech with a roar of derisive laughter. Even though they could not comprehend the speaker's words, they did understand his nonverbal communication. It is said that one cannot lie to an aphasic. Because the aphasic cannot grasp the meaning of the speaker's words, he cannot be deceived by them. But what he does understand he grasps with infallible precision, namely, the affective expression and nonverbal communication.

Their enhanced powers for hearing and understanding primary process communication permit aphasic patients to distinguish between what is authentic and what is inauthentic in a speaker's voice. Sacks (1985) writes, "Thus it was the grimaces, the histrionics, the gestures—and above all, the tones and cadences of the President's voice—that rang false for these wordless but immensely sensitive patients" (p. 29).

Another patient, Edith, a poet of some repute, who suffered from a glioma in her right temporal lobe, also listened to the President's speech and responded as negatively as had the aphasic patients. She had tonal agnosia, a disorder exactly opposite to aphasia. For tonal agnosia patients, the expressive qualities of voices disappear—their timbre, their tone, their affective component—while words are understood. Tonal agnosias (or "atonias") are associated with disorders of the right temporal lobe.

The President's speech did not work for Edith. Owing to her enhanced sensitivity to formal language use, she was easily able to pick out logical mistakes and errors in word usage. Sacks concludes that a good many normal people were indeed fooled by the President's speech, "and so cunningly was deceptive word use combined with deceptive tone, that it was the brain-damaged who remained undeceived" (p. 29).

As this vignette implies, the primary process system is associated with the right hemisphere and the secondary process system with the left hemisphere.

RELATIONSHIP BETWEEN CEREBRAL HEMISPHERIC MODES AND THE PRIMARY AND SECONDARY PROCESSES

Recent studies on the lateralization of the brain cortex show that the left hemisphere operates predominantly according to secondary process modes and that the right hemisphere functions are those of primary process. The right-hemisphere, for example, processes and interprets nonverbal information. These studies, especially those on the so-called split-brain patients, illuminate the neurophysiological correlates of the primary and secondary process systems.

The two hemispheres communicate through the corpus callosum, which joins the hemispheres anatomically. Sectioning of the corpus callosum prevents sensory information entering one hemisphere from the opposite side of the body from being transferred to the other hemisphere. A group of severe epileptics were treated by the "split-brain" operation (commissurotomy), a cutting down the midline of the interconnections between the two hemispheres (Sperry, 1982). Ingenious and subtle tests demonstrated that the operation had clearly separated the specialized functions of the two hemispheres.

The commissurotomy studies indicate that people possess more than a single consciousness. Rather, people have two different consciousnesses, or selves, which in the wake of the surgical intervention become alienated from one another. Each hemisphere has its own sphere for sensation, perception, and other psychic activities; and in split-brain patients nearly all the cognitive activity of one hemisphere is detached from the corresponding activity of the other. Sperry (1964) writes, "Everything we have seen so far indicated that the surgery has left each of these people with two separate minds, that is, with two separate spheres of consciousness" (p. 29).

The split-brain studies provide evidence for psychoanalytic theories of two parallel types of cognitive activity that occur simultaneously. Freud (1940a), Kubie (1954), and others hypothesized that there is an incessant stream of unconscious or preconscious ideation accompanying conscious thought and lending it color, idiosyncrasy, and affective emphasis. Until the split-brain studies were carried out, such a conception of two consciousnesses, attractive as it was in its bold sweep and its capacity to explain many observations, had not been given any satisfactory empirical test.

In some mental processes, the right hemisphere is equal to or superior to the left. The right hemisphere can generate an emotional reaction. In one experiment, a photograph of a nude woman was presented to the right hemisphere of a split-brain patient (Gazzaniga, 1967). At first the patient said that she saw nothing, but then she began to smile and to chuckle. When asked what she was laughing at, she replied, "I don't know . . . nothing . . . oh—that funny machine." Although the right hemisphere could not "say" what she had seen, it nevertheless elicited a lively emotional response. In this and similar tests, a clear split was observed between two cognitive systems that in normal persons are usually integrated and in communication.

Split-brain studies have shown that information stored in the nonverbal mode is inaccessible to consciousness, as we usually define it, unless it is integrated with verbal stores. In tests examining the capacity of the split-brain patients to speak with reference to information specifically lateralized to one or the other hemisphere, very different responses were obtained from the right and left hemispheres. Although spoken descriptions of stimulus material obtained from the left hemisphere showed little or no impairment, the right hemisphere in the same tests was incapable of speech. The right hemisphere, though it cannot "speak," can "understand" language and act intelligently on the basis of what it understands. These findings are consistent with the theory of the primary process system advanced earlier, in which I indicated that primary process activity goes on *nonconsciously*. Only when the primary and secondary process systems are integrated, as when, for example, the corpus callosum is intact, is it possible for the subject to become aware of the primary-process system's end-products and to reflect upon them (e.g., affects and images).

Galin (1974) drew a parallel between hemispheric modes and the primary and secondary processes. He indicated that, whereas the left hemisphere is specialized for verbalization and linear, analytic logic,

> the right hemisphere uses a nonverbal mode of representation . . . a nonlinear mode of association . . . its solutions to problems are based on multiple converging determinants rather than a single causal chain . . . grasping the concept of the whole from just a part" [p. 574].

The right hemisphere senses the forest, so to speak, while the left hemisphere cannot see the woods for the trees (Hoppe, 1977).

The psychoanalyst McLaughlin (1978) built on and expanded Galin's contribution. Both suggested that primary process modes, as conceptualized in psychoanalysis, are formally similar to the cognitive modes of the right hemisphere. McLaughlin's clinical observations support the concept of a congruence between hemispheric functions and their interworkings and those attributed to primary and secondary processes and their interrelationships.

McKinnon (1979) studied the semantic forms in primary and secondary process and compared them with the semantic forms of the right and left hemispheres. He found that they were homomorphic. The descriptive features of the semantic forms of primary and secondary process are logical and structural homologues of, respectively, the right hemisphere and the left hemisphere. The left hemisphere mode is verbal, sequential, detailed, and analytic; whereas the right hemisphere mode is characteristically nonverbal, synthetic, coherent, and spatial.

Hadley (1983) advances the concept of the neural representational system as a bridge between neurophysiology and psychoanalytic theory. She views the neural representational system as a dynamic, evolving one in which one aspect of an experience may be encoded in one area of the brain with one meaning and in another area with an entirely different implication. Split-brain investigations reveal that representations are many faceted: experience is multicoded in several sensory modalities and normally in both the primary and secondary process modes of processing. Human behavior is conceptualized as the result of complementary interactions between the two hemispheres. The balanced and integrated functioning of both hemispheres and both primary and secondary process systems is a requisite for normal cognitive development.

A *dual code model of mental representation,* derived from current work in cognitive experimental psychology, provides a systematic theoretical model of the mind that is more applicable to psychoanalysis than is any single code or common code theory (Bucci, 1985). The dual code model incorporates both verbal and nonverbal processes. Secondary process and its verbal code include the system of language, logic, and communicative speech. The elements of primary process and its nonverbal system include representations of sensory imagery in all modalities as well as representations of affects, of motoric activity, and of visceral and somatic experience. Because of its close link with affects, the primary process system is also the major domain of material that is warded off by defense.

The right hemisphere is involved both in the processing of affective information and in the production of affective expressions to a far greater degree than is the left hemisphere (Izard, 1977; Zajonic, 1980). Abundant evidence supports the idea that affects have a different information-processing system in the brain than does information having verbal referents. As I mentioned earlier, damage to the right hemisphere tends to bring about tonal agnosia. Children who suffer right-hemisphere damage are impaired in their abilities to express emotions and to understand the emotional communications of others. According to Voeller (1985), children with right-hemisphere defects have difficulty in interpreting and expressing emotion, making and maintaining eye contact, gesturing appropriately, speaking with normal pitch and tone, and interacting with other children and adults. Tests that measure their abilities to interpret facial cues and connotations of language patterns reveal severe deficits.

Severing the neural connections between the primary-process system in the right brain from the language centers in the left brain makes it difficult for split-brain patients to verbalize their emotions, and they develop the alexithymia syndrome (TenHouten et al., 1986). Alexithymia, also found in many psychosomatic patients, is characterized by two main features: 1) an inability to describe emotions or feelings beyond some standard, stereotyped word or cliche for it, combined with an inability to differentiate among feelings; and 2) a striking absence of fantasies.

It should not be assumed that one can rigidly dichotomize the left and right hemispheres as subserving strictly linguistic-analytic functions on one hand and spatial-holistic functions on the other. In normal mental life, the two cerebral hemispheres interact with one another in a constantly oscillating, reciprocally balanced relationship, so that even those cognitive functions believed to be the predominant domain of one hemisphere are aided, altered, and shaped by the operations of the other (Miller, 1986).

CHAPTER 3

On Unconscious
Fantasy

My purpose in this chapter is to present arguments from the cognitive sciences and from the psychoanalytic literature concerning theories regarding the existence and function of unconscious fantasy.

Others who have written about unconscious fantasy describe and sometimes deplore the prevalent ambiguity and lack of consensus regarding the meaning of the term (Rycroft, 1956; Beres, 1960, 1962; Sandler and Nagera, 1963; Fossi, 1985; Inderbitzin and Levy, 1990). Freud used the word fantasy to convey a number of different meanings on different occasions, and he used it to refer to conscious daydreams as well as to their unconscious analogues. At times, Freud, and later other analysts, used the term "unconscious fantasy" to refer both to unconscious mental processes and to all unconscious content. The term unconscious fantasy has been applied to normal and to pathogenic phenomena, and it has served also to designate psychic reality in contrast to actual events.

In the psychoanalytic literature, the term unconscious fantasy has come to assume different meanings, including the following: 1) a type of mental representation that is stored in the *Ucs;* 2) either all or some unconscious content; 3) a repressed fantasy that once was conscious; 4) a preconscious fantasy; 5) a mental content which has never been conscious; 6) the direct transformation on to the mental level of a biological entity, an instinct; 7) the Lamarkian inheritance of ancestral experiences; 8) the latent content and proximal cause of dreams and symptoms; and 9) an unconscious mental process.

Often psychoanalytic writers are unclear about which of those or other meanings are intended. Although sometimes the meaning can be understood from the context in which the words are used, oftentimes a reader of the psychoanalytic literature is hard-pressed to understand what is meant by so ambiguous and vague a term as unconscious fantasy.

Unconscious fantasies are said to luxuriate and change in the unconscious, but no one has been able to explain how they know that this occurs or how it happens. Though conscious daydreams are known to be unreal and not to represent reality, this knowledge, according to classical psychoanalysis, does not apply to what are called the "derivatives" of unconscious fantasies. According to classical psychoanalysis, the patient is unaware that his unconscious fantasies cause his apperception of reality to become distorted (Freud, 1912).

What happens when the notion of an erotic daydream fantasy is extended, as in Freud's (1900) writings, to the unconscious, where it becomes an "unconscious fantasy"? Does starting with conscious daydreams and subtracting the feature of consciousness yield Freud's concept of unconscious fantasy? It is not a simple transposition. Rubenstein (1976a) warns that an unconscious fantasy is not simply a fantasy that is not conscious. The existence and activity of unconscious fantasies are inferred by an outside observer. Since, by definition, an unconscious fantasy is not consciously experienced as such by the subject, how, then, can an outside observer know what form the fantasy takes or that it exists at all? (Neu, 1977).

One's understanding of the concept of unconscious fantasy requires distinguishing between the dynamically unconscious and what is merely descriptively unconscious (i.e., preconscious). According to Freud and others, unconscious fantasies are dynamically active rather than sitting in cold (preconscious) storage, and they are alleged to exert a powerful causal influence on one's conscious thoughts, emotions, and behaviors.

Before proceeding to a discussion and critique of psychoanalytic concepts about unconscious fantasy, I shall first review the writings of Freud, Arlow, and the Kleinians on this subject.

FREUD'S WRITINGS ON UNCONSCIOUS FANTASY

From the time Freud (1906) abandoned the seduction theory about the etiology of neurotic disorders until the end of his career, he struggled with questions about the sources of unconscious fantasies. Earlier, he had believed that activated and highly charged unconscious memories of sexual trauma and seduction were the proximal causes of neurotic symptoms. With the relinguishment of the seduction theory, Freud (1906, 1914a, 1925b, 1933) substituted unconscious fantasies for unconscious memories in his formulations about how dreams and neurotic symptoms were formed. Freud (1925b) wrote, "Neurotic symptoms were not related directly to actual events but to wishful fantasies, and that as far as the neurosis was concerned psychical reality was of more importance than material realities" (p. 34).

In Freud's (1917) renunciation of the seduction hypothesis the factual, or *material,* reality of unconscious memories was replaced by the *psychical* reality of unconscious fantasies. In the world of the neurosis, it is the psychical reality that is decisive. For Freud, psychical reality is the reality of basic unconscious wishes and fantasies brought to their truest understanding through the interpretive and reconstructive activity of the analyst.

Freud (1896a, b) did not base his early hypotheses about unconscious memories and his later hypothesis about the causal role of unconscious fantasies in dream and symptom formation on clinical observations of conscious memories or fantasies, but, rather, on inferences drawn from clinical observations (Schimek, 1975b). Most of Freud's (1896a, b) patients did not report conscious memories of seduction, but memories, thoughts, and symptoms that Freud *interpreted* as the disguised and indirect derivatives of unconscious memories of infantile sexual trauma. Referring to such early childhood traumas, Freud (1896a) wrote, "Their traces are never present in conscious memory, only in the symptoms of their illness" (p. 166).

With what he called his "realization" that unconscious fantasies, not unconscious memories, were the underlying basis of neurotic symptoms, Freud (1925b) said he had "stumbled" on the Oedipus complex. He described unconscious fantasies of being seduced by their father as the expression of the typical Oedipus complex in women (Freud, 1933). Freud's abandonment of the seduction hypothesis and his articulation of the theory of infantile sexuality (Freud, 1905b) led to the early mushrooming of writings on drives, on their manifold manifestations, and on their role in psychopathology.

In the first paper in which he publicly rejected the seduction theory, Freud (1906) discussed the reasons for changing his views on the relative importance of unconscious memories of traumatic experiences and unconscious fantasies in the psychogenesis of neurotic symptoms. He believed he had earlier overstated the frequency of actual seduction, and he admitted his difficulty in distinguishing with certainty between traces of real events and the falsifications made by hysterics in their memories of childhood sexual trauma.

Freud (1906) explained some seduction fantasies as attempts to ward off memories of the subject's own sexual activity (infantile masturbation). Freud (1900, p. 491) indicated that hysterical symptoms are not attached to actual memories, but to fantasies erected on the basis of memories. In several papers he repeated the same basic formulation about the formation of unconscious fantasies (Freud, 1900, 1906, 1908, 1909). In his view, some *conscious* fantasies in childhood are formed out of memories of masturbatory experiences in infancy and early childhood. Because of conflict, these conscious fantasies are repressed, only to reappear later in adult life in derivative forms as in dreams and psychiatric symptoms. Freud (1906) wrote:

> Between the symptoms and the childish impressions there were inserted the patient's *phantasies* (or imaginary memories), mostly produced during the years of puberty, which on the one side were built up out of and over the childhood memories and on the other side were transformed directly into the symptoms [p. 274].

According to Freud (1911), two factors—autoerotism and the latency period—bring about a delay in the psychic development of the sexual instincts and their subordination to the reality principle. Consequently, there arises a close connection, on one hand, between the sexual instincts and fantasy and, on the other, between the ego-instincts and the activities of consciousness. Repression remains all-powerful in the realm of fantasy and brings about the inhibition of ideas in *statu nascendi* before they can be consciously noticed.

Freud (1908) discussed two different origins of unconscious fantasies. Some are formed directly in the *Ucs,* and others were once-conscious fantasies during childhood. The latter, because of conflict, are purposefully forgotten and become unconscious through repression. Their contents may afterward either remain the same or undergo modification.

For Freud, unconscious fantasies, in particular repressed erotic daydreams, play a major role in determining the form and content of later daydreams. They also occupy a critical place in the formation of neurotic and psychotic symptoms and in shaping the content of dreams. Unconscious fantasies contribute to all the derivatives of unconscious mental life that are allowed to find expression in consciousness or in motility. The relation of unconscious fantasies to symptom formation in hysteria was discussed in a number of papers (Freud, 1900, 1908, 1909). Freud discussed the part played by unconscious fantasies in delusions in 1907, and his paper on the Rat Man (Freud, 1909) told about the role of unconscious fantasies in obsessional symptoms.

For Freud, the technique of psychoanalysis enables the analyst to infer from psychiatric symptoms the content of the underlying unconscious fantasies and to make them conscious to the patient. The relation between unconscious fantasies and symptoms is the same as that between the latent and manifest content of dreams, and in many of Freud's writings unconscious fantasies constitute all or part of the latent content of dreams, symptoms, myths, slips of the tongue, and the like.

Freud (1911) linked the emergence of fantasy with the development of the reality principle. He indicated that before the development of the reality principle, all mental activity is governed by the pleasure principle. As thought becomes increasingly dominated by secondary process organization, a portion of our thought continues to obey the rules of primary process and wish fulfillment, and this portion he called fantasy. In several papers, he wrote of fantasy as a species of cognition that splits off as the reality principle is introduced during child development (Freud, 1911, 1917a).

Freud (1911) wrote,

> With the introduction of the reality-principle one mode of thought-activity was split off; it was kept free from reality-testing and remained subordinated to the pleasure-principle alone. This is the art of *phantasying*, which begins already in the games of children, and later, continued as *day-dreaming*, abandons its dependence of real objects [p. 222].

Throughout his writings, Freud viewed conscious fantasies and unconscious fantasies alike as wish fulfilling, unrealistic, and detached from environmental interactions.

According to Freud, as the ideational content of instinctual drives, unconscious fantasies find a path to consciousness and motility in a variety of ways. In addition to those already mentioned (such as dreams, daydreams, and symptoms), Freud noted the significance of unconscious fantasies in acting out and in the reliving of past object relationships in the transference. He also discussed how jokes, humor, play, and artistic creations allow for the discharge of unconscious fantasies of forbidden wishes.

FREUD'S THEORIES ABOUT THE INSTINCTUAL SOURCES OF UNCONSCIOUS FANTASIES

Freud's (1916, 1918) later writings on the source of unconscious fantasies shift the emphasis from the repression of conscious childhood fantasies to phylogenetic sources, that is, to inherited racial memories. He believed it might be necessary to postulate inherited memories in order to explain the universality of certain themes that occur in analyses in the absence of relevant real experiences to account for their occurrence. These themes include material related to childhood seduction, to the witnessing of the primal scene, to the phallic mother, to the family romance, to castration fears, and so on.

Freud (1917), discussing the instinctual origins of unconscious fantasies, declared that "primal phantasies" are a phylogenetic endowment. To the end of his life, Freud maintained his belief in the core of "historical truth" contained in social and religious myths (Freud, 1918, 1939) as well as in the unconscious fantasies underlying dreams, conscious daydreams, and delusions (Freud, 1918, 1937).

In Freud's (1900) original model of cognition (the wish-fulfilling theory of cognition), a drive acquires ideational content from the memory image of the object that produced the original experience of satisfaction. This formulation assumes a real object and an actual event that gave content to the drive. Freud's hypothesis of inherited memories was a way of grounding the contents of universal unconscious fantasies on actual events in the history of the race (Schimek, 1975a).

INHERITED SCHEMATA

Freud (1918) described "the core of the unconscious" as an "instinctive knowledge" and "phylogenetically acquired schemata." The idea of inherited memory contents gained little acceptance either in Freud's day or in our own; the concept of inherited schemata shaping and organizing the data from experience is close, however, to contemporary structuralist thought in developmental and cognitive psychology. Although a major point of this chapter is the rejection of psychoanalytic theories about the existence of unconscious fantasies, we do need to retain a modified version of Freud's concepts about innate schemata and their central importance in psychic development. These schemata are not fixed and rigid; they are constantly being modified and supplemented by interactions with the environment, as exemplified in Erikson's (1950) concepts of organ modes and social modalities and Piaget's ideas about sensorimotor and affective schemata. (See Chapter 5 for more on schemata.)

According to Schimek (1975b),

> What is inherited is not so much memory contents but schemata, which, like Kantian categories, have no fixed contents, but act as selective organizers of the data of immediate experience to give them some predetermined configuration and over-all meaning [pp. 855-856].

ARLOW'S CONCEPT OF UNCONSCIOUS FANTASY

Arlow (1969a, b, 1985a, b) extends the concept of unconscious fantasy beyond the confines of Freud's formulation, and he gives it a central position in his theoretical formulations. In his review of Arlow's writings, Kramer (1988) asserts, "Psychoanalysis has become the science of unconscious fantasy" (p. 36). According to Arlow, unconscious fantasies are not exclusively vehicles for the discharge of id instinctual energies. He views the ego and superego as playing a part in the formation of unconscious fantasies. The contribution that unconscious fantasy makes to conscious experience may be dominated by defensive, adaptive, and self-punitive trends, as well as by sexual and aggressive wishes.

For Arlow, a number of unconscious elements (unconscious memory, conflicts, trauma, and the vicissitudes of development) make up the contents of a continuous stream of unconscious fantasy activity. Unconscious fantasy is a persistent concomitant of all mental activity and exerts an unending and distorting influence on how reality is perceived and responded to. In Arlow's view, one's perception of reality is constantly being misconceived because of the distorting powers of unconscious fantasy. He, however, provides no evidence for his claim that there is in all of us a persistent tendency to defy reality that stems from the constant stream of unconscious fantasy and its distorting effects on perception and cognition.

Arlow (1969b) writes,

> while the patients were alert and vigorously involved in reality oriented activity, their judgment of reality and their response to it was completely distorted by the intrusion of an unconscious fantasy. Actually this kind of distortion is one of the essential features of the neurotic process and of the transference' [p. 33].

Arlow's main interest in applied psychoanalysis has been to demonstrate, largely by analogy, the existence and far-reaching effects in textual material (the Bible, a painting, a novel, a play, and so on) of unconscious fantasies and defenses against them on other functions of the mental apparatus. Arlow views myths as shared unconscious fantasies. Both in his clinical writings and in his writings on applied psychoanalysis, Arlow maintains the same basic dichotomy between reality and fantasy; he views both conscious fantasy and unconscious fantasy as the antithesis of reality.

Unconscious fantasy plays a central role in Arlow's theories of symptom formation, of cognition, of intrapsychic conflict, and of the analytic process. Kramer (1988) succinctly summarizes Arlow's opinions thus: "The medium of conflict is unconscious conflict and . . . it is through his unconscious fantasy that an individual lives out his life, a patient lives out his neurosis, and his analysis" (p. 36). What Arlow believes is curative in psychoanalytic treatment is the patient's newly acquired knowledge of unconscious fantasies as expressed in unconscious conflicts.

According to Arlow (1985a), the proper subject of psychoanalytic investigation is not the patient's objective history, but the vicissitudes of the dominant elements of his or her unconscious fantasy thinking and their effects on mental functioning and interpersonal relations. Unconscious fantasies are the source of transference. He writes,

> When the patient wants the analyst to play a role or imagines the analyst to be playing a certain role, he is not treating the analyst as his doctor, but as

an object of some wishful drive stemming from an unconscious fantasy. This is what we mean by transference [p. 247].

Arlow's (1969a, b, 1985a, b) view that unconscious fantasy goes on continuously and accounts for a wide range of both normal and psychopathological phenomena is similar to the Kleinian concept that all primary process content is unconscious fantasy (Isaacs, 1948).

Arlow (1969b) describes the interaction between conscious and unconscious fantasy function and reality perception as similar to the effect that is obtained when two motion pictures flash a continuous series of images simultaneously but from opposite sides on a translucent screen. He writes, "There are two centers of perceptual input, introspection and exteroception, supplying data from the inner eye and data from the outer eye" (p. 48).

Arlow's imaginative but fundamentally erroneous model of two sources of input to consciousness is basically the same formulation that Freud (1940a) made in the "Outline" and that I have elsewhere argued against (Dorpat, 1985). In brief, my argument is that contemporary knowledge in the cognitive sciences demonstrates that there is only one pathway to consciousness and that all input, whether endogenous or exogenous, is processed by the same mechanisms prior to attaining consciousness. Rapaport (1967) and Sandler and Joffe (1969) show that external stimuli pass through the same unconscious and preconscious pathways of processing and organization as do endogenous stimuli on their way to consciousness.

Arlow's formulations, like the Kleinian writings on unconscious fantasy, have broadened and expanded Freud's concepts of unconscious fantasy. Unfortunately, in so doing, Arlow has compounded the errors in the original Freudian theory.

KLEINIAN CONCEPTS OF UNCONSCIOUS FANTASY

Kleinian psychoanalysts make extensive use of the unconscious fantasy concept; for them the primary content of all conscious and unconscious thought processes are unconscious fantasies. Kleinian theory is predominantly concerned with the patient's relationships with internal objects as these are determined primarily by unconscious fantasy. Melanie Klein and her followers view unconscious fantasy as the language of the primary instincts (Isaacs, 1948; Klein, 1952). Kleinians give far less weight to the significance of the child's experience with the environment in determining the child's basic outlook than to the nature of his unconscious fantasy. The major thrust of the interpretive work in Kleinian analyses is the examination of the effects of the patient's unconscious fantasies on internal object relationships that involve the analyst. In my view, as well as Modell's (1984), the concept of an internal object is a failed attempt to retain an object relations theory that is consistent with a one-person psychology.

The notion of "unconscious fantasy" was the source of a lively and prolonged controversy in London between the Kleinian school and the followers of Anna Freud (Glover, 1945; Steiner, 1985). Glover and others asserted that the Kleinians had no justification for extending the meanings and connotations of the term unconscious fantasy far beyond the limits of Sigmund Freud's concept. Anna Freud's group disputed the Kleinian idea of unconscious fantasy as encompassing the totality of unconscious psychic life, and they disagreed that unconscious fantasy begins in the early weeks of infancy.

THE FALSE ANALOGY IN THE CONCEPT OF UNCONSCIOUS FANTASY

No one, including Freud, has explicitly presented a logical argument justifying the inference of unconscious fantasy. The *implicit* argument is a false analogy between conscious fantasy and primary process functioning such as occurs in symptom and dream formation. Freud (1900) drew several analogies between conscious fantasies (especially the erotic daydreams of puberty children) and night dreams, and he used these analogies mistakenly to conclude that the processes and unconscious contents underlying dreams and neurotic symptoms were unconscious fantasies. The false analogy implicitly made by Freud and later by others such as Arlow (1969a, b, 1985a, b) and Isaacs (1948) may be stated in this way: Because some primary process products in dreams and symptoms are similar in their wish-fulfilling aspects to conscious fantasy, primary process is similar in other respects to conscious fantasy. Therefore, the processes and contents of the primary process are those of unconscious fantasy.

One of the fundamental differences between conscious daydreams and primary process functioning is that in daydreaming the subject suspends his reality-testing functions and temporarily withdraws from interactions with the external world. In contrast, as I indicated in Chapter 2, the primary process system functions usually in awake and nonpsychotic people involved in interactions with the external world, and the results of its unconscious meaning analyses of those interactions are represented in the end-products of its functioning.

Though the primary process mode of functioning is similar to conscious fantasy insofar as both concern concrete events (rather than abstractions), the accumulated knowledge (critically reviewed in Chapter 2) about primary process demonstrates fundamental differences between conscious fantasy and primary process cognition. The term unconscious fantasy is a misleading and inaccurate designation for either the content or the mode of functioning of the primary process.

PRIMARY PROCESS COGNITION IN YOUNG CHILDREN

Another kind of evidence supporting the proposition that primary process cognition should not be characterized as unconscious fantasy comes from studies done by psychoanalysts and developmental psychologists on cognition in infants and young children. The egocentric, and (from an adult observer's point of view) unrealistic, characteristics of cognition in young children have led some persons erroneously to describe their thinking as fantasy.

Sandler (1975) has written about the sexual theories of young children (ages 2 to 6) and how these may mistakenly appear to be products of the children's fantasy. He concludes that a child's constructions of sexual theories are perfectly reasonable conclusions reached by the child using the facts at his disposal. What is "reasonable" for a young child is not necessarily "reasonable" for an adult. A three-year-old child who believes that babies are born through the anus is thinking rationally for a child of that age, because he has had the experience that what appears to be part of his body (feces) can be separated from the body through defecation. Similarly, a child who believes in oral conception may have valid and reasonable grounds at the time for believing in that theory.

The sexual theories and other similar ideas of young children should not be considered to be fantasies but rather products of the child's limited cognitive abilities. The apparently unrealistic ideas of young children simply reflect their immature and egocentric cognition in the preoperational stage. Whereas sexual and aggressive wishes may play some role in the creation of a child's sexual theories, they are not the only or necessarily the decisive factors in the formation of such ideas (Sandler and Sandler, 1983).

The Sandlers explain how the repressed sexual theories of young children may later, in adult life, appear as derivatives in symptoms. What once was a conscious idea, say, a child's sexual theory of impregnation through the mouth, becomes repressed and later emerges in derivative form as a symptom or in a dream. The now unconscious and activated idea of oral impregnation may be indirectly expressed in the conversion symptom of vomiting.

ARCHAIC PRIMARY PROCESS COGNITION

The defended-against impulses, wishes, and sexual theories that may in adult life appear in primary process products (such as dreams and neurotic symptoms) reflect the type of cognition characteristic of early childhood before the development of the cognitive stage of concrete operations, which, according to Piaget, begins at about age six. Such archaic primary process cognitions can be thought of as showing the stamp imposed by childhood sexual theories of the preoperational phase as well as other concerns of the child at that time in his or her development. Neither the child's original sexual theory nor its reactivation in dreams or symptoms in later adult life is accurately described as a fantasy, an unconscious fantasy, or the derivative of an unconscious fantasy. The revival or persistence of such developmentally early cognitions in adult life is best described as archaic primary process cognition.

A CASE EXAMPLE

Abend (1990) describes what he purports to be clinical evidence indicating that specific unconscious fantasies are active in a patient's emotional life.

He reports an analytic hour in which a patient complained of her inability to cry and to express her feelings over the recent death of her mother. Abend made the following interpretation,

> You speak as if emotions were like some substance actually inside you that's unable to come out, constipated, as it were, like feces that can't be let out, and you think you'll feel better when the blockage finally breaks up and lets go [p. 68].

I do not challenge the accuracy of the interpretation; the equation of emotional expression with defecation or the riddance of other physical products of the body is a common one.

To speak of emotions as if they were concrete substances within the body is normal and expectable in young children. When this type of concrete thinking persists into adulthood, it should be called archaic primary process cognition. As I indicated in Chapter 2, archaic primary process cognition is cognition that, because of defense, trauma, or other reason has not developed into the more mature and sophisticated primary process cognition typical of adults.

Abend's clinical vignette does not constitute evidence for the hypothesis of unconscious fantasy. He merely describes some examples of archaic primary process cognition, which he mistakenly (in my opinion) interprets as arising from an unconscious fantasy. Abend provides no argument or reasons for supporting his inference that the patient's concrete thinking reflects an underlying unconscious fantasy.

The therapist's attribution of unconscious fantasy to the patient is frequently a projection of the therapist's own subjective images onto the patient. While listening to the patient in a free associative manner, the analyst may form visual and other kinds of images of what he or she imagines is going on within the patient or in the patient's interactions with the analyst. Because they believe their own *conscious* images may capture what is unconsciously going on within the patient, some analysts may mistakenly assume that the patient is having *unconscious* images similar to their own conscious ones. Although the analyst's conscious imagery may be congruent with what is being unconsciously communicated by the analysand, it does not follow that the analysand is having unconscious images or fantasies.

Psychoanalysts commonly refer to primary process or unconscious ideation as unconscious fantasy; in so doing they follow Freud in confusing the intent and experience of the patient with the judgment of the objective observer (Schafer, 1968). The analyst as an objective observer explains certain cognitive distortions as arising from the patient's unconscious fantasies. As Freud himself made clear, however, for the patient these ideas represent reality, not fantasy. Therefore, when an obejctive observer such as the analyst calls them fantasies, he is mistakenly confusing and conflating them with those imaginative activities which the patient recognizes and intends to be fantasy, daydreaming, and the like.

FREUD'S PAPER ON BEATING FANTASIES

Freud (1919), Arlow (1969a, b, 1985a, b), and others who write about the activation of unconscious fantasies in adults trace one of the origins of these unconscious fantasies to the *conscious* fantasies of childhood. For example, in the context of discussing the childhood origin of unconscious beating fantasies in adult patients, Freud (1919) recommended that psychoanalysis should remove the amnesia that conceals from the adult his knowledge of his childhood from its beginnings, that is, from about the second to the fifth year.

The years (two to five) Freud describes as the time period when these conscious beating fantasies are first formed are approximately the same years Piaget (1952) classified as belonging to the preoperational stage of cognitive development. In view of what I have already written about the cognitive limitations of young children and their sexual theories, it is reasonable to question Freud's inference that the ideas young children have about beatings are fantasies. At least in some, if not in all, such instances, childhood ideas about beatings are (like the sexual theories described by Sandler (1975)) the products of the child's limited cognitive abilities and his or her theories about sexuality and interpersonal relationships.

Just as the original childhood ideas that supply the content for unconscious conflicts (such as the sexual theories of young children) are not correctly labeled as fantasies, so, also, the later adult replications of such primary process cognitions should not be called "unconscious fantasies." As Bion (1977) writes, "What psychoanalysts call phantasies are, in some cases at least, the present-day survivals of what once were models that the patient formed to match his emotional experience" (p. 104).

Grossman (1982) wrongly claims, "Infantile fantasies are theories about sexuality. All mental products, then are personal constructions" (p. 923). He even writes of the self as a fantasy and as a "personal myth" (p. 929). Though (as Grossman asserts) all mental products are constructions, not all such constructions are fantasies. That a child's sexual theories are constructions does not warrant their being called fantasies.

In addition to the sexual theories and related ideas of childhood, there is another important childhood source of archaic primary process cognitions in adults. Primitive primary process cognitions in adults can frequently be traced back to various kinds of traumas and developmental deficits. Traumatic parent–child interactions, along with the defenses against those traumas, strongly influence both the formation and maintenance of archaic primary process cognitions. (For further explication of the relationship between trauma and archaic primary process cognition, see Chapter 4.)

STUDIES OF INFANT COGNITION

Stern (1985), challenging the prevailing psychoanalytic idea that the appropriate units of ontogenetic theory are fantasies, disagrees that the most relevant subjective experiences of the infant are reality-distorting fantasies. Current findings from studies of infant cognition oppose the notion that the pleasure principle developmentally precedes the reality principle. Stern persuasively argues that wish-fulfilling fantasies and defenses against reality should not be given a privileged and prior developmental position. He effectively disputes the prevalent notion that the sense of reality should be seen as secondary in time and derivation, as growing out of the loss of the need for fantasy and defense.

According to Stern, a basic assumption of Mahler's concept of "normal symbiosis" is that even if infants could tell self from others, their wish-fulfilling fantasies and defenses would prevent them from doing so. Mahler, Pine and Bergman (1975) postulate that from birth until two months, the infant psyche is protected by the stimulus barrier. After the barrier is gone, infants would be left with all the stresses of being on their own unless they replaced the reality of their aloneness and separateness with the "delusion" of a fused-with mother and thus a protected state. As Stern (1985) demonstrates, Mahler's theory of a normal symbiosis is based on a belief in infantile fantasy and distortion, rather than on a belief in reality perception.

Stern also effectively challenges Kleinian ontogenetic theories of experience as fantasy, not of experience as reality. According to the Kleinians, the units making up the stages of developmental theory are wish-fulfilling fantasies, distortions, delusions, and other defensive formations based on fantasies. Klein postulates that the infant's basic subjective experiences consist of schizoid, paranoid, and depressive positions. Her concepts of these positions wrongly assume that infantile experience operates predominantly outside of ongoing reality perceptions.

Empirical studies of infants show that from the beginning infants mainly experience reality (Lichtenberg, 1983; Stern, 1985). Their subjective experiences are not distorted by wish-fulfilling fantasies or defenses. The so-called cognitive distortions in infants are brought about by cognitive or perceptual immaturity and overgeneralization.

Contemporary investigations of child development show that infants experience only interpersonal realities and not reality altered by unconscious fantasies or conflict-resolving distortions (Stern, 1985). It is the actual shape of interpersonal reality that helps determine the developmental course for infants.

Historically, psychoanalytic theory has maintained that the presence of fantasy activity in infants is indicated by hallucinatory wish fulfillment, which is seen as occurring as early as the third month of life. The observational evidence cited is an awake and hungry baby who begins to cry. The cry is replaced temporarily by a relieved, even smiling, look when the baby begins to suck a finger or a pacifier (Lichtenberg, 1983). Drawing upon his comprehensive review of studies on infant development, Lichtenberg (1983) concludes that the infant does not form internalized images or fantasies, but instead has only memories of action patterns.

PRIMARY PROCESS ACTIVITY
AND THE EXTERNAL WORLD

The standard and erroneous notion that primary process content is unconscious fantasy has contributed to the fallacy that primary process cognition is isolated from interactions with the external world. Freud

(1940a), for example, described the id and the primary processes that take place within the id as cut off from contact with the external world. Similarly, Rycroft (1956) writes about the "fundamentally autistic nature of the primary process" (p. 139), and in his discussion about unconscious fantasy, he describes fantasy "as an antithesis to external reality" (p. 141). Clearly, the terms fantasy and unconscious fantasy in the psychoanalytic literature describe wish-fulfilling mental activities designed to evade reality.

As indicated in Chapter 2, primary process cognition is not isolated from environmental stimuli and interactions with others. On the contrary, the primary process system is immediately and directly involved both in perception of the environment and in communicative interactions (especially affective communication) with other people.

A DISCUSSION OF BOESKY'S CASE STUDY

Little empirical or logical evidence exists for the existence of unconscious fantasy. An exception is Boesky's (1988) clinical report on an analytic patient who supposedly had the unconscious fantasy that the successful termination of his analysis had the meaning of a lethal orgasm. Boesky purports to tender evidence supportive of the influence of unconscious fantasy.

Boesky provides sufficient data, especially from his detailed account of two analytic hours, to demonstrate a coherent and repeated linkage between the patient's thoughts about death, water, explosive discharge, orgasm, and the patient's termination of his analysis. I do not question Boesky's belief that the patient unconsciously equated orgasm with some kind of destructive discharge and that this irrational fear was triggered by the impending termination of his analysis. His inference, however, that the patient's irrational and unrealistic fears stemmed from an unconscious fantasy is not justified. Boesky has done a kind of structural analysis of the patient's communications that demonstrates the existence of a consistent pattern or schema.

The patient's irrational fears stemmed from a schema that contained, as it were, what Weiss and Sampson (1986) call an "unconscious pathogenic idea." A translation of this unconscious pathogenic idea into words would be something like the following: The termination of an important relationship brings about a destructive orgasm. (Chapters 4 and 7 include a more comprehensive discussion of unconscious pathogenic ideas.)

Cognitive Distortion and the Inference of Unconscious Fantasy

On what basis did Boesky draw the inference from the patient's communications that a powerful "unconscious fantasy" was influencing the patient's affects and behaviors? The clinical data Boesky used in making the inference of unconscious fantasy had the common property of being unrealistic and irrational ideas.

The usual reason for inferring an unconscious fantasy in psychoanalysis is the occurrence of some behavior or communication of the patient that the analyst believes demonstrates cognitive distortion (e.g., cognitions that are irrational, inappropriate, or unrealistic). In Freud's theory, as well as in its later modifications by the Kleinians, Arlow, and others, unconscious fantasies plus the distorting powers of primary-process mechanisms account for the distortions in dreams, symptoms, and other cognitions.

Unconscious fantasies play a dynamic role in Freud's hypotheses about cognitive distortion, and in his view, drive-activated unconscious fantasies precede and cause cognitive distortion.

Freud (1915d) wrote:

> Of such a nature are those fantasies of normal people as well as the neurotics which we have recognized as preliminary stages in the formation of both dreams and symptoms and which, in spite of their high degree of organization, remain repressed and therefore cannot become conscious [pp. 190–191].

Traditionally, the judgment that a particular cognition is distorted is made by the analyst, and the patient is said to be unaware of the distortion. This traditional view has been challenged by analysts who stress the degree to which seeming "cognitive distortions," especially within the transference, are not distortions at all but selective and subtle attentiveness to aspects of the analyst-analysand interaction (Gill, 1983, 1984; Hoffman, 1983; Stolorow, Brandchaft, and Atwood, 1987).

Freud (1912) wrote about the cognitive distortions contained in transference manifestations in this way:

> Just as happens in dreams, the patient regards the products of the awakening of his unconscious impulses as contemporaneous and real; he seeks to put his passions into action without taking into account of the real situation [p. 108].

How did Freud and other analysts arrive at the conclusion that unconscious fantasies caused distorted cognitions? My review of the literature on unconscious fantasy indicates that psychoanalytic theories on this subject are not based on an empirical analysis of distorted cognitions, but rather appear to be deductions that follow from Freud's theory of cognition.

Most probably, Freud derived his hypotheses about unconscious fantasy from his primary model of cognition, his theory of hallucinatory wish fulfillment. In his theory of cognition, the capacity for wish-fulfilling fantasy develops out of the prior and infantile ability for hallucinatory wish fulfillment.

In Chapter 1, I argued that Freud's theory of hallucinatory wish fulfillment is not an inductive conclusion based on the empirical analysis of many dreams, but rather a deduction following from his theory of cognition and the psychic apparatus. In support of this argument is Freud's (1900) statement, ''It is self-evident that dreams must be wish-fulfillments, since nothing but a wish can set our apparatus at work'' (p. 567).

The notions of unconscious wish and unconscious fantasy are roughly synonymous, and some authors argue that the idea of a wish implies a fantasy of the self and an object engaged in some interaction. The same arguments I used in Chapter 1 against Freud's theory of cognition and his theory of hallucinatory wish fulfillment also apply to psychoanalytic theories about unconscious fantasies. With the collapse of Freud's theory of cognition and especially his copy theory of perception and hallucinatory wish-fulfillment theory, there are no longer any grounds for constructing valid theories about unconscious fantasies.

Another reason for rejecting theories about unconscious fantasy as a proximal cause of distorted cognition is that psychoanalysis and the cognitive sciences now have more scientifically acceptable and tested hypotheses about cognitive distortion. These proven explanations include ignorance, diminished cognitive capacity such as takes place in neurosis, drug intoxication and brain damage, cognitive dyscontrol, regression, the use of primitive defenses, and developmental defects. The use of the unconscious-fantasy notion to explain cognitive distortion is simplistic.

CHAPTER 4

Unconscious Pathogenic Beliefs or Unconscious Fantasy?

Psychoanalytic Theories on Psychic Trauma

The aim of this chapter is to compare and contrast traditional with contemporary psychoanalytic theoretical approaches to psychic trauma. This study is limited to three topics: unconscious pathogenic beliefs, enactive memory, and defense—all important elements in human responses to trauma. After reviewing the writings of Weiss and Sampson (1986) on the role of trauma in the psychogenesis of unconscious pathogenic beliefs, I shall argue for considering their concept of unconscious pathogenic beliefs as a partial substitute for traditional concepts of unconscious fantasy in reactions to trauma.

In my discussion of enactive memory, I advance the proposition that such repetitions of trauma are not caused by underlying unconscious fantasies but by the organism's need to repeat normal, unexpected, and traumatic experiences. The final section, on defense, presents some reasons for revising the clinical theory regarding the role of defense in reactions to trauma.

The concept of trauma used here is a broad one that includes chronic traumas and what Khan (1963) calls cumulative trauma. The most frequent psychic trauma reactions are psychiatric disorders stemming from persistently disturbing and emotionally destructive parent–child relationships. Much more professional time and effort is expended by psychotherapists and psychoanalysts in treating patients with chronic traumatic reactions arising out of disruptive childhood relationships than is devoted to the treatment of patients suffering from acute trauma disorders caused by stresses, losses, and natural calamities.

In Freud's early writings, he considered psychic trauma to be a major cause of hysteria as well as other psychoneuroses. He believed that hysterical symptoms could be understood only if they were traced to earlier experiences of sexual abuse or "seduction" that had a traumatic effect on the patient (Breuer and Freud, 1893–95).

After Freud (1906) dropped the seduction theory, he tended to minimize the importance of psychic trauma in the pathogenesis of psychiatric disorders. This change, in my opinion, represented an unfortunate and fateful shift that led psychoanalysis to turn its attention away from the personal, mainly unconscious, meanings of actual occurrences such as traumatic events, to a preoccupation with wholly intrapsychic and endogenously created entities such as instinctual drives and unconscious fantasies.

The presumption that most patients' reports of childhood sexual abuse could be ascribed to fantasy is no longer tenable. For instance, in a study of 53 women incest survivors, a large majority of patients who recalled experiences of sexual abuse in childhood were able to validate their memories from other information sources (Herman and Schatzow, 1987).

Along with Ulman and Brothers (1988) and others, I urge psychoanalysis to return to the paradigm of trauma. The clinical evidence indicates that trauma, not psychic conflict, is an important cause of psychiatric illness. Unconscious psychic conflict is ubiquitous; it occurs in everyone, and it is probably always present. The idea of conflict assists us in understanding the *content* of psychiatric symptoms, but it adds little or nothing to knowledge about the *etiology* of psychological disorders.

Freud (1939) classified the effects of trauma into two categories: repetitions and defense. He correctly described defensive reactions as being just as much fixations to trauma as repetitions of trauma. The first category, repetitions, includes those behaviors, such as nightmares, that are involuntary intrusions in thought, emotions, and behavior of aspects of the traumatic experience. Repetitions of trauma are direct or symbolic reenactments of the traumatic event complex. In addition to the foregoing two categories of effects of trauma, there is a third category, pathogenic beliefs, not explicitly noted by Freud. Pathogenic beliefs are the products of individuals' conscious and unconscious meaning analysis of traumatic events and interpersonal relations. Pathogenic beliefs constructed in childhood may later, along with other aspects of their traumatic experiences, become unconscious through defense.

PATHOGENIC BELIEFS:
THE CONTRIBUTIONS OF WEISS AND SAMPSON

Weiss and Sampson (1986) argue convincingly that pathogenic beliefs play a crucial role in the development and maintenance of psychopathology. Pathogenic beliefs should be distinguished from fantasy as Freud (1911) defined it. Freud wrote that a person's fantasies are wishful, regulated by the pleasure principle, and not subject to reality testing. In contrast to fantasies, pathogenic beliefs are not wishful, but instead are grim and constricting. Pathogenic beliefs are not opposed to reality; they are constructed by persons in an effort to represent reality and to adapt to it.

Though Freud did not develop a theory of pathogenic beliefs, he (in Weiss's view) laid down the foundations for such a theory in his discussions about young boys' that the danger of castration is real. Freud believed that it is because of fear of castration that a boy represses his oedipal wishes and so develops a proclivity to neurosis.

Freud (1926) explicitly stated that from the point of view of the boy castration is a real danger. Freud (1940a) emphasized that the belief in the danger of castration, rather than causing pleasure, is shocking, and he asserted that the experiences from which a boy infers that belief provide him with "the severest trauma of his young life" (p. 190).

Weiss shows that Freud repeatedly referred to castration fears as a belief or a conviction, and only on a few occasions as a fantasy. For example, Freud (1940b) wrote that after a boy who has been threatened with castration sees the female genitalia, "he cannot help *believing* in the *reality* of the danger of castration" (p. 277). In Freud's view, if the male patient is to become well, he must become aware of and change his belief that he will be castrated as a punishment for his oedipal impulses. Freud assumed, too, that female analysands must modify their corresponding pathogenic ideas. Freud, however, did not view the working through of pathogenic beliefs as occupying a central position in the therapeutic process.

The conscious fantasies and pathogenic beliefs of children are not equivalent; children derive pleasure from fantasies but not from pathogenic beliefs. Children may be terrified by or severely inhibited by pathogenic ideas. In producing a conscious fantasy, a child ignores the frightening aspects of reality or alters reality so as to view it as the fulfillment of his wishes. In contrast, in forming a pathogenic belief, a child confronts reality.

Weiss and Sampson's theory goes beyond Freudian concepts by asserting that a change in patients' pathogenic beliefs is the essential process of psychotherapy. They modify and enlarge Freud's views in stating that many different pathogenic beliefs exist, in addition to those emphasized by Freud, that are linked with the Oedipus complex.

Pathogenic beliefs and the fear, anxiety, shame, and guilt associated with them and that they elicit provide the primary basic motives for both the development and maintenance of pathological defenses and inhibitions. According to Weiss and Sampson, all kinds of psychopathology are rooted in pathogenic beliefs that are the critical element, the sine qua non, of psychopathology.

Weiss and Sampson (1986) write,

A pathogenic belief contains at least four components: 1) the attitudes, impulses, or goals with which it is concerned; that is the attitudes, impulses or goals it assumes are dangerous; 2) the kinds of dangers it foretells; 3) the kinds of remedies, such as repression or withdrawal, which it enjoins; and 4) the strength of conviction with which it is held. It is possible, by varying these four components, to derive the pathogenic beliefs underlying any kind of psychopathology [p. 325].

Though Weiss and Sampson have made a major contribution to a psychoanalytic theory of psychopathology in their concept of pathogenic beliefs, their theory is mistaken in holding that *all* psychopathology is linked with an underlying pathologic belief. My clinical experience in analyzing enactive memories of patients suffering from psychic trauma plus the contributions of child psychoanalysts Dowling (1990) and Pine (1985), indicate that some, if not all, enactive memories are not attributable to or associated with unconscious pathogenic ideas. It makes sense both clinically and theoretically to distinguish between repetitions of traumatic experiences and repetitions of pathogenic beliefs about those experiences.

DEVELOPMENTAL PERSPECTIVES
ON PATHOGENIC IDEAS

Children develop pathogenic beliefs from their perceptions and experiences of the terrifying and traumatic aspects of reality. Furthermore, in forming pathogenic beliefs, the children are attempting to cope with realistic dangers, frustrations, and traumas.

Pathogenic beliefs are formed by the internalization of conflicts and traumas associated with children's interactions with their parents and others. There are two major sequences by which children may develop pathogenic beliefs (Weiss and Sampson, 1986). One, a child discovers that his attempts to reach a certain goal threaten his all-important ties to his parents. The child then develops a pathogenic belief that causally connects his attempts to reach the goal with the threat to the parental ties. As a consequence of this pathogenic belief, the child needs to defend against the awareness of the goal in order to retain his ties to his parents. For example, an analytic patient came to analysis with the unconscious pathogenic belief that his mother would become unhappy or ill if he acted on his own initiative. Gradually in his analysis the previously unconscious belief could be traced to early experiences with his mother in which she disapproved of his independent and autonomous actions. Probably the patient's childhood observations of his mother becoming unhappy or troubled when he showed initiative led to his pathogenic belief that his steps toward independence caused her to be disturbed and even ill.

The second sequence that leads to the formation of a pathogenic belief is the child's retrospective self-blaming for a traumatic event such as the death of a parent. Prominent examples of this dynamic may be found in cases of survivor guilt.

In the clinical example in the next section, an unconscious pathogenic belief was the major basis for a 46-year-old married woman's profound inhibition of anger. Psychoanalytic treatment revealed that her defenses and inhibitions against anger were triggered by the unconscious pathogenic idea that she would be punished by others if she became angry at them. Though she was not consciously aware of this pathogenic idea prior to her treatment, it had strongly regulated both her feeling states and her interpersonal relations from early childhood. Her unconscious pathogenic belief was formed from her disturbing relations with her parents, who had severely punished her for even the mildest expressions of anger.

THE ROLE OF PATHOGENIC IDEAS
IN THE PSYCHOANALYTIC PROCESS

The psychoanalytic process is one in which the patient works with the analyst, both consciously and unconsciously, to disconfirm his pathogenic beliefs. He does this by unconsciously testing his pathogenic beliefs in relation to the analyst and by assimilating the insights about those pathogenic beliefs conveyed by the analyst's interpretations. Patients seek new experiences with the analyst that are different from their traumatic experiences with their parents (or others) and from which experiences they have formed their pathogenic beliefs. The analyst's primary task is to help the patient in his struggle to disconfirm his pathogenic beliefs.

Patients test the analyst by repeating the traumatic events and relations of their past (rather than by remembering them) in two different ways: by turning passive into active and by transferring. In turning passive into active, the patient behaves as a parent behaved toward him; and in transferring, he behaves as he once behaved toward a parent (Weiss and Sampson, 1986).

In the analytic situation, a patient's goals and plans are directed to overcoming pathogenic beliefs, and they require the patient to test the analyst. Patients are able to progress and gain insight as long as the analyst consistently makes interpretations that patients can use in their struggle to carry out their unconscious plans to disconfirm their unconscious beliefs.

Interpersonal relationships (including the analyst–patient relationship) are therapeutic when they disconfirm the patient's unconscious pathogenic beliefs. Contrariwise, an event or relationship is traumatic to the extent that it confirms and thereby intensifies a person's unconscious pathogenic ideas.

A Case Example

The following case study illustrates and explains the importance of unconscious pathogenic beliefs in psychopathology and traces their beginnings to traumatic childhood interpersonal relations.

The analysand was a middle-aged married woman and mother of two children. A whole cluster of symptoms, character traits, dream symbols, and other behaviors became understandable and interpretable as a single kind of interpersonal schema. The unconscious pathogenic idea contained in the schema could be characterized as, "It is dangerous to reveal to others the good things I own or have inside myself."

Probably most pathological about this pathogenic idea was its inhibitory effects on the patient's thoughts, emotions, and actions. What was kept hidden (sexuality, intelligence) was not available for her conscious use or pleasure.

From childhood until her analysis, she had continued to use the same methods for concealing from herself and others the good parts of herself. As is the case with all defensive actions, she was not only unaware of *what* she was concealing, she was also unaware *that* she was concealing and *how* she was concealing the valuable parts of herself. The working through of the defensive aspects of this schema involved repeated interpretations of the fact *that* she was defending, *what* she was defending against, *how* she was defending, and *why* she was defending.

Early in her analysis, the patient was vague and uncertain about the nature and extent of her financial assets. She was uncommonly reluctant about sharing with her analyst and others what she did know. Once the defensive hiding and inhibition were identified, she could begin to understand and work it through. Only then did she first learn about and acknowledge the full extent of her investments and other financial assets.

She hid from others, and often from herself, her superior intellectual abilities. When teachers or relatives called her bright or even brilliant, she was genuinely surprised and taken aback by their comments. Until late in her analysis, she consistently underestimated her intellectual abilities. By wearing plain and inexpensive clothes, she also concealed her sexuality as well as the fact that she could have easily afforded more expensive and more attractive clothes.

Her pathogenic idea had its roots in different developmental levels. In the anal stage, she had been subjected to rigid toilet training and enemas. Constipation both in childhood and later was another manifestation of this pervasive defense of holding back and concealing from others valued contents within her self. Her unconscious pathogenic idea also had oedipal origins inasmuch as the inhibition of her sexuality and her attractiveness served to allay anxiety and guilt about an "oedipal victory" over her alcoholic mother. In contrast to her mother, whom the patient's father despised and ultimately rejected, the patient felt that she was favored by her father because of her intellectual precocity and her physical attractiveness.

Another important childhood origin of her need to conceal what she valued was to protect herself from her three older siblings, who were intensely envious and jealous of the adoring attention she received from their parents and others.

In summary, this patient's unconscious pathogenic idea regarding the dangers of revealing what she valued about herself was in childhood an adaptive solution to conflicts and traumas arising at different development levels. There is no evidence to support the view that her pathogenic idea was an unconscious fantasy or that it was derived from a childhood conscious fantasy. Rather, it was developed in childhood from her conscious and unconscious appraisals of her actual experiences with her family members.

GEORGE KLEIN'S VIEWS
ON PATHOLOGICAL INTROJECTS

In this section I critically review George Klein's (1976) writings on pathological introjects. Though Klein views introjects as arising from the internalization of traumatically experienced relationships, he, unfortunately, accords a central place to unconscious fantasy in his account of the introject's activity.

Klein describes the cognitive activity of an introject as an unconscious fantasy. He defines an introject as an organized schema with three components: an image of an object, an image of the self in interaction with that object, and an affective coloring of the object-image and self-image at the time of the interaction (such as rage and aggression). His definition of introjects is unobjectionable except that his use of the term "image" to describe unconscious self- and object representations assumes facts not in evidence. Klein, I suspect, is the unwitting victim of the common mistake, discussed in Chapter 1, that imagery is the foundation of thought. In the following quotation, Klein describes the dynamic importance of a repressed interpersonal schema.

> Cognitively, the activity of an introject is an unconscious fantasy. Unconscious fantasy refers to the activity of internalized relationships that have the status of schemata dissociated from the self. The assimilation of a repressed interpersonal mode of relationship results in a repressed interpersonal schema which replicates the dilemma, conflicts, and wishes of that relationship. . . . When such a schema—an unconscious fantasy—gives meaning to

an event or an encounter, defining it as useful or harmful, loving or unloving, these attributes ascribed to the environment are not merely coded but potentiated in the terms of the schema. The environment is endowed, so to speak, with the significance of the unconscious fantasy [p. 299].

Klein goes on to describe the thinking and behavior of a person who is subject to the organizing grip of unconscious fantasy. Such a person behaves as if imaginary events, figures, and relationships were true. Klein views the unconscious fantasy as a repressed interpersonal schema that gives meaning to an event or an encounter. For him, the behavior-inducing activity of an unconscious fantasy is very potent; it has far-reaching effects in structuring reality for the person.

The clinical observations and facts are not in question. As Klein indicates, pathological introjects (i.e., repressed interpersonal schemata) do have far-reaching effects in structuring one's view of the world, and they may bring about distortions in one's perceptions of others. His otherwise sophisticated and informed theory about introjects and their origins is marred by his remarks about unconscious fantasy.

Klein, like many others, infers the activity of an unconscious fantasy from observations of cognitive distortions. The kinds of observations from which Klein infers the activity of an unconscious fantasy include irrational or unrealistic ideation, inadequate affective responses, and distorted or false views about the self and others.

Klein's clinical descriptions of the cognitions and behaviors associated with pathological introjects and his account of the indicators of unconscious fantasy fit the description given in Chapter 2 of archaic primary process cognition. By definition, archaic primary process cognition is concrete, egocentric, and unrealistic. The question, "Why does archaic primary process sometimes persist past its normal developmental stage into adulthood?" has important practical as well as theoretical implications. As I indicated in Chapters 2 and 3, archaic primary process cognition is not fantasy, nor is it derived from unconscious fantasy. It is a developmentally early kind of cognition found normally in young children and under certain conditions in adult life.

Two related elements, psychic trauma and defense, discussed in the last section of this chapter, bring about the pathological persistence of archaic primary process cognition into adulthood. Pathological introjects are formed by the introjection of a disruptive relational mode from a specific traumatic interpersonal relationship. George Klein's study of introjects indicates an uncommon understanding of the part played by both trauma and defense in the formation and maintenance of pathological introjects.

Klein (1976) writes, "What is repressed is not an 'object' but an interpersonal mode—a traumatically experienced relationship. . . . An

introject refers to a relationship associated with danger, anxiety, and fear''
(p. 295).

Elsewhere (Dorpat, 1985) I have discussed the dynamic importance of
psychic trauma in the formation of pathological introjects of five patients.
In all five cases, there was abundant evidence supporting the hypothesis
that the patients' introjects had developed out of traumatic parent–child
interactions. The concept of unconscious fantasy was not helpful in
illuminating the patients' need for repeating or transferring disturbing
object relations either within or outside the analytic situation.

Though Klein gives an illuminating account about the significance of
traumatic interpersonal relations in the formation of pathological introjects, he does not include the role of unconscious pathogenic belief. In my
view, both elements (enactive memory and unconscious pathogenic
beliefs) contribute to the formation of pathological introjects.

CONTRIBUTIONS OF SELF PSYCHOLOGISTS

Though self psychologists, such as the Shanes and Ulman and Brothers,
have made important contributions to the psychoanalytic theory of
trauma, they unfortunately continue to accord a central position to the
concept of unconscious fantasy. To illustrate their claim that self psychology has made important contributions to the understanding of
unconscious fantasy, the Shanes (1990) describe a patient who allegedly
had the unconscious fantasy that he would be forever demeaned by his
mother and forever attached to her because of his inability to give her up.
The Shanes' case study and especially their reconstruction of the patient's
childhood development support the more coherent and plausible explanation that the patient was suffering from the effects of unconscious
pathogenic ideas stemming from the emotional and physical trauma he
sustained during childhood.

From the patient's consistent pattern of irrational masochistic behaviors
they wrongly inferred an underlying unconscious fantasy. Their own
clinical data support the interpretation that the patient's masochistic
behaviors constituted enactive memories and the activity of underlying
unconscious pathogenic ideas.

One of the central aims of Ulman and Brothers (1988) is to formulate a
self-psychological concept of fantasy and to apply it to a psychoanalytic
theory of psychic trauma. Their conception of unconscious fantasy differs
somewhat from Freud's inasmuch as they dispute his notion of unconscious fantasy as solely the product of instinctual drives.

The concept of unconscious fantasy plays a central role in their theory of
trauma as well as their recommendations for the analytic therapy of

traumatized patients. They argue that it is neither reality nor fantasy that causes trauma but, rather, that the unconscious meaning of real occurrences causes trauma by shattering central organizing fantasies of self in relation to selfobject. Their treatment approach relies on the analytic technique of analyzing what they call selfobject transference fantasies of mirrored grandiosity or idealized merger as the means for restoring and transforming shattered and faultily restored central organizing fantasies. Examples of central organizing fantasies are unconscious fantasies of the self as grandiose or of the idealized selfobject as omnipotent. For Ulman and Brothers, central organizing fantasies are unconscious meaning structures that begin to take form early in life and remain active throughout life. They are unconscious narcissistic fantasies that fail to undergo sufficient developmental transformation and therefore remain in their original archaic form. These unconscious narcissistic fantasies involve illusions of personally unique attributes and special endowments, such as a sense of entitlement, of magically uncanny power, as well as merger with idealized selfobjects.

Ulman and Brothers summarize their position in this way:

> We conceive of archaic narcissistic fantasy as the central meaning structures unconsciously organizing the sense of self in relation to selfobject and hence defining the personal significance of events occurring in the social world of shared experience [p. 295].

This formulation is admirable except for the reference to fantasy. What they are writing about when they say "unconsciously organizing the sense of self" and "defining the personal significance of events" is functions served by what we have termed in this book unconscious meaning analysis.

I concur with their view that the understanding, interpreting, and working through of the unconscious meanings of trauma are a major purpose of psychoanalytic therapy for traumatized patients. However, Ulman and Brothers have perpetuated in their theoretical formulations and in their case studies a basic error made by many other psychoanalysts in their writings on trauma. The book by Ulman and Brothers lacks a systematic consideration of the social context of traumatization and how it contributes to both the form and severity of psychological responses to psychic trauma. For example, clinical studies demonstrate how denial of trauma by significant others is often an important part of the psychosocial genesis of pathological responses to traumatic events. The authors apparently do not recognize that most psychological trauma has its origins in the violations or loss of significant relationships and the resultant social isolation, helplessness, and diminished capacity to maintain human relationships. The books extensive case histories show a lack of attention to the actual interpersonal and social world of the traumatized victims. The authors focus on the patients' unconscious fantasies obscures the central, tragic truth that it is the actual (not fantasied) loss or violation of specific relationships that is traumatizing.

Ulman and Brothers claim that psychopathological reactions to trauma stem from the breakdown of unconscious fantasies. In contrast, I hold that what is pathogenic is not the patient's unconscious fantasies but the realities of traumatic experiences and the consequent repetitions of those experiences, as well as the unconscious pathogenic beliefs constructed about those deeply disturbing experiences.

Interpersonal Interactions Are Not Enactments of Unconscious Fantasies

Ulman and Brothers wrongly assume that enactments and other kinds of overt actions are derived from unconscious fantasies. As discussed in previous chapters, their assumption that the manifest content of a person's communications is preceded by and caused by a latent content consisting of unconscious fantasies is an error they share with many classical psychoanalysts.

Ulman and Brothers (1988) describe a traumatized patient in this way:

> The absence of a close father-son relationship prevented Mike from unconsciously enacting a healthy fantasy of idealized merger with an omnipotent paternal imago. This unconscious fantasy enactment could have modulated and tempered his fantasies of grandiosity [p. 44].

The authors erroneously assume that father–son and other similar close male relationships necessarily implicate enactments of unconscious fantasies of idealized merger.

What follows is another example of a similar mistaken kind of inference. In their vignette about a rape victim, Ulman and Brothers write:

> Much as she related to the interviewer as a helpful collaborator, Jean, as a young child, appears to have become her mother's trusted helper and ally. We infer that this behavior was reflective of an unconscious fantasy of idealized merger with her mother . . . [p. 98].

Nowhere in their book do they provide logical arguments for justifying inferences such as that Jean's behavior as a trusted ally of her mother reflected an unconscious fantasy of idealized merger with her. Furthermore, the available evidence from the contemporary cognitive sciences and developmental psychology, as summarized in Chapter 1, argues against such an inference.

In my view, the primary process system nonconsciously appraises ongoing interpersonal relations and represents the products of this meaning analysis of *actual* not fantasy relations. Ulman and Brothers are mistaken in describing a person's representations of interpersonal relations as unconscious fantasies.

ENACTIVE MEMORY

Some of what Ulman and Brothers (1988) call enactments I have called *enactive memories*. One of the hallmarks of trauma, enactive memory stems from the need (*not* the wish or fantasy) to repeat involuntarily in emotions, actions, and dreams the salient aspects of traumatic experiences.

Freud (1914b) distinguished between consciously remembering and repeating the past. He claimed that repeating the past is an unconscious form of remembering. Repeating, in the sense of reenacting past experiences in the present, is remembering by action and affect rather than by thought.

Distinguishing between representational and enactive memory has both theoretical and practical importance. A defining property of the enactive form of memorial activity is that it is unconscious—that is to say, the person is not aware that he or she is repeating something from the past. In contrast, "representational memory" means that the person recalls something from the past that is consciously distinguished from the present. The timelessness and undifferentiated quality of enactive memory classify it as a form of archaic primary process cognition.

After summarizing a vignette presented by Pine (1985), I shall argue that the concept of enactive memory provides for a better description and partial understanding of certain posttraumatic symptoms than does the notion of unconscious fantasy.

Pine's eight-year-old patient, Susanna, was described as a bright and winning girl who had an abstracted, faraway air. School authorities had reported that her faraway quality seriously interfered with her peer relationships and that she periodically engaged in a form of aggressive behavior that gave them much concern. This apparently unprovoked behavior had a driven, repetitive quality; it involved her charging aggressively, at full steam, through a group of her schoolmates, bowling them over, and knocking them aside. The past history revealed that she had been hit by a truck and severely injured at 18 months. Though Susanna could not remember the accident, she was well aware that her family looked upon her survival as miraculous.

Pine tells how almost every psychotherapy session began with some kind of behavior enactment of the accident. Susanna would, for example, drop to the floor suddenly, as though dead, or beep like a truck horn at the most unanticipated moments. It quickly became apparent to her therapist that her trucklike plowing through her schoolmates was yet another enactment of the accident.

In other areas of her life, Susanna functioned remarkably well; the traumatic residue of the accident was compartmentalized to the kinds of aggressive actions just mentioned. The therapeutic work was governed by efforts to help Susanna "talk out" ideas associated with the accident. Therapy progressed well; the symptomatic enactments dropped away, and in their place Susanna developed new age-appropriate interests (skating and bicycle riding). These new interests with moving vehicles were the heirs of the old enactments of the truck accident. One of the core principles of psychoanalytic clinical theory is the active reversal of passively endured traumatic experiences. Susanna's adoption of skating and bike riding were as much repetitions of her passively endured traumatic experiences as were the symptomatic enactments so movingly and vividly described in Pine's (1985) case study.

Pine does not provide any rationale for his inference that his patient's enactments were based on unconscious fantasies. In their efforts to explain posttraumatic symptoms, some authors attempt to fit their explanations into Freud's theories about the causal role of unconscious wish-fulfilling fantasies in symptom formation. To account for repetitive posttraumatic enactments, they postulate "wishes to master," "wishes to turn passively experienced trauma into active repetition," "wishes for punishment," and so on. In my clinical experience with traumatized patients, I have not been able to infer the regular occurrence of such kinds of unconscious wishes to repeat painful experiences, and I do not believe that they play a part in the psychogenesis of posttraumatic symptoms.

The concept of enactive memory advanced here is almost identical to Dowling's (1990) notion of *sensorimotor* or *behavioral memory*. He describes the occurrence of behavioral memories in analysis and elsewhere in patients who underwent traumatic experiences of extreme helplessness during preverbal development. According to Dowling, the occurrence of behavioral memories should not be construed as an indication that the child formed conscious or unconscious fantasies about the experiences from which the behavioral memory derives, because the underlying traumas occur prior to the development of imagery.

ENACTIVE MEMORY AND THE REPETITION COMPULSION

Posttraumatic enactments in nightmares, symptoms, and other behaviors stem, I hypothesize, in part from a biological need (not a wish) to repeat and thus to master novel, unexpected, and traumatic experiences. This need, I suspect, concerns the organism's need to adapt to, and construct meanings about, unexpected and disturbing events by unconsciously repeating them in dreams, emotional reactions, and overt actions.

According to Freud (1920), posttraumatic dreams and other kinds of involuntary replications of traumatic events are "beyond the pleasure principle" and therefore are not manifestations of unconscious wishes. Posttraumatic symptoms stem from what Freud called the "repetition compulsion," which I redefine as the organism's need to repeat and thus to master novel events, including traumatic events. The primacy of needs over wishes in the foregoing explanatory account of enactive memory is consistent with contemporary knowledge of cognitive development in infants, where basic needs activate and shape various behaviors months before repeated experiences of need-gratification allow the child to represent specific needs as wishes. (For a similar concept of the repetition compulsion, see Gedo, 1984, 1988.)

DEFENSE AND PSYCHIC TRAUMA

"Defense" was one of Freud's greatest clinical discoveries, and it continues to play a central role in psychoanalytic theory and practice. Along with his other discoveries, such as transference and the primary process, his concept of defense was derived from his theory of cognition as well as from clinical observations and inferences.

To the extent that Freud's theory about defense was developed from 19th-century concepts about cognition, it is deeply flawed and requires major modifications and corrections. Various mistaken assumptions in Freud's theory of cognition (discussed in Chapter 1) are evident in traditional clinical theories about defense and the effects of defense; in theories about psychological responses to trauma; and in Freud's recommendations for the psychoanalytic treatment of patients suffering from psychic trauma.

Elsewhere (Dorpat, 1983b, 1985, 1987a) I have presented a cognitive arrest theory of defense that modifies psychoanalytic theory in a way that is more consistent with contemporary knowledge about mental functions. In what follows, comparisons between the cognitive arrest theory and classical theory are designed to show the necessity for revising traditional clinical theories about the role of defense in response to psychic trauma.

In the cognitive arrest theory, disavowal (or its synonym, denial) is an aspect of all defensive activity and is one of the essential and defining elements of defense. Disavowal interrupts the normal process of thought formation and thus prevents the verbal representation of whatever is disturbing the subject (Basch, 1981; Dorpat, 1985). To disavow is to reject unconsciously some psychic content as not-self, whereas to avow some psychic content is to accept it as part of the self. Contents that are avowed are those the person experiences and acknowledges as "my feelings," "my ideas," "my memories," and so on.

Clinical as well as experimental studies attest to the universality of denial responses to trauma (Freud, 1939; Horowitz, 1976). Military combat veterans, concentration camp and nuclear holocaust survivors, sufferers of bereavement, and victims of rape demonstrate the same kind of general response tendency to alternate denial and enactive memory despite variations due to differences in personality or event (Horowitz, 1976).

By allowing the subject to attend to other, more pressing problems, denial serves a normal and adaptive protective function immediately following an overwhelming traumatic experience. The prolonged use of denial, however, tends to produce serious pathological effects, which I discuss later.

Both the cognitive-arrest theory and classical psychoanalytic theory acknowledge the role of defense in preventing the arousal of disturbing emotions, and both recognize the significance of defense in symptom formation. The two theories differ, however, in their conception of the effects of defense. The short-term and long-term effects of denial stem from two interrelated but distinguishable dynamisms. Although both theories agree on the first dynamism only the cognitive arrest theory recognizes the second.

The first dynamism concerns what happens to the psychic contents defended against. Both theories agree that such contents remain potentially or actually dynamically active in influencing the subject's thinking, feeling, and overt behavior. The "return" of whatever is defended against in symptoms, dreams, and other manifestations is one example.

The second dynamism is wholly or in part responsible for a class of psychological defects that are the consequences of the denier's failure to avow and to be conscious of whatever he has disavowed. The defects include developmental arrests (Altschul, 1968; Dorpat, 1985), enactive memory (Dorpat, 1985), character malformations (Krystal, 1988), affective and cognitive dyscontrol (Dorpat, 1985), arrested mourning reactions (Altschul, 1968; Dorpat, 1985), alexithymia (Krystal, 1988), and so on. These psychic defects evolve because disavowal suspends the vital regulatory, constructive, and synthesizing functions of consciousness concerning the psychic contents being defended against.

A full understanding of disavowal and how it brings about psychic defects requires an explanation of its opposite, avowal. Becoming fully and explicitly conscious of something requires one to *avow* what one is doing, thinking, or feeling. The structure of the self may be viewed as a product, a synthesis of acts of avowal (Fingarette, 1969). The core principle of defense is an unconsciously active psychic content that is disavowed and thereby dismissed from a person's subjective self. In defense, a dynamically unconscious content is denied the attributes of self-relatedness and is excluded from the self-as-agent, self-as-place, and self-as-object.

The aforementioned psychic defects come about in part because disavowal entails a failure to assume responsibility and control over whatever is disavowed. A mental content defended against by disavowal is deprived of the organizing and synthesizing influence of consciousness, and it is therefore unresponsive to feedback influence. A train of thought or other psychic content that is disavowed is impervious to change by feedback from actions (G. Klein, 1976). This lack of feedback regulation leads to the irrational persistence and dyscontrol over whatever has been disavowed.

Freud was unaware of the formative, regulatory, and integrating functions of consciousness; he incorrectly believed that the only psychically effective entity was the unconscious mind.

The cognitive sciences like psychoanalysis until recent decades minimized the importance of consciousness or dismissed it as a mere epiphenomenon (G. Klein, 1976). After readmitting consciousness as a legitimate area of scientific investigation, cognitive psychology and neurophysiology have performed investigations demonstrating the causal, regulatory role of consciousness in brain function and behavior (Mandler, 1975a; Popper and Eccles, 1977; Sperry, 1982).

THE EFFECT OF DEFENSE ON PERCEPTION AND MEMORY

Freud's notions that perceptions are copies of reality and that memories are copies of perceptions led him to erroneous conclusions both about patients' perceptions of traumatic experiences and about the memories formed from those perceptions.

Though the classical theory of defense and the cognitive arrest theory agree that defense affects perceptions, they differ in *how* and *when* this occurs. Freud (1927, 1940a, b) erroneously assumed that the denier first forms a conscious and veridical perception and then *later* disavows the veridical perception by substituting a distorted idea.

In contrast to traditional theory, the cognitive arrest theory holds that denial affects the perceptual process *before* rather than *after* a conscious percept is created. Denial prevents the construction of veridical and conscious perceptions about whatever is being defended against. In support of this view is the abundant clinical and experimental evidence that denial interrupts the perceptual process prior to the emergence of a conscious percept (Dorpat, 1985).

According to traditional theory, defense blocks the retrieval of fully formed undistorted memories that were conscious before defense caused them to be stored in the unconscious. In contrast, the cognitive arrest theory holds that defense blocks the *construction* of conscious perceptions and of representational memories of whatever is being defended against.

Freud (1914b) greatly overestimated the ability of persons to recover representational memories of trauma in analysis or elsewhere, because his copy theory of perception led him mistakenly to assume that people could accurately perceive and then form undistorted representational memories of traumatic experiences.

He accorded a strategic role to the working through of defenses against trauma so that patients could recover undistorted representational memories of trauma formed at the time of the trauma and later repressed. Actually, there is experimental as well as clinical evidence for the hypothesis that representational memories of disavowed traumatic experiences cannot be recalled or recovered in psychoanalysis or elsewhere, because such memories were never formed (Dorpat, 1985, 1987a)! For experimental evidence demonstrating that psychic trauma interfers with the formation of representational memories see Loftus (1980).

DISAVOWAL PREVENTS THE CONSTRUCTION OF REPRESENTATIONAL MEMORIES

Disavowal at the time of the trauma and afterward, plus the patient's state of emotional turmoil and disorganization during trauma, prevents the patient from forming clear and coherent perceptions and representational memories of the traumatic experience. Moreover, the prolonged use of disavowal following trauma and the consequent failure to form representational memories about the trauma support and maintain the persistence of enactive memories.

How does denial prevent the construction of representational memories? In the act of disavowing the subject turns his focal attention away from whatever disturbs him to something else. In this way, disavowal involves an arrest of cognition with the consequence that what is denied does not attain conscious levels. For a person to form a representational memory of something, he must give his focal attention to it. Cognitive psychologists agree that representational memory formation is dependent on focal attention. Norman (1969) writes, "Events to which we do not consciously attend cannot receive the proper analysis and organization which is necessary for both complete understanding and retrieval" (p. 179).

Frequently patients are unable to recall much about past traumatic events. When they attempt to remember traumas, they tend to become confused and disorganized, because the state of consciousness in which a percept is recalled is similar to the state of consciousness in which the percept was originally formed (Rubinfine, 1973). The processing of external stimuli during a disorganized and traumatized state of consciousness prevents the information from becoming an object of focal attention. Because the formation of representational memory depends on acts of focal attention, few representational memories can be formed during traumatic experiences. The failure to form representational memories at the time of trauma often can lead to gaps in memory and the defensive development of screen memories created to conceal such memory gaps (Dorpat, 1985).

DISAVOWAL PREVENTS PERMANENT FORGETTING

Traumatic experiences defended against by disavowal are both *unrememorable* and *unforgettable*. Both unconscious pathogenic ideas and enactive memories defended against by disavowal remain dynamically active and unconsciously influence in remarkable and diverse ways the person's cognition, feelings, and behavior for a very long time. People who maintain their disavowal defense and who consequently continue to have enactive memories of their traumatic experience are unable to permanently forget their traumatic experience (G. Klein, 1976).

Unconscious pathogenic ideas and enactive memories persist with such freshness and affective strength because they have been blocked from the customary wearing-away process by which most past events are normally permanently forgotten (G. Klein, 1976). Disavowal prevents access to unconscious content, but it also reserves such contents until the defense is lifted and the patient is able to work through and master the traumatic experiences.

The permanent forgetting of most ordinary experiences is expectable and normal, because such experiences have been dissipated through the gradual absorption and integration of the past with the ongoing record of experience. Disavowed experiences are not integrated and are therefore retained unconsciously in a motivating and inhibitory capacity.

IMPLICATIONS FOR PSYCHOANALYTIC TECHNIQUE

A goal of psychoanalytic treatment of traumatized patients is to assist them to *forget permanently* as well as to *remember* aspects of their traumatic experiences. The treatment implications of the axiom "traumatic experiences defended against by disavowal are both unrememberable and unforgettable" are as follows: One short-range strategy is to assist patients, through defense and transference interpretations, to avow rather than disavow the meanings of their traumatic experiences and to construct new representational memories of those experiences; a long-range product is the patient's growing abilities for permanently forgetting some aspects of those experiences that were formerly unrememberable and unforgettable.

An important empirical generalization about the working through of trauma and the disavowal of trauma is that patients in psychoanalytic treatment are thereby able to construct new meanings, ideas, and representational memories regarding their traumatic experiences. In psychoanalytic treatment of patients with trauma one gains the definite and repeated impression that these new ideas and memories have never previously been put into words and that the original experience took place at a level of psychic integration that was not amenable to preconscious or conscious integration.

The construction and reconstruction of disavowed traumatic experiences require, first, the analyst's interpretive construction of new meanings regarding the patient's unrememberable past traumas and, second, the patient's gradual construction of representational memories of the trauma. This constructive task often is optimally carried out by transference interpretations linking current analyst–analysand interactions with traumatizing past interpersonal relations.

A technical implication of Freud's concepts about trauma and defense was the use of interpretations for making what was previously unconscious into something conscious. He mistakenly viewed interpretations as initiating a process in which the working through of the patient's defenses permitted the progressive reinstatement of fantasy images and veridical memory images *that were already there* but had been buried by the distorting power of defenses and drives. Probably Freud's inability to attain his goal of recovering coherent and credible representational memories of childhood trauma from his patients was one reason for his premature and ill-advised abandonment of the seduction theory.

CONCLUDING REMARKS

In classical psychoanalytic theory, nearly all psychopathology was traced to distortions caused by unconscious fantasy and primary process. In this chapter, I have presented arguments for abandoning theories about unconscious fantasy and in its place substituting the concept of unconscious pathogenic ideas. Pathogenic beliefs are the products of a person's conscious and unconscious meaning analysis of traumatic events and traumatic interpersonal relations. Pathogenic beliefs developed in childhood, along with other aspects of traumatic experiences, may become unconscious through defense.

II

Interactional Theory

MICHAEL L. MILLER

A t the end of the 19th century there were no scientific theories that could feasibly explain human cognition. Freud abandoned his early attempt to construct such a theory (Freud, 1895) and over a number of years formulated a metapsychology (Freud, 1900, 1905a, 1911, 1915c, 1920, 1923, 1926) that was to substitute for the lack of an empirically based theory of mental organization and information processing until one could be constructed. Applying the laws of physical science to the operation of the human mind, Freud's metapsychology tried to account for the phenomena he observed in his consultation room. As my coauthor explained in Section I, Freud's speculations were in many respects brilliant and insightful, but, in the light of contemporary science, his basic tenets regarding mental operations have turned out to be incorrect.

Today a revolutionary convergence of empirical research and observational study from the biological, cognitive, and social sciences permit us to begin to fulfill Freud's expectation that such a theory would someday be created.[1] Psychologists and psychobiologists have formulated basic principles of mental organization, functioning, and development to explain human cognition, information processing, and social relations. In Chapters 5 and 6 I present these principles and construct a model of mental organization and information processing that serves as the metapsychology on which I base our interactional theories of psychopathology and clinical process and technique.

---

[1]Freud (1933, 1940a) actually thought that a neurobiological theory would eventually explain human cognitive processes. That dream has not yet been fulfilled.

In using the principles of mental organization, information processing, and human development that have been derived from studies of normal individuals to formulate our clinical theories, we bridge the conceptual gap between normal and abnormal psychological functioning and are, at the same time, able to demonstrate the influence of trauma on the mental structures and functions that organize the human mind. In Chapter 7 I show how trauma at various stages in life affects specific types of deformations in the mental structures that organize the mind and that regulate a person's emotions and relations with others. I describe the types of psychopathology that result from this trauma, the symptoms that reflect it, and the construction of the defenses that protect a patient's psychic organization from reexperiencing traumatic events. By explicating psychopathology, defense, and symptom formation in terms of the mental structures and functions that organize the human mind, our clinical theory directly relates to our metapsychology.

The close interrelationship between our theory of psychopathology and our model of how the mind operates enables us to construct an experience-near theory of psychoanalytic process and technique. That is, our conceptualization of the therapeutic process and of the manner in which analysts construct and implement interventions and interpretations reflect how a patient organizes and interprets his or her interactions with the the social environment. In Chapter 8 I describe how a patient's psychopathology is expressed in the types of interactions in which he or she engages the analyst and in the meaning that the patient assigns to these interactions. I also discuss and demonstrate the kinds of interventions and interpretations that enable a patient to recognize and correct pathological organizations of experience and knowledge.

The reader should be aware that in formulating our theory of meaning analysis I am not simply translating the concepts of classical psychoanalysis into contemporary terminology. As Goldberg (1988) cogently argues, such a translation would merely render the old theory in new terms, adding nothing to the theory that is not there already. Rather, I am proposing a new theory—one that aims, through a new set of axioms and principles, at understanding the phenomena that classical theory describes and the processes and techniques it employs. By applying these same principles of mental organization and process to the clinical phenomena, therapeutic processes, and techniques described by object relations and self psychology theories, we are able to integrate into a single formulation many of the major psychoanalytic theories in use today. By removing the basic incompatibility between the classical models of cognition, psychopathology, and clinical practice and those of object relations and self psychology theories, we are no longer forced to jump from one group of theories to the other (tolerating or ignoring their incompatibilities) in order to understand the extended range of psychopathology amenable to modern psychoanalysis (Gedo and Goldberg, 1973; Chessick, 1990). The utility of our theory in enhancing a clinician's ability to understand the therapeutic process is illustrated in Chapter 9, where we apply our ideas to an actual psychoanalytic hour.

Basic Principles of Mental Organization and Development

What we do clinically with a patient is determined, in large part, by our understanding of how the human mind processes information. Classical psychoanalytic technique, for example, is, the reader will recall from Section I, based on a model of information processing derived from Freud's copy theory of perception and memory. In this model, human beings passively record in memory an exact and true copy of what they perceive such that any thought that does not reflect reality is a distortion. In classical theory, the mind distorts veridical memories into unconscious, wish-fulfilling fantasies to satisfy instinctual drives and then undoes the distortion, through such mechanisms as defense and compromise formation, just enough to adapt to reality. A basic aim of classical psychoanalytic treatment is to restore to a patient his or her undistorted memory by making conscious the unconscious fantasies that led to the distortion.

The interactional theories of psychopathology and of clinical process and technique that we propose here are derived from a model of mental organization and process very different from those of classical psychoanalytic theory and of most object relations and self psychology theories. In this chapter I sketch out some of the basic principles of our model of the mind and highlight their clinical implications. Though the model is a radical departure from traditional psychoanalytic thinking, most clinicians will be familiar with many of the cognitive-developmental principles and concepts on which the model is constructed.

Clinicians acquainted with the research of Jean Piaget (1952) or Daniel Stern (1985) have already been introduced to the most basic concept of interactional theory, which, simply put, is that a person plays an active role in organizing his or her mental structures and in making interactions with the world subjectively real and meaningful. Those authors and others (e.g., Werner, 1948; Sander, 1985) in the cognitive and biological sciences conceptualize human beings as composed of organizations of organs and systems of action and thought. Their studies demonstrate that these organizations and systems are designed from birth to interact with the environment in a manner that enables us to construct our own experience and knowledge of ourselves and of the world.

101

We are endowed genetically with the necessary systems for initial interaction with the environment in personally meaningful ways (e.g., the sucking reflex and the ability to distinguish our own mother's milk from the milk of someone else) and with the self-generative characteristics that ensure our own development and self-actualization. Thus, for example, the experience of coordinating vision, head movement, prehension, and sucking that is required to bring an object into the mouth also serves as a way for an infant to identify the self as a coherent agent of action and then to distinguish himself or herself from other human and nonhuman objects. Contemporary studies of human development (Werner, 1948; Langer, 1969; Piaget, 1971; Sander, 1985; Stern, 1985; Emde, 1988a) suggest that we are designed to keep ourselves adaptively interacting with the environment in a manner that conserves our own organization while simultaneously transforming that organization into developmentally more advanced forms.

In our model, people organize themselves through interaction with the environment in a manner that creates experience and knowledge. The most basic functions of the clinician are to understand the adaptive significance of a patient's experience and knowledge and to articulate this information to the patient so as to enable him or her to evaluate this data and to change those mental organizations of experience and knowledge that are found to be maladaptive.

PSYCHOLOGICAL DEVELOPMENT

Human beings are designed to interact with the environment in such a way as to create mental organization of increasing complexity. The research of Werner (1948; Werner and Kaplan, 1963) and others (Piaget, 1952, 1954; Inhelder and Piaget, 1958, 1964; Sander, 1985; Stern, 1985) demonstrates that a developmentally advanced organization of mental structures is a more differentiated, functionally specific, and internally integrated form of its functional predecessors. The evolving interrelationship between the various systems of mental organization is toward a structural hierarchicalization and functional integration of the parts, both with each other and with the whole mental organization. Developmentally more primitive organizations are not lost with the elaboration of higher forms; typically they become subordinate organizations of the new systems that they comprise. Earlier modes of functioning are continually present through the life cycle. They not only support higher modes of mentation, but also may serve as substitutes for these advanced forms under new or difficult conditions. Faced with a novel situation, a person usually approaches it through a developmental sequence of actions that ranges from the lowest to the highest.

The idea that a person naturally creates mental organization by interacting with the environment is a radical departure not only from classical psychoanalytic theory but also from most object relations and self psychology theories, which are based on the premise that it is only from the frustration of drives, needs, or psychological functions that new mental structures are created. In our model, psychological development is no longer dependent upon intrapsychic or interpersonal conflict; rather, development occurs naturally in the course of interaction with others. Clinically, this means that we can effect changes in a patient's mental organization in more ways than by merely analyzing the processes and products indicative of conflict or frustration. Though conflict in its various forms does occur, psychological development in our model is grounded in the principles of self-regulation and equilibrium.

EQUILIBRIUM AND SELF-REGULATION

Psychological development is a process of formative instability combined with a progressive movement toward stability. The functional relations between the various systems of mental organization are always in a state of disequilibrium, more so early in life and progressively less so as a person develops. The systems are self-regulative in that they strive to establish increasing equilibrium, the ideal state of which is never fully achieved (Werner, 1948; Langer, 1969; Piaget, 1970, 1971; Sander, 1985).

Disequilibrium is brought about by environmental or internal perturbation. Environmentally induced disequilibrium occurs whenever one biologically or psychologically recognizes that something is disturbing one and that one lacks the means (adequate physiological regulations or mental operations) to deal with the perturbation. The person's physiological or mental systems then act to reestablish equilibrium by inducing him or her to perform actions that compensate for the perturbation. The information obtained from the compensatory activity is fed back to the system and usually transforms it. In this way, new mental organizations are forged out of existing systems. The newly created systems functionally anticipate better and deal more efficiently with future perturbations of the same order (Werner, 1948; Langer, 1969; Piaget, 1970, 1971).

Internally induced disequilibrium occurs whenever a person develops a system of mental organization whose functional capacities outstrip his or her present adaptive needs. The person will then develop novel ends (functions) to be served by these means to reestablish equilibrium. Sally, for example, learned to count a few months ago. It has recently become important for her to know how may items of a thing, such as her favorite candy, she has. Sally's need to know how many items she has is a novel end (function) that is served by her ability to count. Reciprocally, whenever a person has functional needs that outstrip the structural capacities of the system, the tendency will be to develop novel means to serve these ends (Piaget, 1952; Inhelder and Piaget, 1958, 1964; Langer, 1969; Stern, 1985). Sally wants to share her candy with her sister. She is concerned that they each have the same number of candies. Sally's needs require her to use her ability to count in a new way: to divide a large number of candies into two smaller groups of equal number. As a consequence of this type of self-regulative operation, the system never remains long in a stable equilibrium but is constantly shifting from one state of disequilibrium to the next.

In this model, psychological development occurs as a result of solving problems in adapting to the physical environment and social surround and as a consequence of the inherent tendencies to utilize skills maximally and to expand knowledge. In contrast to classical, object relations, and self-psychology theories, in which psychological development occurs as a result of a person's mastering frustration to achieve a state of internal peace (i.e., the absence of drive tension or need), our model portrays humans as actively involved with their environment in their effort to achieve optimal adaptation and continuing psychological growth. The clinical importance of this distinction is that what motivates people has changed from drive discharge and wish fulfillment to self-organization and adaptation.

THE INTENTION TO KNOW AS A MOTIVATION FOR DEVELOPMENT

The developmentally most advanced and sophisticated self-regulatory system that evolves is intelligence, and the invariant functions of human intelligence are the mental representations of the two most general functions of the autoregulative process, namely, to organize oneself and to adapt to the world. The principal genetically determined function that motivates human development is, therefore, the intention to know. This intentionality is reflected in a person's progressive tendency to construct knowledge rather than to mirror or react to a preformed reality. From the moment of birth, every person constructs and continually corrects his or her own knowledge, in part under the influence of the environment but in part spontaneously (Werner, 1948; Piaget, 1954; Langer, 1969; Stern, 1985).

If human beings are inherently motivated to organize themselves and to adapt to the world by creating knowledge, what is this knowledge? How is it formed? In other words, how does the mind work?

MEANING—THE PRODUCT OF THE MIND'S OPERATION

The mind is a processing system that transforms data into functionally meaningful units of information. The data to be transformed are the elements that constitute the experience of interacting with the environment. The transformation is achieved by organizing these elements. Organization is defined as the creation of stable relations among the elements of experience. These elements may be sensations, perceptions, thoughts, actions, or feelings, as well as previously organized, higher order elements such as behavior patterns and abstract concepts. These organized sets of related elements form cognitive structures. Meaning, from this perspective, is synonymous with structure in that what is meaningful is the manner in which the elements are interrelated. Events in which the constituent elements cannot be interrelated are not understandable, and actions that are not organized are chaotic. Cognitive structures determine what is perceivable, knowable, or doable (Bartlett, 1932; Piaget, 1952, 1954; Minsky, 1975; Mandler, 1984).

The mind can be conceptualized as an organized system of structures that operates on information gleaned from interaction with the world. It organizes lived experience coherently and interprets it meaningfully. The system provides cues for action and arousal as well as for characterizations of the physical and social surround. The autoregulative nature of the mind insures successful interaction with the environment. The system not only processes inputs from the sense organs, but also adds information or seeks new information from the external world when this is lacking. These autoregulative mental processes and functions are not conscious or available for observation or self-reflection; they must be inferred from the meaning of the feelings, behaviors, and thoughts that are the consequence of the mind's operation. Though the content and effects of the human mind are different for each individual, the form of the mental system and its operation are identical in each person (Piaget, 1976; Nisbett and Ross, 1980; Mandler, 1984).

These principles of mental organization and operation have important implications for our clinical work. First, the idea that the human mind is designed to organize experience into a form that has personal meaning to an individual implies that what a patient communicates to us is his or her unique understanding of an event, not his or her distortion of it.

Second, by conceptualizing the aim of the mind's operation as the organization and interpretation of interactions with the social surround, we, as clinicians interacting with a patient, necessarily cannot help but influence the content and nature of the patient's mental processes. We are no longer blank screens on which patients project their drive-determined fantasies and fears.

Third, the notion that the mental processes we seek to understand and to effect operate outside of both our observation and the patient's self-reflective awareness means that we and the patient must infer the organization and content of the patient's mind from the meanings that he or she attributes to therapeutic interaction and from the types of interactions that he or she enacts with us. The focus of psychoanalytic treatment, therefore, shifts from the analysis of unconscious fantasy to the analysis of the interactions with which patients engage us and the meanings that they attribute to these interactions.

MENTAL PROCESSES

If the mind is a processing system that organizes the elements of lived experience into personally meaningful units of information, how is this transformation achieved? From studying how humans solve problems, psychologists (Werner, 1948; Piaget, 1952, 1954; Inhelder and Piaget, 1958, 1964; Piaget and Inhelder, 1969; Nisbett and Ross, 1980) have determined that humans develop information-processing routines for interrelating the elements of experience. These information-processing strategies are what a person uses to direct his or her physical and/or mental actions upon the environment and to organize the experience that results from these actions into percepts and concepts. They are also the means by which concepts are generalized and transformed.

An explication of these information-processing strategies, called *operational schemes,* is beyond the scope of this chapter. They have, however, been described in detail by Piaget in several volumes of his work (Piaget, 1952, 1954; Inhelder and Piaget, 1958, 1964; Piaget and Inhelder, 1969). What is important for us to know is that operational schemes are the cognitive tools that people use to construct experiential and conceptual knowledge of themselves and of the world. Operational schemes determine the ways in which the elements of experience can be combined to form percepts and concepts. Schemes are also the strategies through which people combine, interrelate, generalize, and transform these experiential and conceptual knowledge structures; schemes are, as well, the means through which new structures are created out of those which already exist. Operational schemes are nonconscious mental operations. They are known to us only from the results they effect in the organizational form of our individual knowledge structures.

> Bill, age five, is presented with a bouquet of flowers, six roses and four a mixture of daisies and tulips. Asked what he has just been handed, Bill answers "a bunch of flowers." How many flowers are there? Bill counts 10. He correctly names each kind of flower and how many there are of each type. Bill is then asked if there are more flowers or more roses. Bill responds that there are more roses.

At this stage in Bill's development, his operational schemes enable him to classify objects according to a common attribute; he can form the concept of a bunch of flowers. His schemes also allow for the differentiation of a subclass from the general class, so he can construct the subclasses of roses, daisies, and tulips. Yet Bill's operational schemes have not become sufficiently independent from his perceptual experience for him mentally to coordinate quality (intension) and quantity (extension) to conclude correctly that there are more flowers than roses. Bill thinks that there are more roses than there are flowers because he perceives a greater number of roses.

In this experiment, Bill's operational schemes were not available for our observation or for his self-reflection. By analyzing his answers to the questions posed, we inferred the operational schemes that enabled Bill to classify objects and to form the concepts of a big bunch of flowers and smaller bunches of roses, daises, and tulips. That is, we determined Bill's operational schemes by analyzing the concepts and conclusions that were the products of these operational schemes. Operational schemes become visible to us only as they are reflected in the way in which the elements of experience are arranged into concepts and percepts.

Piaget and his colleagues have shown that operational schemes coherently interrelate to form organized sets of information-processing strategies that are discernible at particular stages of life. Later sets of operational schemes derive from the differentiation and reintegration of earlier ones. Piaget and Inhelder (Piaget, 1952, 1954; Inhelder and Piaget, 1958, 1964) delineated five classes of operational schemes which they formulated into successive periods of cognitive development labeled sensorimotor, preconceptual, intuitive, concrete, and formal.[1] As products of the operational schemes, the form and character of the experiential and conceptual knowledge structures that organize the human mind and serve as its contents will evidence a sequence of stages dictated by the developmental

---

[1]Piaget also sometimes refers to the combined preconceptual and intuitive stages as the "preoperational" period.

progression of the operational schemes. The following discussion illustrates how the concepts and the reasoning of a child change from one stage
to the next as a consequence of a developmental advance in the child's
operational schemes.

At the preconceptual stage, the child's sensorimotor action schemes are
internalized and so rapidly processed that the child can now think through
a sequence of actions rather than having to enact it as at the previous
sensorimotor stage. By thinking about a sensorimotor action sequence and
the results it obtains, instead of merely acting on a felt desire, the child
frees his or her thinking from the bounds of immediate experience. The
child can now mentally differentiate the means to an end from both the
end itself and the motivation, and he or she can mentally coordinate and
transform these sensorimotor action schemes in order to achieve a desired
result before taking action. The child's sensorimotor action schemes have
thus become mental operational schemes. Reflecting on his or her own
sensorimotor action schemes as means to desired ends, the child uses his or
her own behavior as a model for understanding how the world works. A
child's concept of causality, for example, reflects this change in the
operational schemes: As the child now understands that he or she intends
an action, desires a particular end, or uses effort to achieve a result,
intention, desire, and effort are the causal forces attributed to all animate
and inanimate objects. At two years, one month Piaget's daughter said:
"Moon running" when she was walking by a lake and saw the illusion of
the moon following her. At three years, four months she said, "The sun
goes to bed because it's sad" in reference to the sun's setting (Piaget,
1962, pp. 250-251). In the first instance, the child assimilated the moon's
movement to her own experience of locomotion. In the second, the sun's
setting was assimilated to one of her own motivations for going to bed.
But in both cases, the elements of agency and intention were ascribed to
the object.

At the intuitive stage, the child's operational schemes have developed to
the point where he or she can mentally coordinate representations of
interactions between objects and consider the significance of his or her
actions but only in terms of the immediate perceptual results of these
interactions rather than in terms of the transformations that must have
occurred between them. For example, a child at the intuitive stage
incorrectly concludes that the quantity of liquid changes when it is poured
from a short, squat container into a tall and thin one. The child concludes
that a transformation in the liquid has occurred because he himself has
poured the liquid from one container into the other—so something must
have happened—and because he perceives an apparent change in the
amount of liquid from the first to the second container.

Operational schemes at the intuitive stage are thus egocentric, because they are determined by the child's present action; and phenomenalistic, because they are tied to his or her perceptual experience. Yet these aspects nonetheless represent advances in the intuitive child's operational schemes, and they make it possible for the child to construct physical explanations of phenomena. In terms of the child's concept of causality, he or she now sees the need for contact between objects or continuity of actions, rather than motives and intentions, as the basis of causal relations. At four years, six months, Piaget's daughter, seeing the moon rise over the mountain Saleve, said, "Oh, a moon rise over Saleve! It's moving because there's some wind. It's gliding with the sky" (Piaget, 1962, p. 259). At the same age, she observed Piaget take off on a motorcycle. She put her fingers to her mouth in a special way which was new to her and said to her mother, "I'm putting my fingers like that so that daddy'll come back." During the same period, she stamped her foot in her room and said, "I'm stamping because if I don't the soup isn't good enough. If I do, the soup's good" (p. 256). As is evident in these examples, the magico-phenomenalistic causal reasoning of this stage is an advance over the previous stage, but it is still based on a logic, or set of operational schemes, different from the logic underlying adult causal reasoning. Adult casual reasoning, which appears at the next stage of concrete operations, can take into consideration transformations in objects that are independent of one's own action and perception, and it can coordinate mental operations or physical actions that compensate for or cancel out one another.

Mental development is naturally progressive and hierarchical such that the knowledge a person constructs at one stage of development is reconstructed in new, richer, and more comprehensive configurations at each subsequent stage. The earlier configurations of knowledge and their underlying operational schemes are not lost with development. They are in evidence when a person is stressed, conflicted, or faced with difficulties in adapting to his or her current situation. A person also processes information with operational schemes at a level less advanced than the stage to which he or she has progressed when a developmental deficit or arrest is present as is the case in several types of psychopathology.

> An intelligent and successful marketing executive would explain the child-hood determinants of a particular behavior to me and then wait for me to take an action to make her feel better. She became furious when my interventions and interpretations failed to make her bad feelings go away. She believed that I knew exactly what to do to assuage her bad feelings and that my failure to make them go away was due to her failure to explain correctly the determinants of her problems. This type of affect-regulating object relationship—that her words could get me to take her bad feelings away—and the associated belief—that I would know what her bad feelings were and how to take them away if she performed the right behavior—

derived from the same type of reasoning that Piaget's daughter used when she placed her fingers to her lips to get him to return to her. That is, her reasoning employed operational schemes fixated at the intuitive stage of development. This narcissistically disturbed woman's ideas about her power to influence me and mine to know what was in her mind would be considered fantasies in classical psychoanalytic terms. From the perspective of meaning analysis, they are beliefs and ways of interacting with the world derived from a developmentally arrested type of logical reasoning.

By understanding that certain types of thoughts and particular ways of reasoning about events or interacting with others represent specific stages in the development of a patient's operational schemes, rather than distortions of reality or unconscious fantasies, as we are accustomed to considering them, we can use this knowledge to determine the type of psychopathology or level of developmental arrest or deficit a patient's thinking and behavior reflect. We can then formulate interpretations or interventions that will help the patient to develop or to utilize the more advanced operational schemes required to construct more adaptive concepts and ways of interacting with the world.

In summary, operational schemes are nonconscious information-processing strategies that organize the elements of lived experience into meaningful units of information. The mental structures that are formed by the operational schemes organize the human mind and serve as its contents. They are the configurations of experience and knowledge that we human beings use to organize and to interpret our interactions with the world. In that these mental structures mediate our interactions with others, it is by analyzing these configurations of experience and knowledge that we as clinicians come to understand our patients, and it is by affecting these same mental structures that we initiate in our patients the process of changing these structures and the operational schemes which formed them.

Operational schemes are used to construct many different types of organizations of knowledge. Of particular interest to us as clinicians are those mental structures which embody our knowledge of ourselves and of the social world with which we interact. These mental structures are called *schemata,* and a single mental structure of this type is called a *schema.*[2]

It is unfortunate and confusing that these mental structures are called

---

[2]Whereas organizations of experience and knowledge have been observed to exist in the human mind, neither the anatomical structures of the brain nor the systems of information procesing (the hardware and software) that create these organizations have as yet been delineated. A schema is a heuristic concept formulated by psychologists to describe the mental organizations of experience and knowledge that they have observed in the verbal and nonverbal behavior of individuals (Piaget, 1970; Tulving, 1972, 1983; Stern, 1985).

schemata, a label so similar to the term schemes, which I have employed to describe mental processes. In using these terms, however, I am keeping with terminology that Piaget used to describe information-processing strategies and that other academic and clinical investigators (e.g., Mandler, 1984; Slap and Saykin, 1984) have applied to an organization of mental contents. To avoid confusing these terms, what one needs to remember is that schemes are mental processes and schemata are the products of those processes. As clinicians we work principally with our patients' schemata, since it is through these organizations of experience and knowledge that we learn about our patients' operational schemes, and it is through challenging our patients' schemata that we cause the patients to develop new, more advanced operational schemes.

MENTAL STRUCTURES

Operational schemes organize the elements of lived experience into mental structures called schemata. A schema is a bound, distinct, and unitary representation of an interaction with the environment (Bartlett, 1932; Minsky, 1975; Schank and Ableson, 1977; Tulving, 1972, 1983; Mandler, 1984). A schema is not a carbon copy of the event it represents; rather, a schema is an abstraction representing the regularities inherent in a particular type of person-event interaction. The bedtime ritual of a three-year-old is a good example of a schema. Though the person who puts the child to sleep may vary (e.g., mother, father, or sitter) and the songs or stories at the bed may change, the nature of the activities and their sequence is invariant: the warning that it's time for bed, a period of quiet interaction between the child and the caregiver, saying good night, then the walk up the stairs, putting on the pj's, brushing the teeth, arranging the animals, telling the story, exchanging kisses, and then parting.

Schemata may be conceptualized as memory structures that organize the mind and serve as its contents. A schema functions as a template for organizing and interpreting lived experience. When a person interacts with the environment, data that conform to a schema's prototypical features is selectively parsed from the information available to the senses and organized in a manner that reflects the features of that schema.

During a vacation, I visited a small Egyptian village. There I entered a storefront and saw low tables with cushions around them. I wasn't sure what type of establishment I had entered. A man came up to me with sheets of paper that looked like menus. He said something in Arabic, which I didn't understand, and gestured for me to be seated. The "menus" activated my restaurant schema. Since my restaurant schema includes a set of expected environmental features and a set of basic social interactions that can be executed across a range of possible manners and contexts, the tables, cushions, "menus," and gesturing man were all instantaneously made to conform to this schema. I sat down and by pointing and gestures ordered dinner.

A schema renders lived experience meaningful by organizing it in a way that reflects what a person already knows. If an interaction with the environment is lacking some of the expected features depicted by a schema, a person can use the prototypical features of the schema to interpolate what those missing features would be in order to make the interaction understandable. In the preceding restaurant example, there were no people in the establishment and no plates, silverware, or food to be seen, so I used my schema to fill in these missing attributes. I was then able to conclude that the establishment was a restaurant.

When aspects of an interaction do not conform to the prototypical features modeled by a schema, the schema can be modified to incorporate the novel permutations. A schema can be accommodated to include a novel element as long as the variation does not deviate too much from the schematic prototype. If the permutation is too great, the meaning of the interaction to be assimilated will not be understood, because the interaction would not conform to the general features of the schematic prototype, and it will not be assimilated. If, however, the novel element is but an incremental variation on the theme of the schema, it will be incorporated as another iteration of the schematic prototype. The novel experience will thereby cause the schema to develop into a more complex or advanced form. In the case of the Middle Eastern restaurant, sitting on the floor and eating with my fingers were not too great a deviation from the basic prototype to modify my restaurant schema to include these features. My restaurant schema now includes eating "Middle Eastern" style, along with such other variations as eating at a sushi bar, at McDonalds, and at a four-star restaurant.

The organization of sensory data into a particular schematic form automatically activates those schemata which have a similar content. Activated schemata increase readiness for certain types of environmental evidence to be perceived and decreases readiness for other evidence. Perception and conception at any particular moment in time are limited by the set of potentially activated schemata. Schemata provide a set of general and specific expectations about what is to be encountered in a particular interaction with the social surround.

Each moment of our existence is defined by a set of currently active schemata. Descriptively these schemata have been aptly labeled state-of-the-world schemata by Mandler (1984), and we will follow his usage here. State-of-the-world schemata orient us in time and space and provide us with the information required to adapt to the social and physical demands of the here and now (Tulving, 1972, 1983; Nisbett and Ross, 1980; Mandler, 1984; Stern, 1985). No encounter with the environment is met tabula rasa. State-of-the-world schemata are constantly being updated as a result of every interaction with the social surround.

State-of-the-world schemata reside in what Mandler (1984) and Tulving (1972, 1983) call a preconscious state. Preconsciousness is a state-of-being that is unconscious but capable of becoming conscious under certain circumstances. For example, I am not usually consciously aware of how I run the razor over my face when I'm shaving. I'm usually thinking about what I must do at the office or what I did last night. If, however, I cut myself while shaving yesterday, today I am conscious of the pattern I use in shaving my face and the pressure I put on the razor as I try to avoid the hurt area. In other words, I usually shave preconsciously unless I need to be conscious of how I shave. As I discuss in Chapter 6, schemata operate preconsciously unless problems in processing information require conscious, self-reflective analysis of one's cognitions. From this perspective, the attribution of meaning to experience is a preconscious process. An exception to this maxim is when a schema is the object of defense. As I explain in Chapter 7, these defended-against schemata operate unconsciously inasmuch as they are segregated from the body of schemata capable of being preconsciously activated that constitute the normal range of a person's subjective experience.

In what follows I closely examine two important subtypes of schemata that together organize our experiential and conceptual knowledge of ourselves and of the social world to which we must adapt. They are organizing schemata and conceptual schemata. Organizing schemata are important clinically because they are the templates against which the self is organized and experience regulated. Organizing schemata also determine the nature and function of our object relations. Most character pathology and disorders of the self are the products of maladaptive organizing schemata. Conceptual schemata embody our concepts and beliefs about ourselves and about our social milieu. They enable us to interpret and evaluate lived experience. Conceptual schemata are important clinically because they determine the pathogenic beliefs that cause psychic conflict and neurotic disorders.

ORGANIZING SCHEMATA

Observational research (Spitz, 1965; Brazelton, Koslowski, and Main, 1974; Stern, 1974, 1977; Sander, 1983, 1985; Emde 1983; Beebe and

Lachman, 1988) has shown that from the beginning of life an infant's caregiver attends to the infant's somatic needs, states of arousal, and motor activity in a manner that helps the infant organize his or her behavior and regulate these states. A caregiver who provides this function becomes for the infant a *self-regulating other* (Stern, 1985). The infant's sensorimotor schemes coordinate his or her own behaviors and those of the self-regulating other into an interpersonal schema for organizing and regulating the infant's self-experience (Piaget, 1952; Sander, 1983, 1985; Stern, 1985). I have culled the following interactions from my own observational research to illustrate the process of forming schemata that serve to regulate an infant's experience of arousal:

> Jan's infant son, Charley, is lying on her chest and coos invitingly to her. Jan nuzzles her face next to his. Charley giggles and coos again, and at that Jan nuzzles her face to the other side of his. She matches his giggling with a similarly paced, somewhat exaggerated laughing. He then nuzzles his face to hers, she nuzzles back, and Charley howls with excitement. Jan howls back in a similar tone to his. They nuzzle back and forth between left and right cheeks, faster and faster, until Charley pushes back from Jan by stiffening his arms. He also squints his eyes and turns his head away from her. Jan then slows the nuzzling, hugging him gently from one side to the other. He calms and giggles. Jan then hugs Charley and holds him close to her.
>
> Charley resumes the game by pushing back and forth on Jan's chest so that his nose touches hers; he smiles and laughs and then pulls back. Jan repeats these movements, placing her nose to his and pulling back. They laugh and repeat this interaction again and again until Charley stiffens his arms, squints shut his eyes, and turns his head. Jan then once more slows the interaction to a speed that again produces a smile on Charley's face.

In the games that caregivers and infants play, such as the preceding one, an event is created by the interaction that would not be created by either party alone. The infant is with another who regulates the infant's experience. As Stern (1974, 1977, 1985) and others (Brazelton et al., 1974; Sander, 1985; Beebe and Lachman, 1988) have shown, infant-elicited behaviors are organized by caregivers into a theme and variation format that is ideally designed to enable the infant to identify consistencies in his or her self-experience and to form schemata that regulate these consistencies in self experience out of the infant-caregiver interactions.

In the two variations of the nuzzling game, for example, Charley and his mother adjusted the game to keep him within his range of optimal stimulation. Jan regulated Charley's stimulation by the amount of repetition, variation, and exaggeration she put into the game. Charley regulated the level of excitation by stiffening his arms and by averting his gaze to reduce the stimulation that had risen above his optimal range. Conversely, he used facial expressions, vocalizations, and gestures to seek out and invite new or higher levels of stimulation when the excitation had fallen too low. Together, mother and child formed an interpersonal schema aimed at regulating Charley's experience of arousal.

Regulatory schemata represent real-life interactions with an inherent structure that is encoded in memory as the event is experienced and understood. These schemata form what Tulving (1972, 1983) called episodic memory. Episodic memory is a memory of a coherent chunk of lived experience. The elements of an episodic memory are the sensations, perceptions, actions, thoughts, affects, and goals that are temporally, physically, or causally linked together within a particular context. Let's return to Jan and Charley for an example of the type of lived event out of which an episodic memory is formed:

> Charley is hungry and cries in a particular manner that Jan has come to recognize as his "hunger cry." Jan picks Charley up, and he stops crying. She places him in the high chair and puts a bib on him. When Jan leaves Charley to get the food, he is quiet with anticipation, but if she takes too long, he again cries. Seeing her return with the bowl and spoon, Charley stops crying and smiles. As soon as Jan sits before him, he opens his mouth in anticipation of the spoon. He closes his mouth after the spoon enters. Jan then removes the spoon and scoops another mouthful out of the bowl. Charley smiles again and opens his mouth, inviting the spoon. Jan talks to him as he eats each spoonful. When the dish is empty, Charley's hands and face are wiped clean, and he is removed from the high chair.

This feeding interaction between Jan and Charley is an ordered sequence of feelings, actions, and interactions with a specific aim that occurs in a particular physical setting and within a defined temporal context. If this feeding situation is consistently repeated, Charley will form an episodic memory replicating the elements of the interaction in their causal and temporal order, as well as the contextual features of the environment in which the interaction occurs, to the extent that his operational schemes permit. That is, the event is encoded in memory as Charlie experienced and understood it. An episodic memory is not, however, a memory of a specific instance of an interaction, though specific instances are capable of being remembered. Rather, it is a memory of the invariant features which define a particular type of experience. It is an abstraction formed from the memories of many specific episodes of an experience, each slightly different from the generalized memory structure that their consistent features form (Rummelhardt, 1975; Schank and Ableson, 1977; Ableson, 1978; Stern, 1985).

> As Charley gets a little older he becomes increasingly distracted by the events that are going on around him while he is eating. Jan has to modify the eating

routine in various ways to keep Charley's attention. For instance, Jan has taken to playing airplane with the spoon to get Charley to attend to the spoon and want to take it into his mouth. Charley's father, Bill, also feeds him. Bill's methods of feeding Charley are more abrupt and rigid and involve less play and interaction than do Jan's. Yet, from these variations on the general feeding situation Charley has distilled a generalized memory of feeding: feeling hungry, Charley expresses his desires to his caregiver (in a cry, with gestures, or now with vocalizations). He then is taken to the high chair and bibbed; he sits and waits for the food to come; he is then fed (with or without games); when the food is finished or when he will not take any more, his hands and face are wiped clean, and he is removed from the chair. Charley activates this memory every time he feels hungry. The memory is used to aid Charley in regulating his hunger and in organizing himself in a way that permits him to coordinate his behaviors with those of his parents in order to be fed by them.

Episodic memory is not a conscious experience. It is a preconscious set of expectations about what is to be experienced in a particular type of interaction. Once activated, the episodic memory emerges as an indivisible unit for organizing an ongoing interaction (Mandler, 1984; Tulving, 1972, 1983; Nisbett and Ross, 1980). Self-regulative schemata are episodic memories that depict the self in interaction with a self-regulating other for the purpose of organizing or regulating self-experience. For this reason, I call this type of schema an *organizing schema*.

Organizing schemata become the infant's enduring strategies for constituting a sense of self and for regulating self-experience. They determine the roles that others will play in the regulation and maintenance of self-experience throughout the life cycle (Sander, 1983, 1985; Stern, 1985; Stolorow et al., 1987; Winnicott, 1965). The invariant patterns of experience created by these schemata organize and then maintain a coherent and continuous sense of self.[3] Since this sense of self is mutually created by the regulatory efforts of the infant and the caregiver, the sense of "other" and the sense of "the self with other" are simultaneously formed with the sense of self.

With the cued recall or with the evocation of an episodic memory, the subjective experience of a person is a social experience whether or not the other person is actually present. Each time Charley is hungry he will evoke his feeding schema, which depicts his caregivers feeding him. Charley's parents do not have to be physically present for him to use the schema,

---

[3]In that organizing schemata articulate and regulate arousal and affect in an interpersonal context, affective experience may be thought of as one of the principal dimensions for maintaining the continuity of self-experience across various situational and interpersonal contexts (Emde, 1983, 1988a, b; Stern, 1985). Several examples are given in Chapter 7 of how organizing schemata produce the senses of self-cohesion and self-continuity.

although they will always be psychically present, for they are an integral part of the schema. As episodic memories, state-of-the-world organizing schemata make the subjective experience of self-with-other an ever-present reality.

The regulatory focus of these mutually constructed schemata makes them the primary avenues for communicating affective states as well as for sharing internal experience (e.g., attentional focus, intention, desire, need) between the infant and his or her caregiver (Trevarthan, 1977, 1979; Trevarthan and Hubley, 1978; Stern, 1985; Emde, 1983, 1988a, b). The feelings of intersubjective relatedness and affective attunement that issue from the sharing of internal states and affects make the infant's connections to others meaningful and determine the stability and continuity of his or her affective ties to others (Stern, 1985; Emde, 1988a, b).

The nuzzling games between Charley and Jan illustrate well the sharing of the subjective experiences of intention and affect in the context of a mutually created organizing schema. Sharing intention was exemplified when Charley responded to Jan's touching his cheek with her face by touching her cheek with his own face. In the second iteration of the game, Charley's intention was shared by Jan as she responded to his touching his nose to her nose by touching her nose to his. By sharing the subjective experience of intention, Charley and Jan communicated to one another a subjective experience unique to each of them. In this way, the regulatory schema made it possible to identify and to share similar subjective states-of-mind.

Charley and Jan also shared subjectively experienced affective states-of-being through the pace and rhythm of the cheek-and-nose touching games as well as in the reciprocal demonstration of a happy feeling. Charley signaled this feeling to Jan by giggling, to which she responded by laughing in a similar tone and pace. Charley howled and Jan responded in the same howling tone. Within the context of the schema, these subjectively experienced affects were given a meaning (e.g., happiness), which was communicated in the signals (e.g., Charley's smiling and giggling and Jan's laughing) inherent to the behavioral rhythm and facial expressions of the interaction. In these ways organizing schemata make it possible to share affective states.

Organizing schemata may be conceived of as the medium through which an empathic connection to another is achieved. The tones, shape, timing, and the like, of the behaviors, vocalizations, postures, and facial expression grouped together by an organizing schema make these schemata the means of nonsymbolically expressing one's affective experience of an event (Werner, 1948; Werner and Kaplan, 1963). In the example of affective sharing, Jan's and Charley's facial expressions and the rhythm of their movement made it possible for Jan to capture, experience, and reflect back to Charley the quality of his emotional experience. Similarly, Jan's slowing the cheek-and-nose touching games down to a tolerable level in response to Charley's arm stiffening and gaze aversion demonstrated to him that had understood the meaning of his gestures and the subjective experience they reflected. In these cases empathy was demonstrated by the self-regulating other's responding in a manner that appropriately regulated the person's experience and mirrored the quality of that experience.

Organizing schemata are the blueprints for maintaining a cohesive sense of self, for regulating self-experience, and for relating to others throughout the life cycle. Though these organizing schemata are largely created during the first two years of life, they continue to evolve thereafter into more functionally differentiated forms that are gradually integrated with one another during successive stages in the developmental sequence of the operational schemes. The following examples illustrate some of the different kinds of organizing schemata that can be formed at each stage of development after the sensorimotor period.

At the preconceptual stage, the child's operational schemes create organizing schemata based on a set of specific actions that are required to achieve particular ends. The child's sense of self and other is maintained and developed through the enactment of specific interactions aimed at regulating the child's affect, arousal, and need state. Recall the bedtime schema described earlier. This organizing schema is evoked by the youngster each time he or she prepares for bed at or away from home. The schema aids the child in regulating downward his or her arousal and in binding the anxieties attendant on parting from the parents in order to sleep. The child's sense of self and other is actualized through the enactment of the organizing schema.

The egocentric and phenomenalistic operational schemes of the intuitive stage permit the child to construct organizing schemata that maintain, develop, and integrate a sense of personal identity in terms of the results that his or her behavior has on the environment, particularly as the effects of the behavior are mirrored back to the child in the reactions, behaviors, and judgments of others. Billy, for example, feels like a ball player to the extent that his father affirms his athletic skill when they are playing catch. Billy will consolidate into a ball-playing schema those behaviors which win his father's esteem.

With the onset of concrete operational schemes, organizing schemata are created for the maintenance and regulation of self-experience within a social group. Concrete operational schemes allow for the construction of organizing schemata that coordinate the needs and desires of the self with those of others who have needs and desires that are independent of those of the self and may even conflict with them. Organizing schemata begin to involve rules and conform to social norms and conventions. The mastery of games, such as baseball and jump rope, is an example of the highly structured, rule-bound nature of the organizing schemata constructed at this stage of development.

With the ability to coordinate complex tasks afforded by well-consolidated concrete operations and by early formal operations, the adolescent is able to construct the advanced organizing schemata required to handle the physiological, psychological, and social demands placed on youngsters of this age. For example, it is during this phase of development that young men and women formulate into elaborate regulatory schemata the social intricacies of dating and of relating sexually to one another.

CONCEPTUAL SCHEMATA

It will be recalled from our of discussion of the operational schemes in the toddler that at the preconceptual stage a child's sensorimotor action schemes have been internalized as mental operational schemes that can so rapidly process information that he or she can now think through a sequence of actions rather than having to enact it. By thinking about a sensorimotor action sequence and its results, instead of merely acting on a felt desire, the child at this stage frees his or her thinking from the bounds of immediate experience. The preconceptual child, then, has made the transition from the presentational intelligence of here-and-now feelings and actions to the representational intelligence of reflective thought.

The child can now use his or her organizing schemata to represent an experience that these schemata organized at a time and in a place different from the temporal and situational context in which the experience originally occurred (Piaget, 1952, 1962). The child can now re-present to himself or herself a past interaction for contemplation, and he or she can use this representation as a model against which ongoing experience can be compared and evaluated (Piaget, 1962; Werner and Kaplan, 1963). At one year, eight months of age, Charley exhibited this type of behavior in his play:

> Charley seated his bear in a chair, put a napkin around its neck, and fed it with a spoon. He dug the spoon into an empty bowl, and he played airplane with the spoon before putting it to the bear's mouth. At the end of the feeding, Charley said ''done'' and wiped the bear's face and hands.

In this illustration, Charley evoked from memory his own organizing schema of being fed and used it as a model to guide him in feeding his bear. Charley's present behavior was meaningful to him because the sequence of events matched his schema of being fed.

The operational schemes that enable the preconceptual child to hold both a present and past version of an experience in mind also permit the child to make alterations in the representation of either or both of the events. He or she can transform schemata to represent wishes, fears, desires, and fantasies. The child can formulate schemata that are contrary to experience, undo past actions, compensate for inadequacies, liquidate unpleasant experiences, and represent wished-for interactions with others (Inhelder and Piaget, 1958; Piaget, 1962; Lichtenberg, 1983; Stern, 1985):

> When Charley was three and a half years old, Jan told him not to eat any cookies from the cookie jar before dinner. Angered by the prohibition, Charley went to his younger brother's room and told him that his mother said that he could have all the cookies he wanted so long as he ate his dinner.
>
> At the age of four, Charley got lost at a department store. A security guard found him. Jan was called on the public address system to the shoe department, where Charley was waiting with the guard. That evening, Charley played out scenes in which he was lost but wasn't scared because he knew that security guards were employed to find lost children. He also created scenarios in which his mother, brother, and father were lost and he was the security guard who found them.

The ability to represent, reflect on, and manipulate schemata enables a child to decontextualize the elements of a schema without destroying the schema as a whole in the process. The decontextualization objectifies the elements of a schema by removing them a degree from the subjectivity of immediate experience, thereby making these elements available for the construction of schemata that embody the ideas, feelings, fantasies, and conclusions that result from the child's self-reflective analysis and evaluation of the experience constituted by the organizing schemata (Piaget, 1952, 1962; Kagan, 1981; Mandler, 1984; Fast, 1985; Stern, 1985):

> Charley is a curious child whose attention is easily captured. He has become "lost" on several occasions at department stores, the grocery market, and even at his father's office. One day, Charley told his parents that he was afraid to leave the house because he had a bad brain. Charley said that when he went to the store he would get lost because his brain could not remember where he was. When he is lost his brain is scared and confused, he said.

Out of the several iterations of the lived experience of getting lost, which together form an organizing schema depicting being lost, Charley constructed another schema about having a bad, confused brain that caused him to get lost. Charley formulated this "abstract" schema by reflecting on his experiences of being lost and then by creating an explanation for these experiences. Charley's explanation was composed of elements taken from his organizing schema depicting the experiences of being lost.

I call this type of abstract schema a *conceptual schema*. Conceptual schemata are either transformations of organizing schemata or new schemata constructed from the data provided by an organizing schema. These schemata do not represent lived experience. They are products of a person's creative or logical reasoning about his or her lived experience. Conceptual schemata embody the ideas, concepts, and beliefs formulated by a person to explain his or her perceptions, feelings, and behavior as well as the results of his or her interactions with others:

> Charley's older brother, Joel, was a studious child who earned high marks in his junior high school. The school he attended tracked children according to their abilities. Joel's best friend, Stephen, was tracked below Joel in math. Stephen told Joel that he didn't think it was fair for Joel to be in the Alpha class. Joel advised Stephen that he too could be in the upper class if he would only study harder. Joel explained to Stephen that the students in the Alpha class studied harder than the other children.
>
> Stephen responded that he did study hard, so hard work couldn't be the reason for the tracking. He observed that all but two of the children in the Alpha class were from Roosevelt grammar school, located in a wealthy district of town. Stephen had gone to Lincoln elementary, in the poor area. There were no students from Lincoln in the Alpha class. Stephen believed that the class was selected according to how wealthy the students were.

In this example Joel and Stephen explained the tracking at school according to conceptual schemata that they had each constructed out of their own personal experience. Joel explained the division of the students into groups with his concept that high marks reflect hard work; Stephen explained it according to his belief that a person's wealth determines his place in society.

With the development of advanced operational schemes, conceptual schemata are formed into coherent belief systems and increasingly complex personal theories that represent a person's knowledge of himself or herself and of the social world of which he or she is a part (Nisbett and Ross, 1980; Mandler, 1984; Weiss and Sampson, 1986). Conceptual schemata not only interpret experience, they also direct adaptation by embodying a person's intentions and goals:

> Throughout junior and senior high school Joel earned high marks, particularly in math and science. Joel attributed his high marks more to his study habits and to his willingness to work on weekends and evenings to learn the material than to his being inherently bright. Joel applied to an Ivy League college and was accepted. Joel's belief in his ability to succeed through

applied,, diligent effort gave him the emotional strength to put in the extra studying required to earn superior grades. Joel's academic success made it possible for him to consider a career in medicine and to apply to medical school.

Stephen was himself an excellent student. His belief in the inequity of our social system developed into a concern for the welfare of others, particularly minority groups. Stephen was active in high school politics and held various student body offices. At college, Stephen continued to be interested in politics. He ran for and attained many student body positions, worked at a community shelter for the homeless, and majored in political science. After graduation, Stephen went to live in a poor area populated by several immigrant groups and became a community organizer.

THE INTERACTION OF ORGANIZING AND CONCEPTUAL SCHEMATA

Organizing and conceptual schemata work as an interactive unit to make experience meaningful. Together they form the state-of-the-world schemata that set the parameters of what is likely to be experienced at a particular moment in an interaction with the social environment. Organizing and conceptual schemata interact with one another through a lattice structure of interlocking networks of associated schemata.

Hierarchic associational networks of schemata are formed around a person's conceptual schemata at increasing orders of integration and complexity as the person progresses from one stage of operational schemes to the next. The networks consist of the set of organizing schemata that embody the range of experience out of which a particular conceptual schema was formed. As the structure of the mind becomes increasingly integrated, the conceptual schemata themselves form associational networks of interlocking belief systems (Nisbett and Ross, 1980; Mandler, 1984).

These networks are not only organized around conceptual schemata in the "top-down" fashion just described, they are also structured from the "bottom-up" (Mandler, 1984). Since organizing schemata regulate arousal and define affective experience in an interpersonal context, experiencing the same affect in a number of different contexts will lead to the association of the schemata that organize these experiences. The product of this association is an affectively defined network of organizing schemata (Emde, 1988a, b).

Here is an example of how the system works. An event may be interpreted initially by the currently activated conceptual schema in terms of the ideas, beliefs, and preoccupations that this schema embodies. Joel is in class awaiting the scores of a chemistry test for which he did not study.

Joel's belief that to be competitive with his classmates he must study for each test leads him to the conclusion that he has not done well on this test. As a consequence of the activation of this belief system, a network of associated organizing schemata is called up to process the feelings and thoughts attendant to the receipt of the test that reflect the conceptual schema's thematic predisposition. Joel is sad and feeling angry at himself for not having studied. His conceptual schema has evoked an associated organizing schema that regulates his affective state.

Alternatively, an event may provoke a state of arousal that requires a specific organizing schema for regulating or integrating the experience. The activated organizing schema, in turn, may evoke new conceptual schemata associated with it. While Joel is waiting for the tests to be passed around, he catches Julie's eye. She smiles coquettishly at him. Joel's heart beats with excitement, and he blushes. Julie's behavior required Joel to employ a specific organizing schema to interpret his arousal. In this case it was a schema that organized the exchange of glances as a flirtatious interaction. As Joel's feelings change so do his thoughts about himself. He is elated by her behavior. He thinks about their date the evening preceding the test and the high esteem in which she holds him. Joel winks back at Julie, and he smiles as he receives the test with a grade of C. He thinks that the lower grade was well worth the time spent with Julie. The activation of Joel's flirting schema brought into a ready state the network of sexual organizing and romantic conceptual schemata associated with it. An alternative conceptual schema is thereby made available for interpreting the interaction embodying a belief system that is meaningfully related to the activated organizing schema.

The clinical significance of conceptualizing the mind as an integrated dual-processing system is that it links together into one system what classical and object relations theories have heretofore needed two separate and distinct theoretical systems to describe. Until now, problems related to the organization and regulation of the self and of object relations have seemed to demand one system of explanation while problems that are the result of intrapsychic conflict have seemed to demand another (Gedo and Goldberg, 1973; Chessick, 1990). By contrast, a dual-processing system such as the one we are proposing will enable us to understand both how disorders of the self and of object relations influence the beliefs and concepts about the self and others that cause psychic conflict and how pathogenic concepts and beliefs influence object relations and self-organization. The proposed system will also allow us to assess the impact of classical psychoanalytic interpretations and the kind of psychoanalytic interventions described by self psychologists and object relations theorists (Modell, 1984; Stolorow et al., 1987; Mitchell, 1991) on either or both levels of a patient's psychic organization.

CHAPTER 6

The Mind in Operation

FROM SCHEMES AND SCHEMATA TO PRIMARY AND SECONDARY PROCESS

In the previous chapter I outlined the mental processes and structures that enable us to organize and interpret our interactions with the social environment. The schemes and schemata that underlie this process of meaning analysis are also the mental functions and structures that generate primary and secondary process ideation.

I described organizing schemata as episodic memories that depict the self in interaction with another for the purpose of organizing or regulating self-experience in a specific type of context. These schemata are the templates against which we organize and interpret lived experience and, as patterns of interaction, are the vehicles through which we can communicate to others our feelings and internal states-of-being. So conceived, organizing schemata closely correspond to my coauthor's concept of primary process ideation. By contrast, conceptual schemata were depicted as the ideas and beliefs that we form about ourselves and our universe, which are derived from the experience formed by the organizing schemata. Insofar as these conceptual schemata can be represented as abstract concepts and beliefs, they form the content of what my coauthor has described as secondary process ideation.

Yet these equivalences are only approximate, because the primary and secondary process are composite terms and contain within themselves multiple referents. Depending on the context in which these terms are used, primary and secondary process can refer to a type of thinking (e.g., associational reasoning in primary process and logical reasoning in secondary process cognition), or to a particular kind of mental content (e.g., social interactions for primary process thinking and abstract concepts for secondary process ideation), or to a mode of representing and communicating this content (e.g., nonverbal representation and communication in the primary processes and verbal-symbolic representational forms in the secondary processes). The terms primary and secondary process thus are a useful shorthand for describing frequently encountered constellations of mental processes, contents, and modes of representation employed for processing certain categories of data (e.g., experiential and interpersonal data in the primary processes and conceptual information in the secondary processes). That a given constellation is frequently encountered, however, does not necessarily mean that its elements must always be combined in this way. There are some situations, moreover, in which it is important for the clinician to be able to disassemble the concepts of primary and secondary process according to which components are actually present. Accordingly, it is useful to delineate the components of both primary and secondary process so that we may more easily distinguish them in practice. In what follows, I attempt to restate the usual distinction between primary and secondary process in terms of three different elements. These are schemes and schemata, both discussed in the last chapter, and a third element, the system of representation that is being employed.

Let us begin with schemes. Following Piaget, schemes have been defined as the mental operations that determine the operational possibilities in cognition. Schemes progress through a series of stages during the course of development. The operation of schemes is not conscious to an individual but must be inferred from observing his or her behavior. The developmental stage that has been reached in the formation of schemes determines the relative maturity or lack thereof of a person's mental functioning. All mental life, including both organizing and conceptual schemata, depend on the operation of these schemes, which are themselves nonetheless not conscious. These points were covered in Chapter 5 and are probably familiar to most readers from their previous exposure to the works of Piaget and other developmental psychologists. What is important to realize here in terms of our present discussion is that the operation of schemes affects equally both primary and secondary process. And this is true regardless of the developmental level of the particular schemes being employed. As my coauthor has pointed out, given the history of primary and secondary process thinking in the psychoanalytic literature, we tend incorrectly to associate primary process ideation with more primitive, nonlogical ways of thinking about personal needs and wishes, while associating secondary process with developmentally advanced, logical reasoning about personal issues in a social context. We can restate this important point in cognitive-developmental terms: schemes are logically independent of the primary/secondary process distinction; the schemes being employed in a given instance can, regardless of their developmental stage, equally well affect the manifestations of either primary or secondary process. Thus, secondary process thinking, as in the reasoning of the small child, can be quite primitive, while primary process thinking, as my coauthor has pointed out, can be rich and sophisticated.

The second category we need to consider is that of the schemata, in particular the distinction between organizing and conceptual schemata. If schemes constitute an independent dimension, the distinction between organizing and conceptual schemata by contrast shows a close relation to the usual distinction made between primary and secondary process. That is to say, organizing schemata tend preferentially—though not always—to be expressed in terms of primary process thinking, whereas conceptual schemata tend preferentially—though not always—to be expressed in terms of secondary process. Thus, one can expect that a primary process manifestation during the treatment hour will usually reflect a patient's current organizing schemata, that is, how he or she feels about himself or herself in relation to the analyst. Similarly, one can expect that the secondary process will more likely be used when the patient wishes to communicate something about his or her currently activated conceptual schemata.

Again it is important not to confuse this issue with developmental level. Because an organizing schema is being touched on does not imply a primitive form of cognition any more than the activation of a conceptual schema necessarily implies a more sophisticated level of thought. One can equally have very primitive conceptual schemata and very advanced organizing ones. For example, the organizing schema that permits an experienced therapist experientially to distinguish projective identification from personal countertransference is an extremely sophisticated one. Indeed, unless the therapist has a gift for thinking in terms of very abstract concepts, his practical ability contained in his organizing schemata, is likely to outstrip the conceptual schemata derived from it! Then, too, a conceptual schema may be quite primitive. Recall, for instance, Piaget's daughter, who believed that when the sun set it was going to bed because it felt sad.

The third category we need to examine is the means of representation. As my colleague described in Chapter 2, the lived experience organized by the primary processes is typically represented and expressed by signals and signs, for example, gestures, facial expressions, postures, vocal inflection, and the pitch and rhythm of spoken words. The conceptual information of the secondary processes, on the other hand, is usually represented and expressed in words and symbols. If we think in terms of organizing and conceptual schemata, we can immediately intuit why this must be the case. Organizing schemata, which orient a person affectively to the immediate situation at hand, are indeed likely to be expressed in terms of gesture, vocal tone, and the like. Conceptual schemata, on the other hand, which contain a person's conclusions and inferences based on his or her experiences, seem to require the services of words and symbols, that is, the mode of representation of the secondary process. Indeed, it is just this regular pairing of organizing schemata with one form of representation and conceptual schemata with another that has made the distinction between primary and secondary process clinically useful as a heuristic. But the pairing is neither necessary nor universal. That is to say, it is possible for conceptual schemata to be expressed gesturally, as for example by the nod of one's head to indicate intellectual assent to a proposition. Similarly, organizing schemata can be expressed in verbal and symbolic ways. In short, in thinking about primary and secondary processes, we must be attuned to the fact that while the kinds of information that are being processed are usually represented and communicated in these respective forms, the data of these systems are not exclusively represented or expressed in these ways. The reason for this is that the mode of representation is independent of the mental processes that are to be represented. Thus, though the distinction between primary and secondary process remains clinically useful, we can afford a yet more precise description of the phenomena at stake by keeping in mind the distinction between organizing and conceptual schemata, on one hand, and the means of representation on the other. It is to the latter topic that we now turn.

THE REPRESENTATION AND COMMUNICATION OF EXPERIENCE AND IDEAS

The variety of representational forms available to the primary and sec- ondary processes derives from the fact that the mental system of signs and symbols used to represent and communicate mental processes and con- tents is independent of those processes and contents. Just as the schemes and schemata, which constitute primary and secondary process ideation, develop into independent, but related, mental systems, the system of representation develops into a separate mental system that influences, and is influenced by, these other two systems.

Research in cognitive psychology and psycholinguistics (Werner, 1948; Werner and Kaplan, 1963; Piaget, 1962; Piaget and Inhelder, 1971, 1973; Vygotsky, 1934, 1966; Slobin, 1973; Bruner, 1977, 1983, 1990) dem- onstrates that human beings construct mental images, signals and signs, action symbols (deferred imitations, symbolic play, enactments), graphic symbols (pictures), and verbal symbols (words and stories), and that these images, signs, and symbols evidence a developmental course paralleling that of the operational schemes. Early in development these representa- tional forms are personal, idiosyncratic signs and symbols, very close in form to the mental contents that they represent; but as cognitive development and socialization occur, actions and images, as symbols, become more complex, realistic representational forms, and verbal sym- bols become increasingly abstract and socially defined.

An interaction with the environment is meaningfully organized and interpreted by its assimilation to the currently available organizing and conceptual schemata. The meaning attributed to this event by these schemata is then embodied in a representational form for communication to oneself or to others. The particular symbolic form of a representation is determined by the interpersonal context, the representational capabilities of the communicator, and the nature of the material to be represented. The interpersonal context is defined by such variables as the capacity of the person to whom the communication is being addressed to apprehend the information, the communicator's expectations of how the information will be received, and the purpose and desired results of the communication. The representational capabilities of the communicator concern his or her facility with verbal, graphic, and gestural modes of symbolizing information. The nature of the material to be represented refers to the closeness of fit between the material and the mode of representation. For example, the design concept for an automobile body is best represented by a visual image, whereas words better represent the idea of individual liberties.

The transformation of meaning into a symbolic form is usually a preconscious operation unless problems arise in representing the material or in communicating it to others. This means that most verbal and nonverbal communication between people is preconscious and not the object of conscious self-reflection (Mandler, 1984).

A patient, for example, may express the meaning that he or she has attributed to the analytic interaction in a variety of symbolic forms:

> Mr. L, feeling defeated by his analyst, tells a story about his father beating him in a tennis match. The patient follows this story with a daydream in which a big and a little knight are jousting. The smaller knight is run through by the other's lance. The patient concludes the hour by telling the analyst that he feels weak and inadequate.

In this illustration, the analytic interaction is meaningfully interpreted by its assimilation to an organizing schema that depicts the patient being defeated by a superior person. Mr. L represents the experience of defeat, organized by this schema, in a story (a verbal symbol) of being bested by his father at tennis as well as in a daydream (a visual image employed as a symbol) in which he is lanced in a knightly duel. He also expresses feeling weak and inadequate in words (i.e., a verbal symbolic form). In this example, we can see that interpersonal relations and the affects experienced in these interactions, which are the content of primary process ideation, can be represented and expressed in the form of symbols.

The reality that affects, internal states-of-being, and object relations can be represented with symbols does not alter the fact that these experiences are also expressed by such nonsymbolic representational media as facial expression, posture, gesture, and vocal tone, inflection, and pacing. As I illustrated with the nuzzling games between Charley and Jan in Chapter 5, such nonsymbolic forms of representation are integral to the organizing schemata that regulate affect, arousal, and such internal states-of-being as intention and attention. As such, they serve as the vehicles for communicating these internal states between the self and self-regulating other.

A patient's ideas and beliefs, the content of conceptual schemata, and secondary process ideation are customarily thought to take a verbal symbolic form. Yet ideas and beliefs are not always so represented or expressed:

> Ms. O believes that she is an unlikeable person. She wears a scowl on her face and speaks in a such a whiny and slow-paced manner that her analyst can not stand to listen to her. The analyst begins to hate his time with her.

In this example, Ms. O represents and expresses her belief that she is not a likeable person in the tone and pacing of her voice and by her facial expression. Through these nonsymbolic means she gets the analyst to experience her in a manner that causes him to think of her the way she conceives of herself, as an unlikeable person.

In our clinical work, we must be sensitive to the various symbolic and nonsymbolic forms patients use to encode and communicate the meanings that they attribute to the therapeutic interaction. It is important for us to remember that patients preconsciously translate into a symbolic or nonsymbolic form the meanings they attribute to the patient-therapist interaction. Most meaningful discourse involves the simultaneous use of the symbolic and the nonsymbolic forms of representation and communication. Although it is often assumed that when a patient uses a symbol, such as Mr. L's story about being defeated by his father at tennis, to represent his or her meaning analysis of the analytic interaction the symbol is being employed as a defense against the conscious awareness of the transference (Gill, 1982a), it is more often than not the case that the representation is not being used as a defense. Such representations are, in most instances, merely the symbols preconsciously constructed by a patient to communicate to the therapist his or her experience of and ideas about the analytic interaction. From this perspective, we interpret these symbols as an expression of the transference and not necessarily as a defense against its recognition.

PRECONSCIOUS MEANING ANALYSIS AND THE CONSERVATION OF MENTAL ORGANIZATION

Every interaction with the social surround is made personally meaningfully by its preconscious assimilation to the organizing and conceptual schemata available to the person at the time of the interaction. Organizing and conceptual schemata make events meaningful by arranging the elements of experience into a form that is coherent with what a person already knows. By making lived experience conform to an existing schema, meaning analysis conserves the organizational structure of the mind.

Clinically, this means that a patient will preconsciously organize and interpret his or her interactions with the therapist in a way that reflects and preserves the content and structure of his or her schemata. Hence, the therapeutic interaction can be thought of as a here-and-now representative instance of the patient's organizing and conceptual schemata. Transference, therefore, takes on a new meaning. Rather than being a distortion of the present in terms of the past, transference now becomes the reflection of how a patient organizes and interprets his or her interaction with the therapist. That is, transference is the product of the process of meaning analysis. It can be thought of as a window through which the therapist can infer a patient's organizing and conceptual schemata:

> Ms. T begins her hour by describing an interaction at work that she found difficult; she questions the efficacy of what she did. A short period of silence ensues. She then begins to flirt with the therapist while talking about a male coworker in whom she is interested but whose interest in her she is uncertain of. The therapist interprets her flirtatious behavior as a means of securing *his* interest in her. Ms. T responds with a memory of dancing in front of her father in a pretty dress. She tells the therapist that her father was a high-powered executive who worked very late into the evening. When he came home he would be irritable and interested only in reading his papers. He would avoid her until she danced in front of him or played hide and seek with him. He would then take her on his lap and talk to her about her about what she had done that day.

In this vignette, Ms. T preconsciously organized the therapeutic interaction to reflect her conceptual schema that she was not a person of interest to men; she was only a sexual object to them. Ms. T achieved this result by getting the therapist to participate in an enactment of an organizing schema that was created with her father. Her father would not attend to her unless she acted in a sexually provocative manner. In like fashion, the therapist did not interact with Ms. T until she flirted with him. Ms. T also construed the therapist's interpretation as a confirmation of her belief. The therapeutic interaction thereby became a representative instance of the patient's organizing and conceptual schemata.

Since the therapist's behavior did not deviate from what Ms. T expected, her preconscious cognitive processing of their interaction was not disrupted. Ms. T, therefore, preconsciously represented and expressed to the therapist her meaning analysis of their interaction (the transference) in the form of the memory of her interaction with her father (a verbal symbolic symbol).

Meaning analysis thus can be operationally defined as the process of assimilating an interaction with the social surround to the schemata that organize the interaction into a form that has meaning for the individual. If the process of preconscious meaning analysis preserves the structure and content of the mind, how are the schemes and schemata that organize the mind to be altered? To make effective therapeutic interventions, we must have a theory about how mental contents change.

INTERRUPTION AND ACCOMMODATION

Once initiated, the process of meaning analysis proceeds preconsciously and automatically to completion unless it is interrupted. The interruption of organized cognitive and behavioral processes motivates a person to search preconsciously or consciously for ways of restoring the disrupted organizing activity. The disequilibrium created by the interruption persists until the person alters whatever caused the interruption or accommodates his or her schemes and schemata to incorporate that which interrupted the process of meaning analysis (Zeigarnik, 1927; Werner, 1948; Miller, Glanter, and Pribram, 1960; Piaget, 1970; Berschied, 1982, 1983; Mandler, 1984). If accommodation occurs, a change in the person's schemes or schemata is effected.

Interruption comes about in a variety of ways. In the realm of action, a sequenced or routine behavior is interrupted whenever its completion is physically blocked or temporarily delayed. Examples come readily to mind:

During the night I go to the bathroom, but the door is locked.

A baby sucks on his bottle, but no juice comes out.

Coming to an intersection, I step on the brakes but they fail.

In terms of regulatory interactions, interruptions occur when the self-regulating other behaves in a manner that violates the expected pattern. Here are two examples:

Charley is bibbed and seated in his highchair. Instead of being presented with the expected spoonful of food, Jan gives him a toy.

A patient whose previous therapist said something comforting after she expressed her feelings is taken aback when her new therapist says nothing to mitigate her feelings.

Interruptions in cognitive and perceptual processes are usually experienced as a discrepancy. Discrepant information does not fit our expectations. It interrupts our cognitive processing of an event because what we perceive does not match the schemata we are using to process the data:

> Upon entering a therapist's office I expect to see a couch, chairs, and a desk; seeing a wet bar and stools would interrupt my dominant expectations as determined by my schema of a therapist's office.

Interruptions in cognitive processing also occur when information is introduced that is discrepant with the content of an ongoing stream of thought. Such interruptions usually occur when the data being processed are assimilated to two or more schemata that in some way conflict with one another:

> I was thinking about the vacation I would take with the bonus money I received from work when I remembered that I owed my brother quite a sum of money. The thought that I owed my brother money interrupted my thinking about how I'd spend the money on my vacation.

The removal or modification of an environmental cause of an interruption aside, one of the most common ways to reestablish equilibrium in cognitive processing is to substitute a schema that will resolve the interruption in the current state-of-the-world schema. Substitutability of schemata requires that a similarity exists between the original and the substitute schemata in structure, function, content, and goals. Substitution of schemata is usually a preconscious process:

> When I come to an intersection and my brakes fail, I downshift to stop the car. Without conscious self-reflection, I substitute the schema of downshifting for the schema of breaking.

> The patient whose therapist failed to say something comforting following the expression of her feelings began to talk of suicide. The suicide schema was preconsciously substituted for the schema of emotional display to obtain words of comfort and caring from her therapist.

Accommodation of a schema to incorporate an anomalous behavior pattern or discrepant information is another means of dealing with interruptions in the process of meaning analysis. Though a schema may be preconsciously altered in minor ways, accommodation of a schema involves the reorganization of or alternation in the elements that constitute it such that conscious self-reflection is usually required (Mandler, 1984):

I learned to drive on a car that had an automatic transmission. Several years later I bought a sports car that had a manual transmission. My schema for driving a car was constantly being interrupted by the need to shift. The schema had to be modified to include shifting gears when starting, speeding up, slowing down, turning, and stopping. For quite a while I needed to be consciously aware of how I coordinated stepping on the clutch, shifting gears, depressing the accelerator or break, and steering the car. Now I attend only to the road; all these elements of my driving schema are automatically and preconsciously executed.

When a schema is modified to accommodate novel permutations, the newly created schema is differentiated from the original prototype and then integrated with it. I did not forget how to drive an automatic after modifying my driving schema to include using a manual transmission. In this way, new information is integrated into a schema without destroying the organization or meaning of the original schematic prototype.

This paradigm for altering mental structures and functions has important implications for our understanding of how we effect therapeutic change in our patients. In order to help a patient change his or her organizing and/or conceptual schemata, we have to interrupt the patient's preconscious organizing and interpretative processes.

As clinicians we effect an interruption in these processes whenever we interact with a patient in a way that deviates from how he or she expects us to respond or when we interpret the maladaptive preconscious or unconscious ideas, beliefs, expectations, or consequences of the organizing and conceptual schemata that the patient is using to organize and interpret to his or her interactions with us:

After expressing anger at his male therapist, Mr. Q emotionally withdraws, afraid that the therapist will retaliate. The therapist, instead of retaliating, empathizes with the patient's angry feelings. In deviating from what Mr. Q expected, the therapist is interrupting the patient's preconscious processing of their interaction. Mr. Q not only becomes consciously aware that he expected a hostile response from the therapist, but also is confronted with having to adjust to the therapist's empathic behavior.

Alternatively, the therapist could have interpreted Mr. Q's behavior as a test of his preconscious belief that the therapist could not handle the expression of his anger. The interpretation would have interrupted the patient's preconscious testing by introducing data (i.e., the preconscious belief that is being tested) that was discrepant with the objective of the test, which was to provoke a hostile response. Mr. Q would then be required to reevaluate the premise of his schema in the light of his experience of the therapist's behavior, in order to reestablish an equilibrium between what he believed and what actually happened.

As the examples illustrate, we can enable a patient to alter in his or her schemata not only through our interpretations, but also by interacting with a patient in a new way (Loewald, 1960). In this model of change, it is the patient's activity and not the therapist's interventions or interpretations that produce alterations in the schemata that organize the patient's mind. All that our interventions and interpretations do is set the stage for the patient's problem-solving behavior by inducing a state of disequilibrium. Thus we cause the patient either preconsciously to employ alternative schemata or consciously to accommodate his or her schemata into a new form.

From our clinical experience we all know that patients do not readily change their behavior or beliefs in response to our interpretations or interventions. Patients actively resist altering their schemata, because the human mind first and foremost works to conserve its content and organization. It is only after a period of working through, during which patients test new against old experience and knowledge, that changes in their schemata ordinarily are effected. Interruptions in processing data must occur repeatedly or problems in adapting to a situation must be regularly encountered before patients will engage in behavior aimed at resolving these interruptions and problems and only then by trying to make the discrepant data fit with what they already know. This type of problem-solving activity employs a conscious and deliberate type of meaning analysis.

In what follows, I explain the component processes that make up this type of meaning analysis, beginning with the state of consciousness. I then describe the inferential reasoning strategies that are employed in this conscious form of meaning analysis and demonstrate how these strategies are used by examining the process of introspection.

CONSCIOUSNESS

Contemporary psychologists (Piaget, 1976; Mandler, 1975b, 1984; Kihlstrom, 1987) conceive of consciousness as a mental state that allows the products of different preconscious systems to be evaluated, coordinated, and integrated. It is not a memory system or an information-retrieval system. Rather, consciousness is a mental state that is activated for representing information requiring special processing. The contents of consciousness are the mental representations (i.e., the images, words, and the like described earlier) of the data contained in the organizing and conceptual schemata and the feelings associated with these schemata.

Conscious thinking is initiated when preconscious mental activity has been interrupted. The autonomic arousal that accompanies mental disequilibrium initiates the state of consciousness (Zeigarnik, 1927; Piaget, 1976; Nisbett and Ross, 1980; Mandler, 1975b, 1984). Consciousness permits a review and evaluation of all relevant information, potential outcomes, and alternative means before action takes place. It facilitates decision making, inferential reasoning, and the creation of new ideas and imaginative solutions to problems by enabling a person to manipulate self-reflectively all the relevant variables.

Piaget (1976), Mandler (1984) and others (Tulving, 1983; Nisbett and Ross, 1980) have shown that consciousness is constructed out of one or more preconscious organizing schemata. That is to say, only activated organizing schemata are available for the construction of conscious mental representations. Unactivated schemata and those which are the object of defense remain inaccessible.

Under most circumstances organizing schemata do not enter consciousness directly. They achieve consciousness through the preconscious mediation of a conceptual schema. The mediation is necessary because consciousness has a limited capacity for representing information (Miller, 1956; Mandler, 1975b, 1984). The limit refers to the number of functionally related chunks of data that can be simultaneously held in the conscious state of mind. Conceptual schemata manage the number of related units of information in the conscious state that are required to solve a problem in understanding or in adapting to the social surround (Nisbett and Ross, 1980; Mandler, 1984). A conceptual schema accomplishes this task by selecting those data from the activated organizing schemata which reflect a person's current ideas, beliefs, motives, and goals. What is available for conscious self-reflection are the feelings, thoughts, and behaviors that represent a person's interpretation of his or her interactions with the environment.

> In a halting, affectless manner, Mrs. B is talking about her lack of arousal during intercourse with her husband. The therapist interprets her slow, emotionless presentation as indicating a conflict in experiencing sexual feelings. The interpretation interrupts Mrs. B's preconscious stream of thought. Mrs. B not only becomes consciously aware of how she is presenting her material, but also is flooded with anxiety, fear, humiliation, and sexual arousal. Mrs. B consciously recalls her husband's critical evaluation of her love-making and of the sounds she makes during intercourse. She also recalls her parents scolding her for masturbating. Mrs. B concludes that the therapist's interpretation was critical of how she expressed her sexual feelings and hence that her feelings are wrong and not acceptable to others.

In this example, the therapist's interpretation evoked in Mrs. B the experience of being criticized when expressing sexual feelings. This experience called into play the conceptual schema embodying the belief that her sexual feelings are bad and unacceptable to others. It also made accessible to her conscious awareness the organizing schemata associated with this belief, those of being criticized by her parents and husband for having sexual feelings. To construct her conscious experience, Mrs. B used the belief that her sexual feelings are unacceptable (her conceptual schema) to select particular aspects from her past and current experience (her organizing schemata) that proved this belief true about herself. Also relevant here is that as a child the patient had been sexually molested by her brother. But, since this organizing schema was the object of defense, it was not available for activation and played no part in the formation of the patient's conscious experience of the analytic interaction.

CONSCIOUS MEANING ANALYSIS

The conscious form of meaning analysis is used for solving problems in processing information and in adapting to the social and physical environment, for decision making and conflict resolution, and for speculating about the causes and outcomes of interactions with the social and physical surround. Based on the same inferential reasoning strategies that the preconscious form of meaning analysis uses, conscious meaning analysis enables a person to go beyond the information given in a situation, to formulate hypothesis about unobserved states-of-being, actions, and events and to create ideas about hypothetical situations.

This form of meaning analysis begins with the conscious formulation of a specific hypothesis for solving a problem, making a decision, or inferring a cause or a result. The hypothesis is derived from the concepts, beliefs, or theories embodied in a person's currently activated conceptual schemata. The hypothesis is used to search the person's knowledge structures for organizing schemata that will validate it. The focus of the search is generally quite specific and selective, inhibiting the activation of nonsalient schemata during the process (Nisbett and Ross 1980; Mandler, 1984).

The hypothesis is tested and evaluated against the experience embodied in these related organizing schemata. Data from these organizing schemata are formulated into specific inferences about the causes of the here-and-now event or problem that initiated the process, the probable solutions, and the likely results. These schemata are then employed to scan the environment for data that will support the hypothesis. The following clinical vignette illustrates this process of conscious meaning analysis:

> Mrs. V, a psychotherapist, comes to treatment and hesitantly states that she is glad to be with me in therapy today. She reflects on the difficulty with which she makes this statement and then falls silent. A few minutes later,

Mrs. V talks about her successful handling of a conflict with her husband and about receiving a good review from her supervisor on her handling of a difficult joint therapy session between a pubescent female patient and her father. Mrs. V then describes this session, in which the patient told her father about aspects of their relationship she found difficult. Mrs. V had expected the father to reject his daughter hostilely for what she said. Instead, he was empathically accepting of what his daughter had to say.

I interpret Mrs. V's stories as an expression of her fear that I will reject her for being competent. I also state that I understand that her telling me that she wants to be here today was her way of testing whether I will accept her as a competent person who wants to be with me or treat her as a defective person who needs to be in treatment.

Mrs. V responds that it was very risky for her to say that she wants to be with me because she is leaving herself open to my rejection. It's safer to need to be in treatment. Her mother rejected her when she demonstrated her competence, and her father rejected her for acting independently. Having problems was the safest and easiest way to hold their interest and get their love. Mrs. V adds that her supervisor, like her parents, rejected her for being competent, because at the same session at which she complimented her on how she handled the difficult case she cut their supervisory time in half. Mrs. V feels strongly that she requires the supervisor's continued support.

Mrs. V then says that she feels an acute need to tell me about all the bad things that she has done since her last session. She is conflicted about how I received what she was saying. She interprets my silence after she said that she wanted to be with me as indicating that it's not all right to *want* to be here, but that she is a patient who *needs* to be here. Yet my interpretation told her that I understood what she was experiencing and why. Mrs. V didn't know if she was being rejected or accepted. For her it's safer to connect in the old way by detailing her flaws.

Mrs. V had come to treatment to test her belief that she is acceptable to others only if she is defective or needy. Given her recent experience of feeling rejected by her supervisor for being competent, Mrs. V formulated a conscious hypothesis that I too would reject her for acting in a competent, nonneedy manner. She tested the belief by stating that she wanted to be with me. Although Mrs. V underscored the test by calling my attention to how difficult it was for her to make this statement, she also knew that I would know the meaning of the statement because we had previously talked about needing versus wanting to be in treatment. The patient fell silent waiting for my response. She interpreted my silence as a confirmation of her belief that she was welcome in treatment only if she was needy.

Since my response did not deviate from the response that Mrs. V expected, the conscious form of meaning analysis was no longer required. She fell into a preconscious mode of interacting with me. Mrs. V then communicated her meaning analysis of our interaction in the stories about acting competently at home and at work and in the report of the therapy hour in which she expected a father to reject his daughter for competently expressing her feelings.

My interpretation interrupted Mrs. V's preconscious processing of our interaction because it deviated from how she expected me to respond, given the reaffirmed belief that she was using to organize her experience of our interaction. The interruption brought back into her conscious awareness the belief she had set out to test. Mrs. V then reiterated her belief, the hypothesis she formed about our interaction, and how she tested it. She also expressed the organizing schemata from the past (her parents' behavior) and from the present (her supervisor's behavior) that proved the belief true and that she used to construct the hypothesis.

Mrs. V then consciously reassessed my behavior in terms of this hypothesis. She concluded that she was confused by my responses because they seemed both to support and to deny her being accepted as a competent person. The conscious testing of her belief enabled Mrs. V to become self-reflectively aware of how she defended herself against experiencing rejection by seeing and presenting herself as a flawed person.

Inferential reasoning in both its preconscious and conscious forms seeks to confirm what a person already knows or believes about himself or herself and about the universe (Kuhn, 1962; Snyder and Swan, 1978; Nisbett and Ross, 1980). In this way inferential reasoning works to conserve the content and structure of our conceptual and organizing schemata. It would not surprise us, then, to learn that people tend to adhere to their belief systems well beyond the point at which logical and evidential considerations can sustain them (Nisbett and Ross, 1980). People do not accommodate their theories to new evidence when it is appropriate to do so. Rather, they seek out and more heavily weight evidence that confirms their existing belief system and disconfirms the competing evidence (Snyder and Swan, 1978). They tend to create causal explanations for anomalous data that are consistent with their preexisting belief systems without adequate consideration for the validity of their causal explanations (Wilson and Nisbett, 1978). They also tend to act on their beliefs in a manner that causes those beliefs to be self-fulfilling prophecies (Rosenthal and Jacobson, 1964; Snyder and Swan, 1978).

Without the aid of an external paradigm for correcting this inherent bias in normal human inference, such as the therapist's consistent use of interpretations, the inferences patients form tend to reinforce what they believe about themselves (Nisbett and Ross 1980). As the example of Mrs. V shows, the analytic interaction itself is preconsciously and consciously formulated by the patient to test these beliefs. The repetitive, self-fulfilling quality of the transference is often due to the patient's testing behavior. Since the conscious form of meaning analysis is usually employed following

a therapeutic intervention or interpretation that has induced disequilibrium by interrupting the patient's preconscious meaning analysis, a
process of working through is required to counteract the self-serving,
conservative nature of the patient's inferential reasoning.

The clinical implications of this research lays the basis for reformulating
the concept of resistance in interactional terms. A patient will resist
accepting interpretations—as Mrs. V did when she wanted to reiterate the
bad things she had done in response to my having interpreted the motive
underlying her testing behavior—if the information contained in these
interpretations serves either to invalidate the beliefs that organize the
patient's personal epistemology or else threatens the coherence and
stability of the self. That is to say, resistance preserves the organization and
continuity of the patient's conceptual and organizing schemata.

Earlier in this chapter I argued that patients ordinarily represent and
communicate their meaning analysis of the analytic interaction in the form
of preconsciously constructed signs and symbols. Though this is the case
when the preconscious form of meaning analysis is employed, patients will
make direct, consciously formulated statements about their experience of
and beliefs about the analytic interaction when these are the result of the
conscious form of meaning analysis. Mrs. V, for example, made several
statements directly to me about how she experienced me and my
interventions and what these experiences meant in terms her beliefs about
herself and me while she was consciously testing these experiences and
beliefs in the analytic interaction.

INTROSPECTION

Because meaning analysis is usually a preconscious process, a person is not
normally aware of the internal and external determinants of his or her
behavior, emotional state, or even the contents of his or her conscious
mind. Like an observer, a person must infer the causes of his or her
behavior and mental states. Mandler (1984) as well as and Nisbett and Ross
(1980) persuasively argue that introspective analysis of one's own behavior
is only as accurate as are the methods used in collecting, selecting,
recalling, and representing the relevant data and in forming and testing
causal hypothesis for the behavior. Knowledge of oneself is produced by
the same strategies that issue knowledge of social events and is prone to the
same biases and errors. In what follows, the determination of affective
states exemplify the introspective process.

What a person feels has been shown to be determined by the meaning
that the person attributes to the experience of arousal (Schacter and Singer,
1962; Nisbett and Schacter, 1966; Nisbett and Ross, 1980; Mandler,
1984). As I demonstrated in Chapter 5, the attribution of meaning to the

experience of arousal is usually a preconscious process governed by the organizing schemata. The introspective analysis of one's emotional state, however, is a product of one's theories about what caused the feelings.

Introspection begins with a search for the most plausible causes of emotional arousal. Plausible sources may be events external or internal to the individual. The analysis of the available and plausible sources of the emotional arousal is significantly influenced by the theories (i.e., conceptual schemata) a person holds about what antecedents produce which affective states of being. A person's self-concept and beliefs about his or her personal efficacy, for example, influence the meanings attributed to arousal (Cantor and Mischel, 1977; Nisbett and Wilson, 1977; Wilson and Nisbett, 1978; Lewinsohn et. al., 1980).

Research shows that arousal may be interpreted as anxiety or depression when a person concludes that he or she is not in control of his or her thinking processes or of the situation. Yet, it is the person's assessment of the situation that determines his or her perceived degree of control (Mandler, 1984; Seligman and Maier, 1967; Seligman, 1975; Beck, 1967). Studies reviewed by Beck (1972), Nisbett and Ross (1980), and Mandler (1984) indicate that it is a person's belief in his or her ability to make a situationally relevant action that determines the degree to which he or she interprets himself or herself as effective or helpless. If a person learns that he or she is not able to complete actions or effectively impact others or the environment, as Seligman (1975) has shown, the person develops a belief system in which he or she conceives of himself or herself as helpless and becomes depressed when faced with a problem that needs resolution. Mandler (1984) makes a similar argument for the experience of guilt. Guilt may arise when a person believes that he or she cannot undo what he or she has done.

This research implies that patients do not have privileged information about their internal processes. Patients, like therapists who observe them, must infer the causes of their own feelings, thoughts, and behavior from the context of the here-and-now interaction. The conclusions the patients draw will reflect what they believe produced their thoughts and feelings and not necessarily what actually caused them. Introspection is a form of inferential reasoning and is subject to the same conservative, self-serving biases as are other forms of social judgment. This research does not invalidate psychoanalytic inquiry. From a psychoanalytic perspective, it is through analyzing a patient's experience of the analytic interaction, the beliefs that he or she used to interpret this experience, and the inferences about the self and the analyst that the patient derived from his or her meaning analysis of the analytic interaction that the schemata that organize the mind are revealed and made available for examination and change.

Defense
and Psychopathology

In Chapters 5 and 6, under the rubric of preconscious and conscious meaning analysis, I presented a model of mental organization and cognitive-affective process designed to explain both normal and pathological psychic phenomena. This chapter casts the concepts of defense, symptom formation, and psychopathology in the terms of that model. In reformulating these clinical concepts from a cognitive-affective and interactional point-of-view it is not my aim merely to translate the classical, object relations, and self-psychological conceptualizations of these concepts into the terms of our model. Rather, by using our model to understand the diverse pathogenic phenomena that these theories were constructed to describe, I will formulate a single, integrated theory of psychopathology and will do so in a manner that relates immediately to clinical process.

Classical, object relations, and self-psychological theories were each, to varying degrees, constructed to explain the effects on a person's mental organization of traumatic events (i.e., acute trauma), such as an actual or perceived seduction, and of the cumulative strains and stresses (i.e., cumulative trauma) that result from maladaptive interactions with the person's caregivers over the course of development (Khan, 1963; Sandler, 1967). I shall sketch out how trauma affects the formation of organizing and conceptual schemata, as well as the relationship of these schemata to one another and to the processes of preconscious and conscious meaning analysis. In other words, I shall demonstrate how our model of mental organization and process accounts for alterations in normal cognition and for various forms of psychopathology that are the result of derailments in normal development as a consequence of acute and cumulative trauma.

DEFENSE AND SYMPTOM FORMATION

In some respects the conceptualization of defense and symptom formation embodied in our model of the mind is not new. A cognitive process similar to the concept of preconscious meaning analysis has played a central role in the psychoanalytic theory of defense and symptom formation since

Freud's 1926 reformulation of his theory of anxiety in *Inhibitions, Symptoms, and Anxiety.* In this landmark work, Freud argues that the ego institutes repression in reaction to anticipated danger. The ego judges whether or not instinctually motivated feelings, thoughts, or intentions will lead to a situation of danger. That is, the ego assesses the meaning of interacting with the social surround in a particular way. If the ego determines that a danger situation exists, it generates anxiety to signal the presence of danger. The ego defends against the danger situation by repressing the instinctual wish and then replacing it with a symptom. The symptom can substitute for the conflict between a wish and reality because it is a construct embodying both the instinctual wish and the prohibition against it. From this perspective, the symptom is a symbol constructed to represent the ego's meaning analysis of the interface between instinctual desires and the realities of the social context.

In his *Outline of Psychoanalysis,* Freud (1940a) formalized his theory of defense in a manner comparable to the process of meaning analysis presented here. He proposed that the ego unconsciously assesses the safety of a situation by making decisions about the adaptive consequences of carrying out instinctually motivated actions. Using past experience as a guide, the ego engages in "experimental actions in thought" to decide to carry out a course of action, to delay it, or to defend against it given the realities of the here-and-now situation.

Similar conceptualizations can be found elsewhere in the literature. For example, Sandler's (1960) formulation of defensive activity rests on cognitive processes analogous to the process of meaning analysis as I have defined it. He contends that the perceived safety of a situation is determined by the "meaning" attributed to that situation by the ego. The ego unconsciously transforms incoming excitation from the sense organs into meaningful data by organizing it in terms of past experience. The ego uses instinctual wishes, memories of past experience, and conceptual knowledge as the frames of reference with which to organize the perception of external reality. Successful organizing activity creates a feeling of safety and lowers the potential for anxiety. This sense of safety is not a conscious experience, but it is an unconscious background state that accompanies successful adaptation. If the ego cannot meaningfully organize an event, trauma is experienced and the sense of safety disappears. The ego then utilizes its defenses to correct externally the traumatic situation through motor activity or to restore internally a sense of safety by transforming perceptual data and altering mental representations.

Sandler (1989) and his colleagues (Sandler and Rosenblatt, 1962; Sandler and Nagera, 1963; Sandler and Sandler, 1978) have suggested that the ego organizes its interactions with objects into mental representations consisting of the self, the object, and the interaction between them.

Sandler proposes that the ego, in addition to representing actual, lived interactions, unconsciously transforms these mental representations into schemata representing wish-fulfilling fantasies. By actualizing the realization of a wish in fantasy, reckons Sandler, the ego maintains feelings of safety and well-being. From the perspective of defense, these wish-fulfilling schemata are conceptualized as compromise formations that both gratify a wish and defend against it. Once formed, these schemata are used meaningfully to interpret interactions with the external world, thereby creating consistent and habitual patterns of defense.

Sandler's idea that the ego's organizing activity issues feelings of well-being and safety is similar to what was proposed in Chapter 5 as one of the functions of organizing schemata. The transformation of schemata constructed to represent lived experience for wish-fulfilling and defensive aims parallels the functions attributed to secondary conceptual schemata. Dorpat's (1983a, 1985) cognitive arrest theory of defense is a model for formally integrating these ego functions in terms of the process of meaning analysis.

In the cognitive arrest theory of defense, an interaction with the social environment is preconsciously organized into a personally meaningful event by its assimilation to an organizing schema. If the resulting organization of the event has a meaning similar to a past traumatic situation, a danger signal is issued in the form of a painful affect. The painful affect initiates a process of arresting the transformation of the information contained in this organizing schema into a potentially conscious conceptual schema. In blocking this transformation, the traumatic experience is denied access to consciousness, thereby making it unavailable for self-reflection, and it is segregated from the schemata that make up a person's psychic reality. The inhibition of the transfer of information between the organizing and conceptual schemata is conceptualized as the defensive function of denial.

Though the traumatic experience has been denied, the danger situation still exists. In order for an individual to cope adaptively with the danger situation, the denied information must be restored in some form. If it is not, a gap in subjective experience will exist. This gap will interrupt the person's preconscious organizing activity, thereby initiating the process of conscious meaning analysis. If this were to occur, denial would fail to achieve its defensive aim. The person would become self-reflectively aware of the danger situation.

To prevent a significant disruption in cognitive activity, thereby insuring an effective denial of the traumatic experience, a conceptual schema is preconsciously created to fill the gap in experience produced by the preceding cognitive-arrest phase. The defensive conceptual schema is constructed to compensate for the denied experience. Generally these schemata are alternatives to the actions, thoughts, and emotions that disappeared as a result of the cognitive-arrest phase. They are constructed to contradict painful memories, to substitute for disturbing affects, and to undo upsetting experiences. They may also be restitutive constructions in which a wished-for object relation is substituted for the painful or disappointing one that has been denied.

A defensive schema substitutes for the denied organizing schema and serves as the interpretation of the traumatic event that is used by a person to adapt to the danger situation. It is this defensively constructed conceptual schema that is available to the person for conscious self-reflection and for integration into his or her personal theories and belief systems. The case of Mr. M illustrates this process:

> When Mr. M was six years old, his father, unable to support his wife and child, abandoned the family. Mr. M had believed that his father fled the family because he, Mr. M, was too much of a burden. Mr. M felt both intense anger at his father for leaving and severe guilt for being the cause of his running away. Mr. M's mother, struggling to make ends meet, often worked two jobs. Mr. M was frequently left at home alone while his mother worked her evening job. His mother's work routine recreated over and over again the abandonment that Mr. M experienced with his father. To defend against his feelings of rage and guilt and to deny the schema of being a burdensome person who is abandoned by loved ones that issued these feelings, Mr. M constructed a defensive conceptual schema in which he was the indispensable caretaker of his mother and of his friends. Acting on this defensive construction, Mr. M busied himself during his mother's absences with projects aimed at making her life easier, doing chores for the neighbors, and helping friends with their school work.
>
> This defensive construction became the focus of Mr. M's analysis when he was reminded that the analyst would be away for a month's holiday beginning the following week. On hearing this reminder, Mr. M fell silent for a long time. He broke his reverie to remark that he had completely forgotten about the analyst's vacation. At the end of the hour, the patient told the analyst of a very large bonus he had just received for being the "salesman of the month." At the beginning of the next hour, the patient handed the analyst a check for the month's sessions. The analyst noted that it was not customary for Mr. M to pay for his sessions before the monthly statement had been issued. Mr. M responded that since he had extra money at this time, it was no trouble for him to pay early. He thought that the analyst could use the money before going on vacation. Mr. M said that it made him feel good to be able to do something for the analyst.
>
> Through an analysis of why he felt the need to pay the analyst prior to his vacation, Mr. M realized that he had experienced the news of the impending vacation as an abandonment much as he had experienced his mother's working as an abandonment. To defend against the ensuing rage and guilt

and to deny the schema that had given rise to these feelings—that of being a burden to the analyst—Mr. M enacted an alternative relationship with the analyst—that of being a valued benefactor to the analyst. Mr. M recalled "forgotten" memories of how he used to do chores for his mother in order to control his hateful feelings while she was at work. Mr. M then understood that by making himself into the analyst's benefactor he was forming a relationship with the analyst based on the defensive schema he had constructed in childhood to cope with the feelings of abandonment generated by his mother's absences, a schema in which he was an indispensably helpful son.

Dorpat (1985) proposes that specific defenses, such as undoing, projection, isolation, reaction formation, and repression, belong to the second phase of defense since they are unconsciously used to bolster the self-protective aims of the cognitive-arrest phase. Each of these defenses describes the use of a conceptual schema in a particular manner to fill the gap in subjective experience created by the cognitive-arrest phase. A patient, for example, who denied his anger toward his wife was excessively and inappropriately solicitous of her well-being. The denial of the patient's hostile feelings toward his wife was supported by the reaction formation of inappropriate solicitousness.

Another example is of a young woman who never completed the work of mourning for her mother, who had died of Parkinson's disease. The woman developed a shuffling gait when she entered the analyst's office. The unconscious idea underlying her symptom was, "It is not true that I lost my mother; I have her inside of me." The working through of this conversion symptom in her analysis entailed uncovering both the denial of her mother's death and her identification with her mother's pathological gait.

As the last example illustrates, symptoms are also a form of conceptual schema. They, too, serve as substitute, compensatory constructions formed to support denial. As discussed earlier in this section, symptoms are schemata that are constructed as compromise formations to represent symbolically both that which is denied and the defense against it. Symptoms differ from the other types of defensive schemata in that they are usually expressed in an enactive, symbolic form.

Organizing schemata that have been denied are sequestered from the conceptual systems that form the patient's psychic reality. Though outside the ideas and belief systems that structure a patient's internal world, these disavowed schemata continue to operate as organizing schemata. In this way, they exert a continuous and strong, but unconscious, influence on all aspects of a person's behavior. Cut off from access to consciousness by defense, these organizing schemata form what Slap and Saykin (1984) have called "sequestered consciousness." The concept of sequestered schemata is equivalent to the psychoanalytic notion of the "dynamic unconscious" (Freud, 1915b, c; Burston, 1986).

In summary, meaning analysis is an integral part of defensive activity. The process of meaning analysis serves to isolate a traumatic experience from a person's conscious awareness while simultaneously transforming the experience into a nontraumatic form for integration into the person's psychic reality. (The interactional determinants of denial and defense are detailed in Chapter 12, which examines how a person's meaning analysis of a social interaction determines the initiation of defensive activity and the type of defensive schemata constructed.)

MEANING ANALYSIS AND PSYCHOPATHOLOGY

In Chapter 5 I described how the interactions between an infant and his or her caregivers are internalized to form the organizing schemata through which the infant's self-experience acquires cohesion and continuity and assumes a characteristic shape and enduring organization. Disturbances in the sense of self and in the regulation of self-experience are the result of the internalization of maladaptive patterns of interaction, which form pathogenic organizing schemata. Pathogenic organizing schemata, in turn, result in deficits in the ability to organize a cohesively integrated sense of self and in the capacity to regulate need state and affective experience.

Because organizing schemata represent need-satisfying and affect-regulating interactions with a self-regulating other, disturbances in the organization and regulation of self-experience are accompanied by concomitant problems in object constancy and attachment to objects. These early forms of object relations and the functions that they serve in the formation and maintenance of self-experience determine the types of object relationships and the selfobject[1] functions that will be utilized in the integration and regulation of self-experience throughout the life cycle.

---

[1]The term selfobject refers to one's subjective experience of another person who provides a sustaining function to the self within a relationship, evoking and maintaining the self and the experience of selfhood by his or her presence or activity (Moore and Fine, 1990). In contrast to Kohut (1977), who conceptualized the selfobject relationship as reflecting an experience between the self and the object that is undifferentiated, we think that the data from infant research studies (e.g., Stern, 1985) suggest that the experience of undifferentiation is not the normal state in a selfobject relationship. We conceptualize a person's experience of a selfobject relationship to be one in which a differentiated self and other participate together in the regulation and maintenance of the subject's self-experience.

PSYCHOPATHOLOGY OF THE ORGANIZING SCHEMATA THAT FORM THE SENSES OF CORE SELF AND CORE RELATEDNESS

Early maladaptive experiences with the self-regulating other, and the maladaptive organizing schemata that grow out of them, are a potent source for later disturbances in the sense of self. Recall from Chapter 5 that an infant simultaneously creates an experiential sense of self and an experiential sense of the other out of the interactions with a caregiver that serve to regulate the infant's arousal and need state. Stern (1985) cites four types of experience that must be identified within the interaction between the infant and caregiver and then integrated to form an experiential sense of core self and an experiential sense of core other. These are (1) a sense of being the author and agent of one's own actions as distinguished from the nonauthorship of the actions of others; (2) a sense of self-coherence, which comes from the experience of being a nonfragmented being who is the locus of personal action; (3) a sense of self-affectivity, which derives from integrating patterns of feelings with other experiences of the self; and (4) a sense of self-history, which denotes the experience of regularities in the flow of events such that a continuity of the self with one's own past is created.

Failures of the caregiving surround to regulate adequately the infant's arousal and need states impede the child's identification of the consistencies in self-experience that define the sense of core self as distinct from the sense of core other. In these instances, defensive self-regulatory behaviors are initiated to prevent disintegration, excessive or deficient stimulation, and discontinunity of the self across time.[2] Although these defenses preserve the sense of core self, they create a brittle self-structure and constrict the type and scope of the object relations that an infant will form in regulating his or her internal experience.

Stern (1985) cites the example of Stevie, whose mother was overstimulating and controlling. Stevie would avert his head when his mother's behavior exceeded his tolerance. His mother would respond to this dodge by chasing him with her face and escalating the stimulus level of her behavior to capture his attention. Stevie would then execute another dodge by turning his head the other way. Stevie's mother would follow his head with hers, trying to maintain the level of engagement she wanted. Finally, if Stevie was unable to avoid her gaze, he would become upset and

---

[2]These defensive behavioral regulations should not be confused with the psychological defenses described earlier in this chapter.

end up crying. More often than not, Stevie's aversions were successful and his mother would stop the intrusive behavior before he cried.

Mother's overstimulating behavior with Stevie created the following organizing schema: a high level of arousal is met by maternal behavior that tends to push Stevie beyond his tolerable limits, creating the need to self-regulate downward by persistent evasions of contact. This schema depicts an overstimulated Stevie in interaction with a self-disregulating other in the person of his mother.

Now let us suppose that Stevie is alone or with another person, and he begins to approach his upper level of tolerable stimulation. The feeling of mounting stimulation unconsciously activates the self-with-mother organizing schemata just described to regulate his arousal. The evoked self-with-mother regulatory schema is, however, a representation of a disregulating interaction with mother. Its use will result in Stevie's execution of potentially maladaptive behaviors. He will unnecessarily avoid further contact on the grounds that it will produce further stimulation that threatens to exceed his tolerance. If he is with an appropriately responding caregiver, however, Stevie thereby misses or does not stay open to adjustments on the part of the other that would permit him to remain engaged with the caregiver and successfully manage his level of arousal.

The creation of this maladaptive organizing schema constricts Stevie's developing sense of self and determines the form his object relations may take. In activating a schema that depicts Stevie in interaction with a disregulating mother when highly stimulated, Stevie may inhibit or mute his experience of positive arousal with others in order to maintain a sense of self-coherence. Feeling as if he cannot readily escape his mother's intrusive behavior, Stevie may also develop a damaged sense of agency. He may avoid relationships with others because he expects to be overstimulated and intruded upon.

Organizing schemata created early in life and then elaborated with further life experience determine the types of selfobject functions others will play in the integration and regulation of self-experience. Ms. D, for example, presented with "manic depressive" illness that caused her to have uncontrollable emotional outbursts. She felt constantly on the verge of falling apart. Because few friends could tolerate her emotionality, Ms. D became an isolated woman. Not able to manage the slightest stress in the work place, she could not hold down a job for any length of time. Ms. D was dependent on her mother for financial and emotional support. She remembered her mother as a demandingly rigid and powerfully intrusive person who sought to control every aspect of her daughter's behavior. Her mother's excessive control sapped Ms. D not only of her initiative but also of her ability to regulate her own experience. This was most evident in the selfobject transference that developed in treatment:

During an analytic hour, Ms. D would become mildly emotionally per-
turbed by a memory, an extraanalytic event, or by the analyst's behavior. If
her emotional perturbation was not immediately addressed and assuaged by
the analyst, Ms. D would escalate her feeling state to the point where she lost
control over her behavior. If she was angry, she would have a tantrum,
screaming and thrashing her legs and arms about. If she was happy she would
uncontrollably laugh and giggle. In either case, Ms. D would become
disoriented and temporarily lose self-cohesion. The analyst would then
intervene to assist her in organizing and in regulating her arousal. These
outbursts were frequently accompanied by memories of interactions she had
with her mother or longings for mother to be there to fix the situation she
was in.

In the analysis of the outbursts that occurred within the analytic hours,
the patient's organizing schema became evident. When she felt any sort of
emotion, Ms. D would unconsciously evoke the schema of her mother
regulating her arousal and organizing the situation in which she found
herself. The activation of this organizing schema inhibited Ms. D from
regulating her own emotional experience and from meaningfully organizing and adaptively responding to life circumstances. From interacting
with her mother, Ms. D learned that emotional arousal is not something
that is equally regulated by two people, the self and the self-regulating
other, but that it is the self-regulating other who does all the regulating.
Ms. D expected the analyst, her friends, and her coworkers to regulate her
emotional experience and to organize her social interactions.

The formation of maladaptive schemata for the organization and
regulation of the sense of core self leave a youngster prone to disruptions
in the sense of core self that Winnicott (1965, 1971) called the "primitive
agonies" and "unthinkable anxieties" of early childhood. In adult
patients we observe disruptions of self-cohesion in the experience of
fragmentation, of self-agency in the inhibition of action and will, of
self-continuity in the experience of annihilation, and of self-affectivity in
dissociation. Patients who suffer these disorders are able to maintain a
stable sense of self only with an enormous amount of input from others.
When that input fails, the sense of self falls apart.

PSYCHOPATHOLOGY OF THE ORGANIZING
SCHEMATA THAT FORM THE SENSES OF SUBJECTIVE
SELF AND INTERSUBJECTIVE RELATEDNESS

Infants develop, in addition to the overt behaviors and direct sensations
that constitute the sense of core self, an awareness of their own inner
subjective states of experience (Stern, 1985). Early in life these states are

such experiences as intentionality (e.g., "I go over there"), affectivity (e.g., "I am happy") and attentionality (e.g., "Look at that bear"). Through interacting with others, infants learn that these subjective states are sharable. The sense that what goes on in one's mind is similar enough to what is going on in another's mind for these subjective experiences to be sharable propels the infant into the domain of intersubjective relatedness. As was proposed in Chapter 5, organizing schemata provide the shared framework of meaning and the nonsymbolic means of communication for sharing with another person the content of one's mind and one's affective states.

The emotionally attuned resonance of a caregiver to an infant's inner states-of-being, thoughts, and affects lays down the patterns of intersubjective relatedness and interaffectivity that define the infant's senses of subjective self and subjective other. The infant uses the caregiver's affirming, accepting, differentiating, synthesizing, and containing responsiveness to organize his or her affects and thoughts into an integrated and cohesive subjective sense of self.

An absence of steady, attuned responsiveness to an infant's inner states-of-being or to his or her thoughts and feelings leads to a deficit in the child's ability to integrate his or her internal experience into a cohesive sense of subjective self. This deficit sets up a propensity to deny subjective experience and to disavow affective reactions in order to protect those self-experiences which have already been structuralized. Such children are left vulnerable to self-fragmentation (Kohut, 1971; Stern, 1985; Stolorow et al., 1987).

When a caregiver has difficulty discriminating his or her own subjective experiences, needs, and thoughts from those of the child or when the child's states-of-being and desires come into conflict with those of the caregiver, pathogenic organizing schemata are created in the domain of intersubjective relatedness. Selective attunement, for example, is one of the ways in which a caregiver contributes to the creation of a pathogenic organizing schema. A caregiver's desires, fears, prohibitions, and fantasies determine what the caregiver will respond to in a child and what the caretaker will ignore. The caregiver's selective use of intersubjective responsivity acts as a template to create and to shape corresponding intrapsychic experiences in the child. Selective attunement determines the nature and type of internal experiences, such as joy, sadness, and excitement, that are sharable with another person and those which are not. In this way, selective attunement defines those affects and thoughts that are acceptable and those which are not.

Stern (1985) cites the case of Molly as an example of the pathogenic power of selective attunement in the development of organizing schemata.

Molly's mother loved and valued Molly's enthusiasm such that she emotionally resonated with Molly every time Molly exhibited enthusiasm. Her mother also made attunements with Molly's lower states of interest, arousal, and engagement with the world, but less consistently so. These lower states-of-being were not selected out or left unattuned; they simply received relatively less attunement. In regularly achieving an intersubjective union with mother whenever Molly experienced enthusiasm, Molly learned that her enthusiasm had special significance for mother. Molly began to evidence a certain phoniness in her use of enthusiasm. In order to connect with her mother, she would be enthusiastic instead of expressing whatever subjective state she may have been experiencing. Lower keyed experiences and depressive-like states were not as likely to be shared with mother.

Molly's mother's selective attunement created two types or groupings of organizing schemata: one in which Molly is connected to another person in the sharing of enthusiastic states-of-being; and one in which she suffers alone low-keyed, depressive states. Here we see the beginning of two qualitatively different experiences of the self: a social, enthusiastic self and a private, depressive self. Stern (1985) notes that the division into socially shared versus privately experienced aspects of the self lays the groundwork for disavowing those parts of the self that are not acceptable to others. If Molly's life experience continues along the line of sharing only high-spirited experiences with others she will coalesce two separate and distinct organizations of the self that could develop into what Winnicott (1965) called a true self and a false self. Such a division of the self can lead to an impairment in Molly's capacity to synthesize contradictory affective states. This type of impairment could prevent Molly from constructing an integrated and cohesive sense of subjective self.

By dissociating particular self-experiences in order to maintain a connection to her mother, Molly creates organizing schemata in which she regulates her mother's affective states or gratifies her mother's needs and wishes. These pathogenic schemata place Molly in the role of a need-satisfying selfobject for her mother. By using these pathogenic schemata to organize future interactions with significant others, it is likely that Molly will subjugate her own experience and needs in favor of those of the person with whom she wishes to form a relationship.

The case of Mr. P illustrates well the sequalae of maternal misattunement in the creation of schemata that inadequately organize and poorly integrate the sense of subjective self:

> Mr. P was a successful young attorney who questioned his commitment to a legal profession. He was a chronically dysphoric person who complained of

not being able to "get my feelings behind anything." He felt as if he were going through the motions of life. Though Mr. P frequently engaged in athletic and artistic activities to express his feelings, these endeavors, even when executed at a high level of proficiency, did not effect the integration of feeling and action he so desperately wanted. Mr. P's ambitions to be a creative artist, a star performer at work, and a renowned personality were sequestered parts of his character that achieved realization only in his fantasies and dreams. Mr. P conceived of himself as emotionally inadequate, as a fraud in his relationships, and as a faker in his professional life.

Mr. P repeatedly formed relationships with strong, goal-directed women who would set for him explicit expectations of who he should be, what he should do, and how he should behave. Mr. P often felt inadequate in the presence of these dominant woman; yet he craved their direction because he also felt emotionally alive when he was with them. In his analysis Mr. P would become confused about the analytic interchange and be helplessly overwhelmed by his emotions so as to manipulate the analyst into responding in a fashion that served to organize his experience of analytic interaction and integrate his affect and behavior.

The analysis of the selfobject function required of the analyst revealed a developmental history of maternal misattunement. Mr. P's mother was afraid that her son, like her husband, would lack initiative and self-confidence. In the hope of creating an ambitiously self-directed person who would express himself in a creative way, mother had been acutely attuned to whatever emotions Mr. P expressed or activities he initiated. So over-involved was she in her son's activities that Mr. P's feelings and ideas were swallowed up by hers. Mr. P had become dependent on mother's stimulation of his inner life and her organization of it. He lost the ability to initiate his own experience and the capacities to plan and to direct his expression of it.

Mr. P's mother's overattunement created the very type of passive person she had hoped not to create. Though a talented and accomplished man, Mr. P was not capable of creating his own experience or of planning his life. He felt compelled to form relationships with women who continued his mother's selfobject function of stimulating his internal experience and of directing his life. Mother's overattunement created two groupings of organizing schemata, each of which represents a particular aspect of Mr. P's self-experience and a specific type of object relation related to that aspect of himself. In one set of schemata, Mr. P is bereft of an inner life and demands and expects his object relationships to provide him with feelings, ambitions, and goals. In the other set of schemata, Mr. P is filled with emotion, creative ideas, and personally selected goals but is without a significant other to share in his personal creation and to validate his experience.

PATHOLOGICAL CONCEPTUAL SCHEMATA AND THE CREATION OF PRECONSCIOUS PATHOGENIC BELIEFS

Chapter 4 presented the idea that a patient's psychopathology is rooted not in preconscious fantasies but in preconscious pathogenic beliefs. Preconscious pathogenic beliefs are organized sets of ideas that a patient has constructed about himself or herself and about his or her interactions with others from traumatic experiences (Weiss and Sampson, 1986; Weiss, 1989; Sampson, 1989). By this definition, pathogenic beliefs are conceptual schemata. As such, pathogenic beliefs are used by a person to interpret and evaluate social interactions, to formulate causal inferences about these interactions, and to organize social interactions so as to test hypotheses the person has formed about himself or herself and his or her relationships to others that derive from these beliefs and inferences.

Pathogenic beliefs are different from other conceptual schemata in that they are not benign interpretations of reality nor are they wishful transformations of it; rather, they are painful and constricting ideas. They may be about the way things are or about the ways things should be. Pathogenic beliefs impede normal functioning by giving rise to feelings of fear, anxiety, guilt, shame, remorse, helplessness, and inadequacy. Although they can attain consciousness, pathogenic beliefs preconsciously influence a patient's experience and conceptualization of social reality, determine his or her assessment of the danger or safety of a current interpersonal situation, and direct interactions with others to insure adaptive fit between the patient and the social environment:

> Mrs. F, for example, presented with panic attacks and a fear of dying. A year of analysis revealed that the panic attacks expressed the anxiety Mrs. F felt whenever she experienced strong emotions. Her preoccupation with dying was a manifestation of how dead she felt in her everyday life, particularly in relationship to her husband. Beginning in middle childhood, Mrs. F had inhibited the expression of her feelings and denied her individuality to avoid humiliating admonishment from a punitive and puritanical mother and to escape the hostile ravings of an egocentric, chronically ill father who found his children an irritation. Mrs. F developed the preconscious pathogenic belief that her drives and emotions were disruptive forces that alienated others. This preconscious belief led Mrs. F to live an emotionally constricted existence. She developed few personal interests and pursued no emotionally stimulating activities. She married an affectively flat, undemanding man and settled into a highly structured and routine life style.

Preconscious pathogenic beliefs develop in early childhood from interactions with family members and others that were experienced as traumatic as well as from normal and abnormal events that, due to the immaturity of the child's mental processes, were attributed a disturbing or troubling meaning. The initial traumatic event forms an organizing schema to which successive experiences of a similar nature are assimilated and given a traumatic meaning. The child's interpretation and evaluation of these lived experiences are formed into a conceptual schema, which embodies the child's beliefs about himself or herself, about his or her relationships to others, and about the world in which he or she lives that derive from these traumatic events. This type of conceptual schema forms a pathogenic belief.

The case of Ms. C illustrates the development of preconscious pathogenic beliefs, their use to detect and to defend against danger situations, and their effect on the conceptualization and interpretation of social interactions:

> Ms. C was a chronically depressed and angry woman who mistrusted everyone. She was constantly alert to being taken advantage of and often felt exploited in her dealings with others. Wanting to be connected but feeling damaged, unlovable, and unworthy, Ms. C repeatedly placed herself in degrading situations, formed abusive relationships, and subjected herself to masochistically traumatizing interactions.
>
> Ms. C's mother loved her first-born daughter as a narcissistic extension of herself such that the developmental stage of separation-individuation brought with it mother's wrathful retaliation. Not only was oppositional behavior met with severe beatings, but so were attitudes or characteristics that showed Ms. C to be different from her mother.
>
> Ms. C found solace in her father's loving attention and kindness; yet, she felt conflicted and confused about the nature of their special time together. While comforting Ms. C. her father would inappropriately stimulate her genitals. As Ms. C entered puberty, her mother became envious of her. She forbade Ms. C to dress in a stylish manner, restricted the friends she could have, and confiscated for herself anything nice that Ms. C acquired. To avoid her mother's scrutiny and abuse during adolescence, Ms. C lied to her about what she was doing and whom she was with. Rebelliously, Ms. C ran with a wild crowd, acting out with drugs and sexual activity.
>
> Ms. C consolidated these traumatic experiences into the preconscious pathogenic belief that she was a bad and unworthy person whose good qualities provoked others to envy and exploitation. Her significant object relations were organized to prove or disprove this preconscious pathogenic belief.

Preconscious pathogenic beliefs are also created from experiences constituted by maladaptive organizing schemata. For example, Stevie's experience of being overstimulated when he was with his mother could lead to the creation of a preconscious pathogenic belief that he cannot control himself. Alternatively, his experience of a disregulating mother may foster the preconscious and pathogenic idea that others are so intrusive and controlling that getting close to them is dangerous. By way of contrast, in the case of Ms. D, mentioned earlier, her experience with her overcontrolling mother created the preconscious belief that the only way to achieve a close, intimate connection with another person was to lose emotional control, to merge herself emotionally with another person.

As was illustrated in the cases of Molly and Mr. P, a caregiver's selective attunement or misattunement to particular aspects of a child's behavior creates pathogenic groupings of organizing schemata, each representing a qualitatively distinct aspect of the child's subjective self-experience and leading to the formation of discrete, often mutually exclusive, conceptual schemata about the self and about the child's intersubjective relations to others. The creation of discrete conceptual schemata about the self prevents the formation of a stable and cohesive self-concept and fosters the construction of preconscious pathogenic beliefs reflecting this qualitative split in a person's organizing and conceptual schemata. For example, Molly's creation of one group of schemata representing an enthusiastic self in interaction with others and another group of schemata in which a she is depressed and isolated from others could lead to the formation of the following pathogenic beliefs: (1) that her private feelings and thoughts are bad and unacceptable to others (her true self, in Winnicott's terms), and (2) that her only asset, in the eyes of others, is the enthusiasm and high spirits she can display in social situations (her false self). In a similar vein, Mr. P developed the pathogenic belief that he was a passive, ambitionless person with no direction in life as a result of his mother's overinvolvement in his activities. Her misattuned behavior caused Mr. P to sequester those organizing schemata incorporating his personal ambitions from those schemata embodying his emotional ties to others. Consequently, Mr. P was not able to modify this pathogenic belief by integrating his athletic, artistic, and professional successes, as these experiences were assimilated to a group of organizing schemata defensively separated from those schemata out of which the belief was derived.

Preconscious pathogenic beliefs serve the adaptive function of protecting a person from the anticipated traumatic consequences of attempting to fulfill a wish or attain a goal, of experiencing certain emotions, or of seeing himself or herself in a particular manner. They are the beliefs that form intrapsychic conflicts and thus contribute to the development of compromise formations and symptoms. Pathogenic beliefs attribute meanings to interpersonal events with the aim of detecting and avoiding traumatic or dangerous situations. The case of Mr. B illustrates the relationship between pathogenic beliefs, internal conflict, and symptom formation:

Mr. B was a passive man who presented himself as socially awkward and professionally directionless. Each time he neared success in forming a relationship with a woman or in attaining a career goal he inhibited himself in a manner that caused him to fail. In treatment he deferred to the analyst's interpretations by agreeing with anything the analyst said. These attitudes and behaviors derived from Mr. B's preconscious pathogenic belief that he is a ne'er-do-well who is not good enough to compete in a man's world. This belief was the product of a defensive schema constructed in childhood to fill the gap in his psychic reality that resulted from the denial of his experience of being an extraordinarily special and powerful person.

Mr. B's mother idealized her son and attributed to him extraordinary talents. Mr. B perceived her preoccupation with him and his development as an oedipal victory that had caused the divorce of his parents. In addition to losing his father, whom he experienced as a weak and inadequate person, he had, because of his special relationship with mother and her intense interest in his "talents," alienated his younger siblings, who envied and viciously attacked him. These events caused Mr. B to experience his specialness as a hostile and destructive force from which issued object loss and emotional pain. Mr. B reinforced the denial of his specialness by becoming a problem child with multiple emotional and behavioral problems. Being a problem child was the origin of the pathogenic belief that he was not a good enough person.

With the onset of puberty, Mr. B attempted anew to express his individuality and to direct his own development. His mother met this attempt at separation with such extreme hostility, disappointment, and rejection that Mr. B gave up his drive for independence in favor of living out his mother's wishes and desires. Mr. B developed the symptomatic behavior of working toward the goals he thought would please his mother, then failing to reach them just short of their attainment. These experiences of failure reinforced Mr. B's preconscious pathogenic belief that he was an inadequate, problem-ridden person and transformed this belief into its present form, centering on his failure to compete with others, achieve goals, to secure relationships, and direct his own life.

DEVELOPMENTAL PSYCHOPATHOLOGY

The organizing schemata that constitute a person's senses of self and other and the conceptual schemata that embody his or her ideas and beliefs about the self and other continue to develop throughout life and are vulnerable to the consequences of acute or cumulative trauma at any point in the life cycle. Consequently, as Stern (1985) points out, "the genesis of psychological problems may, but does not have to, have a developmental history that reaches back to infancy" (p. 260). A particular type of psychopathology may be the result of trauma suffered early in life, that has thereby influenced all successive levels of development, or it may be the result of trauma experienced late in life that has been processed by schemata at or below the stage at which the trauma occurred.

There are, however, periods of increased vulnerability to deformations in the various forms of organizing and conceptual schemata discussed in this chapter. These periods of vulnerability correspond to specific stages in the development of the operational schemes described in Chapter 5. The organizational structure of the schemata constructed at each stage of development are vulnerable to specific kinds of deformation, which result in particular types of psychopathology. A complete and detailed discussion of this complex topic is beyond the scope of this chapter. What follows, however, is an overview of the relationship between the effects of trauma on the structure of the organizing and conceptual schemata at a particular stage of development and the types of psychopathology that issue from this trauma.

During the sensorimotor period of development, when the infant is dependent on the activity of the self-regulating other to construct organizing schemata that constitute his or her sense of core and subjective self, the infant is vulnerable to maladaptive patterns of interaction that lead to the formation of defective organizing schemata. These defective schemata inadequately organize and regulate the infant's experience and pervert his or her ability to physically or emotionally connect to others. These infants are disposed to develop psychotic or severe borderline disorders. They may require very specific interactions with human and nonhuman objects in order to organize and maintain their sense of core and subjective self throughout their lives.

During the preconceptual period, the child's normal and maladaptive organizing schemata are freed from the specific contexts in which they were formed and are used to understand novel interactions with the social and physical environments. Though these organizing schemata are used in new contexts and with persons other than the child's caregivers, the child expects these schemata to be responded to in the usual ways and to achieve the ends they were originally constructed to attain. In other words, the child is still dependent on specific actions and attunements of a self-regulating other to maintain and regulate his or her self-experience. Failure of a self-regulating other to perform the expected behaviors or to respond in an emotionally attuned manner leads to simultaneous disruptions in the child's senses of core or subjective self and core or subjective other. The simultaneous disorganization in the sense of self and other is characteristic of what has been described as borderline psychopathology (Kohut, 1971; Kernberg, 1975; Masterson, 1976, 1981).

In contrast to the sensorimotor child, the preconceptual child can reflect on, evaluate, and transform the mental representations of his or her organizing schemata. The abilities to evaluate and transform organizing schemata enable the child to create his or her first conceptual schemata. These nascent conceptual schemata are in may ways still organizing schemata, in that they represent the self in specific interactions with others. With the capability to decontextualize, manipulate, and classify organizing schemata, the preconceptual child can group similar organizing schemata together or keep apart those which conflict in some way. These groupings are made first in terms of affect or hedonic tone (e.g., pleasurable versus unpleasurable) and later in terms of gross conceptual categories such as good self interacting with good mother and bad self interacting with bad mother. When these abilities are used to process traumatic interactions, they define the defense of disavowal. Repeated trauma results in reification of these defensively formed groupings of organizing schemata, which thereby inhibits the later formation of integrated concepts of the self and other.

At the intuitive stage, the child begins to transform the idiosyncratic organizing schemata formed at the previous stage into more socially defined, less egocentric forms and to construct new organizing schemata that embody the personal characteristics and skills required of a member of his or her society. The child's operational schemes have developed to the point at which he or she can fashion organizing schemata that operate without the active participation of self-regulating others. However, the self-regulating others remain vital to the child's well-being. The intuitive child relies on the responses, reactions, and judgments of self-regulating others to determine whether or not he or she has created an organizing schema that is correct or effective in terms of the standards of his or her culture as these standards are represented in the responses of the self-regulating other. These organizing schemata define the child's sense of (core and subjective) personal identity and the role relationships that he or she will have with significant others (i.e., core and intersubjective relatedness). The child's senses of identity and relatedness are maintained and developed by the affirming, validating, mirroring, and empathic responses of self-regulating others. Failure of self-regulating others to provide the requisite attention, attunement, and validation prevent the child from developing a sense of identity, leaving him or her forever dependent on the mirroring responses of others.

At this stage, the intuitive child constructs conceptual schemata embodying the ideas and beliefs that define his or her concepts of self and other out of the experiences constituted by the organizing schemata just described. The form and content of these conceptual schemata reflect the nature and quality of the responses of the self-regulating others to the child organizing schemata. If the self-regulating other is affirming and supportive of the child's personal characteristics and behaviors, the experiences created by these organizing schemata are formed into a positive self-concept. If the responses are negative or disconfirming, the child organizes a negative self-concept.

The effect of selective reinforcement and attunement is to encourage a child to construct a set of conceptual schemata embodying those personal characteristics and behaviors that are acceptable to the self-regulating other and another set of schemata representing those characteristics and behaviors that are not acceptable. Not only does this division promote a true and false self (Winnicott, 1965), but it also prevents the formation of an integrated set of conceptual schemata that define the self. People who are not able to integrate their positive and negative schemata are prone to vacillate between feelings of inferiority and intense shame, on one hand, and grandiosity and perfectionism, on the other. A lack of responsiveness or inappropriate attunement to the child's behavior will lead to a transient fragmentation of these conceptual schemata and a severing of intersubjective relatedness with the self-regulating other. Trauma to and deformation of the organizing and conceptual schemata of the intuitive stage constitute what has been referred to as narcissistic psychopathology (Kohut, 1971; Kernberg, 1975; Masterson, 1981).

With the consolidation of concrete operational schemes, a child's organizing schemata become more differentiated, task specific, and hierarchically integrated. Though these schemata continue to require validation and confirmation, the criteria for acceptable performance changes from the opinions of specific persons, such as the child's parents, to that of others who represent the child's peer group or the group to which the child aspires. The concrete operational ability to understand and approach a task from multiple points of view enables a child to construct organizing schemata independent of any one perspective. As a result of this process, the senses of core and subjective self become both more reflective of the child's individual skills and abilities and of the general culture and particular subculture to which he or she belongs.

The ability to consider multiple perspectives on an issue or a task permits the child to evaluate his or her ideas, characteristics, and performance against those of his or her peers. The child becomes aware of individual differences in abilities and in personal characteristics as well as of prejudices against the child based on the cultural, racial, or ethnic group to which he or she belongs. The child constructs conceptual schemata that reflect these individual differences and prejudices. If the recognition of these differences and prejudices results in trauma for a child or if a child's sense of uniqueness and individuality derives from traumatic interactions, these schemata will embody pathogenic ideas and beliefs that constrict and impede normal functioning.

The cognitive abilities of the concrete operational stage also enable the child to utilize heuristic strategies to resolve differences between himself or herself and others and to solve problems in social interaction. That is, the child can formulate and use rules to regulate social interactions. Rules not only become a way of equalizing differences between people, but, in the form of social convention, they also become the principal avenue for affiliating with social groups. Thus, rules are extremely important to the concrete child, and are valued and internalized more than at any previous stage. Rules are incorporated into the child's conceptual schemata and are used to judge and evaluate his or her own behavior as well as that of others. When applied to the child's own desires, thoughts, and behavior, adherence to the rules and social conventions, which define a child's identity as a member of the family and the social group, generate the intrapsychic conflict that characterizes neurotic disturbance.

In summary, a patient's psychopathology can be defined in terms of the kinds of structural deformations present in his or her organizing and conceptual schemata. Patients who suffer with primitive disorders of the self, such as persons who are prone to psychoses, have formed maladaptive organizing schemata, as have patients with a borderline personality organization. Persons with a narcissistic disorder tend to evidence psychopathology in both their organizing and their conceptual schemata; whereas neurotics suffer from pathogenic or conflicting conceptual schemata.

It is important to remember that organizing and conceptual schemata work together to structure the human mind and to organize and interpret experience meaningfully. Therefore, people with a character disorder will also develop, use, and express conceptual schemata embodying the ideas and beliefs that reflect their pathogenic experiences; and, reciprocally, persons suffering from a neurosis will construct organizing schemata that reflect their pathogenic beliefs. It is through an examination of the structure, functions, and consequences of the schemata employed by the patient to organize and interpret his or her interactions with the therapist that the developmental level of the patient's organizing and conceptual schemata is determined, and thereby the type of psychopathology revealed.

CHAPTER 8

Process and Technique

MEANING ANALYSIS
IN THE PSYCHOANALYTIC SITUATION

Every interaction with the social surround is attributed a personal meaning by its assimilation to a person's organizing and conceptual schemata. As the product of lived experience, a person's psychic reality is composed of both pathogenic and nonpathogenic schemata. Meaning analysis in everyday life, as well as in the psychoanalytic situation, employs both types of schemata in organizing and in interpreting interpersonal experience.

Meaning analysis functions to insure adaptation to a known, reliable, and safe environment. Patients preconsciously organize their interactions with the analyst to maximize adaptation to the analytic setting. From this perspective, patients preconsciously enact with the analyst those object relations that serve to maintain, regulate, and protect their self-experience. The organizing schemata that patients employ to that end can include both pathogenic and nonpathogenic elements. Likewise, patients employ those conceptual schemata, whether pathogenic or nonpathogenic, that will best make sense of the analytic setting while preserving the patients' beliefs about themselves and the world.

Pathogenic conceptual schemata are derived from conflictual and traumatic events and are maintained to protect a patient from again suffering these experiences. Patients will preconsciously and consciously interpret their experience of the analytic interaction in accord with those beliefs about themselves and about their relations to others that will insure their safety. The analytic interaction is assimilated to a pathogenic belief to enable the patient to determine whether or not it is a situation that validates the belief and must be defended against (Sandler, 1976a; Weiss and Sampson, 1986).

Pathogenic beliefs are revealed in the treatment setting in a patient's interpretations of the analytic interaction, in the inferences drawn about the self, the analyst, and the patient's relationship to the analyst from his or her experience of the analytic exchange, as well as in the symptoms, feelings, and attitudes the patient expresses. Patients also tend to recreate with their analysts interactions that prove true their pathogenic beliefs by actuating in the analytic interaction the maladaptive organizing schemata from which these beliefs are derived.

The nature and framework of psychoanalytic treatment encourages patients to enact with the analyst their maladaptive organizing schemata and to test the validity of their pathogenic beliefs. The following clinical vignette illustrates how a patient's preconscious meaning analysis of the analytic interaction transformed the interaction into a representative instance of her pathogenic belief:

> Mrs. L began her hour in a dysphoric mood. She complained that she had nothing to talk about because she leads a boring life. In between periods of silence, she told the analyst that she felt disconnected from her husband. She and her husband are unable to share their time together, because they have nothing in common. He is an intelligent, dynamic business executive, and she is only a mother and housewife. What she does, she said, is of so little interest to him that he never talks to her. She wondered if he would leave her for someone more interesting. Mrs. L was skeptical that treatment would ever make her into an interesting person and lamented her lack of progress to date.
>
> The analyst suggested to Mrs. L that her story about her lack of connectedness to her husband may also have been about her relationship to him. She could have been expressing her fear that she was not an interesting person to him as well. Mrs. L responded that she did have that thought that day. When the analyst came to the waiting area to take her to his consultation room, she had felt that his facial expression was one of boredom. Mrs. L inferred from the meaning she attributed to his expression that he was bored with the repetitive and mundane things she talked about. She thought that the analyst wished she would quit, and she imagined him telling her that they had to terminate treatment.

Mrs. L has a number of negative beliefs about herself that cause her distress. Each time she meets with the analyst, she tests the truth of these beliefs by assessing his emotional demeanor. On that particular day she experienced his facial expression as one of boredom. This experience evoked a specific negative belief: that she is an inadequate and uninteresting person. This belief caused her to interpret the analytic interaction as being as empty and as meaningless as were her interactions with her husband. Mrs. L's dysphoric feelings, self-deprecatory thoughts, and fears of being terminated were a result of this interpretation of their interaction.

In the analytic situation, the process of meaning analysis begins with an actual interpersonal event. In this vignette, the event was the patient's encounter with the analyst in the waiting area. The patient preconsciously assimilated the expression on the analyst's face to an organizing schema that depicted her in interaction with others whom she experienced as bored with her when a facial expression of this type was in evidence. She therefore attributed a specific meaning to his expression: boredom. The conceptual schema to which her experience of their interaction was assimilated represented the patient's pathogenic belief that she is an inadequate and uninteresting person. The patient's interpretation of the waiting room interaction was that the analyst's boredom was due to her being an uninteresting patient. The patient transformed the analytic interaction into a representative instance of this pathogenic belief and made inferences about herself and about the analyst as well as predictions about the outcome of their interaction on the basis of this belief. In linking her worries about her husband to the context of the analytic situation, through interpretation, the analyst made the patient's meaning analysis of the waiting room interaction conscious and available for analysis.

THE PSYCHOANALYTIC INTERACTION

Mrs. L's conclusion that the analyst was bored with her because she is an inadequate and uninteresting person was based on her interpretation of her experience of the analyst's demeanor, affect, and nonverbal behavior. A patient's experience of the analytic interaction is, therefore, codetermined by the analyst's verbal and nonverbal behavior and the schemata to which the patient assimilates this behavior. Likewise, the analyst's experience of the analytic interchange is determined by the patient's behavior and by the organizations of experience and knowledge to which the analyst assimilates the patient's activity. This process of mutual influence is clearly illustrated in the case of Mrs. G.

Patient: [Arrives ten minutes late and is silent for five minutes.]

Analyst:: Do you have some thoughts about being late and your difficulty in starting today?

Patient: [in a whiny voice] I'm having such a hard time trying to manage my time between my child and my job and this analysis. It's hard to be on time and to switch gears on demand. I need a little help and a lot of understanding.

Analyst: How do you mean, help and understanding?

Patient:: What do I mean! I want some sympathy and caring from you. I feel that you don't care about what's going on in my life and that you don't appreciate what I have to do to come here.

Analyst: Tell me more about this.

Patient: Don't you have any feelings? All you do is judge me. You expect me to have no other needs or obligations but to do this analysis. I feel that if I don't do this just right you'll get tired of me and my needs.

Analyst: What are your thoughts about this?

Patient: I feel so angry. I'm afraid to be angry with you because I need you too. I'm afraid that if I show you just how angry I am you won't want to work with me.

Analyst: You feel that I expect you to behave with me in a way other than to express your feelings and thoughts?

Patient: I feel like you are controlling me, telling me what I should talk about. And if I don't take your direction perfectly and do what you want, you're going to tell me I have to leave treatment. It's not exactly in what you say, but it's in the tone you use in talking to me.

In this vignette, the analyst's aggressive, probing, and directive activity may be within the range of his normal style of practice, but these behaviors may also be the result of a countertransference reaction to Mrs. G's coming late to the session, to her whiny voice, or to her tendency to act out rather than to analyze her thoughts and behaviors. Mrs. G's experience of being judged and controlled by the analyst is most likely the product of her assimilating the analyst's persistent questioning to an organizing schema in which her performance is negatively evaluated by a person who wants her to do what she is doing differently from the way she is doing it or wants to do it.

The analyst, like the patient, organizes and interprets the analytic interaction with schemata derived from his or her own personal history. The analyst's organization and interpretation of the analytic interaction, therefore, reflects his or her formative experiences and is as subjective as is the patient's meaning analysis of the analytic interaction (Schwaber, 1983). Since the analyst's subjectivity influences and shapes the analytic interaction, many contemporary psychoanalysts (Langs, 1976; Hoffman, 1983; Schwaber, 1983; Modell, 1984; Atwood and Stolorow, 1984) define the analytic interaction as an intersubjective field generated by the interplay between the subjective universes of the patient and the analyst (i.e., between transference and countertransference). This being the case, these contemporary psychoanalysts correctly argue, the analyst becomes aware of and understands the patient's organizing and conceptual schemata by recognizing and comprehending the impact of his or her activities on the patient and by discovering and interpreting the structures of meaning to which the patient recurrently assimilates these activities—that is, through an analysis of the transference.

EMPATHY AND KNOWLEDGE

Stolorow and his colleagues (1987) suggest that the analyst's interpretations and interventions should be guided by an ongoing assessment of what is likely to facilitate or obstruct the unfolding, illumination, and transformation of the patient's subjective world. They believe that an attitude of *sustained empathic inquiry* is sufficient to enable the analyst to maximally achieve these ends. They define sustained empathic inquiry as an attitude "that consistently seeks to comprehend the meaning of the patient's expressions from a perspective within, rather than outside, the patient's own subjective frame of reference" (p. 10). This attitude creates a therapeutic interaction in which the patient gradually comes to believe that his or her deepest emotional states and needs can be understood in depth. It establishes the analyst as an understanding presence with whom the patient can share vulnerable and previously sequestered regions of his or her subjective life, revive and work through early unmet needs, and rework arrested or derailed developmental processes. In this way the analyst's sustained empathic inquiry creates an environment in which the patient expands his or her own capacity for self-reflection.

We agree with Stolorow that an attitude of sustained empathic inquiry facilitates the unfolding of the transference, controls the influence of countertransference, and is required to comprehend the structures of meaning used by a patient to understand and react to his or her interactions with the analyst. We believe, however, that such an attitude alone may not be sufficient to detect and assess pathological schemata or to select and apply interventions and interpretations appropriately. We suggest that the analyst's attitude of sustained empathic inquiry can be significantly enhanced by augmenting his or her empathy and insight with knowledge of how the human mind processes data and of the normal and pathological schemata that are used in transforming this data into personally meaningful information at the various stages of life that define human development (Basch, 1977, 1981).

In what follows I show how the models of mental organization and information processing, psychological development, and psychopathology, which I presented in the preceding chapters of this section, enhance our understanding of the psychoanalytic process and enable us to formulate more precisely interventions and interpretations that address the various levels and forms of a patient's psychopathology, his or her defenses, and resistances.

From the perspective of the analyst who is engaged in the process of analyzing a patient's meaning analysis of the analytic interaction the term "meaning analysis" takes on a second connotation: the analysis of the patient's organization and interpretation (i.e., meaning analysis in the first sense) of the analytic interaction. We will be examining the process of meaning analysis in this second sense, from the analyst's point of view, and articulating the techniques involved in identifying the structures of meaning to which the patient assimilates the analytic interaction (meaning analysis in the first sense) and in constructing an environment in which the patient can change those schemata that, upon analysis, are found to be maladaptive or pathogenic.

TRANSFERENCE

From our interactional vantage point, the concept of transference refers to a patient's organization and interpretation of his or her interaction with the analyst, or, more generally, to a person's meaning analysis of an interaction with another person. I define transference as the product of a patient's meaning analysis of the analytic interaction, a definition that is compatible with that of contemporary theorists who advocate for a social or an interactional conceptualization of the transference (Ogden, 1982; Gill, 1982a, b, 1983, 1984; Hoffman, 1983; Modell, 1984; Atwood and Stolorow, 1984).

Neither Mrs. L nor Mrs. G distorted what was going on between herself and the analyst. Both patients interpreted the interaction in terms of their current and past experience. Transference is not simply the distortion of a present interaction according to the needs and conflicts of the past, nor is it merely a repetition of a past relationship in the form of a contemporary interaction; it is also a new experience embodying a person's organization and understanding of an ongoing social exchange.[1] For example, Mrs. L believed that the analyst was bored with her because she had no personal substance with which to interest him. This understanding of her interaction with the analyst is the transference. In the case of Mrs. G, her conclusion that she would be abandoned by the analyst if she did not do as he wanted represents the transference. Transference does embrace a person's relationship history since, as the product of meaning analysis, a current interaction is organized and interpreted by its assimilation to schemata that represent the person's past interpersonal experience. Yet these schemata are not relics of the past. They embody a patient's current experience and knowledge.

Although transference is interactively determined by the activated organizing and conceptual schemata, each type of schema makes a unique contribution to the transference. Organizing schemata provide the transference with an experiential component, and conceptual schemata afford the transference a thematic or interpretative component. A vignette from

---

[1]See Chapter 10 for a detailed discussion of various historical and contemporary conceptualizations of transference.

the analysis of Ms. A will highlight these two components of the transference:

> *Patient:* I know that I'm really anxious and frustrated about not being able to feel things. I want to find a way to make myself feel, but I don't know how to do that.
> [A few minutes of silence.]
> *Patient:* I'm really stuck. I just don't know what to do. I don't have a single new thought.
> [Silence again for a short period.]
> *Patient::* I think that I'm back to being angry with you. You just sit there and don't say or do anything! I'm stuck and don't have anything to give you. I know rationally that when I give you something to work with you respond. But when I have nothing to give, how am I going to get anywhere? What's the point?
> [Short silence.]
> *Patient:* I can lie on my couch at home and get in touch with my feelings. You're not helping me. I don't know how to do it. You're not giving me any clues, and I don't know how to get you to help me. It's like you're not even in the room with me. You've left, and left me to deal with this myself. Aren't you the least bit interested? You don't find me interesting. No one finds me interesting. I have nothing to give you or them. No wonder everyone leaves me.

In this vignette the analyst's silence became the object of Ms. A's organizing and interpretative activity. Ms. A's experience of the analytic interaction was organized by the assimilation of the interaction to an organizing schema in which she senses no communicative input from the person with whom she is interacting and no meaningful connection to that person. This organizing schema reflected Ms. A's many experiences as a child with an aloof, narcissistic mother who favored her oldest son and could find nothing in her daughter to interest her. The product of this assimilation formed the experiential component of the transference: the feelings of abandonment, isolation, emptiness, anger, and inadequacy that are associated with this organizing schema.

Ms. A's experience of abandonment was evaluated and given a meaning in the light of her beliefs about herself and about her interactions with others. This meaning came into being with the assimilation of Ms. A's experience of abandonment to two conceptual schemata: (1) her belief that she is not a person of interest or value to others; and (2) her belief that she is empty and without her own thoughts and feelings. Ms. A concluded that the analyst, like others in her life, abandoned her because she has no feelings inside of her to interest him. This interpretation of her experience of the analytic interaction formed the interpretative component of the transference.

Organizing schemata provide the transference with an experiential base that the conceptual schemata interpret to reflect the beliefs a patient holds about himself or herself and about his or her relationships to others. Though one or the other of these aspects of the transference may be the dominant focus of treatment at any given moment, both are always present and available for analysis.

REPRESENTATION AND COMMUNICATION OF THE TRANSFERENCE

It will be recalled from Chapter 6 that meaning analysis is a preconscious process through which organizing schemata are usually, but not always, represented and expressed with nonsymbolic signs and signals, and conceptual schemata with verbal and nonverbal symbols. It follows that the experiential component of the transference is usually expressed by way of such nonsymbolic representational media as a patient's posture, gestures, and facial expression or in the vocal tone, intensity, and rhythm of his or her speech. Mrs. G's whiny tone of voice, for example, communicated her demandingness to the analyst. But primary process communication being a two-way street, and organizational schemata being always brought to bear on current experience, Miss G's organizing schema stood ready to assimilate the analyst's activity as well. Thus, for example, she experienced the analyst's tone of voice as judgmental.

The interpretative component of the transference is most commonly preconsciously represented and communicated with verbal symbols, such as extraanalytic stories about events in the patient's current life or personal history. This type of symbolic representation of the transference has been referred to as a derivative communication by Langs (1973, 1979b) and as an allusion to the transference by Gill (1982a).[2] Mrs. L's story about her concern that her husband will leave her because she is such an uninteresting person is an example of how a vignette from a patient's current life can be used as a verbal symbolic representation of the interpretative component of the transference.

The interpretative component of the transference can also be preconsciously represented in the form of visual images (iconic symbols), such as dreams, daydreams, and fantasies (Kanzer, 1955; Blum, 1976; Langs, 1978b; Sandler, 1976b, 1989), or in the form of enactments. The enactive

---

[2]Whereas Gill and Langs emphasize the defensive quality of these symbolic constructions when they are used as allusions and derivatives, in Chapter 6 I emphasized their function as preconscious symbols that more often than not communicate a patient's meaning analysis of the analytic interaction than defend against its conscious recognition.

representation of the transference is similar to what Langs (1978a) has referred to as a Type B communicative mode, to what Sandler (1976a) describes as the actualization of a particular role relationship with the analyst, and to Ogden's (1982) reformulation of Melanie Klein's (1946) concept of projective identification.

When a patient experiences difficulties in organizing or interpreting an interaction with the analyst, it is usually because the analyst's verbal or nonverbal behavior has in some way violated the patient's expectations. The conscious form of meaning analysis is then employed by the patient to resolve the problem in information processing, thereby enabling the patient to adaptively respond to the here-and-now interaction. When the conscious form of meaning analysis is employed, the patient usually expresses his or her experience and interpretation of the analytic interaction directly to the analyst in terms of the here-and-now interaction. In the case of Mrs. G, for example, the analyst violated her expectation that he behave in an understanding, compassionate manner. She consciously expressed the experiential and interpretative components of the transference to the analyst in terms of her experience of being judged and controlled and in her inference that he would terminate her if she did not behave just as he wanted. Similarly, the analyst's silence violated Ms. A's expectation that he would verbally respond to what she was saying. She then consciously expressed to him her experience of abandonment and her belief that he was not interacting with her because she is not an interesting person.

TRANSFERENCE, PSYCHOPATHOLOGY, PROCESS, AND TECHNIQUE

The developmental level of a patient's psychology determines whether the experiential or the interpretative component of the transference will be the dominant focus of the the analysis. In Chapter 7 I presented the idea that the developmental level of a patient's psychopathology is determined by the kinds of structural deformations present in his or her organizing and conceptual schemata. Psychotic and borderline patients typically have internalized maladaptive organizing schemata that require specific behaviors from a self-regulating other in order for them to maintain cohesive senses of core and subjective self and other. For these patients, the focus of treatment is on the experiential component of the transference. Narcissistic patients, on the other hand, require certain types of affirming and validating responses from a self-regulating other in order to create and maintain the organizing schemata that define their personal identity and to formulate these organizing schemata into conceptual schemata that define their self-concept. The focus of psychoanalytic treatment for these patients may be on either or both components of the transference. For neurotic patients, whose conflicting conceptual schemata or pathogenic beliefs restrict their normal functioning, the emphasis of treatment is on the interpretative (conceptual) component of the transference.

Analysis of the experiential component of the transference, and especially of those elements in it that reflect the activity of pathogenic organizing schemata, requires both a different focus of attention on the part of the analyst and a different class of techniques from that required for the analysis of the interpretative components of the transference. Pathogenic organizing schemata are evidenced in the analytic setting in the kind of interactions that a patient organizes with the analyst and in the nature of the selfobject functions required of the analyst. Since these defective schemata require specific actions by a self-regulating other to prevent or repair disruptions in homeostatic functioning, the analyst employs what I call *psychoanalytic interventions* when working with the experiential component of the transference. As I explain in the next two sections, an intervention occurs when the analyst interacts with a patient in a way that allows the patient to organize more adequately or better regulate his or her self-experience. The intervention is psychoanalytic because the analyst does not intervene in a manipulative, coercive, or educative fashion. Rather, the analyst acts in a manner that provides a context, in the form of an object relationship, in which the patient can accommodate a maladaptive organizing schema into a more functionally adaptive form.

The analysis of the interpretative or conceptual component of the transference, in contrast, involves the mutual exploration of the meanings that the patient attributes to the analytic interaction, the inferences about the self and the analyst that the patient draws from his or her meaning analysis of the interaction, and the behaviors and types of interactions that he or she enacts or does not enact with the analyst. The analyst employs interpretations, confrontations, and observations to articulate and bring into self-reflective awareness the relationship between the patient's experience of the analytic interaction and the pathogenic beliefs he or she used to interpret this experience.

Again, I am speaking about the dominant focus of an analysis. Since both the experiential and interpretative components of the transference are always present, the focus can switch between these components as the patient's attention shifts back and forth from his or her experience of the analytic interaction to his or her evaluation and interpretation of the interaction. Accordingly, the analyst's focus of attention and the kind of psychotherapeutic techniques employed will change to match the patient's concerns of the moment. Over the course of an analysis, the focus of treatment may gradually shift from one to the other dimension of the transference in correspondence with the patient's progressive or regressive movement. It is to an analysis of the therapeutic action of psychoanalytic interventions and interpretations that I now turn.

PSYCHOANALYTIC INTERVENTIONS

As a participant in creating the intersubjective field that defines the analytic interaction the analyst is in a position to affect a patient's pathogenic organizing schemata directly through his or her responses to the patient. The patient expects the analyst to fulfill particular regulatory functions and relates to the analyst as if the analyst knows what response is expected. Or the patient acts in a manner designed to provoke the analyst into fulfilling these functions (Sandler, 1976a; Sandler and Sandler, 1978; Ogden, 1982; Atwood and Stolorow, 1984; Modell, 1984). The analyst is cast in the role of a self-regulating other.

The analyst, however, cannot formulate an appropriate intervention until he or she has determined the form and function of a patient's organizing schemata. This knowledge accrues slowly as the result of many interactions with the patient. Accordingly, the analyst may initially respond to a patient in a role-responsive manner (Sandler, 1976a), thereby reinforcing a maladaptive schema or reenacting with the patient a traumatic interaction. In the case of Mrs. G., for example, her verbal and nonverbal behavior may have provoked the analyst into acting as controlling, directive, and judgmental as Mrs. G's parents were. Later in that hour, Mrs. G recalled an interaction with her mother that may have been the prototype for her interaction with the analyst:

> I'm thinking of the time that my mother and I were cooking dinner together. I must have been nine or ten. She told me to turn the burner off before a pot of pasta boiled over. I couldn't get the gas off and the water boiled over onto the floor. She became furious and screamed at me. She said that I was stupid and careless and that I could never use her kitchen again. I was so angry. It wasn't my fault, but she thought it was. She said that I couldn't follow directions or do anything right. I really tried to do things right, but my parents wanted everything done their way or no way at all. They controlled everything that I did, and I was supposed to know just how they wanted things done. I was always in trouble because I never could do exactly what they wanted.

A role-responsive enactment can be a valuable source of information to the analyst because it can provide data that may lead to a hypothesis describing the organizing schema that the patient employed in initiating the enactment. Such a hypothesis can be constructed by analyzing and then integrating four aspects of the here-and-now analytic interchange: (1) the adaptive context in which the interaction took place, that is, those elements of the here-and-now interaction to which the patient may be reacting; (2) the patient's preconscious and conscious verbal and nonverbal responses to the analyst's interventions, that is, how the patient organized his or her experience of the interaction; (3) the analyst's experience of the patient, his or her countertransference, and the rationale for and the effects of the interventions or interpretations employed; and (4) the patient's interpretation of his or her experience of the analytic interaction.

In the case of Mrs. G, for example, the analyst would begin with an examination of the content of her verbal responses to his interventions, as in her accusing him of being judgmental and controlling, and of the character of her nonverbal responses to him, such as her whiny and hostile tone of voice. Next he would review the nature and quality of his interventions. Why is he asking so many questions and being so confrontational? He would also review how these interventions were employed to address the adaptive context of the analytic interaction. In this case the adaptive context would be Ms. G's coming late to the hour and her requesting of him specific caregiving behaviors and sympathetic attitudes. This analysis may lead the analyst to determine what countertransferential feelings he experienced toward Mrs. G that may have influenced his interventions. Finally, the analyst would listen to Mrs. G's story about cooking with her mother as a verbal symbolic representation of her preconscious meaning analysis of their interaction. By integrating his analysis of these aspects of the here-and-now interaction, the analyst could formulate a hypothesis about the nature of the organizing schema he enacted with Mrs. G. He might then conclude that Mrs. G's hostile demandingness had provoked him into enacting with her an organizing schema in which she was judged and controlled by a critical, rejecting parental figure.

In addition to framing a hypothesis about the form and content of the patient's organizing schemata, the analyst must determine the developmental level of a patient's organizing schemata before an appropriate intervention can be constructed. This knowledge is most often the product of the analyst's inadvertently violating the patient's preconscious expectations of the analyst's responses in a particular context; that is, the analyst does not behave as the patient's organizing schema predicts. For patients who suffer from psychotic, borderline, and narcissistic disorders, these violations may initiate disorganization in the patient's sense of core or subjective self and other; may produce perturbations in the organization and regulation of his or her thinking or affective states; or may lead to a disruption in the patient's ties to the analyst. Therefore, the nature of a patient's response to the analyst's verbal and nonverbal behaviors will reveal, in part, the existence, type, and developmental level of any defects present in the patient's organizing schemata. In addition to this information, the analyst formulates a diagnostic impression of the developmental level of the patient's psychopathology in terms of the type of regulative response that is required of the analyst to enable the patient to regain homeostatic functioning. For example, the analyst must decide whether the patient requires specific regulative behaviors or whether merely validating responses will do. The case of Ms. J illustrates this process:

During a psychotherapy hour early in her treatment, Ms. J was describing an incident that occurred in the lunch room at work in which she experienced herself as alienated from her coworkers. No one initiated conversation with her, and she could not think of what to say to them. Ms. J thought that she shared no common interests or experiences with her coworkers through which they could relate to one another. She felt awkward, inadequate, and angry. She thought that her coworkers were not talking to her because they too found her to be an angry, empty person. She had to leave the lunch room to keep herself from exploding in anger at them.

While she was detailing this event, the analyst had an association to a childhood incident that occurred between Ms. J and her mother in which the two interacted as if they shared the same thoughts and feelings. The analyst's facial expression changed, and his gaze momentarily averted from Ms. J as he thought about how this incident might relate to what she was describing and what might be going on in their interaction.

Ms. J then remarked that what she was talking about was boring. She was just being too sensitive and paranoid. Ms. J apologized for boring the analyst and for not having more interesting things to talk about. She became more and more agitated, fidgeting with her hands and clothing and squirming in her seat. Crying, she loudly said that if the analyst didn't want her to be here, why didn't he tell her to leave? Ms. J felt that he was humiliating her by having her talk about these events so that she'd feel stupid and inadequate.

Analyst: [in a soft but firm voice] You are feeling agitated and very angry at both yourself and at me. You feel humiliated by me because you believe that I was bored by an important and upsetting event that happened to you at work.

Patient: [crying with a hostile tone] It is boring. I'm boring and stupid. You don't have to tell me that. What are you doing, rubbing it in!

Analyst: You may have felt I was bored because I did not say anything after you told me about what happened at work. And you felt stupid and humiliated by my not responding to an event that upset you very much. You may have felt that I didn't think what you were telling me was important or upsetting.

Patient: [in a calmer voice] It wasn't only that you didn't say anything. You looked bored too.

Analyst: While you were describing what happened at work I had a thought about how you and you mother interacted as if you were one and the same person. When I had this thought I recall that I stopped looking at you and my expression may have changed as well. You may have read the expression on my face as boredom.

Patient: I thought you were bored and I got very angry at you. Then I thought you were angry at me for being stupid and uninteresting. Just like I thought the people at work were angry at me for being stupid and uninteresting.

Analyst: When you got upset at me, you thought that I had the same thoughts and feelings that you were having about yourself: that I felt angry at you because you were stupid and uninteresting.

Patient: I did! I get so confused. I can't tell who's thinking what.

Ms. J's preconscious expectation of the analyst was that he have opinions about and reactions to the events she was describing that were similar to hers. She attended closely to what my coauthor refers to as the primary process aspects of the analyst's behavior, such as his facial expression and visual gaze, to detect his compliance with her expectation. The analyst's averted gaze and his contemplative facial expression violated Ms. J's expectations, and she interpreted his nonverbal behavior to mean that he was bored with what she was talking about. Ms. J responded to this violation by becoming angry, agitated, and self-deprecatory. As her agitation increased, her thinking became disorganized, and she became confused about whether these feelings and thoughts were hers alone or whether the analyst shared her anger and deprecatory opinions. Ms. J resolved the confusion by constructing the paranoid experience of the analyst's humiliating her. This level of cognitive disorganization and intersubjective confusion over the origin and residence of her thoughts and feelings led the analyst to hypothesize defects in her organizing schemata characteristic of borderline psychopathology.

The analyst's diagnostic hypothesis was confirmed by the type of interventions needed to stop the deterioration in Ms. J's organizing and regulative processes and return her to her normal state of functioning. His first intervention was to speak in a soft but firm voice to aid Ms. J in regulating downward her agitated emotional state. The content of the intervention acknowledged and affirmed Ms. J's feelings of agitation, anger, and humiliation and the event she believed caused these feelings, her perception of the analyst as bored. The intervention was aimed at reestablishing the analyst's selfobject function as an attentively present listener. The intervention failed to help Ms. J reestablish emotional and cognitive equilibrium. More specific and active regulative behaviors (i.e., the analyst's reconstructively linking Ms. J's experience of him as bored to that aspect of his behavior that may have caused it, namely, his not responding to what she had told him had happened at work) were required to help Ms. J regain control over her thoughts and feelings. Since these more specific regulative behaviors appeared to be necessary for Ms. J to reconstitute her self-experience and her working relationship with the analyst, the analyst concluded that she was operating on a borderline, as opposed to a narcissistic, level.

Ms. J's preconscious expectation was that the analyst, like her mother, shared in her thoughts and feelings and should demonstrate this mutuality of thought and feeling in his nonverbal and verbal behavior. This organizing schema was symbolically represented and expressed in Ms. J's extraanalytic story of the event at work, specifically in her seemingly contradictory reasoning that no interaction had occurred between her and her coworkers because, on one hand, they did not share common interests and experiences while, on the other, they shared her experience of herself as hostile and empty. The analyst's association to the interaction between Ms. J and her mother reflected his "empathic" appreciation of this schema and of what Ms. J was demanding of him. By attending to his own thoughts, however, he ceased to be responsive to her as she expected. When the analyst's behavior signaled to Ms. J that he was not participating in her experience, she began to disorganize. The form and the content of her disorganized experience also reflected the structure of the underlying organizing schema, albeit in a reconstituted, paranoid way. Ms. J now experienced the analyst as angry and as humiliating her by creating a situation in which she appeared stupid: she experienced him, in other words, as actively participating in a persecutory way in her own fury at herself for her social inadequacies.

Although the analyst was aware of the behavior that was expected of him, he did not respond to Ms. J in a manner that replicated the maladaptive organizing schema she had formed with her mother. He did not express her thoughts, enact her feelings, or nonverbally signal to her that he knew what she was experiencing by way of his facial expression or visual gaze. Instead of supplying these regulative functions in the form that Ms. J had come to expect from others, the analyst related to Ms. J in a manner that enabled her to organize her own thoughts and regulate her own feelings within the context of their relationship. In other words, he assumed the role of a self-regulating other at the developmental level appropriate for Ms. J to resume the developmental processes that would lead her to correcting the defects present in her organizing schemata.

The analyst's first intervention thus was aimed at helping Ms. J regulate downward her agitated state. He spoke to her in a soft but firm voice, hoping that Ms. J would match his level of arousal. The analyst recognized and validated her thoughts and contained her feelings by verbally acknowledging her experience of anger, humiliation, and upset at the analyst's behavior. In so doing he demonstrated that he could tolerate her anger without himself becoming angry or uncontrollably hostile. Next, by describing in words her feelings and her impressions of his feelings, the analyst made it possible for Ms. J to experience him as understanding her experience without having to share in it. In other words, the intervention created a relationship in which two persons could communicate their individual experiences of a shared event. Though these two interventions were not successful in enabling Ms. J to gain control over her affective state, they did initiate the holding environment in which the analyst's more active interventions could operate.

The analyst's next intervention was to provide a context in which Ms. J could organize her thinking. He accomplished this by linking as specifically as he could Ms. J's experience of him as bored to that aspect of their interaction which he thought may have given her that impression. He told Ms. J that she may have thought he was bored because he did not verbally respond to the important event she was telling him about. In so doing, the analyst did not dispute her experience of him as bored, but he did not confirm it to be his experience of their interaction either. He treated it as her reaction to a specific behavior of his. By focusing Ms. J on a particular aspect of her interaction with him as the possible precipitant to her current state-of-being the analyst provided a real-time framework for the patient to relate her experience to the actual events that had caused it.

Within the parameters provided by the analyst's focus on the here-and-now interaction, Ms. J was able to organize her thinking well enough to reconstruct that aspect of their interaction that had caused her to think that the analyst was bored with her: the change in the analyst's facial expression. To help consolidate Ms. J's organizing behavior, the analyst confirmed that he had, in fact, changed his expression. Note again that the analyst did not have to agree with Ms. J that he was bored; nor did he apologize for diverting his attention or justify his behavior. He merely noted that his facial expression had changed. The analyst did elect to tell Ms. J that he had had an association related to what she was telling him at the time his expression changed, because he thought that this information might be useful to Ms. J as she continued to organize her experience.

Ms. J's response confirmed the success of the analyst's interventions and the usefulness of the information he had provided in telling her about his association. Her thinking became even more organized, and she used her better organized cognitive processes to sort out her emotional reaction to the analyst and then to relate her experience of the analytic interaction to other similar experiences. Ms. J noted how she became angry when she thought that the analyst was bored and how she then thought that he was angry at her for being stupid and uninteresting, just like she thought that of the people at work when they did not talk to her. In relating the similarities in her experience and interpretation of these two events, Ms. J took her first steps at consciously articulating the preconscious organizing schema that underlay both these events. She began to be self-reflectively aware of how she reacts in a particular type of interaction with others. The analyst then verbalized, in an experientially meaningfully way in terms of their interaction, what he thought to be the organizing schema underlying the similarities between the two events that Ms. J had just described. He noted that when she was upset she thought that he had the same thoughts and feelings she did.

Analytic interventions are formulated to provide a patient with the selfobject functions that were either absent or insufficiently or inappropriately supplied during the patient's formative years. The interventions are designed to create an environment in which the patient can accommodate his or her pathogenic organizing schemata into more functionally adaptive forms. In the case of Ms. J, the analyst's ability to tolerate, absorb, contain, and understand her disruptive affective states assisted her in forming an organizing schema that better regulated her affect and arousal and thereby stabilized her senses of self, other, and self with other (Winnicott, 1965; Bion, 1977; Krystal, 1978; Stern, 1985; Stolorow et al., 1987).

In appropriately fulfilling a selfobject function, the analyst forms a new object relationship with the patient (Loewald, 1960; Stolorow et al., 1987). The experience of enhanced self-regulation that this new object relationship fosters creates feelings of safety and competence that enable the patient to accommodate his or her existing schemata into more adaptively adequate forms (Sandler, 1960; Weiss and Sampson, 1986). Repeated and varied experiences with an analyst who is appropriately responsive to the selfobject needs of the patient provide the working-through process required by the patient to consolidate these newly constructed organizing schemata.

The application of analytic interventions does not have to follow the analyst's unwitting enactment of a patient's pathogenic organizing schema. If the analyst is aware of the patient's psychopathology and of the pathogenic schemata that patient employs, the analyst can craft functionally appropriate interventions at the proper developmental level that will interrupt the execution of maladaptive schemata by creating situations in which the patient must accommodate the schemata into a more adaptive forms. A brief example from the analysis of a narcissistically disturbed patient illustrates this process:

Dr. W curled up on the couch as he described how he had become sexually aroused by one of his patients. He detailed the sexual fantasies he had and how he could barely keep his hands from fondling the woman's breasts and vaginal area. He confabulated a pretext to call his nurse into the exam room to chaperon him. He cried and sobbed, bemoaning both his lack of self-control and his shame in continuing to need others to control his behavior. How could he be a doctor when he so often felt like an uncontrollable child? he puzzled. The analyst quietly listened to Dr. W's confession and to his emotional pain for a very long period before he intervened.

Analyst: It is very difficult for you to experience a loss of control over yourself and to need others to help control your feelings and behavior.

Patient: [now in control of his feelings] I feel so ashamed to have lost emotional control with you. Yet, I'm irritated at you for helping me to control my feelings. It makes me think that you couldn't tolerate them.

Analyst: You think that your expressing feelings was as intolerable to me as it was for you. You experienced me as needing to control you, in order for me not to lose control, like you feel the need for others to help you maintain control.

Patient: That's what my father did; he controlled me. He couldn't tolerate me expressing my feelings, so he'd behave in such a way to get me to shut down my feelings. But sometimes I was so upset that I couldn't. Then he'd get really controlling over where I could be and what I could say. I felt two years old when he did that. Now, I really feel ashamed, you didn't do that. Did you? You didn't tell me what to feel or what to do. You understood me. You only reflected back to me what I said.

Analyst: Your shame may be related to not living up to being the perfectly controlled person you think you should be.

In this example, Dr. W lost control over his emotions as he had in the situation he was describing to the analyst. The analyst's first intervention was to acknowledge verbally and thereby affirm Dr. W's emotional pain over the experience of losing control and needing others to assist him in regaining control. This intervention interrupted Dr. W's preconscious transference enactment because the analyst's empathic understanding of the patient's behavior differed from the controlling response he expected. The interruption in Dr. W's cognitive processing compelled him to employ the conscious form of meaning analysis to resolve the discrepancy between what he had expected from the analyst and how the analyst responded.

Consciously reviewing the analytic interaction, Dr. W expressed his shame at having displayed uncontrollable feelings and his irritability at what he thought was an attempt by the analyst to control his behavior. The analyst responded by empathically reflecting Dr. W's experience of their interaction. He stated that Dr. W thought that he had found the patient's emotional expression as intolerable as the patient did and thus would need to control Dr. W so as not to lose control over himself. The analyst's statement not only made explicit Dr. W's organization of their interaction, but it also related Dr. W's reaction to that aspect of the analytic interaction to which it was a response. In so doing, the analyst formed a new kind of object relationship with Dr. W, one in which the patient's experience was understood and accepted (but not condoned or in other ways evaluated) by the person with whom he was interacting. Within this new object relationship, Dr. W was able to control his own behavior.

The feelings of competence and safety that accompanied Dr. W's experience of self-control enabled him to recall the kind of interaction out of which he formed the pathogenic schema he used to organize his interaction with the analyst and then to compare it with the new relationship the analyst had formed with him. In this way were the behaviors that made up Dr. W's interaction with the analyst analyzed, articulated, and then gradually internalized to form a new organizing schema.

As with most narcissistic patients, Dr. W's psychopathology was the product of pathogenic organizing and conceptual schemata. The last technique in this vignette employed by the analyst, therefore, was to interpret the pathogenic conceptual schema to which Dr. W assimilated his experience of the analytic interaction, thereby bringing into Dr. W's conscious awareness the belief about himself that gave rise to his feeling of shame.

PSYCHOANALYTIC INTERVENTION OR CORRECTIVE EMOTIONAL EXPERIENCE?

Does the analyst in the role of self-regulating other provide a patient with a corrective emotional experience of the type Alexander (1948, 1950) suggested? Technically, an appropriately constructed analytic intervention is not similar to Alexander's idea of a corrective emotional experience. The goal of restructuring a patient's maladaptive patterns of self-regulation through the process of forming a new object relationship with the patient is, however, akin to what Alexander had in mind when he formulated the idea of a corrective emotional experience.

When the analyst acts as a self-regulating other, he or she forms an object relationship with a patient in a manner that functionally responds to the patient's organizing schema in a way that enables the patient to restructure the schema into a more adaptive form. The analyst's specific regulative behaviors will depend on the particular schema that the patient is using to adapt to the analytic interaction. In general, an analyst's regulatory techniques consist of such activities as tolerating, containing, limit setting, and regulating; acknowledging, accepting, confirming, and understanding; clarifying, concretizing, differentiating, and interrelating. Taken together, these behaviors constitute the analyst's attempts to achieve emotional attunement and intersubjective relatedness. In performing these behaviors, the analyst does not take over a regulative function belonging to the patient, nor does he or she organize the patient's experience. Rather, the analyst's regulatory techniques enable the patient to perform better a particular self-regulatory function, or more adaptively to organize his or her experience of an interaction with the social surround, or to consolidate his or her senses of core and subjective self.

In appropriately fulfilling a selfobject function, the analyst does not "role play" a response in order to manipulate the patient into behaving in a particular way, to teach the patient about the consequences of his or her actions, or to get the patient to experience particular affects or states-of-being. The analyst does not, for example, argue with an argumentative patient in order to demonstrate the futility of such behavior or to show the patient that he or she is not afraid of the patient's aggression. Nor would an analyst provoke an argument with a patient in order to get the patient to feel his or her aggression so as not to fear it. The analyst does not contrive an interaction to instruct the patient or to confront the patient with (what the analyst conceives of as) "reality." Rather, the analyst provides a context, in the form of an object relationship, in which the patient can reconstruct his or her organizing schemata into developmentally more advanced forms.

Though the patient may feel "gratified," "reassured," or "taken care of" when the analyst has successfully provided a particular selfobject function, the analyst's behavior is not aimed at providing reassurance, love, or support. If these kinds of feelings emerge, it is because the object relationship that the analyst has formed with the patient has enabled the patient to consolidate more securely a sense of self or to adapt more adequately to the analytic interaction.

PSYCHOANALYTIC INTERPRETATIONS

Analytic interpretations are formulated to make a patient self-reflectively aware of his or her conceptual schemata and to induce the patient to change those concepts, beliefs, and theories that are found to be pathogenic. So defined, analytic interpretations operate on the interpretative component of the transference, that is, on that part of it which derives from the patient's conceptual schemata.

An analyst becomes aware of the interpretative component of the transference in the meanings that a patient attributes to the analytic situation. These meanings are either consciously conveyed to the analyst in the patient's ideas and beliefs about the analytic interchange or preconsciously expressed in extraanalytic stories about events in the patient's current life or from his or her history, in fantasies, and in enactments:

> Mr. R, struggling to make sense of an obtuse dream fragment, was perfunctorily associating to each element but achieving no success. In an unusual maneuver, he asked the analyst for his associations to the dream. After a brief moment of silence Mr. R added that he reckoned that the analyst was holding back his associations because the analyst thought that he had not finished processing the dream himself. Mr. R then fell silent for a long period of time.

> *Patient:* I was just thinking about my piano teacher, Bill. He doesn't seem interested in me any more. He forgot that we had a lesson the other day. And during the lessons he seems distracted. I don't feel that he has a lesson plan or that he's teaching me the music I want to learn. He keeps suggesting that I work on pieces which aren't jazz pieces. But then again perhaps he's frustrated with me. I'm not practicing as much as I want to so I'm not making progress. I just can't get the fingering right, and I'm slow to learn the new techniques he is teaching. He probably thinks that I'm not motivated and that I'm not very talented.

> *Analyst:* Your thoughts about your piano teacher may also reflect your concern that I may not be interested in you. Earlier in the hour you presented a difficult dream that you hoped would capture my interest. You may think I didn't step in to help you analyze the dream because I am frustrated with what you see as your lack of progress. And you may believe that your slowness is turning me off to you.

> *Patient:* I am afraid that you are bored with me. I keep going over and over the same material. I don't know how you stand it. I'm so slow, such a slow learner. I don't feel that I'm doing analysis right. I'm not associating enough or dreaming enough. I find it hard to believe that anything I say is of interest to you.

The analyst was made aware of the meaning that Mr. R attributed to the analytic situation through the patient's extraanalytic story about the piano teacher: Mr. R believed that he had done something to diminish the analyst's interest in him. The analyst understood this meaning to be the interpretative component of the transference because he could relate the content of the story about the piano teacher to a specific incident that had occurred in the analysis, their interaction around Mr. R's presentation of his dream.

The analyst's interpretation made Mr. R conscious of his preconscious meaning analysis of the analytic interchange by linking Mr. R's verbal symbolic representation of the transference, the story about the piano teacher, to the specific event in the analytic interaction to which the representation referred, the analyst's not helping Mr. R analyze the dream. In so doing, the analyst interrupted Mr. R's automatic cognitive processing of the interaction, thereby thrusting Mr. R into the conscious mode of meaning analysis. In this mode, the interpretative component of the transference can be evaluated and tested by the patient. In the present case, Mr. R confirmed the analyst's hypothesis after consciously reviewing his experience of their exchange around the dream.

Analytic interpretations that are designed to make a patient consciously aware of the interpretative component of the transference must be specific and related to the here-and-now interaction. Interpretations that concretely detail the meaning attributed to an ongoing experience are effective because they highlight the linkage between the experiential and interpretative components of the transference. In this way patients become self-reflectively cognizant of the meanings that they have assigned to their experience of the analytic interaction. Genetic interpretations and conceptually abstract interpretations lack the affective urgency attendant on the immediacy of lived experience; they are not well suited for making patients aware of the meanings that they attribute to the analytic interaction.

In making the interpretative component of the transference consciously available to Mr. R for his self-reflective analysis, the analyst had only delineated a specific instance of the patient's conceptual schemata, an instance that reflects the intersection of a conceptual schema and the particular characteristics of the lived event it interpreted. In this case it was Mr. R's belief that he had done something to diminish the analyst's interest in him. In order for the analyst to infer a patient's conceptual schema many specific transference experiences may need to be analyzed. With several iterations of a conceptual schema, the analyst can infer the patient's preconscious theories and beliefs and then, through interpretation, make them available to the patient for his or her conscious self-reflection:

> Mr. R, the man just discussed, developed the habit of arriving five to ten minutes late to his analytic hours. On entering the office Mr. R would scan the analyst's demeanor to detect his mood.

> *Patient:* I have a feeling that you are uncomfortable being with me. When I come to the door you just nod, no smile or friendly greeting. It feels so stiff. I try to break the ice with a passing comment, but that usually falls flat. I feel awkward right off the bat. I try to detect what your mood is so that I will feel safe in being with you.

Analyst: You are afraid that I have uncomfortable feelings about you. Perhaps you are concerned that your comments or your coming late to the hour have created negative feelings in me about you.

Patient: I'm late to everything. I think it is a form of self-protection. I try to see what other people think of me before I enter a situation so I can play it right. I don't know what it is, but people seem to dislike me. The men I know don't want to get close to me. On this last camping trip John, who I hoped to become better friends with, seemed irritated at me the entire time. I don't know why. And it's been this way all my life. In junior high the boys didn't want to play with me, despite the fact that I was a good athlete, and never called me. I remember one kid picked a fight with me for no reason, and the other guys cheered him on. During summer camp I rubbed the boys in my cottage the wrong way too. They didn't like me and shunned me the whole summer. I was so lonely. I remember a time in high school when I was bicycling down the coast. Two huge loggers drove by me, then turned back and got out of their truck. One came up to me, told me that I had given him the finger, which I hadn't, and then he beat me up. I hadn't done anything.

Analyst: You believe that there is something about you that provokes men's hostility so that they reject you, even attack you. You are concerned that you may be provoking me to reject you. Your coming late to the hour may be a way to test this belief.

Patient: I am afraid that I'm making you angry with how slow I am and by my not coming on time. I really believe that there is something about me which makes men angry, drives them away. I don't know what I do. I'm so passive around men. I ingratiate myself to them. I never challenge them. So am I challenging you? The image comes to mind of my sister chiding me as a young child for sitting on the couch twiddling my thumbs day in and day out. My passivity drove her crazy. Maybe I'm passive aggressive. Maybe I use my passivity in an aggressive, manly way!

The analyst inferred Mr. R's pathogenic belief, that there is something about him that provokes men to reject him, from Mr. R's conscious expression of the transference and from his preconscious symbolic representations of the transference in both this vignette and the previous one. In this vignette, the analyst again conveyed to Mr. R his construction of Mr. R's preconscious pathogenic belief in the form of an interpretation. The analyst then related the patient's pathogenic belief to the aspect of the transference that was under analysis at that moment, the meaning of the patient's thoughts about the analyst in the light of his coming late to the session. The analyst not only made Mr. R self-reflectively aware of his preconscious pathogenic belief, but he also demonstrated the influence of that belief in an affectively meaningful way by noting how the belief was used to interpret the here-and-now analytic interaction.

Making the patient conscious of his or her preconscious pathogenic belief is but the first step in effecting a complete, mutative interpretation. The operation of the hypothesized pathogenic belief must then be substantiated to the patient in a meaningful way. A most effective and powerful method for showing the patient the influence of a pathogenic belief is to demonstrate how the belief was used to interpret his or her interaction with the analyst. The more temporally immediate the analyst can make the link between the pathogenic belief and the analytic event around which the interpretative component of the transference was formed, the greater the affective impact and the more mutative the interpretation.

An analytic interpretation is mutative to the extent that it induces a patient to accommodate a pathogenic schema into a functionally more adaptive form. As discussed in Chapters 5 and 6, a person is induced to accommodate a schema when he or she experiences disequilibrium between the data of immediate, lived experience and his or her concepts and beliefs. A mutative analytic interpretation induces disequilibrium by making the patient self-reflectively aware of his or her preconscious pathogenic belief and then by demonstrating the action of that belief in the here-and-now interaction. The patient then acts to resolve the disequilibrium by testing the validity of the interpretation first against that aspect of the transference which the analyst provided in the substantiation of the interpretation and then against previous experience.

Mr. R first tested the now-conscious pathogenic belief against the instance from the analytic interaction cited by the analyst and concluded that he was afraid that he was provoking a hostile response from analyst with his slowness and tardiness. He then tested the belief against past experience with men. Though he felt that the belief was true, he also noted that he perceives himself as passive in relationship to men, including in his interactions with the analyst. Perhaps he isn't so passive, Mr. R hypothesized. His association to his sister's reaction to his passivity enabled him to conclude that he might be using his passivity in an aggressive manner. The analyst's interpretation was mutative because it induced Mr. R to accommodate his pathogenic belief into a more adaptive form: He understood that he is not a passive, weak, and inadequate man, but a man who uses passivity aggressively. It is not something about him that provokes men's dislike and rejection; it was his passive-aggressive behavior, which provokes men's negative reactions.

EVOLUTION VERSUS RESOLUTION OF THE TRANSFERENCE

The mutative effect of psychoanalytic interventions and interpretations is to transform a patient's organizing and conceptual schemata into more functionally adaptive forms. The matured and integrated mental organization that results from successful psychoanalytic treatment will be reflected in transference experiences that enrich and expand the patient's experience and understanding of himself or herself and enhance his or her affective ties to others. From an interactional perspective, transference evolves as the result of analytic treatment. It is not resolved or dissolved, as classical psychoanalysis proposes the aim of successful treatment to be.

AN INTERACTIONAL PERSPECTIVE ON RESISTANCE

Resistance is currently defined as a phenomenon that occurs in psychoanalytic treatment whenever a patient consciously or preconsciously opposes the therapeutic process such that the objectives of insight and change are retarded or defeated. Resistance may take the form of attitudes or actions that defend against the awareness of a perception, idea, or feeling that would recall an early life trauma, uncover preconscious conflicts, or lead to the recognition of unacceptable wishes, fantasies, and thoughts about the analyst or to the renunciation of the gratifications brought about by those wishes and fantasies (Moore and Fine, 1990).

Conceptualized as conscious or preconscious opposition to the therapeutic process, resistance is intimately related to transference. Freud (1912b, 1914b) noted this relationship early in his writing on technique when he described transference as resistance to the work of remembering. The patient acts out with the analyst a past relationship instead of remembering it. When Freud (1920, 1926) made transference the instrument through which psychoanalysis operates, resistance was reconceptualized as a patient's defense against reexperiencing a past traumatic relationship in his or her connection to the analyst or against giving up a gratifying relationship with the analyst.

Racker (1968) noted the contradiction in the relationship of transference to resistance between Feud's early and later writings. In the early works, transference is thought to arise out of resistance while in the later writings resistance is the product of transference. To resolve this conceptual problem, many contemporary theoreticians have dismissed the early relationship between transference and resistance and conceive of resistance solely as a manifestation of the transference (Kohut, 1971; Ornstein, 1974; Gill, 1982a; Stolorow et al., 1987).

From an interactional perspective, resistance does not derive from transference, nor transference from resistance. Both transference and resistance are manifestations of the process of meaning analysis. Transference expresses the content of a patient's organizing and conceptual schemata in the experience of and beliefs about interacting with another person. Resistance reflects a patient's attempt to preserve the content and organization of these schemata by adhering to his or her experience of and beliefs about an interaction when faced with conflicting information. A patient who did not engage in resistance would be forced to accommodate his or her organizing and conceptual schemata whenever data discrepant with the current state-of-the-world schemata was encountered. Such a situation would jeopardize the stability and continuity of the patient's sense of self. To preserve the continuity and stability of the self and to secure a safe and adaptive interface with the social environment, a patient naturally resists altering the experiences and beliefs that issue from these schemata.

In Chapter 6 I cited research supporting the tendency to resist altering one's schemata. The studies reviewed showed that people tend to adhere to their personal theories and beliefs well beyond the point at which logical and evidential factors can sustain them. Rather than accommodate their belief systems to new information, the subjects in these studies tended to seek out and more heavily weight data that confirmed their existing personal beliefs and discredited competing evidence.

As an aspect of the process of meaning analysis, resistance, like transference, can be conceptualized as a universal and ubiquitous mental function. It comes into play whenever the schemata that structure a patient's sense of self and world view are challenged by discrepant information. I am restricting my use of the term resistance to mean opposition to *interpersonally* induced discrepancy. By limiting the definition of resistance to opposition to those discrepancies that are caused by the interaction between the analyst and the patient, I intend to preserve the interactional focus of the contemporary definition of resistance, as opposition to the *process* of psychoanalysis, while distinguishing the concept of resistance from that of defense.[3]

A patient may engage in resistance whenever the analyst's verbal or nonverbal behavior issues information that is discrepant with the patient's expectations, experience, or interpretation of the analytic interaction. In other words, resistance can occur whenever the analyst's behavior introduces data that is incongruent with the patient's currently active state-of-the-world organizing and conceptual schemata. Thus a patient may resist an analyst's interventions and interpretations even when they are well timed, appropriately formulated, empathically executed, and result in improved self-regulatory functioning and enhanced self-understanding. The introduction of discrepant data always runs the risk of provoking resistance instead of accommodation.

---

[3]See Gill (1982a) for a discussion of the distinction between defense and resistance and Langs (1981) for an alternative perspective on interpersonally induced resistance.

The likelihood that a patient will engage in resistance is markedly increased when the incongruous data communicated by the analyst's verbal and nonverbal behavior is the result of misattunement or nonattunement to the patient's self-regulatory needs, to his or her states-of-being, or to the personal meanings that the patient has attributed to the experience of the analytic interaction. In these situations, the patient reacts with resistance because, from the patient's perspective, the analyst's behavior is inappropriately responsive or nonresponsive to the meaning of the patient's communication. The probability of a resistant response is further increased when the patient experiences the analyst's behavior as replicating a past traumatic relationship or as threatening to deny the patient's experience of the analytic interaction or to destroy the meaning he or she has attributed to it.

A patient resists by employing defenses; by engaging in selective perception, biased reasoning, and argument, by withdrawing from the analytic interaction; or by acquiescent compliance. In Chapter 7 I described and illustrated how defenses operate to protect the stability and continuity of a patient's psychic organization by denying a traumatic experience and then by substituting for it one that has been constructed in a nontraumatic form. In a similar vein, a patient protects his or her personal epistemology by denying information that conflicts with his or her concepts and beliefs and by perceiving only that data which supports them. This type of resistance is manifested in clinical situations by such behavior as the patient's failing to understand an interpretation or to perceive the evidence supporting the interpretation cited by the analyst. Resistant patients will often seek out from the analytic interaction or from their life experience evidence that refutes the analyst's point of view and supports their own.

When a patient resists by withdrawing from the analytic interaction he or she ceases to communicate affectively and symbolically with the analyst in a meaningful way (Bion, 1959a; Langs, 1978a, Gill, 1982a; Modell, 1984). In severing all meaningful ties to the analyst, the patient protects the continuity and stability of the self and of his or her world view because the analyst is barred from interacting with the patient in a way that would disrupt his or her subjective experience or invalidate his or her ideas and beliefs.

A strategy correlative to withdrawal from the interaction is for the patient to acquiesce to the analyst's perspective and comply with whatever demands the analyst places on him or her. In complying with the expectations of the analyst, the patient adopts the analyst's perspective on his or her problem and produces whatever material the analyst demands without changing his or her experience and interpretation of the analytic interaction. The patient's experience and beliefs are merely set aside.

Removing the patient's experience and perspective from the focus of the analytic inquiry preserves the patient's sense of self and world view. Meaningful symbolic and emotional communication between the analyst and patient, however, has been severed.

Let us return to the analysis of Mrs. G, the woman who experienced the analyst's interventions as judgmental and controlling, for an example of a situation in which several of these forms of resistance are employed by the patient to protect herself from the analyst's nonattuned behavior:

Patient: I don't know what to do in here. I'm supposed to express my feelings and each time I do you ask for more. I feel like I haven't given you what you want. I'm getting really upset with you. I don't understand what I'm supposed to do.

Analyst: I think that you do understand, but you question what you know because you experience my asking for more as your not giving me what I want.

Patient: I really don't understand this. I feel as if you're trying to get me to talk about something specific, but you won't tell me what it is. It's like you're trying to control me, to manipulate my mind just like my parents did.

Analyst: What comes to your mind about your parent's controlling your mind?

Patient: They'd never listen to what I'd tell them. If I felt one way, they'd say I felt another. They had the idea of what they wanted me to be, and they'd tell me that I had certain thoughts and certain feelings: their thoughts and feelings. It drove me crazy, yet I went along with it. I felt so helpless. Just like I feel with you. I'm afraid that you're trying to control me.

Analyst: Your fantasy is that I'm trying to control your mind, just as your parents did.

Patient: I feel that you are controlling me; yet I don't seem to care. It's like it's not real anymore.

Analyst: How do you mean, not real?

Patient: It's like we're not talking about me anymore. It's like I'm not here. That thought panics me because I need your help. I want your help.

Analyst: I think that your feeling "not here" is a way of keeping more uncomfortable feelings about me out of your mind. Some of these feelings are hostile feelings and some may be sexual feelings.

Patient: [long silence] I don't feel anything. I feel dead. [silence] I saw some dead birds on the way in here today. I couldn't figure out how they died. [silence]

Analyst: Tell me more about feeling dead.

Patient: [long silence and then in a vocal monotone] I . . , I'm afraid of dying. I'm afraid of being alone. [Silence and then with feeling] I guess I do have hostile feelings toward you and perhaps sexual feelings too. I just had an image come to mind that is upsetting. It's difficult to talk about, but I will if I must: I saw myself naked, tied to a bed, face down, being anally penetrated by a faceless man. I suppose the man could be you.

In this vignette Mrs. G adopts a resistant stance because the analyst has not been attuned to her experience of the interaction or to the meanings she attributed to it. The vignette begins with Mrs. G stating that she feels confused by the analyst's behavior. She thought that she had been doing what he wanted in expressing her thoughts and feelings and so cannot understand why he keeps asking for more. The analyst responds by negating the patient's experience, asserting that she knows what to do in treatment but that she doubts herself because she takes his asking for more as an indication that she is not doing what he wanted. Mrs. G corrects the analyst's impression that she misunderstood his behavior by describing her experience of the analytic interaction as a guessing game in which she is supposed to figure out what the analyst has in mind. She tells the analyst that she feels controlled by this type of behavior in much the same way that she felt controlled by her parents. The analyst ignores the here-and-now, interpersonal referent in the patient's communication and redirects her to talk about her parents' controlling behavior. To emphasize the comparison she is making, Mrs. G again directly links her experience of her parents' behavior to that of the analyst. Thus far the patient has been resisting the analyst's nonattunement by continuing to restate her experience and interpretation of the analytic interaction. The analytic interaction has taken the form of an argument.

The analyst responds to Mrs. G's linking his behavior with that of her parents by calling it a fantasy. In so doing, the analyst denies her experience and understanding of their interaction. Mrs. G yet once more corrects the analyst, asserting that she feels that he is controlling her. The analyst ignores her clear, overt characterization of his controlling behavior and redirects Mrs. G to her feeling not real. At this point Mrs. G. is beginning to withdraw from the analytic interaction. She communicates to the analyst that she no longer feels that they are relating to one another about her.

Disregarding Mrs. G's last statement, the analyst shifts the focus of their interaction onto the sexual and hostile feelings and fantasies that he wants her to talk about. Although the analyst's redirection of the content of the hour validates the patient's assumption that he has a hidden agenda and a specific content that he wants her to talk about, the patient cannot appreciate the subtle validation she received. She is so taken aback by the nonresponsiveness of his comment on the content of her previous communication that she withdraws from the interaction. She severs all meaningful contact with the analyst. She talks about feeling dead and about seeing dead birds.

The analyst does not understand that the patient has withdrawn from the interaction and so fails to interpret her resistance. He continues with his questioning of her experience. The patient feels the pressure of the analyst's unabated controlling behavior. She acquiesces to his perspective and complies with his demand to produce sexual and hostile material. It should be noted by complying with the analyst's perspective and content, she has preserved her own experience and understanding of the analytic interaction. It is expressed in the nature of the sexual fantasy she constructed. Through her compliance the focus of the analysis has shifted from the patient's desire to discuss feeling controlled to the sexual fantasies demanded by the analyst. In other words, the patient's experiences and beliefs are not being understood or worked through in the analysis.

The ideas expressed and the behavior patterns invoked by a resistant patient reflect the meanings that the patient attributed to the analytic event that provoked the resistance. The techniques and procedures for analyzing resistance are, therefore, similar to those methods outlined earlier in this chapter for analyzing the transference. To determine why a patient is resisting, the analyst must first understand how the patient experienced what the analyst did or said and the meanings that he or she attributed to this experience. With this knowledge in mind, the analyst is in a position to infer the content of the patient's organizing and conceptual schemata that issued the resistance. The analyst can then attempt to demonstrate to the patient what in the patient's experience or interpretation of the analyst's behavior caused him or her to resist. The analyst can also intervene in a manner that assists the patient to regulate his or her self-experience better, thereby eliminating or alleviating the resistance.

ANALYSIS OF DEFENSE OR ANALYSIS OF TRANSFERENCE?

In Chapter 7 I defined a defensive structure as a schema constructed to substitute for an experience that has been the subject of denial. With the defended-against event (which is itself an organizing schema) sequestered from a person's subjective experience, the defensively constructed schema becomes the content of the person's psychic reality. It is this schema that is used by the person to understand and adapt to similar situations, and it is this schema that is available to the person for conscious self-reflection and for integration into his or her personal theories and belief systems.

Though the unconscious, defensively sequestered schema plays a role in triggering the substitute schema, the defensively constructed schema determines the patient's meaning analysis of an interaction.

This formulation of defense requires a different approach than has been traditionally used in the analysis of defense. With the development of ego psychology, it has been the customary practice of psychoanalysts to confront a patient with those thoughts, feelings, or behaviors (including the transference) believed to be a defense against some other unconscious thought or feeling (A. Freud, 1936). Since, from the patient's perspective, these thoughts and feelings are the product of his or her meaning analysis of the analytic interaction, this approach more often than not is experienced as an attack or criticism that forces the patient into a resistant stance in order to protect the stability and continuity of his or her psychic organization.

An interactional approach to the analysis of defense is to analyze what the analyst believes to be a defensive construction as he or she would any other piece of the patient's behavior, as an expression of the transference. The transference, not the defense, should be the object of analysis. From this perspective the analyst would accept what is believed to be the patent's defensive behavior as a true and valid expression of the schemata the patient employed to organize and to interpret the analytic interaction. The analyst would then engage the patient in an analysis of what in the interaction triggered this response. If during the examination of the patient's meaning analysis of this analytic event the interventions and interpretations employed by the analyst resulted in the patient's enhanced mental and emotional functioning and increased feelings of safety and well-being, those past experiences that were the object of defense in this kind of situation will no longer need to be sequestered from the patient's psychic reality and will become available for conscious self-reflection and analysis (Weiss, 1971; Sampson, 1989). The patient would also become aware of the defensive nature of the schemata that were constructed to substitute for these experiences.

This process was illustrated in example from the analysis of Mr. M presented in Chapter 7. The analyst's understanding acceptance of Mr. M's behavior during their reconstructive analysis of why he needed to pay the analyst prior to the analyst's vacation brought into the patient's psychic reality those experiences of abandonment by his mother that had led him to defend against feelings of guilt at being a burden to significant others and of rage at being abandoned by them, as well as the defensive schema of making himself indispensably helpful to them. Patients' defenses, like their resistances, are understood in the context of their meaning analysis of the analytic interaction and are analyzed as expressions of the transference.

A Clinical Study

In this chapter I will illustrate our interactional approach to psychoanalytic practice by applying to clinical material the theoretical concepts and technical principles introduced. The material comes from the uncensored process notes of the first of four successive sessions of an ongoing psychoanalysis conducted by Dr. Martin Silverman (1987).

We chose Dr. Silverman's case as the vehicle for illustrating our interactional approach because his process notes were used as the clinical material on which eight different psychoanalytic theories and their respective techniques were compared and contrasted. Our aim in using this material is to provide the reader with a means of comparing our theory with the major psychoanalytic theories in use today. In presenting his clinical work for public peer review, Dr. Silverman has made a significant contribution to our profession.

Our critique is aimed at psychoanalytic theories that focus on uncovering a patient's unconscious fantasies at the expense of attending to the dynamics of the interaction between the patient and the therapist. From our perspective, failing to attend to these dynamics prevents therapists from learning about the maladaptive organizing schemata and pathogenic conceptual schemata that organize patients' psychic reality. We believe that these schemata are expressed in the dynamics of the analytic interaction and in the meanings the patient attributes to these dynamics. In the clinical material that follows, Dr. Silverman's adherence to the classical view that unconscious oedipal fantasies are motivating the patient prevents him from understanding and effectively dealing with the patient's psychopathology, which, from our perspective, is clearly presented in how she organizes her interactions with Dr. Silverman and in the meanings that she attributes to these interactions.

THE CASE—A STALLED PSYCHOANALYSIS

Miss K is a 25-year-old, single female whom Dr. Silverman describes in his introduction to the case as suffering from sexual and social inhibitions, masochistic tendencies, and chronic depression. After several years of a slow but progressive psychoanalysis, the treatment has stalled. Whatever improvements the patient made in her self-esteem and social functioning have faded away. Dr. Silverman believes that the patient has settled into an interminable analysis in which she intellectually explores her conflicts, but makes no real changes in herself or in her life style. Dr. Silverman's summary of the hour prior to the sample session provides a window on the interactional issues that may be at the root of this stalemated analysis:

> On Thursday, the day before the first sample session, she was feeling hurt and angry because her father had berated her for saying too much to a salesman who had called. He had never made clear exactly what she should and should not say to salesmen, but she did not protest when he berated her. She answered the phone to relieve her father of the burden of doing it, and she accepts his chastisements, however unfair, without complaint for the same reasons. She lets her father intimidate her and doesn't say anything when he gives her ambiguous instructions and then berates her for not having done what he wanted her to do. She used to get tongue-tied and was not even able to answer him when he asked the simplest questions, thinking he was out to trap her. She reflected on my observation that she was extremely hurt and angry at her father for not recognizing her loving willingness to sacrifice for him, and that, in her struggle with her ambivalent feelings, she had offered her *own* self up to be hurt, erotizing the pain so that she was paradoxically excited by her father's abuse. It was difficult for her, she said, not to reject my observations. She loved and worried about her father. He always acted strong, seemed strong, and claimed to be strong—the whole family did that—but he actually was not a strong person and leaned on her mother. She did not know what to do [Silverman, 1987, pp. 150–151).

In this session Dr. Silverman reports that Miss K complains that she is intimidated by her father because, in his eyes, she cannot do anything right. Miss K's history of failing to meet her father's expectations and her symptomatic behavior of becoming "tongue-tied" and "not being able to answer him when he asked the simplest of questions" lead an analyst with an interactional point of view to hypothesize that Miss K has formulated her lifelong failure to please her father, and men like her father, into a preconscious pathogenic belief that her intellectual and personal inadequacies drive men to berate and reject her. Anticipating rejection when she interacts with men, Miss K feels intimidated by them. Though she recognizes that a man's behavior is often a cause of her inability to perform, for example her father's giving ambiguous instructions, this preconscious pathogenic belief causes Miss K to discount her perception of who is at fault and to accept a man's chastisements as deserved. In this hour Miss K focuses on why she is intimidated by her father and what she does to provoke him to berate her and reject her.

Dr. Silverman has a different understanding of what Miss K is talking about in this hour. In formulating her problem from an oedipal perspective, he interprets Miss K's willingness to do what father wants, but in a manner that provokes his rejection, as a compromise formation expressing her ambivalent feelings toward father. Dr. Silverman tells the patient that she is sexually aroused by her father's abusive behavior. The interpretation implies that Miss K derives sexual pleasure from engaging in conflict with men.

The patient and the analyst appear to be in conflict over what should be the focus of the analysis. Miss K wants to explore why she is intimidated by men and what she does to cause them to behave in ways that intimidate her, whereas Dr. Silverman is set on flushing out the contemporary sequelae of her unresolved oedipal conflicts.

The conflict between Miss K and Dr. Silverman over what is going on within her and in her relations with men can be formulated into a hypothesis about one of the probable causes of the stalemated analytic process: the patient and the analyst are in an unconscious battle over whose reality or point of view should prevail. From an interactional perspective, this battle can be seen as a transference–countertransference enactment aimed at proving true Miss K's pathogenic belief that her inadequacies and personal characteristics alienate men and cause them to reject her. That is, I am hypothesizing that Miss K is preconsciously manipulating the analyst into behaving toward her in as berating and as rejecting a manner as do the other men in her life. It is possible, even likely, that the analysis is stalled because the interactional determinants of the analytic interaction, that is, the various manifestations of this enactment, are not being recognized. Though this hypothesis has been formulated as a point of departure for understanding the first reported episode of the sample hour, my examination of the subsequent episodes tends to support this conceptualization of the case.

To return to Dr. Silverman's summary of the Thursday hour, his report that Miss K struggled "not to reject my observations" takes on a particular meaning with this hypothesis in mind. The patient and the analyst seem to be caught in a vicious circle, each trying to convince the other that his or her point of view is true. Most probably the patient feels intimidated by Dr. Silverman's interpretation because she experienced it as a rejection of her thesis that she does something to make men berate her. Consequently, in line with her pathogenic belief that her own reasoning must be inadequate, she feels as if she has to give up her thematic focus on being intimidated in favor of the analyst's sexualized ideas about her relationship to her father. The hour ends with the patient in conflict over whether or not to accept his interpretation; Dr. Silverman reports that Miss K "didn't know what to do."

Episode One[1]

Patient: The rain woke me up early this morning. It was beating down on my air conditioner so loudly it woke me up. I looked at the clock. It was 5:30. I thought in an hour I have to get up to come here. I didn't want to come today. I've been mad at you all week. It is not that I'm mad at you. I wanted to stay away from all this stuff I think I feel here. I also got angry at R. [her roommate] yesterday. In the bathroom, she takes two towel bars and a hook. And I just have one towel bar. I didn't say anything for a long time. I finally got up the courage and told her we have to change the arrangements in the bathroom. It sounds so silly. I get so worked up over such little things. She was talking about being all worked up because someone called her for a date. She hardly listened to what I was saying. She's so self-centered. Her boyfriend came, and he was there two minutes and he asked about my cousin. She never asks about my cousin. She only thinks about herself. I thought of saying "thanks for asking" to him because I was so grateful he'd asked, but I decided not to say it. Because I'd have been calling attention to her never asking. I get so mad at her [pp. 151–152].

Miss K begins the hour by telling the analyst that she did not want to come to treatment today because she has been mad at him all week. Consciously reflecting on the meaning of her anger, Miss K concludes that she is angry because she doesn't want to experience the feelings she gets when interacting with the analyst. Miss K's association to her anger at the analyst is to her anger at her roommate who takes over most of the bathroom fixtures without regard for her feelings or needs. When the patient voices her concern about the distribution of the fixtures, the roommate fails to hear the patient's perspective because she is preoccupied with her sexual feelings for a man.

From an interactional point of view, Miss K's story about the roommate is understood as a verbal-symbolic representation of her preconscious meaning analysis of her interaction with the analyst on Thursday. In that session the analyst, by interpreting her conduct with her father as soliciting his rejection for her own erotic aims, rejected Miss K's theory that men intimidate her. The analyst, like the roommate, imposed his idea of how

---

[1] I have divided the sample session into eight episodes for the purpose of examining the hour in manageable portions. The text has been silently amended with the inclusion of *Patient* and *Analyst* to indicate who is speaking. Dr. Silverman's references to what he thinks during the hour are indicated by the introductory phrase "Analyst thinks to himself." Dr. Silverman's observations of the patient's affect and significant background information are in brackets within the text, as are his observations of his own affective states. Otherwise, Dr. Silverman's exact language has been preserved as it appeared in the journal.

things are, or should be, on the patient and was too preoccupied with his sexual theories to listen to the issues that she was raising.

Though Miss K is consciously aware of her angry feelings toward Dr. Silverman, a psychoanalyst examining this vignette from an interactional orientation would understand that she cannot connect these angry feelings with her meaning analysis of their interaction because her experience and interpretation of the interaction are not consciously available to her. Dr. Silverman's rejection of Miss K's theory that men intimidate her is consistent with her pathogenic belief that her ideas are not as good as those of a man and will be rejected. Since Dr. Silverman did not violate Miss K's expectation that he would reject her theory and substitute his own, her meaning analysis remains in a preconscious state. With the experiential and interpretative components of the transference not available to her conscious mind, Miss K cannot not use this information to understand why she is angry. Accordingly, utilizing the data consciously available to her (i.e., the bad feelings she has when she is with the analyst), Miss K infers that she is angry because she does not want to experience the feelings she has when she is with the analyst.

Miss K's association to her anger becomes the avenue for the preconscious expression of her meaning analysis of her interaction with the analyst. The story about her roommate's self-centered behavior has an affective quality and a meaning similar to those of her experience and interpretation of her interaction with Dr. Silverman. Miss K's reflections on her roommate's boyfriend asking after her cousin when the roommate herself fails to inquire about Miss K's life is also a symbolic representation of the transference. The story reflects Miss K's experience of the analyst as not attuned to her feelings or to the significant people and events in her life. She interprets Dr. Silverman's nonattuned behavior as indicating that he is too self-centered to care about her.

At the end of this episode, Miss K is still preoccupied with her anger. In connecting her anger with her decision not to call attention to her roommate's failure to show an interest in her, Miss K may be giving voice to her preconscious conflict over whether or not to confront the analyst with his nonattuned behavior.

Episode Two

> *Patient:* I thought about something else in the car on the way here. I went to have my hair cut and it was to be cut at seven o'clock. But I had to wait and wait till nine o'clock. I got angrier and angrier. I told the girl when I paid that I was angry. I told her that I can go to someone else to get my hair cut—or I can wait for him. I don't like either alternative. I don't even know why I go there. I don't fit in. They're mostly older women.

Analyst thinks to himself: She'll get a bill from me in a few days, and it's the end of the week and she has to wait two days to see me again on Monday—like the two hours for the hairdresser—and in two weeks I leave for vacation, and she'll have to wait a month for me. [p. 152].

Miss K's next association to her anger is her anger at the hairdresser for keeping her waiting. Through this verbal symbolic representation of the transference, Miss K preconsciously communicates to the analyst her anger and frustration at having to wait for him to begin listening to her. The story also reflects the patient's continuing conflict about how to deal with the analyst. Should she wait for him to do his job, as she waited for the hairdresser, or should she find a new one. Neither solution is satisfactory to her.

Although Dr. Silverman's self-reflections indicate that he understands that the story about the hairdresser alludes to him, the content of his reflections (i.e., his bill, the weekend, his vacation) suggest that he has not taken the analytic interaction itself as the referent of the patient's communication. Dr. Silverman, therefore, does not understand that what the patient has been conveying is her meaning analysis of their interaction.

Episode Three

Patient: But I didn't say anything to him. I'm intimidated by him the way I'm intimidated by M [the tennis pro]. I don't know why. He's not big and tall like M. He's good looking, but he's not my type. He's married and has children [so does her father]. He has their pictures up. With M, I think it has something to do with my knowing nothing about tennis and his knowing so much about it. And I couldn't understand when he was telling me what to do. "Hold it this way" and "Turn that way," and I couldn't understand anything he said. It was just like with my father all my life. He thinks he gives such good directions and clear explanations, as I said yesterday, but he doesn't. I get intimidated with men. I always feel that they know they have the knowledge. They have the brains, and I'm dumb. And I always feel like I don't know anything and I can't understand and I get intimidated. It's the same thing here. I keep feeling like asking you, "What does it mean?" I always feel like you know. I feel like asking you now. I know you've told me you don't know anything until I've told it to you, but I don't feel that way. I feel you're always a step ahead of me. You *know,* because you're smarter than I am and all the training and experience you have.
Analyst: I don't think that's what it is. I think you feel I know because I'm a man, that as a woman you don't have the brains [pp. 152–153].

In this episode, Miss K reintroduces the problem that she wants to work on in the analysis, namely, why she is intimidated by men. It will be recalled that Miss K's conscious experience of being intimidated by men is the precipitate of her preconscious pathogenic belief that her intellectual and personal inadequacies cause men to berate and reject her. Miss K begins by stating that men intimidate her and cites as examples her interactions with the hairdresser, the tennis pro, and her father. In explaining why she feels intimidated in these situations Miss K is also voicing one aspect of her preconscious pathogenic belief: in comparison with men she feels "dumb," lacking the brains and the knowledge to understand things, particularly how men want things done.

Miss K informs the analyst that he too intimidates her—"it's the same thing here"—and then, as if to underscore the communication, she preconsciously manipulates the interaction to enact with the analyst her specific pathogenic belief that men berate and reject her because she is dumb: Miss K says to Dr. Silverman, "What does it mean?" and then implores him to enlighten her by declaring, "I feel you're always a step ahead of me. You *know*, because you're smarter than I am and all the training and experience you have." Since Dr. Silverman is not attuned to the dynamics of the interaction, he is taken in by Miss K's manipulation and rejects her thesis by stating, "I don't think that's what it is." By adding "I think you feel I know because I'm a man, and that as a woman you don't have the brains," Dr. Silverman substitutes his own interpretation, which centers on what he sees as Miss K's preoccupation with the differences between men and women. Thus, Miss K's preconscious maneuver has succeeded in getting Dr. Silverman to reject her ideas, thereby creating a situation in which she feels dumb and intimidated. She had organized a transference–countertransference enactment that transformed the analytic interaction into a representative instance of her pathogenic belief.

Episode Four

> *Patient:* I get intimidated by men. [anxiously] Do you think I signal it to them and that drives them away? So they think, "Who wants her!" I think it started in a way when my father said to me, "Every man is going to want the same thing from you." I got so angry. Why? Why would he expect that of me? What right does he have? I heard R and her boyfriend kissing just outside the door. She *likes* it! When my father said what he did, first I was mad at them for wanting sex eventually, and then I got mad if I thought they wanted to kiss on the first date. Then I started getting mad that they'd *ever* want to kiss. I got so *angry*. I'm such an angry person.
>
> *Analyst:* As you've said, you get mad to push away other feelings.
>
> *Patient:* With A [the young man she had met on a singles weekend trip, at which she had relaxed her usual guarded stiffness and had danced and smiled and joked, and who had become interested in her and arranged to

come in from out of town to spend two days with her only to stand her up when she went to meet him] I told him when he said he would come down here that he could stay at my apartment. And he got all excited about it and eager to come. And then I got frightened about what I'd said to him, and I said, "Wait a minute," and I made it clear to him I meant he could sleep over at my apartment—on the couch—not with me. [with emotion] Do you think that's why he didn't show up? Did I chase him away? [p. 153].

Miss K responds to Dr. Silverman's interpretation about the differences in brain power between men and women by reiterating her complaint that "I get intimidated by men." In making this statement, she is also informing the analyst that she experienced his interpretation as intimidating. Miss K's question, "Do you think I signal it to them and that drives them away?" communicates to the analyst her preconscious meaning analysis of their interchange, that Dr. Silverman rebuffed her because she felt intimidated, which is the experiential manifestation of her pathogenic belief: men recoil from her when she feels intimidated. From the perspective of her pathogenic belief the question communicates to Dr. Silverman her preconscious awareness that his rejection of her ideas proved true her belief that her intellectual inadequacy provokes men to reject her.

The two stories that follow upon Miss K questioning whether she drives men away further suggest that she experienced the analyst's interpretation at the end of episode three as a sexualization of their interaction. The meaning she attributed to this experience comes from a belief that she internalized from her father: all that men want from women is sex. In the story about overhearing her roommate kissing her boyfriend outside her door, Miss K unconsciously expresses her anger at the analyst for imposing his sexual theories on her.

Dr. Silverman's intrapsychic interpretation, that her anger is being used to push away other feelings, alerted the patient to his failure again to understand that the referent of her story is their interaction. Miss K responds by telling a second story in which she is rejected for correcting a young man's misunderstanding that her invitation to be more intimate was an invitation to be sexual. The story expresses her experience and interpretation of their current interaction. Miss K believes that the analyst has misunderstood her communications as sexual, owing to his own preoccupations, and that if she corrects his misunderstanding, thereby disappointing his expectations, he will reject her.

Miss K again underscores her conscious belief that she drives men away when, in the final lines of this episode, she asks whether her behavior with the boyfriend caused him to reject her: "Do you think that's why he didn't show up? Did I chase him away?" As the question earlier in the hour served a conscious and preconscious aim, these questions also highlight her preconscious experience of behaving in a way that causes the analyst to reject her.

Episode Five

> *Patient:* Men intimidate me. It's like with my father. It's a mixture of excitement and pain and hurt and fear. But wait a minute. It's not only men who intimidate me, I get intimidated about money. Paying and tipping intimidates me. I avoid it if I can. Until lately, when I've been thinking about it here and trying not to avoid the things I tend to avoid. When I left the hairdresser's I looked for the girl who'd shampooed my hair to give her a dollar. But I'd have avoided it if I could. If they had a can with tips in it I would've put it in there. I was too intimidated by the hairdresser who cut my hair and I was intimidated about tipping the girl who shampooed my hair. Why? [slight pause] I can't figure it out. There's no rhyme or reason. I don't understand it.
> *Analyst:* So long as you take that attitude, so long as you don't think it out and find out the rhyme and reason . . .
> *Patient:* Well, *he* cut my hair. He *cut* me. But she just put her fingers into my hair. I don't understand.
> *Analyst:* He stuck scissors into your hair and she stuck her fingers into your hair. You were talking before that about avoiding sexual excitement. Scissors and fingers into your hair *sounds* sexual. You turn away and avoid the excitement, pain, and hurt with men, and when you turn away from men altogether and turn toward a woman you get scared all over again.
> *Patient:* Yes. But there's something that doesn't fit. I had no problem about tipping the woman who gave me a manicure. And she massaged my fingers. And that didn't get me anxious. I liked it. It's relaxing [pp. 153–154].

Continuing with her agenda of analyzing the situations in which she feels intimidated, Miss K realizes that she feels intimidated in circumstances other than interactions with men, such as in tipping the girl who shampooed her hair. This confuses her, and she complains, "I can't figure it out. There's no rhyme or reason. I don't understand it." Dr. Silverman responds with what reads like a scolding, critically exhorting her to change her attitude and to think more clearly: "So long as you take that attitude, so long as you don't think it out and find out the rhyme and reason. . . ."

In reaction to Dr. Silverman's confrontation, Miss K's thinking becomes concrete: "Well he *cut* my hair. He *cut* me. But she just put her fingers into my hair. I don't understand." By focusing on the specific, concrete actions of the hairdresser and the shampoo girl, Miss K inhibits herself from thinking abstractly about the meaning of these actions. She therefore fails to understand what the analyst wants in terms of her reasoning about these interactions. The inability to think or understand is precisely what she told the analyst, during her Thursday session and in episode three, is her response to being intimidated by men and what she has been enacting in this episode and throughout the hour.

Miss K's concrete thinking and inability to understand are defenses against what she experiences as the analyst's dismissive and overbearing response to her. To preserve the continuity and stability of her sense of self, she withdraws from the interaction by terminating affective and symbolic communication with the analyst. The defense of withdrawal from the analytic interaction is an interactional form of resistance that functions to protect a patient's self-experience and psychic reality from externally induced pressures to change.

Dr. Silverman reacts to the patient's symptomatic inability to understand by advancing a sexualized interpretation of her interactions with the hairdresser and the woman who shampooed her hair: "You were talking before that about avoiding sexual excitement. Scissors and fingers into your hair *sounds* sexual. You turn away and avoid the excitement, pain, and hurt with men. . . ." In making this interpretation, Dr. Silverman suggests that she relinquish her focus on being intimidated and accept his lead in reframing her behavior from an oedipal perspective. Implicitly and explicitly he is inciting her to produce sexual material.

Miss K initially agrees to the analyst's interpretation but after testing it against her experience at the beauty salon, she rejects it. Miss K tells the analyst that the interpretation does not fit, because she found the experience of getting her fingers massaged relaxing, not anxiety provoking.

Episode Six

> *Patient*: I thought of something. I told you about it a long time ago and then I dropped it and avoided it. It's a masturbation fantasy. [Now her voice changes, becomes more hollow, tending toward a chilled monotone, drained of all emotion. She speaks this way for much of the remainder of the session, constantly pausing between words. I found her slow, start-and-stop delivery agonizing, and have tried to convey it on the page by the use of dashes to indicate her briefer pauses, reserving the word *pause*, in brackets, for the longer ones.] There's—a doctor—a mad scientist—and his nurse and—he ties me down to—do things to me. I don't know what this has to do with being intimidated by the hairdresser and feeling inhibited tipping the girl who washes my hair but not the manicurist. It makes no sense [pause].
>
> *Analyst:* You've blocked yourself from hearing the answer you gave: the hairdresser sticking scissors in your hair and cutting you; the young woman preparing you for the haircut; they're the mad scientist doctor and his nurse.
>
> *Patient:* The fantasy had to do with something—it had to do with getting bigger breasts. It's foolish—I feel sheepish [pause]. It's so silly [pause].

Analyst: There's nothing silly about it; you mobilize those feelings to push away and avoid looking into the fantasy and the feelings.

Patient: I'd try not to think the fantasy. I didn't want to dig into it. You're right. I feel sheepish to push it away.

Analyst: And what happens to sheep?

Patient: They get sheared, their hair cut off.

Analyst: And so do "fallen women."

Patient: In old times, they did. I know about that. The hairdresser was cutting *my* hair off. Maybe it was my "crowning glory." And sheep certainly get their hair cut off. When I was in New Zealand, I saw the sheep getting sheared. There was one brown one I remember. They held it down and sheared it, and piled the wool, and all that.

[Analyst thinks to himself]: The emotion's gone from her voice; she's shearing the sheep to pull the wool over our eyes [pp. 154–155].

Miss K's presentation of what she calls a "masturbation fantasy" at this point in the hour is, I believe, an attempt to comply with Dr. Silverman's pressure for her to produce sexual material. On a preconscious level, the fantasy conveys to the analyst the patient's meaning analysis of their interaction: she believes that she is being manipulated by a mad scientist who is trying to make her more sexual. Unfortunately, Dr. Silverman fails to sees that the "mad scientist" represents him and that her sadomasochistic fantasy alludes to the analytic interaction.[2]

Although the patient's verbal symbolic representation of the transference, her fantasy about the mad scientist, eludes Dr. Silverman, he does not fail to appreciate emotionally that she does not want to comply with what she perceives as his demands. Miss K nonsymbolically conveys to the analyst her emotional experience of their interaction (i.e., the experiential component of the transference) through her halting, disembodied, and monotonous voicing of the fantasy. In this way the patient preconsciously casts an affective tone of reluctance, almost to the point of obstinacy, to the interaction. Dr. Silverman experiences her reluctance viscerally: "I found the slow, start-and-stop delivery agonizing. . . ."

When Miss K protests the relevance of her "masturbation fantasy" to her problem of being intimidated by the hairdresser, the analyst redirects her thinking by pointing out that the hairdresser and shampoo girl are the mad scientist and the nurse. The analyst's response has a critical edge—"You've blocked yourself from hearing the answer you gave"—which seems to intimidate the patient into continuing with the fantasy. When she expresses her "sheepish" embarrassment in at having to continue with

---

[2]Gill (1987) whose approach to the transference is consonant with our own, pointed this out in his commentary on the case.

this submissive enterprise, the analyst does not accept her feeling "silly" and "foolish," nor does he try to understand why she may feel this way. In the guise of analyzing her defensiveness, the analyst dismisses her feelings, by saying "There's nothing silly about it" and educates her to what he understands to be the self-protective nature of these feelings: "You mobilize those feelings to push away and avoid looking into the fantasy and the feelings."

Miss K struggles to comply with the analyst's implicit demand to adopt his sexualized perspective, but Dr. Silverman's linking her feeling sheepish with "fallen women," in an attempt to connect her associations to his supposition about her sexual inhibition around men, is so disturbing to her that she withdraws further from the interaction to preserve her sense of self. Miss K's associations degenerate into a concrete and emotionless description of shearing sheep.[3] By becoming cognitively concrete and affectively void, Miss K ceases to communicate with Dr. Silverman in a meaningful way, thereby resisting again his attempts to coerce her into altering her psychic reality.

Miss K's resistance derives, in part, from the analyst's failure to accept as valid her affective experience and her interpretation of her behavior and from his insistence that Miss K accept as the only correct interpretation of her behavior his sexualized concept of what is going on with her. A careful analysis of the analytic interaction reveals that the patient has preconsciously provoked Dr. Silverman into a sadomasochistic interaction aimed at confirming her pathogenic belief that she does something that invites men to reject her. Using the behaviors that she reports as upsetting men in her interactions with them, such as being intellectually concrete, ingenuously compliant, and emotionally withholding, the patient evokes in the analyst feelings of impatience; and he begins to adopt a patronizing and condescending attitude toward her.

Inasmuch as Dr. Silverman is not attuned to the interactional determinants of his own or the patient's behavior, he is blind to the sadomasochistic transference–countertransference enactment. Because Dr. Silverman does not appreciate the patient's resistance as a self-protective response to his disturbing communications to her, he cannot deal with the resistances interpretively. These sadomasochistic enactments prolong the analytic stalemate.

---

[3]It is worth noting that in connecting Miss K's feeling sheepish with both sheep and fallen women getting their hair sheared off, Dr. Silverman preconsciously constructs with Miss K a symbolic representation emblematic of what is occurring at that moment in their interaction: with his interventions and interpretations, he is shearing away her experience and thoughts as a sheepshearer strips away a sheep's wool.

Episode Seven

> *Analyst:* You're getting away to avoid uncomfortable feelings.
>
> *Patient:* You're right. That fantasy makes me very uncomfortable. The mad scientist would do something to give me bigger breasts. I wanted bigger breasts very much [pause].
>
> *Analyst:* Notice your interrupting yourself, stopping yourself?
>
> *Patient:* I don't want to talk about it, think about it; I'm afraid you'll think I'm foolish. I had to submit to the mad scientist, like I was his slave and he was my master. When I'm intimidated by men, it's like I have to put up with anything, like I'm a slave and he's a master and it makes me angry [pause]. That slave and master theme in relations between women and men gets me mad. [Her voice changed again.]
>
> *Analyst:* Notice you switched from uncomfortable thinking about the wish for the mad scientist to give you bigger breasts to the slave and master theme?
>
> *Patient:* [back to working voice] There's something about—it's not called S&M—something and bondage—in porno—people waiting to be tied up and things done to them [pause].
>
> *Analyst:* I notice you keep interrupting yourself and stopping yourself.
>
> *Patient:* You've told me several times that you couldn't promise that this would always be easy—but—it's—too hard—[there's tightness in my belly, and I'm getting irritated at her excruciating stopping and starting and hesitating]—if I could find a way to do this without feeling so uncomfortable [pause] [p. 155].

At the beginning of this episode Dr. Silverman's observation "You're getting away to avoid uncomfortable feelings" signals to the patient that he has recognized her discomfort and withdrawal. Encouraged by what she mistakenly understands as Dr. Silverman's recognition and acceptance of her experience of their interaction, Miss K attempts, unconsciously, to express to him her meaning analysis of their interaction by reinterpreting the masturbation fantasy: "I had to submit to the mad scientist, like I was his slave and he was my master. When I'm intimidated by men, it's like I have to put up with anything, like I'm a slave and he's a master and it makes me angry. That slave and master theme in relations between women and men gets me mad."

Dr. Silverman's interpretation, that she has defensively substituted the slave–master theme for her uncomfortable wish to have the mad scientist give her bigger breasts, clearly indicates to Miss K that again he has not understood the referent of her communication to be their interaction. In linking the slave–master relationship between men and women to that of bondage in pornographic films, the patient unconsciously reinforces the connection between the content of this slave and master fantasy and the analyst's sexualized interpretation of her behavior in their current interaction.

The anxiety, frustration, and anger experienced by Miss K are expressed not only verbally in her fantasy, but also in how she communicates the material. The slow, halting, hesitating presentation evokes anger, anxiety, and irritability in the analyst. Dr. Silverman notes the tightness in his belly and his irritation, but he does not use this information to understand what is going on between himself and the patient. Instead, he takes the patient's stammering style of communication as indicative of an internal conflict, while remaining ostensibly unaware that his repeated comments about her hesitations are being taken by her as a verification of her belief that men will find her inadequate.

Though Dr. Silverman continues not to perceive the sadomasochistic nature of his relationship with the patient, Miss K is preconsciously aware of it. In relating her master–slave interpretation of the analytic interaction to "S&M" themes in pornographic movies, she gives expression to this preconscious understanding. One reason Miss K is not consciously aware of the sadomasochistic nature of her relationship with the analyst is that this type of relationship is consistent with her pathogenic belief that she provokes men to berate and reject her.

Episode Eight

> *Analyst:* You want me to make you do it. You're having all that trouble talking about, thinking all those thoughts about pain and hurt, S.&M., bondage, because of a wish to enact the fantasy with me rather than think and feel it out and understand it. You want *me* to be the mad scientist doctor forcing and hurting you and making changes in you.
>
> *Patient:* I want you to use your knowledge and your understanding to change me. Instead of working at this myself and making changes. I want you to do it. But you say it's because I want you to be the mad scientist of my fantasy, that if you force me and hurt me it's exciting. I have to reject that. I can't agree with you on that. That would mean I don't really want to change. But I do want to change. I have to think about it. Maybe I'm undecided and that's why it's so difficult and uncomfortable. I'll have to think about it.
>
> *[Analyst thinks to himself]:* The thing with the tennis teacher was on the weekend; here's another weekend; in a few weeks I'll leave her not just for a weekend but for a month; absence makes the heart grow fonder; she also wants to kill me for leaving her, for not being crazy about her so I can't bear to be without her; masochistic transference; transference neurosis [p. 155–156].

Dr. Silverman's first interpretation in this episode, "You want me to make you do it. . . . [You] wish to enact the fantasy with me . . ," relates the patient's S&M fantasy to the analytic interaction such that she believes that they are now sharing the same frame of reference. She infers that Dr. Silverman accurately appreciates her experience of their interaction and confirms this shared frame of reference by saying, "I want you to use your knowledge and your understanding to change me. Instead of working at this myself and making changes. I want you to do it." But Miss K is confused by the analyst's claim that she *wants* him to be the mad scientist who hurts her and forces her into making changes. Miss K's confusion stems from her initially mistaking what was an intrapsychic interpretation, that her fantasy symbolized an unconscious masochistic wish, for an interpersonal interpretation, that the fantasy represented her experience of their interaction. The patient cannot brook the analyst's intrapsychic interpretation and roundly rejects it.

The inference the patient makes from her conscious meaning analysis of the analyst's intrapsychic interpretation and her rejection of it is that she must not want to change. This inference derives from Miss K's momentary acceptance of Dr. Silverman's assumption[4] that her problem lies solely within herself. For the patient, the frame of reference has now shifted from the interpersonal to the internal causes of her behavior. By unconsciously complying with the analyst's imposition of an intrapsychic cause of her problem, the patient preserves a working relationship between herself and the analyst. The alliance is maintained, however, by the patient's defensive denial of her own experience. The inference that she does not want to change leaves the patient in a state of disequilibrium.

Reflecting on her conscious motivations for treatment, Miss K concludes that she very much wants to change. She desires to understand why she interacts with men in a self-destructive manner and wants to change it. Yet, in the context of the current therapeutic relationship, to change means to abandon her theory of her behavior in favor of the analyst's. Miss K knows that she does not want to do this. So the idea of not wanting to change has intuitive appeal because to change means that she must relinquish her autonomy and freedom. Miss K ends the hour confused about her motivations.

Dr. Silverman's final self-reflections on the oedipal root of the patient's angry feelings about his leaving for the weekend and on his vacation indicate his continuing preoccupation with issues other than those currently between him and the patient. Until what is going on in the analysis is addressed by both participants, the struggle between them is likely to continue to stall the analysis.

---

[4]The assumption is embedded in his intrapsychic interpretation of her fantasy as a masochistic wish for him to excite her sexually.

CONCLUSION

The analysis of Dr. Silverman's hour with Miss K has shown the usefulness of interactional theory in discovering and understanding a patient's psychopathology and in analyzing the efficacy of psychoanalytic process and technique. Several specific theoretical and technical principles of interactional theory were illustrated in this case study, and some major implications for psychoanalytic theory and practice emerge from the interactional analysis of this hour.

From the perspective of psychoanalytic theory, Dr. Silverman's case illustrates how patients consciously and especially unconsciously organize and interpret the analytic interaction in terms of the schemata that structure their psychic reality. The meanings that patients attribute to the actual exchange between themselves and their analysts reflect the content of these schemata and are represented and expressed in verbal and behavioral symbols, such as stories from the patients' current and past life and enactments, and in such nonsymbolic communications as vocal tone and pacing. The case clearly shows how the analytic interaction both influences and reflects the patient's psychic reality.

From this perspective of psychoanalytic process and technique, the clinical material demonstrates the importance of interpreting the symbolic and nonsymbolic representations of the transference in terms of the patient's meaning analysis of the actual analytic interchange. The case clearly documents the consequences of failing to recognize the interpersonal referents of patients' conscious and unconscious communications. It was shown how such failures lead to the imposition of the analyst's point of view on the patient and the resultant increase in the likelihood of a negative therapeutic reaction and resistance to the analyst's interventions and interpretations.

III

Applications and Exemplifications

Theo. L. Dorpat

In this final section, we consider some applications of the theoretical revisions advanced in previous chapters to the understanding of such topics as transference, projective identification, self-fulfilling prophecies, the repetition compulsion, defense, and dreaming.

Countertransference and transference together form an intersubjective system of reciprocal mutual influence. Although the contribution of the patient's transference to the nature of the analyst's countertransference has become well accepted in recent decades, many analysts remain unaware of their contribution to the patient's transference. As indicated in Chapter 10, the countertransference has a decisive impact on the formation of the transference and partially determines which of its dimensions will be manifested in the analytic dialogue. The patient's experience of the relationship with the analyst, that is, the transference, is always shaped both by inputs from the analyst and by the activation of specific schemata into which the analyst's interventions are assimilated.

According to the standard concept, transference feelings and attitudes are distortions of the realities of the analyst, and such distortions are caused by the displacement of feelings and attitudes linked with representatives of the parents onto the representation of the analyst. My views are similar to those of Gill, Schwaber, Stolorow, and others who criticize the concept of transference as distortion because it implies that the patient is producing his or her experience of the analyst out of whole cloth and isolated from the ongoing interactions with the analyst. Another objection to the view of transference as distortion lies in its embeddedness in a hierarchically ordered, two-reality view of the analytic situation—one reality experienced by the patient and the other supposedly "known" by the analyst to be more objectively true.

Chapter 11 discusses self-fulfilling prophecies and especially their significance in projective identifications. In projective identification, the subject manipulates the object in such a way as to evoke attitudes and feelings in the object that confirm the subject's prophecies and expectations. Though some self-fulfilling prophecies can have destructive effects, such destructive effects are not inevitable. A common and salutary product of psychoanalytic treatment is the emergence of patients' ability to disbelieve their own and others' destructive prophecies, thus preventing the prophecy from becoming self-fulfilling.

The traditional psychoanalytic concept of defenses is essentially an intrapsychic, or one-body conception with a nearly exclusive focus on a person's use of internal protective mechanisms activated by signals of danger and mobilized to defend against instinctual drives. Chapter 12 provides an important contribution toward a revised theory of defenses that recognizes the role played by object relations in the development, internalization, and maintenance of defensive activity. Both in childhood and in later life, what is internalized and transformed into defenses as well as other psychic structures are the person's interactions with others.

In Chapter 13, case vignettes are used to illustrate the contribution to dream formation made by patients' unconscious meaning analysis of recent events. Much of the dynamic content of dreams is the product of the dreamer's unconscious meaning analysis of recent events. Chapter 13 argues that what some analysts have called unconscious perceptions are actually the primary-process products of unconscious meaning analysis. They are unconscious judgments and inferences, not unconscious perceptions.

The interactional perspective and the revisions in theory recommended in this book have far-reaching implications for modifications in psychoanalytic technique. In the past, most analysts were almost wholly concerned with what was going on in the patient's mind, that is, the intrapsychic. Though I do not disagree with either the value or legitimacy of the intrapsychic point of view, I would argue that it is only one of several perspectives open to the analyst.

The novelty and success of several new schools of psychoanalysis stem from their implicit recognition of interactional and situational determinants in understanding what is taking place in the analysis. These more recent contributions include Kohut's self psychology, with its strategy of analyzing and interpreting disruptions of the selfobject transference brought about by interventions, empathic failures, and other actions taken by the analyst. Similarly, the writings of Gill and his associates point to the careful attention they give to the actions and behaviors of the analyst that evoke transference responses. In Langs's system of psychoanalytic psychotherapy, interpretations are organized around an adaptive context (usually an intervention made by the analyst) and the conscious and unconscious responses of the patient to the adaptive context. My coauthor and I believe that psychoanalysis, along with other fields of psychology, is entering an exciting era described by the eminent psychologist Bruner (1990) as a contextual revolution.

A systems point of view is valuable for conceptualizing the relationship between the traditional intrapsychic, one-body theory of psychoanalysis and the interactional, two-body theories, which include various object relations theories and self psychology.

My conception of the relationship between the interpersonal and the intrapsychic domains is consistent with Bertalanffy's (1968) General Systems Theory, in which the human organism is conceived of as a multileveled hierarchy of relatively autonomous systems. The organism in its structural aspects is not simply an aggregation of elementary parts such as atoms; rather, each system has a structure or organization of its own, one that is only relatively autonomous from other systems. Each system is an open one that interacts dynamically with other systems and takes in elements and gives off products.

The intrapsychic perspective considers what is going on within the psychic system of the patient, and the interactional point of view focuses on what is going on between the patient and others, most notably the analyst. But since the psychic system is an open system that interacts with others, it is not possible to give a comprehensive or complete description of what is occurring within a patient's psyche without also taking into account his or her interactions with others.

An optimal exploratory attitude for the analyst's understanding of what is taking place in the analysis is one that allows for flexible switching between intrapsychic and interactional perspectives. The interactional and intrapsychic points of view are not contradictory or competitive; rather they complement each other. Both points of view are needed for understanding and interpreting what is occurring in the analytic situation and what is taking place within the patient.

An exclusive use of the intrapsychic perspective precludes an understanding of the significance of the analyst's contributions to the patient's experience. The patient's mind is not a closed system! Similarly, an interactional point of view used exclusively omits consideration of patients' dispositions, their preexisting inclinations to think, feel, and act in certain ways that have their developmental origins in childhood experiences.

The contributions Michael Miller and I are presenting in this book are, along with object relations theories and self psychology, efforts to supplement the almost exclusively one-body theory of classical psychoanalysis with a two-body theory.

Social Versus Asocial Perspectives on Transference

There are extant today two broadly contrasting positions regarding transference. The first, historical position is that transference emanates entirely from the patient. This belief is implicit in Freud's archeological model of psychoanalytic inquiry and in the idea that the analyst serves as a blank screen for the patient's transferences. The second view is that any action, inaction, or restrained action of the analyst can affect the transference on a variety of levels of psychological organization.

Hoffman (1983) proposes the designation "social" for his interactional conception of the analytic situation, and thus of transference and countertransference, in contrast to the historical "asocial" conception. The classical view is asocial in the sense that it conceptualizes a current of experience in each participant, transference, and countertransference, that is essentially unrelated to the present situation and is therefore a distortion of the present.

According to the asocial view, transferences represent distortions of the realities of current interactions by perceptions and expectations that derive from the past and are imposed on and thereby color patients' perceptions of their relationship with the analyst. The asocial view of the transference either ignores or minimizes the impact of the actual attributes and behaviors of the analyst on the formation of the transference. An important technical implication of the asocial view is that analysts, as the more objective party and judge of what is realistic and inappropriate, can through their interpretations assist patients to differentiate distorted perceptions and ideas about the analytic situation from those that are realistic.

According to the social, or interactional, point of view, the transference is constructed out of the interaction of two people, each of whom tries plausibly to construe his or her experience of the other person in that relationship. This construing of the relationship depends on the actual behaviors and attitudes of the other person as they are perceived or inferred from expectations based on past experiences with similar people or similar situations. In the interactional transference, both parties try to make sense of their relationship, each influences the other's perception, and each is either consciously or, more often, unconsciously influenced by the other's actual communications as well as by expectations stemming from past experience.

Those advancing an interactional point of view hold that the analyst is an active participant and regulator of the analytic process whose personal characteristics and interventions powerfully influence the content and shape of transferences. Theorists who advance an interactional view on transference have in common the notion of an inevitable degree of interlocking of transference and countertransference and that transference interpretations must take this interplay into account.

The countertransference and the transference together form an inter-subjective system of reciprocal mutual influence. The countertransference has a decisive impact on shaping the transference and partially determining which of its dimensions will come to the fore in the analytic dialogue. Although the contribution of the patient's transference to the formation of the analyst's countertransference is well known, many analysts are reluctant to acknowledge their contribution to the patient's transference.

DEFINITIONS OF TRANSFERENCE

The concept of transference has a long history and is the subject of a broad literature; a detailed review of the background of this concept is presented by Orr (1954). There is little agreement either on the specific origins and functions of transference or on the observations that are the clinical referents of the term. It is difficult to propose a precise definition of transference because for many authors the term has taken on a very broad extension, even coming to connote all the phenomena that constitute the patient's relationship with the analyst. As a result, the concept has been burdened with each analyst's particular views on the treatment—on its objective, dynamics, tactics, and so on (Laplanche and Pontalis, 1973).

The previously standard definition of transference was provided by Fenichel (1945) as follows:

> In the transference the patient misunderstands the present in terms of the past; and then instead of remembering the past, he strives without recognizing the nature of his action, to relive the past and to live it more satisfactorily than he did in his childhood. He "transfers" the past attitude to the present [p. 29].

Chessick's (1986) definition emphasizes the resistance aspect of transference. He writes: "Transference is a form of resistance in which patients defend themselves against remembering and discussing their infantile conflicts by reliving them" (p. 15). Sandler (1983), discussing how the terms transference and transference resistance have undergone profound changes in meaning as new discoveries and new trends in psychoanalytic technique have gained acceptance, writes, "Major changes in technical emphasis brought about the extension of the transference concept, which now has dimensions of meaning which differ from the official definition of the term" (p. 10).

FREUD'S CONTRIBUTIONS

Freud (1914b, 1917) had three defining criteria for the transference: inappropriateness, resistance, and a repetition of the past. The first criterion, inappropriateness (or distortion), is based on the here-and-now of the analytic situation.

Emplifying Freud's (1912b, 1915a) criterion of inappropriateness in the transference were his hysterical women patients who developed strong reactions of love or hate toward him, along with intense sexual feelings, feared him as a dangerous seducer or abuser, and so on. Though this criterion has some descriptive value in such florid reactions, it has little or no relevance when one is dealing with less dramatic and less openly and directly expressed manifestations of the transference. In the Dora case (Freud, 1905b) and in his later writings (Freud, 1940a), he did not limit the classical definition of transference to its conspicuous and explicit manifestations, though he tended to do so in his more general and theoretical formulations. Most analysts since Freud have included within the transference patient behaviors and communications that do not explicitly and directly refer to the analyst but that are expressed unconsciously and indirectly; thus, their transference meaning rests on the inferences and interpretations of the analyst.

Freud consistently deemphasized the role of the analyst's behavior in determining the character of the transference. He stated, for example, "In every analytic treatment there arises, without the physician's agency, an intense emotional relationship between the patient and the analyst which is not to be accounted for by the actual situation . . . " (Freud, 1925b, p. 42).

Freud's first writings on transference were published in the *Studies on Hysteria* (Breuer and Freud, 1893–1895) where he referred to the patient's establishing a *"false connection"* (p. 302) between the doctor and a figure from the past. He viewed transference manifestations as "a compulsion and an *illusion,"* which melted away with the conclusion of the analysis (p. 304; italics added).

In his *Introductory Lectures,* Freud (1917a) spoke of transference reactions as something distinct from "realistic" reactions to others. In a discussion of negative transference, he wrote that there can be "no doubt that the hostile feelings towards the doctor deserve to be called a 'transference,' since the situation in the treatment quite clearly offers no adequate grounds for their origin" (p. 443).

In his recommendations for how to deal with transferences in treatment, Freud (1917) stated, "We overcome the transference by pointing out to the patient that his feelings do not arise from the present situation and do not apply to the person of the doctor, but that they are repeating something that has happened to him earlier" (pp. 443–444).

Freud's (1900) early, topographic conception of transference lessens the danger of the reductionistic collapse of all aspects of current mental life into their historical precursors:

> An unconscious idea is as such quite incapable of entering the preconscious. . . . it can only exercise any effect there by establishing a connection with an idea which *already belongs to the preconscious,* by transferring its intensity on to and by getting itself "covered" by it [p. 562, italics added].

Freud viewed the transferences in dream formation as occurring through the displacement of cathexis from an unconscious wish onto a day residue. Various authors have extended this formulation in the following way—just as the day residue is the point of attachment of the dream wish, so must there be an analytic-situation residue as the point of attachment of the transference (Loewald, 1960; Gill, 1982a).

CONTRIBUTIONS OF ROBERT STOLOROW
AND ASSOCIATES

Stolorow and his associates join a growing group of psychoanalysts who conceptualize transference in interactional terms and categories (Stolorow and Lachmann, 1985; Stolorow et al., 1987). They view transference as an organizing activity, and their theoretical stance assumes that the patient's experience of the therapeutic relationship is always shaped both by inputs from the analyst and the by structures of meaning into which the interactions with the analyst are assimilated by the patient.

In their view, transference in its essence refers not to regression, displacement, projection, or distortion, but to the assimilation of the analytic relationship into the thematic structures of the patient's personal subjective world. Transference is not a biologically determined drive to repeat the past ad infinitum for its own sake; rather it is an expression of a universal human striving to organize experience and to create meanings.

Stolorow and his colleagues conclude:

The concept of transference as organizing activity, by encouraging an unwavering inquiry into the patient's subjective frame of reference, opens a clear and unobstructed window to the patient's psychological world, and to its expansion, evolution, and enrichment (p. 35).

Stolorow and his associates effectively dispute the traditional view of transference as regression. Diverse clinical as well as experimental studies, including systematic studies of infant development, demonstrate that neither adult psychopathology nor transference regressions can be accurately described as a temporal regressions to an earlier phase of development.

Stolorow and his associates have made important modifications in Kohut's concepts about selfobject transferences. In their view, it is a conceptual error to consider the term selfobject transference to refer to a type of transference. Instead, they use the term selfobject transference to refer to a *dimension* of all transference that may fluctuate in the extent to which it occupies a position of figure or ground in the patient's experience of the analytic relationship. The selfobject dimension of transference is never absent, and so long as it is undisturbed, it operates silently in the background, enabling the patient to make contact with frightening and conflictual feelings.

Stolorow and his associates advance a bipolar conception of the selfobject dimension of transference in which one pole of the transference is the patient's longing to experience the analyst as a source of needed selfobject functions that were missing or insufficient during the patient's formative years. In this dimension of the transference, the patient fervently but anxiously seeks a new selfobject experience that will enable a resumption and completion of an arrested developmental process. The other pole of transference, the fears and expectations of a transference repetition of the original experiences of selfobject failure, becomes a major source of conflict and resistance in psychoanalytic treatment.

ARNOLD COOPER'S CONTRIBUTIONS

Cooper (1987) is among a growing group who believed that analysts cannot fully interpret transferences and transference resistances without acknowledging the contributions made by analyst–analysand interactions. He discusses and compares two major models of transference, the *historical* model and the *modernist* model.

The historical view is implicit in Freud's writings, and it views the transference as an enactment of an earlier relationship. From this perspective, the task of transference interpretation is to gain insight into the ways that infantile relationships are distorting and disturbing the relationship to the analyst.

The modernist model of transference regards the transference as a new experience rather than an enactment of an old one. In this model the infantile neurosis, if acknowledged at all, is an unprivileged set of current fantasies rather than a historical fact. In contrast, the historical view sees the infantile neurosis as a fact of central importance to be uncovered and undone. The historical model views the analyst as a neutral *tabula rasa* upon which instinctual drive derivatives will express themselves. In the modernist model, the analyst is a coparticipant, but in the historical model, the analyst is an observer.

In Cooper's formulation, the historical perspective has become a component part of a larger, more complex conception of transference. In his view, the historical definition of transference is replaced, or at the least subsumed, by modernist conceptions that are more attuned to the theories that abound today.

CONTRIBUTIONS OF MERTON GILL

In his monograph on transference, Gill (1982a) is inconsistent in espousing the "social" or interactional conception of transference. His interactional conception of transference is most clearly and explicitly set forth in papers he wrote (Gill, 1983, 1984, 1986) following the publication of that monograph. In the more recent writings, Gill defines transference as the patient's experience of the relationship with the therapist.

According to Gill (1982a, 1984) the transference plays a central role in both psychoanalysis and psychotherapy. The transference must be interpreted at all phases of treatment, and failure to do so leads to an unmanageable transference situation or premature termination of the analysis. Gill emphasizes the analyst's here-and-now behavior as profoundly influencing the transference that develops. For Gill and his collaborator, Hoffman, transference is the result of the interaction between analyst and patient and is therefore always present. Because the transference is most commonly manifested by allusions in the patient's associations, narratives, and dreams, the analyst must continuously look for it, clarify the contribution of the analytic situation's contribution to it, interpret the patient's resistances to awareness of it, and, finally, translate the disguised and displaced expressions of it into explicit experience and discussion.

In the psychoanalytic literature, the implications are much stronger that the countertransference is intrinsically related to the transference than vice versa. Analysts and therapists tend to protect their self-esteem by separating themselves from their patients and declaring countertransference to be only an occasional phenomenon and definitely pathological, and attributing a significant responsibility to the patient for the countertransference but not to the analyst for the transference (Gill, 1986).

According to Gill (1986), the social conception of the therapeutic situation, and thus of transference and countertransference, enables a therapist, without abandoning the relative restraint on interpersonal interaction with the patient, to be more relaxed and spontaneous in his work and to be more receptive to the cues to transference and countertransference that come both from the therapist's own feelings and from the patient's associations. Thus, the therapist can more effectively use these cues for understanding and interpretation.

Gill recommends a different working conception of transference because in his view the analyst should be concerned first and foremost with aspects of analyst–analysand interactions within the analytic situation. Gill's conception of transference entails a partial shift of emphasis away from the intrapsychic to the interpersonal or transactional, and he acknowledges his debt to Harry Stack Sullivan in this connection.

According to Gill, when conventional Freudian analysts use the concept of transference distortion, they set themselves up as superior or privileged authorities on the nature of reality. He recommends instead that analysts adopt a perspectivist or pluralist view of what is real. They should be prepared to accord some degree of plausibility to the analysand's interpretations of events in the analysis.

Schafer (1985) criticizes Gill for presenting his system as morally superior to that of others, and he argues that Gill's perspectivist attitude rests on his equating perspectivism with a simplified version of egalitarianism. Schafer does not believe that interpreting distortions necessarily depreciates the analysand or establishes the analyst as the arbiter of what is real. According to Schafer, it is

the analyst's responsibility to point out, in appropriate ways, distorted elements in the misperceptions, misrememberings, omissions, exaggerations, *non sequiturs,* polemicizing, and all the other things that can be taken up with a neutral, accepting, curious analytic attitude [pp. 295].

THE INFLUENCE OF CLASSICAL METAPSYCHOLOGY ON THE THEORY OF TRANSFERENCE

Freud's (1912b, 1925b) explanations and theories about transference were derived partly from his clinical observations and partly from his metapsychology, especially his theory of cognition. His clinical observations are not in question, because, as he indicated, patients do develop feelings and attitudes toward their therapists that are repetitious of reactions they once had for their significant others during childhood.

In Chapters 1, 12 and 13, I noted how Freud's theory of cognition influenced his theories of defense and dream formation. This is also true for Freud's theory of transference, and in this section my aim is to discuss briefly how some mistaken ideas in his theory of cognition adversely affected his explanatory theory of transference.

Freud's theory of transference rests on two notions that have been thoroughly studied and decisively rejected by various investigators as untenable and obsolete (see, e.g., Schimek, 1975a; Chaitin, 1978). The first is the concept of unconscious mental representations (unconscious memories and unconscious fantasies), and the second is his theory of displacement as a primary process mechanism that causes cognitive distortion in the service of defense. According to classical psychoanalytic theory, transference is the displacement of affects, attitudes, or other contents belonging to an unconscious mental representation onto the representation of the analyst. As discussed in Chapter 1, Freud incorrectly assumed that copies of perceptions are stored in the unconscious as undistorted mental representations. He believed, for example, that images formed of the father and mother in early childhood persist throughout life and are preserved in the unconscious as unconscious mental representations.

Though Freud (1905b) in his early writings maintained that transferences were caused by the displacement of cathexis from unconscious memories onto representations of the analyst, in his later writings he conceived of transferences as derivatives of drive-activated fantasies that patients mistakenly experience as real. The unconscious fantasy, plus the distorting power of drives and defenses, causes the subject to distort reality.

The conventional psychoanalytic technique for interpreting transference was derived from Freud's (1925b) asocial theory of transference and from his theory of cognition. A central aspect of this technique is the working through of the drive-cathected unconscious fantasy underlying and causing the transference reaction, so that the patient can then perceive and think about the analyst in a less distorted and more realistic and objective way.

Arlow (1985a), emphasizing the importance of unconscious fantasies in the formation of transference reactions, writes:

> When the patient wants the analyst to play a role or imagines the analyst to be playing a certain role, he is not treating the analyst as his doctor, but as an object of some wishful drive stemming from an unconscious fantasy [p. 247].

TRANSFERENCE AS DISPLACEMENT

A psychoanalytic glossary defines transference as: "The displacement of patterns of feelings and behavior, originally experienced with significant figures of one's childhood, to individuals in one's current relationships" [Moore and Fine, 1967, p. 89].

In Freud's (1900) economic theory, a cathexis is displaced from one unconscious mental representation to another one, from a place where discharge is conflicted and blocked to a place where discharge is possible. As I discussed in Chapter 1, there is no evidence supporting Freud's causal explanatory theory of displacement as a distorting process. In Freud's view, distortion is an essential part of the processes involved in the formation of transferences, dreams, and symptoms.

The asocial theory of transference as displacement has little to say about the role of actual patient–analyst interactions in the genesis of transference reactions. It explains transference wholly within an intrapsychic, or closed-system, perspective in which something fully formed and preexisting is simply displaced from one representation to another.

When a person has rebelled against oppressive paternal authority and subsequently adopts the same attitudes toward other people in authority, it does not follow that the person unconsciously displaced such feelings and attitudes from the images of the father onto representations of other authorities. What has occurred is that in relations with the father the person developed a mode of feeling and reacting (a schema) that is generalized in situations that are subjectively analogous (Piaget, 1962).

Though transference manifestations do give the analyst a glimpse of what a childhood relationship was like, this insight into the patient's past history is possible not because an idea or emotion from the past has been displaced onto the present, but because the schemata that were organized in the past either continue to be functionally effective or remain available for periodic mobilization. The concept of transference as displacement perpetuates the mistaken view that the patient's experience of the analytic relationship is solely a product of the patient's past psychopathology and has not been partly determined by the patient's interactions with the analyst.

TRANSFERENCE AS THE DISPLACEMENT
OF EMOTIONS

Some accounts of transference erroneously speak of the displacement of feelings from unconscious mental representations of parental objects onto representations of the analyst. It is mistaken to postulate the preservation of emotions in the unconscious because neither emotions per se nor images are stored in the unconscious. One can, however, justifiably assume that what do persist are modes of actions and reaction, schemata of behavior, and consequently there are certain permanent relationships between the affective reactions of a person in childhood and later as an adult (Piaget, 1962). Piaget writes:

> When the mind ceases to be consciously aware of a feeling which will reappear later on, it is the seat of a virtual feeling, and a virtual feeling is nothing else than a schema of action or reaction. . . . The unconscious is essentially dynamic, and it must be described in terms of reactions if the pitfalls of substantialist language are to be avoided. The explanation of why the subject can be unaware of certain hidden tendencies then becomes much simpler. It is much more difficult to become conscious of a schema of reaction and its intricate implications than of feelings which are already formed and ready to emerge [pp. 186–187].

TRANSFERENCE AS DISTORTION

Another important difficulty with the concept of transference as it is usually formulated and used in clinical work is that it has been so exclusively focused on distortion. Traditional views on transference have, for the most part, excluded other dimensions of transference. Many analysts, beginning with Freud, have written about distortion (or inappropriateness or both) as a primary or defining property of transference.

Anna Freud (1968), for example, defined the transference as "the distortion of a realistic patient–analyst relationship by additions from past unconscious and repressed object relations" (pp. 95–96). Greenson (1967) states unequivocally that "transference reactions are always inappropriate" (p. 152). In a later publication, Greenson (1971) describes the two outstanding characteristics of transference reaction as: "(1) It is an undiscriminatory non-selective repetition of the past, and (2) It is inappropriate, it ignores or distorts reality" (p. 217).

Freud's concept of transference as distortion by displacement had profound implications for classical theories of the analytic process and for psychoanalytic technique. The analytic situation was believed to promote both the *unfolding* and the expression of transference. The reclining posture, the out-of-sight analyst, and the analyst's relative inactivity were believed to foster the patient's regression and the consequent use of the analyst as a blank screen upon which the patient could project his transferences. The analyst's neutrality and minimizing the contact between the analyst and the patient were thought to facilitate the *emergence* of transferences. I have emphasized the words "emergence" and "unfolding" to describe traditional notions about the development of transference, because these and similar terms have been interpreted to mean that transferences are formed somewhere deep within the patient's psyche, where they are immune from interactional influences.

The working through of the transference entails the patient's recognizing the role played in his attitudes about the analyst or the analytic situation by what he brings to the situation. This is often described as the patient's coming to see how he is distorting the realities about the analyst or the analytic situation, or how the real analytic situation differs from what the patient conceives it to be. Gill (1982a) argues persuasively that it would be more correct to say that the patient develops a hypothesis than that he distorts the actual situation.

Insofar as the present is represented in the transference, it is based on as plausible a reaction to the immediate analytic situation as the patient can muster. The term distortion is an applicable and appropriate designation only for those uncommon instances in which the influences of the past contradict the information in the present (Gill, 1982a).

Gill writes:

A more accurate formulation than "distortion" is that the real situation is subject to interpretations other than the one the patient has reached. The analyst suggests that the patient's conclusions are not unequivocally determined by the real situation. Indeed, seeing the issue in this way rather than as a "distortion" helps prevent the error of assuming some absolute external reality of which the "true" knowledge must be gained [p. 118].

The purpose of the analyst's alertness to distortions and inappropriateness is not to correct or educate the patient, but to allow himself to understand the patient's defenses and needs, which are dictating the patient's constructions (Cooper, 1987). Though attention to distortions and inappropriateness is important, it is not the analyst's task to correct these distortions. It is not the analyst's aim to contradict the patient's view. The so-called reality (or lack of it) of the patient's perceptions and judgments of the analyst is, under most circumstances, neither debated nor confirmed. Most often, reality considerations are opposed to the analyst's stance of sustained empathic inquiry. The patient's views and emotional responses about the analyst serve as points of departure for explicating the meanings and organizing principles that structure the patient's psychic reality. The interactional perspective in the main opposes interpreting transference reactions as distortions of some objective reality known by the analyst but not by the patient.

THE "REAL" RELATIONSHIP, THE THERAPEUTIC ALLIANCE, AND THE WORKING ALLIANCE

Conceiving of transference as a distortion of the present by means of a displacement from the past required the introduction of a number of other concepts to account for patients' abilities to perceive and respond to the realities of the analytic situation. Such concepts as the "therapeutic alliance," the "working alliance," and the "real" relationship were designed to address the realistic and supposedly nontransferential aspects of what occurs in analysis (Zetzel, 1956; Greenson, 1965, 1971; Greenson and Wexler, 1969).

There are two kinds of experiences of the patient that even the most traditionalist advocates of the asocial concept of transference recognize as likely to be responsive to something in the analyst's actual behavior rather than as being solely the expression of the distorting influences of unconscious wishes and phantasies.

The first is the patient's perception of the analyst as basically trustworthy and competent, a part of the patient's experience that Freud (1912b) viewed as the unobjectionable positive transference but that others, such as Sterba (1934), Greenson (1965) and Zetzel (1956), exclude from the realm of transference and designate as the "working alliance" or the "therapeutic alliance." The second is the patient's perception of and response to blatant expressions of the analyst's pathology and harmful countertransference.

According to some traditional views on transference, both of those categories of the patient's experience lie outside the realm of transference and thus are also external to the domain of the patient's irrational ideas and his intrapsychically determined derivatives of unconscious fantasies and memories.

The notion that the working alliance or the therapeutic alliance lies outside the realm of transference and thus is immune from influences from the past such as childhood libidinal wishes and conflicts was not supported by Freud. He viewed transference not only as one of the main resistances to treatment, but also as its indispensable facilitator in the form of what he called the "unobjectionable" positive transference, that is, the sublimated, aim-inhibited, affectionate feelings for the analyst.

The working alliance, or the unobjectionable positive transference, is a facilitator of the analysis when its expressions are sublimated and when the patient does not demand immediate gratification, but rather is content with more symbolic, fantasy gratifications. At such times, the positive transference expressions are more tamed, more adaptive, and make the patient more amenable to reason and self-reflection.

This facilitating transference is just as much a transference, just as much a repetition and a reenactment rather than a conscious memory of the past, as the transference resistance is. It has the same origins in the person's schemata contructed out of past experience. The patient's positive transference, the patient's intense emotional involvement with the analyst, can function both as a resistance and a facilitator at different times and in different contexts.

THE REAL RELATIONSHIP VERSUS THE TRANSFERENCE RELATIONSHIP

The standard theory of transference as distortion explains why some authors such as Greenson (1965, 1971) believe it necessary to distinguish between the transference relationship and the *real relationship*. Greenson's idea of the real relationship encompasses both the patient's accurate perceptions of the benign aspects of the analyst, and his perceptions of the analyst's countertransference difficulties. All object relations, according to Greenson, consist of different admixtures and blendings of real and transference components. According to Greenson, the meaning of "real" in the real relationship (1) implies the sense of being genuine and not synthetic or artificial and (2) means realistic and not inappropriate or fantastic.

Although a systematic discussion of the therapeutic alliance, the working alliance, and the real relationship are beyond the scope of this chapter, I would like to present briefly two criticisms about the ways these terms are being currently used. First, they are often employed to connote or denote something that should be deliberately fostered with special techniques—techniques that are, in my opinion, often opposed to the goals and methods of psychoanalysis. Second, in the psychoanalytic literature, these terms are erroneously used to designate object relations in which there is no transference. The real relationship, the therapeutic alliance, and the working alliance are, according to most definitions, nontransference. Because, in my opinion, transference is ubiquitous and occurs in all object relations, it does not make sense to classify some kinds of object relations as nontransference.

Another troublesome problem is that the concept of the real relationship sets up a dichotomy between reality as correctly perceived (presumably by the analyst) and the distortion of that reality in the form of the transference (presumably by the patient). In contrast to that view is the newer point of view advanced by Gill (1983, 1984, 1986), Hoffman (1983), and others that a relationship is continually and plausibly defined by both parties.

It is not a major goal of the analyst to define what reality is and how it is being distorted, but rather to identify the differing plausible ways in which the analyst and the patient are perceiving and thinking about what is occurring in the analytic situation. The analyst's goal is to consider and to evaluate how each party to the analytic dyad is contributing to the other's experience of that relationship.

Stolorow et al. (1987) also caution against the dangers embedded in the concept of a "real" relationship between analyst and patient, of which the transference is presumed to be a distortion. These dangers reside in the fact that judgments about what is "really true" about the analyst and what is distortion are issues left solely to the discretion of the analyst—hardly a disinterested party. In my supervisory experience, I have found that therapists frequently invoke the concept of distortion when patients' feelings about them, whether denigrating or admiring, contradict the therapists' attitudes and judgments needed for their self-esteem and sense of well-being.

NAIVE REALISM

Only the adherence of Freud and others to the assumptions of naïe realism can account for the remarkable persistence in the analytic literature of the sharp distinction between "accurate" and "distorted" perceptions of interpersonal events.

Analysts who advocate an interactional perspective on transference share a view of reality that differs from that of analysts who adhere to the traditional, asocial concept of transference. The former hold a relativistic, perspectivistic, and constructivistic view of reality. The latter, on the other hand, subscribe to a group of fallacies called naive realism; they see reality as preestablished, given, absolute. Freud's naive realism is embedded in his copy theory of perception and his theories of primary process and cognition. For him, perceptions are veridical copies of reality, and memories are copies of perceptions. A major assumption of naive realism is that all humans from infancy onwards naturally and easily form veridical copies of external reality merely by being exposed to it. The copy theory adds that unconsciously people have objective and veridical knowledge of reality and that distortions of reality are brought about by the distorting powers of drives and defenses.

Freud's theory of transference as distortion probably was constructed in this way. Because, according to naive realism, there is a universal capacity for objective and veridical perception, any differences between the views of two persons of what is going on between them must be caused by the defensive distortion of one of the two parties. If, for example, a patient's view of the analyst differs from the analyst's view, the patient's view would be due to a distortion of reality and brought about by the displacement of feelings and attitudes from a prior relationship.

According to Spence (1985), Freud's discovery of transference was an embarrassment to the proponents of naive realism:

> because what is transference but the realization that reality is not simply "out there," waiting to be described, that what the patient "sees" is often a product of his or her own experience, and that the subject matter of psychoanalysis largely consists in disentangling the different faces of what is apparently observed (i.e., in finding flaws with the positivistic model)? [p. 62].

In spite of the challenge to naive realism posed by the discovery of transference, Freud attempted to retain the assumptions of naive realism in his causal explanatory theories of cognition and in his explanation of transference. The notion of transference as a kind of distortion of reality seemed to provide a way of maintaining his theory intact and dealing with the scientific problems and challenges posed by transference. Because he believed that transference was analyzable, once these transference distortions had been identified and worked through the patient could "see" the analyst as the analyst really was. This dissolution of transference distortions by interpretation was thought to restore to the patient his previously established veridical mental representations.

The concept of naive realism implies the idea of an absolute, preestablished, given reality of what is true or accurate (fact) against which transference distortions (fantasy) could be contrasted. Contemporary writers who advance an interactional view of transference are moving toward a perspectivist and constructivist view of reality, especially of affectively significant and interpersonal reality (e.g., Gill, 1984; Stolorow et al., 1987). From a perspectivist and constructivist point of view, the patient's ideas about the analyst are neither simply veridical and objective nor simply unrealistic fantasy.

Naive realism emphasizes the *discovery* of truths, whereas a constructivist approach emphasizes the *creation* of new truths. There is a growing recognition that new truths are constructed through the interaction and joint efforts of analyst and analysand. "Truth" does not simply exist "out there" waiting to be discovered. It is created, and therefore interpretation becomes a creative act.

If we accept the idea that the analytic experience can be both real and illusory at the same time, the distinction between transference and nontransference is no longer meaningful or useful.

THE ANALYST AS A BLANK SCREEN

The asocial quality of earlier views on transference is perhaps epitomized and symbolized in the notion that the analyst serves as a blank screen for the patient. The psychoanalytic literature is replete with attacks on the blank screen idea, on the idea that the analyst is not accurately perceived by the analysand as a real person, but that he serves instead as a screen or mirror to whom various feelings, motives, and attitudes can be attributed. Adherence to the assumptions of naive realism is largely responsible for the previously standard view that these attributions of transference are distortions of reality.

In his review of the literature, Hoffman (1983) finds that the blank screen concept has been pronounced dead and laid to rest many times over the past 35 years. He classifies the critiques of the blank screen concept into two main categories: conservative critiques and radical critiques. Conservative critiques retain the notion that a crucial aspect of the patient's experience of the therapist—the transference—has no relation to the therapist's actual behaviors and attitudes. On the other hand, analysts who share Hoffman's perspective hold that the analyst's attitudes and behaviors do, indeed, influence and contribute to the patient's transference.

The notion that ideally the analyst functions like a blank screen applies only to that part of the patient's total experience of the therapist which is viewed as transference. The remainder, the supposedly nontransference part, is, as we noted earlier, the "real relationship," the "therapeutic alliance," or the "working alliance." By not altering the standard paradigm for defining what is or what is not realistic in the analytic situation, conservative critiques of the blank screen fallacy always end up perpetuating that very fallacy.

Stone (1961), for example, though a conservative critic of the blank screen concept, adheres to the dichotomy of transference and reality:

> "Transference" [is] that aspect or fraction of a relationship which is motivated by persistent unmodified wishes (or other attitudes) toward an actual important personage of the past, which tend to invest a current individual in a sort of misidentification with the unconscious image of the past personage [p. 66].

Radical critiques of the blank screen notion provide cogent arguments for rejecting the dichotomy between transference as distortion of the present by the influence of the past and nontransference as based on current reality. In their view, transference reactions always have a significant basis in here-and-now interactions with the analyst.

Radical critiques of the asocial or blank screen concept are relatively scarce among classical Freudian analysts; they include Sandler (1976a) and Gill (1983, 1984, 1986). Among the Kleinians are Racker (1968) and Heimann (1950). Neo-Sullivanians, whose work leans toward an interactional view of transference and the analytic situation, include Feiner (1979) and Levenson (1972, 1981). Other major proponents to this point of view include Hoffman (1983), Searles (1979), Wachtel (1980), Stolorow and Lachmann (1985), and Stolorow et al. (1987).

CONCLUDING COMMENTS

The revised views of transference advocated here imply a shift to the stance that the analyst is a participant–observer rather than merely an observer. They also imply a sharp, decisive step away from the view of the analytic situation as objectively and realistically definable by the analyst to a constructivist and perspectivistic view of the reality of the analytic situation as defined by the progressive elucidation of the manner in which the situation is experienced by the patient.

An interactional conception of the transference entails, in turn, an altered handling of it. Rather than seeing transference manifestations as having their *only* roots in the past, and being therefore distortions of present perceptions, an analyst might now look first to the current interaction with a patient to see what in it might be plausibly construed by the patient as if it were the same as, or the repetition of, an earlier relationship pattern. It is essential to the analysis of transference reactions to examine in detail the analyst–analysand interactions that evoke them, because transference reactions become intelligible through elucidating and comprehending the *meanings* that these events acquire by virtue of their assimilation to the patient's interpersonal schemas. Unless the analyst acknowledges the role of his own behavior in evoking the patient's reaction, the patient's ability to accept and use the analyst's interpretation will be severely limited.

From the view that the transference is a result of the interaction between the analyst and the patient, it follows that the transference is ubiquitous throughout the analysis. Therefore, analysts need not do anything to develop or create the transference. They should, however, be alert to and interpret, where it is feasible, the patient's resistances to experiencing or expressing transference reactions.

Both the classical and the Kleinian psychoanalytic theories emphasize the intrapsychic and minimize what is variously called the interactional, interpersonal, social, situational, and contextual determinants of behavior. Interactional and intrapsychic factors are not totally separate from one another. There is a fluid and mutually determinative line between "inner" and "outer" worlds. For example, the psychodynamics of the fate neurotic play a causal role in arranging the current environment to which he then reacts. Also one should bear in mind that the neurotic's psychodynamics, like the psychodynamics of everyone else, are a function of still earlier interactions between personality and environment.

Moreover, the two kinds of determinants mutually influence each other. Intrapsychic dispositions determine selective attention to those aspects of the external world that conform to the person's expectations. Also, people behave in such a way as to increase the likelihood that the responses they meet will indeed confirm their expectations. Any genuinely integrated and comprehensive psychoanalytic theory should recognize that behavior is always a resultant of both preexisting intrapsychic determinants and situational, contextual, and interpersonal determinants.

Psychoanalysts holding the asocial, traditional concept of transference believe that the intrapsychic realm is the only one in which analytic expertise applies, and that emphasis on the interpersonal leads to dilution of analytic work, to excessive intrusions of the analyst into the patient's life, or a shallow corrective emotional experience.

The unfortunate attitude persists among many psychoanalysts that the interpersonal interaction is a troublesome interference and complication. To emphasize it either in the general theory or in the theory of technique in particular arouses uneasiness and an apprehension that an interactional perspective will nullify the unique contribution of psychoanalysis to intrapsychic psychology. Intrapsychic and interpersonal are not antithetical, and a truly comprehensive and integrated psychoanalytic theory must consider both.

The terms "social," "interpersonal," or "object relations" do not connote something superficial or readily observable from "outside" or something nonintrapsychic or pertaining only to conscious experience, the pejorative connotations that these terms have unfortunately acquired for many classical analysts. An interactional point of view of the analytic situation, and thus of transference and countertransference, takes into consideration reciprocal conscious, preconscious, and unconscious responses and communications in both participants. The analyst's interactional approach helps provide a safe place for patients to express, understand, and work through their transferences.

CHAPTER 11

Self-Fulfilling Prophecies and the Repetition Compulsion
An Interactional Perspective

The major focus of this chapter is on an in-depth examination of the significance of self-fulfilling prophesies in social transactions and in interpersonal relations such as the analytic dyad. A self-fulfilling prophecy is an expectation or prediction that causes the expected or predicted event to be enacted and thus confirms its own accuracy. For example, if someone assumes that he will be treated by others in a hostile way, he often may, because of this expectation, behave in such an overly sensitive, suspicious, and provocative manner that he will often bring about the very hostility in others that to him "proves" again his firmly entrenched conviction.

One's behavior patterns and psychopathology are often sustained and reinforced by the responses one's self-fulfilling prophecies unconsciously evoke in others. An interactional perspective on repetitive maladaptive behavior patterns thus provides a new and testable explanatory hypothesis for the nature of the repetition compulsion.

We are not passive observers of our respective social and interpersonal worlds, but active forces in shaping and regulating our interpersonal and social relations. In interpersonal situations, a person's attitudes, transferences, communications, and expectancies of the other person often contain a self-fulfilling prophecy. For example, a person's expectation of meeting a friendly response from another person is linked with the kinds of behaviors, such as nonverbal communications, that tend to evoke friendly responses. The predominantly unconscious interpersonal actions and communications that result from a self-fulfilling prophecy produce the requisite conditions for the occurrence of the expected event and in this sense *create* a reality that would not have otherwise occurred. It is this important insight that traditional psychoanalysis often ignores, postulating instead a wholly internal drive or regulatory principle for maintaining intrapsychic patterns without significant reference to the world external to the psyche.

Many, if not all, aspects of the enactment of self-fulfilling prophecies in interpersonal and social relations occur at a preconscious or unconscious level for the participants. Sometimes, however, self-fulfilling prophecies in an interpersonal context can be used deliberately and with a specific, conscious intent. Two examples are illustrative: matchmaking and gaslighting.

Matchmakers in patriarchal societies had the challenging task of arousing a mutual attraction in two young people who probably cared little for each other. The matchmaker's procedure was to talk with the young man alone and ask him whether he had not noticed how the girl often secretly watched him. In a similar way, he would inform the girl that the boy was persistently looking at her when her head was turned. By thus awakening a mutual interest in the two young people, the matchmaker could quickly manipulate the fulfillment of a prophecy of the couple's compatibility.

Gaslighting, a type of projective identification that took its name from the movie "Gaslight," involves both the prophecy that someone will be driven mad and the use of ingenious manipulations to attain that nefarious purpose. In gaslighting, one person engenders mental confusion, even psychosis, in another person by attacking or discrediting the other person's judgment and perceptions. In some cases, the person doing the gaslighting may not be aware of any intention of evoking confusion in another person or that his verbal attacks on the person's perceptions have damaging effects on the mental functioning of another person (Dorpat, 1985).

Self-fulfilling prophecies in interpersonal and social situations can have constructive as well as destructive effects. The self-fulfilling prophecy probably accounts for the therapeutic effectiveness of placebos. Though the chemical substance in a placebo may be inert and therefore without pharmacological effect, its administration may, depending on the relationship between the caretaker and the patient, have demonstrable therapeutic effects. The claim of a physician who administers a placebo that it is an effective, newly developed medicine and the patient's willingness to believe in its effectiveness may create a reality in which the claim actually becomes a fact.

The destructive effects of some types of self-fulfilling prophecies may be observed in cases of what the physiologist Walter Cannon (1942) described as "Voodoo Death." He reported the clinical findings in a number of mysterious, sudden, and scientifically difficult to explain deaths that followed curses, evil spells, malevolent incantations, or the breaking of moral taboos. More recent clinical studies support Cannon's findings and conclusions about the lethal effects of such spells and curses in certain cultures (Jones, 1974).

Similar ideas referring to the effects of such "unscientific" factors as simple expectations and assumptions in the sciences are abundant in the scientific and philosophic literature. Watzlawick (1984) quotes Einstein's remark to Heisenberg: "It is the theory that determines what we can observe." Heisenberg (1958) himself said, "We have to remember that what we observe is not nature in itself, but nature exposed to our method of questioning" (p. 94).

THE "OEDIPUS EFFECT":
THE CONTRIBUTION OF KARL POPPER

In the Greek myth, the oracle prophesied that Oedipus would kill his father and marry his mother and thus played a most important role in the sequence of events that led to the fulfillment of its prophecy. Terrified by this prediction, which he believed to be true, Oedipus tried to protect himself from the impending doom, but his precautions and safeguards themselves led to the seemingly inescapable fulfillment of the oracle's prediction.

According to the philosopher Karl Popper (1957), the idea that a prediction may influence the predicted event is a very old one. Oedipus killed his father, whom he had never seen, as the direct result of the prophecy that had caused his father to abandon him. Popper suggests the name *"Oedipus effect"* for the influence of the prediction on the unpredicted event.

For a time, Popper (1974) thought that the existence of the Oedipus effect distinguished the social from the natural sciences. But then he noted that in biology—even in molecular biology—expectations often play a role in bringing about what has been expected.

CONTRIBUTIONS OF ROBERT MERTON

The self-fulfilling prophecy has been widely recognized in the psychological and social sciences since the time of the sociologist Robert Merton's (1948) classic paper, "The Self-Fulfilling Prophecy."

Merton describes what happened to a successful and solvent bank when rumors of insolvency and the resultant rush of withdrawals by depositors actually caused the bank to become insolvent. Another example from the financial world is the contagious shifts of stock prices that are fueled by supposedly authoritative "predictions" of indeterminate validity. And, Merton explains, the powerful social dynamics of the self-fulfilling prophecy go far toward explaining the dynamics of ethnic and racial conflict.

In the realm of international security, there are many examples of escalating cycles in which the attribution of hostile intentions to a potential adversary induces one country to increase its preparedness for war. These preparations for war have the effect—often unintended and usually undesired—of decreasing the security of other nations and thereby pressuring them, too, into an arms race.

Merton (1948) writes:

> The self-fulfilling prophecy is, in the beginning, a *false* definition of the situation evoking a new behavior which makes the originally false conception come *true*. The specious validity of the self-fulfilling prophecy perpetuates a reign of error. For the prophet will cite the actual course of events as proof that he was right from the very beginning [p. 195].

Although the effects of self-fulfilling prophecies in interpersonal and social situations are powerful, Merton believes it is possible to break the tragic and often vicious circle of self-fulfilling prophecies. The initial definition of a situation that has set the vicious circle in motion needs to be abandoned. Only when the original assumption is questioned and a new definition of the situation is introduced does the consequent flow of events give the lie to the assumption. Only then does the belief no longer father the reality.

Merton (1948) explains:

> *The self-fulfilling prophecy, whereby fears are translated into reality, operates only in the absence of deliberate institutional controls.* And it is only with the rejection of social fatalism implied in the notion of unchangeable human nature that the tragic circle of fear, social disaster, reinforced fear can be broken [p. 210].

The invented or constructed reality of someone's prophecy will become the "actual" reality only if the invention is believed. Everyday experience teaches us that only a few prophecies are self-fulfilling, because only when a prophecy is believed and seen as a fact can it have an actual effect on the present and thereby fulfill itself. This simple fact has far-reaching implications for psychotherapy because one of the major therapeutic strategies of insight therapy is assisting the patient, through interpretations, to disbelieve his own and others' destructive self-fulfilling prophecies. With a better understanding of self-fulfilling prophecies, our ability to transcend them grows. A prophecy or a prediction that we know to be only that can no longer fulfill itself. Building on similar reflections about the role of prophecies in human relations, the mathematician Howard (1967) formulated his *existential axiom*, which maintains that "if an individual becomes 'aware' of a theory concerning his behavior, he is no longer bound by it but is free to disobey it."

THE CONTRIBUTIONS OF SOCIAL PSYCHOLOGY

Social psychologists have used the concept of self-fulfilling prophecy since Rosenthal and Jacobson's (1968) classic studies. Rosenthal and Jacobson's experiments involved more than 650 primary school students, with 18 women teachers. The self-fulfilling prophecy was created in the faculty members at the beginning of the school year by telling the teachers that an intelligence test administered to the students could not only measure intelligence quotients, but could also identify that 20% of the students who would make superior and rapid intellectual progress in the ensuing school year. Although the allegedly superior students were randomly chosen, IQ testing at the the end of the school year revealed that in fact they did better than the students who had not been designated earlier in the year as superior. Reports of the faculty also proved, furthermore, that these children distinguished themselves from their fellow students by their behavior, intellectual curiosity, friendliness, and so on.

The findings of this study are important not merely because they show teachers were able to influence students, but also because the teachers, operating with an incorrect hypothesis, behaved in such a way as to confirm the hypothesis. The teachers created a situation in which the students indeed did perform better by objective measures, even though the teachers were unaware that they had done anything special to create this state of affairs. What occurred first in the Rosenthal and Jacobson experiment and later in others like it was the essence of the self-fulfilling prophecy. Before carrying out these experiments with grade school students and their teachers, Rosenthal (1966) reported a similar experiment with rats that was replicated and confirmed by many investigators in the following years. Subsequent research work with both humans as well as animals has supported the findings and conclusions of Rosenthal's studies (Jones, R. A., 1974; Jones, E. E., 1986).

Over 25 years ago, scientists were amazed by experimental findings suggesting that information stored in a worm's ribonucleic acid (RNA) could be directly transferred to other worms. To transfer the RNA, McConnell et al. (1961) fed untrained worms the ground up bodies of successfully trained fellow worms. An uproar among scientists ensued when worms provided with such food actually turned out to be much more easily and quickly trained than did worms fed a different diet. Alas, the euphoria lasted only briefly; further experiments, conducted under more rigorous controls, were inconclusive. Serious doubts arose among scientists regarding the transferability of worm intelligence through the ingestion of ground worm meat.

Watzlawick (1984) advances the intriguing hypothesis that the results obtained by McConnell et al. (1961) were caused by self-fulfilling prophecies, similar to those in the experiments of Cordaro and Ison (1963), whose laboratory subjects were earthworms (planaria). Because planaria are the most primitive form of life possessing the rudiments of a brain, the researchers assumed that these worms were capable of being trained at the simplest level, for instance, to change direction (to the right or to the left) upon arriving at the crossbeam of a T-shaped grooved track.

Cordaro and Ison induced experimenters to believe the false idea that they were training one group of particularly intelligent animals and another group of especially incapable worms. From the conviction of the experimenters, there developed objectively discernible and statistically significant differences in the experimental behaviors between the allegedly more intelligent planaria and the other worms. The results of this study on the effects of self-fulfilling prophecies on the training of worms were essentially the same as those we previously noted in the experiments conducted by Rosenthal and others on humans and rats.

Rosenthal's experiments are only one example of how deeply and incisively human beings can be affected by the expectations and communications of others. Such investigations indicate the significance of both conscious and unconscious interpersonal interactions in shaping the form and the content of a person's responses.

SELF-FULFILLING PROPHECIES
IN CHILD DEVELOPMENT

What Rosenthal and other social psychologists described as occurring in the teacher–child relationship applies even more powerfully and profoundly in parent–child relations. Over time, parents' conscious and unconscious communications of their expectations, predictions, and assumptions about their children may powerfully shape and mold the child's psychic development. The actualization of the parents' expectations for their children's development may have destructive as well as constructive consequences. Investigations first performed by Johnson and discussed in Kanzer's (1957) panel report demonstrated how children could be unconsciously induced by their parents to act out their parents' disavowed antisocial or perverse impulses. What Winnicott called the "false self" is often the end product of the self-fulfilling prophecies contained in the projective identifications of the parents onto their children.

There is some protection for adults against the results of self-fulfilling prophecies. Psychoanalytic treatment, for example, can help patients master and detoxify the destructive effects of others' projective identifications by enabling the patients to *disidentify* with what has been projected onto them (Dorpat, 1985). And, of course, prophecies become self-fulfilling only when they are believed. Disidentification and disbelief, however, are not available to small children because such defenses are developmentally beyond their cognitive capacities. Therefore, self-fulfilling prophecies and other types of projective identification have even more powerfully enduring and sometimes chronically traumatic effects on children than they do on adults.

THE UNCONSCIOUS EFFECTS OF EXPECTATIONS IN INTERPERSONAL SITUATIONS

It has long been known that people often see what they expect to see and that they frequently select evidence that confirms their own expectations and stereotypes while ignoring information contrary to their expectations. Strong expectancies often shape the way information about another person is perceived and processed.

Research in recent decades (e.g., Rosenthal, 1966; Rosenthal and Jacobson, 1968; Cordaro and Ison, 1963) indicates that strong expectations do more than affect what one perceives. These studies show that *expectancies cause people to act in ways that elicit behavior in others that is interpretable as confirming those expectancies* (Jones, 1986). In other words, expectancies or self-fulfilling prophecies produce, through predominantly unconscious interactions between two or more persons, behaviors that tend to confirm the original expectation or prophecy.

The following account summarize Jones's (1986) example about how expectancies tend to elicit in others the expected behavior. Let us suppose that the subject expects the object to be a friendly person. The object's behavior is ambiguous; it *could* be seen as friendly. The subject's expectancy of friendly behavior is strengthened by perceptual confirmation; feeling encouraged, the subject begins to behave in a warm, friendly manner toward the object. The object, in turn, responds to the subject in a warm, friendly manner. The subject's expectation or prophecy about the object is further strengthened by behavioral confirmation (for example, "I was right. He really is friendly"). There may also be a further interaction in which the object has a self-concept change ("I really am a friendly person").

Ideas such as those advanced by Jones and other social psychologists are congruent with what psychoanalysts have written about projective identification to construct an interactional explanation for what was first called the "repetition compulsion" by Freud (1920).

SELF-FULFILLING PROPHECIES AND THE REPETITION COMPULSION

There are few credible and coherent theories about the repetition compulsion, and only a handful of analysts or scientists accept Freud's biological explanatory hypothesis about a death instinct. The facts as first summarized and discussed by Freud (1920) in *Beyond the Pleasure Principle* are indisputable. He described posttraumatic dreams—dreams that repeat the anguishing effects and memories of some life-threatening trauma. He also told about a game invented by his infant grandson in which the baby threw a spool out of his crib and retrieved with a string. The repetitive playing of this game, Freud postulated, constituted the child's effort to master his physical separations from his mother. At various times he also described other manifestations of the repetition compulsion (Freud, 1933). These behaviors did not make sense from the point of view of either the pleasure principle or the reality principle.

An interactional perspective provides a partial answer to some unsolved questions and problems concerning the repetition compulsion. In my view, social or interactional elements play a much greater role in the formation, and especially the maintenance, of psychopathology than many mental health professionals believe.

Before going into the details about this interactional theory concerning the repetition compulsion, let us briefly review Freudian concepts about the three principles of mental functioning: the pleasure principle, the reality principle, and the repetition compulsion. Psychoanalysts have since Freud's time used the word "principle" to mean a basic trend that regulates mental functioning. At first, Freud (1900) described the human organism's need to avoid unpleasure as a basic motivation. In his writings after 1900 he called this first principle the pleasure principle, but he still emphasized its negative meaning. A primary need and motivation of the psyche is the need to avoid unpleasure, especially anxiety.

The pleasure principle is not enough, however, to insure survival or safety in a hostile world. An organism must find ways not only of avoiding unpleasure but also of maintaining survival and satisfaction in the real world. Hence, Freud (1911, 1915c) also posited a reality principle. His reality principle, however, does not imply deposing the pleasure principle; it, rather, safeguards it. A momentary pleasure, whose consequences are uncertain, is temporarily abandoned, but only in order to gain a more certain and safe pleasure at a later time.

With the pleasure principle and the reality principle Freud thought (as of 1911) that he had arrived at a comprehensive theory of motivation, and he believed he could classify human activities (such as fantasying, religion, science, education, art, dreams, and the like) according to the proportion they had of these two kinds of cognition and these two orientations to reality.

Clinical experience, especially his contacts with soldiers in World War I suffering from traumatic neuroses, indicated that his two-level concept of motivation was not enough. Under certain circumstances, people seem deliberately though unconsciously to seek experiences linked with unpleasure, and all those situations appear to have something to do with repetition. People suffering from psychic trauma, for instance, dream of the original, disturbing experience over and over again. Children repeat in play (such as the doctor game) painful experiences. In the analytic situation, Freud observed that his patients transferred onto him earlier painful and disappointing experiences with their parents.

Freud concluded that the compulsion to repeat was part of a general tendency in all living things to return to an earlier state, ultimately the earliest, inorganic state of nonlife or death. Freud (1920) thus posited a principle opposed to the pleasure principle, one seeking not just equilibrium but zero excitation—a *death instinct*. Few other analysts, with the notable exception of Melanie Klein and some French analysts, have found much evidence or usefulness for the hypothesis of a death instinct. The explanatory hypothesis for the compulsion to repeat proposed here is an interactional one, constructed with the concepts of self-fulfilling prophecies and projective identification. The dynamic explanation rests on the unconscious interactional dynamics of what may be called vicious circles of certain interpersonal transactions.

UNCONSCIOUS INTERACTIONAL DYNAMICS IN VICIOUS CIRCLES

In interpersonal situations, vicious circles occur when the self-fulfilling prophecies and expectations of the first party in an interaction evoke responses from the second party that confirm the prophecies and thus reinforce the first party's psychopathology. In such interactions, each person tends unconsciously to elicit in the other person behaviors that are complementary to his own behavior. For example, one person's sadistic behavior is likely to elicit masochistic behavior in a second person, who, by behaving masochistically, completes the vicious circle by evoking sadistic behavior in the first person.

If others' feedback to a patient could be altered, this would make possible and provide the environmental conditions necessary for disconfirming the patient's prophecies and changing the patient's behavior. But what often prevents both structural change and insight in analysis and in everyday life is that, in fact, the feedback from others is not very likely to change, because the evocative aspects of a person's behavior tend to bring forth the same responses in other persons again and again.

As Wachtel (1987) puts it, every neurosis requires accomplices. Without the feedback from others that intentionally or unintentionally supports or strengthens existing patterns of behavior, changes in neurotically based attitudes and perceptions of self and others could occur. For example, the shy, inhibited young man who tells himself that women are not likely to be interested in him and who fears that he is not handsome or dynamic enough is likely to approach women in an awkward, hesitant manner that evokes responses in women that seem to confirm his views that he is not adequately appealing.

WHAT ARE THE MOTIVES UNDERLYING REPETITION COMPULSION PHENOMENA?

In other words, why do individuals keep doing the same thing over and over again even though what they are doing is not only maladaptive and unrealistic but causes them emotional misery and psychic pain? I believe there are two basic kinds of needs and motives related to those needs that energize the actions and behaviors regulated by the repetition compulsion principle. The first type of needs and motives is linked with the preservation of the subject's identity or self; the second is related to those needs for maintaining selfobjects or other kinds of need-fulfilling object relationships.

Lichtenstein (1977) proposes the term "identity principle" as a substitute for the death instinct. He suggests that

> the capacity to maintain or hold on to an identity is a fundamental characteristic of all living organisms, one to which we refer when we think of "self-preservation" and "self-reproduction." Animals and children deprived of identity maintenance simply die. Hence it is more than an ego function, more even than a drive. Like the death instinct, it overrides the pleasure principle. . . . Thus identity establishment and maintenance can be considered basic biological principles—principles defining the concept of living matter itself. Such an identity principle would be stronger than desire or the drive for pleasure [p. 114].

In the view of Lichtenstein, "repetitive doing"—the very phenomenon Freud sought to explain by the death instinct—serves the biological function of safeguarding the sameness within change that is identity.

The need to repeat certain interpersonal relations as well as painful ego states may be partly explained by the need to maintain a sense of safety by safeguarding one's identity. Siegel (1988) describes patients who at one phase of their analyses tried to heal themselves and complete their body images by their hypochondriacal concerns. Her inspired and novel hypothesis that her patients needed these hypochondriacal states to feel their body boundaries shows a rare understanding of a basic regulatory function of certain intensely disturbing affects and somatic sensations. What she writes about hypochondriacal states holds true also for some other types of highly unpleasurable or even painful states, including some chronic masochistic behaviors and what has been called an "addiction" to painful states.

A masochistic borderline patient who was "addicted" to emotionally painful object relations explained why he persisted in provoking punishment from significant others, including his analyst. He said, "Pain is better than nothing." In childhood and also later in adult life, he preferred punitive people, like his tyrannical father, to people like his schizoid mother, who usually ignored him. Emotionally as well as physically painful interpersonal relations of the kind he first had with his father and later with others helped him to preserve his self–other and body boundaries and maintain his fragile sense of personal identity. Painful feelings helped him to feel real. People addicted to painful states unconsciously prefer feeling states of pain, unpleasure, and even anxiety to states of nothingness, deadness, and emptiness. For infants, a bad or painful mother is better than no mother.

In addition to the need for the maintenance of identity, there is another, more or less unconscious interactional dynamic and complex of motives and affects underlying repetition compulsion phenomena. Unconscious conflicts over object loss and loss of love and the defenses against such conflicts are some of the more important reasons why some individuals become victims of the self-fulfilling prophecies and projective identifications of others.

Why is it that so many persons believe the negative prophecies and predictions of others with the result that the prophecies become self-fulfilling? There is a consensus in the literature that one of the most powerful unconscious motives for sustaining the vicious circles in these pathological symbiotic patterns of relatedness is the participants' anxieties and fears over object loss. (For further discussion of these points see Chapter 12.)

The therapeutic task when patients have identified with or introjected the pathological projective identifications of others is first to assist the patients in recognizing that they have identified with what has been projected upon them and, second, to help them to work through resistances against *disidentifying* with these pathological projective identifications. Similarly, to free themselves from the enslaving and pathogenic power of others' self-fulfilling prophecies, patients must learn to *disbelieve* the prophecies. As mentioned earlier, the expectations and prophecies of others have no influence or pathological effects if the person does not believe them.

INTERACTIONAL SOURCES OF RAGE REACTIONS

The following case vignette illustrates our proposed theory about the role of interactional dynamics in the maintenance of psychopathology. The standard psychoanalytic view is that rage reactions stem from deep and early sources, from internal instincts in the distant past. An interactional perspective adds to that view the contributions made to rage formation by a person's here-and-now interactions with others, and it helps us to understand the role of such interactions in sustaining and reinforcing the patient's psychopathology.

The Woman Who Could Not Say No

A 27-year-old analytic patient had a history of unhappy and disappointing affairs with men. When I say that she "could not say no," I mean it both in the specific sexual sense and in a broader sense to mean that she seldom declined giving to men whatever it was that they wanted of her. Sexual desire played a negligible role in her quasi-promiscuous behavior. Her too easy sexual surrenders were just one aspect of a larger and pervasive difficulty in maintaining her boundaries in the face of another person's desires or needs. She was often masochistic in her relations with men; for a time when she was a senior in college she lived with a man who physically beat her.

After a year of analysis, the analyst and the patient began to discern a pattern in her interactions with her lovers and a repeated sequence of events in her ultimately unhappy if not tragic experiences, which ended with bitter quarrels and the traumatizing breakup of the relationship. Initially she would give herself, her body, her time, and even certain vital ego functions (such as judgment and decision making) over to the man by "losing herself" in him. This meant abandoning her own needs and wishes at the same time that she paid vigilant attention to recognizing and gratifying the desires of her lover. She was defensively self-effacing and compliant, and she characteristically would sacrifice her own needs and pursuits in her efforts to care for and please her lovers.

She was so completely unassertive and subservient that men would begin to take advantage of her and even abuse her. Her frustrations and angry feelings over the slights and abuses she received from men were covered over with reaction formations and masochistic defenses. While her outward behavior appeared excessively nice and self-abasing, her free associations, her dreams, and her inadvertent actions all suggested that behind her polite and even servile façade lay aggressive and rageful impulses.

The false calm of this early stage in her relationships with these men would be shattered when she became jealous of her lover's actual or imagined attentions to some other woman. Uncontrolled episodes of jealous rage and heated quarrels would soon lead to the dissolution of the relationship.

Let us take a look at the interactional aspects of her self-sacrificing attitude and her masochistic compliance with men. Such an interactional perspective allows us to examine the woman's current life for some of the sources of her rage. If we observe how others (including her analyst) react to the unconscious communications and social cues embedded in her behavior, we can discover how she unconsciously provokes others to exploit, deprive, and disparage her. The way she leads her life and relates to men is guaranteed to generate rage, even as she continues to find the rage unacceptable.

Over and over again, she creates circumstances in her relations with men in which her own desires are overridden, her own interests are sacrificed, and her own efforts at self-expression curtailed, inhibited, or suspended. These predominantly self-imposed frustrations generate intense affects of anger and rage, which, in turn, trigger her reaction formations and masochistic defenses.

Her defenses and inhibitions against rage and self-assertiveness stem from unconscious pathogenic ideas, such as her fears of losing the men on whom she depends. Therefore, the rageful impulses she strictly defends against—whatever their infantile, childhood, or instinctual sources—are the paradoxical products of the very defenses constructed to defend against them (Wachtel, 1987). A whole class of aggressive and self-assertive impulses are defended against by her self-sacrificing and masochistic defenses, but these defensive operations include ways in which she unconsciously provokes others to depreciate her and to exploit her. Thus, her *defenses against anger and rage are themselves important causes of her rage.* Impulse leads to defense, defense leads to impulse, and the vicious circle keeps maintaining itself both within this patient's psyche as well as in her interpersonal relations.

Obviously, my emphasis on her current interpersonal relations gives a one-sided picture and leaves out important genetic and developmental elements. My aim is not to discount such childhood factors or the unconscious conflicts arising from them, but to highlight the previously neglected role of her current interactions with others in sustaining both her rage and her defenses against the rage.

Staff at psychiatric facilities who manage repetitively aggressive patients may unwittingly encourage a cyclical and self-perpetuating process of aggression and counteraggression. In this cycle, the hospitalized patient's acts of aggression evoke emotions of fear and anger, as well as protective responses, on the part of the staff. The patient is restrained and then secluded. It is well known that extended periods of seclusion and isolation can exacerbate psychotic symptomatology, self-abusive behavior, and aggression. In such instances, such methods as restraint, social isolation, and seclusion used to manage the aggressive patient tend to promote more aggressiveness.

INTERACTIONAL ELEMENTS IN THE
MAINTENANCE OF OEDIPAL CONFLICTS

Wachtel (1987) argues convincingly for considering interactional elements both in the instigation and the maintenance of psychopathology. Suppose, he suggests, one sees in a particular patient evidence for a strong unresolved oedipal conflict, such as an unconscious longing for a sexual union with the chaste, caretaking mother, and anxiety as a result of such forbidden impulses. Suppose also that, as is commonly the case, there are difficulties such as impotence in the patient's sexual life. Though one could correctly understand the patient's sexual problem as a function of an unresolved oedipal conflict, this explanation is only a partial one because it omits consideration of causally efficacious interpersonal interactions in his current life.

In contrast to the classical psychoanalytic view, an interactional perspective considers the patient's oedipal conflicts not as persisting in spite of how the patient currently lives, but as a *result* of precisely how he is currently living and what feedback he is currently receiving from other persons. The unconscious communications the patient sends as a result of his conflict—that is, his verbal and nonverbal messages and overt actions— lead to consequences that feed back in such a way as to intensify his longings for a fantasied figure who is pure, all-giving, all-protecting, nurturant, and larger than life.

The object relations point of view advanced here takes into account both the patient's predispositions and the interpersonal causes of the patient's behavior. It is on the basis of learned perceptions and learned responses to past experiences that one tends to relate to others in ways that evoke responses that confirm one's expectations and prophecies of the other person's responses.

Learned reactions to childhood conflicts and anxieties play an important role in *starting* a sexually inhibited patient of the kind just described on a pathway in which restrictions and anxious interactions with women are characteristic of his sexual encounters. Once the pattern is started, however, the disturbing and disappointing responses of his sexual partners to the patient's anxious, constricted, or insensitive actions begin to have feedback effects on the neurotic process. These effects tend to confirm his apprehension and conflicts about his sexual experiences and therefore lead him again to approach sex fearfully and once more induce the experiences that confirm his anxieties yet again.

The interactional perspective shares much with the traditional intrapsychic model, but it also differs in important ways. Both emphasize the central significance of unconscious processes, and both hold that early experiences have a major role in shaping later personality. There is a substantial difference between the classical psychoanalytic view, which postulates that many of the most important processes influencing personality functioning are sealed off from influence by current environmental input, and the view presented here, which treats what is currently going in the person's interactions with others as playing a critical role in the subject's unconscious psychic processes.

SELF-FULFILLING PROPHECIES
IN PROJECTIVE IDENTIFICATION

Many, perhaps all, projective identifications contain a self-fulfilling prophecy. For example, paranoid patients often have real as well as imaginary or delusional enemies, and their disturbed interpersonal relations are to a marked degree products of their own expectations and projective identifications. These patients characteristically tend to evoke in others the selfsame aggressive attitudes and hostile emotions that they expect from and attribute to others.

Most persons are unaware that their own projective identifications evoke in others affects and behaviors that confirm their expectations and create self-fulfilling prophecies. For example, the hostile and driven man-on-the-make who tells himself that everyone is out for himself and that no one can be trusted is likely to find that experience confirms this expectation; but he does not realize how his own behavior toward others evokes antagonistic and competitive attitudes in other people. The same persons who persistently try to compete with him and take advantage of his every weakness are capable of acting quite differently with others who have established a more friendly relationship with them and who evoke a different set of emotional reactions.

In Chapter 12 I describe three stages in the process of projective identification. The second stage is the one in which the subject manipulates the object in some way to conform with his projections, and this is done with predominantly unconscious communications designed to make the prophecy self-fulfilling. Through any one or several of a wide variety of interpersonal pressures and manipulations of the object, the subject attempts to *actualize* his projections, expectations, and prophecies.

MUTUAL PROJECTIVE IDENTIFICATION

As described in Chapter 12, the third stage in the process of projective identification is the response of the recipient of the projective identification. There are, of course, a number of possible normal and pathological responses of the recipient. A therapist, for example, who can "contain" (Bion, 1967) or "metabolize" (Kernberg, 1976) what has been evoked in him, may detoxify what has been projected onto him and respond with a therapeutic intervention. In everyday life, however, one of the most frequent and typical types of response is one in which the recipient reacts to another person's projective identification with another projective identification, thus bringing about what Langs (1978a) calls a Type B communicative field or what may also be termed "mutual projective identification" (Dorpat, 1985).

Watzlawick (1984) describes a common type of marital conflict involving mutual projective identification. In this type of situation, each party assumes the conflict to be basically the other's fault, while his or her own behavior is seen only as a *reaction* to that of the partner. The wife complains that her husband is withdrawing from her. He admits withdrawing, but he sees this as the only possible reaction to her constant nagging. She views his withdrawn behavior as the *cause* of her nagging. The vicious cycle in their interaction can be summarized in this way: her nagging evokes his withdrawal, which, in turn, triggers her nagging and so on and on.

Both partners in this marital conflict have constructed two contradictory realities and two self-fulfilling prophecies. By his withdrawal behaviors (e.g., silence, turning his back on her, walking away), he unconsciously manipulates his wife to fulfill his prophecy that she is a nag. Similarly, her nagging effectively provokes his withdrawal behaviors and thereby confirms her expectations of his unavailability.

Most often the dynamically important aspects of projective identification and self-fulfilling prophecies are unconscious for both subject and object. In the example described by Watzlawick, both marital partners correctly identify the behaviors in the other party (such as nagging and withdrawal) that evoke their own responses. However, both parties defensively disavow their own contribution to their turbulent interactions. The husband denies that his withdrawal behaviors evoke his wife's criticisms; and the wife is defensively oblivious to the role her nagging plays in eliciting her husband's withdrawal.

SELF-FULFILLING PROPHECIES AND
TRANSFERENCE

From the study of such self-fulfilling prophecies and vicious circles as just described, one can gain a picture of transference reactions as not merely the residue of some early experience that is being displaced or replayed, but as a part of a *continuous* process that has characterized the patient's life for many years. An interactional perspective both provides a more comprehensive understanding of transference reactions and improved possibilities for insight and structural change.

The path between early childhood experiences and later transference reactions in analysis is more continuous than has been typically presented in psychoanalytic writings. Interactions with many persons throughout a patient's life tend to occur and recur in such a way as to confirm and perpetuate the modes of interpersonal perception and reaction that eventually are manifested as transferences in the patient's analysis.

Transference includes not just a sense of what has happened or is happening, but also a prediction, sometimes even a conviction, about what will happen. A patient's transference often contains a self-fulfilling prophecy together with a fatalistic sense that the outcome of the patient's interaction with the analyst is inevitable (Hoffman, 1983).

Any effort by an analyst to disprove the conscious or unconscious self-fulfilling prophecies included in the patient's transference reactions is always accompanied by an element of uncertainty, because of the analyst's inability to know, in advance, how his own countertransference will govern his response to the patient. Uncertainty also arises from the immense and awesome power of self-fulfilling prophecies contained in projective identifications in determining how patients will repeat destructive or maladaptive modes of interaction with the analyst as they have done so frequently in the past with others.

Patients have good reason for consciously or unconsciously being fearful and uncertain that the countertransference-evoking power of their transferences may be the decisive factor in determining the course of their relationship with the analyst. A patient's ideas and fears about the analyst's countertransference can flow directly and plausibly from what he knows about the evocative nature of his own behavior. On the basis of his prior experiences with other persons, the patient probably has valid reasons for both predicting and fearing that the analyst's all-too-human and constant susceptibility to countertransference will doom the relationship to repeat the very patterns of interpersonal interaction that he came to analysis to change. Sandler (1976a) describes how patients attempt to actualize their transferences by prodding their analysts into behaving in a particular way.

IMPLICATIONS FOR PSYCHOANALYTIC TECHNIQUE

The noxious and sometimes even tragic effects of self-fulfilling prophecies are not inevitable, and the dissolution of behaviors energized by self-fulfilling prophecies is both possible and eminently desirable in psychoanalytic treatment. The art of doing effective psychoanalytic treatment consists in defusing, disconfirming, and finally disarming the pathogenic power of the patients' self-fulfilling prophecies contained in their projective identifications, transferences, and unconscious pathogenic ideas.

As Strachey (1934) noted, the resolution of the transference is accomplished not only by virtue of the shared analytic examination of analyst–analysand interactions, but also because, in the act of interpreting the transference, the analyst behaves differently from how the patient has come to expect and even to provoke. When the therapist behaves in a way that is different than the patient's expectations and self-fulfilling prophecies, the prophecy is disconfirmed. Disconfirmation of the prophecies contained in the patient's projective identifications and transference reactions is a necessary, if not a sufficient, condition for attaining the goals of psychoanalytic treatment—insight and structural change.

CHAPTER 12

Interactional Aspects
of Defense

Mental health professionals often write as if defenses were independent mental operations dissociated from the ebb and flow of interpersonal events. This chapter shows that, in fact, defense is an important aspect of how people communicate with and relate to one another. Until recently, the psychoanalytic literature contained few studies about the influence of object relations on the formation or maintenance of defensive operations. The investigations summarized in this chapter demonstrate how both the form and the content of persons' defensive operations are, throughout life, influenced and shaped by their predominantly unconscious interactions with others.

This chapter is meant to be a contribution toward a revised theory of defenses that recognizes the role played by object relations in the development, sustenance, and internalization of defenses. This approach expands the classical conception of defenses, which is essentially an intrapsychic one, with an overriding emphasis on the use of a variety of inner protective mechanisms mobilized to defend against instinctual drive derivatives.

The overly exclusive emphasis of classical psychoanalysis on defenses against drives has been effectively challenged by a number of investigators writing on defenses from an object relations and interactional perspective (Bion, 1959b; Laing, 1967; Langs, 1981; Muir, 1982; Räkkölainer and Alanen, 1982; Modell, 1984; Dorpat, 1985).

Räkkölainer and Alanen (1982) propose that defensive processes that cannot be accurately conceptualized outside their current interpersonal context should be called "transactional defense mechanisms." Lansky (1985/86) demonstrates both the intersubjective contexts in which defensive activities arise and the function of such defenses in readjusting the intersubjective system so that a sense of safety can be restored.

My emphasis in this chapter on the interactional and interpersonal aspects of defensive activity should not be misinterpreted to mean that persons use defenses only in interpersonal and group situations. Rather, my aim is to demonstrate that defense is fully as much a part of how people communicate and relate with each other in *public* situations as it is an aspect of how and what they think about *privately*.

There is no need for a new category for what others have variously called "transactional" or "transpersonal" or "interactional" defenses. What is needed is a heightened appreciation of the interactional and interpersonal *aspects* of defensive activity, as well as research on the significance of object relations in the development, maintenance, and internalization of defenses. In what follows, I attempt to integrate the findings and conclusions of various studies by psychoanalysts and others concerning the importance of interpersonal interactions in defensive activity.

OBJECT RELATIONS AND THE DEVELOPMENT OF DEFENSES

Defenses are developed from parent–child interactions and other kinds of interactions that children have with nonhuman as well as human objects. The internalization of these interactions provides the dynamic nucleus as well as the forms of defensive activity. Defense mechanisms are not innate; rather, they are formed chiefly out of parent–child relations (Dorpat, 1985).

The term "defense" in psychoanalysis can be considered an analogy to the defense mechanisms employed by the body. These include the protective physiological mechanisms to maintain internal homeostasis as well as the behavioral mechanisms related to riddance, avoidance, flight, and fight. The relationship between psychic defenses and physiological protective mechanisms is, however, more than an analogy. At least in some instances, somatic protective mechanisms and psychic defenses have homologous structures. For example, the physiological riddance reactions of the gastrointestinal and respiratory systems, such as vomiting, defecation, and coughing, are homologous with the psychic defense of projection. This homology comes about because both the somatic mechanisms and the psychic defenses have a common origin in certain innate sensorimotor schemata of infancy.

Child psychoanalysts who have investigated the development of defenses through the direct observation of infants and young children trace a continuous series, beginning with physiological precursors such as riddance and sensorimotor avoidance reactions and ending in the familiar psychic defenses. The infant uses various kinds of physiological avoidance and riddance reactions, either actually or potentially available at birth, for self-protective purposes. These sensorimotor reflexes represent what is available to the infant in the first year or two of life, and they serve as models or prototypes for the later development of psychic defense mechanisms. Avoidance reactions available to infants include eye blinking and turning the head away from noxious stimuli. The nature of the parent–child relations will govern the choice of the particular prototype used for the formation of a specific defensive reaction (Spitz, 1961).

Mahler and her associates (1975) observed the avoidance behaviors in an infant develop later into the defense of denial *in statu nascendi*. Sam, at age four or five months, would protect himself from his overstimulating mother by looking away from her and using his arms to push her away. This looking away and avoidance of excessive stimulation is best described as a precursor of denial, as a protection against noxious or overwhelming stimulation. Sam's particular kind of defensive denial developed later out of this infantile avoidance reaction.

The development of psychic defenses begins in the second and third years of life and is contingent on the child's development of symbolic functions. Several different investigators, using direct psychoanalytically oriented observation of young children, have described the development of denial reactions in the second year. They indicate that these denials are the earliest kinds of psychic defensive reactions (Mahler, Pine, and Bergman, 1975; Galenson and Roiphe, 1980).

Defenses are created and maintained to defend against the arousal of painful emotions associated with pathological introjects. The term "pathological introject" refers to a relationship linked with danger, anxiety, or fear, and denotes an interactional or *relational* mode. Pathological introjects are developed out of traumatically experienced relationships, most often parent–child relationships. From an objective observer's perspective, an introject is a relational mode, but from the subject's conscious or unconscious point of view, an introject is an alien presence with which one feels a dynamic relationship. The following vignette illustrates and discusses the genetic and dynamic relationships between a patient's defensive helplessness and his unconscious introject of an engulfing mother. (For more on the relationships between trauma and pathological introjects, see Chapter 4.)

DEFENSIVE HELPLESSNESS: THE "I CAN'T" ATTITUDE

This patient's defensive attitude of helplessness developed out of his childhood interactions with an overprotective and engulfing mother. His characterological attitude of "I can't" was used defensively to deny his competency and his psychological separateness, first from his mother and later, by transference, from other persons.

The patient was a 33-year-old attorney who started analysis with symptoms of depression and work inhibition. He came to one analytic hour in a state of anxiety over his wife's possible pregnancy; she had missed a menstrual period. His anxiety stemmed from unconscious conflicts over being angry at his wife for risking pregnancy by failing to take her birth control pills regularly. For a time, he actively considered different options, including abortion, for dealing with the unwanted pregnancy. Although disturbed, he was at first able to examine both his mental state and his reality situation. With a tone of helpless resignation, he exclaimed, *"I can't think objectively about my wife and this pregnancy!"* He sighed, and some of the tension seemed to leave his voice as well as his body. Then he became depressed. After saying "I can't," he carried out his self-diagnosis of helplessness and stopped attempting to think or talk about his troubled relationship with his wife. He began to feel overwhelmed with feelings of guilt, worthlessness, and helplessness, and he berated himself for his failure to check on his wife's taking her birth control pills.

In this instance and in many others like it, the patient's "I can't" expression was a signal for the suspension of certain higher level cognitive functions, such as realistic thinking, judgment, and decision making. In suspending these functions, he relieved his anxiety at the same time as he initiated a passive reaction that led to his becoming depressed and relatively ineffective. The patient's defensive helplessness and his denial of his psychic abilities (as in the example described above) were important proximal causes of his depressive episodes.

Often, the patient unconsciously pretended to be helpless when he was not actually helpless. This was not a conscious lie or pretense; rather, his "I can't" attitude was a denial of his capabilities for competent thought and action. He habitually and defensively underestimated and depreciated his abilities. Sometimes the "I can't" attitude substituted for and defended against "I won't" or "I don't want to" or some other unacceptable idea. In interpersonal situations, he frequently used "I can't" communications as a means of manipulating others, including his analyst, into providing attention, help, and other narcissistic supplies.

As a child, he had behaved in a helpless way in order to gratify his mother's unconscious need to keep him dependent and attached to her. In his early childhood (from age two to six), his father was absent from the home while serving in the army. The separation from her husband intensified the mother's need for her son. During his childhood as well as later, she related to him in an excessively solicitous and overly protective manner.

Even after he had started a successful law practice, his mother continued to shower him with unwanted and unneeded gifts of things and attention. From infancy on, she reinforced his dependence on her and supported his defensive withdrawal from disturbing situations. His denial of his abilities derived from the introjection of his mother's mainly unconscious communications of his helplessness and needfulness. The patient's exaggerated and defensive attitude of helplessness was unconsciously used to maintain his pathological symbiotic tie to his mother and to deny his separateness from her.

The "I can't" attitude had its beginnings in conflicts and fixations from both oedipal and preoedipal periods. He unconsciously feigned helplessness, and even incompetence, in order to reduce his anxieties over forbidden sexual strivings and to disarm actual or imagined rivals. Separation-individuation phase conflicts and fixations also contributed to his defensive attitude of helplessness. The unconscious pathogenic idea underlying his "I can't" attitude was the guilty and frightening idea that being competent and independent would be hurtful to his mother. He feared saying no to his mother's insistent offers of help and care, because he believed she needed him to be her grateful and "needy" little boy. During the analysis, his progressive movements toward separation and independence from his mother evoked intense feelings of separation anxiety and separation guilt.

This patient's defensive helplessness defended against the awareness of the unconscious introject of a smothering and engulfing mother. His characterological and defensive attitude of helplessness both warded off awareness of sexual and aggressive impulses and, at the same time, unconsciously gratified those impulses. His "I can't" communications often led his mother, or surrogates for her, to do things for him and take care of him.

In summary, the patient viewed himself as helpless and incompetent in a manner that was similar to the way his mother had treated him. His "I can't" attitude served as a defense against the introject of an engulfing mother at the same time that it unconsciously replicated and gratified his childhood object relation with his mother. The patient's learned helplessness both expressed and defended against the awareness of the unconscious pathogenic idea that his mother would suffer if he became competent and independent.

SHARED DENIAL AND SHARED DEFENSES
IN GROUPS

Madness, said Nietzsche, is the exception in individuals, but the rule in groups. Freud (1921) agreed. He viewed people in groups as regressing to an infantile state as a consequence of their group membership.

Though it is a common phenomenon, there are few clinical studies about shared defenses and shared denial. Silverblatt (1981) reports six cases of denial of pregnancy in which physicians and others unconsciously colluded with the pregnant women in denying the fact of pregnancy. The *folie a deux* syndrome is based on a shared denial of psychotic proportions, in which a more disturbed and psychotic person induces a less disturbed person to believe some delusional idea. Elsewhere (Dorpat, 1974), I have written about the relatives and physician of a young suicidal woman who, together with the patient, denied the serious intent and lethal meanings of her suicidal attempts. Their shared denial kept them from taking the kinds of preventive and therapeutic actions that might have prevented her ultimate suicide.

SHARED SCHEMATA AND SHARED DEFENSES

In a group as as with individuals, schemata shape the flow of information. In any group, the relevant schemata are those that are shared by members, the subset of schemata that is the "we." Groups, whether small or large, are as vulnerable as individuals to self-deceptions. The motivating force behind the formation and maintenance of shared defenses in groups is identical to that in individuals: to minimize painful emotions such as anxiety, guilt, and shame.

Bion (1959b) describes the group self in terms of a "group mentality," which he sees as the shared pool of members' wishes, attitudes, opinions, and emotions. Any contribution by an individual to the group mentality must conform to the contributions made by others—only those schemata that are shared are incorporated into the group self. The most crucial aspect of this group mentality, according to Bion, are the basic assumptions about how to handle anxiety-evoking information. These assumptions often include an unconscious collusion by the group members about what to deny.

People in groups come to share a vast number of schemata, most of which are communicated indirectly. Foremost among these shared, yet unspoken, schemata are those which designate what is worthy of focal attention, how it is to be attended to—and what the participants of the group are tacitly enjoined to ignore or deny. When the individuals in a group make the choice (usually made tacitly or unconsciously) about what they will deny, they have established a shared defense.

Shared schemata reside not only in the minds of individual members, but also in the *interactions* among them (Reiss, 1981). Shared schemas are embedded in daily activity; they are the unseen regulators of what goes on in the group or family. Groups are ordinarily unaware of these shared schemata, although they play a crucial role in regulating and shaping the group's interactions and awareness.

The family constructs a reality through the joint schemata members come to share. Such shared schemata are expressed in the family's rituals and routines, as well as in how the members take in, interpret, and share or don't share information. Families, like other groups, have their shared schemata about what aspects of shared experience can be acknowledged and talked about, and what must be denied. These shared schemata direct attention *here* and away from *there;* they embody how this and that are to be construed.

The rules that govern what is talked about in families and other groups and what is not talked about, what is acknowledged and what is denied, are implicit. And even the rules are denied. Laing (1969) codifies the functioning of such invisible rules about rules in this way:

Rule A: Don't.
Rule A1: Rule A does not exist.
Rule A2: Do not discuss the existence or nonexistence
of Rules A, A1, or A2.

For example, an implicit family rule that was rigorously enforced for at least four generations in a wealthy New England family of a patient was that children were never to raise their voices in anger. Rigid, uncompromising control of emotional expression, especially anger, was promptly enforced by spanking the hapless offenders. There was also a relentless suppression of verbal aggression, such as tantrums, quarrels, or other verbalizations of anger. Only in analysis was the patient able to articulate and understand his family's rule against verbal anger.

Goleman (1985) illustrates the collusive evasion and shared denial that typically exists in families where child abuse, incest, or alcoholism occur. Weissberg (1983) describes the kind of strong shared defenses that operate in families in which there is incest, that prevent the family members from acknowledging to themselves or others what is taking place in the family. Multiple clues to what is happening are apparent to persons within and outside the family, but they are ignored or explained away.

"GROUPTHINK" AND SHARED DEFENSES

Compelling evidence for the collective defenses and shared illusions at work in groups comes from Janis's (1983) research on "groupthink." Famous examples of groupthink include major fiascos like the Bay of Pigs invasion and Watergate. In these instances, a small group of key decision makers tacitly conspired to ignore crucial information because it did not fit the collective view. The result of their mutual evasion of reality by a shared denial was disaster.

When the small number of invaders at the Bay of Pigs was quickly overwhelmed by the much larger Cuban army forces, the president, John

Kennedy, was stunned. "How," he asked, "could I have been so stupid to let them go ahead?"

Janis offers a detailed answer to that question based on reports by members of Kennedy's inner circle, recalling what happened during the 80 days of discussion before the brigade of Cuban exiles set sail for Cuba. Janis traces the answer to the development of a number of illusory group schemata and shared defenses that the group of presidential advisors unconsciously evolved to protect those illusions against disconfirming information.

The impetus for groupthink is to minimize anxiety, protect self-esteem, and preserve group cohesiveness. The term "groupthink" denotes the deterioration of a group's mental efficiency, attention, and judgment that results from implicit constraints and pressures. Subtle constraints, which leaders may unconsciously reinforce, prevent a member from openly expressing criticisms and doubts when others in the group appear to have reached consensus. The first victim of groupthink is critical thought!

Janis formulated his notion of groupthink from his research on groups as diverse as infantry platoons and executives in leadership training. In all the groups he studied, he observed some degree of trade-off between preserving a sense of cozy group solidarity and the willingness of individuals to face facts and express opinions that challenged key shared schemata of the group.

Loyalty to the group and the group leader may require that members not raise embarrassing questions, attack weak arguments, or counter vague, wish-fulfilling thinking with hard facts. Janis summarizes his conclusion in this way.

> The more amiable the esprit de corps among the members of a policy-making in-group, the greater is the danger that independent critical thinking will be replaced by group-think, which is likely to result in irrational . . . actions [p. 13].

INTERACTIONAL ELEMENTS IN THE DENIAL OF ILLNESS

Mental health professionals, as well as nonpsychiatric physicians, have become increasingly aware in the past several decades of the phenomenon of denial of illness. Less well known is the importance of interpersonal relations both in the instigation and the maintenance of denial reactions in physically ill patients. Several investigations of seriously ill and disabled patients reveal that interactional factors profoundly influence patients' denial of their illnesses.

Denial of illness is by no means restricted to patients—many relatives, nurses, and physicians show varying degrees of denial of patients' disability or illness. In nurses, for example, denial may take the forms of ignoring, minimizing, or excusing behavior changes (Weinstein and Kahn, 1955).

Weinstein (1980) emphasizes the importance of social and interpersonal elements in the denials of brain-damaged hospitalized patients and demonstrates how denial responses serve an adaptive function in dyadic interactions. He claims that such denials would not exist if not created or solicited by the hospital situations or staff. For example, equivocation on the part of physicians produces uncertainty in patients, which in turn creates an excess of denial.

In his study of denial reactions of seriously ill and terminal patients, Weisman (1972) notes that a common threatened danger that evokes denial is a jeopardized relationship with a key person. He writes, "The distinctive quality of denying and denial is that it occurs only in relation to certain people, not to all, and has the main purpose of protecting a significant relationship" (pp. 75–76).

Weisman tells of a patient with an inoperable carcinoma who showed considerable denial of her impending death with various hospital personnel, including physicians, nurses, and social workers. Only with the consulting psychiatrist was the patient able to speak frankly and openly about her dying and death. Severely ill patients, according to Weisman, often have an overriding need to preserve and stabilize their relationship with persons essential to their well-being. They unconsciously deny their illness to these persons because to admit it, they assume, would jeopardize their relationship with them.

Weisman's conclusions about the critical role of interpersonal relations in denial reactions are similar to Rubinfine's (1962) formulation that denial in young children is needed to preserve object relations when aggression threatens object loss. Those who have studied denial reactions in seriously ill and terminally ill patients argue that both the quality and the quantity of such patients' denials are strongly affected by the communications and attitudes of their physicians, nurses, and social workers. These investigations underscore the importance of free and open communication by medical personnel in alleviating their patients' pathological denial reactions. Most clinicians, however, tend to overlook their own contribution to their patients' denials (Kübler-Ross, 1969; Weisman, 1972).

SUICIDE SURVIVORS' DENIAL
OF PARENTAL SUICIDE

Several studies of the traumatic effects of parental suicide on surviving children reveal that the child's denial of parental suicide is augmented and supported by similar denials and evasions used by adult surviving relatives to conceal from themselves and others both the facts and the affective significance of the suicide (Rosen, 1955; Wallerstein, 1967; Cain, 1972; Dorpat, 1972). The shared denials and other defensive actions against acknowledging and accepting certain meanings of the suicide were fostered by failures of communication and by distorted communication between the surviving parents and children.

Cain (1972) notes that surviving parents, to an extent difficult to imagine, avoid communicating with their children about the suicide. Distortions of communication between surviving parents and children are even more profound. Not to be given opportunities to talk about the parental suicide deprives surviving children of opportunities for appropriate mourning and for testing and correcting their distorted ideas and fabrications about the suicide (Dorpat, 1972).

Rosen (1955) describes a borderline patient with derealization symptoms and severe disturbances in reality testing, who had struggled since childhood to carry out the command of his father to deny his mother's suicide attempt, which he had witnessed when he was three-and-a-half years old. His father had denied the traumatic episode and had treated any mention of the event by the patient as something he had imagined or as a "bad dream." The patient's derealization symptom could be traced back to the trauma of witnessing his mother, hanging, and his denial was supported and sustained by his father's deceptions and denials of the mother's suicide attempt.

These investigations of suicide survivors revealed that the patients' denial of the parental suicide was a prominent and long-lasting defense that was associated with arrested mourning reactions and developmental fixations. Clinical studies of these survivors, including the psychoanalysis of some of them, agree on the central importance of interactional factors in the formation and sustenance of the patients' denials. The evasions and distorted communications of the surviving parents about the parental suicide played a critical role in causing, supporting, and perpetuating the surviving children's denial of the parental suicide.

DEFENSE AND MODE OF COMMUNICATION

Langs (1978a, 1981) has made an important contribution in his formulations about the relationships between defense and modes of communication. He describes three communicative modes and types of bipersonal field (Types A, B, and C) that are related to specific kinds of defensive activities and interactions. The Type A mode, characterized by a predominance of symbolic imagery, communicates the most meaning and is geared to attaining insight. Type A communication contains interpretable and mature primary-process products, such as images, metaphors, and modulated affects. Defensive activity in Type A communication can be inferred from the content of the patient's verbal communications. This is not true of Type B and Type C communicative modes, in which the patient's defensive activity is expressed mainly in the communicative mode itself, rather than in the verbal content.

Defense in the Types B and C modes occurs much more in *how* a person communicates rather than *what* is explicitly and verbally communicated. The Type B mode is characterized by persistent efforts at projective identification and action discharge. In the Type B field, both patient and therapist extensively employ projective identification and use the other member of the dyad as a container for disruptive projective identifications.

The occurrence of a Type B field in psychotherapy and psychoanalysis is far more frequent than many realize. Langs's (1976, 1978a, 1979a, 1980, 1981) psychotherapy seminars for psychiatric residents clearly demonstrated that major contributions to the formation of a Type B field often came from *both* the therapist and the patient. My supervision experience with psychotherapy trainees and with psychoanalytic candidates indicates that a Type B field is common in both psychotherapy and psychoanalysis and that frequently therapists and analysts unconsciously either initiate or maintain this kind of shared defensive activity.

In the Type C mode, the essential links between the patient and the therapist are broken, and both verbal and nonverbal communications are designed to destroy meaning and relatedness (Bion, 1959a; Modell, 1984). In this mode, there is a relative absence of interpretable and sophisticated primary process products.

PROJECTIVE IDENTIFICATION

The most intensely studied type of explicitly interactional defensive activity, projective identification, was first described by Melanie Klein (1946). Bion (1959b) views projective identification as the single most important form of interaction between patient and therapist, parent and child, and in groups of all kinds.

Projective identification has been investigated in individual and group therapy sessions, in families, and in other kinds of groups. It has been described by different investigators with disparate theoretical orientations. Some of the various labels attached to the different variants of a broadly defined concept of projective identification are "trading of dissociations" (Wynne, 1965); "irrational role assignments" (Framo, 1970); "symbiotic" (Mahler, 1952); "externalization" (Brodey, 1965); "dumping"

(Langs, 1982b); "actualization of wished-for object relations" (Sandler, 1976a); "evocation of a proxy" (Wangh, 1962); "merging" (Boszormenyi-Nagy, 1967). The colloquial expressions "laying a trip" and "mind-fucking" describe different kinds of projective identification.

Ogden (1982) views projective identification as a psychological process that is simultaneously a type of defense, a mode of communication, and a primitive form of object relationship. For him, projective identification is a type of defense in which one can distance oneself from an unwanted or endangered part of the self while at the same time unconsciously keeping that aspect of oneself "alive" in another.

As a mode of communication, projective identification is one in which the subject makes himself or herself understood by exerting pressure on another person to experience a set of feelings similar to his or her own. Projective identification can also be seen as a type of pathological symbiotic object relationship, in which the subject experiences the object of the projection as separate enough to serve as a receptacle for parts of the self, but sufficiently undifferentiated to maintain the illusion that one is literally sharing a given feeling with another person.

In one type of transference reaction, the patient unconsciously manipulates the therapist in order to actualize some wished-for relationship. Transference reactions, according to Sandler (1976a), may include the patient's attempts to manipulate the analyst into responses that represent an unconscious repetition of old object relations. He views countertransference as a compromise between the analyst's own tendencies and his responses to the role that the patient attempts to force on him. The relationship between transference and countertransference is conceptualized as a specific instance of the general phenomenon of *actualization*. In psychotherapy as in everyday life, people consciously or unconsciously attempt to actualize the particular object relationships inherent in their dominant unconscious wishes (Sandler and Sandler, 1978).

DENIAL AND PROJECTIVE IDENTIFICATION

An implicit denial is an essential component of projective identification, and it profoundly affects the subject's representations of self and others. What the subject denies as some aspects of the self, he or she projects onto the object. What are the denied aspects of the self that are projected in projective identification? Clinical reports reveal that a wide range of unconscious contents, conflicts, and affects may be denied and then projected. When the object is idealized, "good" parts of the self are projected; and when the object is denigrated it "receives," as it were, the "bad" parts of the self. Thus, whole objects, part objects, selfobjects, introjects, conflicts, emotions, superego elements, drive representations, and many other contents have been identified as the projected elements in projective identification. Often, projection is used as a means of distancing conflicting parts of the self. A person may marry a person with the ego-dystonic aspects of his or her unconscious psychic conflicts. A man, for example, who is unable to tolerate the passive-receptive aspects of himself may project such feelings and attitudes onto his wife. His choice of a mate may be determined in part by the need to find a passive woman whose character fits his own projections.

Many studies emphasize the presence of conscious or unconscious hostile wishes toward the object in patients' projective identifications (Brodey, 1965; Ogden, 1982). Though I do not dispute that this is a common dynamic, I do disagree that hostile wishes toward the object are either a necessary or defining feature of projective identification. In several patients reported elsewhere (Dorpat, 1985), the unconscious wishes underlying their projections were loving wishes to give, to please, and to sacrifice some function or part of themselves for the analyst. These patients had denied certain psychic abilities of their own; and then, in what they considered to be a loving action, they attributed to the analyst these functions and the moral authority to regulate them. In so doing, they were replicating with the analyst earlier pathological symbiotic relationships in which they had consciously or unconsciously viewed their attribution of idealized powers and abilities to the object an act of love and surrender. Over time in these cases, it became clear that their self-sacrificing "gifts" of parts of themselves had been unconsciously shaped by the need to bolster the fragile self-esteem of their earlier symbiotic partners, whether spouses or parents.

In projective identification, the object is perceived and related to as a distanced but not separate part of the self, and any behavior of the object that does not fit the subject's projection is frequently ignored or discounted. The reality of the object, which cannot be used to verify the projection, is not consciously perceived, and, as Brodey (1965) has demonstrated, the subject has a negative hallucination for whatever there is about the object that is discordant with the subject's expectations and wishes for the object.

THE EVOCATION OF A PROXY

Wangh (1950, 1962) discusses an interactional defense in which persons attempt to mobilize in others unwanted aspects of themselves. He calls this defense the evocation of a proxy, which as I indicated earlier, may be considered a kind of projective identification. In an article on Shakespeare's *Othello,* Wangh (1950) underlined the point that Iago needs to rid himself of an intolerable jealousy and partially succeeds in doing so by arousing the same emotion in Othello.

Selected unconscious contents and functions not only are assigned to another person, but are actively evoked in the other person instead of the self. Wangh (1962) correctly emphasized that there is something more than projection involved here. The subject's unconscious motive is to mobilize and activate the object's feelings and reactions, and these motives are acted out by manipulating the other person. The evocation of a proxy has the purpose of preserving a good relationship with a narcissistically cathected object. Wangh stresses the importance of both denial and projection in the evocation of a proxy. Whatever a person denies within himself, he projects onto the object. Then the person uses his perception of the activated emotional and instinctual drive manifestations in the proxy object to deny those impulses and contents in himself.

PROJECTIVE IDENTIFICATION IN THE FAMILIES OF DISTURBED ADOLESCENTS

Zinner and Shapiro (1972) report on 45 disturbed adolescents and their families studied at the Clinical Center of the National Institute of Health. Their observations focused on parents' perceptions and attitudes toward their children, and they refer to the parents' acts and statements that communicate to the adolescent the parents' image of him as *delineations.* Some parental delineations are determined more by their service on behalf of parental defensive needs than by their capacity for appraising the actual attributes of their adolescent children.

Family group behavior, as well as subjective experience in family members, is determined by shared schemata and unconscious assumptions. Role allocations for the collusive acting out of these shared schemata and unconscious assumptions are communicated and evoked in family members by the mechanism of projective identification. For projective identification to function effectively as a defense, the actual nature of the relationship between the self and its projected part in the object must remain unconscious, though the subject may feel an ill-defined bond with the recipient of his projections (Zinner and Shapiro, 1972).

STAGES OF PROJECTIVE IDENTIFICATION

The common threads noted in the various studies just cited can be summarized in terms of three stages of projective identification.

Stage 1. Denial and Projection

Whatever the subject denies as some part of the self is projected onto his or her representation of an object. The subject then perceives the object as if the object contained the disavowed aspects of the subject's self. Thus far I have summarized what occurs *within* the subject—the next two stages deal mainly with what occurs in the interactions and relations between the subject and the object of projective identification.

Stage 2. Interactional Manipulation

Through any of a wide variety of interactional conscious or unconscious manipulations (for example, persuasion, coercion, intimidation, gaslighting, idealization, denigration) the subject evokes or provokes conflicts and emotions in the object that conform with the subject's unconscious projection. Through these manipulations and interactional pressures, the subject seeks to control the responses of the object and to actualize an unconsciously wished-for kind of pathological symbiotic relationship. These interactional manipulations are conveyed by both conscious communications and (more frequently) unconscious verbal and nonverbal communications.

Stage 3. The Object's Response

The object of the projective identification receives the subject's verbal and nonverbal communications and responds to the interactional manipulation. There is a broad spectrum of both normal and pathological kinds of reactions to projective identification. When the object of a projective identification "contains" (Bion, 1967) and "processes" (Langs, 1978a) the induced thoughts and feelings in a more mature way than did the projector, the recipient's methods of handling the projected thoughts and feelings become available for constructive internalization by the projector by way of therapeutic introjections and identifications.

The recipients of projective identification may unconsciously identify with whatever has been attributed to them, a reaction called projective counteridentification by Grindberg (1962). Depending on how much and how long the person has identified with what has been projected onto him, counteridentification could have (as it did in the adolescents studied by Zinner and Shapiro, 1972) pathological consequences.

MUTUAL PROJECTIVE IDENTIFICATION

The object of the projective identification may respond by communicating with another projective identification. In so doing, he will be participating in what Langs (1978a) calls a Type B communicative field, which may also be called *mutual projective identification* (Dorpat, 1985). Interpersonal interactions containing mutual projective identification involve the enactment of pathologic symbiotic modes of relatedness and communication. In such interactions, each party unconsciously colludes with the other to verify and validate the other's projections. In other words, each party acts out rather than contains and internally processes the contents and roles projected onto him by the other member of the dyad.

Interactions characterized by mutual projective identification contain *complementary* modes of communicating in which the subject's mode of communicating evokes a complementary communication from the object. Compliant communications, for example, tend to elicit directive communications from the object. Similarly, in other interpersonal contacts, passive-dependent and masochistic modes are apt to evoke, respectively, active-independent and sadistic modes of response.

In the sadomasochistic type of mutual projective identification, the sadist unconsciously denies the masochistic aspect of himself; projects the disavowed aspect of himself onto an object; and, by means of his sadistic mode of communicating, manipulates the object to behave masochistically. Then the object introjects what has been projected onto him and acts out the masochistic role by behaving in a weak, demeaned, or submissive manner. These masochistic behaviors and communications may, in turn, provoke the sadist again to behave sadistically. By responding sadistically, the sadist completes and renews the vicious cycle in mutual projective identification in which the communication of each party functions both as a signal and a provocation for the complementary behavior of the other party. (Chapter 9 provides an in-depth examination of such sadomasochistic interactions occurring in a stalemated psychoanalysis.)

How is it that the object of projective identification may collude in this defensive activity and act out the role or psychic content ascribed to him? In such instances, the subject's projections are to some extent actualized in the object's behavior. Those who have studied this phenomenon in the psychotherapy dyad, in families, and in other groups generally agree that one of the most powerful unconscious motives for sustaining these shared defenses and pathological symbiotic relations is the participants' anxieties over object loss.

Brodey (1965) notes that the terror of abandonment perpetuates these kinds of narcissistic relationships. Adolescents studied by Zinner and Shapiro (1972) feared they would lose their parents' love if their actions did not verify their parents' defensive projections. These adolescents were afraid not to collude, not to comply, and not to identify with what had been projected onto them by their parents. Räkkölainer and Alanen (1982) found that the primary target of transactional defense mechanisms was separation anxiety. According to Wangh (1962), anxiety over separation from objects experienced as part of the self was a critical element in both initiating and maintaining relationships based on the "evocation of a proxy."

THE DEFENSE OF AFFECTIVE NONRELATEDNESS

In the psychoanalytic treatment of patients suffering from disorders of the self as well as of more seriously disturbed borderline and psychotic patients, there is a characteristic form of defense that has as its focus a struggle against affective communication and interpersonal relatedness. Modell (1984) describes how such patients retreat into a self-sufficient cocoon reinforced by fantasies of omnipotence. This defense takes the form of protracted states of affective nonrelatedness and often leads to corresponding states of boredom, "deadness," and indifference in the analyst. By blocking the expression of affects, the patient also at the same time blocks interpersonal relatedness.

In an obvious case of affective nonrelatedness, the analyst may observe a massive inhibition of affect as the patient fills the hour with talk that has been depleted of affective charge. Though such patients may sometimes report experiencing anxiety, guilt, or sadness, their tone of voice does not convey such emotions.

The defense of affective nonrelatedness occurs most frequently in the opening phases of the analysis of patients with narcissistic disorders and tends to diminish after the emergence of a stable selfobject transference. This defense may later recur at times of stress or when there has been a disruption of the selfobject transference by such events as the analyst's vacation breaks or his empathic failure.

It should be emphasized that this defense may be used to protect against any kind of relatedness and not only against libidinal, whole-object relations. Especially in the early stages of the analysis of narcissistic disorders, affective nonrelatedness protects the patient against the disturbing object relations conflicts linked with the emergence of need-fulfilling selfobject transferences.

The conflicts engendering this defense are summarized by Modell (1984) as follows:

> The wish to maintain the autonomy of the self versus the fear and wish to merge; the affirmation of the self in the mirroring response of the other versus omnipotent self-sufficiency; the need to communicate versus the fear that an unempathic response will shatter the sense of self [p. 78].

These are all conflicts leading to defensive activities occurring within an interpersonal interaction, and, as Modell argues, the defense of affective nonrelatedness cannot be understood or explained as an internal or intrapsychic defense.

The defense of affective nonrelatedness can be traced to traumatically experienced object relations and constitutes an effort to avoid repeating such painful relations. It is, in essence, an attempt at flight, an effort to remain hidden. Affective nonrelatedness is a reaction to fears of fragmentation and annihilation of the self. It is prompted by the need to preserve the integrity and cohesiveness of the self. The defense process itself is not an internal event, but one occurring between two people. Modell (1984) asserts:

> Unlike repression it [the defense of affective non-relatedness] is not an internal process that defends against heightened instinctual tension within a psychic apparatus, but a defense directed against a danger that is perceived in the present, within the context of a group of two. Defenses that are purely intrapsychic, such as repression and isolation, can and do co-exist with defenses such as I have described that are entirely within a two person context [p. 78].

Affective nonrelatedness and projective identification cannot be accurately described in intrapsychic terms because they are defenses occurring within what Modell calls the context of a two-person psychology.

AFFECT "DEAFNESS"

In his description of the defense of affective nonrelatedness, Modell (1984) emphasizes the patient's noncommunication of affects and makes only a brief mention of the fact that patients with narcissistic disorders block their *reception* as well as their *transmission* of affective messages. Elsewhere (Dorpat, 1985), I have focused on the negative hallucination of affective messages, the defensively motivated blocking out of awareness of others' affective communication commonly observed in patients with narcissistic disorders.

An analyst in a case conference reported that he had become increasingly frustrated by his patient's unconscious need to ignore him and to "blank out" many of his interventions. Partly because of his unconscious wish to merge himself with an idealized and omnipotent selfobject, the patient often misinterpreted the analyst's interventions as some kind of directive. For several years, he did not comprehend the analyst's communications as interpretations and apparently did not "hear" the affective significance of what had been said to him. Often the analyst had the impression that the patient had not paid any attention either to the analyst's verbal or to his nonverbal communications. With him and similar patients with disorders of the self, the defense of affective nonrelatedness was manifested not only in the affectless way he talked, but also in his affective deafness to the analyst's messages. The patient ignored nearly all the analyst's verbal and nonverbal communications and especially those that were discordant with his wishes for an idealized selfobject. His negative hallucination for the analyst's communications was not total; if the analyst said anything that the patient could construe as some kind of directive, he would use the analyst's words as a *prescription* for how he should behave. For him, the analyst was predominantly a need-fulfilling person, and the patient did not attend to any of the analyst's communications that did not conform with his needs. The patient's habit of ignoring others typified many of his object relations since early childhood. It had been formed by a defensive identification with his borderline mother, who since his infancy had ignored many of his needs. Ignoring others enabled him to deny his needs for others and protected both him and others from the arousal of frustration and rage.

The affective "deafness" in this patient and other patients with narcissistic disorders is not a global one, nor is it necessarily a fixed and unchanging unresponsiveness to others. They hear and respond to some affective communications, but not others. These patients "turn off" more with some persons than with others, and the immediate and most critical determinant of their affective deafness is the interpersonal context. Their affective deafness is like a variable threshold or gate that is regulated in part by their defensive need not to hear or respond to the affective communications of others.

The defensive quality of affectless communication and affective deafness is most readily recognizable and interpreted after a stable selfobject transference has been established, because then the ebb and flow of this defense is determined predominantly by the nature of patient–analyst relations. Recurrences of this defense are triggered by disruptions of the selfobject transference, and the defense recedes or even disappears once the selfobject transference is reestablished. An overall strategy for analytic treatment of patients with disorders of the self is the systematic interpretation and working through of disruptions of the selfobject transferences. Frequently the study of such disruptions begins with an examination of what the therapist did to trigger the disruption.

SOME USES OF COUNTERTRANSFERENCE

My aim here is to discuss the uses of countertransference in understanding the interactional aspects of defensive activity in the psychoanalytic and psychotherapy situations. The term countertransference is used here in the broad sense to include all of the analyst's attitudes and affective responses to the analysand. Countertransference is an amalgam of the analyst's preexisting tendencies and conflicts and those affective reactions which are elicited or evoked by the patient's communications and manipulations.

In the analytic treatment of patients who communicate predominantly in the Type A mode, there is usually no pressing need for the analyst to use his countertransference reactions to understand the patient's communication. Because such patients express themselves with sophisticated primary process cognitions, there are usually sufficient images, metaphors, and narratives for the analyst to use in making interpretations. In the analysis of patients who communicate in Type B and Type C modes, there is a relative scarcity of interpretable and mature primary process products. For such patients, the analyst's recognition of his countertransference emotions and attitudes is frequently not only a desirable, but a necessary, approach for understanding both what is unconsciously occurring in the patient–analyst interaction and whatever is being defended against.

The analyst must be able to use his countertransference feelings and attitudes for identifying the unconscious meanings of the patient's Type B communications. The important and interpretable meanings are not, for the most part, contained in the verbal content of projective identifications. Therefore, the clues to and indicators of what is going on unconsciously may often be obtained by attention to the countertransference. That is to say, the analyst's understanding of the patient's disavowed affects as well as various other disavowed contents comes about through his recognition of the affects and contents that have been evoked in himself by the patient's projective identification.

Modell (1984), Kohut (1971), and others have described the different typical countertransference responses that occur in the analysis of patients with disorders of the self. The most common countertransference reactions that develop in response to patients who develop a mirror transference are boredom, indifference, and inattention (Kohut, 1971).

The countertransference responses that typically occur in response to the defense of affective nonrelatedness should be distinguished from the affective responses engendered in the analyst when a stable selfobject transference has been established. Differences in the countertransference responses can be accounted for by the different kinds of frustration obtaining in the two situations.

The patient's defense of affective nonrelatedness deprives (at least temporarily) the analyst of any affective exchange or meaningful relation with the patient. At such times, the analyst is treated as if he did not exist; patient neither speaks nor listens to the analyst in any affectively meaningful way. On the other hand, establishing a cohesive and relatively stable selfobject transference implies the formation and acknowledgment of an attachment and a relationship to the analyst. Then the analyst is treated like someone important to the patient for filling certain personal needs and functions. Except for times when there has been a disruption in the selfobject transference, patients who have established a stable selfobject transference are ordinarily able both to transmit and to receive affective communications.

CONCLUDING REMARKS

A comprehensive theory of defense should take into account interactional dynamics, the mainly unconscious ways in which people influence and contribute to both the conscious experience and the unconscious psychic functioning of other people. An object relations element is an essential aspect of all defensive activity, whether that defensive activity is carried out privately in one's thinking and imagination or publicly in one's interactions with others. In summary, from the perspective of the interactional concepts pervading psychoanalytic theorizing in recent years, psychological phenomena, including even unconscious conflicts and defenses, are understood as properties of an intersubjective system and thus as taking shape at the interface of interacting subjectivities.

Unconscious Meaning Analysis, Unconscious Perception, the Day Residue, and Dreaming

UNCONSCIOUS MEANING ANALYSIS AND DREAM DORMATION

This chapter is an extensively modified and enlarged version of an earlier paper entitled, "Unconscious Perception, the Day Residue and Dreaming" (Dorpat, 1978b). The title has been changed because months after the original paper was published I discovered that I was mistaken in labeling certain clinical phenomena as "unconscious perception." My studies have convinced me that what many writers, including Goodheart (1987), Langs (1980, 1981, 1982a, 1982b), Mendelsohn (1985), Searles (1965, 1979), and others, have called unconscious perception is actually the end-product of a process of unconscious meaning analyses rather than a perceptual process.

As currently used in psychoanalytic writing, the term "unconscious perception" has two different meanings, one literal and the other metaphorical. The literal meaning of unconscious perception is similar to the meaning of the term perception as it is used in everyday life, that is, as sensory reception. The word "unconscious" in the term unconscious perception describes the perceiver's lack of awareness of a particular perception. In its most prevalent usage, "unconscious perception" is a metaphor that has been misinterpreted in a literal way. It is a misnomer because it does not actually refer to a perceptual or observational process. So-called unconscious perceptions are the end-products of an unconscious process of meaning analysis. They are judgments or inferences, not percepts.

An example of this metaphorical and mistaken use of the term unconscious perception is the therapist who speaks about a patient's unconscious perception of the therapist–patient relationship. This therapist is using

An earlier version of this chapter appeared in *The Yearbook of Psychoanalysis and Psychotherapy* (1987, Gardner Press). Adapted by permission of the publisher.

unconscious perception as a figure of speech because relationship is not something one literally perceives by using one's eyes and ears.

A judgment about the nature of a relationship is formed by evaluating what is going on between the two persons engaged in the relationship. This, of course, can be done consciously. People can and do reflect on and make conscious judgments about the nature and quality of their own and others' relationships. The claim made in this book (see especially Chapters 2, 5 and 7) is that a similar process of evaluation, of meaning analysis, can and often does occur unconsciously.

An analyst is mistaken in interpreting a patient's primary process derivative as "expressing his unconscious perception of the therapist's lack of commitment" in that lack of commitment is not something one literally perceives with one's senses. The idea that someone lacks commitment is a judgment made after we have consciously or unconsciously evaluated the person's activities and behaviors.

Clinical Vignette #1

Langs (1982b, pp. 198–215) writes about a patient who reported a frightening dream in which a man was chasing her. The man cornered her in a motel room and wanted to rape her. The patient felt furious. Langs traces the entrapment element of the dream back to the therapist's extension of the patient's previous hour by ten minutes. In Langs's view, the dream of being chased and cornered was a valid, unconscious perception of one implication of the therapist's frame error, because the therapist had indeed attempted to entrap the patient, even if momentarily and unconsciously. Langs adds that the patient's dream of being chased and cornered also symbolized the patient's own involvement in self-punitive rape fantasies, which she tended to act out unconsciously in her everyday life.

Let us assume that the therapist's extension of the psychotherapy hour with the patient was represented in the dream by the scene in which the patient was cornered in a motel room by a man who wanted to rape her. There is no good reason for believing that her awareness of this implication of the therapist's frame error derived from a perceptual process. It was a judgment unconsciously made on the basis of her observations of the actions made by the therapist and her knowledge about the rules or "frame" of therapy. Clearly her representation of the therapist's violation of the frame was a judgment derived from a *conceptual* process rather than a *perception* formed from an observational or *perceptual* process.

Clinical Vignette #2

A 41-year-old divorced professional woman was given her monthly statement at the beginning of the analytic hour. She looked at the statement and noted a charge for an appointment she had missed. She seemed angry and began questioning the analyst about the charge. He replied, "Well, let's talk about it," and with a motion of his index finger he indicated that she should get on the couch. She reclined on the couch and continued to discuss her feelings about the statement and about being charged for the missed analytic hour. The patient appeared to feel somewhat relieved upon recalling the original contract with the analyst and its provision about paying for missed appointments. Late in the session she mentioned feeling humiliated by getting on the couch rather than facing the analyst while they settled the issue about the payment.

At the next day's session, she reported a dream in which she was doing a striptease in front of the analyst, who became emotionally and physically aroused by her nudity and her erotic dancing. In the dream, each time he arose from his chair to move toward her, she put her index finger on his shoulder and pushed him back in his chair. Several times in the dream she told him to "shut up." She wanted him to beg her for sexual intercourse, which she would then triumphantly refuse. Associations to the dream concerned her fear that she would be rejected if she told him about her sexual wishes for him. While growing up, she had thought her mother was rejecting her when actually, she realized, it was she who had rejected her mother. The patient spoke about her wish in the dream to humiliate the analyst in much the same way as she had felt humiliated about having to get on the couch to discuss the missed analytic session.

The patient's use of her index finger in the dream to control the analyst was a derivative of her unconscious meaning analysis of the analyst's directive gesture of the day before. In the dream, there was a defensive reversal of roles wherein she became the one who controlled and directed the analyst's behavior rather than being the passive victim of his power over her. Her pushing the analyst back into his chair with her index finger in her dream represented her temporary and defensive identification with the analyst's aggressive and controlling attitude expressed in his gesture indicating that she should get on the couch.

In this instance, as in the other vignettes presented here, a powerful stimulus for the patient's unconscious meaning analysis was the therapist's commission of some kind of frame error. In all the vignettes, these disruptive frame infractions evoked intense, but mainly unconscious, disturbances in the patients, which they defended against by denying, and thus not becoming consciously aware of, both the fact of the frame error and their affective responses to it. Their dreams and their associations to the dreams, however, showed that they had unconsciously analyzed the meaning of what the analyst had done and that they unconsciously "recognized" the analyst's behavior as a violation of the psychoanalytic frame. (For more discussion of the significance of frame errors see Dorpat, 1984.)

Clinical Vignette #3

A 35-year-old analysand had a long history of alternating periods of compliance and rebellion toward authority figures, beginning with his punitive and authoritarian father. In the sixth month of his analysis, he spoke to his analyst-candidate about his plan to seek marital therapy for his wife and himself. The candidate abruptly forbade the patient to go to a marital therapist. He impatiently interpreted the patient's wish to see another therapist as a defensive need to displace his feelings for the analyst onto someone else. The patient compliantly agreed. In the following analytic hour he reported a dream in which he was sitting in the front seat of an automobile driven by the analyst.

His associations to the dream indicated that the dream images of the analyst and himself in the automobile represented his unconscious evaluation of what had taken place in the previous day's analytic hour. The image of the analyst driving the car stood for his unconscious recognition of the analyst's controlling intervention in forbidding family therapy. The dream image of his sitting beside the analyst in the passenger seat symbolized the passive and compliant role he had adopted in his relation to the analyst, a role he had taken previously in relation to his father as well as to other persons in authority.

In this instance, the patient was not conscious of the inferences and ideas he had used to form the judgment of his passive and compliant role in relation to the controlling analyst. Not only was he unaware of how he had reached this judgment, he was also unaware how that the events of the previous day (i.e., his compliant response to the analyst's prohibition regarding marital therapy) were represented in the dream. I do not mean to imply that people are always or necessarily unaware of the significance of the products of their unconscious meaning analyses. Sometimes a moment of self-reflection permits a person to understand the previously unconscious meaning of such primary process manifestations.

Clinical Vignette #4

One Sunday, a middle-aged, recently divorced analysand inadvertently drove past her analyst-candidate's house and happened to see him working in his yard. During the following Monday morning analytic hour, she reported seeing him on his front lawn but dismissed the incident with, "Oh well, it doesn't matter." She went on to talk about her teen-aged son, who, according to her account, attempted to dominate her as his father had done while married to her. The candidate was silent in the Monday hour except for some nonverbal utterances, to be discussed later.

During the next analytic hour on Tuesday, the patient recounted a dream in which a man was using a garden tool to turn over pieces of turf on a lawn. There was no pattern or system to his performance, and he seemed to be working on the turf in a willy-nilly, disorganized manner. He turned over some pieces of lawn and others he left alone. While associating to the dream, she recalled seeing the analyst working in his yard during the previous weekend.

Later in the hour, the analyst responded to something the patient said with what the patient earlier had described as a "grunt," a short "aah, aah" kind of vocalization. The patient complained about the analyst's "grunts," stating that she no longer liked this type of intervention. At the beginning of the analysis, his "grunts" seemed to be reassuring to her. Later he had stopped doing this. The patient felt puzzled over why he had resumed these supposedly reassuring nonverbal sounds. About a year previously, the candidate's supervisor had actively worked with the candidate on this same type of interaction and had demonstrated from the patient's communications that the candidate's nonverbal "aah, aah" interventions were unnecessary and even antianalytic.

Early in the analysis, the patient had been unconsciously using the candidate's nonverbal intervention as a directive for what she was supposed to talk about. In this way, the analyst/candidate and the analysand were enacting the same kind of pathological symbiotic and eroticized relationship the patient had previously and unconsciously enjoyed with her seductive father.

About six months after the events reported in this vignette took place, memories gradually began to emerge of her sadomasochistic and incestuous sexual activities with her father during her puberty and adolescent years. Her acute sensitivity to the analyst's intrusions and frame errors was strongly shaped by her traumatic incestuous experiences with her father.

Unconsciously she had viewed the analyst's "grunts" as disruptive intrusions on her autonomy. His inconsistency in expressing this vocalization was unconsciously symbolized in the dream by the haphazard, willy-nilly way in which he was turning over the pieces of turf in the lawn.

After the candidate recalled that on the previous day (Monday) he had uttered several "grunts," he made the following interpretation to the patient: "You were troubled yesterday by my grunts, especially since we had talked about this before and I had stopped doing it. I think my going back to the grunts puzzled you, and you symbolized your puzzlement and consternation in the dream about a man who was turning over the pieces of turf in a disorganized manner."

The patient spoke about feeling troubled after the Monday hour. She said she had struggled, with the analyst's help, to grow away from her disturbing relationship with her father. In his interactions with her, she explained, her father had assumed an apparently benevolent but actually directive and intrusive attitude toward her.

The patient's conscious perceptions of the analyst working on his lawn provided images she later used in the formation of her dream. These perceptions, plus the products of her unconscious meaning analyses of the analyst's directive actions, constituted what Freud called the "day residue." The candidate's relapse into using the antitherapeutic nonverbal communications was correctly, though unconsciously, evaluated by the patient and symbolized in her dream by the image of a man turning over pieces of turf in a disorganized manner. The products of her unconscious meaning analyses of the analyst's frame errors (i.e., his nonneutral grunts) and their meaning as disorganized and disruptive intrusions on her autonomy were represented in the dream. These unconscious appraisals of what was taking place in her relations with the analyst contributed dynamically important elements to the formation of her dream.

Both the present and the past contributed to the construction of the dream, and both played a part in the patient's valid though unconscious meaning analysis of the therapist's use of the grunts and his inconsistency in so doing. His intrusive communication activated the schema established out of her traumatic experiences with her father, and they constituted minitraumatic stimuli both because they disrupted the psychoanalytic frame and because they replicated similar, more damaging violations made by her father.

DISCUSSION

Recent investigations into dreaming recognize the inadequacy of the traditional psychoanalytic theory and advance alternative theories about the functions of dreaming. The concept of unconscious meaning analysis proposed in this book is consistent with theories that dreams are involved in the adaptation or solution of focal problems in the current life of the dreamer (Noy, 1979; Fosshage, 1983; Winson, 1985; Weiss and Sampson, 1986). Certain dreams provide wishful solutions to these problems; others are a search for a solution or an adaptive response based on the experience of the dreamer from childhood onward.

Both clinical and experimental studies reveal the organizing, interpretive and synthesizing functions of dreams (Erikson, 1954; Bonime, 1962; Noy, 1969, 1979; De Monchaux, 1978). Others have described the importance of dreaming in the internalization process and in memory formation (Meissner, 1968; Palombo, 1978).

The traditional and metapsychological view of dreams as predominantly a product of regression to infantile hallucinatory wish-fulfillment levels of functioning has tended to obstruct recognition of the constructive and synthesizing functions of dreaming. Fosshage (1983) argues persuasively that *"the superordinate function of dreams is the development, maintenance (regulation), and, when necessary, restoration of psychic processes, structure, and organization"* (p. 65).

The meaning analysis functions in dreaming, as in other primary process activities such as art, humor, and play, are states of emotional concentration that promote creative and constructive solutions of unresolved psychic conflicts.

DERIVATIVES OF UNCONSCIOUS PERCEPTION IN DREAM FORMATION

To the best of my knowledge, Searles (1965, 1979) and Langs (1980, 1981, 1982a, 1982b) were the first to describe what they call unconscious perceptions occurring in the analytic situation. As noted earlier, my examination of their publications on this subject shows that what they were describing was not, literally speaking, unconscious perceptions, but rather the products of a process of unconscious meaning analyses of emotionally charged events. These products arise from *conceptual* not *perceptual* processes. In Langs's view, the derivatives of unconscious memory, unconscious fantasy, and unconscious perception are fused. From their inner worlds of unconscious memory and fantasy, patients (according to Langs) add elements derived from unconscious perceptions. He believes that the role played by valid unconscious perceptions of other individuals has been neglected in the etiology of emotional disturbances.

Earlier I argued that what Langs, Searles, and others call unconscious perceptions are actually the products of unconscious meaning analyses. Still, there is a correct usage of the term unconscious perception, though, in my opinion, it has a more limited scope than the usage employed by Searles, Langs, and others. I suggest restricting the term to its literal meaning, that is, perceptions about which the subject is unaware.

A Clinical Vignette

Basch (1974) reports an analytic patient's dream that contained derivatives of an unconscious perception from the previous day. He describes the patient as a graduate student whose sexual frigidity and fear of marriage was the characterological outcome of an hysterical conflict. Though the patient's analytic hours demonstrated her genuine involvement with the analyst, consciously she experienced the transference only in displaced form. She was convinced that one of her professors was the hidden object of her erotic dreams and fantasies.

One day, the patient and the analyst found themselves entering an otherwise empty elevator, and after greeting each other they rode a few floors in uninterrupted privacy. They were then joined by a man who knew the analyst and greeted him. The three soon reached street level and went their separate ways.

The next day the patient reported a dream that expressed (according to Basch) in thinly disguised form her anger at the interruption of their privacy of the previous day and her jealousy of the other passenger. Though Basch does not describe the manifest content of the dream or the patient's associations to the dream, he generously provides an account of the patient's dream and her associations to it.

In the dream, the patient is leaving Basch's office, and he follows her. Though she calls him "Dr. Basch" he is really, according to the patient, a 23-year-old young man in a white coat. The young man catches up with her, turns her by the shoulders, and, laughing gaily, kisses her. She and the young man are laughing and going down on an escalator. The young man (who also represents the analyst) pushes her from behind, saying, "Come on." Then the patient and the young man are in a doctor's staff dining room and behind them is an older man who does not want to be seen by the patient and the young man. There is a feeling in the dream that the analyst is very young, and she wonders if he knows his field.

Her associations to the dream were as follows: the young man was someone who had a crush on her when they were kids. The episode in the dining room gave her the same feelings she had had when was on a ship and a young man courted her. While they were dancing, she had stumbled and seen her father looking at her in disgust. Then, associating to the escalator, she recalled that she and the analyst had gone on the elevator together the previous day. She had been surprised to find herself in that situation and had wondered whether or not she should talk with him. She questioned aloud about whether the analyst was younger than she previously thought, although, as far as she knew, she had not doubted his skill. She also wondered if the older man in the dream was her father. She found herself feeling angry while associating to the dream, but did not know why. The patient's later associations led to her rage at being excluded by her parents on various occasions.

Eventually Basch suggested to the patient that her dream may have been a response to the interruption of their elevator ride by a third party. She replied matter of factly, "No, that couldn't have been so. No one else got on the elevator. We were alone."

Basch describes the patient's failure consciously to perceive the presence of the third party in the elevator as a negative hallucination. She did unconsciously perceive the interruption by the third party, and her unconscious perception was represented in the dream image of the older man in the doctor's staff dining room. Another probable manifestation of her unconscious perception of the third party in the elevator was the conscious memory of her father looking at her when she stumbled while dancing.

According to Basch, her negative hallucination symptom was related to her disavowal of the analyst's significance to her. As long as she could ward off anxiety by disavowing the meaning of her relationship to the analyst, her insights, though valid, remained intellectual; and the disappearance of many of her symptoms was the effect of an unanalyzed transference cure.

Basch does not mention the possibility that another disturbing stimulus for the dream was the frame disruption of his extraanalytic contact with the patient in the elevator. The image of the young man who pushed the patient on the escalator and the feeling in the dream that the analyst is very young could be products of her unconscious meaning analysis of the frame disruption. Her doubts in the dream about the analyst knowing his field could also be a product of this meaning analysis.

THE UNCONSCIOUS PERCEPTION OF SOMATIC STIMULI IN DREAMS

Another example of unconscious perceptions appearing in dreams is somatic sources of stimulation occurring during sleep. Exogenous stimuli may be represented in dreams by an immense variety of ideas; dreams contain symbolizations of bodily organs and functions (Freud, 1900). Somatic stimuli that are symbolized in dreams may include such noises as the sound of an alarm clock, bright lights, digestive disturbances, and the like. These external stimuli are not represented in dreams in their true character but invariably by some other image. The ringing of an alarm clock, for instance, is represented by something else, and the symbol of water in a dream frequently represents a urinary stimulus. Somatic sources of stimulations, according to Freud, play a part in the formation of dreams that is similar to the part played by recent impressions left over from the previous day (i.e., the day residue).

For Freud, the dream is a reaction to everything that is currently active in the sleeping mind, including childhood fantasies and memories, the day residue, and somatic stimuli. In Freud's view, somatic stimuli undergo the same kinds of primary process transformations as does the day residue. The products of these transformations appear in dream symbols.

EXPERIMENTAL STUDIES
ON UNCONSCIOUS PERCEPTION

A large number of experimental studies demonstrate that unconscious perception does occur and that fragments of such perception may appear in the subject's dreams as well as waking imagery (Poetzl, 1917; Fisher, 1954, 1956, 1957; Shevrin and Luborsky, 1958; Fisher and Paul, 1959; Silverman, 1976). Fisher (1954, 1956, 1957) and others have demonstrated that stimuli exposed tachistoscopically at a speed so great that nothing more than a flicker of light can be consciously perceived will nevertheless register in the brain and affect behavior. When subjects were asked to free associate or "free-image" (i.e., draw whatever came to mind) immediately after such subliminal exposures, aspects of the stimulus would often appear in their productions.

Silverman (1967) discovered that if the subliminal stimulus has "psychodynamic content" (e.g., content related to unconscious wishes or anxiety) in addition to its content becoming retrievable, the person's level of psychopathology would be affected. The subliminal content would unconsciously stir up motives congruent with the particular stimulus, and symptoms rooted in those emotions would emerge or become intensified. For example, the subliminal message evoking a fantasy of symbiotic gratification, "Mommy and I are one," led to reduced thought disorder and more adaptive ego functioning in a group of schizophrenic patients.

In a pioneer laboratory investigation of dream imagery, Poetzl (1917) discovered that his subjects dreamed about the originally unreported parts of a previously exposed picture. He flashed slides of everyday scenes at 1/100 second and asked subjects to describe and draw what they saw. Then he told them to record any dreams they had that night. On the following day, when he asked the subjects to describe and draw their dreams, he found that their dream imagery borrowed extensively from the unreported portions of the picture. Other investigations have confirmed Poetzl's findings (Fisher, 1954, 1956, 1957; Shevrin and Luborsky, 1958; Silverman, 1967).

Both Poetzl and Freud were aware of the parallel between Freud's theories of dreams and Poetzl's findings. The "indifferent" perceptions that Freud identified as day residue represented in the manifest content of dreams, Poetzl equated with the unreported parts of the picture that were later dreamed.

According to Fisher (1954), findings from experiments on subliminal perception necessitate a very great expansion of the role of the day residue in the process of dream formation. Fisher and Paul (1959) argue persuasively that the first phase of the "Poetzl phenomenon" (i.e., sensory registration outside of awareness) cannot be considered preconscious in the psychoanalytic meaning of the term. By definition, "preconscious" refers to contents not in consciousness but that may, with varying degrees of difficulty, merge into it. Subliminal perception and the first phase of the "Poetzl phenomenon" involve unconscious, not preconscious, perception.

DISCUSSION

The foregoing clinical and experimental findings argue for a revised theory about the importance and function of recent events in dream formation. Freud's theory on this topic is incomplete. A major omission in Freud's (1900) writings on the day residue was his failure to account for the contribution made by the products of unconscious meaning analysis to dream formation.

In what follows, Freud's (1900) views on the day residue are summarized, and some modifications and additions to the theory about the role of recent events on dream formation are offered. According to Freud, dreams are triggered by events occurring shortly before the dream. He called these events the "day residue" and the "preconscious residue." Dreams pick up the "indifferent refuse" left over from the previous one or two days, and these trivial and indifferent impressions provide some of the manifest content of dreams (p. 589). What is "subsidiary" and "unnoticed" in the previous day may appear in the manifest content.

Freud described a number of different thought impulses carried over from the previous few days that persist in sleep. They include "unsolved problems," "tormenting worries," "overwhelming impressions," "indifferent" daytime impressions, and whatever has been "suppressed" during the daytime. He did not attach much dynamic importance to the day residue. He believed that it was the "innocent" and "unimportant" actions and perceptions of the previous day that are repeated in dreams (p. 21). That is, what is "indifferent" and consequently unnoticed, appears in dreams. The fact that the content of dreams includes remnants of trivial experiences he explained as a manifestation of censorship through primary process distortion. He asserted that the neutral or indifferent character of the preconscious day residue permitted it to serve as a "cover" for unconscious infantile wishes that would not otherwise escape dream censorship.

According to Freud, the preconscious residues must connect up with infantile wishes from the Ucs. The "motive force" dreams require is provided by infantile unconscious wishes (p. 561). There occurs a transference (by displacement) of psychical intensity from these unconscious wishes onto the preconscious residues, and the latter provides part of the manifest content. Preconscious trains of thought left over from waking life are relegated to a secondary and subsidiary position with respect to dream formation (p. 554).

Freud admitted that there is a whole class of dreams whose "instigation" arises principally from residues of daytime life, although "the *motive force* which the dream required had to be provided by a wish" (pp. 560–561). Not until much later, in *Beyond the Pleasure Principle,* did Freud (1920) modify his theory of unconscious wishes being the only type of motive force in dream formation. There he noted that dreams that occur in the traumatic neuroses and dreams that bring to memory the psychical traumas of childhood are exceptions to the rule that dreams are wish fulfillments.

Though Freud's comments about the repetition compulsion, trauma, and dream formation indicated the necessity for major changes in the theory of dream formation, few analysts since Freud's time have assimilated insights about the relationship between the repetition compulsion and dreaming into their concepts of dreaming. Sharpe (1937) follows the earlier views of Freud (1900). Few since Freud have considered this topic, and there appears to be a general unawareness about the importance of reality experiences in dream formation and a concomitant excessive and almost exclusive emphasis on the role of repressed wishes and unconscious fantasies.

An exception to the neglect of reality experiences in dream construction is a 1971 paper by Langs. His hypothesis that day residues derive from actual experiences that are a significant part of an ongoing interaction between a person's psyche and reality is one of the few in the psychoanalytic literature stressing the role of reality experience in dream formation. As my coauthor explained in Section II, reality experiences interacting together with schemata established in the past create a totality out of which neuroses and dreams develop.

Freud's theory on the role of recent events in dream formation was mistaken or incomplete on several counts. First, Freud, like others of his time, was unaware of the existence of unconscious meaning analysis and of the fact that the products of this process could appear in dreams and other primary process manifestations. Second, Freud and other scientists of his day did not know about unconscious perception. As I explained in Chapter 1, they mistakenly believed that perception is a sensory given and immediately known to the subject—for example, Pcpt = Cs (Freud, 1900). Freud held that sensory stimuli, in contrast to drive derivatives from the *Ucs,* have direct access to consciousness.

A third error made by Freud in his theory about the role of recent events in dream formation was his consistent tendency to minimize their dynamic importance. He recognized that preconscious residues played a part in dream formation, but he assigned them the relatively unimportant and subsidiary function of contributing to the dream's manifest content. He believed that recent events making up the day residue were of a trivial and indifferent kind and that their function in dream formation was simply to provide images for the manifest content. The major thesis advanced in this chapter is that unconscious meaning analyses and unconscious perception of recent events are dynamically important in dream formation and that they contribute to the unconscious meanings (i.e., latent content) of dreams.

Goodheart (1987) argues persuasively for the proposition that Freud's turn toward intrapsychic sources of dreams and symptoms and away from reality interactions was defensively motivated. Consequently, Goodheart claims, the entire thrust of Freud's therapeutic and investigative efforts was to probe for unconscious, forbidden wishes and fantasies within himself and his patients rather than also to explore for unconscious perceptions of interactions with others that could serve as an important stimulus for the formation of dreams, associations, and symptoms.

UNCONSCIOUS MEANING ANALYSIS AND FREUD'S THEORY OF THE DREAM-WORK

As I noted in Chapter 1, Freud's theory of how dreams are formed was based on his theory of cognition and especially his concepts about primary process distortion and censorship in the second stage of cognition. The demise of Freud's theory of cognition as discussed in Chapter 1, plus the overwhelming evidence from research on dreaming, points to serious errors in the classical Freudian theory of dreaming.

Freud's basic error in his theory of dream formation was his presupposition that the dream possesses two different contents: (1) the manifest content representing a real and distinct transformation of (2) a latent content. The dream has only one content, and it has this sense immediately, not prior to a nonexistent process of censorship through primary process distortion (see Piaget, 1962; Politzer, 1974). The only proper use of the term latent content is in referring to the meanings of a dream that the dreamer does not initially understand.

Freud's explanation of the distortion in dreams was an attempted causal explanation: the distortions, the absurdities, and the bizarre properties of dreams are caused by the occurrence of the processes Freud (1900) called the dream-work. The most important dynamic in his theory of the dream-work is that the undistorted cognitions in the latent content are censored, disguised, and distorted by primary process mechanisms of displacement and condensation.

The so-called distortions, the strangeness, and the often bizarre quality of dreams do not, in my opinion or that of others such as Fossi (1984), Foulkes (1972, 1978), Hall (1966), Hobson (1988), Holt (1976), Jones (1970), Piaget (1962), and Winson (1985), arise from a process of primary process distortion and censorship. Dream researchers and others have suggested other more plausible explanations for the so-called distortions and cognitive peculiarities of dreasm. Distortion and disguise do not enter into the process of dreaming as such. The process of dreaming involves the transformation of recent as well as infantile mental contents into new forms. Whether it be slight or massive, the onus of defensive distortion falls upon the waking state, a state in which dreams may be interpreted but not formed (Jones, 1970). The bizarreness, distortion, and other cognitive characteristics of dreams are merely the consequence of their expression in analogical, primary process form. The process of dream formation is *transformative* rather than distortive.

The latent content of the dream is some meaning the dreamer does not initially understand but can understand through self-reflection and free association. The latent content is not something that exists prior to dream formation. Nor is it something that the dreamer or analyst finds or discovers; rather, it is something that the dreamer, with or without the aid of a therapist, *constructs* by applying different categories of understanding to the manifest dream. The process of meaning analysis is carried out unconsciously in dreaming itself and then it may also be continued consciously in waking life when, with or without the aid of a therapist or analyst, the now awake dreamer creates new interpretations of the manifest dream.

References

Abelson, R. (1978), *Scripts*. Invited address to the Midwestern Psychological Association, Chicago, May.

Abend, S. M. (1990), Unconscious fantasies, structural theory, and compromise formation. *J. Amer. Psychoanal. Assn.*, 38:61–73.

Adrian, E. D. (1934), Electrical activity of the nervous system. *Arch. Neurologic Psychiat.*, 32:1125–1135.

Alexander, F. (1948), *Fundamentals of Psychoanalysis*. New York: Norton.

——— (1950), Analysis of the therapeutic factors in psychoanalytic treatment. *Psychoanal. Quart.*, 19:482–500.

Altschul, S. (1968), Denial and ego arrest. *J. Amer. Psychoanal. Assn.*, 16:301–318.

Arlow, J. (1969a), Unconscious fantasy and disturbances of conscious experience. *Psychoanal. Quart.*, 38:1–27.

——— (1969b), Fantasy, memory and reality testing. *Psychoanal. Quart.*, 38:28–51.

——— (1985a), Consensual analysis: A clinically focused discussion. In: *New Ideas in Psychoanalysis*, ed. C. F. Settlage & R. Brockbank. Hillsdale, NJ: The Analytic Press.

——— (1985b), The concept of psychic reality and related problems. *J. Amer. Psychoanal. Assn.*, 33:521–536.

Asaad, G. (1990), *Hallucinations in Clinical Psychiatry*. New York: Brunner/Mazel.

Atwood, G. E. & Stolorow, R. D. (1984), *Structures of Subjectivity*. Hillsdale, NJ: The Analytic Press.

Bacal, H. A. & Newman, K. M. (1990), *Theories of Object Relations*. New York: Columbia University Press.

Balint, M. (1965), *Primary Love and Psycho-Analytic Technique*. London: Tavistock.

Bartlett, F. C. (1932), *Remembering*. Cambridge, UK: Cambridge University Press.

Basch, M. F. (1974), Interference with perceptual transformation in the service of defense. In: *The Annual of Psychoanalysis*, 2:87–97. New York: International Universities Press.

——— (1976a), Theory formation in chapter VII: A critique. *J. Amer. Psychoanal. Assn.*, 24:61–100.

——— (1976b), The concept of affect: A reeaxmination. *J. Amer. Psychoanal. Assn.*, 24:759–777.

——— (1977), Developmental psychology and explanatory theory in psychoanalysis. *The Annual of Psychoanalysis*, 5:229–263. New York: International Universities Press.

——— (1981), Psychoanalytic interpretation and cognitive transformation. *Internat. J. Psycho-Anal.*, 62:151–176.

Bateson, G. (1955), A theory of play and fantasy. *Psychiat. Res. Rep.*, 2:39–51.

——— (1972), *Steps to an Ecology of Mind*. New York: Chandler.

Beck, A. T. (1967), *Depression*. New York: Harper & Row.

——— (1972), Cognition, anxiety and physiological disorders. In: *Anxiety, Vol. 2*, ed. C. D. Spielberger. New York: Academic Press.

Beebe, B. & Lachmann, F. M. (1988), The contribution of mother–infant mutual influence to the origins of self and object representations. *Psychoanal. Psychol.*, 5:205–338.

285

Beres, D. (1960), Perception, imagination, and reality. *Internat. J. Psycho-Anal.*, 41:327–334.

⸻ (1962), The unconscious fantasy. *Psychoanal. Quart.*, 31:309–329.

Berscheid, E. (1982), Attraction and emotion in interpersonal relationships. In: *Affect and Cognition*, ed. M. S. Clark & S. T. Fiske. Hillsdale, NJ: Lawrence Erlbaum Associates.

⸻ (1983), Emotion. In: *Close Relationships*, ed. H. H. Kelley, E. Berscheid, A. Christenson, J. Harvey, T. Huston, G. Levinger, E. McLintock, A. Peplau & D. R. Peterson. San Francisco: Freeman.

Bertalanffy, L. von (1968), *General Systems Theory*. New York: Braziller.

Bion, W. R. (1959a), Attacks on linking. *Internat. J. Psycho-Anal.*, 40:308–315.

⸻ (1959b), *Experiences in Groups*. New York: Basic Books.

⸻ (1967), *Second Thoughts*. New York: Aronson.

⸻ (1977), *Seven Servants*. New York: Aronson.

Blum, H. P. (1976), The changing use of dreams in psychoanalytic practice. *Internat. J. Psycho-Anal.*, 57:315–324.

Boesky, D. (1988), Criteria of evidence for an unconscious fantasy. In: *Fantasy, Myth and Reality*, ed. H. P. Blum, Y. Dramer, A. K. Richards & A. D. Richards. Madison, CT: International Universities Press.

Bonime, W. (1962), *The Clinical Use of Dreams*. New York: Basic Books.

Boszormenyi-Nagy, I. (1967), Relational modes and meaning. In: *Family Therapy and Disturbed Families*, ed. G. H. Zuk & I. Boszormenyi-Nagy. Palo Alto, CA: Science & Behavior Books.

Bowers, K. S. (1984), On being unconsciously influenced and informed. In: *The Unconscious Reconsidered*, ed. K. S. Bowers & D. Meichenbaum. New York: Wiley, pp. 227–272.

Bowlby, J. (1969), *Attachment and Loss, Vol. 1*. New York: Basic Books.

Brazelton, T., Koslowski, V. & Main, M. (1974), The origins of reciprocity: The early mother infant interaction. In: *The Effects of the Infant on Its Caregiver*, ed. M. Lewis & L. Rosenblum. New York: Wiley.

Breuer, J. & Freud, S. (1893–1895), *Studies on Hysteria. Standard Edition*, 2. London: Hogarth Press.

Brodey, W. M. (1965), On the dynamics of narcissism: I. Externalization and early ego development. *The Psychoanalytic Study of the Child*, 20:165–193. New York: International Universities Press.

Brown, J. W. (1972), *Aphasia, Apraxia, and Agnosia*. Springfield, IL: Charles C. Thomas.

Bruner, J. S. (1977), Early social interaction and language acquisition. In: *Studies in Mother–Infant Interactions*, ed. H. R. Schaffer. London: Academic Press.

⸻ (1983), *Child talk*. New York: Norton.

⸻ (1990), *Acts of Meaning*. Cambridge, MA: Harvard University Press.

Bucci, W. (1985), Dual coding: A cognitive model for psychoanalytic research. *J. Amer. Psychoanal. Assn.*, 33:571–608.

Burston, D. (1986), The cognitive and dynamic unconscious: A critical and historical perspective. *Contemp. Psychoanal.*, 22:133–157.

Cain, A. C. (1972), Children's disturbed reactions to parental suicide: Distortions of guilt, communication, and identification. In: *Survivors of Suicide*, ed. A. C. Cain. Springfield, IL: Charles C. Thomas.

Cannon, W. B. (1942), Voodoo death. *Amer. Anthropol.*, 44:169–181.

Cantor, N. & Mischel, W. (1977), Traits as prototypes: Effects on recognition memory. *J. Personality & Social Psychol.*, 35:38–49.

Cassirer, E. (1960), *The Logic of the Humanities*. New Haven, CT: Yale Universities Press.

Chaitin, G. D. (1978), The representation of logical relations in dreams and the nature of primary process. *Psychoanal. Contemp. Thought*, 1:477–502.

Chessick, R. D. (1986), Transference and Countertransference Revisited. *Dynam. Psychother.*, 4:14–30.

_____ (1990), Psychoanalytic listening III. *Psychoanal. & Psychother.*, 8:119–131.

Cooper, A. M. (1987), Changes in psychoanalytic ideas: Transference interpretation. *J. Amer. Psychoanal. Assn.*, 35:77–98.

Cordaro, L. & Ison, J. R. (1963), Observer bias in classical conditioning of the planaria. *Psychol. Reports*, 13:787–789.

Dahl, H. (1965), Observations on a "natural experiment": Helen Keller. *J. Amer. Psychoanal. Assn.*, 13:533–550.

De Monchaux, C. (1978), Dreaming and the organizing function of the ego. *Internat. J. Psycho-Anal.*, 59:443–453.

Dewald, P. A. (1972), *The Psychoanalytic Process*. New York: Basic Books.

Dorpat, T. L. (1971), Phantom sensations of internal organs. *Comp. Psych.*, 12:27–35.

_____ (1972), Psychological effects of parental suicide on surviving children. In: *Survivors of Suicide*, ed. A. C. Cain. Springfield, IL: Charles C. Thomas.

_____ (1974), Drug automatism, barbiturate poisoning and suicide behavior. *Arch. Gen. Psychiat.*, 31:216–220.

_____ (1983a), The cognitive arrest hypothesis of denial. *Internat. J. Psycho-Anal.*, 64:46–58.

_____ (1983b), Denial, defect, symptom formation—and construction. *Psychoanal. Inq.*, 3:223–258.

_____ (1984), Technical errors in supervised analyses. In: *Listening and Interpreting*, ed. J. Raney. New York: Aronson.

_____ (1985), *Denial and Defense in the Therapeutic Situation*. New York: Aronson.

_____ (1987a), A new look at denial and defense. In: *The Annual of Psychoanalysis*, 15:23–48. New York: International Universities Press.

_____ (1987b), Unconscious perception, the day residue and dreaming. In: *The Yearbook of Psychoanalysis and Psychotherapy*, Vol. 2, ed. R. Langs. New York: Gardner Press.

Dowling, S. (1990), Fantasy formation: A child analyst's perspective. *J. Amer. Psychoanal. Assn.*, 38:93–111.

Eagle, M. N. (1983), A critical examination of motivational explanation in psychoanalysis. In: *Mind and Medicine*, ed. L. Laudan. Berkeley: University of California Press.

Edelson, M. (1984), *Hypothesis and Evidence in Psychoanalysis*. Chicago: University of Chicago Press.

Emde, R. (1983), The representational self and its affective core. *The Psychoanalytic Study of the Child*, 38:165–192. New Haven, CT: Yale University Press.

_____ (1988a), Development terminable and interminable I: Innate and motivational factors from infancy. *Internat. J. Psycho-Anal.*, 69:23–42.

_____ (1988b), Development terminable and interminable II: Recent psychoanalytic theory and therapeutic considerations. *Internat. J. Psycho-Anal.*, 69:283–296.

Erikson, E. H. (1950), *Childhood and Society*, rev. ed. New York: Norton.

_____ (1954), The dream specimen of psychoanalysis. *J. Amer. Psychoanal. Assn.*, 2:5–56.

Fast, I. (1985), *Event Theory*. Hillsdale, NJ: Lawrence Erlbaum Associates.

Feiner, A. H. (1979), Countertransference and the anxiety of influence. In: *Countertransference*, ed. L. Epstein & A. H. Feiner. New York: Aronson.

Fenichel, O. (1945), *The Psychoanalytic Theory of Neurosis*. New York: Norton.

Fingarette, H. (1969), *Self-Deception*. New York: Routledge & Kegan Paul.

Fisher, C. (1954), Dreams and perception: the role of preconscious and primary modes of perception in dream formation. *J. Amer. Psychoanal. Assn.*, 2:285–445.

_____ (1956), Dreams, images and perception: A study of unconscious-preconscious relationships. *J. Amer. Psychoanal. Assn.*, 4:5–48.

_____ (1957), A study of the preliminary stages of the construction of dreams and images. *J. Amer. Psychoanal. Assn.,* 5:5–60.

_____ & Paul, I. H. (1959), The effect of subliminal visual stimulation on images and dreams: A validation study. *J. Amer. Psychoanal. Assn.,* 7:35–83.

Fisher, S. & Greenberg, R. P. (1977), *The Scientific Credibility of Freud's Theories and Therapy.* New York: Basic Books.

Fosshage, J. L. (1983), The psychological function of dreams: A revised psychoanalytic perspective. *Psychoanal. Contemp. Thought,* 6:641–669.

Fossi, G. (1984), *Le teorie psicoanalitiche.* Padua, Italy: Piccin.

_____ (1985), Psychoanalytic theory and the problem of creativity. *Internat. J. Psycho-Anal.,* 66:215–230.

Foulkes, D. (1972), *Children's Dreams.* New York: Wiley.

_____ (1978), *A Grammar of Dreams.* New York: Basic Books.

Framo, J. L. (1970), Symptoms from a family transactional viewpoint. In: *Family Therapy and Transition,* ed. N. W. Ackerman. Boston, MA: Little, Brown.

Freud, A. (1936), *The Ego and the Mechanisms of Defense.* New York: International Universities Press.

_____ (1968), Acting Out. *The Writings of Anna Freud,* 7:94–109. New York: International Universities Press, 1971.

Freud, S. (1895), Project for a scientific psychology. *Standard Edition,* 1:295–397. London: Hogarth Press, 1966.

_____ (1896a), Further remarks on the neuro-psychoses of defense. *Standard Edition,* 3:159–184. London: Hogarth Press, 1962.

_____ (1896b), The aetiology of hysteria. *Standard Edition,* 3:189–221. London: Hogarth Press, 1962.

_____ (1900), The interpretation of dreams. *Standard Edition,* 4 & 5. London: Hogarth Press, 1953.

_____ (1901), On dreams. *Standard Edition,* 5:631–685. London: Hogarth Press, 1953.

_____ (1905a), Three essays on the theory of sexuality. *Standard Edition,* 7:125–134. London: Hogarth Press, 1953.

_____ (1905b), Fragment of an analysis of a case of hysteria. *Standard Edition,* 7:7–124. London: Hogarth Press, 1953.

_____ (1906), My views on the part played by sexuality in the aetiology of the neuroses. *Standard Edition,* 7:271–279. London: Hogarth Press, 1953.

_____ (1907), Delusions and dreams in Jensen's Gradiva. *Standard Edition,* 9:7–93. London: Hogarth Press, 1959.

_____ (1908), Hysterical phantasies and their relation to bisexuality. *Standard Edition,* 9:157–166. London: Hogarth Press, 1959.

_____ (1909), Notes upon a case of obsessional neurosis. *Standard Edition,* 10:153–318. London: Hogarth Press, 1955.

_____ (1911), Formulations on the two principles of mental functioning. *Standard Edition,* 12:215–226. London: Hogarth Press, 1958.

_____ (1912), The dynamics of transference. *Standard Edition,* 12:99–108. London: Hogarth Press, 1958.

_____ (1914a), On the history of the psycho-analytic movement. *Standard Edition,* 14:3–66. London: Hogarth Press, 1957.

_____ (1914b), Remembering, repeating and working through. *Standard Edition,* 12:147–156. London: Hogarth Press, 1958.

_____ (1915a), Observations on transference-love. *Standard Edition,* 12:157–174. London: Hogarth Press, 1958.

_____ (1915b), Repression. *Standard Edition,* 14:143–158. London: Hogarth Press, 1957.

_____ (1915c), The unconscious. *Standard Edition*, 14:161–204. London: Hogarth Press, 1957.

_____ (1916), Some character-types met with in psycho-analytic work. *Standard Edition*, 14:311–331. London: Hogarth Press, 1957.

_____ (1917), Introductory lectures on psycho-analysis. *Standard Edition*, 16:243–256. London: Hogarth Press, 1963.

_____ (1918), From the history of an infantile neuroses. *Standard Edition*, 17:3–122. London: Hogarth Press, 1955.

_____ (1919), A child is being beaten: a contribution to the study of the origin of sexual perversions. *Standard Edition*, 17:177–204. London: Hogarth Press, 1955.

_____ (1920), Beyond the pleasure principle. *Standard Edition*, 18:3–64. London: Hogarth Press, 1955.

_____ (1921), Group psychology and the analysis of the ego. *Standard Edition*, 18:67–143. London: Hogarth Press, 1955.

_____ (1923), The ego and the id. *Standard Edition*, 19:3–59. London: Hogarth Press, 1961.

_____ (1925a), Negation. *Standard Edition*, 19:235–239. London: Hogarth Press, 1961.

_____ (1925b), An autobiographical study. *Standard Edition*, 20:3–70. London: Hogarth Press, 1959.

_____ (1926), Inhibitions, symptoms and anxiety. *Standard Edition*, 20:77–172. London: Hogarth Press, 1959.

_____ (1927), Fetishism. *Standard Edition*, 21:149–157. London: Hogarth Press, 1961.

_____ (1933), New introductory lectures on psycho-analysis. *Standard Edition*, 22:3–157. London: Hogarth Press, 1964.

_____ (1937), Constructions in analysis. *Standard Edition*, 23:257–629. London: Hogarth Press, 1964.

_____ (1939), Moses and monotheism. *Standard Edition*, 23:3–56. London: Hogarth Press, 1964.

_____ (1940a), An outline of psychoanalysis. *Standard Edition*, 23:141–206. London: Hogarth Press, 1964.

_____ (1940b), Splitting of the ego in the process of defense. *Standard Edition*, 23:273–278. London: Hogarth Press, 1964.

Galenson, E. & Roiphe, H. (1980), The preoedipal development of the boy. *J. Amer. Psychoanal. Assn.*, 28:805–828.

Galin, D. (1974), Implications for psychiatry of left and right cerebral specialization. *Arch. Gen. Psychiat.*, 31:572–583.

Gardner, H. (1983), *Frames of Mind*. New York: Basic Books.

Gazzaniga, M. (1967), The split brain in man. *Scient. Amer.*, 217:24–29.

_____ (1985), *The Social Brain*. New York: Basic Books.

Gedo, J. E. (1979), *Beyond Interpretation*. New York: International Universities Press.

_____ (1984), *Psychoanalysis and Its Discontents*. New York: Guilford Press.

_____ (1988), *The Mind in Disorder*. Hillsdale, NJ: The Analytic Press.

_____ & Goldberg, A. (1973), *Models of the Mind*. Chicago: University of Chicago Press.

Gill, M. M. (1982a), *Analysis of Transference I*. New York: International Universities Press.

_____ (1982b), Merton Gill: An interview. *Psychoanal. Rev.*, 69:167–190.

_____ (1983), The distinction between the interpersonal paradigm and the degree of the therapist's involvement. *Contemp. Psychoanal.*, 19:200–237.

_____ (1984), Transference: A change in conception or only in emphasis? *Psychoanal. Inq.*, 4:489–524.

_____ (1986), Discussion of "Transference and Countertransference Revisited" by R. D. Chessick. *Dynamic Psychother.*, 4:31–33.

_____ (1987), The analyst and participant. *Psychoanal. Inq.*, 7:249–259.

Glover, E. (1945), Examination of the Klein system of child psychology. *The Psychoanalytic Study of the Child*, 1:75–188. New York: International Universities Press.

Goldberg, A. (1988), *A Fresh Look at Psychoanalysis*. Hillsdale, NJ: The Analytic Press.

Goleman, D. (1985), *Vital Lies, Simple Truths*. New York: Simon & Schuster.

Goodheart, W. B. (1987), Towards an understanding of Freud's overlooking unconscious perception. In: *The Yearbook of Psychoanalysis and Psychotherapy, Vol 2*, ed. R. Langs. New York: Gardner Press.

Greenson, R. R. (1965), The working alliance and the transference neurosis. *Psychoanal. Quart.*, 34:155–181.

_____ (1967), *The Techniques and Practice of Psychoanalysis*. New York: International Universities Press.

_____ (1971), The real relationship between the patient and the psychoanalyst. In: *The Unconscious Today*, ed. M. Kanzer. New York: International Universities Press.

_____ & Wexler, M. (1969), The non-transference relationship in the psychoanalytic situation. *Internat. J. Psycho-Anal.*, 50:27–40.

Grindberg, L. (1962), On a specific aspect of countertransference due to the patient's projective identification. *Internat. J. Psycho-Anal.*, 43:436–440.

Grossman, W. I. (1982), The self as fantasy. *J. Amer. Psychoanal. Assn.*, 30:919–937.

Hadley, J. L. (1983), The representational system: A bridging concept for psychoanalysis and neurophysiology. *Internat. Rev. Psycho-Anal.*, 10:13–30.

Hall, C. (1966), *The Meaning of Dreams*. New York: McGraw-Hill.

Hartmann, H. (1939), *Ego Psychology and the Problem of Adaptation*. New York: International Universities Press.

_____ (1964), *Essays on Ego Psychology*. New York: International Universities Press.

Heider, F. (1958), *The Psychology of Interpersonal Relations*. New York: Wiley.

Heimann, P. (1950), On countertransference. *Internat. J. Psycho-Anal.*, 31:81–84.

Heisenberg, W. (1958), *Physics and Philosophy*. New York: Harper.

Herman, J. L. & Schatzow, E. (1987), Recovery and verification of memories of childhood sexual trauma. *Psychoanal. Psychol.*, 4:1–14.

Hobson, J. A. (1988), *The Dreaming Brain*. New York: Basic Books.

Hoffman, I. Z. (1983), The patient as interpreter of the analyst experience. *Contemp. Psychoanal.*, 19:389–422.

Holt, R. R. (1967), The development of the primary process: A structural view. In: *Motives and Thought*, ed. R. R. Holt. *Psychological Issues*, Monograph 18/19. New York: International Universities Press.

_____ (1976), Freud's theory of the primary process—present status. *Psychoanal. Contemp. Sci.*, 5:61–99.

Hoppe, K. (1977), Split brains and psychoanalysis. *Psychoanal. Quart.*, 46:220–244.

Horowitz, M. J. (1976), *Stress Response Syndromes*. New York: Aronson.

Howard, N. (1967), The theory of metagames. *General Systems*, 2:167–169.

Inderbitzin, L. B. & Levy, S. T. (1990), Unconscious fantasy: A reconsideration of the concept. *J. Amer. Psychoanal. Assn.*, 38:113–130.

Inhelder, B. & Piaget, J. (1958), *Growth of Logical Thinking from Childhood to Adolescence*. New York: Basic Books.

_____ & _____ (1964), *Early Growth of Logic in the Child*. New York: Harper & Row.

Isaacs, S. (1948), The nature and function of fantasy. *Internat. J. Psycho-Anal.*, 29:73–97.

Izard, C. E. (1977), *Human Emotions*. New York: Plenum Press.

Janis, I. (1983), *Victims of Groupthink*. Boston, MA: Houghton Mifflin.

Jones, E. E. (1986), Interpreting interpersonal behavior: The effects of expectancies. *Science*, 234:41–46.

Jones, R. A. (1974), *Self-fulfilling Prophecies*. New York: Halsted.
Jones, R. M. (1965), Dream interpretation and the psychology of dreaming. *J. Amer. Psychoanal. Assn.*, 13:304–319.
_____ (1970), *The New Psychology of Dreaming*. New York: Grune & Stratton.
Kagan, J. (1981), *The Second Year of Life*. Cambridge, MA: Harvard University Press.
Kanzer, M. (1955), The communicative function of the dream. *Internat. J. Psycho-Anal.*, 36:260–266.
_____ (1957), Panel report: Acting out and its relation to impulse disorders. *J. Amer. Psychoanal. Assn.*, 5:136–145.
Keller, H. (1908), *The World I Live In*. New York: Century.
Kernberg, O. F. (1975), *Borderline Conditions and Pathological Narcissism*. New York: Aronson.
_____ (1976), *Object Relations Theory and Clinical Psychoanalysis*. New York: Aronson.
Khan, M. M. R. (1963), The concept of cumulative trauma. *The Psychoanalytic Study of the Child*, 18:286–306. New York: International Universities Press.
Kihlstrom, J. F. (1987), The cognitive unconscious. *Science*, 237:1445–1452.
Klein, G. S. (1976), *Psychoanalytic Theory*. New York: International Universities Press.
Klein, M. (1946), Notes on some schizoid mechanisms. *Internat. J. Psycho-Anal.*, 27:99–110.
_____ (1952), Some theoretical conclusions regarding the emotional life of the infant. In: *Envy and Gratitude and Other Works, 1946–1963*. New York: Delacorte Press/Seymour Lawrence, 1975.
Kohut, H. (1971), *The Analysis of the Self*. New York: International Universities Press.
_____ (1977), *The Restoration of the Self*. New York: International Universities Press.
Kolb, L. C. (1951), Disturbance of the body image. In: *American Handbook of Psychiatry, Vol 1*, ed. S. Arieti. New York: Basic Books.
_____ (1954), *The Painful Phantom*. Springfield, IL: Charles C. Thomas.
Kramer, Y. (1988), In the visions of the night: Perspectives on the work of Jacob A. Arlow. In: *Fantasy, Myth and Reality*, ed. H. P. Blum, Y. Kramer, A. K. Richards & A. D. Richards. Madison, CT: International Universities Press.
Kris, E. (1952), *Psychoanalytic Explorations in Art*. New York: International Universities Press.
Krystal, H. (1978), Trauma and affects. *The Psychoanalytic Study of the Child*, 33:81–116. New Haven, CT: Yale University Press.
_____ (1988), *Integration and Self-Healing*. Hillsdale, NJ: The Analytic Press.
Kubie, L. S. (1954), The fundamental nature of the distinction between normality and neurosis. *Psychoanal. Quart.*, 23:167–204.
Kübler-Ross, E. (1969), *On Death and Dying*. London: Macmillan.
Kuhn, T. S. (1962), *The Structure of Scientific Revolutions*. Chicago: University of Chicago Press.
Lacan, J. (1968), *The Language of the Self*, trans. A. Wilden. Baltimore, MD: Johns Hopkins University Press.
Laing, R. D. (1967), Family and individual structure. In: *The Predicament of the Family*, ed. P. Lomax. New York: International Universities Press.
_____ (1969), *The Politics of the Family*. Toronto: CBC.
Langer, J. (1969), *Theories of Development*. New York: Holt, Rinehart & Winston.
Langer, S. K. (1942), *Philosophy in a New Key*. Cambridge, MA: Harvard University Press.
Langs, R. (1971), Day residues, recall residues, and dreams: Reality and the psyche. *J. Amer. Psychoanal. Assn.*, 19:499–523.
_____ (1973), *The Technique of Psychoanalytic Psychotherapy, Vol. 1*. New York: Aronson.
_____ (1976), *The Bipersonal Field*. New York: Aronson.
_____ (1978a), *The Listening Process*. New York: Aronson.
_____ (1978b), *Technique in Transition*. New York: Aronson.
_____ (1979a), *The Therapeutic Environment*. New York: Aronson.

_____ (1979b), The formation and timing of interventions. *J. Amer. Academy of Psychoanal.*, 7:4, 477–498.

_____ (1980), *Interactions.* New York: Aronson.

_____ (1981), *Resistances and Interventions.* New York: Aronson.

_____ (1982a), *Psychotherapy.* New York: Aronson.

_____ (1982b), *The Psychotherapeutic Conspiracy.* New York: Aronson.

_____ (1986a), A new model of the mind. *The Yearbook of Psychoanalysis and Psychotherapy,* 2. New York: Gardner Press.

Lansky, M. (1985/86), Preoccupation as a mode of pathologic distance regulation. *Internat. J. Psychoanal. Psychother.*, 11:409–425.

Laplanche, J. & Pontalis, J. B. (1973), *The Language of Psychoanalysis* (trans. D. Nicholson-Smith). New York: Aronson.

Levenson, E. (1972), *The Fallacy of Understanding.* New York: Basic Books.

_____ (1981), Facts or fantasies: The nature of psychoanalytic data. *Contemp. Psychoanal.*, 17:486–500.

Lewinsohn, P., Mischel, W., Chaplin, W. & Barton, R. (1980), Social competence and depression: The role of illusionary self-perceptions. *J. Abn. Psychol.*, 89:203–212.

Lichtenberg, J. (1983), *Psychoanalysis and Infant Research.* Hillsdale, NJ: The Analytic Press.

_____ (1989), *Psychoanalysis and Motivation.* Hillsdale, NJ: The Analytic Press.

Lichtenstein, H. (1977), *The Dilemma of Human Identity.* New York: Aronson.

Loewald, H. (1960), On the therapeutic action of psychoanalysis. *Internat. J. Psycho-Anal.*, 41:16–33.

Loftus, E. (1980), *Memory.* Reading, MA: Addison-Wesley.

Lorenz, K. (1965), *Evolution and Modification of Behavior.* Chicago: University of Chicago Press.

Mahler, M. S. (1952), On child psychosis and schizophrenia: Autistic and symbiotic infantile psychoses. *The Psychoanalytic Study of the Child,* 7:286–294. New York: International Universities Press.

_____ Pine, F. & Bergman, A. (1975), *The Psychological Birth of the Human Infant.* New York: Basic Books.

Malitz, S., Wilkins, B. & Esecover, H. (1962), A comparison of drug-induced hallucinations with those seen in spontaneously occurring psychoses. In: *Hallucinations,* ed. L. J. West. New York: Grune & Stratton.

Mandler, G. (1975a), *Mind and Emotion.* New York: Wiley.

_____ (1975b), Memory, storage and retrieval: Some limits on the research of attention and consciousness. In: *Attention and Performance, V,* ed. T. M. A. Rabbit & S. Dornic. London: Academic Press.

_____ (1984), *Mind and Body.* New York: Norton.

Masterson, J. F. (1976), *Psychotherapy of the Borderline Adult.* New York: Brunner/Mazel.

_____ (1981), *The Narcissitic and Borderline Disorders.* New York: Brunner/Mazel.

McConnell, J. V., Jacobson, R. & Humphries, B. M. (1961), The effects of ingestion of conditioned planaria on the response level of naive planaria: A pilot study. *Worm Runner's Digest,* 3:41–45.

McKinnon, J. A. (1979), Two semantic forms: neuropsychological and psychoanalytic descriptions. *Psychoanal. Contemp. Thought,* 2:25–76.

McLaughlin, J. T. (1978), Primary and secondary process in the context of cerebral hemispheric specialization. *Psychoanal. Quart.*, 47:237–266.

Meissner, W. W. (1968), Dreaming as process. *Internat. J. Psycho-Anal.*, 49:63–79.

Melzack, R. & Loeser, J. D. (1978), Phantom body pain in paraplegics: Evidence for a central "pattern generating mechanism" for pain. *Pain,* 4:195–210.

Mendelsohn, R. M. (1985), The concept of unconscious perception. In: *The Yearbook of*

Psychoanalysis and Psychotherapy, Vol. 1. Hillsdale, NJ: New Concept Press.

Merton, R. J. (1948), The self-fulfilling prophecy. *Antioch Rev.,* 8:193–210.

Miller, G. (1956), The magical number seven, plus or minus two: Some limits in our capacity for processing information. *Psycholog. Rev.,* 63:81–97.

———— Galanter, E. & Pribram, K. (1960), *Plans and the Structure of Behavior.* New York: Holt.

Miller, L. (1986), Some comments on cerebral hemispheric models of consciousness. *Psychoanal. Rev.,* 73:129–144.

Minsky, M. (1975), A framework for representing knowledge. In: *The Psychology of Computer Vision,* ed. P. H. Winston. New York: McGraw-Hill.

Mishkin, M. (1982), A memory system in the monkey. *Philosophical Transactions of the Royal Society of London,* B298:85–95.

Mitchell, S. A. (1991), Contemporary perspectives on self—Toward an integration. *Psychoanal. Dial.,* 1:121–147.

Modell, A. H. (1984), *Psychoanalysis in a New Context.* New York: International Universities Press.

Moore, B. E. & Fine, B. D., Ed. (1990), *Psychoanalytic Terms and Concepts.* New Haven, CT: Yale University Press.

Moore, M. S. (1983), The nature of psychoanalytic explanation. In: *Mind and Medicine,* ed. L. Laudan. Berkeley: University of California Press.

———— (1984), *Law and Psychiatry.* Cambridge: Cambridge University Press.

Muir, R. C. (1982), The family, the group, transpersonal processes and the individual. *Internat. Rev. Psycho-Anal.,* 9:317–326.

Neisser, U. (1967), *Cognitive Psychology.* New York: Appleton-Century-Crofts.

Neu, J. (1977), *Emotion, Thought and Therapy.* Berkeley: University of California Press.

Nietzsche, F. (1986), *Beyond Good and Evil.* New York: Random House, 1966.

Nisbett, R. & Ross, L. (1980), *Human Inference.* Englewood Cliffs, NJ: Prentice-Hall.

———— & Schachter, S. (1966), Cognitive manipulation of pain. *J. Exper. Social Psychol.,* 21:227–236.

———— & Wilson, T. (1977), Telling more than we can know: Verbal reports on mental process. *Psycholog. Rev.,* 84:231–259.

Norman, D. A. (1969), *Memory and Attention.* New York: Wiley.

Noy, P. (1969), A revision of the psychoanalytic theory of the primary process. *Internat. J. Psycho-Anal.,* 50:155–170.

———— (1973), Symbolism and mental representation. *The Annual of Psychoanalysis,* 1:125–158. New York: International Universities Press.

———— (1979), The psychoanalytic theory of cognitive development. *The Psychoanalytic Study of the Child,* 34:169–215. New Haven, CT: Yale University Press.

Ogden, T. H. (1982), *Projective Identification and Psychotherapeutic Technique.* New York: Aronson.

Ornstein, A. (1974), The dread to repeat and the new beginning. *The Annual of Psychoanalysis,* 2:231–248. New York: International Universities Press.

Orr, D. W. (1954), Transference and countertransference: A historical survey. *J. Amer. Psychoanal. Assn.,* 2:621–670.

Palombo, S. R. (1978), *Dreaming and Memory.* New York: Basic Books.

Penfield, W. & Rasmussen, T. (1950), *The Cerebral Cortex of Man.* New York: Macmillan.

Peterfreund, E. (1971), Information, systems, and psychoanalysis: An evolutionary biological approach to psychoanalytic theory. *Psychological Issues,* 7, Monogr. No. 25/26. New York: Basic Books.

Piaget, J. (1952), *The Origins of Intelligence in Children.* New York: International Universities Press.

_____ (1954), *The Construction of Reality in Children*. New York: Basic Books.

_____ (1962), *Play, Dreams, and Imitation in Childhood*. New York: Norton.

_____ (1970), *Structuralism*. New York: Basic Books.

_____ (1971), *Biology and Knowledge*. Chicago: University of Chicago Press.

_____ (1976), *The Grasp of Consciousness*. Cambridge, MA: Harvard University Press.

_____ & Inhelder, B. (1969), *The Psychology of the Child*. New York: Basic Books.

_____ & _____ (1971), *Mental Imagery in the Child*. New York: Basic Books.

_____ & _____ (1973), *Memory and Intelligence*. New York: Basic Books.

Pine, F. (1985), *Developmental Theory and Clinical Process*. New Haven, CT: Yale Universities Press.

Poetzl, O. (1917), Experimentall erregte traumbilder in ihren Beziehungen zum indirekten gehen. *Ztschr. f. d. ges. Neurol. und Psychiat.*, 37:278–349.

Politzer, G. (1974), *Critique des Fondements de la Psychologie*. Paris: Presses Universitaries de France.

Popper, K. R. (1957), *The Poverty of Historicism*. New York: Harper & Row.

_____ (1974), *Unended Quest*. La Salla, IL: Open Court.

_____ & Eccles, J. (1977), *The Self and Its Brain*. New York: Springer.

Pribram, K. H. & Gill, M. M. (1976), *Freud's Project Reassessed*. New York: Basic Books.

Racker, H. (1968), *Transference and Countertransference*. New York: International Universities Press.

Räkkölainer, V. & Alanen, Y. O. (1982), On the transactionality of defensive processes. *Internat. Rev. Psycho-Anal.*, 9:263–272.

Rapaport, D. (1954), On the psychoanalytic theory of affects. In: *Psychoanalytic Psychiatry and Psychology*, ed. R. P. Knight & C. R. Friedman. New York: International Universities Press.

_____ (1960), The structure of psychoanalytic theory. *Psychological Issues*, Monograph 6. New York: International Universities Press.

_____ (1967), *The Collected Papers of David Rapaport*, ed. M. M. Gill. New York: Basic Books.

Reiser, M. F. (1984), *Mind, Brain, Body*. New York: Basic Books.

Reiss, D. (1981), *The Family's Construction of Reality*. Cambridge, MA: Harvard University Press.

Rogers, R. (1980), Psychoanalytic and cybernetic models of mentation. *Psychoanal. Contemp. Thought*, 3:21–54.

Rosen, V. H. (1955), The reconstruction of a traumatic childhood event in a case of derealization. *J. Amer. Psychoanal. Assn.*, 3:211–221.

Rosenblatt, A. D. & Thickstun, J. T. (1970), A study of the concept of psychic energy. *Internat. J. Psycho-Anal.*, 51:265–278.

Rosenthal, R. (1966), *Experimenter Effects in Behavioral Research*. New York: Appleton-Century-Crofts.

_____ & Jacobson, L. (1968), *Pygmalion in the Classroom*. New York: Holt, Rinehart & Winston.

Rubenstein, B. B. (1976a), Hope, fear, wish, expectation, and fantasy: A semantic-phenomenological and extra clinical theoretical study. *Psychoanal. Contemp. Sci.*, 5:3–60.

_____ (1976b), On the possibility of a strictly clinical psychoanalytic theory: An essay in the philosophy of psychoanalysis. In: *Psychology Versus Metapsychology*, ed. M. M. Gill & P. S. Holzman. New York: International Universities Press.

_____ (1980), On the psychoanalytic theory of unconscious motivation and the problem of its confirmation. *Psychoanal. Contemp. Thought*, 3:3–20.

Rubinfine, D. (1962), Maternal stimulation, psychic structure and early object relations. With special reference to aggression and denial. *The Psychoanalytic Study of the Child*, 17:265–282. New York: International Universities Press.

_____ (1973), Notes toward a theory of consciousness. *Internat. J. Psychoanal. Psychother.*, 2:391–410.

Rummelhardt, D. (1975), Notes in a schema for stories. In: *Representation and Understanding*, ed. D. Bobrow & A. Collins. New York: Academic Press.

Russell, B. (1940), *An Inquiry into Meaning and Truth*. London: Allen & Unwin.

Rycroft, C. (1956), Symbolism and its relationship to the primary and secondary processes. *Internat. J. Psycho-Anal.*, 37:137–146.

_____ (1962), Beyond the reality principle. *Internat. J. Psycho-Anal.*, 43:388–394.

Sacks, O. (1985), The president's speech. *New York Rev. Books*, 32:29.

Sampson, H. (1989), How the patient's sense of danger and safety influence the analytic process. Paper presented to the Seattle Institute for Psychoanalysis.

Sander, L. W. (1983), To begin with—reflections on ontogeny. In: *Reflections on Self-Psychology*, ed. J. Lichtenberg & S. Kaplan. Hillsdale, NJ: The Analytic Press.

_____ (1985), Towards a logic of organization in psychological development. In: *Biologic Response Styles*, ed. K. Klar & L. Silver. Washington, DC: American Psychiatric Press.

Sandler, J. (1960), The background of safety. *Internat. J. Psycho-Anal.*, 41:352–356.

_____ (1967), Trauma, strain and development. In: *Psychic Trauma*, ed. S. S. Furst. New York: Basic Books.

_____ (1975), Sexual fantasies and sexual theories in childhood. In: *Studies in Child Psychoanalysis*. New Haven, CT: Yale University Press.

_____ (1976a), Countertransference and role-responsiveness. *Internat. Rev. Psycho-Anal.*, 3:43–47.

_____ (1976b), Dreams, unconscious fantasies and the identity of perception. *Internat. Rev. Psycho-Anal.*, 3:33–42.

_____ (1989), On internal object relationships. Paper presented to Seattle Institute for Psychoanalysis.

_____ & Joffe, W. (1969), Towards a basic psychoanalytic model. *Internat. J. Psycho-Anal.*, 50:79–90.

_____ & Nagera, H. (1963), Aspects of the metapsychology of fantasy. *The Psychoanalytic Study of the Child*, 18:159–164. New York: International Universities Press.

_____ & Rosenblatt, B. (1962), The concept of the representational world. *The Psychoanalytic Study of the Child*, 17:128–145. New York: International Universities Press.

_____ & Sandler, A. M. (1978), On the development of object relationships and affects. *Internat. J. Psycho-Anal.*, 59:285–296.

_____ & _____ (1983), Reality and unconscious, the second censorship, the "three-box model" and some technical implications. *Internat. J. Psycho-Anal.*, 64:413–425.

Schachter, S. & Singer, J. (1962), Cognitive social and physiological determinance of emotional state. *Psycholog. Rev.*, 69:379–399.

Schafer, R. (1968), *Aspects of Internalization*. New York: International Universities Press.

_____ (1985), Wild analysis. *J. Amer. Psychoanal. Assn.*, 33:275–299.

Schank, R. & Abelson, R. (1977), *Scripts, Plans, Goals, and Understanding*. Hillsdale, NJ: Lawrence Erlbaum Associates.

Schimek, J. G. (1975a), A critical re-examination of Freud's concept of unconscious mental representation. *Internat. Rev. Psycho-Anal.*, 2:171–187.

_____ (1975b), The interpretation of the past, childhood trauma, psychical reality, and historical truth. *J. Amer. Psychoanal. Assn.*, 23:845–865.

Schur, M. (1966), *The Id and the Regulatory Principles of Mental Functioning*. New York: International Universities Press.

Schwaber, E. (1983), Psychoanalytic listening and psychic reality. *Internat. Rev. Psycho-Anal.*, 10:379–392.

Searles, H. (1965), *Collected Papers on Schizophrenia and Related Subjects*. New York: International Universities Press.

_____ (1979), *Countertransference and Related Subjects*. New York: International Universities Press.

Seligman, M. E. P. (1975), *Helplessness*. San Francisco: Freeman.

_____ & Maier, S. (1967), Failure to escape traumatic shock. *J. Experimental Psychol.*, 78:1–9.

Shane, M. & Shane, E. (1990), Unconscious fantasy: Developmental and self-psychological considerations. *J. Amer. Psychoanal. Assn.*, 38:75–92.

Sharpe, E. F. (1937), *Dream Analysis*. London: Hogarth Press.

Shevrin, H. & Luborsky, L. (1958), The measurement of preconscious perception in dreams and images: An investigation of the Poetzl phenomenon. *J. Abn. Social Beh.*, 56:285–294.

Siegel, E. E. (1988), *Female Homosexuality*. Hillsdale, NJ: The Analytic Press.

Silverblatt, H. (1981), Denial of pregnancies extended to physicians. *Psychiat. News*, November 20.

Silverman, L. H. (1967), An experimental approach to the study of dynamic propositions in psychoanalysis: The relationship between the aggressive drive and ego regression—initial studies. *J. Amer. Psychoanal. Assn.*, 15:376–403.

_____ (1976), Psychoanalytic theory: "The reports of my death are greatly exaggerated." *Amer. Psychol.*, 31:621–637.

Silverman, M. (1987), Clinical material. *Psychoanal. Inq.*, 7:147–165.

Slap, J. W. & Saykin, A. J. (1984), On the nature and organization of the repressed. *Psychoanal. Inq.*, 4:107–124.

Slobin, D. I. (1973), Cognitive prerequisites for the development of grammar. In: *Studies of Childhood Language Development*, ed. C. A. Ferguson & D. I. Slobin. New York: Holt, Rinehart & Winston.

Snyder, M. & Swan, W. (1978), Behavioral conformation in social interaction: From social perception to social reality. *J. Exper. Soc. Psychol.*, 14:148–162.

Spence, D. (1982), *Narrative Truth and Historical Truth*. New York: Norton.

_____ (1985), Roy Schafer: Searching for the native tongue. In: *Beyond Freud*, ed. J. Reppen. Hillsdale, NJ: The Analytic Press.

Sperry, R. (1964), Problems outstanding in the evolution of brain function. James Arthur Lecture, American Museum of Natural History, New York.

_____ (1982), Some effects of disconnecting the cerebral hemispheres. *Science*, 217:1223–1226.

Spitz, R. (1961), Some early prototypes of ego defenses. *J. Amer. Psychoanal. Assn.*, 9:625–651.

_____ (1965), *The First Year of Life*. New York: International Universities Press.

Steiner, R. (1985), Some thoughts about tradition and change arising from an examination of the British Psychoanalytic Society's Controversial Discussions (1943–1944). *Internat. Rev. Psycho-Anal.*, 12:27–71.

Sterba, R. (1934), The fate of the ego in analytic therapy. *Internat. J. Psycho-Anal.*, 15:117–126.

Stern, D. (1974), Mother and infant at play: The dyadic interaction involving facial, vocal and gaze behaviors. In: *The Effects of the Infant on Its Caregiver*, ed. M. Lewis & L. Rosenblum. New York: Wiley.

_____ (1977), *The First Relationship*. Cambridge, MA: Harvard University Press.

_____ (1985), *The Interpersonal World of the Infant*. New York: Basic Books.

Stolorow, R. D. & Lachmann, F. M. (1985), Transference: the future of an illusion. *The Annual of Psychoanalysis*, 12/13:19–37. New York: International Universities Press.

_____ Brandchaft, B. & Atwood, G. E. (1987), *Psychoanalytic Treatment*. Hillsdale, NJ: The Analytic Press.

Stone, L. (1961), *The Psychoanalytic Situation*. New York: International Universities Press.

Strachey, J. (1934), The nature of the therapeutic action of psychoanalysis. *Internat. J. Psycho-Anal.*, 15:127–159.

Suler, J. R. (1980), Primary process thinking and creativity. *Psychol. Bull.*, 88:144–165.

Swanson, D. (1977), A critique of psychic energy as an explanatory concept. *J. Amer. Psychoanal. Assn.*, 25:603–633.

TenHouten, W. D., Hoppe, K. D., Bogen, J. E. & Walter, D. O. (1976), Alexithymia: An experimental study of cerebral commissurotomy patients and normal control subjects. *Amer. J. Psychiat.*, 143:312–316.

Tinbergen, N. (1953), *Social Behavior in Animals with Special Reference to Vertebrates*. London: Methuen.

Trevarthan, C. (1977), Descriptive analysis of infant communicative behavior. In: *Studies in Mother–Infant Interaction*, ed. H. R. Schaffer. New York: Academic Press.

—— (1979), Communication and cooperation in early infancy: A description of primary intersubjectivity. In: *Before Speech, The Beginning of Interpersonal Communication*, ed. M. M. Bullowa. New York: Cambridge University Press.

—— & Hubley, P. (1978), Secondary intersubjectivity: Confidence, confiders and acts of meaning in the first year. In: *Action, Gesture and Symbol*, ed. A. Lock. New York: Academic Press.

Tulving, E. (1972), Episodic and Semantic Memory. In: *Organization of Memory*, ed. E. Tulving & W. Donaldson. New York: Academic Press.

—— (1983), *Elements of Episodic Memory*. New York: Oxford University Press.

Ulman, R. B. & Brothers, D. (1988), *The Shattered Self*. Hillsdale, NJ: The Analytic Press.

Voeller, K. K. S. (1985), Children with right hemisphere deficits need special therapy. *Psychiat. News*, 20:16.

Vygotsky, L. (1934), *Thought and Language*. Cambridge, MA: M.I.T. Press, 1962.

—— (1966), Development of the higher mental functions. In: *Psychological Research in the U.S.S.R., Vol. 1*, ed. A. Leontive, A. R. Luria & A. S. Smirnov. Moscow: Progress.

Wachtel, P. L. (1980), Transference, schema and assimiliation: The relevance of Piaget to the psychoanalytic theory of transference. *The Annual of Psychoanalysis*, 8:59–76. New York: International Universities Press.

—— (1987), *Action and Insight*. New York: Guilford Press.

Wallerstein, R. S. (1967), Reconstruction and mastery in the transference psychosis. *J. Amer. Psychoanal. Assn.*, 15:556–569.

Wangh, M. (1950), Othello: The tragedy of Iago. *Psychoanal. Quart.*, 19:202–212.

—— (1962), The evocation of a proxy: A psychological maneuver, its use as a defense, its purpose and genesis. *The Psychoanalytic Study of the Child*, 17:463–469. New York: International Universities Press.

Watzlawick, P. (1984), Self-fulfilling prophecies. In: *The Invented Reality*, ed. P. Watzlawick. New York: Norton.

—— Beavin J. & Jackson, D. (1967), *Pragmatics of Human Communication*. New York: Norton.

Weinstein, E. A. (1980), Affects and neuropsychology. *The Academy Forum*, 24:12.

—— & Kahn, R. L. (1955), *Denial of Illness*. Springfield, IL: Charles C. Thomas.

Weisman, A. D. (1972), *On Dying and Denying*. New York: Behavioral.

Weiss, J. (1971), The emergence of new themes: A contribution to the psychoanalytic theory of therapy. *Internat. J. Psycho-Anal.*, 52:459–467.

—— (1989), The nature of the patient's problems and how in psychoanalysis he works to solve them. Presented to Seattle Institute for Psychoanalysis.

—— & Sampson, H. (1986), *The Psychoanalytic Process*. New York: Guilford Press.

Weissberg, M. (1983), *Dangerous Secrets*. New York: Norton.

Werner, H. (1948), *Comparative Psychology of Mental Development*. Chicago: Follett.

_____ & Kaplan, B. (1963), *Symbol Formation*. New York: Wiley.

West, L. J. (1962), A general theory of hallucination and dreams. In: *Hallucinations,* ed. L. J. West. New York: Grune & Stratton.

Westerlundh, B. & Smith, G. (1983), Perceptogenesis and the psychodynamics of perception. *Psychoanal. Contemp. Thought,* 6:597–640.

Wilson, T. & Nisbett, R. (1978), The accuracy of verbal reports about the effects of stimuli on evaluations and behavior. *Social Psychol.,* 41:118–131.

Winnicott, D. W. (1965), *The Maturation Processes and the Facilitating Environment.* New York: International Universities Press.

_____ (1971), *Playing and Reality.* New York: Basic Books.

Winson, J. (1985), *Brain and Psyche.* New York: Anchor Press.

Wittgenstein, I. (1921), *Tractus Logico—Philosophicus.* London: Kegan Paul.

Wolff, P. H. (1967), Cognitive considerations for a psychoanalytic theory of language acquisition. In: *Motives and Thought,* ed. R. R. Holt. *Psychological Issues,* Monogr. 5. New York: International Universities Press.

Wynne, L. C. (1965), Some indications and contraindications for exploratory family therapy. In: *Intensive Family Therapy,* ed. I. Boszormenyi-Nagy & J. L. Framo. New York: Hoeber.

Zajonic, R. B. (1980), Feeling and thinking: Preferences need no inferences. *Amer. Psychol.,* 35:151–175.

Zeigarnik, B. (1927), Das behalten erledigter und unerledgtier handlungen. *Psychologische Forshung,* 9:1–85.

Zetzel, E. R. (1956), Current concepts of transference. *Internat. J. Psycho-Anal.,* 37:369–376.

Zinner, J. & Shapiro, R. (1972), Projective identification as a mode of perception and behavior in families of adolescents. *Internat. J. Psycho-Anal.,* 53:523–531.

Index

THE SECRET
OF
STONEHENGE

I. L. COHEN

58541

New Research Publications, Inc.
GREENVALE-N.Y.

Inquiries should be addressed to:

New Research Publications, Inc.
P.O. Box 231
Greenvale, NY. 11548

Printed in the United States of America, 1982

Library of Congress Cataloging in Publication Data

Cohen, I. L., 1922–
  The Secret of Stonehenge.

  Includes bibliographical references.
  1. Stonehenge (England)   I. Title.
DA142.C63 1982   936.2   82-19107
ISBN 0-910891-01-X

Dedicated to

YAHWEH

with deepest respect

Table of Contents

List of Illustrations

INTRODUCTION

We are all aware, by now, of the existence of a huge stone structure in the Salisbury Plain, north of Southampton, England. This structure, Stonehenge, has been the subject of innumerable studies, theories, comments, measurements, etc. for the past thousand years, at best. An exact explanation as to who built it and why is not available on a direct basis. All the theories proposed are deductions based on apparent facts and historical comments known to us. Obviously, as our level of knowledge advances, more scientific information will be amassed, and with it, newer theories and understandings will develop to explain the existence of Stonehenge.

An historical review of past attempts to explain this marvel would not be within the scope of this book. The subject has been discussed at length by a great many authors, and is so well known that additional repetition in detail is hardly necessary. Let it be said only that Stonehenge has been widely referred to as a temple of the ancient Celts. Later on, the Druids held their religious processions and incantations to the midsummer sunrise in this "temple." Despite all attempts, nobody has been able to scientifically pinpoint the actual background of these stones.

The first truly comprehensive theory was expounded by Professor G.S. Hawkins in 1963, in an article in *Nature,* and in 1965 in his famous book *Stonehenge Decoded.* In it, he submits evidence of the meaningful existence of certain very specific astronomical alignments within some of the stones found in Stonehenge. These alignments point to very important movements of the sun and the moon. Thus, Stonehenge is considered as a computer or measuring device for events taking place in the heavens. This theory and its proof did make sense, although there are certain aspects of it that are still not satisfying to logic.

It is the purpose of this book to review some of the findings of Professor Hawkins, along with those of other scientists and to analyze their meanings. By introducing information supplied to us by historical reports, and by critically evaluating certain recent findings in Stonehenge, I have reached quite unexpected conclusions. These results will shed an astonishingly different light on the reason for the existence of this incredible structure.

The present book submits a new theory that will also shed a light on a great many mysteries of antiquity besides Stonehenge. However, let us remember that a theory is an expression of a new thought that tries to explain an unknown situation, and by its very nature and by its "newness", cannot be perfect as we are probing our hazy and misunderstood past. Nevertheless it is a useful tool in order to research further along the newly discovered path. Naturally drastically new explanations can be regarded as "odd," since they do not fit into known and accepted patterns of thought. Thus, the tendency is to disallow the possibility that such theories reflect the actual truth. However, theories that have the possibility of being backed up by controlled scientific experiments and proofs will withstand the initial display of incredibility. Science has learned to respect established facts and test results, even though the connotations and meanings derived might appear far fetched, based on the knowledge to which we have become accustomed—rightly or wrongly. Hard facts and test results cannot be denied and overlooked, even if they upset our old established values, understandings and beliefs.

Science is continually trying to probe into the forces that exist in the universe. It is trying to find what *is*. If we can understand a small portion of what *was*—no matter how small that portion might be—it will surely help us realize what *is*.

In my previous book *Urim and Thumim—the Secret of God,* I submitted a new theory on the past historical events of humanity. This new evaluation, if proven to be correct, can impart an enormously different meaning to a great many aspects of our past—meanings that will reverberate onto various other disciplines, such as for example: archaeology.

The present book is a follow-up to my previous publication. It is meant to submit the first of several tangible proofs to support my thesis, and by doing so, it unravels enigmatic aspects of some of our archaeological inheritances.

There are other proofs that are just as important and valuable. We have a multitude of inscribed clay tablets from the Sumerian, Akkadian, and Assyrian eras, some of which report most important facts. These are awaiting to be properly understood and evaluated by us. We have archaeological artifacts from the same areas, depicting a great many activities that took place 4000–6000 years ago. A careful examination of old maps sheds a new light—a new understanding that differs from the one to which we have been accustomed until now. Ancient writings, to be found throughout various continents, lead us to new evaluations of past events. Most of these additional proofs will be submitted and detailed in future volumes.

Certain of the information supplied in *Urim and Thu-*

mim—the Secret of God had to be repeated in this volume, so as to render it independently cohesive in meaning.

We are enormously lucky that we still have on hand some remnants of the activities of past generations. These are priceless treasures that have to be meticulously safeguarded, especially as we need them desperately in their original state so as to apply additional and very sensitive scientific tests, performed by trained technicians and scientists.

After reading this book, perhaps interested readers might be inclined to run out to the general Stonehenge area, or other similar sites around the countryside, and start digging or performing other investigative activities. Such a haphazard attempt would destroy a great many tell-tale signs and negate the results of future scientific tests that will be performed. Unknowingly, one can deal a deadly blow to our chances to perform exact measurements and tests of the grounds in question. I urge the general public to hold back from even stepping onto the meadows surrounding Stonehenge, or other stone circles, barrows, stone chambers, etc. There are a great many aspects that do not meet the eye and which have to be preserved. The biggest help we can extend to our scientists is to stay away from those areas.

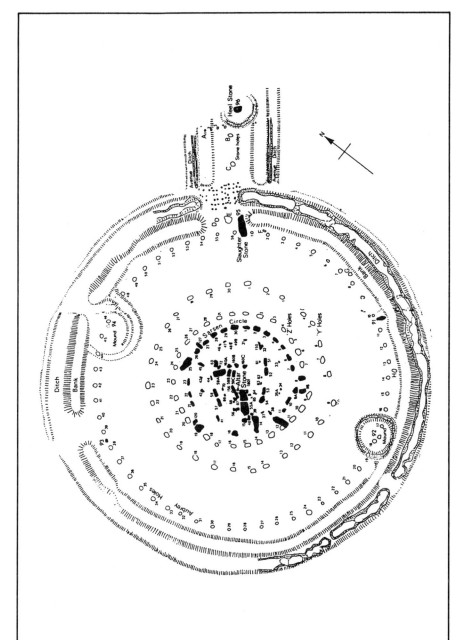

FIG. 1 — OFFICIAL GROUND PLAN OF STONEHENGE

(British Crown copyright — reproduced with permission of the controller of
Her Brittanic Majesty's Stationery Office.)

1

Construction Effort

Reliable dating methods have pinpointed the existence of three different construction eras within the complex known as Stonehenge. These three periods are generally defined as:

Stonehenge I . . .   built about 2300 B.C.
Stonehenge II . . .   built about 2100 B.C.
Stonehenge III . . .   built about 1900 B.C.

It is naturally understood that these figures have to be taken on a slightly tentative basis as there could be variations of a few hundred years forward or backward in time. In fact, recent studies made on carbon-14 indicated the necessity of re-evaluating all the datings (because of new measurements made on the bristlecone tree.) Professor Fred Hoyle in his book *On Stonehenge* indicated that new carbon-14 datings pushed each date back by about 500 years. Thus, a newer version of the dating figures would suggest that:

Stonehenge I . . . was built from about 2500–3000 B.C.
Stonehenge II . . . was built from about 2300–2800 B.C.
Stonehenge III . . . was built from about 2100–2600 B.C.

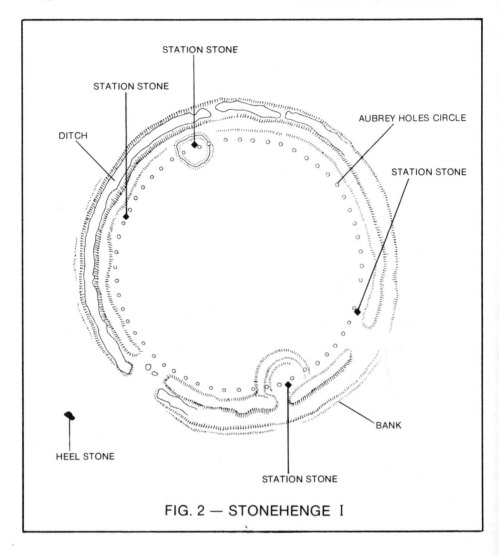

STATION STONE

STATION STONE

DITCH

AUBREY HOLES CIRCLE

STATION STONE

HEEL STONE

BANK

STATION STONE

FIG. 2 — STONEHENGE I

No matter what calibration dating is chosen, the fact remains that most people will concede to 2500 B.C. as the
approximate building date of Stonehenge I.

STONEHENGE I: It is now generally agreed that the construction of this period consisted of the following:

A) A circular ditch varying in width from 10 to 19 feet with a depth of about 4½—7 feet.

B) On the inside of the ditch is a circular bank of white chalk measuring about 6 feet high by about 20 feet in width. The diameter of this bank, measured from crest to crest, is approximately 320 feet.

C) Inside the bank is a circle of large holes known as Aubrey Holes, named after a Mr. Aubrey who discovered their existence about 300 years ago. There are 56 of these holes, varying in diameter from between 2½ feet to 6 feet each and located around a perfect circle measuring 285 feet in diameter. Each of these holes has a depth varying from 2 feet to 4 feet, with straight sides dug into the ground and a flat bottom. All of these holes are filled with fine white chalk. The distance between the center of each Aubrey hole is almost exactly 16 feet (within a variation of a few inches).

D) Outside these circles there is a large Heelstone weighing approximately 35 tons. It leans towards the circle at an angle of about 30 degrees from the vertical. It doesn't appear to be a dressed stone, but instead gives the impression of being in its raw state. It is 20 feet high, 8 feet wide, and 7 feet thick. It is located almost in the center of what is called the Avenue. (The actual fact is that it is off-center towards the right.) The Avenue is a broad lane bordered on each side by a ditch and a bank. The width between the center of the ditches is roughly 72 feet and the width between the two banks is about 40 feet. Measurements have shown that it is a perfectly straight and parallel avenue, running for several hundred yards. At present, not much of the Avenue remains since it is cut by the modern road and then appears lost among the fields beyond the road. Nevertheless, it is discernible, especially when viewed from the air.

The amazing fact remains that 4500 years ago "bar-barians" were able to build a ditch and bank absolutely parallel in a straight line for a distance of at least 2000 feet. This, in itself, is quite surprising as anybody dealing with the movements of earth will realize the difficulty in generating two parallel lines for such a length. The precision is the amazing aspect that repeats itself continuously in every facet of the Stonehenge construction. It is logical to expect that the bank was formed by the chalk dug from the ditches. This means that originally there probably were two strips of white gleaming chalk running for 700 yards, at least.

E) Near the Aubrey Holes, in certain specific positions, are small mounds around which we find small ditches. In the middle of these mounds there are stone markers. These positions have been numbered as position 91, 92, 93 and 94.

F) Eight holes were catalogued as A, B, C, D, E, F, G, H. There is no agreement as to whether these 8 holes once contained stones or wooden posts, or whether they simply were unfilled holes. A diagram of these various items is shown in Figure 1.

STONEHENGE II: A few hundred years after the construction of Stonehenge I it appears that a new construction activity was begun on the same spot. It would seem that they tried to erect 2 concentric circles of Bluestones, each weighing about 5 tons. These 2 circles are 6 feet apart. The holes in each circle were placed in such a way as to be positioned along a radial spoke from the center of the circle. Some researchers noted that the Bluestones in the inner circle appear shorter than the corresponding stones on the outer circle. It is acknowledged that only a number of these Bluestones were placed in position and that the project was most likely abandoned as the circle was never completed. Although we do not know the exact number of stones that

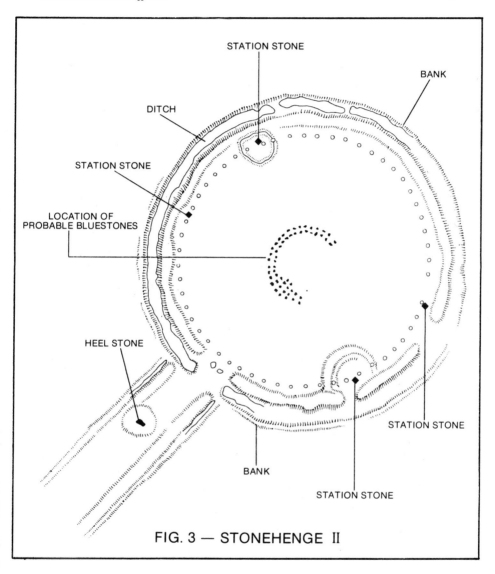

STATION STONE

BANK

DITCH

STATION STONE

LOCATION OF
PROBABLE BLUESTONES

HEEL STONE

STATION STONE

BANK

STATION STONE

FIG. 3 — STONEHENGE II

were to be placed, it is estimated that about 38 pairs were to be used. The position of these 2 concentric circles of blue stones is shown in Figure 3. At present, the only traces we have found are those of a number of holes located in a double circle. This circle was not completed, giving the impression that the construction was halted before the work was finished.

STONEHENGE III: A few hundred years after the construction of Stonehenge II a new construction effort was undertaken, much larger and more powerful in design and execution. A huge circle was formed from upright Sarsen stones, each weighing about 25 tons. The stones are partly imbedded in the ground to a depth of approximately 4 feet and are all joined to each other at the top by horizontal stones, called lintel stones. Between each Sarsen stone there is a gap or passage. The whole structure gives the impression of a colonnade in a circular design. The lintel stones are connected to the vertical Sarsen stones by means of a system called mortise and tenon. In essence, the vertical stones each have 2 large knobs (tenons) protruding from their top so as to fit perfectly into the holes carved underneath each horizontal lintel stone. Furthermore, each horizontal lintel stone is tied to each other by means of a tongue-and-groove system.

Five huge trilithons are placed in the position of a horseshoe. Each trilithon consists of 2 large upright stones with a third horizontal stone on top. The vertical stones are so close to each other as to allow a space of only about 10 inches. These trilithons are taller than the Sarsen Circle and each unit of trilithon has a different height.

In front of these trilithon groups, towards the center of the area, are a number of Bluestones placed in a horseshoe shape. Also, in front of all the Sarsen stones is a closed circle of Bluestones, most of which are no longer available.

Twenty-nine "Z" holes were dug in a circle on the out-

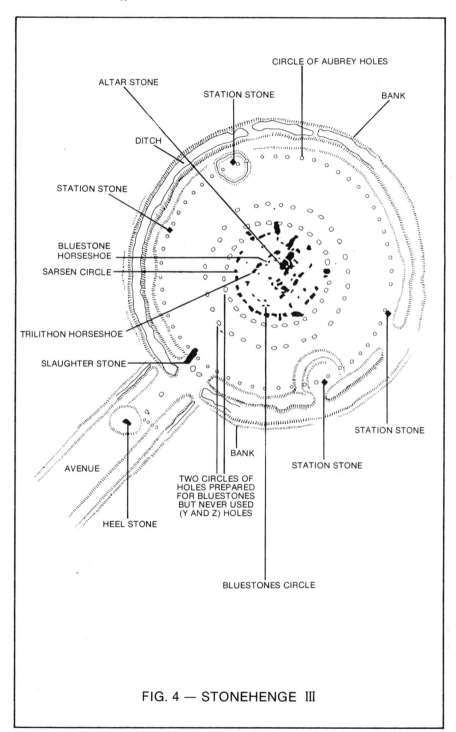

FIG. 4 — STONEHENGE III

side of the Sarsen Circle. Thirty "Y" holes were placed in a circle further out on the outside of the "Z" holes. Both groups of holes are usually rectangular in shape and average a depth of approximately 3 feet for the "Y" holes. The impression is that the holes were readied to receive rectangular stones. The "Z" holes are about 5 feet deeper. None of these seem to have been filled, nor have any traces been found showing the presence of upright stones that might have been inserted in them.

In front of the largest trilithon stone is a rectangular boulder, lying horizontally on the ground, partly imbedded in the ground. It has been named, the Altar Stone—on the assumption that perhaps it was used for religious services —whatever they might have been. Whether this stone was once in an upright position is not known.

Another large rectangular stone is found where the Avenue enters the Aubrey Circle. It has been named the Slaughter Stone for some theoretically inspired reason. We do not know whether it ever was in an upright position, or whether it actually belonged to that spot.

A diagram showing the positions of the various stones and holes in this portion of the construction is indicated in Figure 4.

This, then, represents Stonehenge essentially as we see it today.

This structure is located on the Salisbury Plain, near Amesbury, about 25 miles northwest of Southampton. We believe that the Bluestones used in this construction must have come from the Prescelly Mountains in Wales, approximately 240 miles west (or about 130 miles as the crow flies). We also believe that all the Sarsen stones came down from the Marlboro Downs about 25 miles north (as the crow flies).

Salisbury Plain, as the name implies, is an open plain with no mountainous regions around its horizon. It is acknowledged that this region of England was very sparsely populated 4500 years ago, at the time when Stonehenge was built. It is estimated that the general area around the Salisbury Plain could not have contained more than about 1500 people. That population is considered to have been living in the English Stone Age; that is, at a period when that society had only stone, bone, or wood as tools.

Rough calculations made by Professor Hawkins indicate that it would have taken these people 1,500,000 days of physical labor to erect Stonehenge. This is in addition to the enormous amount of time that would have been spent in organizing, designing and focusing on the intellectual work necessary to coordinate the entire project.

We must consider that for each working person there must have been a large number of other people ready to support this effort by hunting, agriculture, preparing the food, the shelter, etc. This, in itself, would have constituted considerable exertion of energy. When we start thinking through the step-by-step motions necessary to perform this task, we reach immediately the first enigma: How could a very sparsely populated society find the human power and the time to perform such an arduous task? This question has never been answered satisfactorily and is still up in the air, searching for a logical and plausible answer.

We are faced with a second dilemma: How could these "primitive" people arrange to transport such huge stones, weighing up to 50 tons each? How could they arrange to erect them in the exceedingly solid and powerful way demonstrated by the Stonehenge structure?

Many people have tried to indicate a logical method that could have been used to transport the stones. They have drawn pictures and sketches of how such a transport might have been performed by means of logs and ropes. Of course, the undertaking looks quite possible as rendered by an artist's sketch and, theoretically, it appears plausible. The reality would have been quite different as it would have been an extraordinarily difficult job to perform if we consider the distance, the weight involved, the terrain, the manpower available, and the logistics of the entire procedure. We have to ask where these primitive people would have obtained thousands upon thousands of ropes of such strength that they could be wound around a 40-ton stone and pull it over miles and miles of rough terrain without being cut by its sharp edges? What type of fiber or leather could they possibly have found in that region of England in such massive quantities as to create the enormous numbers of ropes required? We must seriously question the validity of such a theory as it is unlikely they could have produced hawsers strong enough to withstand the pull of a 40-ton stone, over long distances of rough terrain.

As a result, although artists' sketches show it to be a seemingly possible proposition, a thorough step-by-step evaluation of the logistics involved indicates that this job would hardly have been possible. Its probabilities are exceedingly small to be even considered as a likely procedure to have been applied 4500 years ago.

There are other difficult questions that must be faced and answered.

In 1963 Mr. C. A. Newham announced his findings concerning the alignments of stones 91-92-93-94 forming a perfect rectangle with 90-degree angles in each corner and lined up in such a way that the short sides point to the midsummer sunrise. Independently in 1963, Professor G. S. Hawkins published his important findings suggesting that various alignments had astronomical significance, including the parallelogram of stones 91-92-93-94. The extraordinary fact is that this situation holds true only at the particular spot at which Stonehenge was built, namely latitude 51.17N and longitude 1.83W. If Stonehenge had been built 15 miles farther north or farther south, it could not have contained this precise parallelogram; instead, positions 91-92-93-94 would create a nonrectangular parallelogram with corner angles other than 90 degrees. Sir Fred Hoyle made the following interesting remark in his book *On Stonehenge:*[1]

"In order for the station positions to have such a relation at other latitudes, they would need to be set in a nonrectangular parallelogram that had pre-constructed corners, a task beyond the capacity of the builders equipped with only sticks, ropes and stones. The precise measurement of angles, like 87 degrees, calls for a technique that would probably require the use of metal instruments."

It is obviously unlikely that this is a mere coincidence since there are thousands of sites in England that could have been chosen on which to erect such a structure. Yet these "barbarians" chose the only spot that gave them this very exact alignment. This suggests an enormously sophisticated knowledge of earth geography, as well as sky geometry.

Logically, one must expect that in order to pinpoint this specific location, these barbarians had to measure and test a great many other sites before deciding on this particular location. To test a number of different sites would necessitate the capacity of measuring—in other words, instrumentation. Furthermore, it would require a substantial amount of time to erect and test a number of sites until the proper parallelogram form was found, aligned to the midsummer sunrise at a 90-degree angle. In the third place, it implies the capacity of traveling widely throughout the countryside in order to take measurements and experiment with various locations. This

[1]*On Stonehenge*, by Sir Fred Hoyle published in 1977 by W.H. Freeman and Company.

implies mobility capacity. In the fourth place, it presupposes that they knew exactly what they were after and why they were looking for such a specific site. It follows that their theoretical knowledge had to be exceedingly advanced, to predetermine the relationship of the sun, moon, the earth, and their exact relative positions at various times during the year. It also means a deep sense for evaluating the problems, and an advanced planning capacity for the construction. We must keep in mind that they had no writing facility and that all this astronomical observation and the development of the theory, with its many calculations, were simply performed in their heads without any permanent records being available (except possibly for signs scratched on stone, as on stone walls of caves). Additionally, all these complicated details had to be transmitted from generation to generation by word of mouth!

If we keep in mind the fact that the original inhabitants of that region were Stone Age people without sophisticated instruments capable of measuring, without capacity to widely and speedily travel throughout the countryside, and without writing ability to generate and transmit the necessary theory from generation to generation, then we must ask ourselves how it was possible for them to pinpoint this particular location for Stonehenge? There are two obvious answers:

A) These barbarians were extraordinarily lucky and by sheer coincidence happened to hit on the one spot that would result in the above stated geometric situation. The probability that this choice was simply a coincidence is so minute that it must be considered negligible.

B) These "primitive" people knew exactly what they wanted and had the capability to measure, travel and perform the theoretical studies in advance. This means that they must have been a group of very sophisticated people having a high degree of intelligence, completely in advance of the Stone Age we know.

I am inclined to believe this last conclusion, since the stones used in Stonehenge were not found in its immediate vicinity. If these people were really primitive and living under difficult conditions, they would most likely have decided to erect their "temple" or "observatory" near their quarries. Instead, they went to the great hardship of dragging those huge boulders over most impressive distances. Obviously, it means that this enormous amount of work was performed in order to erect the structure at a very specific spot. Thus, the amount of work involved doesn't seem to have been important; the result to be achieved by erecting Stonehenge at a given specific spot was much more important. We could also make the bold statement that this extreme effort, exerted over a span of a great many years, might not necessarily represent the astonishing achievement that it appears to us. Perhaps it was relatively easy for them to perform this very considerable task. If so, then these people were not the Stone Age inhabitants of that region.

Be it as it may, I believe the location of Stonehenge was definitely not a haphazard choice. Instead, it was a predetermined, well-thought-out, chosen site to achieve a very specific result.

There is another aspect that baffles me. For these "primitive" people to have erected this structure, they must have known the exact source of the stones required. This implies a thorough knowledge of the entire region of southern England and Wales—a huge area to be surveyed on foot by a relatively small group of barbarians. After all, we must consider that these builders did not immediately hit upon the Prescelly Mountains in Wales or Marlborough Downs as being the only sources available for their raw material. They must have certainly roamed throughout the territory to locate various sources of stones, evaluated those sites and compared them with other far-off sites. A decision must have been reached at some point, at which time they agreed to quarry the mountain, remove quantities of stone and lug them all the way to the predetermined site on the Salisbury Plain. All of this implies an extraordinary amount of travelling back and forth and a mobility for surveying and investigating such a huge territory. It would have been well beyond the capacity of one generation to perform. Theoretically, it means that the project was of such extraordinary importance that generation upon generation of Stone Age people simply concentrated on that task. If we keep in mind that the biggest problem for those people was gathering food and creating shelter for themselves, we must be amazed that they even found the time to consider the construction of so huge an undertaking, let alone to put it into operation.

If the above several enigmas are not sufficient to question our previous understandings, then we have a still greater mystery facing us. How did these barbarians produce the theoretical work behind the astronomical computer represented by Stonehenge? The fact that Stonehenge is a very sophisticated structure for pinpointing the various positions of the sun and the moon can hardly be contested after the brilliant work performed by Professor Hawkins and C.A.Newham. Twenty-two key alignments were established as determined by specific stones, each indicating an important and specific direction of the moon and the sun. The Aubrey Holes were explained by Hawkins and Hoyle as a computing device to predict eclipses. Whether the explanation for the Aubrey Holes is correct or not is still debatable, but the fact remains that it seems to work out properly.

With today's scientific methods we know that the only system we have for generating a theory is to collect a substantial amount of data in order to see an overall picture, to evaluate the data, and then to create the type of theory that fits these specific conclusions. We must see a continuity and a predictable repetition of results before we can be certain that the theory works. For any sort of people—primitive or sophisticated—to decide that a specific type of moon eclipse has an 18.67-years cycle or a 56-years cycle or any other cycle, would require a collection of data extending back centuries upon centuries, especially if they did not know that they were looking for a recurring periodicity. It could be only on the basis of accumulated and precisely recorded information that Stone Age people would have been able to ascertain and be aware of a regularity of occurrence. This means that these "barbarians" would have needed to rely on exact data, transmitted to them by their ancestors for 500 or 1000 years before.

The southern part of England is not known for its clement weather throughout the year. We must consider the fact that on a great many crucial days, when the occurrences should have repeated themselves, the sky might not have been perfectly clear. If clouds were covering the sun or the moon or the stars, etc., then the whole crucial moment would escape detection. It is fair to assume that over a span of 1000 years, every night of the 56-years cycle or the 18.67-years cycle would not have been perfectly clear and visible. Astronomers, watching the sky every single night, and not knowing yet that a specific lunar eclipse cycle existed, would have been at a fantastic handicap if they could not see the moon on a great many nights during the year because of unsatisfactory weather conditions. This means that data would be nonexistent for those particular nights and thus the result of observation incomplete and inconclusive.

What's more, this project must have been extraordinarily important to the Stone Age people for them to have kept it alive for generations upon generations, all of them working towards the same goal over a span of centuries. Assuming that these "barbarians" were the ones who collected this data, we must conclude that they considered it of immense importance to sit and watch the sky every single night of the year over a span of hundreds or thousands of years. Generations upon generations must have had enough stamina and singletrack-mindedness to continue this project of collecting data, without weakening in their determination, and certainly without skipping readings.

Even though this is an exceedingly remote possibility, at least they might have performed this project if they had possessed some sort of writing capacity in order to transfer information from generation to generation. Without any writing, it becomes impossible to conceive that this type of very precise scientific data could have been followed through over a span of so many centuries and then produced the basis for a precise theory with astronomical connotations. We must keep in mind that in order to pinpoint the various equinoxes and movements of the sun and the moon, these barbarians had to maintain the same location or observatory over a span of a thousand years (at least) so as to observe the sky and the moon from the very same spot! Otherwise their observations would have differed in the event that they changed sites.

The more we think about these step-by-step occurrences that must have taken place, the more we must realize that it is quite against reason to expect primitive people to generate, with certainty, any theory on sun and moon cycles. How these Stone Age people were able to create the theoretical background and arrive at very specific conclusions is certainly a most baffling question. Nevertheless, the facts are clearly in front of us. We have a Stonehenge structure—its existence cannot be denied. It displays some very specific and meaningful sighting directions connected with astronomy.

No matter how we look upon Stonehenge—whether it is the construction, or the pinpointing of the site, or the measuring of the stones, or the alignments, or the theoretical background—each and every aspect indicates the presence of a far superior intelligence, way beyond the level known to us of the Stone Age people.

2

Decoding

For a great many centuries, numerous theories have been advanced attempting to explain the reasons for the existence of Stonehenge. The fact remains that none of these theories have really satisfied completely the situation.

The first breakthrough came when C.A.Newham announced, in 1963, his findings that alignments of stones 91-92-93-94 formed a perfect rectangle with the short sides pointing to the midsummer sunrise, the longer sides pointing to the summer moonrise and the winter moonset. Also in 1963, Professor Hawkins published an article in *Nature* and in 1965, a book, *Stonehenge Decoded,* in which he developed, step by step, his findings and his calculations to prove the different alignments found in Stonehenge. For the first time a plausible scientific explanation was submitted. This book is quite important, not only for the facts it depicts, but also for the meaning that ensues from these facts.

Professor Hawkins developed and proved a number of points:

A) He suggested that the Heelstone was placed in the exact position where the midsummer sun would

rise on the one specific day of the year when the
sun produces the longest day of the year. This
exact position is marked by the Heelstone when
viewed from the center of the Aubrey circle.

B) When connecting stones 91, 92, 93, 94, he got a perfect parallelogram. The most interesting aspect is
the fact that it is a parallelogram and that line
91-94 is exactly at a 90-degree angle to the line
drawn from the center of the circle of the Heelstone. This is an extraordinary occurrence since
there are very few spots on earth where this can
occur; to be specific, it is only on latitude 51.17 (either N or S) that these two lines will be perpendicular to each other. Line 92-93 is exactly parallel to
line 91-94. Thus, the observation of Newham was
confirmed.

C) the direction obtained when connecting 91 to 94
points exactly to the midwinter moonset.

D) The direction created by the extension of a line
drawn from 93 to 94 points to the midsummer sunrise.

E) The direction created by the extension of a line
drawn from G to 94 points to the midsummer sun-
set.

F) The direction created by the extension of a line
drawn from 93 to 92 points to the midsummer
moonrise.

G) The direction created by the extension of a line
drawn from 91 to 92 points to the midwinter sun-
set.

H) The direction created by the extension of a line
drawn from 93 to H points to the midwinter sunrise.

I) The direction created by the extension of a line
drawn from 93 to 91 points to the midsummer
moonrise.

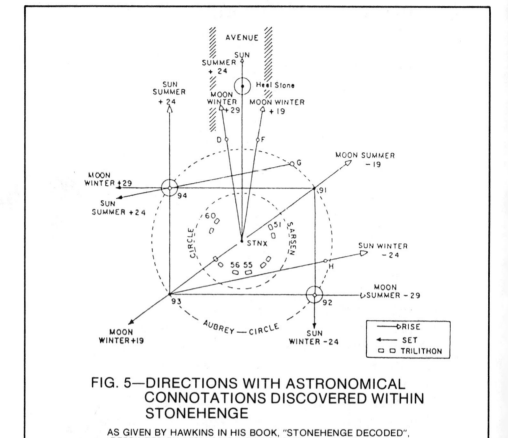

FIG. 5—DIRECTIONS WITH ASTRONOMICAL
CONNOTATIONS DISCOVERED WITHIN
STONEHENGE

AS GIVEN BY HAWKINS IN HIS BOOK, "STONEHENGE DECODED",
REPRINTED BY PERMISSION OF DOUBLEDAY & COMPANY, INC.

J) The direction created by the extension of a line drawn from 91 to 93 points to the midwinter moonset.

K) The direction when connecting the center of the circle with D points to the midwinter moonrise (plus 29).

L) The direction when connecting the center of the circle with F points to the midwinter moonrise (plus 19).

M) He proposed that the 56 Aubrey holes were a measuring device to compute the exact occurence of sun and moon eclipses taking place every 18.67 years.

These directions are depicted in Figure 5.
Professor Hawkins had the following to say:[1]

"By using them to count the years, the Stonehenge priests could have kept accurate track of the moon, and so have predicted periods for the most spectacular eclipses of the moon and sun. In fact, the Aubrey circle could have been used to predict many celestial events. It could have been done quite simply if one stone was moved around the circle one position, or Aubrey hole, each year, all the extremes of the seasonal moon and eclipses of the sun and moon at the solstices and equinoxes, could have been foreseen. If these stones spaced 9,9,10,-9,9,10 Aubrey holes apart were used, each of them moved one hole counter-clockwise each year, astonishing power of prediction could have been achieved. With 6 stones—3 white 3 black—the Aubrey hole computer could have predicted—quite accurately, every important moon event for hundreds of years."

"I have recently found that the Aubrey circle computer can be worked with 3 instead of 6 stones; the winter or summer eclipses occur when any stone is at hole 56 or 28; i.e. on the axis. Actually, the predicting can be done with one stone only, if 12 positions are marked around the circle."

These discoveries of Professor Hawkins have been proven since some of the stones are still there, and since

[1]*Stonehenge Decoded* by Gerald S. Hawkins Copyright © 1965 by Gerald S. Hawkins and John B. White. Reprinted by permission of Doubleday & Company, Inc.

the sun and the moon still perform exactly as they did 4000 years ago (with an exceedingly small deviation, hardly noticeable to the naked eye).

Later on, Professor Fred Hoyle rechecked the various calculations used by Professor Hawkins and confirmed their accuracy. Hoyle went a step further and described the workings of the Aubrey "computer." In his book *On Stonehenge* he gave us a very technical explanation of how this layout of 56 holes could be used in a slightly different manner than that suggested by Professor Hawkins. Nevertheless, the end result would be the same; namely, the prediction of the eclipses with a periodicity of 56 years (3 times $18.67 = 56.01$).

3

Peculiarities

Although a great many theories have been advanced in the past, none of them have given satisfactory answers to certain peculiar features that can be observed in the Stonehenge complex. I consider that there are at least eight exceedingly important occurrences that have not been properly analysed or explained to satisfaction. The answers to these eight enigmas will possibly give us the clue to the real function of this particular structure built 4500 years ago, even before the great pyramids of Gizeh.

AUBREY HOLES: Fifty-six holes were dug around a perfect circle having a diameter of 285 feet. Each hole measures about 2½ to 6 feet in diameter, and 2 to 4 feet in depth. Each was dug straight down into the ground with almost perpendicular sides and a flat bottom. Each was subsequently filled with white chalk. The center of each hole is almost exactly 16 feet away from the center of the next hole (with a variation only of a few inches, if at all). These holes represent the first construction, or what is called Stonehenge I. It is estimated that it was built sometime during the years 2500–3000 B.C. along with a ditch and a bank of dirt that encircle the 56 holes. It is only 500

years later that the Sarsen Circle of huge upright and horizontal stones was added (Stonehenge III). This means
that for 500 years all that was on hand was a circle of
holes filled with white chalk and set in the middle of a
plain, (plus the other few stones, ditch and bank mentioned before). For 500 years these masterful "primitive"
people were perhaps satisfied with such a layout and able
to perform whatever function they had in mind. Obviously, the 56 holes must have had a satisfactory meaning
of their own, to remain without addition for 500 years.

Professor Hawkins has cleverly given us an explanation of these 56 holes in stating that they represent a measuring device, or computer, to predetermine the solar and
lunar eclipses that take place regularly every 18.67 years.
Multiplying this figure by 3 we get 56 (or 56.01 to be exact).
Since certain specific eclipses take place at regular intervals of 18.67 years, and a very precise periodicity occurs
every 56 years, then $3 \times 18.67 = 56.01$ seems close enough
to determine the time when such an eclipse would take
place. According to Professor Hawkins (and later
confirmed by Professor Hoyle), a marker or a small stone
could be moved progressively from hole to hole until it
reached the specific point that indicated the occurrence of
the eclipse. This method works, resulting in a prediction
of future eclipses, every 56 years.

Although we must be impressed with the solutions
submitted by these two learned astronomers, there remains the possibility that 20th-century minds are possibly
reading something into the Aubrey circle not necessarily
consistent with the original objective. Possibly this solution might be part of the answer. It is true that $18 + 19 +
19$ is equal to 56. By the same token, however, 8×7 is also
equal to 56. Possibly these "barbarians" needed a counting
device for the periodicity of eight weeks' time. Thus, the
figure 56 could have a number of other meanings and
could have been used as a different type of computer.

However, be it as it may, there remain several very basic matters that concern me when considering the picture of Stonehenge I: the size of the holes, the way in which they were dug, the white chalk put into them, and the huge circle around which they were located. Performance of the functions suggested by Professor Hawkins does not require holes that are up to 6 feet in diameter. Nor do they need to be around a huge circle 285 feet in diameter, and certainly they do not need to be 4 feet in depth with straight walls and flat bottoms. What's more, they do not have to be refilled with fine white chalk. It is true that the region contains an underlayer of hardened chalk beneath the regular dirt. It is a very difficult process, however, to dig up that hardened white chalk; why in fact, dig a hole and then fill it up again? And why perform such an exercise 56 different times?

Performance of the exact function suggested by Professor Hawkins does not require so huge an undertaking. It could be accomplished by digging, for example, 56 little holes, 2 inches in diameter and 2 inches deep, placed around a circle of 3 feet, inside a protected cave. In fact, it does not even have to be a circle—an ellipse, or even a nondescript roundish shape would perform the very same function. If the only purpose were to move a little stone or three little stones, or a piece of wood, etc. from one hole to the other, then the small version I suggested, would succeed admirably well, and would perform exactly as required by Professor Hawkins' calculations. Obviously, it makes no logical sense to expect the Stonehenge builders (who were by no means simple-minded people) to over-build on such a huge scale and go through the tremendous trouble of performing the job—if they could have done exactly the same thing in a much simpler way. I cannot readily accept the premise that the Aubrey holes were built solely for the purpose of moving a marker from one hole to the next. What's more, the Aubrey circle is not even a collection of "holes" in the true sense of the word. These are holes that were refilled and thus are even with the surrounding ground; there is no depression as with a hole. I can possibly conceive that Hawkins' theory might be a part of the answer, but the main function could not be as described by him. We must logically expect that there was a very important reason for the existence of these 56 Aubrey holes, each filled with white chalk, and each of such huge dimension. It behooves us to critically analyze these holes further, and determine whether there could have been any other functions for them.

There is also another peculiar aspect of the holes that must be kept in mind: A person of about 5 feet, standing in the middle of this circle, can hardly see these Aubrey holes. It is known, from skeletal remains, that the height of the people of southern England 4500 years ago was on average about 5 feet. Therefore, a stone-age individual standing in the middle of that circle would have very little visual contact—if any—with these 56 holes. Especially during the Stonehenge III period, the huge Sarsen Circle, the five Trilithons, and all the other stones would almost completely interfere with the line of sight when standing in the center. The only time these holes become visible is when standing at a height of 20 feet or more, or when viewed from the air.

Why are these Aubrey holes filled with white chalk? It can be argued that the region has white chalk and as a result that would be one of the most accessible materials. This may be so, but it does not completely satisfy the logic of digging such large holes and filling them up again.

Then there is the fact that the builders found it necessary to erect a bank (or a wall), about 6 feet high and 20 feet wide also of white chalk, all around these holes as though they wanted to protect them. Why would they want to protect holes filled with chalk (since there was nothing else of permanence to protect within that circle)?

Theoretically, we can answer the question by pointing out that the bank was to keep people from running across the circle, or animals, or even dirt and leaves from being blown in by the wind. I cannot think of anything else they would want to hold back from entering this circle. If so, we must ask the question of why it was so important to protect these Aubrey holes? What could anybody do to these chalk-filled holes that they would need protection? It is farfetched to imagine people running to these holes to scoop out white chalk, especially as this raw material is available throughout the vicinity. Consequently, the original builders might not have been worried about a possible theft of the chalk. If we think in terms of stray animals removing it, that too, would hardly make sense as animals are not interested in chalk. At most, they might enter the big circle to graze or claim territory: this might have presented a displeasing aspect to the users of Stonehenge, but it is doubtful that this aspect was important enough for them to exert such tremendous effort to create a ditch and a bank, for its protection. What's more, animals can climb banks and ditches.

Let's keep in mind that, theoretically at least, Stonehenge I was used only to determine the midsummer sunrise over the heelstone. This is a once a year occurrence. Even if we consider the other sightings, we can conceive, at best, a usage of Stonehenge for a total of about only fourteen days during an entire year. Therefore, to keep animals away from this circle during a two week period is certainly not weighty enough to create such a big ditch and bank construction.

As far as dirt and leaves blown by the wind are concerned, although the bank would have a tendency to stop part of such blowing debris, it could not serve as a completely satisfactory barrier. Leaves and dirt driven by the wind would have cleared the bank.

Summing it up, I find it difficult to believe that the

bank was built in order to physically protect whatever was inside the circle.

We can turn the question around, however. We can ask why they might have attempted to protect people and animals from these holes filled with chalk? Why was it important to attempt to keep living creatures from a contact with the holes? Possibly such a question might sound unnecessary at first, yet was it necessary to have 56 holes, each one about 4 to 6 feet in diameter and 4 feet in depth, aligned in a perfect circle of 285 feet in diameter, and filled in with chalk?

There must be something more to the Aubrey circle than the creation of a simple device to count the passing years and thus predict the eclipses that will occur in the future.

It is good to keep in mind the fact that the construction of such a large ditch and bank would be an enormous undertaking; it has been estimated that about 30,000 human hours must have been expended in its construction. No grouping of peoples will spend this amount of time and effort, unless they consider it of the utmost importance for their Stone-age communities and survival.

CONSTRUCTION: When we examine the step-by-step process of building a monument like Stonehenge, we reach a point of great difficulty. We are told that Stonehenge III was the last phase of the construction, at which time all the stones within the Sarsen Circle were erected. Actually, we are not absolutely certain as to the exact datings when these various stones were erected. We do not have a scientific method of dating to tell us whether the trilithons were erected before the Sarsen Circle or after. We have no laboratory means or testing procedure (such as Carbon-14) to pinpoint the age of the construction, since we are dealing with stone, a nonliving matter. The logical assumption has been that all these stones were erected at the same time, starting with the trilithons, for the simple reason that they could not have been brought into the circle after the erection of the full Sarsen Circle. At least this is what normal logic would induce us to think.

If we accept this premise, then we must ask ourselves how these primitive people proceeded to erect this structure? There are a great many questionmarks that cannot be answered with just plain logic. Let us review a few of these. We know that the stones had to be carried from a great many miles away to converge on the specific construction site. The dragging of so many stones, weighing up to 50 tons each, is in itself, astonishing. Although plausible explanations have been advanced, on paper, and although a few practical experiments have been performed to prove their possibility, the explanations still do not address themselves to the overall problem, especially in view of the magnitude of the undertaking. It is one thing to experiment with the dragging of one stone, and it is a completely different matter when you are dealing with more than 100 stones.

We know that Stonehenge I was a ditch, a mound and 56 Aubrey holes with the Heel Stone in location. 500 years or more thereafter, we understand that the construction of the center part was started. If we suppose for a moment that each stone was being hauled into the construction site, we realize that it had to move over the ditch which measures about 10 to 18 feet wide and 4 to 7 feet deep. It is hardly likely that the primitive people could have negotiated such a barrier with 100 stones. Immediately after the ditch, is the bank whose dimensions are about 6 feet high by 20 feet wide. This is another extraordinary obstacle and no primitive people, equipped with ropes and logs, could possibly move 50-ton stone over the two obstacles.

The next possibility would be to consider that the stones entered the construction site through the Avenue connecting the Aubrey Circle to the Heel Stone. That is theoretically possible, but it means that all these huge stones had to enter through the same spot. Even if we consider that there might be another flat opening near stone 92, it would indicate a second possibility of entrance to the construction site. However, we must not forget that immediately after the bank are the large Aubrey holes, each measuring up to 6 feet in diameter. This means that a horizontal trilithon stone, weighing about 50 tons, would have had to cross the Aubrey holes in order to enter the center of the construction site. It is unlikely that they could proceed with so much weight and cross a soft spot, such that presented by the Aubrey holes. Logically, the workers should have experienced a tremendous difficulty as the stones would have a tendency to sink or slip into or near the open Aubrey holes. The soft chalk could not extend a great support to a movement of so many tons. Furthermore, they were not faced with the passage of one stone; but with dozens upon dozens of huge boulders that had to enter into the inner circle.

Summing it up, we are faced with a very considerable problem of movement when we realize that all the stones had to enter through very few openings and had to jump, so to speak, over the Aubrey holes in order to reach the center of the construction site.

Suppose we consider that they were able to bring all these huge stones into the circle. We can then proceed to follow their movements to erect the entire complex. We would expect that the first stones to be erected would be the innermost ones, namely the trilithons with their lintels, the Bluestones, and then the Sarsen Circle with its lintels.

According to our theoretical reconstruction of the events, these stones could only be pulled rather than pushed. This means that hundreds of people had to tug on ropes to pull the stone forward. For them to perform this task they had to have hundreds of feet of room ahead of the stone in order to be able to pull in that direction. Such a job, if performed at all, could only have meant the concerted muscle effort of several hundred people all pulling at the same time. We cannot conceive that these stones could possibly be pushed from the back, as there would be no means to apply the pressure of 200 people to inch the stone forwards. Keeping in mind the fact that they needed a few hundred feet of straight headroom, we can consider what might have happened during construction.

The first stones would probably be the center trilithon because, theoretically, it would be the easiest stone to put in place. The next ones would most probably be trilithons number 53, 54 and 57, 58. Observe that these stones are already in a different direction than the center trilithons. This means that the primitive people had to turn around; thus, with every stone that they moved, they needed a sizeable arc, a few hundred feet away, so that the haulers could twist and move the stone in a different direction. This, in itself, indicates the necessity of a huge amount of space to maneuver around. Let us give them the benefit of the doubt and consider that they were able to perform exactly this function. The next step would be to position for arguments' sake, trilithons 59, 60. This also could be performed since the tugging line would still have some room to maneuver in. However, when it came time to position trilithon 51, 52, they should have encountered problems as there would not have been enough room in front of them to properly haul the stones into place and turn them around. Stones 59, 60 would have been in the direct line of action (see Figure 1).

A much greater problem can be detected when thinking through the erection procedures of the upright Sarsen stones. We will consider even the possibility that the original builders alternated the erection of trilithons and Sarsen stones. It is possible that Sarsen uprights 12 to 18 might have been the first ones erected, before trilithons 55,

56. If we continue this process of thought, we will never-theless reach a point where the circle narrows and a quan-tity of the Sarsen stones could hardly have been pulled into the circle any longer, as there would have been no room to maneuver. By that point the circle would have become very crowded and the last number of stones would have presented great difficulty in being towed into place, turned around into the proper position, and then erected. In fact, the probabilities are that they simply could not have pulled any further stones into the center, as there would have been no room left for the hundreds of people to pull the boulders into place. Of course, the situation would have been quite different if they had possessed the capacity to push a stone into place instead of pulling it; they would then have been acting from the outside to-wards the center. Even if we consider that the stones were pulled in and left on the ground until all of them were in place and then erected, we still face the same basic prob-lem that there would have been no room to move around.

This problem is greatly compounded if we go one step further and realize the necessity of pulling in and erecting the entire Bluestone Circle. At the present time, 20 of these stones are in place. We do not know exactly how many were originally placed; various figures have been pro-posed, going all the way up to 40. An educated guess would indicate that there were probably 30 Blue stones, corre-sponding to the number of Sarsen stones. This Bluestone Circle is positioned inside the Sarsen circle, between the Sarsens and the trilithons. These stones vary in height from between 2½ to 6½ feet. It certainly would have been an additional problems to pull these Bluestones into the circle along with the rest of the boulders.

As though this were not enough, we have to consider also the Bluestone Horseshoe. These stones appear to have been 19 in number, weighing an average of 3½ tons each and measuring about 6 to 9 feet in height. The average diameter of these stones is about 2 feet; a peculiarity is the fact that they are sort of conically-shaped towards the top. These are placed in the form of horseshoe and are to be found in front of the trilithon group which were also placed in a horseshoe shape. They form the innermost row of stones that had to be pulled into place.

Finally, there is the Altar Stone, which lies on the ground, slightly buried. It is sandstone, a completely different material from the rest of the stones. It is about 15½ feet long × 3 feet wide × 3 feet high; we do not know whether it was ever in an upright position or whether it has always been lying on the ground.

Summing it up, we realize that a great number of very heavy stones had to be pulled towards the center and positioned. Since these had to be pulled rather than pushed, it is doubtful that the stone-age people had enough room to maneuver in order to pull all these boulders to the center and erect them in place.

And, yet the construction has been performed and the stones have been put in place. How they achieved this feat remains a mystery. It leads one to speculate that these primitive people might possibly have had a different means of moving the stones, rather than simply pulling them with ropes towards the center of the construction site.

MISSING STONE: In all the reports and studies I have read, hardly any mention has ever been made about the fact that the most important stone is missing and doesn't seem to have ever been set in place. Most of the previous studies do not mention the fact that there had to be a very important stone in a specific spot, without which most of the sightings could not be pinpointed. This missing stone is the center stone that should have been located in the center of the Aubrey Circle. We have no traces of such a stone, nor do we have any indication that there ever was one, since the ground doesn't show any telltale signs of having contained such a stone.

It is an elementary concept that one needs at least two specific points in order to draw a line and determine its precise direction. The heelstone is a specific point. However, it needs a second point (or stone) to connect to and generate the exact direction of the midsummer sunrise. Without this center stone we do not have a precise location and cannot connect it in a correct manner to the heelstone. Therefore, these "primitive" people could not have pinpointed the exact direction of the midsummer sunrise over the heelstone if they did not have another point of reference to guide their sight. If this missing center stone was never placed in position, then their sightings would have been haphazard. Each time they wanted to look at the heelstone they might have looked from a different spot in the center of the circle. This, of course, would negate all their precise work, and would have been definitely out of character with their actions as indicated by the astonishing amount of work and preparation that went into the construction of Stonehenge. We must concede that they were a very sophisticated group of people, very precise and knowledgeable in their behavior, who knew exactly what they wanted and how to perform the precise operations. Obviously, the center stone is the most important pivotal spot in this observatory.

We also must keep in mind that the center stone had to be used for aligning the winter moonrise (+ 29 moon high) by connecting it to position A. The center stone had also to be used to determine the direction of the midwinter moonrise (+ 19 moon low) by connecting it with position F (see Figure 5).

The same center stone had to be used to determine the direction of the summer moonrise by connecting it to position 91.

The same center stone had to be used to pinpoint the

direction of the winter moonset by connecting it to position 93.

All these directions could be precisely determined only if they had a fixed point of reference, namely the center stone. We must discard the idea that the builders involved did not consider the necessity of a center stone. They were too precise and sophisticated to overlook such an important position. We must also discard the idea that each time they wanted to take a sighting they preferred to locate anew the center of the circle and then determine the position. It would not make sense for these sophisticated, hard-working "primitive" people to go through the trouble of searching and determining the center of the circle each time they decided to use their observatory. The conclusion must be reached that somehow they used a center stone of some fashion, or a very precise marker that would pinpoint for them the exact position of the center of the circle. Without this center stone, the heelstone would have no meaning and would not generate a precise direction.

In some of the studies I have seen, Aubrey hole number 28 is used as a direction finder. This would not yield precise measurements, especially as it is not a stone aligned more or less at the same height as the heelstone; furthermore, the exact center point of Aubrey hole number 28 connected to the heelstone does not pass through the center of the circle. In other studies, the opening between Sarsen stones 30 and 1 was considered the direction finder. Although a line connecting the heelstone to the center would extend through the opening 30-1, it is still not a precise pinpoint location as the movement of the observer's head, by a few inches, would create a substantial error in the angle of sight. At best, it would be an approximation. And yet, we observe that nothing is approximate with these builders of Stonehenge. On the contrary, they seem to have accomplished a tremendous

amount of work in order to create a very precise computer.
Furthermore, during the periods of Stonehenge, I and II

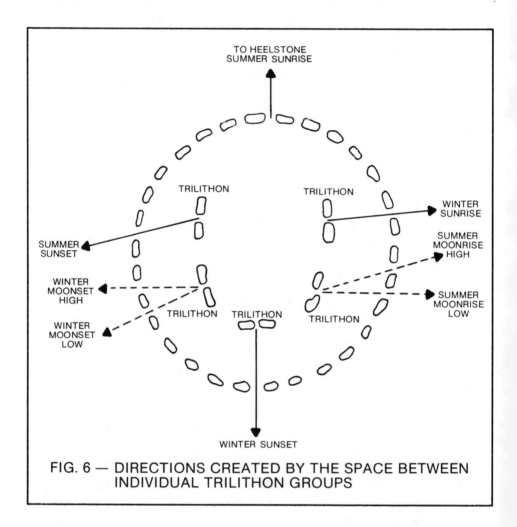

FIG. 6 — DIRECTIONS CREATED BY THE SPACE BETWEEN
INDIVIDUAL TRILITHON GROUPS

there was no Sarsen Circle, but only an empty large circle
of land.

We must, therefore, conclude that these "barbarians"

definitely possessed a center marker of some sort. The peculiar observation must be made and analyzed as to why we do not find any trace of such a center stone having ever been placed in its proper position.

TRILITHONS: When studying these five huge trilithons we are immediately impressed by their heights. Each of these units of three stones is higher than the Sarsen circle. They vary in height from 21 to 24½ feet. The two vertical stones are placed very close to each other and allow a small opening of a maximum of 10 inches as though they wanted to guide the observer's sight in a very precise direction and shut out the rest of the area.

Indeed, it has been found that these openings do direct one's view to very specific directions, as shown in Fig. 6. Yet, there is a very peculiar aspect that should generate a question in the minds of modern viewer's. Why would 5 foot-tall individuals erect 24-foot high structures simply to look through a small slit towards the horizon? If the only purpose were to determine a given direction, these "primitive" people could have selected two 6 foot high stones, placed them in the exact direction of sight, and saved themselves a tremendous amount of labor. After all, by any stretch of the imagination, it certainly could hardly have been a pleasureful pastime for these stone-age people to lug huge boulders weighing up to 50 tons each over distances of 20 miles, then erect them in place! It does not appear to make sense to generate tremendous trilithons structures that are 24 feet high simply to direct the sight of a 5-foot tall individuals to a very specific direction on the horizon. Again, let us remember, that these original builders knew exactly what they were doing, and performed their task in a most elegant, yet simple way, by using elementary tools available on the spot: stones, chalk and holes. There was sense and reason for every single hole and for every single position they created in that observatory. Nothing was haphazard.

It is thus more likely that these 24 feet high channel of

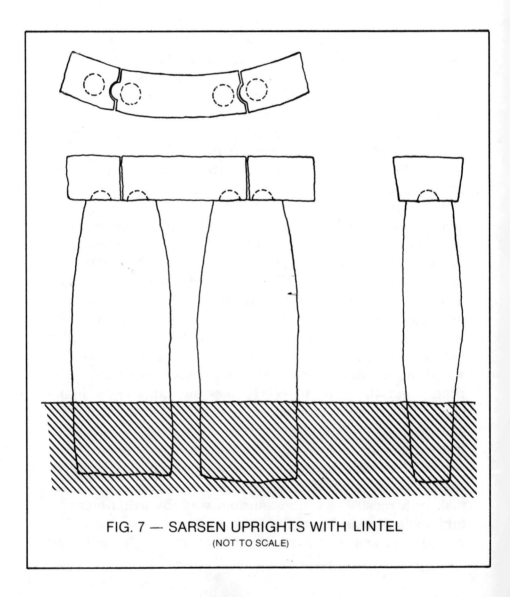

FIG. 7 — SARSEN UPRIGHTS WITH LINTEL
(NOT TO SCALE)

sight of the trilithons had a specific meaning that has not been understood up to now. Perhaps these channels are not strictly sighting tools.

SARSEN CIRCLE: This structure consists of a solid circle built with 30 vertical stones, each weighing about 25 to 35 tons. They are connected to each other on top by horizontal stones, called lintels, weighing about 7 tons each. These lintels are connected to the vertical stones by means of a "mortise and tenon" system. In essence, the vertical Sarsen stones each have two knobs (tenons) protruding from their top that fit perfectly into holes carved into the bottom of each lintel (see Fig. 7.) Furthermore, each lintel stone is connected to the neighboring lintel stone by means of a "tongue and groove" setup. This must have been a complicated procedure to shape and tailor exactly such a quantity of Sarsen stones with the proper tongue shape so as to fit the corresponding groove. It had to be done in such a way that corresponding pairs fit properly to each other. Is it too much to expect that a certain testing had to be performed so as to ascertain that the fit was satisfactory? Such a testing presupposes that these unwieldy stones had to be put together and taken apart a few times in order to experiment with the "fit". If these activities were performed by mere muscle power, one must feel really sorry for such a backbreaking exercise undergone by these poor Stone Age people. And yet, these people seem to have performed it. This means that the difficulty (or at least what we consider difficulty) was basically not too important, nor difficult, as long as they achieved their specific goal.

This combination of tongue and groove on one hand, and mortise and tenon on the other hand is certainly surprising. The only conclusion to be drawn is that the Stone Age people were extraordinarily keen in insuring that the top lintel circle should not move and should withstand a tremendous amount of pressure. The tenons alone should have been sufficient to hold the lintels in place and not permit them to move and fall off. Even though this should have been enough for normal circumstances, they went through the most difficult step of producing the tongue-and-groove construction as an additional factor of safety. Why such a tremendous sturdy construction on top?

It is important to consider that we do not come across, anywhere else in England, this type of system for tying stone to stone. Especially the tongue-and-groove system in a triangular shape is most extraordinary. We must again consider that they used different methods and different tools than the ones we think were available to them 4500 years ago.

One thing is certain: We have here an enormously sturdy and strong construction. Such a structure can withstand a great pressure, or stress and strain, from the elements or otherwise, because of its interconnected truss-work.

These lintel stones display an additional characteristic. They have been shaped so as to create a curvature on the outside and inside surfaces, in line with the curvature of the general Sarsen circle. What's more, they have been vertically tapered so that the top surface is about 6 inches wider than the bottom surface. Again, we realize that it must have been an exceedingly difficult job for these primitive people to dress 30 lintel stones and chop them down in such a way as to generate the various desired effects. And yet, this is exactly what they did.

Oddly enough, when analyzing the Sarsen Circle, none of the scientists—such as Hawkins, Hoyle, Atkinson, etc.— were able to determine any relationship between the Sarsen Circle and the astronomical sightings. If the basic function of Stonehenge was that of an observatory, then the Sarsen Circle with its lintels seem to be an immense structure placed there out of context with the main function. To be sure, these Sarsen stones were placed in such a manner that there would be an opening between them in order not to interfere with the sightings generated by the other stones. However, the stones of the Sarsen Circle themselves do not seem to have any meaning or function within these sightings.

It could be argued that this was a Temple and, as such, represented only an imposing structural edifice. Just as the Parthenon in Greece had a majestic group of colonnades, so would the Stone Age people produce a regal edifice with their primitive type of colonnades. This doesn't make too much sense in this particular context especially if we consider that the Stone Age people had to devote the greatest portion of their time to their everyday survival and could hardly afford the inordinate expenditure of time and effort needed to erect such an immense structure. In the second place, there is no real determination that this was truly a temple—instead, there is a determination that this was partly an observatory or computer, tied to astronomical events.

As such, it must be considered most peculiar that such a huge, extraordinarily sturdy construction should be built, having no observable connection to the movements of the sun or the moon or the stars. Instead, it looks like a frame erected with the idea of generating sturdiness and massive strength to resist all sorts of stress and strain, specifically on the horizontal lintel stones.

When analyzing the construction of this Sarsen Circle, we observe another very important and amazing aspect. Professor Hawkins, after an aerial survey called photogrammetry, which measures the elevation of every spot, observed that the area on which Stonehenge is built is not even. There is a slight drop in altitude from the southwest to the northeast. The diameter of this Sarsen Circle is about 100 feet. The ground drops off by about 2 feet from one end of the circle to the other. From the middle of this structure, such a slope is hardly apparent. However, a drop of 2 feet in 100 feet is a serious matter.

The extraordinary aspect observed is that the top, or the upper surface, of the horizontal lintel stones is level with the horizon. Disregarding a few of the irregularities of the stone itself, it was found that the top surface of the various lintels is exactly at the same height above sea level. This means that the original builders created a level surfaced structure on a slanted ground! To perform this feature they used stones of different heights and imbedded them in the ground at varying depths. If we consider that there are 30 Sarsen stones placed in a perfect circle of 100 feet diameter, we can appreciate the amazing accuracy and engineering capacity that went into creating a level surface all around such a massive structure. This, in itself, is an extraordinary achievement, as they were dealing with tons upon tons of stones that were very unwieldy to move around. Not only did the stones have to be placed in proper position, but the builders had to constantly reset them so that all the top surfaces of the lintels would be level.

All of this is assumed to have taken place about 4500 years ago, at a time when that section of England was considered to have been still in the Stone Age! It is simply amazing to consider that utterly "primitive" people, with limited tools, no machines, very short of manpower, were able to generate so sophisticated a precision while working with simple muscle-power, on hundreds of tons of unwieldy boulders. The procedure in modern times would be to level the ground and then set stones that had been pre-cut to uniform heights. Of course, we have today the proper machinery such as scrapers, bulldozers, trench diggers, leveling instruments, etc.

There are some very baffling questions that face us:
A) If Stonehenge was an observatory for sun and moon

alignments, why was it so important for these massive lintels to be perfectly level on top?

B) Why was it important that the top of the lintel stones be level and not the ground on which they stand? Why could the tops not have been slanted in the same general proportion of 2 feet in 100 feet as is observed on the ground?

C) Why was it easier for the Stonehenge builders to work via the most difficult method—at least from our point of view—rather than to level the ground and work with similar size stones?

The more one thinks about it, the greater the mystery becomes. We are faced with an extraordinarily difficult job of setting up 30 vertical stones in such a way that the 30 horizontal stones will fit perfectly with each other, creating a tight circle and yet be completely level on top. Imagine the hardship that would be involved if the builders found, for example, that stone number 105 was not level and had to be reset or moved. These "barbarians" could not possibly have performed these adjustments by simply using muscle power.

SARSEN No. 11: The next baffling observation deals with the upright Sarsen Stone No. 11 (see Fig. 9) Most reports on Stonehenge do not specify the fact that the Sarsen Circle is not perfectly uniform. 29 upright stones seem to follow the same general rule, namely, they are stones, well-anchored in the ground, and supporting the horizontal lintel stones at a height of about 14 feet by means of the "mortise and tenon" method. This is true for all of them— except for stone No. 11.

In the middle of this utter uniformity and perfection, we discover, all of a sudden, a small stone, almost half the size of the other Sarsen uprights. Instead of being about 14 feet high, this stone is only 8 feet high. Instead of measuring about 7 feet by 4 feet in cross section, as the other 29

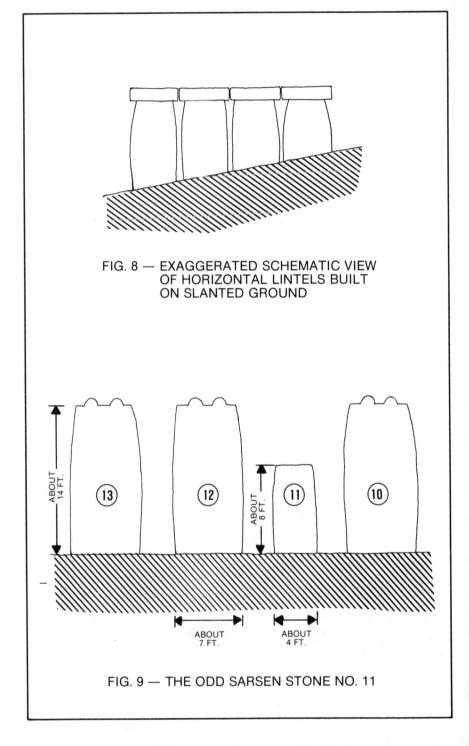

FIG. 8 — EXAGGERATED SCHEMATIC VIEW
OF HORIZONTAL LINTELS BUILT
ON SLANTED GROUND

FIG. 9 — THE ODD SARSEN STONE NO. 11

Sarsen upright stones average, this one has a dimension of about 4 feet by 2 feet. Why?

One can argue that this might have been an accident, and suggest that sometime during the past 4000 years, half of the stone was broken off. But if that were the case, how do we explain that the cross-section is so much smaller? Obviously, half of the width and depth of the stone were not also sheared away!

We must again revert to the same observation we posed before: Nothing in this extraordinary structure was done haphazardly; every stone, every hole, every alignment had a very precise meaning, and was the end result of finely precalculated moves. Thus, Stone No. 11 cannot be a mere coincidence, thrown in haphazardly within a perfect plan. If Sarsen upright No. 11 is smaller in size— there must be a meaning to it. We must assume that it was purposely set that way, from the very beginning. Just because we did not have a plausible explanation until now is not sufficient reason to overlook this obvious, yet surprising, anomaly in the construction of the Sarsen Circle.

LINTEL STONES: In the particular case of the Sarsen stones and their corresponding lintels, we must keep in mind that these are tailor-made stones. Not only must every stone have been carefully selected ahead of time, but each was shaped and dressed with some sort of tool so as to generate the proper fit and alignment in conjunction with the rest of the massive stones. What's more, each lintel stone was exactly dressed down to form a proper curvature on the inside of the circle, as well as on the outside of the circle. In addition to this fact, each lintel had to have two holes drilled beneath the surface, at a proper depth, to fit satisfactorily on top of the protrusions left on the vertical Sarsen stones.

The holes in the ground had to be dug in such a way that they fit the particular stones to be placed in them so as to achieve the proper height for the lintel stones to be level with the horizon, as well as with its neighboring stones. Obviously, there must have been tremendous intelligence and engineering capacity in performing this feat. It cannot be achieved by simply pushing around massive stones with the hope of adjusting and readjusting them all by so many inches in order to finally achieve a perfectly level circle of stones. The magnitude of the problem is much too big to consider that the task was performed with simple muscle power supplied by the Stone Age inhabitants of that region. Again, we must conclude that the original builders either found it easier, or felt it absolutely imperative to perform an extraordinarily difficult task with clumsy, massive stones, since their most important objective seems to have been a level surface for the top side of the lintel circle, at a height of about 20 feet from the ground. Obviously, their specific aim was to create such a level surface on top and not a level ground on the bottom. Thus, the whole purpose of the Sarsen Circle must have been the creation of an absolutely flat surface at a height of about 20 feet.

If the whole purpose of such an observatory was to determine the exact point of the midsummer sunrise or the precise direction of the equinox moon, it could have been achieved by placing two small stones located in specific spots. They did not need such a massive structure with stones weighing about 35 tons each, to pinpoint a specific direction. Obviously, the Stonehenge builders must have had other plans in mind besides pinpointing the various movements of the sun and the moon. To be sure, their plans included the capacity of specifically determining the movement of the moon and the sun, etc. However, besides this, the structure must have had some very important additional functions which we have not yet deciphered.

It could be argued that the lintel stones were first

placed in position and then dressed down by chopping off pieces with flintstones and mallets until the top surfaces were level. If such a possibility is considered then it would mean an enormous amount of additional work had to be performed while perching on top of the stones. It would certainly mean a measuring capacity, so as to be sure that an even surface was achieved on all lintels. Besides having each lintel stone level, it would have been necessary to measure so that each horizontal lintel stone be at the same height as the other 29 stones! Since there is a drop in altitude of about 2 feet from one end of the circle to the other, it follows that they must have chopped off 2 feet of surface from those lintel stones that were on the higher side of the circle. Or else we could consider that they started with the same thickness of lintel stones but used different heights of vertical Sarsen stones in order to make up for the difference in height. If we accept this to be true, then these "barbarians" must have known ahead of time that the entire ground within the Aubrey Circle was not even, but was subject to an incline of 1:50. This infers again a capacity of measurement—it also infers measuring devices that would be precise enough to give them a correct reading of the ground slope. Can we thus consider that these Stone Age people had the knowledge and capacity to precisely survey the elevation of a circle of land, 300 feet in diameter?

We will probably not be able to answer this question with any degree of accuracy. Yet, we can confidently state that before starting the entire structure, these Stone Age people knew exactly what they wanted to achieve, namely: an exceedingly sturdy, round platform with an exactly level surface on top, standing at a height of about 20 feet above ground. We observe that this is precisely what they achieved and performed with toolings unknown to us and with methods that still baffle our understanding.

The lifting of the lintel stones from the ground up to

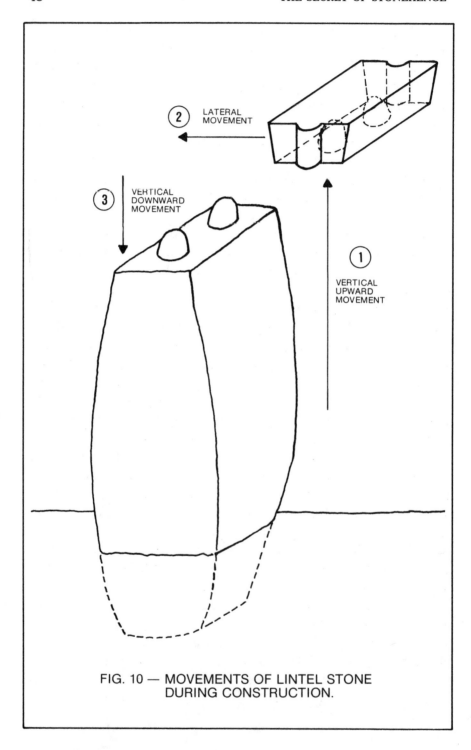

FIG. 10 — MOVEMENTS OF LINTEL STONE
DURING CONSTRUCTION.

about 16 feet, must have represented an enormous under-taking. We have been shown various artist's sketches de-picting possible methods by means of which these "bar-barians" lifted 7 ton lintel stones up in the air. By means of wooden scaffolding, we are told, they could inch it up and theoretically reach an altitude of 16 feet. We are not shown, however, what happened after bringing each stone to that height. At that point they had to arrange to move each lintel stone to the side, on a lateral movement over the vertical Sarsen stone. This side movement must be considered to have been immensely difficult, if not impos-sible, when starting with a stone lying on a wooden sca-ffolding. Plain muscle power can hardly be expected to have moved the stones in an horizontal direction.

Once the lintel stone was situated above the tenon of the vertical Sarsen stones, hanging in air so to say, they had to arrange to drop it exactly in place. This is a second vertical movement, downwards in direction. The lintels must not only have fitted on top of the tenons, but at the same time must have fitted perfectly into the grooved openings of the "tongue and groove" arrangement. If, per chance, a stone did not fit perfectly the very first time, then those unfortunate people would have encountered the considerable problem of pushing the stone into posi-tion, or lifting it and resetting it properly.

In Fig. 10 we observe that there are three movements to be performed with each lintel stone so as to fit it in place; namely, a vertical upwards movement, a lateral movement, and a vertical downwards movement. It is hardly believable that Stone Age people could have per-formed this miracle of construction.

DESTRUCTION: We have considered the extraordinary difficult job involved in erecting the Sarsen Circle. We should also ask how this structure was partly destroyed. It is almost as difficult a job to dismantle and move these

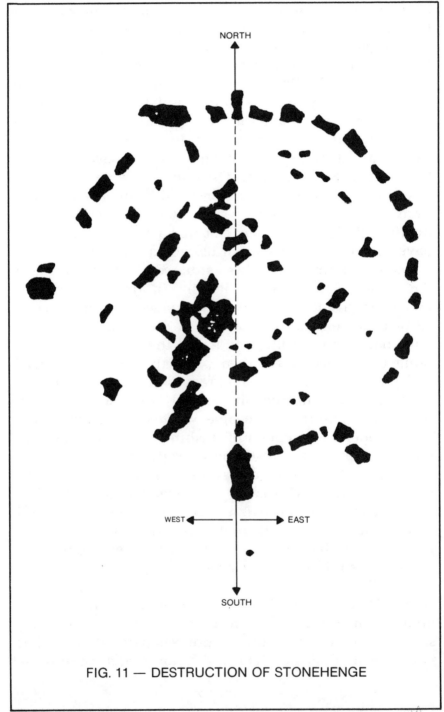

FIG. 11 — DESTRUCTION OF STONEHENGE

huge stones, as it was to bring them in and put them in place. To start with, the lintel stones had to be lifted out of their tight tongue-and-grooved circle, as well as out of their sockets before the vertical Sarsen stones could be dislocated from their imbedded positions. This would have necessitated a tremendous amount of effort and, again, there is serious doubts that it could have been done strictly by muscle power.

The people who wanted to destroy the structure must have gone to a tremendous amount of effort in order to break up the Sarsen Circle. This must have been an effort that lasted an appreciable amount of time, especially when we realize that a number of these stones were apparently dragged away and are no longer to be found on the spot or in the neighborhood. In fact, none of these large missing stones have ever been found. There could be various explanations for this loss of certain stones. Nevertheless, the important thing to realize is that somebody must have felt the urgency or the necessity of dismantling and moving a great number of these stones out of the locale. The tremendous effort exerted to do this must have been worthwhile to this group of people, for reasons best known to them.

Yet, a complete destruction did not take place, only a partial one. A number of vertical Sarsen stones and lintels are still in place although they represent the easiest portion to destroy since they are free-standing and would require less effort to topple. The peculiar aspect is that this dismantling crew did the most difficult part of the job but seemingly got tired of it and decided not to finish the job even though the remaining part would have been much easier to dismantle. There is something peculiar about the destruction of this edifice as it does not seem to follow the logical pattern to be expected from a group anxious to destroy the whole structure.

A closer look at a top view of Stonehenge, as it stands

today, reveals a peculiar picture. As we see from Fig. 11, only a certain portion of the monument seems to have been destroyed, with a number of stones lying scattered about the area. If we draw a line in a north to south direction, passing roughly through the center of the circle, we observe that the greatest destruction has taken place to the west of this imaginary line. Almost all the stones to the east of this line seem to be yet in place. This indicates that the people bent on dismantling the structure started their work on the west and proceeded towards the imaginary north-south line. It is in this half of the monument that almost all stones have felt the fury of the destructors. It is in this section that we see the greatest number of missing stones that cannot be located at the present time.

It is also interesting to observe that although the eastern section does not seem to have experienced this wave of destruction, most of the lintels have disappeared. Yet the vertical Sarsen stones are still in place in this half of the circle. These lintels were extraordinarily well tied-in to each other and to the uprights—and yet they seem to have disappeared, while the uprights are still in place.

In conclusion, we observe a peculiarity in Fig. 11: roughly half the structure seems to have undergone a destruction effort by people whose origin we do not know. Nor do we know when this destruction took place or why they were so single-mindedly bent on destroying Stonehenge.

Summing up the preceding observations, I consider the following meaningful peculiarities:

1) AUBREY HOLES: Their physical construction.
2) CONSTRUCTION: The step-by-step construction process does not satisfy plain logical expectations.
3) MISSING STONE: The fact that the all-impor-

tant center stone is missing, and was perhaps never put in place.

4) TRILITHONS: Their physical construction and their varying heights.

5) SARSEN CIRCLE: The extraordinary sturdiness of the construction and the seemingly meaningless positioning of the stones, in relation to the astronomical alignments of the rest of the stones.

6) SARSEN UPRIGHT No. 11: The peculiar size of this stone in comparison to the other Sarsen stones.

7) LINTEL STONES: The surprising fact that the top of the lintel stones are level with the horizon and create a tight circle.

8) DESTRUCTION: The partial destruction that does not follow the logical expectation of fury in a group of people bent on destroying the edifice.

These peculiarities must be given careful consideration. We must try to find, if possible, meaning behind these facts. It is my firm belief that the original builders of Stonehenge did not do anything haphazardly. We observe the existence of markedly pronounced intelligence and knowledge, both on theoretical ground and on the ground of technical construction. We must admit that each move, each stone and each hole, was predetermined so as to become part of a master design to fit a very specific purpose. What was that purpose?

4

MY

For a number of years, Professor Alexander Thom of England has been actively inspecting and measuring stone circles and standing stones (menhirs) throughout the British Isles, as well as in the northern part of France. Mr. Thom, an engineer by profession, has written a number of scientific articles and books on this subject, in which he delineates his important observation, namely that throughout the surveyed area he was able to determine a very precise unit of measurement employed continually by the builders of the stone circles, of which a thousand or more remain. He called this unit of linear measurement, the magalithic yard—or MY.

He also determined that the builders—whomever they were—used mostly full lengths of the MY. It is only in unusual cases that ½ or ¼ MY was used in the various constructions examined and surveyed by him. A great many of the circles had diameters of either 8 or 16 MY. Such circles would generate circumferences that are very close to 25 or 50 MY. Whether there was a determined effort made so that the circumference would be a full number is debatable. Nevertheless, established data shows that a great many of these circles have diameters that are whole units of MY, without any fractions.

A wealth of data was accumulated to back up these determinations. Mr. Thom submitted his findings in his book *Megalithic Sites In Britain*[1] without drawing any further conclusions.

Normally the presence of a measuring stick would not be surprising since any builder—unsophisticated or not—would have to use some measuring device. When we consider the important construction effort of stone circles that took place throughout England and Ireland, it is reasonable to presume that these builders used such a measuring stick. However, one of the amazing discoveries of Mr. Thom was the precision of the MY, which he was able to determine after collecting a very substantial number of measurements and data. In fact, Mr. Thom reported that throughout the British Isles, the stone circles seem to have been constructed on the basis of a MY whose exact length was:

$$2.720 \pm 0.003 \text{ feet}$$

The fact that the MY was correct to the third place after the decimal indicates an astonishing display of precision.

When we enter the realm of precision, we automatically infer a high degree of sophistication. It would have been possible for a Stone Age person, whose only tools were stone and wood, to create a specific length of measuring device to be used repeatedly to determine distances. A stick of this character could certainly measure considerable distances, but could, under no circumstances, be considered a precision measuring device. If that individual had to duplicate the measuring device and produce a second identical unit, it is almost certain that the second stick would have a different length than the first. When we refer to precision represented by the third place after the

[1]Megalithic Sites In Britain, by A. Thom published in 1967 by Oxford University Press, Oxford, England.

decimal, we can hardly be talking about a wooden plank
or a length of rope. Even if we disregard the precision
indicated by Mr. Thom's measurement, even if we consider a measurement of 2.72 feet only, it still reflects a
surprising precision to be constantly duplicated by mere
Stone Age people. This type of precision requires, at least,
the use of metal such as brass, bronze, etc. Even then the
person in charge has to be quite sophisticated to be able to
reproduce the measuring stick with a mediocre degree of
accuracy. Naturally, this completely disregards the effect
of temperature changes which would certainly influence
the exact length of the measuring device due to contraction and expansion of the metal.

What's more, we know from historical and archaeological data that the section of England in question had
not entered the Bronze Age 4500 years ago. It is usually
acknowledged that the first crude samples of bronze artifacts in the area are dated, at best, at 2000 B.C. Even if we
consider that the Stone Age people in southern England
had acquired the technology of casting bronze, they would
have been at the very early stages of the art. At such a
stage, it is doubtful that they would have been able to reproduce measuring sticks displaying the sophisticated
precision in question.

The baffling problem becomes still more enigmatic if
we consider that the very same precise MY measurement
seems to have been used on almost all stone circles
throughout England, Ireland, Scotland, etc. We are talking
about a very large area, all the way from the southern tip
of England to the Orkney Islands up north. Throughout
this entire region, there are hundreds upon hundreds— if
not thousands—of stone circles of different sizes and
shapes, flattened circles, ellipticals, etc. It is certainly
amazing to realize that the Stone Age people in the southern tip of England could possibly have used the very same
exact measuring yard as the Stone Age people building a

stone circle 600 miles to the north. When we consider that the precision to the third place after the decimal is present in the one place, as well as in the other, we must reach the conclusion that:

A) Perhaps there was a central organization that produced a quantity of extraordinarily precise measuring sticks and distributed them throughout the British Isles from south to north, from east to west, and on to Ireland and France. In that case it must be expected that this central organization was powerful enough to impose its will and convince these "barbarians" to use this particular measuring device in all their construction efforts of stone circles. The historical data we have certainly has not hinted at the existence of such a society with a centralized organization somewhere in England. What's more, its existence would also imply substantial mobility which is also very doubtful. And yet the facts speak for themselves.

B) Or else, we must consider that a very bright Stone Age individual created such a measuring stick and ran up and down virtually the whole territory of the British Isles, convincing the local population to buy and use it in their construction enterprises. This hardly makes sense if we consider the distances involved.

If this Stone Age person had used a specific length of a stick (such as, for example, a 2.72 feet long piece of wood) it would have been necessary to put a number of them end to end in order to measure 8 lengths or 16 lengths. Such a process would certainly defeat the precision of ±0.003 previously mentioned. There is no chance of having used one measuring stick and to mark off 8 lengths with this degree of precision.

The next possibility would have been for this individual to have produced 16 separate yardsticks which were laid down on the ground, end to end. Here, the chances are infinitesimal that the end product would have displayed the degree of precision involved. Or, we can consider that this individual generated a 16 MY long measuring stick. This would allow the measurement only of distances of 16 MY, but not any other lengths as pinpointed by Thom. Here again, it is impossible to conceive so precise a measuring result.

We could also consider that a rope was used for measuring purposes, instead of wood. Again we reach the conclusion that the degree of precision involved could not have been generated with a rope. One of the inherent characteristics of any rope is its elasticity, which changes constantly depending upon the pull exerted. Whether this rope is made of leather strips or vegetation fibers, the end result would be a course measuring capacity and certainly not a sophisticated precision that repeats itself, over and over again.

It is true that when adding a number of nonprecise measurements and averaging them, one could get a mean figure with a certain degree of precision—at least arithmetically. Actually, we know that the average result cannot be more precise than the component parts. Even if we take this aspect into account, we still cannot account for the repetitive precision that shows up in almost all the circles measured by Thom. Again we must conclude that these results cannot be haphazard since we have a constant duplication of the same precision in hundreds of samples, and potentially thousands.

The more one thinks about the actual steps that must have been taken by a Stone Age person to reach the precision in question, the more one is led to believe that we are probably faced with a completely different type of measuring capacity than wood, bronze rods, strings, etc. The constant repetition of this precise measuring capacity indicates the existence of some other type of very sophisticated technique. The fact that we saw it displayed over and over again throughout a large territory leads to the conclusion that this MY measurement had to be the product of an advanced intelligence, out of context with the type of society known to exist in that part of England 4500–5000 years ago.

Since these original builders had the obvious capacity to create whatever size circle they wanted, and since a preponderant number of these circles measure exactly 8 or 16 MY, it follows that stone circles of 8 or 16 MY must have had a very definite meaning to them. They must have felt the need for many stone circles to measure exactly 8 MY or 16 MY, distributed throughout a very large area. One is led to ask: Why did they need so many repetitive constructions of precisely 8 or 16 MY, scattered throughout the wide territory of England, Scotland, Wales and Ireland? There must have been a very specific reason.

Summing it up, in my estimation, Thom's discovery of the MY is exceedingly important. In his book *Megalithic Sites In Britain,* Thom has supplied us with a large amount of surveying data and has pinpointed the facts. He did not want to draw any conclusion, nor did he submit a plausible theory for the existence of the repetitive precision. I believe we have to go one step further and draw conclusions from the implications ensuing from the existence of the MY. Let us remember that a repeated display of precision is a mark of sophistication, which means an expression of knowledge, intelligence and scientific purpose.

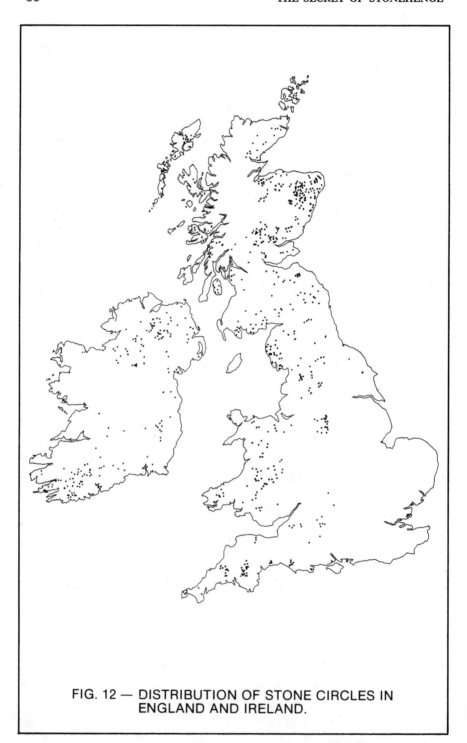

FIG. 12 — DISTRIBUTION OF STONE CIRCLES IN
ENGLAND AND IRELAND.

5

Stone Circles

There have been a great many studies of the hundreds of stone circles to be found on the British Isles. We have to be thankful to Professors Burl and Thom, among others, for the incredibly detailed surveying they performed over a long span of years in order to pinpoint the exact locations and dimensions of these circles. Both of them have written very valuable books, quite technical in nature, yet showing very clearly the variety of circles to be found in that part of the world. Although the most important one is a perfect circle, there are other shapes that have been determined: the ellipse, the flattened-out circle, the egg-shaped circle, etc. A detailed description of the various stone circles is naturally beyond the scope of this book, although the subject is tremendously interesting. A careful study of the various circles, their locations and their constructions should throw an important light on all the activities of these Stone Age people of the British Isles. Possibly, a meaningful interrelationship can be established.

We observe that the entire territory of England, Scotland, Wales, Ireland, etc. is dotted with hundreds upon hundreds of these stone circles, some larger, some smaller.

(see Fig. 12) These are the ones that can be distinguished today. Undoubtedly, a large majority of additional circles must have been destroyed over the past 5000 years, either by neglect, or by design, by being plowed under, or used for construction material in new housing, or destroyed for other reasons. Thus, the remnants that we observe today should be considered only a portion of the original construction effort.

It is also prudent to consider that among these thousands of circles, some might have been created by later generations of local population who wanted to emulate the existing circles they found in place. From time immemorial the local folklore had it that these stone circles had special powers. Although the exact nature of these powers is quite hazy, the general indication seems to have been that the stones in question had specific healing powers. People with ailments who were exposed within the circle, or who touched certain stones, were reported to have been miraculously cured. Thus it is logical to expect that at certain other times, especially during difficult years, there could have been a tendency among the local population to erect such stone circles in the hope that they would attract the attention of "God" or of "spirits" and produce the type of blessings that had been known to emanate in the past from such stone circles. It is questionable whether these copies ever performed the miracles expected. Yet it is not too far-fetched to consider that some of the remaining circles are not the original ones created 4000 to 5000 years ago at about the time when Stonehenge was constructed.

If we disregard a certain proportion of these circles as being fake copies, and if we concentrate on the originals (at least, hopefully, consider them to be originals), we still observe that a great many of these were built throughout the countryside, on flat territory (very few are on slopes of mountains, possibly for a good reason.) In a great many instances where we can still reconstruct and study the situation, it has been found that the telltale signs are still there: namely, a sighting stone to pinpoint the direction of the midsummer sunrise and, in certain cases, the midsummer moonrise. Again, in the vast majority of these circles, there is no center stone—as was the case in Stonehenge. Where foresights cannot be located, Thom, very astutely, discovered that specific natural characteristics on the horizon (such as sharp mountain tops), surprisingly replace the outlying boulders, and performed the same function of pinpointing the desired direction. In other cases, where no foresight stone has been found, it is possible to consider that it was destroyed or carted away by the local populations that lived there during the ensuing centuries.

We also observe that these stone circles are not necessarily bunched in clusters, but are spread out, to a good extent, throughout flat land. It is only here and there that

FIG. 13 — STONE CIRCLES IN BEAGHMORE, TYRONE, NORTHERN IRELAND.

small colonies of circles can be found in proximity to each other, such as the ones in Beaghmore, Tyrone (see Fig. 13). In very few isolated cases, we find stone circles placed on the slope of a mountain.

It is worthy to note, that all of these circles are made of upright stones. We do not encounter trilithon type structures with horizontal stones lying on top of two vertical stones.

Aside from these stone circles, we also observe in England, a quantity of parallel rows of smaller stones. It is true that we do not encounter a great many of them at the present time, although we have no way of knowing whether many more existed 4500 years ago, and were destroyed during the intervening years; their present numbers are relatively small and are found in Bodmin and in Scotland. These are the ones that we can still observe today. Chances are that most probably a great many other parallel rows were destroyed or moved out of place during the past several thousands of years. These rows are not necessarily made from huge boulders as are the stone circles. Instead, they have a tendency of being much smaller in size and much shorter in height. They, too, constitute an enigma. No plausible explanation has ever been put forward to explain their existence.

As a third occurrence within the same general family of megaliths, we observe individual large stones standing in the middle of "nowhere". These menhirs do not seem to follow a very specific pattern, although not enough studies have been performed to pinpoint their relative positions and plot them on an overall map. Again, old legends indicate that these menhirs possessed mysterious powers. We do not know precisely what these powers were and how the stones displayed their powers. We only know that there was something "special" about them, something "holy" so that people had a tremendous respect and awe for them. They repeatedly reported healing powers, and,

CIRCLE
ROLLRIGHT (OXFORDSHIRE)
MERRY MAIDENS (CORNWALL)
TRIPPET STONES (BODMIN)
SHERBERTON (DARTMOOR)
ASTLERIGG (CUMBERLAND)

FLATTENED CIRCLE
DINNEVER HILL (CORNWALL)
BURNMOOR (CUMBERLAND)
BLACK MARSH (SHROPSHIRE)
CAMBRET MOOR (KIRKCUDBRIGHT)
BAR BROOK (DERBYSHIRE)

ELLIPSE
KILLIN (PERTH)
DAVIOT (INVERNESS)
POSTBRIDGE (DEVON)
CLAVA (INVERNESS)

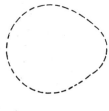

EGG-SHAPE
ALLAN WATER (MIDLOTHIAN)
DRUID TEMPLE (INVERNESS)
BURGH HILL (ROXBURGH)

COMPOUND RING
KERRY POLE (MONTGOMERY)
E. DELFOUR (INVERNESS)
MOEL TY UEHA (MERIONETH)

FIG. 14 — VARIOUS SHAPES OF STONE CIRCLES

at times, lightning effects. What ever it was, it is important to realize and keep in mind that there was "something" connected with them in the earlier centuries—and,
perhaps, even today.

Aside from these circles, we also observe a quantity of
stones set in slightly different configurations, such as elliptical or flattened circles. The shapes have been pinpointed
by various archaeologists, such as Atkinson, Burl, Thom,
etc. Usually these special shapes are larger in size than
the normal round circles of 8 MY or 16 MY.

Summing it up, we acknowledge a tremendous construction effort throughout a wide territory, repeating certain aspects over and over again. Naturally, the obvious
question must always be raised:

What were these stone circles and why did the people
need so many of them?

Stone Rows: The greatest concentration of stone rows
in the British Isles is to be found in Dartmoor in Devonshire where about sixty independent rows have been pinpointed. Aside from this, Thom was able to analyze
thoroughly and to supply a great many details about the
four main stone rows found in northeast Scotland: namely,
those in Mid Clyth, in Dirlot, in Lock of Yarrows and in
Camster. In his book *Megalithic Lunar Observatories*,[1]
Thom analyzes the numerous aspects of the construction
of these stone rows and supplies thought-provoking data.
In the four Scottish sites mentioned above, Thom considers that the rows were laid out in a fan type shape, as
though they were segments of a large circle. Figure 15 is
a reproduction of Professor Thom's diagram in which he
indicated the exact location of the stones, as they are
found today. On top of the diagram he superimposed a
grid, which clearly shows the alignments of these parallel

[1]Alexander Thom, *Megalithic Lunar Observatories*, published in 1973 by
Oxford University Press, London, England.

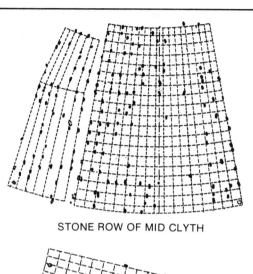

STONE ROW OF MID CLYTH

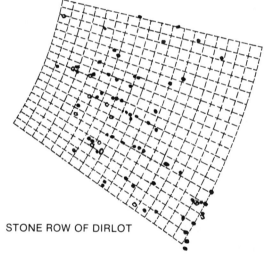

STONE ROW OF DIRLOT

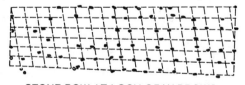

STONE ROW AT LOCH OF YARROWS

FIG. 15 — STONE ROWS IN ENGLAND
BASED ON OBSERVATIONS BY A. THOM
FROM HIS BOOK—"MEGALITHIC LUNAR OBSERVATORIES"—OXFORD UNIVERSITY PRESS.

rows. To be exact, the word parallel is not correct. The rows seem to converge and thus are not parallel in the true sense of the word. The most important aspect is to observe that the dimensions determined by Thom continue to be based on the MY. This is another indication that the same people who built the stone circles were involved in laying out these stone rows.

According to Professor Thom, the rows appear to have been a calculator device for solving extrapolation problems, especially when connected with lunar alignments. He offered a number of mathematical formulas that would indicate a pattern among the four Scottish sections. It is well to note, however, that the major unit, the Mid Clyth, does not seem to fit correctly into the pattern, even though it is the largest and best preserved structure among the four.

As far as the 60 known stone rows in Devonshire are concerned, they are much less imposing than the ones in Scotland, as they contain usually one or two rows, while a few of them have three rows. At least these are the remnants we see at the present time. Perhaps, originally, there were a great many additional parallel rows that have been destroyed in the meantime. The rows vary in length, with the longest one about 2 miles and the shortest about 100 feet.

A most interesting observation has to be made: the Devonshire rows are very near to the vicinity of an outlying standing stone. In some cases, a standing cairn seems to be placed at the termination of the row. In other cases, the stone rows have large boulders between them at one end, as though indicating the closure of the construction. Similarly, the 4 fan-type stone rows studied by Thom are close by to standing menhirs. These rows do not consist of very large boulders; they vary in size between 1 and 2 feet at most. In the case of the Mid Clyth stone rows, we also observe that the left section contains a bent line (see Fig. 15).

6

Morbihan

In the northern part of France, in Brittany, there is a section, Morbihan, that contains a great number of megalithic remnants. It is generally known as the region of Carnac and faces south towards the Gulf of Morbihan. In this general region we observe a type of stone structure that is quite unique and not duplicated in England. There are huge parallel rows of stones that extend a number of miles. Fig. 16 indicates the main characteristics of this general area.

These parallel rows of stones, unlike the ones that we find in England, contain a great many more rows and extend for 3000 to 4000 feet. At least these are the remnants we presently find. Furthermore, we observe three distinct groups which can be classified as follows:

A) LE MENEC: It is the biggest field containing 1,099 standing boulders, which vary in height from about 13 feet to 2 feet. It is composed of 11 almost parallel rows covering a width of 100 meters (about 330 feet) and extending for a length of 1167 meters (3850 feet). At the beginning of this field there is a sort of circle that contains accumulations of 70 tall monoliths. At the end of these rows there is evidence of a stone circle.

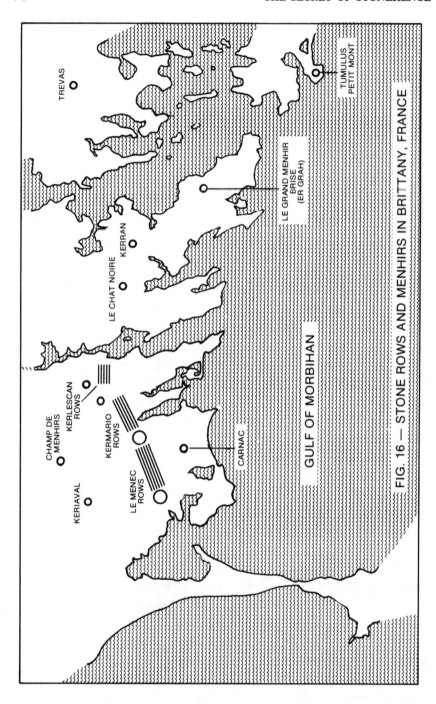

FIG. 16 — STONE ROWS AND MENHIRS IN BRITTANY, FRANCE

B) KERMARIO: This is the second largest field containing presently 1029 stones aligned in 10 semi parallel rows. The area covered is about 101 meters wide (333 feet) and 1120 meters long (3696 feet). Here again, we observe the same general characteristic of large menhirs appearing at the beginning and measuring about 6½ meters (21 feet). They progressively decrease in size and end in stones whose height is about 50 centimeters (1.6 feet).

C) KERLESCAN: This is the smallest unit of the three with 13 parallel rows about 880 meters in length (2904 feet) by 139 meters in width (460 feet). At the present time, we can only count 594 stones, although the obvious indications are that there were originally a great many more megaliths in place. Here again, we observe the fact that at the beginning of this field there is a type of stone circle or accumulations made up of 39 large stones.

Around this general area we also observe a quantity of big boulders placed in different spots. Fig. 16 pinpoints some important ones that have been observed, and shows the relative positioning of these stone rows on the south shore of Morbihan. The whole region is dotted with all sorts of additional stones, mounds, etc., giving us definite proof that a tremendous activity must have taken place in this region during prehistoric times. Those megaliths that we now encounter are the remnants of what must have been a large construction effort. During the ensuing centuries, a number of stones have been taken away for construction purposes, or plowed under, or simply moved to other spots. It is also interesting to note that none of these stones are dressed. They consist of all sorts of shapes, as though their form was completely immaterial to the original builders. As long as they had a huge boulder in a specific spot, they did not seem to care at all about the type of form that was involved. As a result, these huge rows of stones give a very eerie feeling with each stone displaying

FIG. 16a — STONE ROWS IN BRITTANY.

its own individuality and its own shape.

The only stone that appears to have been somewhat shaped to size is called Le Grand Menhir Brise. This is the largest stone in the whole area, and shows an almost oval cross section throughout its entirety.

The most important characteristic is the type of construction involved in the 3 distinct fields of parallel stone rows. On the one hand, there is a gradual reduction in height of the stones starting at one end with a big boulder, with succeeding boulders progressively becoming smaller towards the center, then increasing slightly in size again. What's more, these rows are not exactly parallel lines. Instead, the distance between the rows becomes narrower towards the end; we can compare the space to a trough or funnel that begins with a wide end and then narrows to a smaller end. Furthermore, these rows seem to have been placed around an imaginary arc; it gives the impression that they form a segment of an arc whose center was a few thousand yards away. Part of this curvature was achieved by an angular break in the straight line of the stone rows. Finally, each parallel row does not seem to have the same height of stones nor the same relative proportions from one end to the other. One gets the impression that, although the passing of time and the interference of various people have naturally obscured the exact sizes, certain outer rows on one side have a tendency to be higher than the inner rows. All in all, we can detect a type of concave area at an angle around the segment of an arc and flowing downwards from one end to the other.

Centuries of studies have proposed all sorts of reasons for their existence. The truth of the matter is that we really do not know what this huge accumulation of megaliths signifies. It could certainly not be a display of the caprice or the fancy of prehistoric individuals, who had nothing else to do but move so many huge stones all over the place and implant them in certain specific positions. Stone Age people are acknowledged to have been hard-pressed to survive and perform their immediate duties of creating food and shelter with most primitive tooling. It is difficult to imagine that a small Stone Age society in this particular section of France spent such an extraordinary amount of time and effort just collecting boulders and carrying them to Morbihan. The amount of human hours that must have gone into producing this huge display of stones is considerable. Again, we must ask ourselves the same questions we did in the case of Stonehenge: Where did the engineering knowhow come from to devise and create these specific alignments? How was the transportation capacity generated? It is difficult to believe that primitive people could have moved so many thousands upon thousands of huge stones about the countryside by sheer muscle power. Obviously, there was a plan, a program, a definite will to create structures with a specific meaning. That meaning has escaped us all along—we don't even know who the people were to whom such structures were of such importance.

Le Grand Menhir Brise is estimated to weigh in the vicinity of about 660,000 pounds and to have an overall dimension of about 72 feet. Eight to nine feet must have been placed underground, and the above ground height would be roughly 65 feet. This stone is made of a type of granite whose nearest source has been located in the area of the Finisterre, a distance of roughly 55 miles.

If we consider that a 40-ton stone was certainly a problem to transport for the builders of Stonehenge, imagine what it meant to transport and erect a 300 ton stone! There is simply no possibility that any society during the Stone Age, or even Bronze Age, had the physical capacity of quarrying such a menhir from a granite mountain, and then transporting it 55 miles over land to its site to be erected in a perpendicular position. The terrain is certainly not flat land. With all its hills and valleys, rivers and woods, it is unthinkable that they could have moved such a megalith. In fact, even for modern builders, it would be a huge undertaking requiring all sorts of mechanical equipment to lift and transport a single piece weighing 660,000 pounds (330 tons).

As in the case of Stonehenge, we are faced with an unanswered question when considering that this stone could be toppled by muscle power, and would break as it did. In order to bring the stone down, an enormous amount of power had to be applied. Even then, it is most doubtful that a Stone-Age group of people would be in a position to spend so much time and energy simply in order to destroy the stone. If so, the destruction of this lonesome stone must have been one of the priorities of that society—there must have been a tremendous urgency and necessity to bring it down. As in the case of Stonehenge, we must consider that an outside force (perhaps an explosion?) of considerable magnitude must have been applied to throw down a 330-ton megalith.

7

The Old Testament

For more than 3000 years, the Old Testament has been regarded as a religious document and has been evaluated from that point of view. It is my contention that this document is actually a factual report handed down to us by our Hebrew forefathers. They tried to put in writing the various actual occurrences that they experienced during their lifetimes. These happenings were of momentous proportion and impressed them with a tremendous awe concerning the "apparition" they saw; namely, the presence of their God, YAHWEH. They tried with all humility to describe and report what they saw, what they heard, what was said and what they experienced. Thus, the Old Testament should be considered as an enormous gift from our forefathers, telling us what happened so many centuries ago.

If we read the Old Testament as it was written 3000 or more years ago, and try to project these words onto a 20th-century technological background, we obtain an incredible picture that starts making sense for modern people. Our forefathers did not understand what was going on, nor what was happening to them. They were only able to describe with their level of understanding and with their own words, experiences that were completely beyond their own grasp. These very same experiences translated with our today's technical and scientific understanding generate a completely different picture.

In my previous book entitled *Urim & Thumim—the Secret of God,*[1] I tried to analyze a number of chapters of the Old Testament, and tried to understand them with today's terminology and technology. I reached some very unexpected and startling conclusions that can shed a completely different light on various aspects of our history.

In the following pages, I would like to give a very concise description of some of the highlights analyzed in that book.

Towards the beginning of the Old Testament we read that God extended to Moses exceedingly detailed and specific instructions about how to prepare the proper clothing to be worn by Aaron, the head priest (Exodus, chapt. 28) His clothing was supposed to be made strictly of linen with no admixture of any other fiber-and especially no wool. On top of the chest he was to wear a breast pocket attached to his tunic with gold rings and gold chains. In the breast pocket he was supposed to place the "Urim and Thumim".

On the other hand, Moses—who was definitely the much more important personality—received no instructions at all as to how he should dress himself. Instead, all the precise instructions given, concerned the head priest and his assistants.

The priest's function was simply to take care of the inner sanctum of the Tabernacle, a room where the Ark was placed and where none of the people were allowed to enter with the exception of the priest, his assistants and

[1]I. L. Cohen, *Urim & Thumim—the Secret of God*, published in 1982 by New Research Publications, Inc.

Moses. This was the room where god's presence was "observed" or "felt," since his seat was supposed to be on top of the Ark.

The first puzzling passage detected was the one in which YAHWEH gave instructions to weave gold wires within the cloth for Aaron's attire. Why would anybody want wires to be woven into the clothing of a priest? And why only in the priest's clothing, and in nobody elses?

The second puzzle was the fact that despite detailed descriptions for each part of the attire, no description whatsoever was extended in the case of the "Urim & Thumim" except for an order to place "it" inside the breast pocket. For all these centuries theologians have been unable to explain exactly what the "Urim & Thumim" represented, since no description was available and the phrase itself did not represent a specific meaning for an object known to the Hebrews throughout the ages. The exact translation of these two words is: lights and perfections (Fig. 16b).

In the Old Testament, there exist the exact instructions issued by God concerning how to construct the Ark (EX. 25:8/24). It represented a wooden box lined with gold plates on the inside and the outside. On top was a golden lid which supported two large golden statues representing two angels with outstretched wings, pointing towards the sky.

A further puzzle was that according to the Old Testament each time the Hebrews went to the battlefield they had to take along the Ark, accompanied by the priest who would blow the trumpets, ordering the troops to advance or withdraw. Whenever the Ark was with the Hebrews they won their battles against their superior enemies. Without the Ark, they usually lost.

The Ark was known to have some very unusual characteristics; in fact, YAHWEH had warned the Hebrews ahead of time: to touch the Ark meant to die! The only

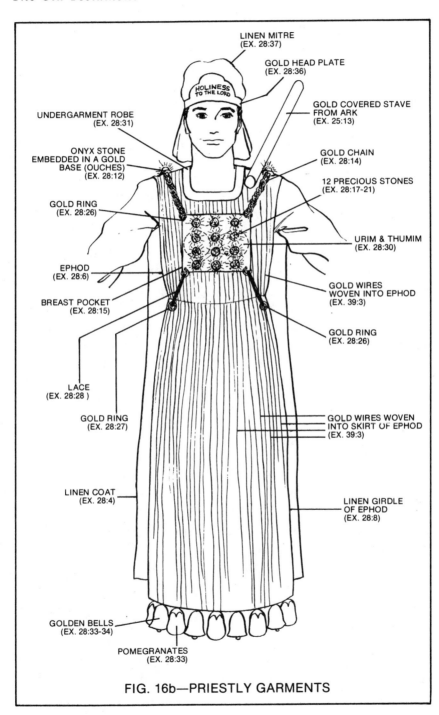

LINEN MITRE
(EX. 28:37)

GOLD HEAD PLATE
(EX. 28:36)

HOLINESS TO THE LORD

UNDERGARMENT ROBE
(EX. 28:31)

GOLD COVERED STAVE
FROM ARK
(EX. 25:13)

ONYX STONE
EMBEDDED IN A GOLD
BASE (OUCHES)
(EX. 28:12)

GOLD CHAIN
(EX. 28:14)

12 PRECIOUS STONES
(EX. 28:17-21)

GOLD RING
(EX. 28:26)

URIM & THUMIM
(EX. 28:30)

EPHOD
(EX. 28:6)

GOLD WIRES
WOVEN INTO EPHOD
(EX. 39:3)

BREAST POCKET
(EX. 28:15)

GOLD RING
(EX. 28:26)

LACE
(EX. 28:28)

GOLD RING
(EX. 28:27)

GOLD WIRES WOVEN
INTO SKIRT OF EPHOD
(EX. 39:3)

LINEN COAT
(EX. 28:4)

LINEN GIRDLE
OF EPHOD
(EX. 28:8)

GOLDEN BELLS
(EX. 28:33-34)

POMEGRANATES
(EX. 28:33)

FIG. 16b—PRIESTLY GARMENTS

persons allowed to come near the Ark were the priest and his assistants, since they would be properly dressed up for the occasion and had been trained for that activity.

During one trip to the battlefield, the Ark, being drawn by oxen, was shaking too much over the rough terrain and a well-meaning person by the name of Uzzah tried to hold it with his hands. The Bible tells us that he immediately fell dead to the ground—(II Sam. 6:6 and 6:7). The explanation given, of course, is that he disrespected the specific order given by God. If we believe the exact wording of the Bible, we must consider that a man fell dead by simply touching the wooden box lined with golden plates. In 20th century parlance the only way we can conceive of this is in the event the box were electrically charged sufficiently to electrocute the person.

In the Old Testament, a battle is mentioned with the Philistines, who were able to capture the Ark and bring it to their headquarters in Ashdot. We are told of the extraordinary havoc the box heaped on the Philistines, killing numbers of people and creating a considerable panic. The terror of the Philistines was such that they tried desperately to get rid of the Ark and return it to the Hebrews. (I Sam. Chapter 5). Again, the classical answer has been that the wrath of YAHWEH was aroused and that he brought destruction onto the Philistines. On the other hand, if we try to analyze this event with 20th century understanding, it must seem peculiar that a plain box, lined with gold plates, could create havoc among people who were near it or who touched it. Or is it?

In elementary physics taught today in our Junior High schools, metal plates that are separated from each other by some sort of insulation, perform a very specific function. A box produced from such insulated plates and having outstretched extentions on top, is well-known in physics as a condenser. It has the capacity to absorb and store static electricity (i.e. electrically charged particles), retain the charge up to a certain threshold point, and then discharge it in the form of a lightning, accompanied by a loud noise—a thunder. Such an experiment is constantly being performed in our beginner's classes of physics.

Depending upon the potential capacity of that "box", its electrical discharge can certainly electrocute a person. The dimensions of the Ark, as given to us by the Bible (Ex. 25:10) indicate a very large sized box, and thus a very powerful capacity to absorb and store electrical energy of high potential.

Consequently, the devastating experiences of the Philistines with the Hebrew Ark, are quite understandable, as they were dealing with an electrically charged condenser that was discharging onto people who were not properly insulated against it. Of course, the question arises: Who charged and discharged this Ark with electricity?

Although we don't know what the Urim and Thumim actually was, we know how it was used. It was "something" placed in the breast pocket of the High Priest. Individuals would face him and ask an important question to be answered by God. Aaron, the priest, would then receive the answer from God through the Urim and Thumim. Furthermore, we also know that YAHWEH specifically indicated that one of his means of communicating with the people was through the Urim & Thumim (I,SAM. 28:6). In other words, we have a direct confirmation from YAHWEH, that this was a communication device.

There is a further puzzling matter when we realize that the commander-in-chief, so to speak, of the Hebrew armies, seems to have been the High Priest himself, since he directed the battles by blowing the trumpets to indicate the withdrawal of the left flank or the advance of the right flank, etc. It is surprising that an unknowledgeable person such as the priest, who was hardly versed in warfare matters, could be the one to direct the battles. If we keep in mind that these battles were not small affairs, but involved 20-30,000 troops on each side, plus a very hilly terrain, it follows that one person, located in a specific spot, could not possibly have an overview of the complete battlefield and know what action should be taken at what time. And yet, each time the priest was on the battlefield with the Ark, he was able to successfully direct the action and win the battles, even against very superior forces. We must naturally ask ourselves: How did the High Priest have the knowledge to issue orders by blowing his trumpet? and why was the Ark on the battlefield?

In my previous book, I tried to show that these occurrences represented a complete interconnected electrical system by means of which "God" directed the battles of the Hebrews. The Urim & Thumim seem to have been a microphone and speaker (possibly also a battery). The dress worn by Aaron and his assistants (his four sons), with wires running throughout, was basically an antenna and conductor set-up grounded on the bottom by means of small gold metal bells (EX. 28:33). The Ark was a condenser, charging or discharging, depending upon the circumstances. The High Priest on the battlefield received his orders via the Urim & Thumim (microphone and loudspeaker) and transmitted them through the signal of his trumpet. The Ark had to be with him as the source of energy that kept the whole communication system going. YAHWEH was flying in his "cloud", overlooking the battlefield and thus had a complete view of the movement of the various enemy troops. Depending upon the circumstances, he would order Aaron, via the Urim & Thumim, to sound the trumpet for an advance on the left flank or a withdrawal on the right flank.

This concept of God sitting in a "cloud" is reported over and over again in the Old Testament. We read that he flew from spot to spot and made his presence felt at various places. We also read that he was constantly surrounded by an aura of light called "glory," "splendor," etc. Each one of these terms used by the ancient Hebrews denotes some connection with light, with brightness, which, in other words, suggests electric energy.

In various other chapters of the Bible we read of a capacity to lift people and transport them through the air. Although these unknowledgeable Hebrew tribes did certainly not understand the exact meaning of what was happening, they nevertheless reported it in their own words. These reports are utterly amazing and depict similar occurrences. A few examples would suffice to indicate the existence of a lifting capacity for YAHWEH—the God of the Hebrews (also known as Jehovah; the difference in names occurs because the Hebrew alphabet does not contain vowels and readers would have a tendency to use different vowels.)

> "II Kings 2:11—There appeared a chariot of fire, and horses of fire, and parted them both asunder; and Elijah went up by a whirlwind into heaven."

> "Ezekiel 3:14—So the spirit lifted me up, and took me away . . ."

> "Ezekiel 8:3—And he put forth the form of a hand and he took me by a lock of mine head; and the spirit lifted me up between the earth and heaven. . . ."

> "Ezekiel 11:1—Moreover the spirit lifted me up, and brought me onto the east gate of the Lord's house . . ."

> "Job 4:15—Then the spirit passed before my face; the hair of my flesh stood up."

In these and other passages we observe a similar occurrence. Certain people were being lifted up in the air and transported. In fact, there is also a surprising indication that when this occured it seemed to have been preceded by the hair standing up, as specified by Ezekiel and Job. Today that would mean to us that the object or person was electrically charged.

In *Urim & Thumim—the Secret of God,* I tried to show a relationship among these occurrences, which when considered together, suggest that 4000 to 5000 years ago there was on earth the presence of some very scientifically advanced people, who were way ahead of the time and who had technological capacities utterly misunderstood and unknown to the people of that era. They had the power to fly in vehicles, some of which were clearly described in detail by Ezekiel (Ez. 1:1 onwards). They had a propulsion means that seems to have been connected with some sort of electromagnetic field; they also seemed to have had the capacity to charge a nonmetallic body and then lift it into the air (most probably via reversed polarity). This electrical field (?) appears to have displayed itself optically by means of an aura of light, or "glory" etc. The commander of this group seemed to have been YAHWEH, who acted as the God of the Jews, guiding them out of Egypt and fighting their battles for survival and establishing their homeland.

One of the extraordinary books of the Old Testament is the one of the prophet Ezekiel (who lived around the year 600 B.C.). For centuries, theologians have debated the real meaning of this book since it referred to occurrences that were outside of their normal understanding. The simple fact was that they did not quite grasp what Ezekiel had described.

Historically, Ezekiel was a Jewish priest who was deported from Israel into Babylon by King Nebuchadnezer in the year 597 B.C. along with a portion of the Hebrew population. As such, it meant that he had a certain social status and education.

In his book he described his experiences and what he observed during a few extraordinary encounters with

"God" who descended from heaven in some sort of vehicle with legs, wings, arms, wheels, etc. His report was in amazing detail as he described what he perceived and tried to compare it to things he knew by referring to colors, shapes, sizes, etc. of known products. All told, he had four encounters, at various times over a span of 20 years. His book has to be considered with amazement since it is the first time that we have such recorded details about the "spaceship of God"—provided we consider that this was YAHWEH in person or some of his assistants, the "Sons of God."

Ezekiel reported that he saw a great cloud with fire coming from its inside, a tremendous brightness surrounding it, with whirlwinds and some shiny, amber-type thing in the midst of the fire. Out of this cloud he thought he saw four "living creatures," each having four faces and four wings. The wings, at times, rotated in an horizontal plane, or else at times dropped to the sides in a vertical position whenever the vehicle was not moving. He observed straight legs with large calflike feet of gleeming brass color. Under the wings he saw the "form" of a human hand.

While looking at this apparition, he observed, all of a sudden, that each "living creature" had a huge wheel. All four wheels looked exactly alike, yet they were not regular type wheels. He described them as "wheel and its work." Translated in today's terminology, this would mean a whole wheel assembly including the spokes and whatever appurtenances were included on the inside. Furthermore, he observed that this wheel was of very large dimension (Ez. 1:18) and notes his amazement at the fact that the wheel did not always turn regularly forwards, but instead at times turned inside out. He called it a "wheel within a wheel." Whenever the whole structure with the four "living creatures" moved, the wheels went along; but when the whole thing lifted up into the air, the wheels did not turn anymore but rose into the air at the same time. In addition to these "living creatures" with their wings, he observed a "likeness" of a firmament; in other words, he tries to compare it to a firmament covering and protecting the four "living creatures" and their wings. Whenever these wings turned, they made noises like the "rushing of water."

On top of the firmament he observed a "likeness" of a throne having the same color as a sapphire stone; and above that throne he saw the "likeness" of a man with a glow surrounding him. Not surprisingly, he concluded that he was in the presence of God, since from his previous education he understood that YAHWEH always appeared from the sky and had a glow or brightness surrounding him. This has been traditional teaching among the Hebrews for a great number of centuries since Moses, and it had been reported throughout the religious teaching of the Hebrew nation. This type of apparition seemed to have appeared to Moses and continued to appear intermittently after the death of the prophet.

Ezekiel was so overtaken with this encounter that he fell on his face, prostrating himself in awe, and/or emotional shock. He continued to report that the "spirit" entered him, spoke to him and set him upon his feet (Ez. 2:2). Then he heard a very distinct voice telling him of the inequities of his people and asking him to talk to his tribe.

He continued to give us a description of his first liftoff and stated as follows:

Ez. 3:12—Then the spirit took me up, and I heard a great rushing, saying, Blessed be the glory of the Lord from his place.

Ez. 3:13—I heard also the noise of the wings of the living creatures that touched one another and the noise of the wheels over against them, and a noise of a great rushing.

Ez. 3:14—So the spirit lifted me up, and took me away, and I went in bitterness, in the heat of my spirit; but the hand of the Lord was strong upon me.

These three paragraphs are of great importance as they are couched in very clear language and give us an exact description of what happened to him. He reported that he was lifted into the air and taken away. At the same time, he heard the noise of the rotating wings, similar to a "great rushing." He was taken away and felt a great "bitterness." That means he must have been scared out of his wits at being lifted into the air, although he felt that the "hand of the Lord was strong upon me." In other words, he felt that he was tightly held during this trip through the air. His going in "bitterness" is most natural and indicates his capacity to describe accurately what he felt and what he saw. In fact, he also reported how he returned to his people and "I sat where they sat and remained there astonished among them seven days." (Ez. 3:15). This means, he must have been utterly dazed and still emotionally upset from the extraordinary experience of this free-floating trip through the air.

He continued to explain in very exact details his various other encounters and what he observed with the various assistants of YAHWEH who performed certain jobs, including the measuring of certain buildings and areas with a special meter. There were some very important and interesting details given by him, among which we read the following:

"Ez. 8:3—And he put forth the form of an hand, and took me by a lock of mine head; and the spirit lifted me up between the earth and the heaven, and brought me in the visions of God to Jerusalem, to the door of the inner gate that looketh toward the north. . . ."

The important observation here is that he considered
being lifted in the air through a pull of his hair. In other
words, he realized somehow that his hair must be standing up and because of this, he was lifted into the air. He
seemed to make a connection with the hair standing vertically and his moving vertically up into the air.

This entire book of Ezekiel has been read over and
over again millions of times by past generations. The general concensus was that it contained certain mystical revelations which we could not understand up to now, as they
did not accord with known experiences, with the fact that
a person could fly through the air, or that the hair of a
person could stand up on end, or that a spaceship with fire
and noise could land, etc., etc. Nevertheless, it was considered a "sacred" book that had some sort of connection
with YAHWEH—the God of the Hebrews. As such, it was
included into the Old Testament even though generations
upon generations of Jews did not quite understand its
meaning. Yet, tradition had given them this book of
Ezekiel and tradition demanded that it be maintained. We
must consider ourselves today very lucky that the Jews
have had such a pronounced feeling for tradition and kept
the book of Ezekiel for us to be able to read it in the 20th
century. If it had been discarded and forgotten 2500 years
ago, if it had not been included in the Old Testament,
today we would not have an enormously important link to
the understanding of history.

In 1973 Mr. Josef F. Blumrich wrote a most remarkable book entitled *The Spaceships of Ezekiel.* This book
has the distinction of being written by a man who certainly should know what he is talking about. Mr. Blumrich
was Chief of the Systems Layout Branch of NASA, Hunts-
ville, Ala., a holder of many patents, and a recipient of the
NASA Exceptional Services Medal. He wrote a good many
technological articles and was a member of the team that
built Saturn V. The greater part of his professional life

was spent in design and analysis of aircraft and rockets. Consequently, his knowledge of the field can certainly not be considered to be marginal or insubstantial.

Originally, Mr. Blumrich started analyzing the book of Ezekiel as a lark as he wanted to prove how silly it was to consider these biblical reports, which seemed to indicate the presence of some sort of spaceship. The more he read the book of Ezekiel, the more amazing a picture he discovered, especially because a great many statements of

FIG. 17 — THE SPACESHIP AS DEDUCED BY
J. F. BLUMRICH WHEN FOLLOWING
THE DESCRIPTION OF EZEKIEL.

Ezekiel made plenty of sense to him—even though they had made little sense for the past 2500 years. To a man like Blumrich, with his professional background and activities within the NASA organization, the statements of Ezekiel started fitting into a pattern. He realized that he was reading a report by an intelligent and very precise person, even though ignorant and naturally unknowledgeable about the thing he was seeing. Of course, the words used by Ezekiel were not in the exact technical terminology we are accustomed to in the 20th century. Yet, this prophet seemed to have had a very keen observation capacity for details; he could not have described what he saw in better terms, considering his educational background.

Mr. Blumrich evaluated the entire book of Ezekiel and decided to publish his analysis as a book. Instead of belittling Ezekiel's statements, as he originally intended to do, Mr. Blumrich concluded by having a tremendous respect for what Ezekiel had said. Although there are a great many most interesting details connected with this entire matter, the following highlights of Blumrich's analysis will suffice to give a general idea. By simply following the descriptions given by Ezekiel, Blumrich was able to reconstruct a spacecraft having the following characteristics:

A) A main body
B) 4 extensions, or legs, equipped with helicopter blades
C) A top capsule for the commander, his crew and control instrumentations.
D) A power plant underneath the capsule and between the rotating blades

A picture of his reconstruction is shown in Fig. 17. Even though this particular shape has not yet been used by NASA, it had been studied by them and was developed by Roger A. Anderson of the NASA Langley Research Center, who published his findings in December 1964.[1]

To use Mr. Blumrich's own words on this subject:[2]

"This configuration was the result of an attempt to combine high aerodynamic drag and low structural weight. Both requirements were made in a brilliant fashion. The use of a concave profile to obtain a lightweight structure is a particularly elegant solution because, with proper selection of the profile, only tensile stresses will occur in the surface structure which can therefore be made of thin sheet metal with a minimum of reinforcement . . ."

"The helicopter units can be located at the maximum distance from each other, which is very important for good flight characteristics. It even becomes possible to fold the rotor blades upward within the arch of the concave body. With this arrangement the main body is located between the helicopters. This solution reduces to a minimum overall height of the spacecraft and the total center of gravity is located as low as possible to provide the desired in-flight stability and landing properties."

"At this time,[3] no other spacecraft configuration is known which would reconcile the operational and structural requirements of this spacecraft. In this context we may think of the well known shapes of the Mercury, Gemini and Apollo capsules. It becomes immediately clear, however, that their configurations do not allow the inclusion of helicopters in the general layout."

"In view of the mission that the spaceships described by Ezekiel obviously had, and given the level of technolog-

[1] "Structures Technology—1964" published in *Astronautics & Aeronautics*—Dec. 1964
[2] *The Spaceships of Ezekiel* by Josef F. Blumrich. Originally published in German by Econ Verlag GmbH. Copyright © 1974 by Econ Verlagsgruppe. Text quoted in this book, as well as Fig. 17 are reprinted by permission of Bantam Books, Inc. All rights reserved.
[3] Originally written in early 1973.

ical capacity apparently available to those unknown engineers, the configuration they chose was undeniably the key to realization . . ."

"The main items involved are: the rocket engine (consisting of reactor, plug nozzle and radiator), the propellant tank and the propellant, the central power plant for the helicopters, additional units such as the environmental control system, and the propellant reliquefaction unit."

"Just as the shape of the lower body was the key to our reconstruction, so the reactor is the key factor in the actual design. It is located in the lowest portion of the main body. This reactor is the reason why we are not yet able to build such a vehicle . . ."

"Our propulsion systems of today use oxygen or an oxidizer in combination with a fuel so as to produce high combustion temperatures. Depending on the propellants used, such systems today can reach ISP values up to and above 400 seconds. With the use of reactors, this value reaches levels exceeding 900 seconds because of their high temperatures. However, the analysis in the appendix of this book shows that Ezekiel's spaceship becomes a possibility only when ISP values of 2000 seconds or more are available. That is why a spaceship of this kind cannot be built today. Such values, however, are not as hopelessly beyond our grasp as comparisons with present figures seem to suggest. One may rather assume that it will become possible to design and build such propulsion systems within a few decades."

"The reactor of the spacecraft is certainly not a system which lies—as far as we are concerned—in some dreamy and fantastic remote future; we are, in fact, quite close to it. When we say "close" we mean, in this case, close in terms of time. This assessment of closeness is based on the experience-supported expectation that a continuing intensive effort will bring about the technical success pursued. But in purely technical terms we are still quite far from the goal."

"These considerations on the comparison of our present knowledge that all alien technology are of much relevance to the evaluation of Ezekiel's observations. They give us a new and much closer relationship to the biblical spacecraft . . ."

"The radiator is located above the plug nozzle . . . there is no doubt, however, that a large surface is needed. The radiator has accordingly a considerable upward extension and constitutes a part of the aerodynamic surface. While the size is an unanswered question, fairly safe estimates can be made of the operational temperature of the radiator. Fundamental considerations of material properties let us expect temperatures on the order of 1000–1300 degrees centigrade (1800–2300 degrees F). This determination is important insofar as it indicates that the radiator glows when in operation . . ."

"The radiation shield protects the crew in the capsule from the harmful radiation of the reactor. The crew spends most of its time in the capsule and the radiation dose in that direction must therefore be kept at as low a level as possible. Although the propellant in the tank does provide some shielding, most of the radiation must be blocked by a special shield."

The above represents some of the technical explanation presented by Blumrich. He offers a great number of additional details, also of a technical nature, to explain the proper functioning of this spaceship and the various elegant solutions in the design incorporated by the builders—whoever they were.

This entire matter of Ezekiel and his proverbial "wheels" was analyzed in *Urim & Thumim—the Secret of God.*

Summing it up, we have a remarkable report by a person who lived about 2500 years ago, concerning a spacecraft whose aeronautical characteristics accord well with today's technology. In fact, it is somewhat more advanced than our present technology even though we are almost at the stage where we can duplicate this structure. In my estimation, there is at least one aspect that we are not able to duplicate as yet and that is the electromagnetic (?) power that this spaceship seemed to radiate in connection with its various activities. As time goes on, and as our scientific knowledge improves, it is almost certain that we, too, will reach the point of controlling the same type of electromagnetic forces displayed by YAHWEH.

When comparing this description of a spaceship with the other occurrences we read of in the Old Testament, we can discern a very specific pattern weaving its way throughout the Old Testament. Our Bible is certainly not a collection of "fairy tales," or a religious book to be connected with unseen divinity. Instead, the Old Testament is a most important historical source as a report handed to us by our forefathers, concerning things they saw and experienced with their "Living God." For so many thousands of years it was read without objective analysis necessary to understand its meaning, since it depicted situations that were always beyond the technical knowledge level of the reader. It is only during the second part of the 20th century, when mankind is improving its technological capabilities and knowledge, that we are finally able to lift a small corner of the curtain and understand, with modern terminology, the various experiences reported to us by this incredible heritage called the Old Testament.

WATCHERS

A most interesting feature is the continuous reference in the Old Testament to the "Sons of God." This indicates that YAHWEH was not alone but had various assistants who helped him perform his job of civilizing the Hebrew tribes. The concept of additional help is woven throughout the Old Testament over and over again, with various words such as "angels," "fallen ones," "giants," "saints," etc.

A most important and revealing concept is found in the *Book of Jubilees,* which is an apocryphal writing. The same concept is also reported in the Dead Sea Scrolls, recently discovered in Jordan, in the Caves of Qumran. In one of these scrolls appears a report about the birth of a son to Lamesh, one of the early patriarchs who was upset to observe that his newborn baby did not have at all the average Hebrew physionomical traits, but instead seemed to look very much like one of the "Sons of God." In those days (as stated in the Bible, Gen.6:2), the "Sons of God" who descended to earth found the earthling women very attractive and seemed to have had children with them (Gen.6:4) Lamesh was in effect accusing his wife of having had intercourse with the "Sons of God," a fact she vehemently denied as follows:

"I swear to thee by the great Holy one, the King of heaven . . . that thine is this seed and from thee is this come and from thee was the fruit formed . . . and it know no strangers nor is it of any of the watchers or of the sons of heaven . . ."

We observe that she introduced a new word: the "Watchers." Not only that, she seemed to make a distinction between the "Watchers" and "the Sons of Heaven" as two separate groups. This is a very interesting matter since it indicates to us that the "Watchers" had a special function, separate and distinguishable from the activities of the "Sons of God." As the word implies, the "Watchers" must have been engaged in observing or watching something.

The *Book of Jubilees* refers elsewhere to angels with most interesting abilities. When describing the life of

Enoch, another of the important Hebrew patriarchs, the *Book of Jubilees* has the following to say:

"And he was moreover with the angels of God these six Jubilee of years, and they showed him everything which is on earth, and in the heavens, the rule of the sun, and he wrote down everything and he testified to the watchers who had sinned with the daughters of man . . ."

In reference to the life of Kainam, still another Hebrew patriarch, the *Book of Jubilees* reports:

And the son grew and his father taught him writing and he went to seek for himself a place where he might seize for himself a city. He found a writing which former (generations) had carved on the rock and he read what was thereon and he transcribed it and sinned owing to it; for it contained the teaching of the watchers in accordance with which they used to observe the omens of the sun and moon and stars in all the signs of heaven.

These two passages shed very interesting light on the activities of the "Watchers." Their duties apparently were the observation of the sun, moon, sky and stars—that means they were involved in astronomy and recorded the movements of these celestial bodies, as seen from earth. Obviously, they made certain records of this data since Kainam was able to read some of this information. The indications are that they were teaching some of this new science to Enoch and possibly to a few other educated Hebrews in a position to read, write, and intelligent enough to grasp the meaning of astronomy.

For the first time in our evaluation of our history, do we now have a clearcut indication that astronomy, in our prehistoric time, was not necessarily a science hit upon by the astute observations of primitive people during the Stone Age, or even later on. Instead, it was a science taught to the earthlings by the "Watchers" or the "Sons of God" who may have descended to earth for specific reasons, such as bringing education and civilization to the various peoples they encountered, as well as collecting data about the solar system, as seen from earth, and about earth itself.[1]

My analysis in my previous book, has opened the way to some far-reaching conclusions. These theories, when applied to the peculiarities we observe in Stonehenge, suggest some very basic and important possibilities and lead us towards a new approach to the mystery of Stonehenge.

Following are some of the conclusions I reached in *Urim & Thumim—the Secret of God:*

A) There was present on earth a group of very highly advanced people, small in numbers, but possessing an enormous amount of technical knowledge and intelligence, completely beyond the level of civilization known in the past 6000 years.

B) The leader apparently was YAHWEH, whose name is mentioned in the Old Testament. At least we can conclude that he was the leader at a certain point in time. Perhaps there were other similar leaders, at different times or at different places.

C) Their greatest ambitions seems to have been the proper civilization of planet Earth by introducing advanced standards of morals and ethics. They did not want anything for themselves but tried to create a more advanced civilization among earthlings. They were disappointed by the results they obtained and by their failures to educate humans.

[1] The Old Testament refers to the "Watchers" only on three occasions: Daniel 4:13 - 4:23 - 4:17

D) YAHWEH moved around this world through the air. He flew spaceships from place to place. To my mind, there is little doubt about this subject, as there are so many aspects and examples that point in this direction.

E) Their flying machine had a light aura surrounding it, shining brightly—thus blurring the details of its structure most of the time. It was referred to as a "cloud" during the day—or a "light" at night (see Ex.13:21) However, Ezekiel, who seemed to have been the only one to have had a good look at it, gave us detailed descriptions. His report was analyzed and evaluated by Blumrich, who should know what he is talking about since he was the chief engineer of the systems branch of NASA, working on the same type of spaceships described by Ezekiel. In fact, the advanced nature of the information given by Ezekiel, 2500 years ago, led Blumrich to apply for and obtain a patent in the year 1974 of our modern era! (patent No. 3789947.)

F) This aura of light (or "spirit" or "glow" or "splendor" or "glory") was a result of some type of luminescent high-energy radiation emitted by the spaceship—or anything connected with it. I don't believe that our level of science is advanced enough to understand this particular radiation energy or electromagnetic force, or whatever type of energy was involved.

G) This special energy seemed capable of lifting non-metallic objects into the air. Possibly YAHWEH first impregnated and charged the objects with his special energy, then pulled them up by applying opposite polarity. We observe that people such as Job or Ezekiel seemed to have felt this force. Consequently, it is important to basically note that YAHWEH had the capacity of lifting things by somehow energizing them first, then lifting them, just as a magnet would perform.

H) YAHWEH used this source of energy, or a similar one, as a means of propulsion, as well as to establish an electrical communications system with the Hebrews, by means of the Ark, Ephod, and the Urim & Thumim.

I) The Ark was nothing else but an electrically charged condensor capable of absorbing, storing, and discharging high voltage of this special type of radiation. It was likely the same source of energy that activated the Urim & Thumim.

J) YAHWEH was not alone in these activities. He was accompanied by various "Sons of God" or "angels" or "Watchers" or "giants," etc. The Old Testament reported some of their activities, although it was certain that the greatest portion of their work on earth and the exact nature of their activities with the Jews is not well known or understood. As yet we do seem to have understood that the "Watchers" were busy observing and recording astronomical events as seen from earth, and teaching earthlings.

Keeping these possibilities in mind, it is interesting to analyze now the situation of Stonehenge.

8

The Theory

It is my contention that Stonehenge was not built by any Stone Age people living about 4500 years ago in the southern part of England. Possibly some of these inhabitants may have been used as hand laborers to perform certain menial tasks. However, the entire engineering, construction, and theoretical work behind this structure was the brainchild of much more sophisticated people than the ones we believe to have inhabited the region of the Salisbury Plain. The intelligence and capacity displayed was beyond the level of sophistication we believe inherent in Stone Age cultures. Every aspect of this structure and every facet of it, displays characteristics that indicate the presence of an enormously advanced intelligence.

It is my contention that Stonehenge was designed and built by YAHWEH and his assistants for purposes that will be explained later on.

If this theory is accepted for a moment, we must be able to test it against the known aspects of the problem and see whether the various peculiarities we encounter accord with the theory. Such a theory is only meaningful if it stands the tests of various unsolved characteristics of the problem. The more points that seem to fit into the greater picture, the more meaningful the probability becomes that the theory could be correct. Let us keep in mind this theory and analyze the various aspects observed in Stonehenge.

AUBREY HOLES: The first wave of construction apparently was a circular ditch with its bank and the 56 large holes filled with white chalk. As indicated earlier, a person of about 5 feet, standing in the center of this huge circle, could hardly observe any of the holes. Yet they become very obvious when viewed from the air. This is precisely the capacity which YAHWEH and his group appeared to have. They were able to fly in the air or hover over a given spot. To them, hovering at a certain distance above the ground on top of the circle, they would have a complete view of the 56 Aubrey holes with the bank and the Avenue leading to the Heelstone. At this stage of the research, I do not believe that the figure 56 has any specific meaning. Possibly it might have included the aspects mentioned by Professor Hawkins, who considered Stonehenge a computer to predict future moon eclipses. However I am inclined to doubt this theory, at least for the present. Fifty-six was the number of holes that fit around the circumference of this large circle. If there had turned out to be 37 or 75 or 91 holes, etc., we would have tried to find a meaning in that specific number.

The important consideration, in my estimation, was the fact that YAHWEH needed a reflective area that could be easily seen from the sky, to pinpoint the exact location of the landing circle. We have seen in our previous research of the Old Testament that YAHWEH had a capacity to emit a certain type of radiation from his "cloud." This radiation had specific properties that were visual to Moses and the Hebrew tribes. It had at least the property of luminescence, since our forefathers were always able to observe a brilliance or glow in everything connected with the "cloud" of YAHWEH. We have also observed that he had the power of seemingly "impregnating" nonmetallic objects with this type of radiation. The object in question would retain the luminescent effect for sometime and was normally recharged by exposure to YAHWEH or his "cloud" or his men, etc. This was clearly described by the glow shining from the face of Moses whenever he came down from the mountain after talking to YAHWEH (Ex.34:29/30). If we imagine that the Aubrey holes, filled with white chalk, were impregnated with this special radiation, we can then realize that they would emit a luminescent effect for some time to come. In other words, they could act as spotlights emitting a glowing light. I am inclined to believe that the 56 Aubrey holes performed at least the function of 56 spotlights shining vertically into the sky and also illuminated the whole area. The soft chalk filling of these holes might be conducive to better absorption retention, and emission of the rays in question.

If we were flying in an helicopter over a plain having no significant characteristics, we would naturally want to have a visible landmark in order to direct our landing to the proper spot. Especially if such a descent were to take place at night, or during foggy or cloudy periods, it would greatly help if the landing pad were properly illuminated and could be seen from a few miles above. Such a circle of 56 large holes would perform this exact function and would brightly illuminate the spot, much as a lamp or a beacon would.

It is also possible that these 56 holes might have had a specific connection to the astronomical orientations involved, although our present state of research does not lead us yet to such firm conclusion.

The flat ground within this circle may have been the landing pad for the original spaceship, and naturally also the liftoff spot whenever they decided to move away. The bank measuring 6 feet high and 20 feet wide would have provided an additional refractory surface to maintain the light within that specific circle and to appear as a lit circle when viewed from the sky. The ditch would have no significance except that it was a by-product necessary when creating the bank, as the earth taken from the ditch produced the bank.

Such a bank could have served an additional purpose. It could have warned local people not to walk into the circle, especially as we have come to realize through the study of the Old Testament that YAHWEH's rays possessed a certain radio-activity. A concentration of such rays could very possibly be harmful, even fatal, to human beings. The fact that a spaceship was resting in the center of the circle, or the fact that light was shining from the ground, must certainly have been awe-inspiring to the Stone Age people living in that vicinity. A bank would delineate the "holy" spot of the presence of "God" and would warn the inhabitants of the region not to come too close or certainly not to enter onto that "divine" ground.

It is most interesting to observe that when some of these holes were dug up cremation remnants were found in them, as well as within the silting of the ditch. This would indicate that certain human beings (and possibly animals, too) were cremated and their ashes then inserted in these Aubrey holes or in the ditch.

It is, of course, peculiar that on one hand we should have a system of cremations to bury the dead, while parallel to it, outside the circle, exist round and long barrows, which, theoretically, were supposed to be graves to bury the dead. A number of skeletons have been found in these barrows. It is surprising that a small society of Stone Age people would have two different types of burials, side by side. Logically one would expect that such a primitive society would either cremate all their dead, as a matter of principle or religion, or else inter them.

This, in itself, should indicate to us that something special happened within the circle, requiring cremation, while something usual and normal took place outside the circle which needed only regular burial. It is my contention that the cremations we see inside the circles are the result of people having been exposed to a serious dosage of YAHWEH's radio-active rays.[1] These people had to be burned and their remains were then inserted in the Aubrey holes or within portions of the circle—the "holy" ground. These people could have been some of the workers enlisted to perform the menial jobs such as digging the circular trench or digging the Aubrey holes—a job possibly performed with antlers or animal shoulder blades. They could also have been local inhabitants, such as children who strayed into the circle and were exposed to the radiation and electrocuted. They could even have been YAHWEH's own assistants who died accidentally or naturally.

In the specific case of Stonehenge, a skeleton was also found buried within the inner circle. This seems to have been an isolated case as it was not apparently repeated in the other stone circle throughout Britain. We must naturally differentiate between the various centuries when these burials took place. It is my impression that the cremations belonged to the early period when Stonehenge was a functioning base inhabitated and used by YAHWEH and his assistants. The one skeleton that was found could well belong to a completely different century, at a time when this structure was no longer used by the originators but had become only an archaeological relic. Carbon-14 dating methods, if applied to the skeleton in question and to the cremation remnants, would indicate to us whether this contention is correct. In general, the fact is that cre-

[1]It is interesting to refer to the Old Testament; Joshua, chapter 7, where cremation was performed due to exposure to these rays. Also refer to *Urim & Thumim —the Secret of God.*

mations do exist specifically within stone circles, while the preponderant burials of skeletons are always outside the circles. This should be significant.

The remnants that are within this fine chalk should also be significant as they would provide the basis for future testing. Both the animal bones, ashes, or any other objects found within the Aubrey hole could possibly contain remnants of that radiation absorbed so many thousands of years ago. We know for a fact that 22 of the Aubrey holes have not been dug up as yet, and could be the basis for further tests.

If this ground was basically used as a landing spot of YAHWEH's spaceship, it then follows that the center part of it must have been exposed to other types of radiation, such as exhaust or radiation from the engines used to propel this spaceship. On the other hand it is also possible that such exhaust traces might not be found as the design proposed by Blumrich indicated the presence of helicopter rotors. Thus, liftoff and landing would have been performed by means of helicopter blades rather than by other conventional engines. However, the design proposed by Blumrich included a reactor working on some sort of atomic power and located in the center of the blades (see Fig. 17) If the same type of unit was flying at Stonehenge, then radiation from this reactor would have penetrated at least the center spot of the circle. Whether traces of radioactivity can still be detected is a question to be determined by atomic scientists, or radiation experts.

Theoretically, too, this entire center portion exposed to radiation, should have been bare and should not have been able to sustain plant life—unless enough time had elapsed to wear off the effects of the radioactivity and/or radiation.

It is important to remember that the long Avenue runs from the Aubrey holes circle, in the direction of the midsummer sunrise. This Avenue continues for 2000 feet or more and is at least 70 feet in width. The construction is similar to that of the circle—namely, a ditch with a bank. The earth taken from the ditch was used to create the bank. Since that region has an underlayer of white chalk, the banks were solid chalk. When viewed from above, the observation would be of a white circle with two parallel white lines running for a distance of 2000 feet.

There is an additional aspect to be considered. This region of England has never been known to experience consistently good weather. The majority of the year there is mist, rain, overcast skies, etc. Consequently, the visibility of a spaceship preparing to land would certainly have been impaired. At a greater height, visual contact could not be made through the clouds in order to pinpoint the Avenue and the circle. Obviously, other methods had to be used if this sighting was to have been made.

For a number of years we have had a system in our instrument flight techniques in which beeps are emitted at certain specific spots along a corridor. These sounds are received by the pilot whose function becomes to navigate precisely into the center of the beeps. If the pilot is off-course, too much to the left, the beeps to the left will be much stronger than those to the right. The pilot can consequently maneuver to the right until the intensity of the beeps from left and right are equal. In this manner, a flight in low visibility weather is directed into the landing strip. If we apply this system to the Aubrey Circle and the Avenue, we could conceive that it could have produced the same effect for the landing of the spaceship. The white chalk, being impregnated with the special radiation of YAHWEH, would have constantly emitted radiations. The pilot of the spaceship could have had a means of capturing the radiation coming from below and navigated accordingly. Simple instrumentation could have directed them, even in complete darkness, to the center of the circle. During clear weather, the system would still have functioned and given them the additional visual contact of the gleaming white chalk.

We can also conceive that these impregnated parallel lines of the Avenue and the Aubrey Circle would have registered on a radar-type receiving screen situated in the control room of the spaceship, providing a visual picture of the landing area.

MISSING STONE: If we imagine that the center of the Aubrey Circle was frequently covered by YAHWEH's spaceship, then we realize a possible reason why there was no center stone. As deduced by Blumrich, the space-ship in question had to have a top bubble that contained the controls and the crew. Such a control room, situated at a height of about 50 to 100 feet (and perhaps even more) above the ground would replace the center stone. Observers inside the bubble could easily use a simple pointing device in order to align themselves towards the Heel Stone and towards markers 91, 92, 93, or 94, especially as they knew that the angle between the Heel Stone direction and position 92 was 90 degrees. In this manner, while the spaceship was covering the center part of the ground, the crew had the means of pinpointing the direction towards the Heel Stone while sitting in their cabin. Thus, no center stone was necessary since the sighting was not being taken from the ground but instead from the control room of the spaceship, above the ground.

This can perhaps explain one of the problems encountered in pinpointing the exact direction of the mid-summer sunrise over the Heel Stone. In view of the fact that no center stone has been found, it has become a question of determining the exact spot that had to be aligned against the Heel Stone when standing in the center of the Circle. Various measurements have been taken in the past. It was observed that the center of the Aubrey Circle was different than the center of the center of the Sarsen Circle: These two points are in fact, about three feet apart.

Another study tried to align the center of the space created by Sarsen stone 1 and 30 with the center of the Avenue on which the Heel Stone is located. It was found out that the center of the Avenue was not the center of the Heel Stone.

The additional problem involved was to determine whether sunrise as seen from the center of Stonehenge should be considered the point at which the first top arc of the sun appears over the Heelstone, or whether it should be when half of the sun shows above the horizon of the Heel Stone, or whether the bottom arc of the fully-raised sun should be considered. Naturally, with each increase in altitude of the sun, we also have a lateral movement; that means that we have different locations of the sun along the horizon as it moves upwards.

Additional suggestions were made to consider the left side of the Heelstone as the alignment point. Although the sun has hardly changed its relative movement with respect to the earth, it is still a fact that over a long period of time, a very minute movement takes place. In other words, the exact point where the sun came over the horizon in 4000 B.C. would not have been precisely the spot seen by an observer during the year 1000 B.C. Granted, the difference is quite small and for practical purposes might not be serious, yet if we are discussing an astronomically precise instrumentation, then this slight difference could be germaine. It all depends upon the necessity of precision required by the observer.

This, then, was the problem when we looked upon the present structure of Stonehenge, especially when no center stone could be located. The obvious indication was that the point of alignment had shifted as time passed. Of course, the time span had to be an important one to make any difference.

Let us now consider that a spaceship is resting on the lintel platform. On top of it is the bubble containing the crew and its instrumentations. If we visualize that they have a desk marker to align with the Heelstone, we can logically deduce that they would be in a position to move that marker slightly to the left or the right in order to compensate for the slight change of position of the sun, depending upon the year when the sighting was being taken. Yet, one fact remains unshaken: we need two points so as to determine the exact direction of a line. Originally, YAHWEH's crew had to start with a given line of direction that was preset in advance. Subsequently, the marker in the command module would then align itself with that predetermined direction. Slight variations occuring over a span of a great many years would then be adjusted as required. We acknowledged the Heelstone to represent one of the points. Where was the second fixed stone marker?

We can consider these space people to have been of extraordinarily sophisticated intelligence with a deep understanding of the relative positions of the sun, the moon, the stars and the earth. In view of their prolonged stay on earth, or their continuing visits to specific spots over a span of thousands of years, it is understandable that they required a moveable marker in the center in order to align it towards the Heel Stone. The value of such a marker would have been temporary and would have needed to be shifted over a long period of time.

Naturally, the next obvious question we have to ask ourselves is: Why might precise alignment to the midsummer sunrise have been so important to these people?

CONSTRUCTION: We have considered various theories submitted in order to make some sense out of the astonishing construction job performed at Stonehenge. In an attempt to understand how Stone Age people could have transported such large quantities of stones weighing up to

50 tons, various theories have been developed. We have considered how those barbarians might have transported those heavy stones over all sorts of terrain, over waterways, over mountains, through marshes, etc. We have considered their building capacities and how they could theorectically have put such a structure into place.

Actually, none of the attempted explanations are truly satisfying. They might have been theoretically possible, yet they are not probable. Especially when we think in terms of the tools being principally flintstones and mallets, we must question their capacity to have quarried those large amounts of stones and dressed them down to required size and shape.

If we apply now my theory of YAHWEH, we realize that the whole matter is exceedingly simplified, and possibly much more plausible. We have recognized the powers of YAHWEH to lift objects.[1] In various reports of the Old Testament we read of the lifting of people through the air after being "impregnated" (i.e. the spirit entered them) with some sort of radiation emanating from the "cloud" of YAHWEH. My explanation has been that YAHWEH possessed the capacity to saturate a nonmetallic object with electromagnetic (?) radiation (whose scientific nature we do not know as yet) by charging these bodies with a specific polarity, let's say positive, and then being able to lift up the object by applying a reversed polarity, namely negative. If the center of power in the "cloud" were strong enough, there is no telling how heavy an object could possibly have been lifted.

Applying this same trend of thought to the movement of stones in the southern part of England, we realize that it would have been a relatively simple matter to carry these stones through the air and then place them in readymade holes. If the stones had been lowered from the air, they could

---

[1]Cohen: *Urim & Thumim—the Secret of God.*

have been let down precisely in the holes desired without interference with the other stones in the immediate vicinity. This would have been possible in the case of the horizontal lintel stones, as it would have been an exceedingly easy matter to have insert them from the top into exact position, if guided by a person on the ground. Stones that are suspended in air can easily be moved- in this case with the help of the electromagnetic forces at the disposal of YAHWEH and his group. This explanation can now possibly shed light on some of the construction features and peculiarities observed not only in the Sarsen Circle, but in the trilithons and the Bluestones.

The accounts in the Old Testament do not specify that people or objects traveling through the air were actually carried "within" the "cloud." Instead, reports indicate that the objects in question were simply traveling through the air (as though they were hanging from some sort of threads), tightly held by the "hand of God." (EZ 3:14) We can conceive of this movement as though the stones were actually hanging in air with no visible means of support, except for the unseen polarity of the invisible electromagnetic lines.

As far as quarrying such huge boulders out of mountains is concerned, it is easy to conceive that YAHWEH and his group had the technological means to cut such stones away from a mountain. This performance was perhaps not simply a chiseling operation as we have come to believe for so many centuries. Primitive people with Stone Age tools, such as flintstones, would have needed to work an extraordinarily long time under all sorts of handicaps, to possibly quarry such quantities of stone and dress them down to the sizes and shapes desired. On the other hand, YAHWEH and his group with enormously advanced technology, electrical power, and tooling, such as laser beams, could have performed the same feats within a matter of minutes.

Surveying the countryside and locating sources of stones, would be a relatively simple matter for YAHWEH with the flight capacity that could take the craft within minutes from area to area. He would have an overview of the terrain and could easily have pinpointed sources for stones without spending the enormous amount of time otherwise necessary for the Stone Age people.

Summing it up, we see that the location of the stones, the quarrying of same, their transport, and the erection of all of these boulders, would have been a simple matter for a technologically advanced group, possessing the power to fly and to lift very heavy objects. This offers a reason why the structure erected in Stonehenge displays enormously complicated and difficult construction processes, if applied via normal and regular means. That is perhaps the reason why we imagine that certain aspects were produced in what we consider to be the most difficult manner, instead of having been produced via the easiest manner. What we regard as enormous difficulties would certainly not have been considered in the same light by YAHWEH and his group.

Their first and foremost objective might have been a solid platform to give a greater permanence to their visits in that part of the country, in a very specific and predetermined spot. It is understood that part of their purpose was likely involved with astronomical sightings and connected to the relationship of the sun, the moon, the stars, and the earth—as seen from the earth. This was very clearly indicated by our Hebrew forefathers more than 3500 years ago—in the Book of Jubilees.

STONEHENGE II: We have been told that the second stage of construction involved two concentric circles of blue stones in such a way that two stones would be positioned on the same radius. Figure 3 shows the layout. Archaeologists have been able to locate a number of these holes and determine that Bluestones were once inserted in some of them. Yet it was found that this circle was not finished, as though the builders had abandoned the project for reasons still not clear to us.

Certain researchers have gone so far as to indicate that these pairs of stones along the radius must have had lintel stones on top. Some of the blue stones were perhaps used later on and inserted in the center of today's Stonehenge structure. When a few of these blue stones were dug out, it was observed that the bottom of the stones had single mortises—that is the spherical-shaped protrusions we see in the vertical Sarsen stones and on the trilithons. This was the standard Stonehenge method of connecting a vertical stone to a horizontal stone. The suggestion has been made that the Bluestones originally used in the construction of Stonehenge II were dismantled and placed upside down in the center of the Sarsen Circle. A good many of them are still there today. If we accept this point of view, then we can conceive that this double circle was created as a platform for the spaceship. However, after part of the construction was performed, the builders may have realized that it would not be suitable for their purposes. Possibly they realized that the height was not satisfactory for the type spaceship being used at that moment, or the sturdiness was not sufficient. Possibly they might have found out that a different, bigger, or smaller more powerful unit would be flying in, necessitating a stronger and taller platform. Under the circumstances, they perhaps decided to dismantle this construction and build the whole thing as seen in Stonehenge III. (see Fig. 4)

Naturally, since we know so very little about the true construction of Stonehenge II, all of these theories and possibilities represent thoughts not based on well-founded facts. Nevertheless, it is interesting to consider that, in case the construction of Stonehenge II was as described by some archaeologists, my present theory would include a logical meaning for its past existence.

SARSEN CIRCLE: We know from research that Stonehenge I continued in existence for about 500 years. This means that during this time YAHWEH and his crew could have found the layout satisfactory for their purposes. It is to be expected that they were not sitting there on a constant basis, but must have been flying out to different directions. After awhile they may have felt the necessity for a more permanent base with better "equipment." This may be when the Sarsen Circle was built. We have considered the most important aspect of the Sarsen Circle as the flat absolute level top surface of the lintels. This would make sense if the Sarsen Circle were nothing else but a resting platform for YAHWEH's spaceship. We have considered that there were no astronomical sightings connected with the vertical, and certainly not with the horizontal stones of this huge construction. However, every aspect of this construction would accord with the purpose of such a platform. It would have been necessary to have an exceedingly sturdy construction so that the spaceship could land and rest on it. The construction of the Sarsen Circle indicates that it was an extraordinarily sturdy construction. The use as a landing platform would presuppose that the top lintel stone surface had to be well-grounded in place with no possibility of the craft shifting or sliding off the top of the vertical Sarsen stones. The construction we observe would perform exactly this function by means of its tongue-and-groove construction, plus the mortise-and-tenon system. Normally, one of these systems would have been sufficient for sturdiness. Yet the builders included an additional factor of safety by building in a second system to insure that no accident would occur. It is understandable that a big space vehicle like the one described by Mr. Blumrich must have weighed a substantial amount. In fact, Mr. Blumrich's calculations indicate that the spacecraft in question must have weighed at least 220,000 pounds to include the weight of its own structure and sufficient propellant for the return trip. Such a lintel platform would have needed to be extraordinarily sturdy and secure in order to withstand a very heavy spaceship for a prolonged period of time and create a solid footing for it. Naturally, it had also to be strong enough laterally to withstand the constant pressure exerted on it during the time when the spaceship was resting upon the lintels. That, too, can be deduced by the interconnected lintels that form a basic truss.

Another necessity would have been for that spaceship to land on a very flat and even surface, especially as very accurate measurements would be taken from its command module. This, too, would have been achieved by the great care taken in building the top surface of the lintels.

It is worth noting that a force acting on the top surface of the lintel and applied at an angle (as the legs of a spaceship would) could have a tendency to twist the lintel stone out of its position, were it not for the "tongue-and-groove" construction: Even if the lintel stone could be made to rotate out of its sockets (mortise and tenon) along its outer ledge, when pressure were applied at point A (Fig. 18), the vertically running tongue-and-groove surfaces would thwart such a twist. As each lintel stone is securely connected to its adjacent stone, the Sarsen Circle forms a very tight grid with no possibility for it to rotate out of its sockets. We thus see an ingenious construction: The mortise-and-tenon system would stop the lintel stone from sliding laterally, while the tongue-and-groove setup would interfere with a rotational movement.

Interestingly enough, the calculations made by Mr. Blumrich indicate that such a spaceship (as seen by

Ezekiel) would be about 59 feet in diameter. This dimension would fit almost perfectly on top of the Sarsen Circle, which is about 100 feet in diameter. If we consider that the spaceship in question had a quantity of landing legs, most probably situated at an angle, we can then observe

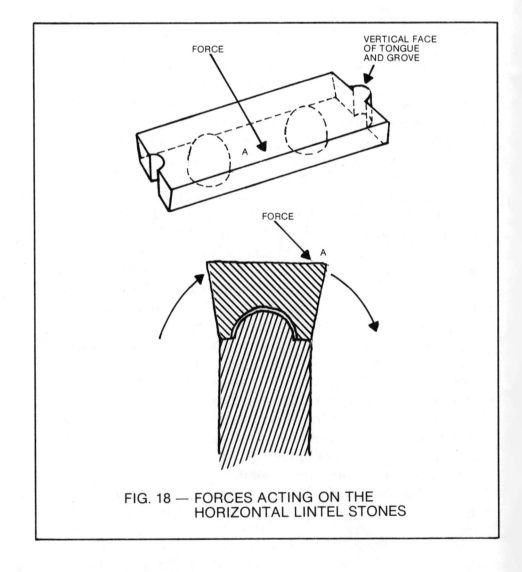

FIG. 18 — FORCES ACTING ON THE
HORIZONTAL LINTEL STONES

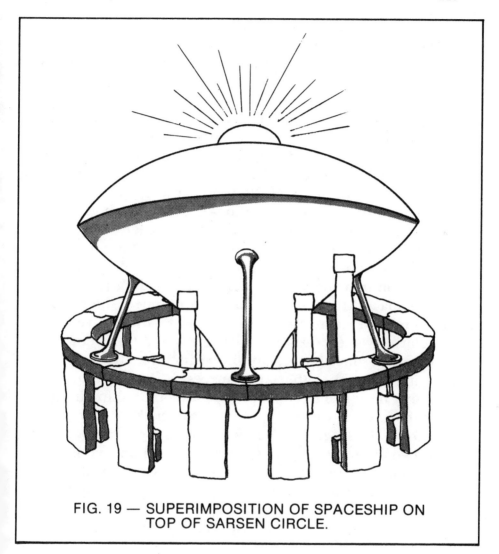

FIG. 19 — SUPERIMPOSITION OF SPACESHIP ON
TOP OF SARSEN CIRCLE.

the necessity for a 100 foot diameter landing platform (see Fig. 17)

In Fig. 19 I have superimposed the spaceship described by Blumrich on top of the Sarsen Circle. By placing the lintel circle at a certain height, we observe that the center reactor has room to remain inside the Sarsen Circle without touching the ground.

Of course, this represents only one possible design of a spaceship that might have been involved, based on the precise description deduced by Mr. Blumrich's research. It is understood that other types and sizes of spaceships could also have been involved, since we are talking about a considerable span of time. It is to be expected that at various periods there might have been different types of spaceships that landed in the southern part of England.

What's more, the indications derived from the Old Testament and the studies made by Blumrich hint at the probability that the top bubble containing the crew was detachable and had its own flight capacity. We have the impression that the bubble was actually riding piggyback on the spaceship. Once the spaceship landed, the bubble (or command room) could take off on its own power and fly relatively short distances away. It would then return to its base and place itself again in position for liftoff. Blumrich indicated that the large spaceship in question was probably designed to connect with a mother ship circling in space, around the earth. If we consider these probabilities, then we recognize the fact that we are dealing with at least two different types of spaceships, each one having its own propulsion capacity. The larger unit was probably the one that would have been resting on top of the lintel circle, while the smaller individual bubble would either rest on top of the spacecraft or else fly on local reconaissance flights.

It is naturally possible that the larger spacecraft contained more than one bubble and could thus have afforded independent flight capacity to various teams of researchers flying in different directions. At the present stage of our research, we can certainly not determine the type of unit involved, except that this theory opens certain channels of thought that are worthwhile pursuing.

There is also the possibility that there might have

been more than one type of spacecraft that landed in that region of England. The fact that Stonehenge is unique-that no other similar struction is to be found anywhere in England, Ireland, Scotland, Wales, the Continent, etc., is an indication that this was the prime base for a specific type of aircraft. What's more, it must have been of a semi permanent nature with periodic flights and extended stays. At the same time, it is quite probable that additional types of smaller spacecraft could have been visiting and landing on different sites. These particular units did not necessarily need to have the same tremendous type of support structure we see at Stonehenge.

It is most interesting to note that Stonehenge is not the only stone circle or circular ditch-and-bank construction to be found in England. Some very important sightings have been made by scientists such as Atkinson, Thom, Burl (and many, many others), who have catalogued and pinpointed at least 700 stone circles throughout England, Scotland, Ireland, Wales, etc. These are found throughout the country, in scattered locations, but are much smaller in size, and apparently in importance. One exception, however, is the circle in Avebury, about 18 miles northeast of Stonehenge. In that site are a ditch and a bank, much larger than the ones at Stonehenge, as well as the remnants of a quantity of stone circles, and stones.

Thus, it is logical to conceive that the Stonehenge structure represented the main base for the large spaceship, at least the one that was perhaps semi-permanently located on earth and had to take precise astronomical readings and coordinate all the other readings collected throughout the entire territory. The other circles scattered throughout the countryside, could have represented the temporary landing spots for the smaller crafts.

SARSEN UPRIGHT NO. 11: Sarsen stone No. 11 is peculiarly different than all the other Sarsen stones; it is almost half the size. As Upright No. 11 is not 14 feet tall,

it could not have helped support the horizontal lintel stone
between positions No. 12 and No. 10. For this circle to be

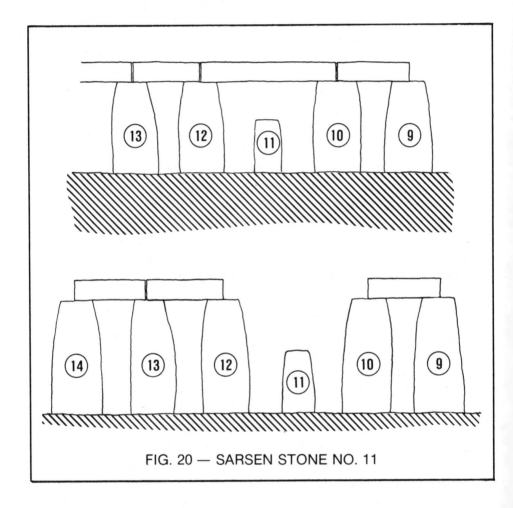

FIG. 20 — SARSEN STONE NO. 11

complete, there must have been a double length lintel
stone supported only by Sarsen Uprights 10 and 12. While
all the other horizontal lintel stones measure about 10 feet

6 inches (3.2 meters), this particular one must have measured 21 feet (6.4 meters) as it had to span the double distance. What's more, this would indicate a certain weakness in the structure, since such an extended span could not support the same direct weight on top, as the other lintel stones. Or it could mean that this particular spot did not have to support as much weight as the other sections of the Sarsen Circle.

There is another alternative: Perhaps there was no lintel stone at all between positions 10 and 12—instead the circle might have been broken at that spot (see Fig. 20).

In using such a stunted stone, the original builders seemed to have required a specific opening, or room, above and on the two sides of Upright No. 11. We could not exactly call it an entrance door, as that would imply an unhindered passage—which it is not. Yet, it is obvious that a certain additional opening was generated by inserting such a small Sarsen upright, leaving space in between.

Why was such a space needed? If we consider that the spaceship would have rested on top of the Sarsen Circle, then it becomes obvious that further stones (or other heavy large objects) could not have been brought in to the inner circle. The usual transport method used by YAHWEH and his assistants was through the air. With the spaceship in place, they could not have let down a blue stone or even a trilithon lintel stone. Such an object would have had to be brought in through some opening in the Sarsen Circle, provided the opening was big enough for the object. It is possible that Bluestones, and/or other stones presently found inside the circle, were brought after the spaceship was anchored on top of the Sarsen Circle platform. What's more, there could have been other objects that had to be placed underneath the aircraft—such as maintenance equipment for the reactor? Whatever the case might have been, a specific entrance space would have needed to be created, as a passageway into the circle.

The above thoughts are based on the assumption that there was a double length lintel stone between uprights 10 and 12. However, we must also consider the possibility that there was no Lintel stone at all, as shown in Fig. 20 In such a case, the entrance space would have needed to be much larger and even trilithon boulders could have been "floated" horizontally through such a space. We can conceive that after the entire Sarsen Circle and its lintels were in place the necessity was felt to arrange for an opening. Sarsen Upright No. 11 could have been cut in half to allow for such a space. At that point, either a double length lintel stone was placed, or else it was taken away altogether, leaving the space empty. With their lifting technique an unhindered opening would not have been necessary, since they could just as easily have lifted their objects 9 feet in the air and floated them horizontally over the stunted Sarsen Upright No. 11. Of course, we earthlings would do it differently. We could need a completely free passage—such as a door opening. We would have taken Upright No. 11 completely out of the way, since our usual movements of heavy objects proceed on top of the ground.

Among other alternatives, one must also consider the fact that the operators of the spaceship/observatory, sitting all the way on top in the command module, had also to descend to the ground, from time to time. A ladder would have to lead over the top part of the space ship and over the ledge of the circular part of same, since the underneath part was taken up with the reactor and its radiator. Thus, at some spot, there had to be an exit possibility for the constant movement of the crew. Possibly, the open space between Uprights 10 and 12 might have been the spot where the overhanging ladder ended. Incidentally, it is interesting to observe that at this exact spot, we also find a break in the ditch and bank. Fig. 1 shows a top view of the entire circle. Opposite Upright No. 11, we observe that there is no depression in the ground, that means that the builders did not continue the ditch but left the ground even, as though it formed a bridge over the ditch. Thus there is ground level entrance from the outside area directly towards Upright No. 11. This indicates that this stone was not an afterthought or a haphazard occurence, but was planned that way to be used as an entrance and exit for material and/or crew.

TRILITHONS: Five pairs of trilithons are positioned in the center of the structure (see Fig. 1). Each of the units has a different height, with the tallest one being placed on a center line connecting with the Heelstone. It measures about 24 feet in height. The side pairs are about 1 to 2 feet shorter. These units are composed of two huge boulders placed very close to each other so as to allow a small channel of space of about 10 inches. These two stones are connected on top by a lintel—or a horizontal stone. Each one of these boulders weighs roughly 50 tons. In essence, we have 20 to 24 feet channels in a vertical position. Professor Hawkins has indicated certain sightings that can be made by looking through this space and through the Sarsen Circle openings. Fig. 6 illustrates his findings.

Although we can naturally not question the directions it is nevertheless doubtful that these sophisticated builders would have produced such a huge construction simply to pinpoint five different directions. It is my contention that they did not need a 24 feet high channel of space, 10 inches wide simply to pinpoint given directions. This could have been achieved very simply with the positioning of two small stones. Logically the trilithons must have had a meaning beyond the one we have been able to ascertain. Persons of about 5 to 6 feet would certainly not need a 24 foot-high channel to make an observation at eye level, unless they wanted to make sure to direct their view towards the sky in a very specific direction. We suspect that nothing pertaining to Stonehenge was performed in a haphazard manner. If the original builders created this narrow space, 24 feet in height, there most likely was a very good and sound reason why it was built thus.

On the basis of my theory, it is interesting to note that the positioning of the spaceship on top of the lintel circle would not have interfered with the height of the trilithon horseshoe. The design deduced by Mr. Blumrich indicated a concave center portion that contained, at the bottom, the radioactive reactor and above it, the radiator and the propellant. This concave space would not have interfered with the trilithons as they would have fit nicely underneath the spaceship as illustrated in Fig. 21.

It is to be noted that the crew, situated on top in its control room would not have been able to see these trilithons from where they sat, since the boulders would be hidden under the body of the spaceship. Yet, there must have been a very good reason for YAHWEH and his assistants to want such a channel, or five lintels at a very specific height.

Theoretically, we can conceive that a tube could have been lowered from under the spacecraft with a light nozzle emitting light rays or some other type of radiation. Such a source could be lowered in the exact direction of the channel so as to direct that particular ray in a very specific direction. Thus, a light ray shining through this channel of the top part of the trilithons, would proceed through the channel, pass over the top of the lintel circle and then into the outer area. In other words, we can conceive that the necessary useful space of these trilithons was actually the top part and not the bottom part. Of course they had to be built 24 feet high, to produce the necessary effect on top. The bottom part could possibly be considered as unimportant or as a by-product necessary to the contruction.

This leads naturally to the question concerning what

these directions represent. Theoretically, we should connect the center of the circle to these channels and try to deduce what that direction represented. There are serious problems involved, however, as we can never be sure of the exact location of the center since we have realized that there may have been no center stone, that instead even the center stone of the control room might have been an adjustable one.

What's more, we cannot be certain that the direction of any of these rays actually followed a radial path along a line connecting the center of Stonehenge to the center of the space between the two trilithon uprights. For all we know, the tubes that descended from the spacecraft could have directed their beams along a different line. Thus there would have been a great many possibilities within this channel of about 10 inches.

As research progresses, we may discover the probable directions in question, if that should have been the case. For the moment, this explanation is not probable.

There is an additional aspect that should be analyzed. Why are the five trilithons of different heights? It is difficult to conceive that the trilithons have different heights simply because those stones were of different lengths. The builders knew how to cut stone, how to set them deeper or higher in the ground, and how to transport any size of stone they desired. It is my impression that the different heights of the trilithons are not haphazard occurrences.

If the 24-foot channel does not have a meaning, then perhaps the height of the top surface of the lintel stones (atop the trilithons) served specific functions. It is conceivable that YAHWEH and his assistants needed small ledges or platforms at a given height. There might have been protrusions in specific spots around the lower part of the spaceship that could rest on top of the given lintel stones for additional support.

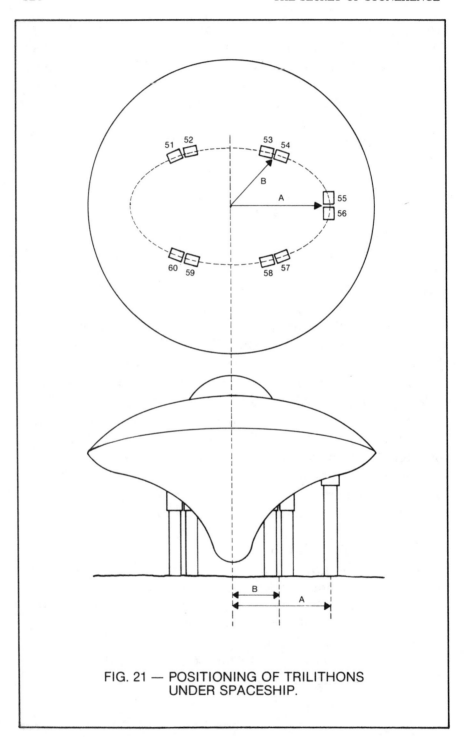

FIG. 21 — POSITIONING OF TRILITHONS
UNDER SPACESHIP.

The height and locations of the five trilithons tend to suggest such an impression. These five sets of massive stone are located almost around an eliptical path inside the Sarsen Circle. The tallest unit (Stones 55–56, as shown on Fig. 21) is the one situated the furthest from the center of the circle. Keeping in mind the shape of the underbelly described by Blumrich, we observe that the further away we move from the center, the greater the distance between the ground and the body of the spaceship. The nearer we are to the center, the smaller this distance becomes. Fig. 21 clearly illustrates that Trilithon Group 55–56 would properly fit under the spaceship. On the other hand, Trilithon Groups 51/52, 52/54, 57/58, 59/60 are much closer to the center, and thus should be of shorter height to fit underneath the spaceship. Surprisingly enough, this is exactly the case.

Tentatively, we could consider that these five trilithon groups might have been support pillars, fitting under the spaceship at very specific spots in order to align it in place, and give it the necessary additional support strength required for a more extended residence on top of the Sarsen Circle.

If we connect the top lintels of these five trilithons to each other, via curved lines, we might be able to determine the approximate curvature of the undersurface of the spaceship.

Excavations made at Stonehenge revealed another baffling mystery. Upright Trilithon Stone No. 56 is the standing stone of the central unit, which means the tallest of the five units. It was discovered that starting at the footing of Stone No. 56 and proceeding at 90 degrees to its central axis, there is a long trench eventually filled with chalk. This trench has the characteristics of a ramp, as it becomes deeper when approaching the base of the upright stone. Numerous question marks have been raised, trying to determine a plausible reason for such a peculiar occurrence.

With my theory of YAHWEH, perhaps a logical answer can be obtained—at least tentatively. I have tried to show that the trilithons were probably supports for the semi-permanent anchoring of the main spaceship observatory, situated on top of the Sarsen Circle. By having a slanted trench at a 90-degree angle to the axis of the trilithon, they may have used it as a ramp to move into place, or remove, Upright No. 56 (and possibly No. 55 as well). However, the surprising fact is that such a ramp exists only in the case of the Center Trilithon, while the other four pairs do not have a trench. This can mean that the 55–56 Trilithon Unit was incorporated later on, after the spaceship was already sitting atop the Sarsen platform and atop the other four trilithons. It is as though, they realized that they needed one additional support, that had to be slid from under the spaceship. At the same time, such a trench would have given them the possibility of removing this underpinning whenever necessary—as though this were the removable part of an in-place rigid truss. The other 4 trilithons were likely inserted from above—from the air—in a perpendicular direction, since the spaceship was not in place as yet. The fifth one, however, would have had to be set in place through the ramp and then pushed up into place, starting from an horizontal position, moving up at an angle, and eventually reaching the vertical position to fit underneath the spaceship. If this were so, then it tends to indicate that the spaceship in question was almost permanently set in place atop the Sarsen Platform.

DESTRUCTION: Finally, we reach the point where this structure, having fulfilled its purpose over a long period of time, had to be abandoned or destroyed. History does not report the exact occurrences that took place for the destruction of this monument. We only inherited rumors; some of them indicated that "in the olden days" certain groups of people (of vague origin) wanted to rid themselves of the remnants of that "pagan" existence—they decided to destroy Stonehenge. Personally, I doubt the historical veracity of such a report, especially if based on practical considerations of a step by step destruction procedure. We have seen how enormously difficult it was to construct Stonehenge; in my estimation, its destruction is still more difficult. For example, the lintel stones were kept in place by a tongue and groove, as well as a ball and socket system. Thus to take these apart, one would need to *lift* them out of their sockets and grooves—a very difficult task indeed. Stones that stayed together for 1000–2000 years, do not part easily from each other, especially not with simple human muscle power. Furthermore, once dismantled, the lintel or sarsen stones had to be carried away, since they are not to be found in the immediate vicinity of Stonehenge. In fact, none of the missing stones have ever been located in any other region of England. They simply vanished!

As shown in Fig. 11 one half of the circle disappeared almost completely, while the eastern half is—to some extent—still in place. In my estimation such a destruction does not indicate to be the result of a dismantlement, lead by the pronounced hatred of some unknown tribe. Instead, I am inclined to believe that a man-made explosion took place somewhere in the western half of the circle—an explosion that pulverised a number of stones and threw a few of them to the ground, where they are presently lying.

Interestingly enough there are certain telltale signs that support this theory of explosion.

During excavations undertaken at the site, a number of Bluestone stumps were discovered buried just beneath the surface of the ground. A schematic illustration is submitted in Fig. 21a. It has been hinted that these Bluestones

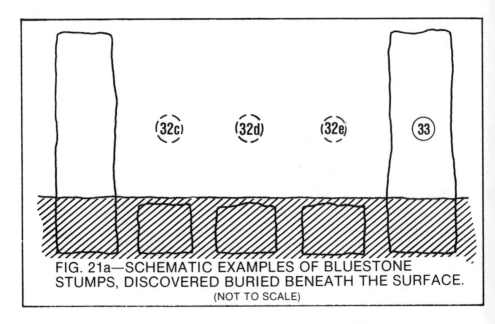

FIG. 21a—SCHEMATIC EXAMPLES OF BLUESTONE
STUMPS, DISCOVERED BURIED BENEATH THE SURFACE.
(NOT TO SCALE)

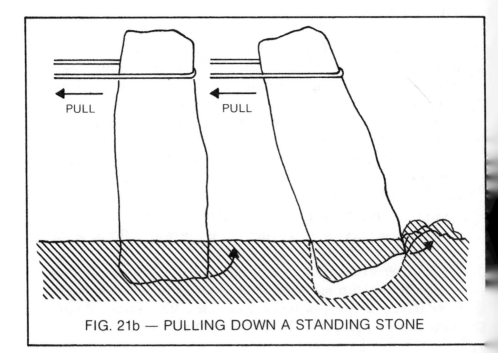

FIG. 21b — PULLING DOWN A STANDING STONE

were broken off by the same group of ancient people who were determined to destroy Stonehenge. Such an explanation is not logical.

Let us imagine a group of people desperately determined to push down a standing stone. How would they proceed? They would push or pull at the top end of the stone. A Bluestone, weighing about 4-5 tons, will offer a great resistance to a pull exerted by mere human force. If the force applied is great enough, then, at best, the chances are that the entire stone will tilt and the underground portion of the stone will push up the adjoining ground (Fig. 21b). The entire Bluestone—including its buried lower end—will then come to rest on the surface of the ground. A clean fracture of the stone at ground level is unlikely to occur, since the hardness of the Bluestone and its thickness are such that not enough force could be exerted by humans. It takes much less strength to push up two cubic feet of dirt, than to fracture a stone having a cross section of about two square feet.

There is another practical aspect to this matter. Why would a group of people exert such an inordinate amount of strength and effort to break off a standing stone when they could achieve their goal by much simpler means? All that had to be done was to dig out a small amount of soil from next to the base of the stone. When such a small trench were dug up, even a child could have pushed down the Bluestone. It does not make sense for a team of destruction-minded people to spend such an inordinate amount of energy if the same result could have been obtained by less strenuous methods.

For a 4-5 ton stone to fracture at ground level, at least two factors have to be present:

a) The force applied must be exceedingly powerful so as to fracture a two square foot area of stone.
b) The maximum force must be applied suddenly so

as not to give enough time to the stone to push up
the soil

In my estimation, such a sudden application of a tremendous force can only be achieved through a powerful
explosion.

There is additional evidence about the after-effect of
such an explosion. If an explosion took place, it follows
that a standing stone would either fall down or be pulver-
ized. Amazingly enough, this is exactly what we find. We
see that a number of stones fell to the ground. However
what is not too well known is the fact that, distributed
throughout most of the area outside the Sarsen Circle, we
find a layer of small stone chips. These are estimated to
count in the tens of thousands and are composed mainly of
Bluestones—a type of stone that is softer than the hard
Sarsen stones. The surprising aspect is that these stone
chips are almost evenly strewn all the way to the ditch
and bank surrounding Stonehenge—and even beyond. We
find a horizontal distribution of these stone chips throughout the area rather than a concentration in a few places.
As we are dealing with tens of thousands of small chips, it
is not logical to expect that the destroyers of Stonehenge
were the ones who sprinkled stone chips throughout the
area in an almost uniform manner.

A powerful explosion, however, could break some of
the Bluestones into small chips and forcefully throw them
all over the surrounding area.

At the present stage of our research, we have no way
to determine whether this explosion was performed by
YAHWEH's crew, or by some other group of space people,
or whether it took place accidentally.

STONE CIRCLES

In my estimation, there are at least three main possibilities to reflect the necessity for such stone circles.

Possibility A: If we accept the thesis that a master laboratory or a main observation vehicle, rested on the platform of Stonehenge, we can deduce that smaller vehicles had to fly around the countryside in order to perform local tests and investigate the area—exactly as we earthlings would do if we set foot on another planet. The drawings suggested by Mr. Blumrich include a capsule atop the vehicle. This capsule could have been capable of independent flight capacity. Even if we do not consider the existence of these independent capsules, we must admit that a research team landing in England would likely be equipped with more than one vehicle, especially as the area of land under consideration is rather large. It is my tentative theory that the individual stone circles in other locations were individual landing pads for the smaller vehicles sent throughout the countryside. In each instance they probably created the landing areas and inserted the necessary stones in order to pinpoint the all-important directions of the midsummer sunrise and moonrise. By measuring the angle between the sighting of this stone and the sunrise on that particular day, they would have been in a position to calculate immediately the position of the earth in its orbit around the sun. Thus they would have been able to pinpoint each day their whereabouts in space, as well as the relative position of the earth's satelite—the moon.

The stones in question were then most probably merely delineating features of the grounds used as a landing pad. The shape and the size of the stones thus would not have been important as long as they were sturdy enough to withstand the elements and remain observable from a distance. The stones of various sizes and shapes that were used in the construction of these circles were well-embedded in the ground and withstood the ravagement of the elements during the past several thousand years.

Why did these space creatures want to especially delineate the grounds on which they placed their spaceship? It is my impression that they wanted to make sure of using the same spot over again upon their return to that region. It is to be considered that they must have made a great number of flights back and forth so that one specific area would have been visited on various occasions. We have observed that the design deduced by Mr. Blumrich suggests that the spaceships were powered by some sort of radioactive reactor, which would naturally emit radioactive radiation. If this were the case, then it would have been most commendable of YAHWEH's team to have landed constantly on the same spot so as not to contaminate various other locations. By using the same landing pad, they would have been recontaminating an already contaminated area and therefore reducing the chances of spreading deadly radiation throughout the countryside.

Furthermore, the presence of the large stones could also have been a deterrent to unknowledgeable Stone-Age people of the region (if there were any) attracted to such an incredible apparition as a spaceship during the year 5000 B.C. By creating an imposing stone structure, they might well have warned the local population not to venture too close as this was "holy" ground.

It is also to be expected that YAHWEH and his team would have required illumination during the night for their landing pads. It is possible that these stones might have been impregnated with the type of radiation we have considered in the accounts of the Old Testament: namely a sort of luminesence or "brightness" or "glory." In order to generate this type of illumination, YAHWEH would have required stones as the base for impregnation.

Finally, there is an important reason for having used circles as tools to perform the functions of the "Watchers." Since these people had to make constant readings and observations of the sky to determine and understand the precise relationships and periodicities existing between the moon, the sun, and the other stars, it is natural that a great many readings had to be collected. For this data to be meaningful at all, the readings had to be taken from the very same spot, at different intervals over a great number of years. It is most important to have placed an observer exactly in the same position in order to observe the particular astronomical phenomenon of a particular night. The Watchers, who were there theoretically, to collect precise data, had to pinpoint their observation points to insure that they could return to the very same spot. A collection of meaningful readings must, by necessity, be taken from the very same spot (today, we earthlings use precise longitudes and latitudes to reestablish our exact bearings). By arranging for sturdy stone circles of a permanent nature, they would have had exact points of reference.

By including certain very specific stones for their foresights, such as the midsummer sunrise or the midsummer moonrise, they would have had a permanent point of reference or departure to be used in their calculations, and could then have compared their subsequent readings accordingly. It is quite important to consider the work performed by Professor Thom who physically measured dozens and dozens of stone circles all over England. He was able to determine that these stone circles either had stones used as foresights, or else that there was on the horizon some very specific, outstanding characteristic that pinpointed the exact direction of the midsummer sunrise and/or moonrise. In other words, if the Watchers were able to locate a specific mountain top that could be used as a precise foresight for the direction of the midsummer moonrise, they would have used it, instead of creating for themselves a new foresight by inserting a boulder in the ground.

At any rate, their probable modus operandi appears clear: they needed a stone circle and they needed the all-important direction of the midsummer sunrise, a direction that was the basic point of departure of all their space exploratory work.

Once they had this direction pinpointed, they would have been on the same coordinates with all their other stone circles and especially with the mother-unit, Stone-henge. Now any sightings taken by the various field units would have been meaningful, as they would have related to the same set of celestial occurrences, placed on the same common denominator. In most of the stone circles there is no center stone (there are but very few excep-tions.) Such a situation is logical as the spaceship would have been sitting in the middle of the circle and thus would not have required a marker in the center of the landing pad. The sightings were not necessarily taken when the observer was standing on the ground and look-ing at the foresight stone. Instead, it is quite probable that the readings were taken from inside the spaceship capsule while looking at the foresight stone.

Possibility B: The stone circles could also have been used as part of a system to capture, generate, and transmit energy. It is likely that these people had a technology to capture power in the radiation coming from space. Al-though our knowledge in space radiation is seemingly ad-vanced, we must certainly consider it to be at an early stage of the discipline, as we must acknowledge that there could be a great many other radiations still unknown to us. As science advances, we will learn more and under-stand newer facets of the radiation systems that exist in outer space and in our atmosphere.

We have discovered much during our past 100 years, starting with Madame Curie and others, who introduced us to the X-ray or Roentgen radiations. We have since discovered a number of additional radiations—such as alpha, beta, gamma, ultra violet rays, micro waves, etc., etc. Yet we can be certain that we are not at the end of our discoveries and that a great many additional rays will eventually be discovered.

It can be expected that these space creatures possessed the technology of rays other than the ones known to us today. It can also be expected that a scientifically most advanced group of people, such as YAHWEH's crew, would also have had the knowledge to capture these rays to advantage and thus generate power for their local purposes.

During the past few years quite a bit of work has been performed in capturing the energy of the sun's radiation. We have succeeded to a certain extent, although we are at the clumsy beginning of this technological solution to our energy problem. Basically, we are trying to follow two paths. We are trying to capture the heat generated by the sunlight and warm with it liquids so as to transfer heat energy. And, we are working on the technology of cells that captures the sunlight and transforms it directly into electrical pulses that, in turn, mean electrical current. In other words, we are using mechanical devices and exposing them to the interaction of sun radiation coming from outer space. Instead of doing this YAHWEH's men could have had a much more advanced, yet simpler, method of generating power. The stones could have been impregnated by YAHWEH's special radiation. They would thus have created a circular field or a large flat disc of the given radiation. If we consider that the sun rays would hit this field, and if we consider that YAHWEH possessed the necessary technology, it is possible to conceive that he had the means of transforming this sun energy into practical

power energy, or even electricity. In order to create a large
field of his given radiation, he would have required stand-

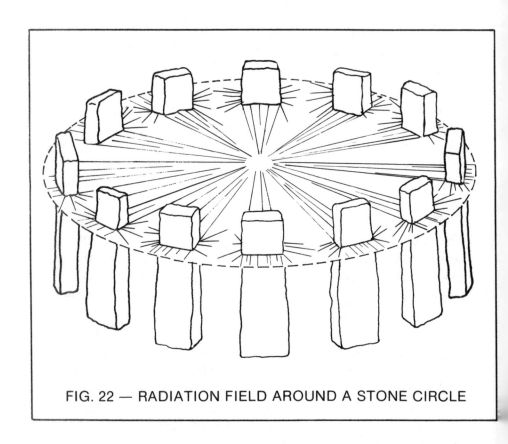

FIG. 22 — RADIATION FIELD AROUND A STONE CIRCLE

ing stones as the basis of the radiation disc. (similar to
Figure. 22)

The interaction of the sun's rays with this field could
conceivably have produced direct electrical current or
other types of power. It could have been a more advanced,
and certainly more elegant way, of generating power than

our present attempts to attract the sun's rays via certain mechanical devices.

It is well to realize that possibly YAHWEH was not dealing with the sun's rays. Possibly there are other types of radiations emanating from outer space that have the capacity to interact with a manmade field. From the accounts in the Bible, there is an indication that YAHWEH dealt with an electromagnetic field. Whether it was a true electromagnetic field as we understand it today, or whether it was some similar but different type of field, is a question that cannot be answered as yet.

Possibility C: Finally we have to consider that as a third possibility YAHWEH might have used a combination of the above mentioned two alternatives. In other words, that the stone circles were used for both as power collecting fields, as well as landing spots for data collection of the "Watchers". If these electromagnetic (?) fields were really in use, then it follows that they had to have a system of transmitting the power from place to place. Power generated in a certain spot cannot always be used at that particular spot. It has to be transmitted to the place which requires the usage. It is within the realm of possibility to consider that the standing stones, or menhirs, which we find throughout the countryside, could have been used as standing poles for accumulating and transmitting power. Let us look to our today's technology. We generate power in a certain spot and often have to transmit it for miles to some locale that requires the power. We accomplish this by using high voltage wires supported by tall poles or towers. Our electric current, or ions, flows along the copper wires stretched for miles upon miles on our countryside.

In the case of YAHWEH, it is possible that the technology was advanced enough so as not to require copper wires. It is conceivable that electric current, or a stream of ions, could have been directed and can pass along through a field created for that purpose, such as the special electro-magnetic (?) field perhaps used by YAHWEH throughout his contact with earthlings. Thus we can conceive of these standing single stones as having been the posts around which these fields were stretched. Power could then have passed from one menhir to the other, depending upon the requirements of YAHWEH. He could have tapped the specific electromagnetic (?) field of a given menhir and pulled the power into that spot at will.

If we had the opportunity to reconstruct the exact positions of these menhirs throughout England (and throughout Europe, as well as other parts of the World), possibly we could come to realize that there was a very specific pattern in the positioning of the individual stones. Unfortunately, the data is not conclusive enough as a number of stones are missing. For all we know, later generations of Englishmen or Scotsmen or Irishmen might have decided to erect such individual stones—because of the legendary "powers" they knew had existed in such stones. It is my impression that if enough correct data can be collected, and if we can pinpoint the exact position of true menhirs, we will probably find a pattern in the positioning of these stones.

We cannot completely rule out the possibility that some of the menhirs could have been foresights for the use of its corresponding stone circle. The latter might have been plowed under or otherwise destroyed, while the vertical stone showing the direction of the midsummer sunrise remains in place today—although we consider it an independent, lonesome menhir.

There is another possibility explaining the existence of these individual standing stones—a possibility that is suggested by a study of the Hebrew prophets. In *Urim and Thumim—the Secret of God,* I tried to analyze how God used the prophets and how these functioned. That analysis indicated that YAHWEH used a specific individual (called a prophet) to transmit a vocal message to the Hebrew crowds. We know that these prophets did not generate their own messages. They were simply mouthpieces activated from the "cloud" above by YAHWEH. That analysis also indicated that before a person could act as a prophet, a certain "something" had to "enter" him—and that something was called "spirit" by our forefathers, for lack of a better word to describe the occurrence. If we use modern terminology, we could suggest that a certain radiation was being directed towards that person. Once he was impregnated with this field (electromagnetic?), he was able to receive YAHWEH's message (and clearly hear it), and then could repeat it to the crowd. Only he could hear this given message and not other individuals in the crowd who were standing nearby. This set-up was connected with some aspects of electricity since we have examples of heat having been generated, singeing effects having been observed, and above all, abnormalities having resulted from the force involved.

It is quite possible that in England and Europe, instead of having used humans as receiving poles for voice messages, YAHWEH could have impregnated the standing stones and forwarded messages, in the form of directed ion streams, from one stone to the other. His assistants, or his "Watchers", standing near such a stone, could have tapped it and received a voice message.

Naturally, a bothersome question has to be asked: if we earthlings, who are at a lower stage of development than YAHWEH, have radio cummunication capacities, why would YAHWEH not have it too? First, such a question presupposes that radio is an advanced communication capacity, which it might not be. There could well be more scientifically elegant and more advanced systems. Secondly, we know for a fact that electromagnetic pulses or fields interfere with radio communication, so as to render them useless. As we seem to have detected, some sort of electromagnetic presence was in and around YAHWEH. Thus, the lack of radio communication usage could be considered a natural consequence.

There could be still another purpose for these circles —to have been used as an electric fence around the spaceship in order to keep away curious inhabitants of the region. We have repeatedly found cremations of young children within these circles—and not skeletons. What is more normal than to expect young children (and not grown-ups) to display a curiosity to enter the "circle" to see or to touch the apparitions? Grown-ups would have displayed a much greater degree of suspicion and self-restrain, and would have tried to stay away. Children (as we so well know) do not always listen to the admonitions of their elders. Thus, playful or super-curious youngsters would have had a much greater probability of trying to enter these forbidden circles—unfortunately being electrocuted or exposed to lethal doses of radioactivity. Once that happened, it is possible that the "Watchers" would have been forced to burn the small victims and bury them, rather than inter them as whole bodies.

Professor Thom, having discovered the MY measurement that underlines the construction of these circles, has gone a step further in pinpointing the basic geometry used by the builders. Although the observations of Professor Thom are correct, in my estimation the sequence of events he suggested is the reverse of what may have happened. If we find a specific shape of triangle that could have been used as a basis for the construction of a flattened-out circle, for example, we cannot state that they laid out a triangle first and then built the circle around it, to satisfy the geometry in question. We can turn the matter around and suggest that a specific shape of flattened circle was built and because of that shape, a certain type of triangle was inherent in its basic foundation. For example, we can place a compass on a piece of paper and draw a circle. We can then take the radius and position it exactly six times around the periphery and thus obtain six specific points. When these are connected to each other we obtain a hexagon. On the other hand, we can reverse the procedure. We can first draw a hexagon and find its center. Using as a radius the distance between this center point and one of the corners of the hexagon, we can draw a circle. All the six corner points of the hexagon will be found to be located on the circle. This effect is most natural, since these are fixed relationships. Therefore, the geometry involved within circles or ellipses or egg-shaped contours is inherent to the shape itself.

In my belief, YAHWEH and his crew did not begin by laying out different triangular forms in order to reach the shape of the circles we now observe. Instead, they started with the circle itself and the geometric figures we now discover and read into it are inherent and part of the whole geometric relationships.

The next question to be asked is how YAHWEH and his crew went about constructing these shapes, be they perfect circles or ellipse shapes, or flattened circles, etc. If we keep in mind the type of technological and electromagnetic capacities they most likely had mastered, then we might be able to hint at a probable means of construction. We have considered that YAHWEH and his group had certain very specific capacities in lifting nonmetallic objects. We read of certain amazing occurences in the Old Testament, all of which started to make sense to us in the latter part of the 20th century because of our advancement in technology and science. The understanding of these types of technological events has occurred only during our lifetime.

STONE ROWS

We can apply the same thinking to the case of the parallel stone rows in England and especially in France. It is my impression that these stone rows were another means of performing the same functions as the stone circles and the standing menhirs. They were an alternative in collecting energy from outer space by creating a large surface of the special (electromagnetic (?) field displayed by YAHWEH.

In the case of the stone rows, we can conceive that after being impregnated with this special field force, they would have generated an elongated area facing the source of radiation. Since we find only a few of these parallel rows in comparison with the multitude of stone circles, we can conceive that they were less efficient and less attractive to the "Watchers". It is possible that both systems were in use. After a certain period they might have decided that electromagnetic (?) fields implanted around stone circles served the purpose better than long stretches of parallel rows of stones. Naturally, this is only an assumption but the fact is that there are many more stone circles on hand in England than parallel rows. The fact that these parallel rows are composed of much smaller stones seems to indicate that the height of the field away from the ground was not an important consideration. In the case of the stone circles, the construction could have had multiple uses as the base for the field, and as a landing pad and observation spot of the "Watchers." In the case of the parallel rows, they would have needed somewhere a menhir to receive the energy collected from the electromagnetic (?) field.

When we look at the fanlike layout at MID CLYTH, we get the impression that something was collected there and pushed towards the narrower end into a standing pole—a large boulder. The layout gives the impression of having been a trough that was ready to absorb radiation from space—be it sun rays or other radiation unknown to us. This imaginary electromagnetic (?) field seems to have directed the flow of the radiation into a standing stone or cairn or other vertically sitting large boulder. This aspect is quite clearly observable in the case of the Devonshire rows, which seem to end with some sort of a large boulder.

The situation is much more pronounced and more perfected in the case of the parallel rows we find in Brittany, in France. At the beginning and end of these fields of parallel rows we seem to detect stone circles or at least accumulations of huge boulders placed in a circular position. Not far away from these stone rows, huge monoliths stand lonesomely in the field.

All these alignments generate the thought that they were created in the form of a segment of an arch having a concave-type area and whose rows were progressively closer to each other at the end of the alignment. If we could connect the tops of all these stones, we would probably generate a curved trough that stands higher at the beginning and lower at the end.

If we imagine that this entire area was impregnated by YAHWEH with his special electromagnetic (?) field, then we could conceive a concave band at a certain angle facing a spot in space as though it were a rounded pan to collect radiation from space and to direct it towards the lower end of the field.

In the big field of LeMenec, at one end is a circle and at the other another circle, or at least standing stones giving the impression that they might have been part of a stone circle. Possibly they were the areas where the "Watchers" were stationed. These could have been the collection focus of whatever radiation was gathered. We observe a certain quantity of standing stones, large ones as well as small ones, and it is conceivable that some of the large ones were used as transmission poles or "storage batteries." It is interesting to observe that around the general area of Carnac, Brittany, we do not find a great many stone circles as was the case in England. Here the construction effort was much more directed to creating these huge fields of parallel stones. It is possible that in the case of Brittany only a few circles were originally installed to be used as bases. This general area instead was used much more as the main "power plant" of YAHWEH in collecting energy from space.

This possibility of having been the main "power house" is further suggested by the fact that in this region occurs the tallest standing stone we have ever come across. It is located on a small peninsula southeast of the huge stone rows and is called the *Er Grah* (which in Briton means the stone of the fairies), or to use the French expression, *Le Grand Menhir Brise* (the large broken menhir). At present it lies on the ground and is broken into four sections. It is estimated that its weight is about 330 tons. Its entire length is about 70 feet; probably part of it was set into the ground. Such a huge standing stone could indicate a usage as the main transmitting post for the energy collected in the various fields of parallel rows. In modern setups, we require straight unobstructed direct lines to transmit waves from one spot to the other; in certain regions we have to install taller poles in order to transmit. In hillier terrain we require relay stations in order to surmount the mountain contours of the terrain. Thus, transmission of TV, power, etc. must flow in a direct line. The same principles could probably have been applied to YAHWEH's energy transmission problems.

Is it too far-fetched to consider that these stone rows were actually the base for a field to receive radiation from outer space? Not necessarily—if we consider that modern technology has reached the point of doing almost precisely the same thing: We are presently building huge stone rows! Only, our modern builders, rather than using raw stones, are pouring concrete and erecting monolithic-shaped units, extending for 13 miles. And what is the purpose of this huge construction effort? Almost exactly as for the same general usage suggested for YAHWEH—only we are much less advanced than he was, and as a result, we are only experimenting in a different direction, while he actually applied his technology to good use. We are using these units as a basis for a field intended to capture radio waves from outer space. Fig. 23 and Fig. 24 show portions of this huge construction effort near Socorro, New Mexico. Especially Fig. 24 gives the impression of an almost modern duplication of the stone rows in Brittany, France.

In the middle of the New Mexico desert, far away from population centers, in a remote section of land, our scientists have decided to erect an immense construction complex of concrete pillars. The stone rows likewise were in remote regions, far from population centers. This huge project, undertaken by the National Radio Astronomy Observatory, is expected to create the most sensitive and the largest radio telescope in the world. Labeled the "very large array" (VLA), it is expected to direct batteries of huge antennas towards space in order to capture whatever radio wave emissions are being sent out by the various celestial bodies. The concrete pillars shown in Fig. 24 are actually the base of the footings of the enormous antennas that will stretch out for about 13 miles (!) into the desert. Not only did they create one stretch of 13 miles, but also a second similar stretch of 13 additional miles, as well as a "shorter" one extending only 11 miles into the desert.

After 4500 years, we seem almost back to the situation from which YAHWEH functioned. We have reached the point of surmising that space has an enormous reservoir of energy, and that various bodies in our sky seem to be "alive" and emitting all sorts of rays and/or waves. 4500 years ago, YAHWEH perhaps knew exactly what waves or rays were involved, how to capture them, and how to put them to use, when he was stationed on planet earth.

FIG. 23 — LAYOUT FOR THE LARGEST RADIO TELESCOPE IN
THE WORLD AT SOCORRO, NEW MEXICO.

FIG. 24 — PILLARS FOR THE RADIO TELESCOPE OF SOCORRO,
NEW MEXICO. PLEASE COMPARE WITH FIG. 16a.
(FIG. 23 and 24 — COURTESY THE NATIONAL RADIO ASTRONOMY
OBSERVATORY, OPERATED BY ASSOCIATED UNIVERSITIES, INC. UNDER
CONTRACT WITH THE NATIONAL SCIENCE FOUNDATION.)

9

Midsummer Sunrise

One of the first things that attracted our attention in Stonehenge was the existence of the Heelstone. After years of experiments and theorizing, we have reached the con- 'clusion that the Heelstone was used as a marker to pin- point the exact direction of the midsummer sunrise, on June 21st of every year. This is the date on which the longest period of daylight occurs during the year. As a result, the tendency had been to consider Stonehenge a sort of temple dedicated to the worship of the sun, espe- cially on the longest day of the year. There have been many another explanation, among which agricultural consideration was preponderently acknowledged. Some- how it was thought that the Stone Age people needed to know this precise date in order to perform their planting accordingly.

Although this is, theoretically, a plausible explana- tion, it is not too likely since a small society, such as the Stone Age culture, would not likely have been able to spend such an enormous amount of energy, time and work to construct so huge a structure. The pinpointing of the midsummer sunrise could have been achieved with much simpler means and did not require the extraordinary effort displayed in Stonehenge. What's more, it is certainly quite unimportant whether a seed is planted six days before June 21st or three days after June 21st. Agricultural success depends upon so many other factors besides a scientifically precise dating. There are a great many imponderables such as rain, temperature, humidity, soil condition, etc., which would make for a successful or unsuccessful crop. Thus, a precision instrument that would provide the "scientifically" correct date of the midsummer sunrise could not logically have been the most important requirement of a Stone Age society. Nevertheless, the fact remains that Stonehenge is definitely oriented towards the midsummer sunrise and has a very specific and precise foresight to pinpoint this exact direction. Naturally, there are a great many other astronomical directions that are also pinpointed; but the most important one is still the Heelstone.

When we review the various other stone circles found throughout England, Scotland, Ireland and Wales, we observe a repeated pattern; namely, we are able to determine the fact that most of these circles also seem oriented towards the direction of the midsummer sunrise and/or moonrise. There are hundreds upon hundreds of circles throughout the British Isles, some of them in good shape and a good many of them in dilapidated condition. In certain cases, we find the majority of the stones properly placed around the circle, while in other cases we only find a few. Throughout the past 4000 years, it is natural that a good many of these stones would have been moved, destroyed or plowed under. Yet a good many of the circles that are in place today, as well as the projections we can make from the existing part-circles, give us a very clear indication that the direction of the midsummer sunrise was most important to these people—almost an obsession. In most of these cases, the painstaking work of people such as Professors Thom, Hawkins, Atkinson, Burl, Newham, etc. clearly indicates the existence of a foresight to the midsummer sunrise and especially moon rise. Of course, the logical conclusion reached by most people involved with the subject has been that all of the circles were, somehow astronomical observatories for the determination of the midsummer sunrise and/or moon rise. It must be admitted that this extraordinary one-track mindedness of the builders displays some peculiarities.

A great many of these circles are not considerably far apart, and yet each one of them seems to have been concerned with those particular directions and has the means of determining them.

To find that direction they did not need so many hundreds upon hundreds of circles performing the same function over and over again. We must logically conclude that this direction and their related circles had a much more important meaning to these builders than the simple curiosity of pinpointing the midsummer sunrise and moonrise. The fact that most of these circles (if not all) have the necessary "equipment" to precisely determine the midsummer sunrise or moonrise is indicative of a society that subscribed to the very same sets of rules and had the same purposes. In other words, we are confronted with a unified society. We could almost state that there seemed to be a centralized plan and program being respected by all these circles. The circles occur from the very southern tip of England all the way to the northern tip in the Orkney Islands, as well as from the western part of Ireland all the way through to the eastern part of England (see Fig. 12). A tremendous construction effort took place thousands of years ago from one end of the islands to the other. And all of them seem to be lined up in one very specific direction; all of them seem to have been built along the same general master plan, measured with the same measuring stick so ably determined by Professor Thom (the megalithic yard (MY)).

In view of the fact that this alignment repeated itself continually throughout a large territory, we must conclude that the specific directions must have been of great importance.

In order to understand the meaning of this importance, it is well to consider the workings of our present-day society. We earthlings have agreed among ourselves to a very specific set of rules so as to pinpoint our positions, draw the proper maps, guide ourselves in our travels from spot to spot, and report to each other our exact position. For each one of us to understand what the others are doing, saying, and where they are going, we have agreed to draw all our maps of the earth on the basis of the "north" being shown on top of the page. On the basis of this premise then, our south is at the bottom of the page, while west is to the left, and east on the right. To pinpoint our north we have discovered that we can use a magnetic needle that will always be attracted towards the magnetic north pole. We have also discovered that the magnetic north pole is not exactly in the same spot as the geographical north pole of this earth. The Chinese, on the other side of the world, who use the same set of principles and the same compass, can understand and follow our maps exactly because we all use the same directional specification. Humankind has agreed to orient itself on this earth by taking north as a reference point. From that position we calculate or describe all the other directions. By using this simple set of rules, all the world is exactly aware of directions correctly described and can guide itself accordingly. Thus, for us earthlings, the chief direction that counts is north.

If we apply the same type of logic to YAHWEH and his people who were involved in constructing and running Stonehenge, as well as hundreds (perhaps thousands) of stone circles throughout the British Isles, we can easily understand why they would deploy such precise align-

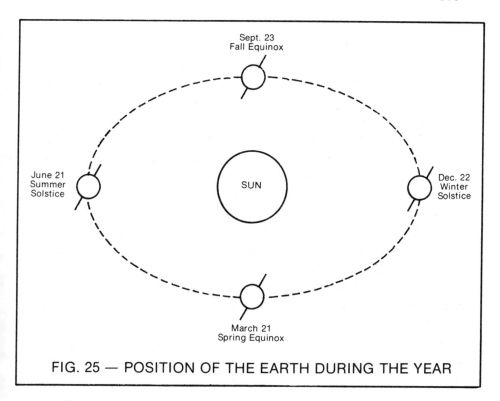

FIG. 25 — POSITION OF THE EARTH DURING THE YEAR

ments towards the direction of the midsummer sunrise and moonrise. We must understand that YAHWEH and his people were not earthlings and, as a result, they were not especially interested, at the beginning, in establishing a direction relative to the geography of the earth. Instead, they were mainly concerned with establishing a direction relative to space, and then in exploring the relationships in the solar system, as seen from earth. It was only in the context of the relationship between the position of the earth, moon and the sun, and the other stars and/or planets that YAHWEH was interested in locating himself.

The direction of the midsummer sunrise indicates a

very specific position in the orbit of the earth around the sun. This position is reached only on the one day of the year when the earth is in a very specific spot along its elliptical orbit around the sun. Fig. 25 will show the exact position in which the earth on that day finds itself in relationship to the sun. YAHWEH and his crew were space-oriented people who had to establish their bearings in relationship to the exact position of the earth in space. Thus, the considerable effort invested in each stone circle in the British Isles tends to indicate that crew members at each stone circle were concerned with aligning themselves in a very precisely given direction so that observers at any of the circles could take readings of the solar system, based on the same coordinates, and would understand where they were located at that very moment.

At least, this must have been their partial purpose. In my opinion, this vast effort to locate the direction in question, has no bearing with planting, with crops, or with sun worship. Instead, it is simply the direction-finding method of space people who would naturally want to know the positioning of the Earth, in relationship to space, and who are trying to understand and discover the periodicity of the relative movements within our solar system.

Since YAHWEH and crew were possibly a society that traveled through space and descended to earth, it would have been essential for them to know exactly when they could rejoin their mother ship in space. We follow this pattern when we send missions into space, place a mother ship in orbit around a heavenly body, then eject a smaller vehicle from it, to land on the celestial body under observation. Meanwhile, the mother ship continues circling in a very specific orbit. When the observer capsule is ready, it can then lift off into space and rejoin the mother ship in its orbit in a very specific position.

YAHWEH and his crew would have needed to know their exact positions at all times in relationship to the orbiting mother ship. In view of the fact that these people likely spent such an extended period of time on earth, perhaps as long as 1000 years, it is also conceivable that their orbiting mother ship did not constantly remain in orbit, but took off for other planets, then returned to place itself back into orbit around the earth.

The moon is in constant orbit around our planet and circles it with a very specific periodicity. A space mothership that placed itself in orbit around the earth would have to choose a similar orbit to that of the moon in order to place itself at the disposal of the astronauts returning from earth. As a result, YAHWEH and his crew would have had a constant interest in knowing the exact position of the moon in relationship to the earth and the sun. That could have been the reason they went to all the trouble of pinpointing the one and only spot in the northern hemisphere that would give them an easily determinable relationship between the sun and the moon as seen from earth. That particular spot is Stonehenge with a latitude of 51.17N and a longitude of 1.83W. It is precisely at this spot that the positioning of the sun versus the moon creates exactly a 90-degree angle. As a result, YAHWEH and crew perhaps arranged to pinpoint the direction of the midsummer sunrise by installing the Heelstone and at the same time pinpointed the direction of the moonrise at a 90-degree angle by erecting and maintaining Stones No. 91, 92, 93, 94. By having these two directions fixed, they had the means of knowing at all times the position of their mother ship circling in an orbit around the earth. They also had then the means to determine the exact position of the earth in relationship to the sun throughout the 365 days of the year. Most probably the speed of that mother ship was synchronized with that of the moon so that the crew living and working on earth would follow simply the position of the moon and know when to lift off from the earth in order to join the mother ship.

Summing it up, just as the direction of north is essential for us earthlings, so would the direction of the midsummer sunrise have been the most important direction for YAHWEH and crew to locate themselves in relationship to space.

This leads to the tentative conclusion, that YAHWEH and his Watchers did not originate from within the immediate vicinity of the solar system, since they were out to investigate and understand the laws of nature governing our solar system. If these individuals had existed on planets near our solar system, they should have known the exact periodicities taking place within this system, including the earth. This means that, at best, they likely originated from another planet in our galaxy, a planet far enough from our solar system so as not to afford them normal visual access to the basic and relative movements of the bodies within that system. For them, this must have been a new experience, a new world to be discovered, understood, and plotted. For them, it must have been a new discovery to pinpoint the periodicities of the various planets in our solar system. It would have been an extensive and time-consuming job, and must have required an extended stay on planet earth. Periodicities or the laws governing the movements of each planet cannot be determined in a week's time. It takes centuries of painstaking data collecting, collating same, and then generating an overall picture. That's exactly what YAHWEH and his Watchers may have been doing at the beginning of their visit to planet earth.

We must remember that the most important reason for their one-track mindedness in pinpointing the midsummer sunrise direction was as a proper, stable coordinate in nature that could be used as a point of reference for all the subsequent readings to be taken. It becomes a very simple matter to determine the direction of the sunrise on any given morning. The angle between that direction and the established direction of the midsummer sunrise gives a precise indication of how far the earth has moved along its orbit from the spot it occupied during the midsummer sunrise period. They would have known where the earth was in its orbit on that particular day. When this reading is plotted and the sightings of all the other celestial bodies are taken, the entire three-dimensional solar system starts displaying its periodicity.

Finally the question could be asked as to why these individuals were basing their directions on the midsummer sunrise and not the midwinter sunrise. A system of reference based on the midwinter sunrise would have given them the exact same possibility of plotting the position of the earth in its orbit. Obviously they preferred to use the midsummer sunrise which is more logical since the overcast sky during the winter months would certainly hide the sunrise. During the summer months, the chances for a clear sky are much greater than in winter. From a practical point of view, the Watchers would have been correct in choosing the midsummer sunrise, and not the midwinter one.

10

What's in a Name?

In 1969 Mr. John Phillip Cohane wrote an interesting book entitled *The Key*, [1] which contained uniquely challenging ideas worth being investigated further, a thought supported by Professor Cyrus Gordon of Brandeis University.

Cohane's thesis is that certain specific names, or roots of these names, appear and reappear throughout the world as common geographical names for cities, towns, mountains, valleys, rivers, etc. This conclusion was reached after an extensive research on all continents leading to a compilation of names and their roots. According to him, the root of most of these words go back to two specific ancient words, namely: Hawe and Oc. His research indicated that Hawe (Haue) was originally Ava, representing the godess of fertility, or Eve, the first woman encountered in the Old Testament. Furthermore, the site on which Avebury has been built, used to be known in ancient time as "Ava."

Mr. Cohane went on to expound his theory quite interestingly and demonstrated the same common roots in a variety of sites throughout the world, all of which seem to

---

[1] *The Key*, published in 1976 by Schocken Books

hint to some sort of common interest, as well as a common semitic heritage.

With all due credit to the pioneering work generated by Mr. Cohane, I respectfully suggest that probably the root of Haue (or Hawe) was not at all Ava (or Eve) as indicated by him, especially as he was tying it to old "deities." In my mind, it would make much more sense to consider that the basic root would have been YAHWEH, so well known and defined throughout history as the Hebrew God and the most important deity, and certainly much more important in stature than Eve.

Please note that the phonetic pronunciation of Hawe (Haue) and YAHWEH is identical. If Mr. Cohane would substitute YAHWEH instead of Ave, I am certain that he would realize a new dimension and a different picture that would make much more sense—throughout the world.

The related affinity becomes much more pronounced when we consider the fact that Avebury seems to mean Haue-village, since "bury" means village. Avebury, about 18 miles north of Stonehenge, is a most interesting place in its own right, as it contains probably the biggest stone circle in England, even though it is not a structured edifice as we consider Stonehenge to be. Besides, Avebury is the nearest village to a number of other immense and puzzling structures found in the proximity, namely: West Kennet, Silbury Hill, Windmill Hill, Sanctuary, Ogbury Camp, etc. Each one of these still presents a baffling problem for archaeologists who do not have a precise answer concerning the historical origins of the sites.

I suggest that the origin of the word Avebury is YAHWEH-bury. It is naturally understood that if this were a solitary fact, with no other connections involved, it would not have an important meaning. Accidentally, two words can have a similar pronunciation without having been connected in their history. However, it is very peculiar, to

say the least, that just in Avebury we should find a surprising correlation between the root of the word Haue-bury
and YAHWEH. It is surprising that it is in this spot, where
the various mysterious stone structures and mounds are
found, that we should hit upon a coincidence of this magnitude. We must admit that considering the possible connection of Stonehenge with YAHWEH, it would be logical
to expect that a certain close-by village would have been
named after him, especially as his presence was felt perhaps for centuries upon centuries in that part of England.

Indirectly Mr. Cohane's research might shed some additional light on the general theory expounded here. YAH-
WEH, with his assistants, had the capability to fly from
country to country and from continent to continent. Thus,
the fact that a number of sites throughout the world seem
to have the same root as *HAUE* (-YAH-WEH) is significant
and can be logically expected, if he actually once were
present in various countries. This aspect should be further
investigated and could indicate various other places visited by YAHWEH during his centuries of activity on this
earth.

In relationship with Stonehenge, there is a second
baffling connection in the roots of the word. It seems that
the word Stonehenge is derived from some very old local
language meaning "hanging stones." This could be understood in two different ways: a) Stones for hanging or b)
Stones that are hanging One of the explanations used in
the past hinted that the lintel stones had been used as
gallows to hang people. It must be considered far-fetched
that primitive people would go to the extreme trouble of
erecting such an enormously heavy structure to use it simply for the hanging of people. Theoretically, it is possible
that at a later stage in history it was used as a ready-made.
gallows.

According to an additional legend persisting in history, the magician Merlin is credited with having erected

the Stonehenge structure within one night. In this oft-repeated tale, this monument was constructed somewhere in Ireland. Word circulated concerning the enormity of the structure and its extraordinary powers (usually connected with special healing powers effective against many ailments).

It seems that King Arthur wanted to possess this structure and to use it as a monument to the slain noblemen of his court. They dispatched a small army of men to Ireland to capture this monument; however, they were not in a position to move the stones in question and King Arthur felt very frustrated. At that moment he asked advice from the legendary Merlin, present at his court. Merlin promised to bring the stones to England. Using his "magical" powers, Merlin was apparently able to carry the whole structure overnight from Ireland to its present site in Salisbury Plain. How he was able to move this entire structure within one night over such a long distance has always been one of the engaging mysteries connected with the legends circulating about the magician Merlin. Some say that it was carried through the air.

Considering my theory, the term "hanging stones" could have a connection with very ancient times. I have proposed that these stones were placed in position by YAHWEH and his crew and were transported through the air. Seen through the eyes of an unknowledgeable Stone Age person, it certainly would appear that these stones were hanging in air, as there was no visible support. The local Stone Age people who could have observed the movement of stones transported by air and let down perpendicularly into a prepared hole, would be inclined to name them "hanging stones." At least there seems to be a logical connection in applying such a name.

It is also quite noteworthy to observe that the root of the names of the two most significant sites—namely; Stonehenge and Avebury—should seem to have very pronounced connections and relationships with YAHWEH. Names by themselves do not necessarily paint a full and true picture. However, when the connection is so closely intertwined, and when they fit in with a greater band of events, then they start generating an important meaning of their own.

In my estimation, "Haue-bury" and "Hanging Stones" are not mere accidental names. They had a meaning to the original inhabitants of the region; both names seem to fit within the theory submitted in this book.

11

The Reconstruction

The way I reconstruct the events that might have taken place 5000–10,000 years ago, leads me to the following tentative picture:

A group of people—humanoid in nature and structure —coming from outer space, entered our solar system for investigative purposes. At the beginning they surveyed from the air the various planets—including ours—just as we did when we initiated our various space probes. Their first order of the day would have been to collect atmospheric data and to take pictures of the earth—similar to the tasks our satelites are performing at this very moment. Such activities, intersperced with carefully attempted periodic and temporary landings on planet earth, must have lasted for an appreciable span of time, until enough data was gathered and analysed to reach the conclusion that a landing in larger numbers would be safe and advisable. Naturally, all the photographs taken from space would be analysed to determine satisfactory landing areas. If this happened during our last Ice Age (about 10,000 years ago), it is possible that a more permanent landing attempt might have been postponed for several thousand years, until the atmospheric conditions on planet earth were more conducive for such a landing program.

About 6000 years ago, they may have finally decided to land in greater numbers and establish a more permanent base on planet earth. At the beginning they may have tried to investigate the territory in greater detail and collect samples and data about the earth. One of their first attempts would certainly have been the collection of data concerning the relationships between the earth, the moon, the sun, and the other planets and stars in space. To do that, it is logical to expect that they would have had to make a variety of observations from different spots on earth in order to take the necessary readings. Such a job, by its very nature, had to be stretched out over a long period of time, in order to determine a periodicity of occurrence. Data had to be collected from a great many spots, collated, and depending upon the results, a more permanent observatory established. Thus we can assume that part of the stone circles were the first to be constructed throughout England. Readings of the sun, the moon, the planets, and the stars would have been taken over a prolonged period of time from the stone circles. The first attempt must have been to learn about the interrelationship existing in our sky. As this data commenced to create a meaningful picture, the locations were further refined and narrowed down. Eventually a specific spot would have been pinpointed for a more permanent central observatory. It had to be a spot that had certain specific advantages—astronomically speaking, so as to correlate all future readings of the planets in a systematic and easy manner. The precise location of Stonehenge, situated at latitude 51.17N and longitude 1.83W, would have given them such an advantage, as it was the spot where an exact 90-degree relationship existed between the midsummer sunrise and moonrise.

After Stonehenge was functioning, it is likely that they built additional stone circles (as small observation posts) to collect additional data.

The functions of collecting data had to be entrusted to a group of trained personnel. The Bible suggests that they actually performed the function of astronomers and data collectors, and that the "Watchers" were the group entrusted with this function. These "Watchers," who had to spend months upon months on earth, probably did not have enough to do during the daytime since a good part of the readings must have been taken at night. During their extended free time, these Watchers must have been utterly bored. They may well have disrespected the order of their superiors against "fraternizing with the local population," mingled with earthlings, and even had affairs and/or married local women. This fact is reported to us by the Old Testament and by the Apocryphas.[1]

Through the accounts in the Old Testament, we get the impression that the data-gathering activities took place not only in England, but also in Israel, where the Watchers were active. Obviously such activities must have taken place in other countries. It is an almost foregone conclusion that YAHWEH and his Watchers may have been actively collecting data from other countries as well: for example, Greece, Egypt, Persia, Europe, India, China, America.

These same "Watchers" seem also to have had the function of teaching the more knowledgeable earthlings, some of the science of the relationships of the sun, the moon, the earth, etc. Today termed astronomy, in the days of Abraham it was not a defined science, but regarded only as the expression of the will of God displayed through the movement of the stars and the planets.

A study of history shows us that in certain ages and in certain spots on earth, there all of a sudden mushroomed a surprising knowledge of astronomy. If we go back 4000 to 5000 years ago, we know for a fact that no instrumentation was available. Astronomy without precise instrumen-

[1]See "Book of Jubilees", "Dead Sea Scroll," "Book of Enoch" and Genesis 6:2—6:4

tation is hardly possible as a precise science. Everybody can see with the naked eye that a certain star is on the horizon. These general observations can certainly not be classified as precise scientific data. The magnitude of the movements of the stars and planets, the precision of reoccurrence, the minute variations of these movements, are so important and so delicate that the naked eye cannot possibly detect them and generate a precise scientific theory—let alone a precise established fact. Precise astronomy can only be expected with the application of precise instrumentation used with scientific methods and purposefulness. Yet, our ancestors 5000 years ago did not have any instrumentation at all—at least that is what we believe, based upon the known facts acknowledged for so many centuries.

Despite this tremendous handicap, we observe the fact that certain groups of people—be it the Chinese, the Arabs, the Mayans, the Egyptians, etc., generated an incredible precision, all tied in with the exact movements of the solar system.

It is interesting to note that these different cultures were not in contact with each other so as to transmit information from one to the other, nor were they living during the same period of time. Yet, in each case they displayed an extraordinary sophistication and intelligence beyond the normal capacity of that particular society. In each case, we have always wondered how these scientifically primitive people were able to reach incredible precise conclusions which they did in this particular field while remaining relatively unsophisticated in the other aspects of their civilization. We have always marveled at how the Egyptians were able to determine the precise length of the solar year—with a precision that went beyond the fourth decimal. By the same token, we have always marveled at how the Mezo-Americans were able to create, for instance, intricate computations generating a still higher degree of precision when calculating the exact number of days within a solar year. When we consider, for example, that the Mezo-Americans had not even invented the wheel, it becomes difficult to believe that they had enough science, sophistication, and intelligence to discover or understand the intricate precision of the solar system.

We also observed in history, that this "knowledge" displayed by these societies, mysteriously died out, just as suddenly as it was born. There does not seem to be a continuity in science in these societies, such as we display today. Oddly enough, that sprouting of scientific knowledge simply fades away. It does suggest that these societies received an infusion of knowledge from a "teacher"—and when the "teacher" left, the local students, when left to their own devices, could not support and sustain scientific thought and methodology.

If we now apply the theory of the existence of the "Watchers", we then obtain a different picture. We now see the implantation of a very sophisticated and advanced humanoid group who is coming in touch with primitive societies. They have the necessary equipment, tools, instruments, theoretical knowledge and travel possibilities, to gather the necessary data on a scientific basis. They would then turn over some of this information to the more intelligent type of earthlings within the local society (usually the priestly class). They would have the possibility of teaching these backward people some of the facts relating to mathematics, astronomy and the movement within the solar system. As those "Watchers" descended on various spots on earth, or traveled from area to area at different times, they would be able to train and educate different groups within the local population—groups that were completely disconnected from each other; and who would grasp the new teachings with a different absorption capacity, at different times.

The degree of sophistication of the Egyptian astronomers, in comparison with the sophistication of the Chinese astronomers, would naturally have differed, depending upon the time at which "Watchers" resided with the local population, and depending upon the capacity of the local intelligentsia. The knowledge of astronomy displayed by the Incas in Peru might have differed slightly from that displayed by the Babylonians, who, surprisingly, also understood an incredible amount of astronomy. Yet these two societies lived centuries apart, thousands of miles separated their countries, and thus they had no contact.

After performing a number of sighting tests, after using data received from various spots around the country, they finally pinpointed the specific spot that met their requirements: an exact spot in the Salisbury Plain—and accordingly prepared the grounds for what we call STONEHENGE I.

When this first stage was created, their main purpose seemed to have been the exact pinpointing of the midsummer sunrise together with an exact sighting of the moonrise at that spot. This was achieved by installing the Heelstone that gave them a permanent foresight to the direction in question.

At a later stage of their research on earth, they must have felt the necessity for a more permanent base. This is when we seem to detect a construction effort which we call Stonehenge II. In this instance we believe that they were trying to build two concentric circles made out of bluestones, about 6 feet apart from each other. They positioned them in such a way so as to place them along a radial line. There is a suspicion that the stones used in the inner circle seem to have been smaller in height than their corresponding partners of the outer circle. There is also an indication that these two Bluestones were then connected by a lintel stone that must have been on a slant (see Fig. 26). It indicates that this construction was trying

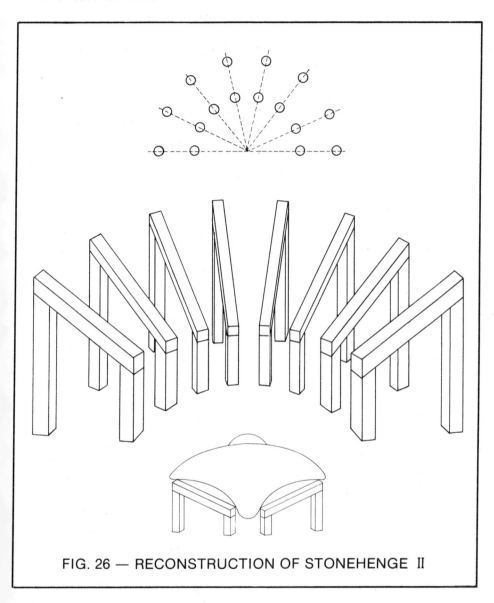

FIG. 26 — RECONSTRUCTION OF STONEHENGE II

to create a type of trough in the form of an inverted cone. The assumption can be made that such a construction was probably the first design to create a secure stand for a spaceship observatory. This flying laboratory would then place itself in that cone and would be supported by the slanted lintel stones. After part of this construction was terminated, we observe that the balance of the circle was discontinued and no further construction was undertaken. On the contrary, those bluestones that had been put in place were dismantled and taken away. We could deduce that they realized the construction in question was not satisfactory or had certain serious flaws. Since they could not perform the desired function they had in mind, they decided to dismantle the half-built construction and start again with a completely new design.

We now enter the third phase of the construction effort which we call Stonehenge III as represented by the structure we presently have on hand. Here we see a much stronger construction, enormously solid, generated to create a very level circle of stones at a height of about 20 feet. This platform was now ready to receive the semipermanent spaceship that was to act as a main observatory and data collecting center. The design proposed by Mr. Blumrich (see Fig. 17) would fit perfectly on top of this platform and would perform the functions of an observatory for astronomical events. Consequently, the structure as seen by us today, was nothing else but a landing platform and observation base for YAHWEH's spaceship, placed on a level plane, in order to collect precise astronomical data and collate it with the other readings being received from all various outposts.

Unlike in the case of Stonehenge II with its inverted conical stone trough, this time the spaceship does not touch any stone. Instead, its legs get supported by the lintel platform, while the entire flying unit is simply suspended in air. This is certainly a marked advantage over the previous design, where, most probably, it had to rest on top of the slanted lintel stones. If so, they could have run the risk of damaging the undersurface of the space-ship. By using the Stonehenge III design, they achieved a semi-suspension in air of the spaceship, and yet generated a firm anchoring of the unit, so as to create an absolute level position with the horizon. Possibly there also was a fine tuning device on the legs, so as to create an absolutely level positioning of the spaceship.

The next point to be answered by the theory on hand, is how the construction of Stonehenge took place. The details of the construction as described previously, clearly indicate that we are dealing with a very sophisticated type of construction, having very subtle intricacies, one that was certainly beyond the mental and physical capacities of the stone age people living in that area 5000 years ago.

YAHWEH had displayed capacities for lifting non-metallic objects up into the air and carrying them through the air.

By applying this capacity, it is simple to realize how he is able to move huge boulders over long distances without the assistance of the local population. Thus, after surveying the area and testing the type of stones that would satisfy his particular requirements, he pinpoints the source of the Sarsen Stones (which happen to be Marlborough Downs in Salisbury). With his technology it would be a simple matter to quarry these boulders and cut them loose from the ground or the mountain. They would then be carried through the air to the Stonehenge base and let down into a prepared hole. This operation would be repeated for all the subsequent stones. The proximity of each stone to one another is no longer a problem as they are coming down from above and can easily fit into their holes without touching the other stones. The same situation is repeated when placing the Lintel Stones, whose tongue and groove portion has to fit in perfectly, with one another, and must be set in place from above.

We observed the incredible construction capacity in

order to generate a completely level top of the Lintel platform. With such a technique it is easy to see that if stones
did not fit properly, if they were too high or too low to
generate the proper level, they could easily be lifted up
into the air, additional ground could be dug or filled in,
and then the stone could be let down with hardly any
human effort being expended. When the Sarsen Circle and
the lintel platform were in place, they would then slightly
shave off the top at given spots in order to make sure that
it was level with the horizon.

This explains to us why a seemingly very difficult job
(at least for us) seems to have been performed via the
more difficult route than the one we, earthlings, would
have expected. What we had considered to be a burden-
some and awkward construction effort, meant a very simple action for YAHWEH and his construction men.

It is interesting to note, in this connection, that any
chiseling performed on these stones, does not seem to have
been done with metal tools. Usually stones that are quarried or cut with metal tools always show certain traces of
the metal. In this particular case, up to now, we have been
led to believe that only stone mallets were used in order to
dress down the stones, since no metal traces, however
minute, had ever been discovered.

It is interesting to recall, at this stage, the special instructions that YAHWEH gave to the Hebrews for the construction of the altar stone. No metal tools were to be used
when dressing it down, as though the presence of metal
would be most undesirable.[1] In those days, naturally, the
reason was not understood. Today, although we still do not
know the very precise reason, the possibility exists that
the type of electromagnetic(?) field generated and used by
YAHWEH applied to nonmetallic objects and not to metal.
Perhaps even traces of metal would have interfered with
the proper action of this field.

[1]Exodus 20:25

Naturally no metal traces would be found on the stones at Stonehenge if this group of builders did not use metal hammers or chisels. Perhaps their technology was able to cut stone by completely other means, such as with rays. We have started to realize such techniques by applying laser-beam technology in a variety of ways. Consequently, it is certainly not unlikely that YAHWEH and his men might have mastered such a technology, or even a more advanced one.

At this point we can ask ourselves whether or not local labor might have been used in the construction effort of YAHWEH. It is difficult to answer that question as there are indications on the affirmative side and yet there are reasons to believe the contrary.

The fact that we find antlers and oxen shoulderblade bones at Stonehenge, led us to believe that they were used by the Stone Age population. It might very well be, although there is no reason to believe that the more advanced "Watchers" would not themselves have used these same bones found in the countryside. If they used local labor, it must be realized that these people would eventually have perished as a result of their extended exposure to the radioactive fields surrounding YAHWEH and his crew members. Even if the indigenous population were expendable elements, it still is a moot question whether they could have been induced to perform the menial tasks perhaps desired by the space people. Yet, it is easy to imagine how enormously overwhelmed these Stone Age minds would have been to see the presence of advanced, peculiarly dressed beings with flight capacity and spaceships. The first reaction would likely have been that "God" had landed. And if God wanted them to dig holes, with a trembling hand, they would probably have performed. Whether these laborers, after being exposed to radiation, eventually died and represent the cremations we find within those circles, can naturally not be answered.

Although there are certain indications that local labor

was used, yet, there is no way of tying it to the Stonehenge construction effort. Outside Stonehenge, graves were found that contained a number of simple and primitive artifacts. Among them, most surprisingly, were a quantity of blue beads. This is most significant as we know from experience that blue beads were manufactured only in Egypt. The technology to produce the particular type of blue bead in question apparently was the well-guarded secret of a few families in ancient Egypt. These beads were greatly valued and were sought after throughout the Middle East. It is a well-known fact that the blue beads in the Middle East region are today considered barriers against the "evil eye." Newborn children, and grown ups for that matter, carry some sort of a blue bead as a lucky charm or as a protection against the evil spirits that are directed through the looks of the "evil eye." This is, at present, an almost standard practice for millions of people in the Middle East. It is quite possible that the same valuation was given to these blue beads in ancient times.

For these beads to have appeared in prehistoric England has been a considerable enigma that has baffled archaeologists and historians. Naturally, the first tentative explanation was to consider that an Egyptian expedition had landed in England, colonized that place and left behind the blue beads. Others have it that Phoenicians who, we are told, were sea-faring trading people, might have roamed the European and British countryside in search of trading opportunities. They would have brought along blue beads and perhaps have exchanged them with the local population. It is not quite certain what they would have received in exchange, as it is difficult to conceive Stone Age people possessing valuables that would have attracted the keen business interests of the Phoenicians.

It is possible that YAHWEH and his crew would have picked up the beads in Egypt, brought them back to England, and gave them to the local laboring population as a reward for their menial help. We must not forget our own immediate past when the white men met the red Indians of North America. One of the first things he paid him with were trinkets and beads. Tons of beads were, in fact, exchanged with the American Indians for land or furs, etc. It is not too far fetched to imagine that YAHWEH too might have brought small trinkets from his visits to Egypt that were attractive and valuable to the primitive Stone Age laborers in England.

On the negative side, however, we must consider that he would not really have required a large local labor force since he possessed the necessary technology to accomplish what he wished much faster and simpler. And, if we consider that exposure to their radiation would definitely have harmed and killed the indigenous people, then there is a tendency to doubt that YAHWEH would have greatly used them during his construction efforts in Stonehenge.

As a next step we could try to reconstruct the way the stone circles were built. As stated before, one of the possibilities would be that they represented the outside limits of the grounds on which the smaller spaceships were placed. The electromagnetic(?) field would follow, at a given distance, the contours of the spaceship placed in the center. Thus, it should not be considered unusual that we observe so many circles that have an exact measurement of 8 MY or 16 MY. It could mean that those particular circles were the base for smaller flying units of, let us say, 6 MY and 14 MY. The larger circles would have contained the larger flying units. The distance between the circumference of the small spaceships and the stone circle would be predetermined by the "Watchers" to fit their particular requirement. Thus, it is logical to expect Professor Thom's observations that there was a very precise measuring unit used in the construction of all the stone circles and that a very great number of these circles measure 8 MY or 16 MY.

It is my belief that the precision as indicated by Professor Thom, namely; 2.720 ± 0.003 feet, could not be the result of regular measuring techniques such as yardsticks or ropes, etc. Even if we disregard the degree of precision incorporated and consider the measuring unit to have been simply 2.7 feet, it would suggest much too advanced a measuring capacity to have been achieved by our typical types of measuring devices. It is possible that the "Watchers" used a much more advanced technique (such as wavelengths) in order to determine the exact location where the stones were to fit. In view of the possibility that YAHWEH may have used an electromagnetic(?) field to move the stones around, it is understandable that this magnetic force (if we can call it a magnetic force) could have been finely adjusted from a gauge in the spaceship. As a result, the stone could have been held in a precise position, at a very exact distance from the opposite stone, as regulated by an adjustment of the gauge. For all we know, all the stones of the circle might have been inserted at the same time and held in the air together as a circular unit. Since they were controlled from an overhead magnetic power source, they would have followed the forces as directed from above. Professor Thom's precision factor could have been built into their gauge or their tool—whatever it was.

If we can imagine that these stones were the outside border for the smaller spaceships that periodically sat in the center of the stone circles, we can go one step further and suggest a reason why we observe other types of stone circles in the form of flattened circles, compound rings, egg-shaped rings, and elliptical rings. The circles would have been created as a limiting border for the spot containing the spaceships, or possibly as the outer limit of the electromagnetic field around that particular space vehicle. An ellipse is a geometrical figure that contains two centers. We could conceive then that an elliptical stone circle

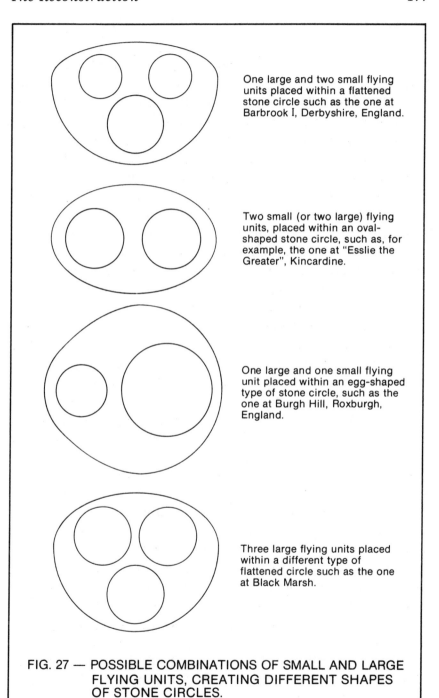

One large and two small flying units placed within a flattened stone circle such as the one at Barbrook I, Derbyshire, England.

Two small (or two large) flying units, placed within an oval-shaped stone circle, such as, for example, the one at "Esslie the Greater", Kincardine.

One large and one small flying unit placed within an egg-shaped type of stone circle, such as the one at Burgh Hill, Roxburgh, England.

Three large flying units placed within a different type of flattened circle such as the one at Black Marsh.

FIG. 27 — POSSIBLE COMBINATIONS OF SMALL AND LARGE FLYING UNITS, CREATING DIFFERENT SHAPES OF STONE CIRCLES.

might have contained two small spaceships placed at the two centers—as shown in Fig. 27.

In the case of the egg-shaped stone circles, it could have contained a small and a bigger flying unit as depicted in Fig. 27. In the case of flattened circles or compound rings, we could imagine that two small units, along with a larger one, or two larger ones, along with a smaller one, or three small ones, etc., were "parked" there. In those cases, and depending upon the distances between the flying units stationed at the site, the builders would have generated bordering stone circles to fit the particular requirements of the station. It is my impression that the layout of these odd-shaped stone circles did not follow an exact geometric pattern, that the shape followed the general contours of the flying units stationed there, in order to create the required fencing.

All of this suggests an enormous building activity throughout the region and throughout the British Isles. YAHWEH, even with all his powers and technical knowhow, would have needed a substantial amount of help. The Old Testament reports the existence of a multitude of "angels," "giants," "Sons of God," etc., thus giving clear-cut support to the notion that YAHWEH was not alone, but had a large group of helpers.

The region around Stonehenge is enormously interesting—and yet, quite enigmatic. The structure of Stonehenge, itself, is only one manifestation of the activities. We encounter a great many other remains (see Fig. 28). Slightly north of Stonehenge, we find the Cursus—parallel ditches and banks that extend for a considerable distance. South of Stonehenge, we encounter the largest example of ditch-banks: the Dorset Cursus, extending for about 7 miles—truly an enormous earth-moving undertaking.

Northeast of Stonehenge, we find the remains of a great many concentric holes, dug around elliptical paths.

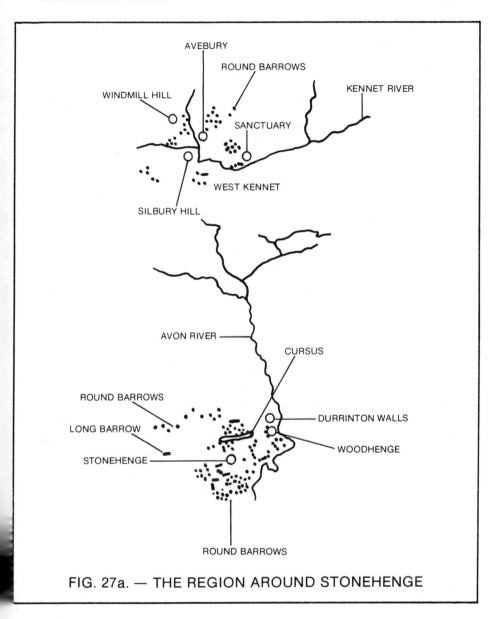

FIG. 27a. — THE REGION AROUND STONEHENGE

It is generally acknowledged that these holes did contain—
at one time or another—wooden posts. Thus, we came to

name the site Woodhenge. Its purpose is really not known for certain.

Again, further north, we observe with amazement the largest earthen mound ever encountered in Europe. This man-made mountain takes the shape of a rounded pyramid with a flat top—or a truncated cone. It is about 120 feet high (40 meters) and covers an area of about 5.5 acres (2.2 hectars). It certainly was an immense construction effort, if one realizes that they must have moved about half a million tons of earth in order to create and shape it. Indications are that it was built between 2500 BC and 3000 BC which means slightly before the large pyramids of Egypt. What was the purpose? Again, we must openly confess our ignorance—we do not know for certain. One thing is established: this was not a burial mound. No skeletal remnants were ever found.

Excavations determined that rocks were placed inside, in such a manner as to give the proper base and strength to the mountain of earth that was piled on top. This construction was in the form of steps, as shown in Fig. 29 The entire step-pyramid was then covered with earth. It has been estimated that about 18,000,000 man-hours must have been spent to complete Silbury Hill. If we consider that a person worked 2000 hours per year (50 weeks at 40 hours per week) it means that 500 people must have labored for 18 years in order to finish this mountain. It is certainly questionable that a stone age society in England of 5000 years ago, possessed enough people and time to devote exclusively to this task. If we keep in mind all the other construction efforts in and around Stonehenge, it becomes incredible that such a primitive group of people could have produced them all.

A look at this step-pyramid construction of Silbury Hill, leads one to compare it with similar structures found in other parts of the world. For example: in Egypt we have the Saqqara pyramid (Fig. 30) while in Mexico

FIG. 28 — THE BIGGEST MAN-MADE MOUNTAIN
IN EUROPE—SILBURY HILLS,
WILTSHIRE, ENGLAND.

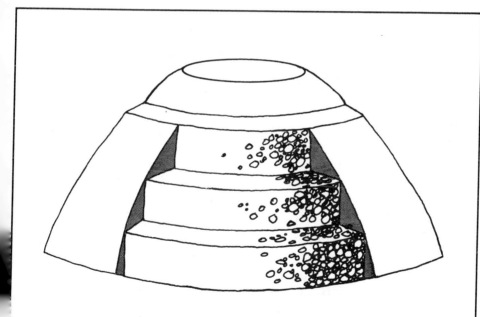

FIG. 29 — SCHEMATIC CUT THROUGH EARTH
COVER OF SILBURY HILL.

we encounter the Teotihuacan pyramid (Fig 31.) It is
certainly amazing to observe the very same construction
and design in all three of them. The same principle of
supporting the sides with stones and generating a step
effect, was applied in England, in Egypt, and in Mexico
—countries that are located in three different continents
and are separated from each other by thousands of miles
of oceans.

Yet, all three have a certain common aspect: they are
huge in size and end up with a flat top—as though the
entire purpose was to create a large flat surface area at a
given height.

Involuntarily a thought comes to mind: could it be that
these were flat landing pads for a certain type of space
ships?

Throughout this entire Stonehenge region, we see dozens upon dozens of barrows—or "burial" mounds. These
were either made completely out of earth, or contain elaborate stone structures within the mounds—such as tun-
nels, chambers, etc. The long barrows, as the name implies, were elongated in shape, while the round barrows
were circular. This Stonehenge region has probably the
greatest concentration of barrows in England—thus hint-
ing that at one time in our antiquity, it was a very populated area.

It is surprising to observe that a tremendous construction effort was spent to create all the corridors and chambers that appear within the mound. These were constructed with the judicious use of stones, boulders, etc.,
placed so as to generate walls, ceilings, rooms, alcoves, etc.
If these were to have been used strictly as burial chambers, then these Stone Age people must have had an enormous amount of time on their hands that allowed them to
divert so much time and energy to these underground
habitations. These are not small, timid affairs; on the contrary, they display a very sophisticated capability to create

FIG. 30 — THE SAQQARA STEP PYRAMID, EGYPT

FIG. 31 — PYRAMID OF THE SUN, TEOTIHUACAN, MEXICO

housing units with very course and simple material: stones.

What is still more surprising is the fact that archaeologists have never unearthed any rich artifacts in these long barrows; instead very few skeletons with meager remains are all that have been found. One would think that such an enormous construction effort would have been undertaken to extend a "regal" burial to their chiefs, or kings, just as the Egyptians did. It appears not to have been so at all.

The long barrows give the impression that they were actual underground living quarters for a multitude of people, and that the skeletons found there were only incidental to the main purpose.

Why would "primitive" people have gone through all the trouble of creating such elaborate underground housing projects? Especially as such an attempt is not universally found as a characteristic of Stone Age societies?

One is led to remember the admonitions extended to us by our authorities in the early fifties when an atomic war was considered possible. We were then told that the best defense against contamination by radiation was to reside underground behind thick layers of cement or stone walls, which have the capacity to thwart the penetration of radiation waves. The best protection, in fact, were stones buried behind a mountain of earth.

Be it as it may, the least that we can say is that all of these remains indicate that they were the center of beehive activities. To perform all the constructions in the area, man-power is required, and man-power needs living quarters—it needs a camp. This is exactly what we find slightly north of Stonehenge: a site known today as Avebury (see Fig. 32) It is the largest known circle and henge in England. Not only does it consist of a huge ditch and bank, along with a standing stone circle, but inside that area are additional smaller stone circles. Today almost half the entire village of Avebury lies within this enormous enclosure. Here, hundreds (perhaps thousands) of YAHWEH's helpers may have made their camp and lived during the centuries they spent on earth. The smaller stone circles within the enclosure were possibly used as the boundary for the smaller spaceships.

Avebury is acknowledged to be the largest stone circle in England. Its construction effort is a story in itself, with especially interesting aspects to amaze the thoughtful onlooker. Since all of these details would be beyond the scope of this book, only a few facts will be submitted to illustrate the huge effort exerted here.

It is estimated that about 4000 tons of large boulders were moved into place (about 200 uprights weighing up to about 45 tons each). This, in itself, must have been an herculian task. And to top it all they moved approximately 200,000 tons of chalk/dirt to create the ditch and bank around Avebury. Some sources estimate it to have been about 4,000,000 cubic feet of earth that had to be moved! This task is supposed to have been achieved—we are told —by a limited group of Stone Age laborers, whose only tools were stone picks, and oxen shoulderblade bones. Hardly any stretch of the imagination can accept such a premise.

At any rate, Avebury (Yahwehbury, or the village of YAHWEH) was created and functioned for an untold number of years.

From here perhaps radiated all their activities and plans. From here they may have determined their new explorations, their future trips, and coordinated their arrivals and departures. We could consider Avebury the nerve center and capital of YAHWEH in that part of the world.

After Stonehenge was established and functioning as the central observatory, numerous sorties must have been made with smaller flying units—the ones that used the

FIG. 32 — AERIAL VIEW OF AVEBURY AND VICINITY. SILBURY HILL SHOWS UP ON THE LOWER RIGHT HAND CORNER OF THE PICTURE.

(COURTESY WILTSHIRE COUNTY COUNCIL, WILTSHIRE, ENGLAND.)

FIG. 33 — VIEW OF STONE CIRCLE AND DITCH/BANK CON-
STRUCTION AT AVEBURY, (WILTSHIRE, ENGLAND.)

FIG. 34 — ANOTHER VIEW OF THE STONE CIRCLE OF AVEBURY
(WILTSHIRE, ENGLAND)

FIG. 35 — LARGEST INDIVIDUAL STONE WITHIN THE AVEBURY
STONE CIRCLE. TO REALIZE THE ENORMOUS
SIZE, COMPARE WITH THE 6 FT. (1.80 m) TALL STANDING
PERSON

smaller stone circles of 8 MY and 16 MY. Probably prede-termined routes were established so that individual space ships could visit consecutive stone circles on consecutive dates and collect astronomical data from each of these spots.

While these activities were going on throughout the British Isles, it is certainly to be expected that they started extending their explorations to other continents, to its in-habitants, and to astronomical data-collecting activities in other parts of the world. Europe must have been one of the early territories to be investigated. In France, they may have decided to build their main power collecting units—the stone rows of Morbihan—so as to supply their power requirements throughout the entire region. Of course, we could ask: Why France? Why not set it up in England it-self, or in Spain, or Germany? For the present, we are not yet in a position to have an exact answer to this question.

We can guess that the northern region of France is more centrally located and can feed both England to the north, Spain to the south, and the rest of Europe to the east. Also, perhaps the particular area of France in ques-tion was better situated to capture from space whatever radiation was involved. If we consider that the sunrays were the source, then it could be that the region of Morbi-han had more clement weather than the region of Salis-bury. Naturally, there is also the possibility that the sun might not have been the source of the energy being col-lected. For all we know, there could have been other im-portant radiation sources somewhere in space that were more efficiently harnessed with a collecting trough situ-ated in the region of Carnac, France, rather than in En-gland.

As they proceeded further and further away from En-gland, they would have encountered larger and larger groups of populations. 4000 years ago England, northern France, northern Germany, etc. were very sparsely populated regions. Archaeological studies indicate the presence of very primitive life styles: Stone Age existence, the first step of our movement up the ladder of civilization. In contrast, the Near East, the Meditterranean basin, India, etc. had reached a higher plateau, with infinitely larger populations, organized in more determinable groupings.

As YAHWEH and his crew perhaps met these separate civilizations, they would first have needed to observe and understand the workings of these multitudes. Possibly, at first, they did not try to play God (although the local population might have considered them gods). Instead, they may have wanted to understand local habits, then, possibly introduce cleaner concepts of living—and/or teach basic elementary ideas to the local "intelligentsia." They may not have interfered with the local activities in an overt manner, but tried to guide local rulers and teach them scientific knowledge. At places where they needed the help of the local laboring force, they would probably have camouflaged their project under the guise of local necessities and induce the kings and their courts to perform and apply their plan. They would have found, with time, that the concept of "God" was a catchy one, and that with such a tool they could obtain greater obedience. For example, the large pyramids in Egypt were built supposedly as regal tombs. Nothing so big, so extraordinary, so well engineered, and yet so complicated and mysterious had ever been built before—and certainly not since. Yet, they were perhaps able to convince the Egyptian kings to allow the building of these huge stone pyramids with all their internal passages and rooms. Outwardly, these were patently graves for a specific pharaoh. In actuality, I have serious doubts that this was the true purpose. YAHWEH may have had other needs that required such enormous structures to have been built in stone. We are only at the threshold of our research, but exciting discoveries can be expected in that direction.

Greece, Egypt, Crete, Babylon, India, Persia, etc., are

all civilizations that, somehow or other, flourished suddenly—as though there were a sudden influx of knowledge and technology that appeared on the scene. It is my suggestion that these civilizations were the results of the intermittant relationships of the local population with YAHWEH and his crew.

In the beginning, little civilizations would likely have been impressed with the extraordinary appearances of the beings capable of flying—whom they probably considered gods. In fact, they would have perhaps perceived a multitude of "Gods" simply because of the multitude of helpers or Watchers who came in contact with the local population. These unknowledgeable people naturally would have considered that there existed more than one God (as believed in Greek mythology, and others). While YAHWEH was busy with his plans and travels to other parts of the world, local kings and their "magicians" would have been left to their own devices for stretches of time, during which the tenets and teachings of the outsiders would have been diluted and even forgotten.

With the years, YAHWEH's contacts with the local population, made through their established leadership, would have created certain advancements, but perhaps not produced the type of moral and ethical society desired by YAHWEH. The despotism of the ruling class persisted since they thought they possessed now all the powers and could subjugate everybody else—after all "God" was in touch with them! However, since YAHWEH and his assistants were not constantly present and did not live with these specific groupings, the ruling class did not enjoy a constant guide to prevent them from misusing their new powers, derived from the new teachings. These intermittent contacts would have started the mental process for the existence of divinities. Yet, if not properly digested, this new teaching would degenerate into the creation of golden statues—idols—and would misdirect the tenets of decency, ethics, civilization, as well as the concept of a single omnipotent God. YAHWEH's message was lost and forgotten.

It is at this stage in world history that YAHWEH may have decided to attempt new tactics: to develop a new group of people who would be continually in touch with him and who would be devoted to him so as to follow religiously his teachings and life style. It would have to be a new group of people that were not tarnished with the existing slant on religion or ethics, a group of people who would completely underplay material wealth, but instead, would uphold the moral law as dictated by Him.

He selected a downtrodden, miserably abused group of slaves—the Hebrews—to create out of them[1] the core of a "Nation of Priests" in order to become their God and in order to make His home with them. From there on we are basically aware of what happened and how it did happen. We are aware that YAHWEH had now changed his approach—now he was in the forefront, leading the Hebrews, fighting their battles, imposing his laws, his statutes, displaying directly his fury and his admonitions—he was the "Living God." He accepted the title of God—but under the one condition that the Jews never draw a picture or make a sculpture of him. The Hebrew monotheistic concept required the anonymity of the face or shape of God. We were supposed to consider our God to be a spiritual entity and not a physical one (even though YAHWEH was certainly a physical appearance to our early Hebrew forefathers). He handed over to them the "Law", the Ten Commandments, and helped them elevate themselves into a much higher level of moral and spiritual existence—one that underplayed the physical but stressed the moral and the ethical.

The rest is known as history; the Old Testament reports much that happened from then on.

[1]Exodus: 25:8

12

Myths & Legends

Much has been said in historical writings about a report given by Diodorus of Sicily.[1] There is a passage in which Diodorus quoted Hecataeus, who lived roughly in the year 350 B.C. This report reads as follows:

"Of those who have written about the ancient myths, Hacataeus and certain others say that in the regions beyond the land of the Celts there lies in the ocean an island no smaller than Sicily. This island, the account continues, is situated in the north and is inhabited by the Hyperboreans, who are called by that name because their home is beyond the point whence the north wind blows; and the island is both fertile and productive of every crop, and since it has an unusually temperate climate it produces two harvests each year. Moreover, the following legend is told concerning it: Leto was born on this island, and for that reason Apollo is honored among them above all other gods; and the inhabitants are looked upon

[1]Diodorus Siculus
Translation by C.H. Oldfather
Harvard University Press, 1960

193

as priests of Apollo, after a manner, since daily they praise this god continuously in song and honor them exceedingly. And there is also on the island both a magnificent sacred precinct of Apollo and a notable temple which is adorned with many votive offerings and is spherical in shape. Furthermore, a city is there which is sacred to this god, and the majority of its inhabitants are players on the cithera; and these continually play on this instrument in the temple and sing hymns of praise to the god, glorifying his deeds. The Hyperboreans also have a language, we are informed, which is peculiar to them, and are most friendly disposed towards the Greeks, and especially towards the Athenians and the Delians, who have inherited this good-will from most ancient times. The myth also relates that certain Greeks visited the Hyperboreans and left behind them there costly votive offerings bearing inscriptions in Greek letters. And in the same way Abaris, a Hyperborean, came to Greece in ancient times and renewed the good-will and kinship of his people to the Delians. They say also that the moon, as viewed from this island, appears to be but a little distance from the earth and to have upon it prominences, like those of the earth, which are visible to the eye. The account is also given that the god visits the island every nineteen years, the period in which the return of the stars to the same place in the heavens is accomplished; and for this reason the nineteen-year period is called by the Greeks the "year of Meton." At the time of this appearance of the god he both plays on the citheria and dances continuously the night through from the vernal equinox until the rising of the Pleiades, expressing in this manner his delight in his successes. And the kings of this city and the supervisors of the sacred precincts are called Boreades, since they are descendants of Boreas, and the succession to these positions is always kept in their family."

There has been a general tendency to consider that these statements referred to events in England. It seems that in those centuries England was considered inhabited by Hyperboreans. Whether this report truly refers to the region of England or not, is still a question. Nevertheless, there are some very interesting aspects of the report that accord well with the thesis I have proposed concerning Stonehenge.

The first such statement refers to a magnificent sacred precinct and a noteable temple with its spherical dome. Commentators have interpreted this as a structure that has vanished in the meantime. In the theory I have proposed concerning YAHWEH, there would have been a domed shaped "temple" or structure located in England: the main spaceship, or observatory, stationed atop the Sarsen Circle. Figure 17 shows the type of spaceship suggested by Mr. Blumrich after evaluating the Book of Ezekiel. It did incorporate a spherical dome: the command module of the vehicle. To a person not knowing otherwise this would certainly look like a magnificent sacred temple, spherical in shape.

It is also interesting to observe that the presence of a "god" was considered to have manifested itself in this region. Since the report was written by a Greek scholar, it is natural to expect that he would have borrowed from his own background and conceived of the type of god he was familiar with. And so he called the god Apollo. It is difficult to know why he chose to call him Apollo, as there are a great number of other gods in Greek mythology. Yet, Apollo was the god of healing and was one of the sun gods worshipped by the ancient Greek culture. As we know from our flight patterns, pilots usually keep the sun behind them when landing. An observer on earth watching a descent might sense that the craft was coming from the sun's direction. As a result, unknowledgeable people who witnessed the extraordinary event of a "god" landing on earth, would naturally have considered that the visitors had come from the sun—that their chief was the sun God.

There seems to be a connection between the healing capacities attributed to Apollo and the healing capacities attributed to YAHWEH. As advanced technological persons, it is reasonable to imagine that the Watchers had medical knowledge and would have displayed their prowess by performing regular medical services to the earthlings with whom they came in contact.

A most interesting aspect in the report of Diodorus is the sentence that indicated that on this island the moon appeared to be only a short distance from the earth, and to have mountains and valleys like those of the earth. In modern terminology, the only way a person could observe the moon as especially close to the earth, and to determine the type of surface it has, would be through a telescope. Yet the Greeks in those years did not know what a telescope was and certainly did not have one. Despite this fact, Diodorus correctly described the effect of looking through a powerful telescope. This suggests that on the island (England) at the temple of Apollo (Stonehenge) there were instruments that allowed the eye to see the moon as being close by, and to determine the nature of its surface. Those instruments, or telescopes, would have been naturally found in the "domelike" structure of this supposed "temple": in other words, in the command module atop the spaceship.

Another thought-provoking passage in that report of Diodorus indicated that the god visited the island every nineteen years, which was the period required for the stars to return to the same place in the heavens. The Greeks apparently called this period the "year of Meton."

In modern astronomy we used the phrase "Metonic Cycle" to describe the periodicity of the sun eclipse that takes place at regular intervals of 18.67 years. When re-reading this passage of Diodorus, one can draw a different conclusion than the one tying the 19-year period to the sun eclipse cycle—as was hinted by Professor Hawkins. Diodorus indicated that this was the period necessary for a complete cycle to be performed by the stars in order for them to return to the same place in the heavens as they had occupied before. He is consequently not talking strictly about a connection with the moon and the sun alone. Instead, he seemed to be referring to a movement of a certain star (or star systems) that return to their original position every 19 years. Of course, the term "star" is vague and does not convey a precise meaning as to which stars he was referring to. Yet, the term is quite distinct from sun or moon—words whose meaning and difference were well known to the Greeks. Were these stars within our solar system or were they stars outside our solar system? If they were within our solar system, there are millions of them that might have been meant. Despite the lack of precision in the word, it is compelling to ponder this statement of the Greek historian.

He was referring to "God's" periodic return visits to the temple every nineteen years.[1] This might mean that YAHWEH or his "Watchers" resided for a certain period on earth and returned to their planet (or star). This could indicate the reason why it was important for the "Watchers" to determine the movement of the moon in relationship to the earth and thus pinpoint the entry into the earth's atmosphere of a space vehicle that would place itself in orbit around the earth—just as the moon is orbiting the earth.

The reason given for the importance of this periodic

[1]Should we understand it to mean 19 light-years?

nineteen-year cycle can induce one to presume that when certain stars or star systems were in a specific position vis-a-vis the earth (every 19 years) there was travel possibility from there to earth (and/or vice versa). It seems to indicate that until a certain specific positioning or relationship existed between planet Earth and those other unidentified stars, that the god (YAHWEH) perhaps was not able to easily leave or return to earth. The next question to be asked is: which stars or star groups return to the same position vis-a-vis the earth every nineteen years? Perhaps our astronomers can indicate the existing possibilities.

A further statement in this historical report indicates that there was a magnificent sacred precinct of Apollo, a city sacred to this god. As stated before, close to Stonehenge, we have the largest stone circle in the British Isles. We know it as Avebury. As I tried to show previously, the name Avebury is possibly connected to Hawebury or YAHWEH-bury. Since "bury" means village, it may have been YAHWEH's village. The theory that Avebury was the main living quarters for the group in question would tie in quite readily with the description found in the history of Diodorus.

The suggestion that the Hyperboreans had a language peculiar to them is what we would expect.

All in all, the various descriptions given to us by this surprising report do coincide quite well with the theories presented in this book. We cannot yet be certain that we are talking about the same place. Nevertheless, the probabilities are there.

Indirectly, this report of Diodorus suggests confirmation of what the Bible mentioned, that YAHWEH and his aides were humanoid. The report continues to refer to them in most normal terms as though they were little different from neighbors. That is, there is nothing unusual enough about them to merit comment. Certain Greeks went to the island for a visit—and a reciprocation of previous visits was made by those people to Greece. The whole matter was related as a most natural coming and going of acquaintances, without the slightest remark about any peculiarities concerning the physical appearances of the "Hyperboreans." If these inhabitants had any visible variations from the norm (such as having three eyes, or three legs, or being twenty-five feet tall) this would have been reported as the most obvious and extraordinary observation of this class of gods. Yet, nothing of the sort is happening—that means that there is nothing unusual to report, since these are by all means of judgement, ordinary looking normal human beings.

And finally, a very interesting word was given to us by Diodorus: the Hyperborean who visited Greece was *Abaris.* I believe that etymologists will agree with my analysis of the word:

```
   A-BA—    RIS
   A-VA—    RIS
  YA-VA—    RIS
YAH-WAH—    RIS
```

The ending *is* is the usual ending found in Greek names. Depending upon the previous vowels used, Greek names end in *s.* For example:

> ending in . . . us (i.e. Diodorus)
> ending in . . . es (i.e. Socrates)
> ending in . . . is (i.e. Filipidis)

The *r* used in between is actually a connecting consonant to render the pronounciation more phonetically pleasant. In this particular case, the ending *ris,* is the hellenized termination for YAHWEH.

It is also interesting to evaluate a footnote that appears in Oldfather's translation of *Diodorus Siculus* (Book II). The editor and/or the translator had the following to say in connection with the word *Abaris:*

> "*Abaris* is apparently a purely mythical figure, who, in some authors, sailed on his arrow, as on a witch's broomstick, through the air over rivers and seas."

This means, that the mythical concept of *Abaris* (YAHWAH-RIS) is that of a person flying through the airs. It is certainly interesting that this very particular person should be the one about whom so little is known, except that he was able to fly through the air, over rivers and seas. We know that "myths" are often modern versions of slightly recalled aspects of antiquity. The basic knowledge is hazy and gets blurred, fading into the distant past—yet, there is almost always a core of truth in it. As far as the Greeks were concerned, *Abaris* was not a personage (or God) who was constantly on hand, or allowed himself to be in close touch with them (as YAHWEH had in the case of the Hebrews). Thus not much information has come down to us, although there are other reports about Abaris to be found in Greek mythology—also most interesting. The chief information that survived thousands of years is that he flew through the airs! It fits perfectly with the capabilities of YAHWEH as I have suggested them to this point.

In *The History of the Kings of Britain,* Geoffrey of Monmouth indicated that the stones carried by the magician Merlin had various properties with medicinal powers. In case of sicknesses, it seems that water was poured over these stones to run down the sides and was then collected at the bottom in a tub. The sick would then sit in that water and be cured. Unfortunately, we are not told the type of sickness that was treated thus nor the length of time, etc. Yet there is a very interesting sentence in Geoffrey of Monmouth's account that states: "There is not a single stone among them which has not some medicinal virtue." Can that be taken to mean that all these stones were impregnated with some sort of radiation which, in turn, had healing capacities? This is, of course, what my theory of YAHWEH suggests.

We have repeatedly read of the "healing" powers displayed by these menhirs. People with ailments (which ones—we are not told or vaguely understand) touched the stone, or slept next to it, or danced around it, etc.—and, miraculously, they were healed. This display of "special power" is found not only in British legends—but also in Europe. For example, across the channel from England, the French Bretons insistently repeat the old stories circulating in Brittany: couples that could not have children spent the night dancing around and sleeping next to the stone rows near Carnac. Some stories have them dancing naked—others do not specify that point. But all of them seem to end with the same result: they were cured! How can an inanimate object like a stone have any powers—unless it emits certain radiations? These emissions could be from radioactive ore, intrinsically present in the stone itself—such as uranium, etc. Or else they could also be radiations that were implanted in it.

Electromagnetic fields can be powerful, can be luminescent, can discharge electricity, can emit certain rays. Could it be that YAHWEH and his special radiation is at the basis of all these stories about stones with special powers? We know that certain types of radiation have the capacity to cure various illnesses—we are using such techniques constantly in modern medical treatments.

13

Pictures That Are Worth
a Thousand Words

If my contention is correct, concerning the existence of a powerful central observatory atop the Sarsen Circle then it follows that the immediate area around Stonehenge must have been teeming with activity. A unit such as this would have required numerous deliveries to the spaceship, supplies for its crew, and materials for its reactor. If an extended stay was involved, there must have been constant goings and comings during the centuries in question.

This type of traffic might have left behind some telltale signs that we can locate and decipher. Surprisingly enough, such signs are there.

It is a well-known fact that the techniques of aerial photography have advanced to the extent that such photographs can pinpoint the minutest detail in a picture taken dozens of miles above the earth. In fact, our defense establishments are constantly relying on pictures taken from our satellites in orbit around the earth. It is through this method that we are able to monitor the ground activities and military preparations of our enemies. A well-trained team of interpreters can determine an enormous amount of information from aerial photographs, and describe in detail the occurrences taking place, or having taken place, on the ground. And, if different types of films are used, we are able to obtain a still greater spectrum of data, which can lead to finer adjustment of the interpretation.

Even without the introduction of these advanced modern techniques, simple aerial photography displays details that cannot be discerned from the ground. The chapter at hand presents a series of pictures taken during the past seventy-five years, depicting the general area around Stonehenge.

Before examining these pictures, it is important to have an overall idea of what "barrows" are. This term is used to denote mounds of earth, usually circular in shape. Elongated "long" barrows, or elliptical ones, are also encountered around the English countryside, although much less frequently. The round barrows have been classified according to their cross sectional forms. A few of these classifications are indicated in Fig. 36. Their sizes vary from an overall diameter of about 165 ft. (50 m.) to about 42 ft. (13 m.)

Most of these barrows are surrounded by a ditch-and-bank construction. It has been estimated that at one time the British Isles contained over 100,000 units. A great many of them are still visible today, although large numbers have been flatened and plowed under.

In general, barrows have been considered to represent burial mounds for one or more human beings. A good many of these sites have produced traces of human internments, be it in the form of inhumations, or cremations. However, the internment sequence assigned to these findings has generated doubts. Whether the skeletal remnants were of a primary or of a secondary nature, has been a moot question. In other words, one is not completely certain whether the internment took place at the same time as the construction of the barrow, or whether the body was placed into the ground long after the barrow

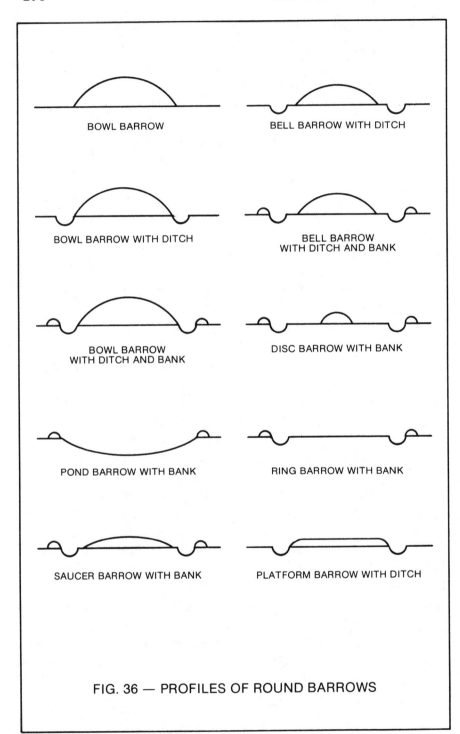

FIG. 36 — PROFILES OF ROUND BARROWS

was in existence. While some barrows have not contained internments, a great many of them have yet to be opened, and, as a result, their contents are unknown.

Fig. 37 represents an aerial photograph taken from a balloon in 1906 by Lt. P.A. Sharp of the Royal Engineers of England.[1] The first aspects that stand out are the roads that cross the Stonehenge grounds. Whether these were created 5000 years ago, or whether they are the result of the constant traffic during the past 500 years or so, cannot be answered with any degree of accuracy. The obvious fact remains that a number of roads did pass through the general circled area of'this monument.

The surprising aspects revealed in this photograph are the various individual small circles that appear throughout the area. These circles are clearly defined by the contrast in the shading of the ground.

Fig. 39 is another photograph taken in 1906 by the same Lt. Sharp and showing an oblique view of the grounds. Once again we observe very sharply defined circles, which have been reproduced on the accompanying sketch (Fig. 40) for greater clarity. Although picture-taking techniques in 1906 were naturally not as advanced as today's techniques, nevertheless they did bring out details that could not escape the mechanical impartiality of the lens.

With the advent of the fixed-wing airplane, new pictures were taken in the 1920s, displaying a greater degree of clarity. In Fig. 41, another oblique shot, we can discern again the same enigmatic circle formations around the general area of Stonehenge; these have been enhanced in the accompanying sketch Fig. 42.

[1]Figs. 37–39–41–43–45–47–52—53–56–60–67 have been supplied by the British Government from their National Monuments Record Collection of the Royal Commission on Historical Monuments (England). I am indebted to them for their gracious permission to reproduce and publish them, as well as to Terry Betts of their Air Photographs Units, for the patience in answering my inquisitive questions. (Crown Copyright reserved)

FIG. 37 — AERIAL PHOTOGRAPH OF STONEHENGE TAKEN FROM A BALLOON IN 1906 BY LT. P. A. SHARP OF THE ROYAL ENGINEERS OF THE BRITISH ARMY

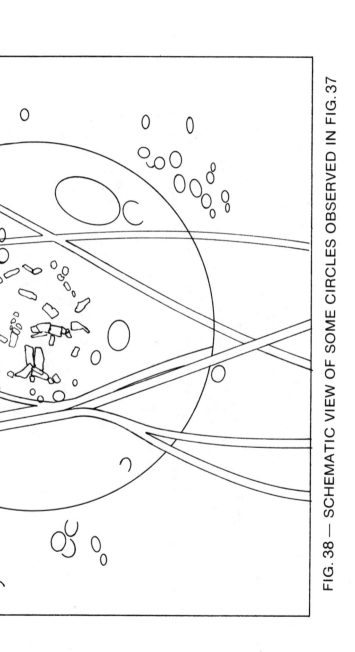

FIG. 38 — SCHEMATIC VIEW OF SOME CIRCLES OBSERVED IN FIG. 37

FIG. 39 — OBLIQUE AERIAL VIEW OF STONEHENGE, AGAIN TAKEN FROM A BALLOON IN 1906 BY LT. P. A. SHARP

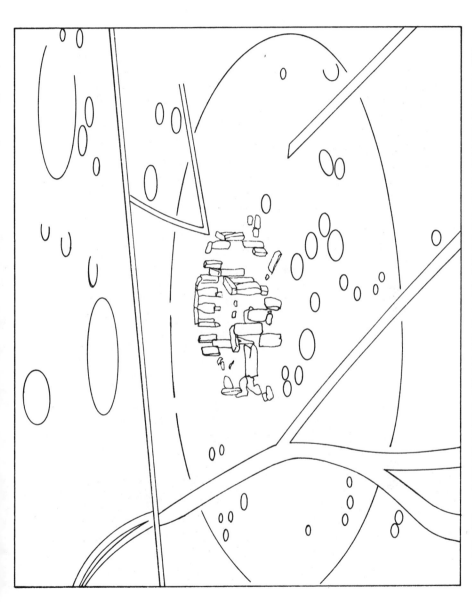

FIG. 40 — SCHEMATIC VIEW OF SOME CIRCLES OBSERVED IN FIG. 39

FIG. 41 — AERIAL VIEW OF STONEHENGE TAKEN IN THE 1920's

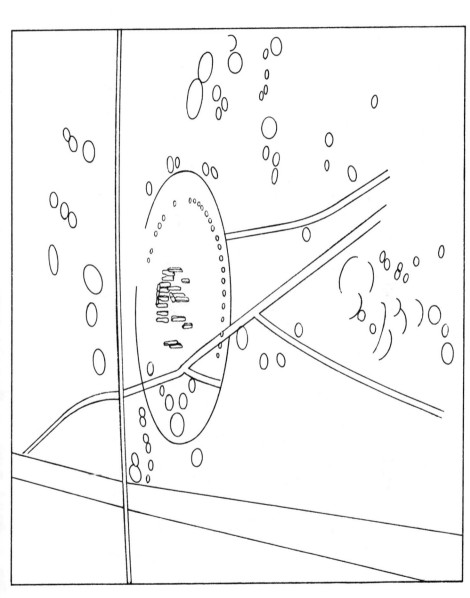

FIG. 42 — SCHEMATIC VIEW OF SOME CIRCLES OBSERVED IN FIG. 41

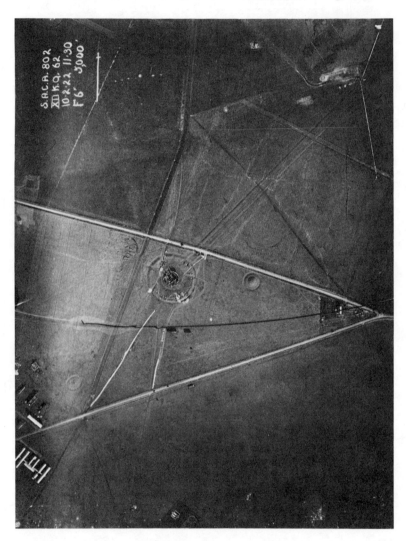

FIG. 43 — VIEW OF STONEHENGE AND ITS SURROUNDINGS TAKEN IN 1922 FROM AN ALTITUDE OF 5000 FT. (ABOUT 1500 m.)

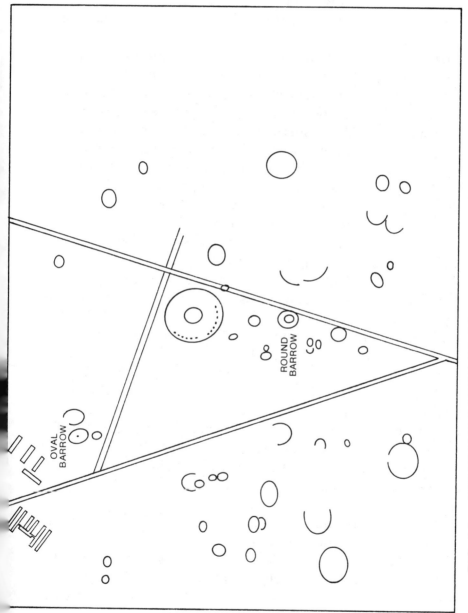

FIG. 44 — SCHEMATIC VIEW OF SOME CIRCLES OBSERVED IN FIG. 43

Fig. 43 was taken in 1922 from an altitude of 5000 ft. (1500 m.) and shows additional clear details of these same circles. As the area covered in this photograph is larger, we observe that such "circles" also prove to be present further away from the center of the monument, all the way on the meadows that surround it. This picture also depicts for us, in a very sharp manner, two barrows near Stonehenge. Barrow No. 1 is a very well-defined circular mound with a ditch surrounding it. However, barrow No. 2 is a much shallower oval mound encompassed by a precisely designed oval ditch. Oddly enough it also reveals some sort of object on top of the mound that casts a shadow in the same direction as those created by the upright Sarsen stones of Stonehenge. This gives the impression that the object in question is a small upright stone. Two aspects are thought provoking:

a) The perfection of the ovalness of the ditch is remarkable. Primitive people, using oxen shoulder blades as picks and shovels, would have had a very difficult time creating a ditch, let alone worrying about the perfect geometrical precision of an oval, especially one of such large size. We know that the Sarsen Circle is about 100 ft. (about 30 m.) in diameter. In comparison, the oval barrow seems to be about 90 ft. (27 m.) on its small axis and about 110 ft. (33 m.) on its long axis—a very impressive dimension for an oval barrow. Such a perfection of the oval shape leads one to believe that it must have been created by mechanical means—a luxury that these primitive stone age people did not, to our knowledge, enjoy.

b) The existence of an object, or stone, in the middle of the oval mound opens up new possibilities that we had looked for, but not found, in the past (see page 109.) If a point atop this object is connected by a straight line to the center of the Sarsen Circle, its extension will intersect the Heel Stone. Could it be that this is the missing second point that would have determined the direction of the midsummer sunrise? As stated in previous chapters, the direction of a line can be determined only by connecting two points. Previous archaeological research did not uncover any traces of the existence of a center stone in the middle of the Sarsen Circle. Thus, the Heel Stone, being one of the points of this imaginary line, could not have performed by itself, but would have needed an accompanying stone. This second stone could not have been in the middle of the circle, since that center would have been covered by the spaceship and its radioactive power plant. Instead, the marker could have been located inside the command module, on top of the vehicle. Yet, it also follows that the operators of the vehicle had to guide themselves—originally—by an existing marker that had already pinpointed the direction of the midsummer sunrise, in conjunction with the Heel Stone. If such a marker had been placed in the center of the Sarsen Circle, it would have been useless to the operators sitting above it, since they would not see it. However, a stone placed atop the oval barrow could have been seen easily from the command module. Thus, the crew would have been given the possibility of lining their desk marker with the exact line connecting the Heel Stone to the oval barrow's stone. This suggestion should be checked in the field since the present analysis, performed on paper, is not sufficiently accurate to prove the existence of a scientifically correct alignment.

In 1923 another photograph (Fig. 45) was taken, this time from an altitude of 3000 ft. (about 900 m.) Again we observe a very clear rendition of the enigmatic "circles." This particular picture displays some very clear details throughout the entire area. Possibly the angle at which the lens took the picture, combined with the light direction of the sun, might have created an ideal condition to enhance the details of these "circles." As shown on the corresponding sketch (Fig. 46), a great number and variety

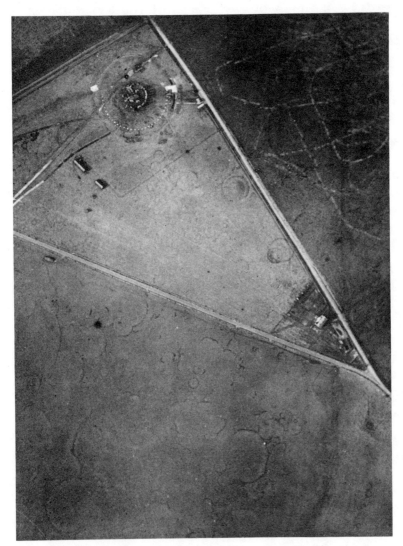

FIG. 45 — AERIAL VIEW OF STONEHENGE TAKEN IN 1923 FROM AN ALTITUDE OF 3000 FT. (900 m.)

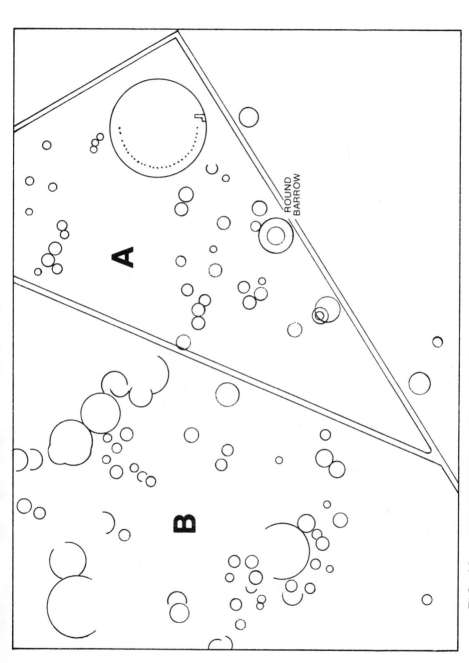

ROUND
BARROW

A

B

FIG. 46 — SCHEMATIC VIEW OF SOME CIRCLES OBSERVED IN FIG. 45

of sizes of circles appear, some of the circles being superimposed on other circles.

In the lower right-hand corner of the picture we observe certain criss-crossed white lines. They seem to be the product of vehicle tracks that must have dug deeply enough into the topsoil so as to lay bare the chalky ground that covers the entire region underneath the surface. We do not know who made these tracks and what sort of vehicle was used. It is possible that a modern tractor roamed aimlessly in this meadow, although farmers are not known to have been particularly keen during the 1920s on killing time by driving around haphazardly, especially on grounds that they were not tilling for their crops. Whatever the explanation, the fact remains that these peculiar lines show quite clearly on this particular picture.

Moreover, a closer look through a magnifying glass indicates that the shape observed has not been created by straight lines. Instead there appears a sequence of dotted lines, as though a tractor's plow (if it was a plow!) jumped and skipped, up and down, as it moved along. Toward the lower right-hand corner of the picture, one can observe additional dotted lines, without discerning a pattern.

However, a pattern emerges quite clearly in the next photograph (Fig. 47) taken also during the 1920s. Unfortunately, the exact date could not be determined, although it was probably taken at about the same time as Fig. 45. The criss-crossed lines we observed in the lower right-hand corner of the previous picture, do not show up as clearly, while other lines (that remained outside of the frame of Fig. 45) indicate new forms. Again we find the same phenomenon as before: namely, dotted lines that seemed to have bared the white chalky underground beneath the surface of the topsoil. As in a Rorschach ink test, different individuals would see various objects formed by these lines. To me they give the impression of a bird in flight.

The fact remains that some sort of shapes appear to

have been "etched" on these grounds. Naturally, one's mind immediately connects this with other similar sites to be found in England: the Cerne Abbas giant of Dorset, the Long Man of Wilmington (East Sussex), the Uffington white horse (Berkshire). In all these cases, shapes and forms were cut into the topsoil so as to bare the underground chalk and thus produce the desired effect. At the present stage we do not understand the significance of these forms.

Fig. 47 is quite important from a different point of view. It supplies a very clear rendition of the enigmatic "circles" that can be seen all around the Stonehenge area. There are dozens of these circles, some of which were redrawn on the corresponding sketch Fig. 48. There is a peculiar difference between Fig. 45 and Fig. 47. In the latter, within triangle "A," formed by the roads, the circumference of the "circles" is dark, with the center being lighter. On the other hand, in the left area, "B," we can observe that the periphery of these "circles" is white, while the centers are dark.

In Fig. 45 the area "B" to the left proves to be the opposite. Here, the periphery is dark, while the center is lighter. However, when it comes to the "circles" within triangle "A," we see again the same situation we encountered in Fig. 47; namely, a dark circumference delineating a less dark center. This means that the photographs shown in Fig. 45 and Fig. 47 are identical as far as the "circles" inside triangle "A" are concerned—yet, they are different as far as the circles in area "B" are involved. Why is that so? Could it be the result of the refraction of the sun's rays acting variously on different types of ground? Or could it be that the character underlying the creation of these "circles" in area "A" was different than that of area "B?"

Another picture taken in the 1920s also reveals this phenomenon (Fig. 52) Similar characteristics are observ-

FIG. 47 — ANOTHER AERIAL VIEW OF STONEHENGE TAKEN IN THE 1920s

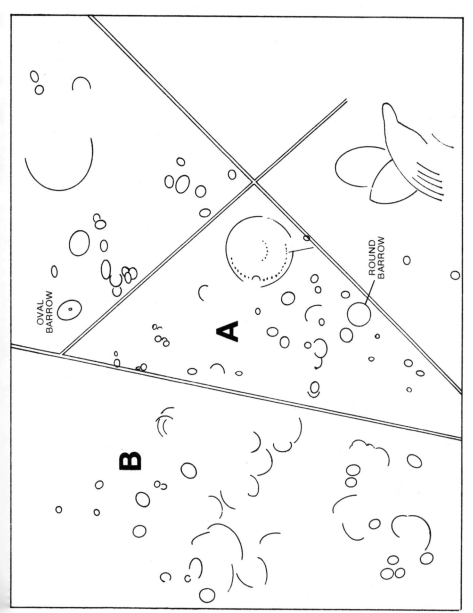

FIG. 48— SCHEMATIC VIEW OF SOME CIRCLES OBSERVED IN FIG. 47

able: the "circles" have the same black and white scheme as the ones in Fig. 45. We also observe that the criss-crossed lines are again visible. The "bird-in-flight" is discernable, as well as additional unrecognizable lines under its feet.

The same details appeared again in a picture taken in 1928 (Fig. 54). The oval barrow observed in Fig. 43 and in Fig. 47 is less defined here and does not display as sharp a characteristic as it did in those earlier pictures. Although the general oval shape does show up, it is difficult to determine whether that barrow continued to exist. Nevertheless, the important consideration is the fact that a number of circular imprints continued to appear in this photograph.

Again the mysterious circular imprints show up in another aerial photograph of the Stonehenge area, taken in 1930 (Fig. 56). The section within the immediate vicinity of the monument displays these circles in such an obvious manner that a separate sketch was actually not necessary. Interestingly enough, some of these circles are sharply defined; others are not—they are much less discernable, as though they were "older" imprints that were fading away. Some circles have an almost geometrically precise circular periphery, while others have a roundish form that is not exactly a perfect circle. Finally, we observe a variety of sizes among the various circles.

Even in 1962, when another picture was taken, (Fig. 57) a repetition of the same manifestation appeared. This particular picture restricted the general area of sight; nevertheless, it clearly displays a number of circular imprints within Stonehenge's immediate vicinity. The interesting aspect to be remembered is that by 1962 the ground within the Aubrey Circle had probably undergone a number of disturbances, such as diggings, resodding, levelings, etc. Despite these upheavals, the enigmatic circles continued to appear, as captured through the lens of an aerial camera.

FIG. 49 — THE LONG MAN OF WILMINGTON
(EAST SUSSEX, ENGLAND)

FIG. 50 — THE UFFINGTON WHITE HORSE
(BERKSHIRE, ENGLAND)

FIG. 51 — THE CERNE ABBAS GIANT (DORSET, ENGLAND)
THE HEIGHT OF THE FIGURE IS 180 FT. (55 m.),
THE CLUB IS 120 FT. (36 m.) LONG

And finally, in 1981, newer aerial pictures were taken during a land survey study performed by the Wiltshire County Council. Fig. 58 displays interesting aspects. In the first place it reestablishes the existence of the myterious circles observed as far back as 1906 (Fig. 37 and 39). This means that during the past 75 years, these circles continued to exist and are still showing up in our today's aerial photographs.

A comparison of Fig. 43 with Fig. 58 points to a visual reconfirmation of the above tentative conclusion. In the earlier picture, taken in 1922, we observe, in the upper left corner of the triangle produced by the roads around Stonehenge, the existence of a number of buildings or barracks (also depicted in Fig. 53). These belonged to an air force airfield that functioned during World War I and a few years thereafter. Sometime after 1922, these buildings were destroyed and the ground flattened out, thus returning it to its original state of empty meadows, as now shown in Fig. 58. The interesting aspect, however, is the fact that the ground once covered by these barracks displays again the existence of circles. In other words, even though the topsoil has been mightily disturbed by constructions and destructions of buildings, by constant vehicular and personnel traffic, the circles could simply not be destroyed. They have reappeared very clearly, irrespective of what activity has taken place on the topsoil.

Additional pictures taken in 1981 for the Wiltshire County Council indicate the same phenomenon of the circles, on other sites in the general area around Stonehenge.

Naturally, we have to ask ourselves: what are these circles?

The first obvious explanation that comes to mind is that they were the result of a careless handling and washing of the negatives during the development process. Theoretically it is possible that drops of fixing or developing solutions were left to dry on the negatives, thus resulting in circular specks. Such an explanation is not satisfactory since photographs developed over decades show the same positioning of many of the circles. An imperfect developing of different negatives could not duplicate the positioning of the circles.

If these circles are not the byproducts of faulty developing processes, then what are they, how were they created, and who could have produced them?

At this stage of the research, an exact answer is not forthcoming without at least additional tests of the grounds, using special aerial photography techniques, soil sampling, and radiation tests. Nevertheless, there are a few answers that could be considered, even though they are hypothetical, at present:

We have suggested that a spaceship, circular in form, was positioned atop the Stonehenge monument. Yahweh and his helpers may have commanded these circular

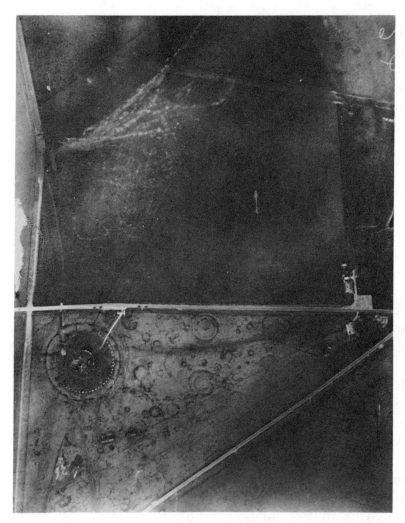

FIG. 52 — STONEHENGE, AS SEEN FROM THE AIR, IN THE 1920s. THE AUBREY HOLES APPEAR VERY SHARPLY AS WHITE DOTS

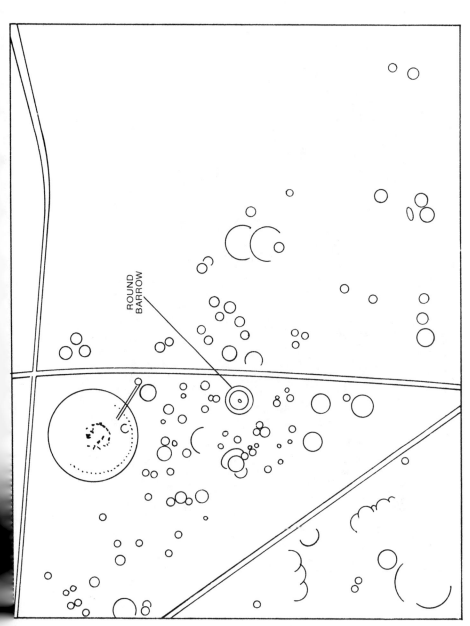

ROUND
BARROW

FIG. 53 — SCHEMATIC VIEW OF SOME CIRCLES OBSERVED IN FIG. 52

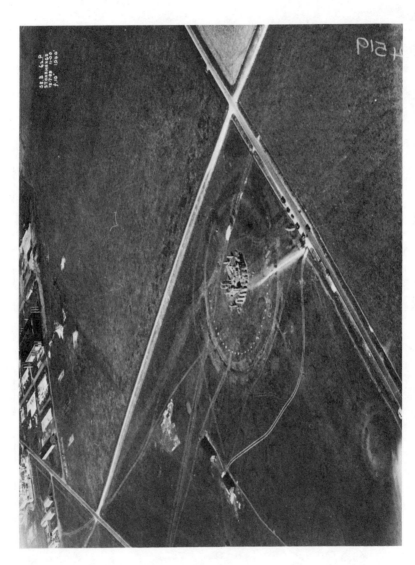

FIG. 54 — AN OBLIQUE AERIAL VIEW OF STONEHENGE AND ITS ENVIRONS TAKEN IN 1928

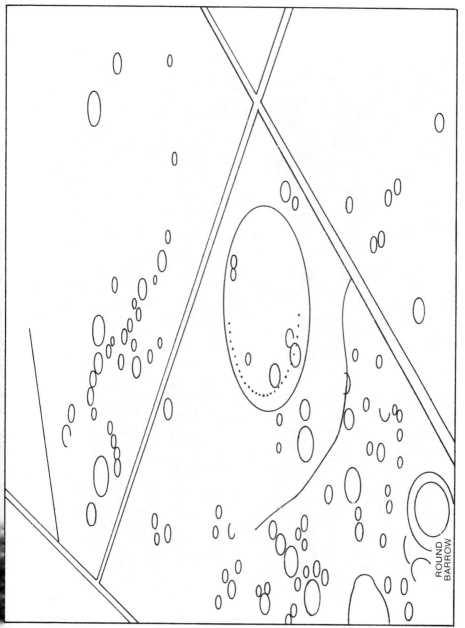

ROUND BARROW

FIG. 55 — SCHEMATIC VIEW OF SOME CIRCLES OBSERVED IN FIG. 54

FIG. 56 — AERIAL PHOTOGRAPH OF STONEHENGE TAKEN IN 1930. THE AUBREY HOLES ARE REGISTERING VERY CLEARLY AS WHITE DOTS ALONG THE ARC OF A PERFECT CIRCLE.

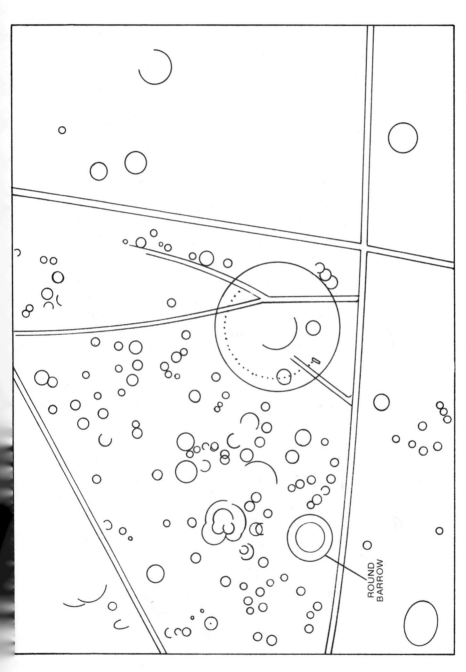

FIG. 56a — SCHEMATIC VIEW OF SOME CIRCLES OBSERVED IN FIG. 56

ROUND
BARROW

shaped flying machines. Because of the importance of Stonehenge to the entire system possibly developed by this group, acting as it did as the nerve center of all their activities on this planet, it can be deduced that a major activity must have occured there. A tremendous amount of traffic must have taken place there over a span of at least 2000 years. These comings and goings would have consisted of sorties of various smaller individual spaceships, each circular in shape. The ground of the landing spot would not have been especially important, so that the marks left by each subsequent landing might have been superimposed on those made by a previous touchdown. Thus, the signs we see today could be the last impressions left before the group finally departed from this planet.

Why is it that such flying spaceships would leave circular imprints that are discernable on the ground after so many thousands of years? It gives us the impression that during landing (and/or take off) these flying units or their legs must have been rotating themselves onto the ground and thus crating perfectly round ditches, some of which we call disc barrows. The perfection of the round shapes we now see on the ground indicates the impressions of mechanically perfect circular shapes of the flying units.

It is also possible that small jets (or other types of propulsion systems) around the circumference of these flying ships emitted thrusts that created the circular ditches. One thing is certain: A study of a good many barrows— including the one so clearly shown next to Stonehenge in Figs. 43, 45, and 47—induces us to think that such perfect circular shapes could have been generated only by mechanical means; they could not be, it would seem, the product of human hand labor. The perfection of the shapes, and their constant repetition throughout the British countryside, in the form of thousands of barrows, hint at the presence of a machine.

Some of the circles we now see in these photographs,

could possibly be the traces of ditches originally created by circular space ship, then subsequently overgrown by vegetation and partly flattened out. These shapes are not easily observed from the ground, but become much clearer when viewed from the air. Naturally the refraction of the light at the moment of picture taking could play a role in giving us a better or worse contrast. This means that what we see today, could be the faint traces of the ditches around the barrows.

There is a second theory that could be advanced. We have had indications that some sort of radioactive radiation was emitted by YAHWEH's flying machines. If that were so, then, during a landing period, the soil and vegetation under the circular space ship would have been affected. If the radiation was strongest around the periphery, then grass or shrubs in those particular spots would have been exposed to a higher degree than that in the center of the circle (or vice-versa). As a result there would have been a mutation in the cellular structure of the plants. This could translate itself, even after a long period of time, into darker or lighter, denser or sparser, shoots of grass or plants. If that were so, then tests performed today on the vegetation of those areas could possibly give us some substantiation. Whatever the original cause might have been, the fact remains that as late as 1981, there appeared light and dark areas in the form of circles.

A third theory could be submitted to explain this mysterious occurrence. When looking at the various pictures presented up to this point, one is struck by the haphazard location of the circles. Although some of these are of almost identical size, there are a good many that vary considerably in dimension. There is no real uniformity, especially in the circles appearing in Figs. 43, 45, 47, and 52. The ones further from Stonehenge tend to be much larger than those nearer the monument.

The way these circles appear brings to mind an every-

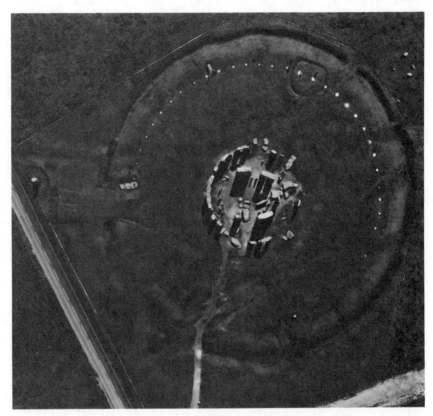

FIG. 57 — OBLIQUE AIR PHOTOGRAPH OF STONEHENGE, TAKEN IN 1962 (COURTESY OF MERIDIAN AIRMAPS, ENGLAND)

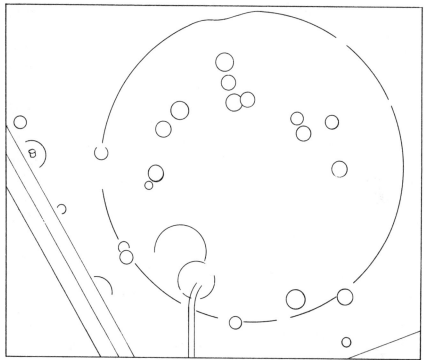

FIG.57a — SCHEMATIC VIEW OF SOME CIRCLES OBSERVED IN FIG. 57

day home occurrence. In washing dishes, we usually splatter drops of water onto the plastic kitchen counters. These drops of water, falling as they do from above the countertops, hit the surfaces in circular shapes, since the water drops have a round cross-section. They then spread over the surface of the countertops and become diffused. Depending upon the surface characteristics of that top (such as the presence of oil, grease, dirt, etc.) the water drops spread in a slightly irregular manner, producing a generally roundish form, although not necessarily a perfect circle. If the surface is of truly uniform consistency, we find round moist areas. The same type of phenomenon is created when individual raindrops splash against the glass of a car's windshield. They produce roundish circles.

The photographs in Figs. 43 through 56 suggest a similar occurrence. One gets the feeling that large drops fell from above onto the ground and spread in a circular manner.

In earlier chapters we surmised that the destruction of the original Stonehenge structure was not due to the fury of some unknown tribes who wanted desperately to dismantle it, stone by stone. After half the dismantling process was accomplished, those in charge seemed to have tired, since they ceased any further destructive activity. I had suggested that the destruction was the result of some man-made explosion.

In old mythological reports from various parts of the world, we read about "wars of the Gods" who were out to destroy each other through fierce and terrible combat. (One would have thought that true "Gods" would have had more sense than to wage wars—a stupidity usually reserved for earthlings! Or are we to conclude that those whom ancient peoples called "Gods" were nothing else but technologically advanced human beings?) If we consider that such wars could have been waged, then YAHWEH—as a "God"—could have had his enemies too, determined to destroy him and his nerve center of Stonehenge. Could it be that these circles and/or near circles were the after-effects of a concentrated bombardment from the air? Under familiar twentieth-century procedures, such an action should have produced craters in the ground. But we do not encounter such craters around Stonehenge. However, we might consider that people controlling radioactive capacities could possibly have used bombs that spread radiation over the surface of the ground from the point of impact, thereby producing the circles. Although such a theory is naturally far-fetched—at least at the present stage of our research—it does support the previous conclusion of the destruction of Stonehenge through an explosion.

Finally, we could combine the various above-mentioned theories, and consider that the mysterious circles seen in the pictures presented, were partly the result of attempts at destruction and partly the result of the activities of spaceships. The perfect circles could be attributed to the landing of circular objects, while the diffuse roundish forms might be the after-effects of radioactive bombardment, and perhaps partly the optical effect of superimposition of various circles at different times.

Parenthetically let it be noted that these pictures were submitted to experts in aerial photography and photogrammetry for their evaluation. They were baffled and could not explain the circles, since they had never encountered them before in their disciplines or in their professional activities.

In due time we will find the answers to these enigmas.

We can go one step further in our analysis and consider the following:

If there really were round flying ships that landed around the Stonehenge area, then, logically speaking, these same units must have lifted off and landed in other

FIG. 58 — AERIAL PICTURE OF STONEHENGE AND ITS VICINTY TAKEN IN 1981

(COURTESY WILTSHIRE COUNTY COUNCIL, WILTSHIRE, ENGLAND)

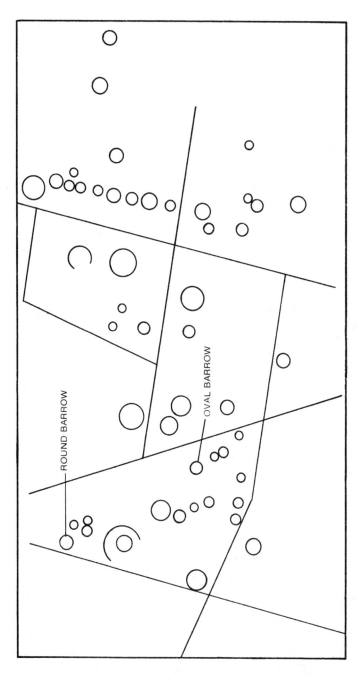

FIG. 59 — SCHEMATIC VIEW OF SOME CIRCLES OBSERVED IN FIG. 58

spots. The chances are that a flying unit will not remain permanently grounded in one spot, or remain constantly flying through the air. Thus, for this theory to be valid, this phenomenon of circular imprints must repeat itself on other sites. We should be able to detect them in other areas that show the remnants of the megalithic construction effort: stone circles, barrows of all kinds, tumuli, dolmen, henges, etc. And amazingly enough, this is exactly what we observe when we carefully scan aerial photographs of other areas.

Fig. 60 shows an aerial photograph taken in 1930 of the Winterbourne Stoke barrow group, in Wiltshire, England, depicting the various acknowledged round barrows as well as the famous long barrow. The interesting parts of this photograph are the innumerable "circles" that appear throughout the picture. Surprisingly enough, they resemble very much the dense circular imprints we observed around Stonehenge in Figs. 45, 47, and 52. Winterbourne Stoke is only about 2½ miles (3.75 kilometers) northwest of Stonehenge.

In 1933, another picture of the Winterbourne Stoke (Fig. 62) was taken. Again, a large number of circular imprints show up in the same general positions as in Fig. 60. There are so many of them that it becomes logically very difficult, if not impossible, to consider them remnants of old, leveled barrows.

In 1950 a very clear photograph of the Lambourn Barrows in Berkshire, England, (Fig. 63) was taken. It depicts the same circular pattern, in addition to the obvious round barrows. Yet, the interesting aspect is the fact that these circles now appear in the plowed fields. Fig. 64 offers a schematic drawing of the circles.

A very similar display can be observed in Fig. 65, which represents an aerial picture of Arbury Banks, Hertfordshire, England, taken in 1937, of plowed fields revealing sharply defined circles. The fact that the ground was cultivated, plowed and turned over, did not destroy some of the circles.

Fig. 67, taken in 1926, presents the area around the famous Woodhenge circular monument, located slightly north of Amesbury in Wiltshire, England. The same phenomenon observed throughout the previous pictures is repeated: very clear circular imprints that show up throughout plowed fields. In some instances, certain circles appear to intersect other circles—an indication that these might not have been true barrows with their characteristic individual ditches since we have not previously encountered round barrows whose ditches intersect.

Near Amesbury, Wiltshire, England, and within sight of Stonehenge, there lies a plowed field, aerial photographs of which were taken in the 1920s and thereafter. (Fig. 69) These pictures depict the existence of an oval shaped circle, about 180 ft. (55 m.) by 150 ft. (45 m.) as measured along its two axis. It was classified as a Class I henge, which, by definition, meant a bank-and-ditch construction whose circumference is interrupted by one "entrance." Historical reports have never referred to the existence of an earthen construction in this particular spot. Since 1562 it has been known as a plowed field under the name of Middle Field. In other words, we have here a field that has been constantly plowed for over 400 years—and yet, we can still observe a sharply defined oval shape when seen from the air. The constant turning over of the topsoil was simply unable to destroy or obliterate the traces of this very old henge earthwork! Or was it really a henge earthen construction to start with?

And finally, the clearest and most electrifying picture showing circular imprints within plowed fields: Fig. 70. It displays the Wilsford Barrows in Wiltshire, England, roughly 1½ miles (about 2½ kilometers) southwest of Stonehenge. The accompanying schematic drawing (Fig. 71) pinpoints for us the great many additional

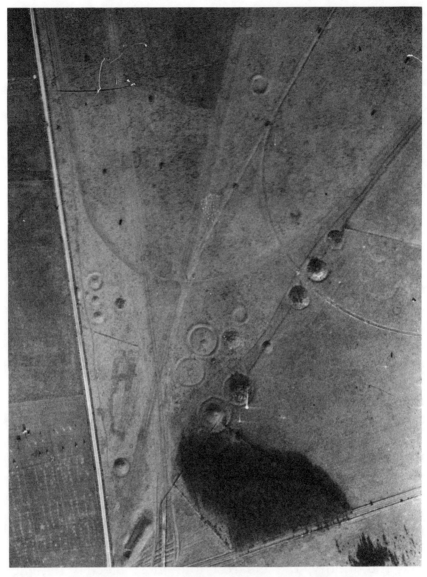

FIG. 60 — WINTERBOURNE STOKE BARROW GROUP (WILTSHIRE,
ENGLAND). THIS PHOTOGRAPH WAS TAKEN IN 1930.

FIG. 61 — SCHEMATIC VIEW OF SOME CIRCLES OBSERVED
IN FIG. 60

FIG. 62 — AERIAL PHOTOGRAGH OF WINTERBOURNE STOKE BARROW GROUP TAKEN IN 1933 (COPYRIGHT ASHMOLEAN MUSEUM)

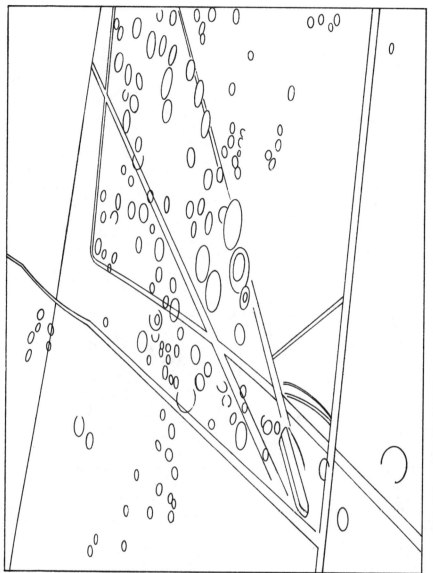

FIG. 62a– SCHEMATIC VIEW OF SOME CIRCLES OBSERVED IN FIG. 62

FIG. 63 — BIRD'S EYE VIEW OF LAMBOURN BARROWS (BERKSHIRE, ENGLAND) TAKEN IN 1950 (COURTESY UNIVERSITY OF CAMBRIDGE—CROWN COPYRIGHT RESERVED)

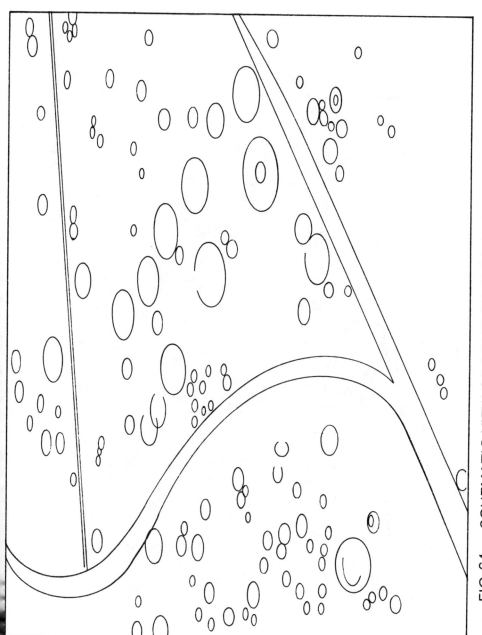

FIG. 64 — SCHEMATIC VIEW OF SOME CIRCLES OBSERVED IN FIG. 63

FIG. 65 — AERIAL PHOTOGRAPH OF ARBURY BANKS (HERTFORDSHIRE, ENGLAND) TAKEN IN 1937 (COPYRIGHT ASHMOLEAN MUSEUM)

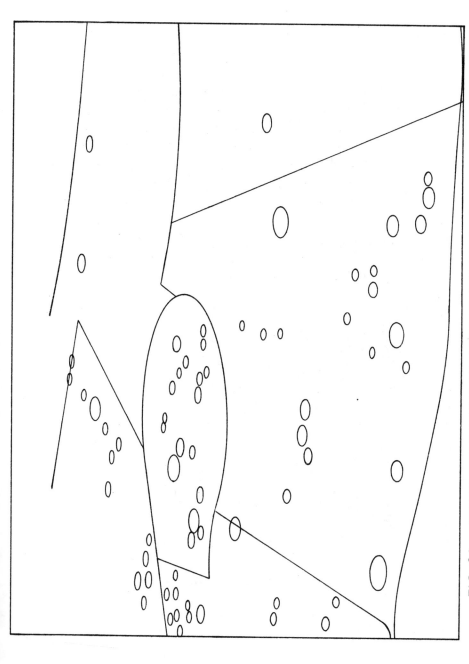

FIG. 66 — SCHEMATIC VIEW OF SOME CIRCLES OBSERVED IN FIG. 65

FIG. 67 — AERIAL PHOTOGRAPH OF WOODHENGE AND ITS IMMEDIATE ENVIRONS, TAKEN IN 1926.

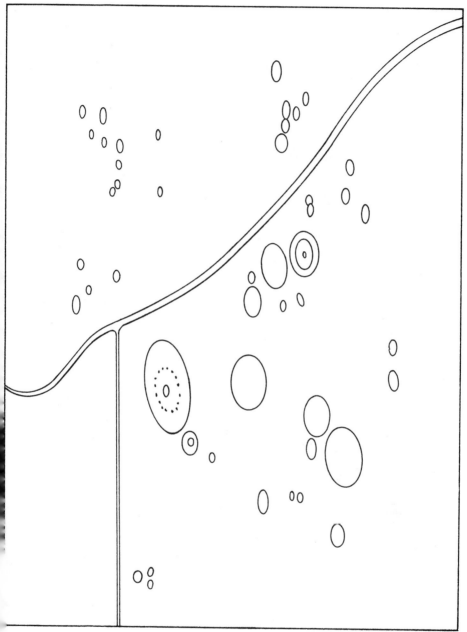

FIG. 68 — SCHEMATIC VIEW OF SOME CIRCLES OBSERVED IN FIG. 67

circles that can be observed in this aerial photograph.

There are a good many other aerial photographs of various sites that duplicate, again and again, the same occurrence. It is naive to believe that stone-age inhabitants of the area had the free time to create thousands of circles on the ground, throughout a wide region of the countryside.

The fact that enigmatic circles are clearly discernable in plowed fields is thought provoking. Initially we considered that these round shapes might merely be the remaining traces of ditches characteristic of barrow constructions. The slight undulations of the ground, representing the different heights of the ditches and the banks, in relation to each other, might have been responsible for the optical effect that appeared in previous photographs. Such a theory could have been defended, had the circles appeared only on virgin land—meadows—that had not been tampered with during the past centuries. But since the topsoil has been cultivated, hoed, turned over, dug into, and leveled, it should have played havoc with these circles; and these activities should have destroyed most, if not all, of the unevenness of the surfaces. And yet, nothing of the sort seems to have occurred. These circles appear very clearly on the photographs of the plowed fields, as though the physical characteristics of the surface are completely immaterial.

This could mean that what we see today is the effect of some sort of radiation that penetrated these grounds 4000–5000 years ago—radiation that was generated by the circular shapes of the flying vehicles of Yahweh and his assistants.

We do know, as a matter of fact, that in certain sites there are discolored portions of the ground as well as soil marks. However, we cannot positively state that all displays of circles in aerial photos are the result of discolored

FIG. 69 — BIRD'S EYE VIEW OF A HENGE ON CONEYBURY HILL, WILTSHIRE, ENGLAND, CLEARLY SHOWING AN OVAL SHAPE WITHIN A FLATTENED PLOWED FIELD. THIS PICTURE WAS TAKEN IN 1954.

topsoil. There are indications that a number of these circles are not observable from the ground, but become visible only when viewed from the air. Consequently, one is inclined to believe—at least at the present stage of the investigation—that we are confronted with both types of situations: those displaying discolored ground and those appearing despite uniform coloration of the topsoil. There could be two distinct logical explanations:

1) In the case of the discolored ground, the photographs may have simply registered the light and dark areas of the topsoil. Considering that these circles originally may have been created by radiation emitted from circular flying ships, it is possible that the areas in question indicate the saturation of radiation through the changes in the coloring of the ground. Vegetation in those areas might have been affected by this radiation, and as a result, have become darker, denser, or sparcer.

Such an explanation is plausible for regular meadows —that is, virgin land that has not been disturbed over a long span of time.

In the case of cultivated fields that have been plowed again and again over dozens of years—if not hundreds of years—it is logical to assume that by now the top surface has been continually reworked and rearranged to the extent that any original dark and light areas on the surface must have been thoroughly mixed so as to generate today a relatively uniform grey surface. Previously appearing circular shapes in such locations should have certainly disappeared. Also, considering that chemical fertilizers have probably been added to the surfaces of the plowed fields, a more uniform coloration of the topsoil might be expected. Yet, the circular patterns are still visible in the aerial photographs.

Although the original circular imprints may have vanished as a result of plowing and leveling of the ground, and although past discolorations of the earth should have blended by now into a uniform color, there might still be a reason for the persistant appearance of the circles: the original flying units may have emitted radiation that penetrated deeply into the ground, impregnating a considerable depth of earth. Each time farmers have replowed, they have destroyed the coloration of the upper surface. However, this discoloration could possibly have been renewed by radiation emitted from the full depth of the saturated ground beneath. Thus, while on one hand, the upper surface continues to be rearranged, on the other hand, the circular patterns may be replaced by radiation from beneath the surface layer. If such has been the case, then the film emulsions have captured again the light and dark aspects of the regenerated circles.

2) In the case of topsoil that is not discolored and shows no signs of soil marks, we are confronted with the enigmatic situation of being able to photograph and discern these circles only from the air. If such a fact is positively established, it would suggest that rays are being emitted from the spots where circles once existed, and are registering on the silver emulsion of standard films. It is well to remember that all these photographs were taken with standard film having a silver emulsion base. As far as we knew before now, this type of film was sensitive only to light. The object to be photographed had to possess in itself different degrees of shading so as to register accordingly on the film. Discoloration of the topsoil would naturally register on film. However, when no discoloration can be observed on plowed fields, but still the film registers a circular shape, one can easily speculate that the emulsions used in regular films may be sensitive to both normal light as well as to the type of radiation emitted from these locations on the ground!

Extensive soil and radiation tests will have to be performed so as to generate a clearer understanding of the phenomena.

FIG. 70 — AERIAL VIEW OF THE WILSFORD BARROWS IN
WILTSHIRE, ENGLAND, TAKEN IN 1972.
(COURTESY UNIVERSITY OF CAMBRIDGE)

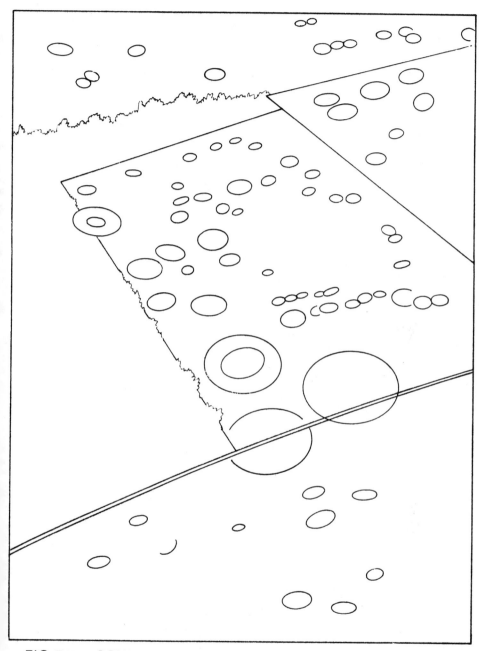

FIG. 71 — SCHEMATIC VIEW OF SOME CIRCLES OBSERVED
IN FIG. 70

One fact is clear and undeniable: after so many millenia, we can observe very sharply defined circular imprints on various sites of meadow lands, plowed fields, and in the immediate and neighboring vicinities of Stonehenge, etc. as registered on regular silver emulsion films.

The sum of the above mentioned observations leads to a prediction:

In a previous chapter, I referred to the peculiar construction characteristics of Silbury Hill, inducing one to speculate that the main purpose of this immense earthen structure was the creation of a flat-top surface at a given height, to be used as a landing spot for YAHWEH's circular space vehicles. If such a theory has any merit to it, then one can predict that proper aerial photographs taken above Silbury Hill will display a circle, or circles, on the top flat, truncated portion of the mountain.

Moreover, one can also predict that similar circular imprints will be found in England—and in other countries —wherever megalithic constructions were involved, which, in turn, means: the sites where extraterrestrial activity took place.

14

Picture That Is Worth
a Million Words

A very clear and interesting picture of Stonehenge is found in the library of the Museum of Natural History in New York City (Fig. 72). At first sight it is a beautiful picture depicting the still existing portion of the Sarsen Circle with the Lintel Stones in place. In front of the vertical Sarsen Stones we still see the smaller Bluestones.

This picture also shows clearly the existence of a "shadow" thrown on the base of the Sarsen Stones. That is, we observe a whitish area on each Sarsen Stone—an area almost equivalent to the contours of the Bluestone standing in front of it.

The peculiar aspect is that this "shadow" is white. An object usually casts a shadow when it is hit by a source of light. A shadow is not of a permanent nature, but will disappear when the source of light is cut off. Invariably, it is darker in nature than the object itself, since the rest of the area is lit by the same source. In this particular case, we have exactly the opposite—a white "shadow," and what's still more important, a permanent one!

In our experience a white "shadow" suggests one cause. During World War II, Hiroshima was the recipient of the first man-made atomic bomb explosion in modern times. That event opened the door to numerous studies in connection with the after-effects of the radiation generated during the exposure. Subsequent testing performed in the U.S. deserts confirmed the findings.

For the first time we came in contact with atomic radiation, with its after-effects, with its deadly power, and with its deadly invisible rays emanating from the enormous radioactivity and heat generated.

During these studies certain basic factors were observed and understood. When a source of atomic explosion throws into the atmosphere a stream of radiation, such a stream will hit, along with the heat it produces, any object in its path. If the object happens to be human, animal or vegetation, the impact of the atomic radiation, as well as the extreme heat, will simply destroy that living tissue. When such a radiation hits, for example, a person standing in front of a wall, that human being protects the wall for a split second, during which he absorbs the on-coming radiation instead of letting it pass through and hit the wall behind it. The whole area taken up by the contour of that person acts—for a split second—as a barrier, stopping the radiation from proceeding. The space outside the contour of the object experiences no interference so that the radiation rays and the heat continue straight into the wall. This means that for a short period of time when the object acts as a shield, less radiation and heat penetrate the wall behind it, in comparison with the amount of radiation and heat that flows directly onto the wall along the path that experiences no interference (that is, beyond the contour of the man). As a result, we find in Hiroshima and other atomic explosion sites, white "shadows" along walls that reveal exactly the contour of the objects that were standing in front. White "shadows" have become tell-tale indications that both the object and the wall behind were exposed to a source of radioactive radiation and tremendous heat.

FIG. 72 — PART OF SARSEN STONES WITH THEIR LINTELS AND BLUESTONES, SHOWING THE "WHITE SHADOW" EFFECT. THIS PICTURE WAS TAKEN IN THE EARLY 1960s BY MR. M. LOWENFISH. (COURTESY AMERICAN MUSEUM OF NATURAL HISTORY NEW YORK).

This seems to be the situation we encounter at Stonehenge. We see very clear areas of white "shadows" reflecting the objects in front of them, the Bluestones. In this particular case, the stone is not disintegrated by radiation and thus the object is still there to be seen and tested. In the other cases at Hiroshima, etc. the objects were, to a great extent, human and have thus vanished, leaving only the white "shadows" behind on the wall.

In order for such a situation to cccur, there must have been a source located somewhere in the center of the circle which constantly, or perhaps intermittently, generated and emitted radioactive radiation and heat. Theoretically, we could connect the general contour of the shadow area with the Bluestone standing in front of it and extend such an imaginary line towards the middle of the circle. We would probably reach a point about 10 to 15 feet off the ground located in the center of that circle. This would be the spot where the atomic reactor of a spaceship would have been located since it was placed under the spaceship as shown in the diagram of Mr. Blumrich (see Fig. 17). It is expected that such a source of radiation would have constantly or intermittently thrown off radiation and heat into all directions and would have hit the ground or the stones of the supporting platform.

It is interesting to observe that in front of every vertical stone (such as the Sarsen Stones or the Trilithons) there's a much smaller Bluestone, as though YAHWEH and his crew wanted to protect the lower portion of the standing stones from receiving too much radiation and heat. Furthermore, these protective devices—if we may call them that—are of a different type of stone than the Sarsen Stones or the trilithons. They are known as dolerite (and some are rhyolite), both of which are especially hard in texture.

Under normal circumstances, builders who had to

erect such a structure would not be especially concerned about the special type of stone to be placed in front of the Sarsen uprights—unless they had a very good reason to go out of their way, to lug the stone all the way from the Prescelly Mountains, more than 200 miles away! Yet, we realize that the effort was made, seemingly without regard to distances and difficulties in transportation, to bring in a different consistence of stone from a completely different direction to perform a very specific job: namely, as I suggest, to absorb radiation and heat and protect the standing bases of the platform on which the spaceship was sitting —the upright Sarsen stones, as well as the upright Trilithon stones. It is interesting to note in this respect that according to the calculations made by Blumrich, temperatures of 1800–2300 degrees F (1000°–1300°C) would have been experienced in such a situation. Also, the cooling radiator would have had a "glow" when in operation. This means that the stones in Stonehenge would have been exposed to very large dosages of concentrated heat and radiation. The absorption capacity of the Bluestones would be less than the absorption capacity of the Sarsen stones, and there would have been a drawback in allowing the base of the Sarsen stones to absorb too much radiation and heat. Since, in my estimation, the purpose of the vertical Sarsen stones was to support a flat platform at a height of about 20 feet, it follows that the radiation in question would have had a tendency to weaken the solid footing of the Sarsen stones. For all we know, these smaller Bluestones used as protective shields might have been constantly replaced, depending upon the degree of radiation and heat they absorbed. This is a possibility, although I don't believe remnants of Bluestones lying around the countryside outside of the Stonehenge complex have yet been found. They might, however, have been buried.

It is to be expected that other portions of the entire

structure would have been exposed to the same radioactive radiation and heat. As such, remnants would probably show us today other white "shadow" areas. We could subsequently reconstruct their position and the objects that protected them and generated the white "shadow" areas in question.

15

The Proof

I started this book by mentioning that a theory is an expression of a new thought that tries to explain an unknown situation. By its very nature, it cannot be perfect, since it results from a new exploration into the dark. It is useful in opening the way to new channels of thought, to new directions for investigation in the future. Yet, if at a later date, the theory proves basically correct, it is still to be expected that certain aspects of it could prove to be wrong or partially wrong.

As we progress, we learn more, and as we think deeper into the problems, we will probably make a number of changes and correct ourselves along the way. The thoughts, or even the direction of the thoughts expressed in this book, must be taken with a certain degree of flexibility; there may be a core of important truth giving us a tremendous breakthrough in understanding our whole past. It is important that we continue "digging."

However, every theory has to be proven. There is no end to speculations, to thoughts, to scientific or semi-scientific possibilities and/or probabilities that can be expressed. It is good to tred new ground and test how new thoughts can possibly explain old enigmas. Yet positive and scientific proof is necessary to give any theory a lease on life until it can be dissected, digested, debated and eventually—and hopefully—proven correct.

There are two basic ways to prove a theory:

A) The logical sequences and the preponderance of the probabilities have to be of such weight that they can lead to the sober evaluation of correctness—or at least within the boundaries of present scientific knowledge. Deductible results can be meaningfully obtained, if our thought process is correct.

Even so, the fact that a given problem is solved by a proposed theory is not enough in itself to substantiate it as "truth." We can always generate some sort of a theory to fit a given occurrence. We can even cover two or three occurrences with the same theory—and still not be able to really substantiate our theory. The more points we cover with the same theory, the greater our probabilities of being correct. It is only when we see that a great number of diverse and unconnected enigmas start fitting into the same theory, that we can assume our research direction to be correct. In other words, objective evaluation of probabilities and sheer logic can tend to prove a theory.

B) On the other hand, more convincing proof is obtained through actual scientific testing, in which physical data and results can be verified. This sort of proof takes the conclusion out of the realm of logic and inserts it in the domain of experimentation. It is much easier to "see" than to "think" in the abstract. Naturally not all theories can be physically tested. We require a variety of factors to lay the foundation for a proper testing procedure.

A great many books have been written about Stonehenge and other megalithic circles. Each one of these writers had some personal explanation. Unfortunately, all of these remain in the same realm of speculation and theory since most of them suggested no aspects that could be physically proven by scientific methods, or were able to answer a multitude of questions with the same theory.

The theory I am submitting here contains the ingredients necessary to be tested scientifically. If this theory, in part or in whole, reflects actual happenings and displays the correct situation of 5000 years ago, then we should be able to perform very specific tests today and obtain certain answers to substantiate our theoretical evaluation. For this theory of YAHWEH to be correct, it means that the following tests should display positive results:

Sarsen Circle: I advanced the thought that the Sarsen Circle was nothing else but a support for a level platform that had to be about 20 feet in the air in order for YAHWEH's spaceship to land there on, and subsequently become the headquarters and nerve center of his organization to collect and collate astronomical and geological data. The physical construction of the structure supports this theory as tremendous strength was built into it. If this were the case, then scientific testing involving radiation traces left in the stones and in the ground by the centrally located radioactive core of the spaceship would lend strong support to the point. It means that the surface of the Bluestones that face the center of the circle should display a very pronounced degree of radiation penetration. However, the back side of the same stones should prove to have absorbed far less radiation since the source emitting these rays was in the center of the circle.

It also follows that the area of the white "shadow" shown on the bottom of the Sarsen stones should show a lower degree of radiation than the outer area which was not "protected" by the Bluestones. As we proceed upwards in testing the stones, the radiation penetration should also decrease. The Lintel stones should show less of a radiation factor than the rest of the structure. The top of the Lintel stone should display very little, if any, radiation. The outside facade of these standing Sarsen Stones, however, should reveal hardly any traces of radiation, since they were not facing the center of the circle—that is, the spaceship itself.

There is another important aspect that can be tested. The three standing Sarsen stones, with the three Lintel stones on top, are the ones that should display the greatest radiation (these stones are the ones shown in Fig. 72). A look at a top view map of Stonehenge will show immediately that this section was in full view of the center of the circle where the spaceship's reactor would have been. There were no Trilithon stones in its path, and thus they could not have interfered with the direct movement of radiation rays emitted from the center of the circle. Since these particular stones (numbered 28-29-30-1-2-3 on the official plan Fig. 1) were fully exposed to the source of radiation, they would now show a much higher degree of radiation penetration than other vertical Sarsen stones that were protected by Trilithons. For example, Sarsens 6 and 7 were mostly protected from a direct line connection with the center through the interference of Trilithons 51 and 52. Likewise, Sarsen 16 was "hiding" behind Trilithon 56, or Sarsen 21 was protected by Trilithon 58. Therefore, these Sarsen stones should display a much lower degree of radiation—if any at all.

The only exception would be if the Trilithons were installed later on, and after the Sarsen Circle had been used for a given amount of time. That would mean that all the Sarsen stones and all their corresponding Bluestones were exposed to constant radiation during a certain period. Later on, when the Trilithons were installed, they would have cut down the amount of radiation received by the Sarsen stones that were located behind them. Thus, a different degree of radiation could also be found on the Sarsen's Bluestones located directly in the path of the radiation, than on the Sarsen's Bluestones hidden behind the

Trilithons. Perhaps this could even pinpoint for us the dating of the Trilithons.

On the other hand, outlaying stones that are at a fair distance from the center of the ground should display a much lower degree of radiation. For example, the Heel stone, or the Corner stones 91-93-94 should fall in this category.

It also means that the very same situation has to be found with the Trilithon stones and their corresponding Bluestones. Here again, the side of each Trilithon's Bluestone facing the center of the circle is the one that should show an even greater penetration, since it was closer to the source (the center), while the white "shadow" area of the vertical Trilithon stone should show less penetration. The Trilithons themselves, being nearer to the center, should display a much greater degree than some of the Sarsen stones that were much further away.

Also, if this concept is correct, then deadly radiation must have penetrated into the grounds—at least around the base of the Bluestones. Depending on whether or not there was a protective shield in the center, which stopped radiation from penetrating straight down into the earth, we should also be able to find traces in that center area. Theoretically, no grass or vegetation should have been able to grow in these spots. Of course, since several thousand years have elapsed, it is possible that the ground is no longer radioactive and will support vegetation, such as grass, at present. However, thousands of years ago vegetation should not have existed there since we know for a fact that radioactivity will kill any living organism, be it a plant or an animal or a human being. In the case of the stones, the situation is different since stones do not die.

Our experiences with our space technology have led us into techniques that can detect the previous existence of radiation. For example, we are in a position to detect today the path traveled by energized particles (such as alpha, beta, gamma, etc.) when they penetrate an inanimate object such as stone. The path traveled by these penetrating particles remain in the stone just as fossils remain imbedded in their surroundings. Through techniques known as tracking, we can determine today whether a stone was previously exposed to radioactivity. Possibly we can even determine the period of that exposure and even perhaps the magnitude involved, and its dating.

The next logical step would be to test the grounds within the inner circle and compare them with the grounds outside the Sarsen Circle which, in turn, should be compared to the grounds outside the ditch and bank circle. Each one of these areas would have been exposed to a different intensity of radiation. The center of the circle should show the most pronounced traces. As we proceed out towards the Salisbury Plain, that radiation should decrease. In fact, the area outside the bank should be mostly neutral; that is, it should have continuously supported plant growth.

As for the Aubrey Holes, and even the bank, it is most likely that they would have been impregnated with the type of luminescent radiation perhaps used by YAHWEH on other occasions. Exactly what type of radiation this might have been is impossible to state at the present stage. It could have been the type of radiation that interacts only when exposed to some other rays, such as ultra-violet rays, in which case it would glow in the dark—something similar to our present-day fluorescence display. Since a few Aubrey Holes have not been opened up as yet, it might be worthwhile to test their contents for radiation, with the hope that the chalk has not been disturbed for a great many centuries and still contains some of the absorbed radiation it received in the past.

In this connection, artifacts that were found inside the

Aubrey Holes can also be exposed to such testing, as they should display the presence of radiation. Especially the cremation remnants that were discovered could indicate to us the existence of such absorption.

Aside from these radioactive radiations that I theorize were emitted by the spaceship, we have to consider the partial destruction of Stonehenge. In my estimation, this destruction did not take place because of the hatred, the fury, or the animosity of later generations who were bent on destroying the structure. The destruction of such an enormous number of boulders, the movement and rear-rangement of 30 to 40 tons of stones, all compacted in a relatively small area, would certainly not have been an easy job. It would have taken a great many hours of labor to dismantle the Lintel stones and topple the Trilithons. In my opinion, the partial destruction resulted from a willful or accidental "man-made" explosion. Whether this explosion was triggered by YAHWEH and his crew before leaving the grounds and returning to their homes, or whether an unwanted accident happened that destroyed part of the structure is a question that needs further investigation. It is important to remember that most of the destruction took place on the left side of an imaginary line drawn in a north to south direction. In other words, the western portion of the structure would have absorbed the brunt of this explosion, while the eastern section of the circle escaped, to a great extent, the full fury of the detonation. This means that the western section of the field might possibly contain telltale traces of an explosion. These can perhaps be detected on the fallen stones themselves or in the grounds surrounding the area. Thus, this portion of the circle, theoretically, would display two layers of radiation: the regular one emitted from the spaceship and the secondary one resulting from the explosion. Whether the explosion was radioactive in character or not is a moot question that requires specific testing. Experts should be in a position to study the resulting damage and determine the epi-center of such a detonation.

There seems to be a certain anomaly in the magnetic field around Stonehenge. On a September day, I walked for a few hours around the outer ditch/bank with a compass in hand. I obtained peculiar readings. Instead of having the magnetic needle point to north, most of the time it would be deflected and point only towards the center of the Stonehenge monument. The other part of the time it would act normally and point constantly north.

A few days later, I repeated the same procedure. This time the needle would point upwards and hit the glass of the compass, as though a magnetic force was pulling from above. This situation was not a constant one but would reoccur from time to time as I walked around the periphery of Stonehenge.

I do not know what these two displays of magnetic anomaly mean. It might be important to keep them in mind and repeat them with more refined testing procedures.

I requested permission of the British Government to have a group of scientists from some English University perform the tracking test—similar to the one performed on the stones brought back from the moon. Unfortunately, permission was denied because small samples of stones had to be taken from the Stonehenge monument so as to subject them to very sensitive laboratory tests. The concern displayed by the British authorities is quite understandable and commendable. Yet, we are dealing here with an enormously important aspect, covering all of mankind's past history. If the theories submitted in this book are even partially correct, we are then opening a completely new chapter in our understanding of our antiquity. For the sake of science and history, it is fervently hoped that the British Government will reconsider its decision and allow me to perform the suggested scientific tests on a few of the Stonehenge stones.

So much for Stonehenge, itself.

Additional tests, however, can be performed on the other stone circles and individual stones that remain from the activities of YAHWEH and his "Watchers." In the case of the stone circles, we should again meet the following radiation possibilities:

1) The center ground should have been saturated with some sort of radioactive radiation.

2) If so, grass or other plants should not have been able to grow—thus, we should have had bare spots that did not support life.

3) The upright stones would display a certain radioactivity, although much less than in Stonehenge.

4) Since these stones were inserted from the air, they would have been impregnated by the type of field used by YAHWEH for lifting nonmetallic objects.

5) If the stones were used as bases for an impregnated field to collect energy from space, they should reveal traces of that particular field.

The boulders that were used as foresights to pinpoint the movements of the sun and the moon, should display the least amount of radioactivity—if any at all. In their cases, the only exposure would have been lifting-field type radiation. Those boulders that were used as transmitting poles would, however, display traces of two separate radiations. They would have been exposed to the lifting-field, and to the energy collecting field, (which also included the energy transmission field, probably of the same nature).

The standing rows of stones would fall exactly into the same category. Naturally, the ones in Brittany would display a much more pronounced presence of these types of radiations, especially as they were so much more powerful and used more intensely for their energy-collecting capacities.

Up to now the discussion has centered around the stone circles of England and the stone rows in northern France. However, we can go one step further and predict that if this theory is correct, it is likely that YAHWEH and his "Watchers" may have performed the basic same functions in other parts of Europe, and in other parts of the world. Stone circles, individual standing stones, and stone rows must have existed in various parts of Europe, Africa, Asia, and America. It is not logical to expect that explorers landing on planet Earth would limit their investigations only to the territory of England and northern France, especially as they would have had flight capacity that could take them to any part of the world within a very short time. Furthermore, a proper collection of data relating to astronomical problems cannot be generated through an observatory located in one spot only. Our modern methods indicate to us that we need observatories in various parts of the world to coordinate our sightings and pinpoint with a scientific accuracy the occurrences in the sky. Consequently, it is to be expected that YAHWEH and his "Watchers" must have taken sightings from other parts of the world. Unfortunately, it is quite possible that a great majority of these stone circles in other parts of the world have been destroyed. Yet a certain number of them should still be on hand. Especially in the case of standing stones, the probabilities are that a greater portion of them are on hand. They have infrequently been reported as existing in other countries such as France, Germany, Baltic area, etc., although their presence has never aroused a very great interest. The considerable number of stone circles still in existence in the British Isles today has called the constant attention of generations upon generations of the English— thus became a national enigma challenging the inhabitants for a solution. The other countries, with far fewer

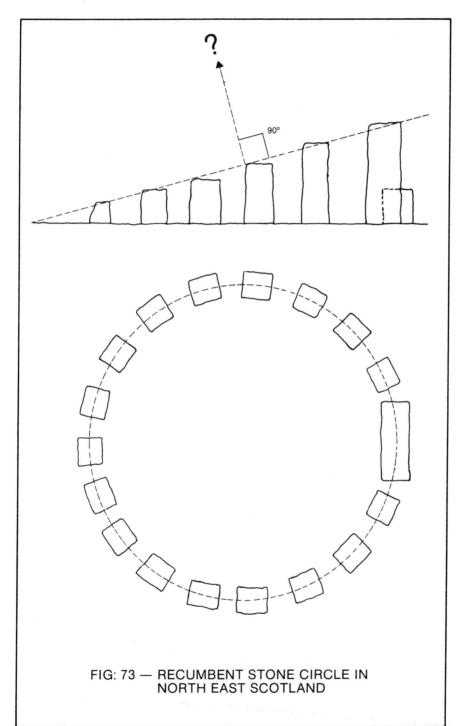

FIG: 73 — RECUMBENT STONE CIRCLE IN
NORTH EAST SCOTLAND

remnants to show would naturally extend less attention and display less curiosity about their existence than England.

Despite this lack of awareness in other countries of the world, it is still to be expected that standing stones (perhaps ones having had "special powers") and stone circles must exist. It is a matter of locating them, realizing their historical importance, and testing them properly for radiation. By pinpointing their exact location and preparing a unified map, we can possibly generate a meaningful relationship for an interconnected grid.

Another interesting test that could be performed concerns recumbent stone circles in North East Scotland. In this particular case, we see groups of two large upright stones with a third one lying flat on the ground. As we proceed along the circle, each subsequent stone is smaller until we reach the end where they are at a very low height. A side view of this circle would look approximately as shown in Fig. 73. If we connect the top of all these stones, we would create a flat surface at a given angle facing the sky. It would be interesting to determine the spots in the sky that would be pinpointed by a 90-degree direction facing this slanted surface of the circle. Naturally, a good amount of trial and error would have to be performed since there will be angle variations in the slanted area when connecting the various points of the stone circles. Nevertheless, a general direction can be pinpointed. Astronomers could determine the celestial bodies in those particular directions. Chances are that a radiation-emitting body would be found in that direction. We can conceive that YAHWEH and his "Watchers" here also created their electromagnetic(?) field at a given angle in order to face the direction of the source emitting the radiation.

In certain cases, the same effect was possibly achieved by them by erecting a number of stone circles on the slope of a mountain. In these cases, they used uniform stones, which when placed on an inclined plane, created a slanted surface at a certain angle facing the sky.

The same general procedure could be performed on the stone rows of Carnac, France. As the stones are quite weather-beaten and irregular in shape, a precise projection of the field can probably not be generated. Nevertheless, a general idea could be obtained by connecting all these points and observing the type of curvature created by a field lying on top of stone rows. It could give us some sort of indication as to the source of radiation the Watchers were perhaps trying to capture.

The second group of testing procedures is via films. If there really were radiation, or impregnation by a certain type of electromagnetic(?) field, then such a phenomenon would, theoretically, be discernible on film. It is possible that the existing impregnation is still reacting today with radiation coming from space. Or else, it is possible that remnants of this impregnation continue to exist today on these stones—naturally quite reduced in power—but still discernible. Then film exposures could give us a printed proof of this existence. There are, of course, various emulsions of films that can be used. A certain trial-and-error procedure would have to be followed in order to determine the correct type of film that would react to the types of radiation emitted by these stones.

We must also realize that we would probably be faced with different types of radiations—a review of the theories suggested to this point show the following possible classifications of radiations:

1) A field to permit the lifting of nonmetallic bodies
2) A field to collect energy from space
3) A field to transmit energy from stone to stone

4) A field to transmit sound
5) Regular radioactive radiation
6) Luminescent radiation

Whether these would be the same or different fields cannot be answered as yet, at the present stage of our research. Possibly various films will capture the same field or indicate different types of fields.

We have also to consider that if these fields really exist today on these stones, they may still be interacting with the sun's light or other unknown radiation sources from space. Each different interaction might generate a different type of print. For example, if the sun light hits a certain spot at a certain angle, and if our camera is situated in a specific position, we might not observe anything unusual on the film. Yet, if the camera were moved so that the angle of reception were different, we could quite well generate a special effect on our film.

At any rate, the fact remains: If there really is some sort of radiation on these stones, then (provided all other conditions are ideal) we should be able to generate a certain number of prints depicting the existence of these radiation fields. Probably their existence would be suggested by some bluriness in the picture, some streaks, some "halos" around the stone, or some lighted spots, etc. Pictures taken with different types of films (such as ultraviolet, infra-red, X-ray, etc) or using different picture taking techniques and/or developing procedures, could display traces of such an existence. Perhaps, Kirlian photography might give us the proofs.

There is a third group of testing procedures that can be performed: by means of instrumentation. If these stones trully radiate certain types of radiation, or if they are presently interacting with present day space radiation, then sensitive meters should be able to register the flow of charged particles. After all, radiation can be boiled down, in its simplest form, to represent the flow of some sort of charged particles from one location to another. Any movement of particles, or any differential in potential (which in turn creates the flow) should be discernible through instrumentation. There are a great many types of meters and testing procedures that can be applied to determine the existence of the field(s) or even the constant emission of radiation.

For example, we have been told of electric shocks experienced by certain people when touching these stones. They insist that they feel a strong reaction in their bodies, as though a shock of low voltage is passing through their bodies. To test these reactions of theirs, we could easily wire them and connect them to proper instruments so as to observe the reaction registered on these meters.

And lastly, we could perform a series of radiation, soil, and vegetation tests on the areas that display circles, as observed in our aerial photographs. Perhaps such tests would determine for us the character of the radiation involved.

Unfortunately, there might be a pitfall in these testing procedures, because of our possible limitation of knowledge in radiation. We know how to perform a "tracking" test and thus determine the past existence of alpha/beta/-gamma rays. But, how about the fact that YAHWEH's radiation might have been different than our well-known and understood radiations? We have seen that this very advanced person used types of rays that are still puzzling and foreign to us, at the present stage of our knowledge. A possibility exists that the radioactive display of YAHWEH's spaceship might have been completely different in nature than the ones we came to know up to now. Certainly, there can be various types of radiations and/or radioactivities which we did not discover as yet, and thus are incapable of testing for the moment. With every year that passes, our scientific knowledge is advancing, and, hopefully, we will uncover and realize the existence of additional types of radioactivity—different than the ones we know today.

Consequently, although the presence of a "white" shadow is a definite tell-tale sign for the previous exposure to alpha/beta/gamma rays, there is a possibility that our tests might give us negative results—if YAHWEH used different radiations than the ones known by us up to the present time. In that case, these tests should be repeated after our knowledge of radiation improves and progresses.

16

Conclusions

I have tried to reconstruct a series of occurrences and facts that unite in a theory—the theory of YAHWEH, and shed an extraordinary light on our historical past. Isolated facts, of course, do not necessarily mean a great deal, and from them often little inference can be drawn. However, the cumulative effect of same tend to greatly enhance the value of each of the component parts, so that solitary happenings, which in themselves would not carry much weight, become exceedingly important since they form an integral part of an overall pattern. It is through the creation of an interconnected grid that the value of each individual occurrence is considerably enhanced.

Through a step-by-step evaluation of known facts, through a critical analysis of historical writings, through scientific data, we realize that Stonehenge may have been created by YAHWEH and his group about 4500 years ago.

If this is true—or even if only part of it is true—then we are faced with an astonishing new picture of our antiquity, a picture that sheds a completely different light on our understanding of our history. In fact it could have a tremendous influence on our future approach and research in all scientific and space matters. It could have an effect on our success in harnessing unlimited amounts of energy from outer space.

These space people may have tried to bring civilization to many parts of the world, being in touch with Egypt, Babylon, Greece, Israel, Persia, Sumer, India, China, the Americas, etc. Wherever they went, they left an imprint in one form or another, even though the traces were not previously obvious to us. They were the ones who tried in different ways to introduce the concept of religion (that is, selfimposed restraint for decency); when this failed they took a direct hand in establishing an organized tradition and religion—at least the one we so well know as the Hebrew religion.

Our interconnected grid leads to speculate that the numerous civilizations that started about 6000 years ago had a common denominator: YAHWEH and his group. For example, when we consider that the Aztecs had a white God —Quetzalcoatal; the Incas had a white God—Viracocha; the Mayans had a white God—Kukulcan; the Tupis in Brazil had a white God—Sume, we realize that a common denominator may well have existed. Could it be that it was the same white God?

What does it all mean?

It means that, even if only a portion of my theory proves correct, we may have to rewrite our history. We may need to rethink and reevaluate all the occurrences that took place between 6000 B.C. and 2000 B.C. (at least). The results can be extraordinarily far-reaching.

We are dealing with a huge mosaic puzzle having hundreds of scattered tiles throughout the world. In fact, we never before may have even suspected that all these pieces belonged to the same puzzle.

Every tile we analyzed in the past, did not mean too much in itself, nor did it give us an indication that it belonged to one and the same puzzle. With this new theory, however, all the pieces are starting to fall in place and are meshing into one general picture. For the first time, a meaningful reason is emerging to answer dozens of questions that have occured throughout the study of our historical records—throughout our antiquity, a span shrouded in a deep mist and about which we know hardly anything. For the first time, we now discern the possible existence of a central source from whom radiated all the teachings, all the beginnings of recent civilization on our planet—at least for the past 6000 years. We perhaps can now understand a multitude of events that continually baffled us in the past. I have suggested that YAHWEH and his crew were possibly the unifying core that spread knowledge, civilization, ethics, and religion to many different peoples of the world—and not only to the Hebrews. We can now perhaps start to understand the surprising similarities in various parts of the world.

For a good many years, thoughtful archaeologists, historians, scholars, and other thinkers have realized the existence of a very surprising interrelationship between the Hebrews and the Celts, between the Egyptians and the American Indians, between the Greeks and the Hebrews, between the Basques and the Iroquois Indians, and so on. They were intrigued enough to pose questions, since they were scientifically objective enough to realize that something unusual and mysterious was hidden behind these obvious facts.

When Professor Cyrus Gordon of Brandeis University, the acknowledged authority on ancient Near Eastern history, realized a common background between the Hebrew and the Greek civilizations, he was pinpointing the results of his learned research; yet, he had no specific answer.

When Henrietta Mertz explained the surprising similarities she found between the Hebrews and the Mandan Indians of North Dakota, she was putting her finger on an amazing enigma without being able to realize how it came about.

When my friend, Dr. Robert Stieglitz, deciphered the writings on the Bat Creek, Tennessee, stone tablet, found in a grave, and expressed amazement that it read legibly in Hebrew, he was establishing an undeniable fact. As for the answer, only guesses abounded: Somehow or other, 2000 years ago, a group of Hebrew people were placed in a grave in Tennessee. Naturally the first reaction was to belittle such a decipherement of the Hebrew letters on the tablet. The second reaction was to rationalize a possible trip by a hearty group of Hebrews who had taken to the seas, sailed through the Meditterrannean, past the Straights of Gibraltar, into the huge unknown Atlantic and eventually landed on the shores of North America. Either they continued their trip from the Atlantic coast on foot, despite untold miles of hardship until they reached the mountains of Tennessee, or they entered through the Gulf of Mexico (another long voyage) into the Mississippi, and sailed up river until they branched off into the Tennessee River. Some trip! Stieglitz realized the impossibility of it—yet the alternative answer was then not clear.

When Professor Barry Fell of Harvard University, discovered Egyptian hyrogliphic inscriptions among the Micmacs, and the Libian alphabet being used by the Zuni Indians in Iowa as well as by the Maoris of the Pacific, he put his finger on the heart of the puzzle.

Again, when Professor Fell observed that the language of the Pima Indians of the American Southwest has an almost identical root with Semitic/Arabic languages, he posed a very big question—even though the answer was not forthcoming.

When Dr. LePlongeon, in 1896, pointed out the surprising resemblance between the Mayan language (in Central America) and Akkadian (in the Near East), he raised our curiosity without being able to really understand the reasons for the similarity.

When the Catholic Church revealed to us the enigmatic Shroud of Turin, kept for centuries in a vault in that city, and suggested that it was the one used by Christ, we were able to look at it with amazement and observe the two images of a person (front and back)—images that appear on the linen, as though they were photographic emulsions. We did not know how this could have happened. Perhaps, today, we can realize that YAHWEH's radiation might have penetrated from above into the body of Jesus, as it possibly had with previous Hebrew prophets. Jesus would have glowed with this radiation, which, in turn, would have penetrated the Shroud that covered his body. This might have been similar to that observed on the face of Moses, for example, when he returned from his meeting with "God" on the mountain (Ex:34:29).

Perhaps, today, if we could experiment with various types of radiations that leave a photographic negative picture on a linen, or if we could scientifically analyze the radiation on this Shroud we might come a step closer to understanding one of the types of radiation used by YAHWEH.

When we think back to the recent history of the Great Pyramids of Egypt, we know that, surprisingly enough, a great many people involved with their original reopening and the reentering into the inner chambers died mysteriously, without apparent reason. This fact has been, for the most part, either brushed aside, or considered superstitiously connected with the "curse" of the Pharaohs.

A dead corpse cannot enact a curse. And, scientifically speaking, what is a curse? Radiation trapped in the stone chambers of these incredible structures for 4500 years could have escaped upon the moving of the huge stones that had kept it tightly confined for centuries. Radiation, of course, can penetrate humans, and in time, destroy them "mysteriously." The internal ravage of radiation is not always apparent, especially when one is not even looking for it, and is not aware that it could be the possible cause of death. We call something "mysterious" because we do not understand the cause. Once we know the law of physics that govern it, then it is no longer mysterious. The enigmatic Pyramids may, sooner or later, tell us their secret and the reason for their construction (which is quite likely not simply as tombs for kings).

When the Turkish admiral Piri Reis drew his famous map in 1513, showing exact shore lines of South America, as well as the South Pole, while the rest of the world had no idea of the very existence of these lands, we asked ourselves: Where did he copy it from? He openly told us that he had copied it from very old maps—without knowing who the original draftpersons were. For the type of precision that was involved, it would seem that aerial photography and spherical trigonometry had to have been employed.

When Professor Hapgood, of Keene University, New Hampshire, analyzed the maps drawn in the fourteenth to sixteenth century by Haji Ahmet, Zeno, Dulcert, Piri Reis, Benincasa, Yehudi Ibn Ben Zara, etc. and exclaimed his amazement at the surprising precision that was involved, at a time when not even longitudes and latitudes were applied, he discovered a very important tile of the mosaic puzzle.

Also, when Mr. Cohane's research indicated a common root for a great many names throughout the world, appearing over and over again, in one form or another, he made another connection within the same mosaic.

This list could be continued for many pages, and still we would not have mentioned all the parts of the puzzle that scholars know exist—yet have no plausible explanations for.

Perhaps today, the answers are on hand, or should I

say, *The* answer itself, since many of these occurrences may lead back to the same common denominator: YAHWEH and his group. It is possibly because of his physical presence, because of his interest in humankind, and his desire to raise our level of civilization that we now begin to understand and appreciate the immense work he may have tried to perform for us earthlings. He tried desperately to elevate the ethical level of groups of semi-savage tribes all over the world. He tried to introduce a moral code to be used by humanity on its way up the ladder of civilization. If he failed it was because we earthlings were too retarded to even understand what he was trying to tell us and to explain to us.

Our solar system appears to contain one life-supporting planet: the earth. But there are literally millions of similar solar systems in our galaxy, to say nothing of the other galaxies. The probability is substantial that somewhere in that vastness, in those millions and millions of miles of space, life exists. 5000 years ago, when our civilizations on earth were only in their primitive infancy of their potential, YAHWEH and his group may have been at least, 6000 years ahead of us. Progress is not a linear equation but an exponential one, with the momentum carrying it further and faster with every passing year. If YAHWEH's group returned to earth today—a fact which is not so impossible to entertain—they might well be as much as 25,000 years ahead of our present technology.

In all this time that YAHWEH has left us to handle our own destinies and run our own affairs, we have achieved, in the final analysis, the ability to kill more people faster and more efficiently. Our savagery, our inhumanity to humanity, could possibly have become proverbial among the various space-people communities throughout the universe.

YAHWEH may have left this world in disgust—we were too insubordinate and too dumb to understand his

repeated admonitions and messages. If we have a modi-
cum of wisdom left, we should diligently search all the old
records written by our forebearers. For thousands of years,
they set in writings accounts of what they saw and what
they heard—even though they may not have understood a
number of their experiences. YAHWEH—the "living God"
—was real, was true, was alive, was flesh and blood. His
intellect, his ethics, his morals, his technology were so
much above that of our forebearers of 5000 years ago, that
they could not possibly grasp the meaning of his teachings. Now, in the 20th century, we can finally understand
his consuming frustration and bitterness when he la-
mented his failure, as reported in Hosea 4:6

> My people are destroyed for lack of knowledge; be-
> cause thou hast rejected knowledge. . . .

In all these ancient writings—such as the Bible, the
Apocryphas, the reports of early historians, volumes hidden in caves, monasteries, museums, libraries—there lies
an incredible wealth of information. It depends upon us to
properly interpret these writings and extract the meaning
hidden within these reports. If we reread these texts, keeping in mind the theory suggested here, we may discover a
completely different dimension. Up to now, we have evaluated and understood our history in a two dimensional
plane. We have considered that our forebearers could
move only over land, and by sea—and even that, with
great difficulties. Now, we are suggesting a third route—
travel by air. If YAHWEH moved people around through
the air, we can understand how some Hebrews may have
ended up in the middle of Tennessee.

I suggest that I may have discovered only a key—
which started to open certain doors that were shut to us
for 5000 years. But, this is only the beginning; there are

very many more enigmas to understand, and many more doors to be opened.

"Seek, and you shall find" is an age-old saying.

We *must* seek—and quite likely—we *will* find the various answers handed down to us by YAHWEH.

There are astonishingly immense forces in the universe, about which we know nearly nothing. YAHWEH may have known of some of them and wanted to teach us part of that knowledge. We did not understand, nor were we able to understand. He may have realized that fact and asked us to have faith in his statements. Even that did we find difficult to perform. For example when YAHWEH told us that there is a God—a Creator; when YAHWEH told us that human beings were "created"; when he told us that they were created on the bases of the image of God—these were not necessarily idle words. It behooves us to stop and think—to research the possibilities with a greater determination than before.

While performing this immense research, it would be well to remember the words of Einstein:

> Science without religion is lame
> Religion without science is blind.

Science wishes to determine what *Is* by using experimental processes and thereby accumulating facts. Religion also wants to ascertain what *Is,* but asks us to accept certain "beliefs" unquestioningly because our power of comprehension is yet too primitive to understand what *Is.*

Theoretically, there is little difference in the goals of these two disciplines. With time, with knowledge and wisdom, we may realize this and allow the knowledge of each discipline to contribute to the understanding of the other, to a far greater degree. In my estimation, the two are one and the same and will fuse into each other in what I choose to call "scientific religion." We can survive as a planet, only if we live by "knowledge" and "faith".

Science is essential for us, to discover and understand the astonishingly tremendous forces that govern nature and the universe. The more we discover, and the more we understand, the more we may come to realize that there is a Creator, as we were told by an enormously knowledgeable and awe-inspiring YAHWEH—an intermediary perhaps between us and our Creator.

In the coming years, it is certain that our scientific knowledge will expand, but will our ethical and moral values expand in the same proportion? Will humankind be wise enough to finally, finally grasp how microscopically insignificant we all are, in the context of nature and the universe and God? Will humankind become mature enough to finally, finally, apply and respect the true spirit of the message conveyed to us by YAHWEH through the Ten Commandments—DECENCY?

There are many more enigmas to understand—many more doors to open.

17

Epilogue

Well-meaning scientists have always looked upon the probable existence of spacemen with a great measure of scorn. Any reference to such a possibility has been usually disdainfully labeled "science fiction." Yet science has certainly not been able to come forward with positive proof that there are no other human civilizations in outer space. If such scientific proof is not available, then we certainly have to maintain an open mind on the subject and be willing to search all plausible avenues of thought and evidence.

There are literally billions of planets in the various galaxies that fill outer space. Is it not somewhat presumptuous and immature to believe that our Earth is the one and only life-bearing planet among billions of other planets? There is no logical reason to think so.

Basic scientific principles require that we discard our subconscious disdain for anything pertaining to spacepeople. Instead a very careful and diligent search should be allowed to proceed so as to scientifically prove or disprove the thought-provoking theories advanced in this book.

FIG. 74 — THE HEELSTONE OF STONEHENGE.

FIG. 75 — STONEHENGE — LOOKING TOWARDS
THE HEELSTONE.

FIG. 76 — STONEHENGE, AS SEEN FROM THE HEELSTONE.

FIG. 77 — MERRY MAIDENS STONE CIRCLE,
CORNWALL, ENGLAND.

FIG. 78 — SECOND HURLER STONE CIRCLE,
CORNWALL, ENGLAND.

FIG. 79 — ROLLRIGHT STONE CIRCLE, OXFORDSHIRE, ENGLAND.

FIG. 80 — A LARGE BOULDER STANDING IN THE MIDDLE OF
A FIELD, CORNWALL, ENGLAND.

FIG. 81 — TWO LARGE BOULDERS — PART OF THE INNER STONE
CIRCLE AT AVEBURY.

FIG. 82 — PART OF THE OUTER STONE CIRCLE AT AVEBURY.

FIG. 83 — TRETHEWY QUOIT, CORNWALL, ENGLAND —
AN IMPOSING MASSIVE STONE STRUCTURE.

FIG. 84 — A SIX FOOT TALL PERSON DWARFED BY
THE MAJESTY OF TRETHEWY QUOIT.

FIG. 85 — LANYON QUOIT, CORNWALL, ENGLAND —
REMNANTS OF ANOTHER STONE CONSTRUCTION.

FIG. 86 — STONE "PANCAKES" STRUCTURE, BUILT ON A
SLOPE OF A MOUNTAIN — FRONT VIEW,
CORNWALL, ENGLAND.

FIG. 87 — REAR VIEW OF SAME "PANCAKES" STRUCTURE.